MACMILLAN
A Prentice Hall Macmillan Company
15 Columbus Circle
New York, NY 10023

Library of Congress Cataloging-in-Publication Data

Tuleja, Tad, 1944–
    The New York Public Library book of popular Americana/Tad Tuleja.
    p. cm.
  ''A Stonesong Press book.''
  Includes bibliographical references and index.
  ISBN 0-671-89987-2
  1. Americana—Dictionaries. 2. Americanisms—Dictionaries. 3. English language—United States—Terms and phrases—Dictionaries. 4. United States—Civilization—Dictionaries. I. New York Public Library. II. Title. III. Title: Book of popular Americana.
E169.1.T83   1994   94-22672
973'.03—dc20   CIP

Designed by Rhea Braunstein

Manufactured in the United States of America

10 9 8 7 6 5 4 3 2 1

THE NEW YORK PUBLIC LIBRARY®

— BOOK OF —
POPULAR
AMERICANA

TAD TULEJA

A Stonesong Press Book

MACMILLAN · USA

.

In memory of the folks
who threw me
into the melting pot

my grandparents

Gertrude Bastling
Elizabeth Meagher
Edward Stokes
and
Maximilian Tuleja

CONTENTS

ACKNOWLEDGMENTS

In pulling together the threads of this American tapestry, I have used more sources, both primary and secondary, than convention permits me to mention in a book of this nature. For readers whose thirst for Americana it stimulates rather than slakes, I can recommend a short shelf of specialized sources that have been invaluable in the course of my research.

For social and political history generally, the Reader's Digest *Family Encyclopedia of American History* (1975) is an intelligent and comprehensive reference work, as effective as Thomas Johnson's better-known *Oxford Companion to American History* (1966). Of the many U.S. history textbooks that have crossed my desk over the years, Henry Steele Commager and Samuel Eliot Morison's *Growth of the American Republic,* first published in 1931 and endlessly reprinted, deserves its classic stature. For wit and style, I have yet to find a text more graceful than Thomas A. Bailey's *The American Pageant* (1966). Two sound sources for the less sedate aspects of our history are the Reader's Digest *Story of the Great American West* (1987) and Carl Sifakis's *Encyclopedia of American Crime* (1982).

For matters literary, the best first stop is still William Rose Benet's *Reader's Encyclopedia,* frequently reprinted since its appearance in 1948. For the popular American works or writers not covered there, one repairs wisely to Max Herzberg's *Reader's Encyclopedia of American Literature* (1962) or James Hart's *Oxford Companion to American Literature* (1983). For genres often facilely dismissed as "subliterary," I can recommend Humphrey Carpenter and Mari Prichard's *Oxford Companion to Children's Literature* (1984), Chris Steinbrunner and Otto Penzler's *Encyclopedia of Mystery and Detection* (1976), and Ron Goulart's *Encyclopedia of American Comics* (1990).

The doyen of American folklore until his death was the irascible and irrepressible Richard Dorson. Of his many publications, those most accessible to a general audience are *American Folklore* (1959) and *America in Legend* (1973). A sound introduction to "folkloristics" is Jan Harold Brunvand's *The Study of American Folklore* (1978). Useful compendia include another Reader's Digest volume, *American Folklore and Legend* (1978), and the regional "treasuries" edited by Benjamin Botkin, beginning in 1944 with *A Treasury of American Folklore.*

My main source for Tinseltown biographies is Ephraim Katz's masterly *Film Encyclopedia* (1979). Also invaluable for movie buffs are Scott and Barbara Siegel's *Encyclopedia of Hollywood* (1990), Paul Michael's *American Movies Reference Book: The Sound Era* (1969), and two hardy perennials by Leslie Halliwell: his *Film Guide* (1977) and *Filmgoer's Companion* (1965). Jeff Lenburg covers Bugs Bunny & Co. ably in his *Encyclopedia of Animated Cartoons* (1991). *The International Dictionary of Films and Filmmakers* (1985), edited by Christopher Lyon, gives a limited but lively selection of movie reviews.

For the "golden age" of radio, I consulted John Dunning's usefully chatty survey *Tune In Yesterday* (1976). For television, my channel surfer's Bible is Tim Brooks and Earle Marsh's *Complete Directory to Prime Time Network TV Shows* (1992). Robert LaGuardia's *Soap World* (1983) is an entertaining guide to daytime television, while the weekend diversions of the toddler set are warmly recalled in Gary Grossman's *Saturday Morning TV* (1980).

The standard guide to national foot-tapping is the *New Grove Dictionary of American Music* (1986), edited by H. Wiley Hitchcock and Stanley Sadie. Daniel Kingman's *American Music: A Panorama* (1979) is a more accessible and equally lucid survey. Among the guides to particular genres that I have found useful are Alan Lomax's *Folk Songs of North America in the English Language* (1960), John and Alan Lomax's *Folk Song U.S.A.* (1966), Sigmund Spaeth's classic study of Tin Pan Alley, *Read 'Em and Weep* (1945), Sheldon Harris's *Blues Who's Who* (1979), Bill Malone's *Country Music U.S.A.* (1985), Stanley Green's *Encyclopedia of the Musical Theatre* (1976), and *The Rolling Stone Encyclopedia of Rock & Roll* (1983), edited by Jon Pareles and Patricia Romanowski. For the dates and stories of individual hits, one must perform judicious juggling among several sources. My preferences are Roger Lax and Frederick Smith's *Great Song Thesaurus* (1989) and David Ewen's *American Popular Songs* (1966).

For the stories behind American inventions, one may consult Harry Harris's *Good Old-Fashioned Yankee Ingenuity* (1990). The background of U.S. advertising symbols is presented engagingly in Hal Morgan's *Symbols of America* (1986). John Mariani's *Dictionary of American Food and Drink* (1983) does the same, equally engagingly, for our national cuisine. For other minor genres—in fact, for *anything* in the field of popular Americana—the indispensable scholarly guide is the *Handbook of American Popular Culture* (1989), edited in three volumes by M. Thomas Inge.

For the student of American verbal expression, especially slang, everybody's port of first call is H. L. Mencken's *The American Language* (1919–48). Mitford Mathews's *Dictionary of Americanisms on Historical Principles* (1956) remains unsurpassed for its intelligence and ample citations. For those willing to forgo the citations, Robert Chapman's *New Dictionary of American Slang* (1986) is an excellent alternative. For the social matrix of language in historical perspective, the indispensable works are by Stuart Berg Flexner. His companion volumes *I Hear America Talking* (1976) and *Listening to America* (1982) present decades of his formidable labors in an agreeable format.

Lastly, some personal notes, with pride of place, as always, going to my family. Thanks first to my wife, Andrée, who throughout this bear of a project provided her customary warmth, insightful humor, and firm anchorage. My enduring love to our children, Noah, Adriana, and India, who continue to remind me of Sandburg's definition of a child: "God's opinion that the world should go on." To my parents, back in New Jersey, a heartfelt thanks for the Davy Crockett costumes, the Everly Brothers records, and letting me stay up late for *Your Show of Shows*. For broadening a Yankee's perspective, my gratitude to Jeanne and Claude and to the Cleghorn clan of Villa Rica, Georgia. (Thank you, Onie, for those wonderful summers.)

My seduction by popular culture began in earnest in the midnight TV room of Timothy Dwight College. For introducing me there to *Casablanca,* my thanks to the usual suspects: Walter, Otis, Greg, and John. David Morse, at the University of Sussex, supervised my continued decline into B-moviedom by directing my thesis on the postwar outlaw. At the University of Massachusetts, years later, George Carey stimulated my interest in American folklore. Angus Gillespie, at

Rutgers, and Jay Mechling, at the University of California at Davis, had the reckless courage to solicit my first scholarly paper; they have been solid mentors and good friends ever since. Finally, three of my professors here at Texas have considerably improved my understanding of the popular. My appreciation to Steven Feld, Douglas Foley, and Roger Renwick.

To the many friends and editors who have suggested inclusions, or deletions, for this volume, my gratitude for your help in sharpening its focus. Particular thanks to Bill Betts for his able and insightful copyediting and to Curtis Townsend for his help in the realm of sports.

Finally, my thanks to the person who has done more than anyone else to make this book a reality. Paul Fargis, president of The Stonesong Press, not only brought the concept to my attention and provided useful feedback on the manuscript, but he arranged to have it published in a Stonesong reference series that is produced in cooperation with the New York Public Library. As a longtime reference writer and a former New Yorker, I am delighted to be associated with an institution that has been in the vanguard of making New York a community of readers. Eight decades after the Library's opening in 1911, its staff continues to honor the public weal in what can aptly be called a citadel of democracy. It is an honor to be associated with New York Public, and I am especially grateful to Paul for making it possible.

Tad Tuleja
Austin, Texas

INTRODUCTION

Honoring the People's Choices

"The throne we honor is the people's choice."
—Richard Sheridan

In 1987, a University of Virginia English professor, E. D. Hirsch, lit fires throughout the groves of academe with a call for educational reform entitled *Cultural Literacy*. In it he made the seemingly innocent observation that "literate Americans" share "a minimal core of background information" that enables them to "thrive in the modern world." Possession of that information he called "cultural literacy," and he specified it, in detail, in the book's Appendix—a "thinking American's list" that trundled graciously from "abominable snowman" down to "Zürich."

The list—and its underlying "canonical" assumptions—were instantly attacked by diverse partisans. Some believed that Hirsch was on to something, but that he hadn't gone nearly far enough. How could you call yourself literate, they asked, and not know the meaning of "semiotics"? Others, waving the banner of multiculturalism, denounced Hirsch and his ilk as cryptically elitist. If there *was* a canon, they observed, it was loaded—and pointed at the heads of the Third World. Still others mocked the very idea of canons. "What every American needs to know," they proclaimed, could never (and should never) be frozen; a plural nation needed plural truths.

Wherever one stands on the merits of these vociferous, if sometimes puerile, cultural positions, one basic lesson remains clear: Canons are *always* loaded. Anyone with the temerity to define what every American knows, or should know, does so subjectively, that is, under the burden of social background, educational experience, and personal taste. That is as true of Professor Hirsch's critics as of his champions. Whether you put Descartes before *houris,* or vice versa, you do so because your past has bred you so, has made you *that* type of cultural literate and not another.

For someone about to push his own canon into the fray, this lesson suggests an important corollary: Make it clear to your readers not only (as the 1960s had it) "where you're coming from," but also (as my wife is fond of saying), "where you bought your ticket." The savaging of Professor Hirsch might have been ameliorated, I suspect, had he checked his Ivy League credentials at the starting gate rather than touting them as "every American's" heritage. People take less umbrage at the Great Tradition when you don't represent it as universal writ.

Which brings me to my own subjective slant—one that focuses, unabashedly, on a Lesser Tradition. There's a certain irony in this, because Professor Hirsch and I got our educational tickets at the same stations. Indeed, in the mid-1960s, we haunted the very same alcoves in Yale's Sterling Library, and my senior essay there, on Wordsworth and Hölderlin, was much indebted to his book on Wordsworth and Schelling. By the late 1960s, however, as he was beginning his tenure at Mr. Jefferson's university, I was becoming addicted to popular culture. A master's thesis that I wrote in 1971 was a jejunely populist account of the Hollywood Western, and my doctoral work, as I write this, is in American folklore.

The *New York Public Library Book of Popular Americana* reflects this training. Its aim is to cover not what every American *needs* to know, but what the average American once knew and has since forgotten. It is an aid less to *Hochkunst* than to popular memory, because I have tried to record here the background information of Americans at large, not just the "thinking" ones. Thus I omit dignitaries like the logician Charles Sanders Peirce (who would not ring a bell with, say, Roseanne Arnold) to give more space to *Ozzie and Harriet* and Minnie Pearl.

This is not to snipe at the Great Tradition, for I do not condemn as elitist the modest supposition that high school graduates should be able to identify Appomattox. But our cultural heritage is more than battles and books. It includes not only "I have not yet begun to fight" but also *I Love Lucy;* not only Roger Williams but also Esther, Hank, and Ted. A book of "the popular" must take that into account. It must take seriously the interests of the great unwashed even if that means slighting, relatively speaking, the classics that appeal to Milton's "fit though few." That is the organizing principle of this collection. You will find brief and I trust helpful comments here on *American Gothic* and Andy Warhol's soup cans, but scant news of minimalist or conceptual art. There's more on Elizabeth than on Zachary Taylor, more on Burl than on Charles Ives, more on Harold Robbins than on Henry James.

The reader must not conclude from such comparisions than I find Harold Robbins more significant than Henry James. I don't. But the American people at large do not agree. They have voted with their feet at countless bookstores to make Robbins one of our all-time best-selling authors. I have yet to encounter anyone outside of an English class who will read *The Golden Bowl* without benefit of thumbscrews.

As its title indicates, *Popular Americana* focuses on those facets of culture that are at once distinctively American and broadly recognizable. It provides the basics on U.S. history from Sam Adams to the XYZ Affair; literary figures from Captain Ahab to Frank Yerby; folklore from John Alden to Yankee Doodle; Hollywood from Fred Astaire to X rating; popular music from "After the Ball" to "Zip Coon"; broadcasting from *Amos 'n' Andy* to *Wheel of Fortune;* "fine" art from the Ashcan school to Whistler's mother; sports from Henry Aaron to Babe Zaharias; and slang expressions from "aces and eights" to "zoot suit."

In addition to entries on individual people and works of art, I also include discussions of creative genres that have come to fullest flower on these shores. Many have been "enriched" by the media—a typical process in the home of Barnum and Edison. Our very folklore, indeed, is commercially massaged. Davy Crockett and Ichabod Crane, for example, survive in the collective consciousness via Walt Disney, while "poplore" heroes like Pecos Bill and Bugs Bunny are even more straightforwardly media inventions. I attend to them, as I attend to other "lowbrow" amusements like vaudeville, because to slight them is to slight the people themselves. Hence the entries on Tin Pan Alley and the comics, the Hollywood Western and the soaps, country music, show tunes, and rock 'n' roll. Here, as throughout the book, small capitals ("See Buddy HOLLY") indicate cross references to full entries.

A word on chronological scope. While I favor terms with a currently high "recognition factor," I modify that benchmark in two senses. First, I include many items which, although now obscure, were universally known in their time— like the Hall-Mills murder case and jumper Sam Patch. Second, with few exceptions I avoid the contemporary scene, with its intensely hyped, fifteen-minute wonders. A future volume, perhaps, might gauge the cultural impact of the Branch Davidians, Whitney Houston, and Jerry Seinfeld. Because it would be premature to do so now, I concentrate on stars with some patina.

I do not pretend that the result is either exhaustive or objective. In foraging through the thickets of our past, I have more than once felt kinship to Buridan's ass—that proverbial creature who, unable to choose between two piles of hay, starved to death while weighing their relative merits. Nettling choices, inevitably, had to be made, and this has meant that my intuitive sense of things, my subjective judgment calls, have been enlisted to recommend some haystacks over others. *Faute de omniscience,* it could not be otherwise.

No doubt the resulting coverage will pique some readers—tennis experts, perhaps, or fans of the Whigs. I ask them to remember, by way of apology, my commitment to chart the taste of the general public rather than that of the aficionado or partisan. I am sufficiently partisan myself to feel the costs here in fields untrodden and culture heroes unsung, but I have aimed for the nation's taste, not my own. *Popular Americana* covers those phenomena that have most broadly and deeply touched the national mood. Some of them have earned Pulitzer Prizes, others only the sniffs of sherry tipplers. All, in one way or another, are the people's choices. Woven together, they are the fabric of the streets and the fields, the still evolving tapestry of our everyday lives.

A&P The Great Atlantic and Pacific Tea Company, founded in 1869 by tea merchant George Huntington Hartford. Named in honor of that year's transcontinental railroad, it became the nation's first grocery chain.

Aaron, Hank (1934–) Baseball player. Born Henry Louis Aaron in Alabama, he played first for all-black teams, then in the major leagues for the Milwaukee (later Atlanta) Braves. He made sports history on April 8, 1974, when he broke Babe RUTH's 39-year-old career record by hitting his 715th home run. (The pitcher was the L.A. Dodgers' Al Downing.) Aaron retired two years later, leaving a new record of 755.

Abbott and Costello Bud Abbott (1895–1974) and Lou Costello (1906–59), one of Hollywood's most popular comedy teams. With lanky, debonair Abbott playing straight man to Costello's cherubic bungler, the pair headlined on vaudeville in the 1930s, then made over thirty hit farces in the 1940s and 1950s. Their most famous routine, "Who's on First?," appears on a plaque in the Baseball Hall of Fame.

Abdul-Jabbar, Kareem (1947–) Basketball player. After leading his UCLA team to three straight intercollegiate titles, Lew Alcindor joined the professional Milwaukee Bucks in 1969, adopted an Arabic name during the BLACK MUSLIMS' rise to prominence, and played spectacular ball for the ensuing decade. In his career with the Bucks and later with the Los Angeles Lakers, he averaged almost thirty points a game, retiring with still-standing records of most games played (1,560) and most blocked shots (3,189). With a career total of 17,440 rebounds, he is third behind Wilt CHAMBERLAIN and Bill RUSSELL.

Abie's Irish Rose A 1922 comedy by Anne Nichols about the problematic romance of a Jewish boy and Irish girl. After a record 2,327 performances on Broadway, it generated a novel, a radio series, and a Hollywood film.

Abilene Kansas railhead which, in the 1860s, became the major shipping point for Texas cattle bound East. As the northern terminus of the CHISHOLM TRAIL, it became one of the wildest western cow towns, with Wild Bill HICKOK serving as marshal in 1871. Abilene was also the birthplace of Dwight D. EISENHOWER.

abolitionists Those who, in the decades preceding the Civil War, advocated an immediate and total end to the institution of slavery. Notable abolitionists included William Lloyd Garrison, who edited the antislavery paper *Liberator;* his lieutenant, Wendell Phillips, who banned all slave-grown products from his home; escaped slave turned lecturer Frederick DOUGLASS; Harriet Beecher STOWE; Julia

Ward Howe; and John Brown. Many of the abolitionists also supported wo-men's suffrage.

Abraham Lincoln Brigade   Popular name for the American volunteers who fought on the Republican side in the Spanish Civil War (1936–39). Part of the antifascist International Brigades, they were the first U.S. troops to be fully integrated.

Academy Awards   Awards presented annually by the Academy of Motion Pic-ture Arts and Sciences for excellence in the making of films. Nominees are chosen by their peers (actors nominate actors, designers nominate designers), and winners are selected by secret ballot. The actual winners' award, a gold statuette of a knight standing on a reel of film, has been called Oscar since 1931, when an Academy member noted its resemblance to her uncle Oscar. The awards cere-mony, televised each spring with considerable ballyhoo, is itself frequently re-ferred to as the Oscars. Winners' names, announced by celebrities, are kept in sealed envelopes until the event, and the revelation follows the ritualized request "The envelope, please."

Acadia   See Cajuns.

aces and eights   In poker, a pair of aces and a pair of eights. Known as the dead man's hand because Wild Bill Hickok was supposedly holding it when he was murdered by Jack McCall.

acid   Lysergic acid diethylamide (LSD). From the 1960s, "to do acid" or "drop acid" is to ingest LSD; an "acidhead," or simply "head," is a devotee of the drug. The musically inclined played "acid rock."

Acres of Diamonds   An inspirational book by Baptist minister Russell H. Con-well (1843–1925), who delivered it thousands of times as a lecture before its publication (1888). Like Andrew Carnegie's "Gospel of Wealth," it promoted the philanthropic virtues of accumulation. Conwell also founded Temple University.

Acuff, Roy   (1903–92) Singer. Often called the King of Country Music, Acuff was the Grand Ole Opry's first major singing star. The son of a Tennessee Baptist preacher, he performed with the Smoky Mountain Boys, favoring tradi-tional and sacred tunes such as "Wabash Cannonball" and "Great Speckled Bird." Through performances and income from Acuff-Rose Publications—the nation's first country music publishing house—Acuff built a personal fortune as solid as his following. Country-bred G.I.s were among his greatest fans, and Ernie Pyle related that during a Japanese attack on Okinawa, entrenched Marines heard the insulting battle cry "To hell with Roosevelt, to hell with Babe Ruth, to hell with Roy Acuff!"

Adams, Andy   (1859–1935) Writer. His novelistic depiction of an 1882 cattle drive, *The Log of a Cowboy* (1903), was so realistic that many readers took it for autobiography. Although not a professional cowboy himself, Adams was inti-mately familiar with the cattle country, and his attempt to counter DIME NOVEL mythmaking with factual description was thoroughly successful. Folklorist Richard Dorson called the book the "first and classic narrative of the trail drive."

Adams, Ansel (1902–84) Photographer. With Imogen Cunningham and Edward Weston, Adams was a founder of Group f/64, which revolted against the impressionistic softness of the pictorialist school and brought high-contrast, "straight" photography into vogue. Born in San Francisco, Adams was known for his brilliant black-and-white scenes of the American West, especially the natural grandeur of the national parks. His various "moonrise" images, including one taken at Yosemite, are among the most widely reproduced of photographic images.

Adams, John (1735–1826) Second president of the United States (1789–97), a believer in government by "the rich, the well-born, and the able." A Boston lawyer, he defended British troops against murder charges after the BOSTON MASSACRE, helped to draft the DECLARATION OF INDEPENDENCE, and in 1789 became George Washington's vice president—a post he called "the most insignificant office that ever the invention of man contrived or his imagination conceived." The Adams administration saw the XYZ AFFAIR and the passage of the Alien and Sedition Acts (1789), whose unpopularity signaled the end of the Federalist era (see POLITICAL PARTIES).

Adams, Maude (1872–1953). Actress. One of the turn of the century's most adored female performers, she specialized in melodrama, especially the plays of James M. Barrie. His PETER PAN, in which she played Peter, was her crowning achievement.

Adams, Samuel (1722–1803) "Penman of the Revolution." After graduating from Harvard, Adams nearly ran his father's beer business into the ground before finding his métier in political propaganda. An ardent foe of British tax policies, he denounced them in so many pamphlets and inflammatory speeches that colonial Governor Thomas Hutchinson called him an "incendiary." He also organized both the Committees of Correspondence and the SONS OF LIBERTY, fanned public ire over the BOSTON MASSACRE, and was a ringleader of the BOSTON TEA PARTY. Once the war began, he railed in Congress against reconciliation with the Crown, and after independence he served a term as Massachusetts's governor. Given his poor showing as a brewer, it is ironic that Samuel Adams ale has borrowed his name.

Addams, Charles (1912–88) Cartoonist. Addams's whimsically macabre cartoons, featuring a mansion full of breezily eccentric ghouls, started appearing in THE NEW YORKER magazine in the 1930s and were collected in *Drawn and Quartered* (1942) and other volumes. The continued appeal of Addams's warped humor led to television's *Addams Family* (1962–64) and two feature films (1991 and 1993).

Addams, Jane (1860–1935). Social worker. Influenced by British settlement houses, which provided social activities, education, and day care to the poor, Addams founded an American counterpart, Chicago's Hull House, in 1889. Her story of its work, *Twenty Years at Hull House* (1910), is a classic document of the social gospel. She won the Nobel Peace Prize in 1931.

Adler, Polly (1900–62) Madam. In the 1920s and 1930s, Adler ran New York City's most famous house of prostitution—a finely appointed twelve-room apartment on the fashionable East Side. Among her friends was the writer Robert

Benchley. Among her girls' customers were gangsters like Lucky Luciano and Dutch Schultz as well as prominent members of New York high society.

affluent society Catchphrase for the economic exuberance of the post–World War II era. From *The Affluent Society* (1958), in which liberal economist John Kenneth Galbraith questioned the growth of production at the expense of "social" values.

African Queen, The A 1952 film directed by John HUSTON, based on a novel by British writer C. S. Forester. It depicts the comic though hazardous attempt by a missionary spinster (Katharine HEPBURN) and a grizzled boat captain (Humphrey BOGART) to destroy a German gunboat on Africa's Lake Victoria. Bogart's performance earned him an Academy Award.

afro A "natural" hairdo popular among black men and women in the 1960s and 1970s. The hair was allowed to grow free and full, rather than being "processed" down to simulate Caucasian styles. The name reflected the wearers' belief in the style's African origin.

"After the Ball" A waltz composed in 1892 by Charles K. Harris. Thanks partly to plugging at the following year's Chicago World's Fair, it became the sheet-music wonder of its day, selling an estimated 10 million copies.

aggie (1) An agate marble. Prized by children as "shooters" between the world wars. (2) A student at an agricultural college or a university with an "ag school" tradition. The aggie is frequently depicted, on rival nonaggie campuses, as the ultimate numskull. At the University of Texas, for example, "aggie jokes" denigrate the intelligence of students at neighboring Texas A&M: "How many aggies does it take to change a lightbulb? Four: one to hold the bulb and three to turn the chair." "Professor: How many seconds are there in a year? Aggie: Twelve: January second, February second . . ."

Ahab, Captain The tortured protagonist of Herman Melville's novel MOBY-DICK. His monomaniacal pursuit of the white whale that has crippled him results in disaster for himself and his crew. Gregory PECK portrayed him with hooded intensity in John HUSTON's 1956 film.

"Ain't Misbehavin' " See Fats WALLER.

air guitar The mimicking of a rock guitarist's hand and body motions by someone without an instrument. Typically "performed" to recorded music for theatrical or humorous effect.

Alamo A Spanish mission in San Antonio, Texas, site of the most famous battle in the Texas war for independence. After being besieged by forces under Mexican dictator SANTA ANNA, about two hundred Americans lost their lives there in a final onslaught (March 6, 1836), with their martyrdom making "Remember the Alamo!" an instant rallying cry. Texas won its autonomy from Mexico six weeks later. Among those who died at the Alamo were Davy CROCKETT, James BOWIE, and the garrison commander, lawyer William B. TRAVIS.

As the end approached, Travis is said to have drawn a line in the compound sand with his sword, offering the chance to escape to anyone who refused to cross it. According to some sources, the one man who chose escape, Moses (or Louis) Rose, ended his life in obscure debauchery in New Orleans; popular legend says that no one refused to stay. The battle is the subject of John WAYNE's directorial film debut, *The Alamo* (1960), starring Wayne himself as buckskin-clad Davy Crockett.

Alamogordo   Town in New Mexico near which the world's first atomic explosion took place in a test on July 16, 1945. It remains the site of Holloman Air Force Base and White Sands Proving Ground.

Alcatraz   A notorious federal prison, nicknamed the Rock, which sat on rocky Alcatraz Island in San Francisco Bay. Originally a Spanish fortress, then a military prison, it became a federal penitentiary in 1933. Until its closing thirty years later, it housed such dignitaries as Al CAPONE and the BIRDMAN OF ALCATRAZ, earning a reputation as an escapeproof internment center. The handful of convicts who did get over its walls were believed to have drowned in the rapid currents of the surrounding bay. *Alcatraz* is the Spanish word for "pelican."

Alcott, Louisa May   (1832–88) Writer. The daughter of utopian reformer Bronson Alcott, Louisa May knew Ralph Waldo EMERSON and Henry David THOREAU as a child, served as a nurse in the Civil War, and spoke widely in her later years on women's suffrage and temperance. She achieved renown with her letters from the front, *Hospital Sketches* (1863), and although she wrote hundreds of other works and was a regular contributor to THE ATLANTIC MONTHLY, she is popularly remembered for a single novel, LITTLE WOMEN. Its success led to the sequels *Little Men* (1871) and *Jo's Boys* (1886).

Alden, John   (ca. 1599–1687). In tradition and in Henry Wadsworth LONGFELLOW's poem, the Puritan paramour John Alden is an unwitting swain who pleads his friend Miles STANDISH's case to Priscilla Mullins and is met by the coy response "Why don't you speak for yourself, John?" The historical Alden was Priscilla's husband, Standish's friend, a signer of the MAYFLOWER COMPACT, and a respected leader of the PLYMOUTH COLONY.

Aldrich Family, The   A sitcom inspired by a Clifford Goldsmith play and scripted by him for *The Rudy* VALLEE *Show* before entering a long run (1939–53) on radio and a shorter one (1949–53) on television. Henry Aldrich was a genial adolescent whose gift for SNAFU generated humorous predicaments. The show popularized Mrs. Aldrich's call "Henreee! Henry Aldrich!"; Henry's response, "Coming, Mother"; and his expression "Golly jeepers!"

"Alexander's Ragtime Band"   A dance tune (1911) by Irving BERLIN. More a rapid march than a rag, it was the young composer's first success.

Alger, Horatio   (1834–99) Writer. A Massachusetts-born Unitarian minister, Alger moved to New York in 1866 and the next year had his first literary success with the serialized novel *Ragged Dick*. Its endearing formula—poor but industrious lad makes good—sustained Alger through over one hundred books, including the best-selling *Luck and Pluck* (1869) and *Tattered Tom* (1871); it also contributed to the national myth of the self-made man. Hence "Horatio Alger story" for any rags-to-riches tale.

Algonquin (1) Broadly speaking, a native American language group whose members stretched from the Eastern seaboard to the Rocky Mountains, including peoples as culturally distinct as the CHEYENNE and the DELAWARE. (2) Narrowly, an eastern contingent of this group which occupied the area between the St. Lawrence River and Virginia; it included the Narraganset, Mohican, Delaware, Shawnee, and Powhatan peoples. Traditional enemies of the IROQUOIS LEAGUE, they sided with the French in the FRENCH AND INDIAN WAR, then with the British in the WAR OF 1812.

Algonquin Round Table A group of writers who met informally from the 1920s to the 1940s in the dining room of New York's Algonquin Hotel, providing endless merriment for gossip columnists and quip enthusiasts. Frequenters of the booze-and-banter fests included George S. Kaufman (see KAUFMAN AND HART), Harpo Marx (see MARX BROTHERS), Dorothy PARKER, and Alexander WOOLLCOTT.

Ali, Muhammad (1942–) Boxer. Among the most colorful personalities in sports history, Cassius Clay won a gold medal at the 1960 Olympic Games, took the heavyweight championship away from Sonny Liston four years later, and then embarked on a professional career that was as notable for his politics and theatrics as for his skill in the ring. Converting to the BLACK MUSLIM faith and changing his name to Muhammad Ali, he was stripped of his title in 1967 when he refused army service on religious grounds. Reinstated in 1970, he lost and then regained the crown twice in fights with Joe Frazier and Leon Spinks—becoming the first man to win the title three times. His self-confidence was most succinctly announced in his signature boast, "I'm the greatest," while his fluid but hard-hitting ring style was aptly described in his promise (before the Liston fight) that he would "float like a butterfly, sting like a bee."

Alibi Ike One who makes excuses for incompetence or misbehavior. From the title character of a Ring LARDNER story (1924), which also inspired a popular comic strip.

All About Eve A 1950 film that won the best picture and five other Oscars, including two for writer/director Joseph Mankiewicz. The backstage story about the rise of an ambitious actress sparkles with venomous gems from leading lady Bette DAVIS. As aging star Margo Channing, she delivers the film's most famous line to a roomful of partygoers: "Fasten your seat belts. It's going to be a bumpy night." Best supporting actor George Sanders appears as a jaded critic, a young Marilyn MONROE as his "companion."

All in the Family See Archie BUNKER.

All the King's Men A Pulitzer Prize novel (1946) by Robert Penn WARREN. The model for its protagonist, southern demagogue Willie Stark, was Huey LONG. Filmed in 1949, it won Academy Awards for producer/director Robert Rossen and actor Broderick Crawford as Stark.

"All the News That's Fit to Print" See NEW YORK TIMES.

All the President's Men See WOODWARD AND BERNSTEIN.

All-American (1) Designating an athlete, or a team of athletes, selected for superior performance. The first All-Americans were football players chosen for a sports weekly in 1889 by Walter CAMP. (2) Displaying the high spirits and competence thought to be typically American qualities, as in the expressions "All-American boy" and "All-American girl." See, for example, Frank MERRIWELL.

Allen, Ethan (1738–89) Revolutionary War hero and leader of Vermont's GREEN MOUNTAIN BOYS, Allen achieved notoriety in 1775 when, with the assistance of Benedict ARNOLD, his Yankee irregulars captured FORT TICONDEROGA from the British; legend has him asking for its surrender "in the name of the great Jehovah and the Continental Congress." A mythically outsize figure even in his lifetime, he was known for his physical prowess, his fondness for drink, and his blatant impiety—the latter trait making the Jehovah line highly unlikely. In one legend, he severs a nail with his teeth. In another, surprised by white-sheeted pranksters on a dark road, he invites the "devils" home because "I married your sister." In a third, bitten by a rattlesnake while asleep, he wakes up complaining of mosquito bites—as the snake emits a loud belch and passes out. Ironically, given his national status, Allen was an ardent Vermont separatist, vocally championing its independence in negotiations with the British. That the Green Mountain State was briefly an independent republic (1777–91) was due in part to his efforts.

Allen, Fred (1894–1956) Pseudonym of John F. Sullivan, a juggler and comedian whose quip-filled radio show ran first as *Town Hall Tonight* (1934–39), then until 1949 as *The Fred Allen Show*. A comics' comic, Allen promoted a humorous feud with Jack BENNY, wrote skits for the Mighty Allen Art Players (a name later adapted by Johnny CARSON on THE TONIGHT SHOW), and used mythical Allen's Alley to introduce such comic antiheroes as farmer Titus Moody and Senator CLAGHORN. He once defined communism as a system where "nobody's got nothing, but everybody's working."

Allen, Gracie See BURNS AND ALLEN.

Allen, Woody (1935–) Filmmaker. Born Allen Konigsberg, he began as a writer for Sid CAESAR and moved to stand-up comedy in the 1960s. His films explore the nuances of insecurity among rattled but sophisticated contemporaries. His film *Annie Hall* was the best picture of 1977, winning further Oscars for Allen as writer and director and for his leading lady, Diane Keaton, in the title role.

alligator A large, much-feared crocodilian indigenous to the southeastern United States. Unknown in Europe, the creature became an early emblem of America, and then of American "wildness." Davy CROCKETT and other frontier boasters claimed to be "half alligator, half horse." The creature's menacing nature is evoked in the expression "up to your ass in alligators" (meaning to be in serious trouble) and the recurrent legend that pet baby alligators, brought from Florida by vacationing New Yorkers and then flushed down toilets, have grown to monsters in the city's sewers. "Alligator wrestling" by SEMINOLE Indians has been a Florida tourist attraction since the 1920s.

almanacs See Davy CROCKETT; THE OLD FARMER'S ALMANAC; POOR RICHARD'S ALMANACK.

almighty dollar Struck by the commercial energy of his fellow Americans, writer Washington IRVING coined this phrase to describe "that great object of universal devotion throughout our land." It appeared first in his travel sketch "The Creole Village."

aloha   Hawaiian for "love." Hawaii, where the term is used as a greeting, is the Aloha State. Its prestate anthem, written by Queen LILIUOKALANI, is "Aloha Oe" (Love to Thee).

alphabet agency   Any of various agencies established under the NEW DEAL, for example, NRA, CCC, WPA, FDIC.

alphabet soup   A hodgepodge or potpourri. From a CAMPBELL'S SOUP Company product containing pieces of pasta shaped like letters as well as various vegetables.

Amana   See UTOPIAN COMMUNITIES.

"Amazing Grace"   Hymn written in the eighteenth century by English minister John Newton. In country, folk, and gospel versions, it is a performance perennial with American musicians.

America   (1) Popular term for the United States of America, and more broadly for the two American continents. From Amerigo Vespucci (1445–1512), a Florentine navigator who sailed to South America shortly after Columbus and who, unlike Columbus, recognized the true import of the 1492 discovery: Vespucci was the first to identify the Western lands as a *mundus novus,* or "New World." The term "America" dates from a 1507 map on which German cartographer Martin Waldseemüller showed the southern continent as having been "discovered by Amerigo." Notwithstanding many Americans' disdain of Vespucci for supposedly filching the Genoan's laurels, his contemporaries thought him, in Columbus's words, a "most worthy man." (2) "America," a patriotic song more commonly called (from its opening line) "My Country, 'Tis of Thee." Written by Massachusetts clergyman Samuel Francis Smith, it follows the same tune as the British anthem "God Save the King" and was first sung publicly in Boston on July 4, 1831.

America, Miss   See MISS AMERICA PAGEANT.

"America the Beautiful"   The country's unofficial national anthem, celebrating the physical wonders of the North American continent "from sea to shining sea." The words are those of an 1893 poem by Wellesley College English professor Katharine Lee Bates, who was inspired by a climb up Pikes Peak; the music is by Samuel A. Ward. Lovers of the song periodically tout it as a replacement for the notoriously "unsingable" "STAR-SPANGLED BANNER."

American Bandstand   Television show. The first rock 'n' roll hit parade show, *American Bandstand* presented records and lip-synching live acts in a studio full of grinning, dancing teenagers—a format that made it the ABC network's longest-running show (1957–87). The host, former Philadelphia disc jockey Dick Clark, midwifed dozens of pop stars into national prominence. Among the acts that debuted on *Bandstand* were SIMON AND GARFUNKEL, Frankie Avalon, and Chubby Checker (see THE TWIST).

American dream The attainment of material and social success. The United States' democratic tradition makes it an article of national faith that such success is available to all who are willing to work for it. Among the quasi-sacred formulas encoding the idea are "upward mobility," "rags to riches," "pulling yourself up by your bootstraps," "land of opportunity," and "self-made man." See also Horatio ALGER.

American Expeditionary Force The American troops sent to Europe in 1917 upon the United States's entry into World War I. The AEF was under the command of John J. PERSHING.

American Gothic A 1930 portrait of a midwestern farm couple by the regionalist artist Grant Wood (1891–1942). One of the most widely recognized—and widely parodied—of American paintings, it employs a stark, wittily stylized realism to evoke the rugged simplicity of rural life.

American in Paris, An A 1928 composition by George GERSHWIN which inspired Vincente MINNELLI's Oscar-winning 1951 musical. It featured imaginative choreography by Gene KELLY and marked the screen debut of his costar, Leslie Caron.

American Legion The United States's largest veterans' organization. Founded in 1919, it champions veterans' causes, promotes civic awareness through speaking contests and model congresses, and stands for military preparedness and national pride.

American Party See KNOW-NOTHING PARTY.

American Revolution See REVOLUTIONARY WAR.

America's Cup In 1851, after the New York Yacht Club's schooner *America* bested British opponents in a race around the Isle of Wight, the crew took home a large silver cup as a prize. Dubbed the America's Cup, it has remained the symbol of sailing supremacy ever since. American vessels defeated all challengers for the cup until 1983, when the yacht *Australia* beat the American *Liberty* off Newport, Rhode Island. Subsequent races have been won by the United States (1987), Australia (1988), and the United States (1992).

America's Sweetheart (1) Nickname for Mary PICKFORD. (2) In the plural, America's Sweethearts, a nickname for Nelson EDDY and Jeanette MacDonald.

Amish One of various Mennonite sects that immigrated to the United States in the eighteenth century, they are also called Old Order Mennonites. Followers of the seventeenth-century Swiss reformer Jakob Amman, they are known as Plain People from their commitment to a simple farming life, which rejects commercial products such as store-bought clothing, automobiles, and electricity. Concentrated in Lancaster County, Pennsylvania, the industrious Amish have accommodated slowly to the "world," and still drive horse-drawn buggies to the local markets. See also PENNSYLVANIA DUTCH.

Amos 'n' Andy A radio, then television, series about two black men which, after decades of controversial popularity, left the networks because of political pressure. Quiet, steady Amos and ambitious, gullible Andy were the creations of Freeman Gosden and Charles Correll, white actors who did their voices on radio (1929–48) and oversaw the TV series (1951–53) until its demise. Since the main characters were constantly looking for extra income, the radio show struck a chord with Depression audiences, and at one point the number of fans reached 40 million. On television, with black actors replacing Gosden and Correll, the show's racial stereotyping became more evident, and in 1951, the NAACP condemned it as a "one-sided caricature" of black Americans. The focus of resentment was less Amos, a family man, than the bumbling Andy and his exuberant mentor, the scheming Kingfish. After two seasons the show went into syndication, having made broadcasting history as the first all-black TV show.

"Anchors Aweigh"   The U.S. Navy's official service song, composed in 1906 by Charles Zimmerman and Alfred Miles. It was originally a fight song for the Army-Navy football game.

Anderson, "Broncho Billy"   (1882–1971) Actor. The movie industry's first cowboy star, Max Aronson played several roles in the landmark GREAT TRAIN ROBBERY and then, as Broncho Billy Anderson, made the 1907 *The Bandit Makes Good*. This led to hundreds of shorts with titles like *Broncho Billy's Redemption, Broncho Billy's Indian Romance,* and *Broncho Billy and the Revenue Agent.* He retired from films after World War I.

André, John   (1750–80) Spy. Major André was a British army officer hanged on October 2, 1780, for conspiring with Benedict ARNOLD to accept the surrender of West Point. Refined and worldly, he went to the gallows so stoically that he was later romanticized as a "gallant" officer.

Andretti, Mario   (1940–) Race car driver. The Italian-born Andretti was a fixture on the INDIANAPOLIS 500 track throughout the 1970s and 1980s. He won that event in 1969 and placed in 1981, 1985, and 1991. He is the only Indy 500 winner also to win the Daytona 500 stock car championship (1967) and the World Grand Prix title (1978).

Andy Hardy   See Mickey ROONEY.

Anglo   A Mexican-American term for a non-Hispanic white American, especially one of Anglo-Saxon descent.

animal crackers   Developed in 1902 by the National Biscuit Company, Barnum's Animal Crackers were originally a seasonal promotion: The box's carrying string was designed for hanging it on a Christmas tree. Named for P. T. BARNUM, they inspired the 1930 MARX BROTHERS film *Animal Crackers* and the song "Animal Crackers in My Soup," which Shirley TEMPLE sang in *Curly Top* (1935).

Annapolis   The capital of Maryland and the site of the U.S. Naval Academy, started there in 1845. "Annapolis" also refers to the academy itself, whose students are referred to as midshipmen. The Annapolis degree leads to a commission in the U.S. Navy or Marine Corps.

Annie   See "LITTLE ORPHAN ANNIE" (2).

Annie Get Your Gun   See Irving BERLIN; Dorothy FIELDS; Ethel MERMAN; Annie OAKLEY.

Anthony, Susan B.   (1820–1906) Women's rights pioneer. Raised a Quaker, Anthony began her life of activism in the temperance and antislavery movements, turning to women's issues when she experienced discrimination from male reformers. The generally acknowledged mother of the suffrage movement, she helped to found the National Woman Suffrage Association and was arrested in 1872 for voting illegally in a city election. In 1979 the U.S. government honored her efforts by putting her likeness on a silver dollar.

"Any man who hates small dogs and children can't be all bad"   Writer Leo Rosten's estimation of W. C. FIELDS, often erroneously attributed to Fields himself.

Anything Goes   (1934) A Broadway musical that was LINDSAY AND CROUSE'S first collaboration. The Cole PORTER score, interpreted winningly by Ethel MERMAN, included the title song, "You're the Top," and "I GET A KICK OUT OF YOU."

Apache   A native American people of the Southwest. Traditionally hunters, gatherers, and farmers, they attained a reputation as fierce warriors in the nineteenth century under the Chiricahua leaders COCHISE and GERONIMO. Second only to the SIOUX in popularity among moviemakers, Apaches figure in such western classics as John Ford's *Fort Apache* (1946) and Delmer Daves's *Broken Arrow* (1950). Their alleged wildness inspired the term "apache" for Parisian ruffians.

Apollo   In 1961 President John F. KENNEDY proposed that a U.S. manned space flight reach the moon within a decade. The subsequent space effort, dubbed the Apollo program, reached its goal on July 20, 1969, when the flight commander of *Apollo 11*, Neil ARMSTRONG, stepped onto the moon's Sea of Tranquility. "Apollo" itself was a misnomer: The Greek Apollo was a solar, not a lunar, god.

Apollo Theater   A burlesque house turned variety theater in New York's HARLEM, the Apollo showcased mainly black talent for almost fifty years (1934–83). Before World War II, amateur nights sparked the careers of Lena HORNE and Sarah VAUGHAN; later, the fare shifted toward RHYTHM AND BLUES and SOUL music. Before it began to decline in the 1970s, the Apollo was as well known for popular music as the COTTON CLUB had earlier been for jazz.

Appalachia   Although geographically coterminous with the APPALACHIAN MOUNTAIN system, "Appalachia" refers more exactly to the impoverished uplands of Kentucky and West Virginia, long victims of extensive coal-mining and government neglect. The region's poverty became a cause célèbre in the 1960s, although its reputation for backwardness was then a century old. Since the days of the HATFIELD-MCCOY feud, the area's "mountaineers' have been derided by outsiders as MOONSHINE-swilling rubes, and the barefoot HILLBILLY remains a stock figure in media stereotyping (see L'IL ABNER).

Appalachian Mountains   A system of gently contoured mountains that runs from Newfoundland into Georgia and Alabama. Before the CUMBERLAND GAP was opened in the 1770s, it inhibited westward expansion, especially from the South, and thus indirectly contributed to the growth of the eastern seaboard. Rich in scenery and folklore, the Appalachians include such ranges as the White, Green, CATSKILL, Blue Ridge, and Great Smoky. The system's highest point is Mount Mitchell (6,684 feet) in North Carolina. The Appalachian Trail, a 2,000-mile-long hiker's path, runs from Springer Mountain in northern Georgia to Maine's Katahdin.

Appaloosa   A white or light gray horse dappled with brown ''pawprint'' markings. Bred by the NEZ PERCÉ Indians along the Palouse River of Washington and Idaho, Appaloosas were popular in the WILD WEST SHOWS.

apple   Hardy and prolific, apple trees were so widely planted in colonial America that they came to symbolize the country itself: hence ''American as apple pie.'' Apple cider, the alcoholic drink of choice for most Americans into the nineteenth century, gave us the term ''applejack'' by around the War of 1812. ''Apple-pie order'' appeared at the same time, while the fruit's versatility inspired such kitchen delicacies as apple brown Betty, apple cobbler, and applesauce. The last came to mean ''foolishness'' in the first decade of this century, at the same time certainty was first expressed by the simile ''as sure as God made little green apples.'' The 1920s insult ''apple polisher,'' for a fawning subordinate, reflects the student custom of bringing an apple for the teacher in communities where teachers were paid in farmers' produce. See also BIG APPLE.

Apple Annies   Women who sold apples on street corners during the Great Depression. Such unlicensed vending was a not uncommon means of support in the lean thirties.

Appleseed, Johnny   (1775–1847). Itinerant preacher. Born John Chapman in western Massachusetts, this mild Swedenborgian eccentric spent forty years tramping barefoot in the Ohio wilderness, warning settlers of Indian attacks, rescuing ill-treated animals from their owners, wearing a coffee sack tunic and a tin plate hat, and everywhere planting apple seeds. Many of today's Ohio apple orchards sprang from forebear trees grown by this American St. Francis.

Appomattox Courthouse   A small Virginia town where, on April 9, 1865, Robert E. LEE surrendered the Army of Northern Virginia to Ulysses S. GRANT. Although fighting continued elsewhere for two weeks, the action effectively ended the Civil War. Painters have frequently depicted the signing of the surrender papers, and a legendary aura has become attached to Grant's magnanimity. One popular tale says that Lee offered the Union leader his ceremonial sword and that Grant refused it. That much is probably fiction, although Grant did allow Confederate officers to keep their side arms and prohibited his own troops from celebrating the somber occasion.

Arbuckle, Fatty   (1887–1933). Actor. One of the comedy kings of the silent-film era, Roscoe ''Fatty'' Arbuckle had plied a 300-pound frame and a gift for slapstick into a reputation second only to Charlie CHAPLIN's and Buster KEATON's when, in 1921, he was accused of raping a young starlet, Virginia Rappe. When she died of internal injuries, he was indicted for manslaughter, and although the jury acquitted him, the ensuing scandal ruined his career. It also encouraged the film industry, already nervous about Hollywood's image as a city of sin, to set up the HAYS OFFICE the following year.

Arcaro, Eddie   (1916–   ) Jockey. In a 31-year career, Arcaro won the Kentucky Derby a record five times and brought two mounts (Whirlaway and Citation) to the Triple Crown. When he retired, he had jockeyed 4,779 winners.

Archie   Cartoon character. Often called the oldest teenager in America, Archie Andrews was created in 1941 by cartoonist Bob Montana. Comic book appearances over half a century have been supplemented by news strips and animated films, all set in the squeaky-clean atmosphere of Riverdale High. Archie's friends are levelheaded Betty, wealthy Veronica, and the gently ingratiating oddball Jughead.

archy and mehitabel   A cockroach and cat, respectively, they were the creations of journalist Don Marquis (1878–1937), who published humorous, often versified accounts of their adventures in New York newspapers in the 1920s and 1930s. His conceit was that archy, a reincarnated poet, wrote the columns by jumping onto typewriter keys—without capitalization because he could not work the shift key.

Arkansas toothpick   The Bowie knife. The term was first recorded in 1836—the year of James BOWIE's death at the ALAMO.

"The Arkansas Traveler"   A traditional comic song relating a traveler's difficulty in getting food, shelter, or even conversation from an Arkansas backwoodsman until his fiddle-playing transforms him into an honored guest. The story inspired several CURRIER & IVES prints, and the fiddle tune is a bluegrass standard.

Arky   A Depression-era migrant from Arkansas. See also OKIES.

Arlen, Harold   (1905–86) Songwriter. Best remembered for Judy GARLAND's signature tune, "Over the Rainbow," he also produced many other nightclub standards, including "STORMY WEATHER," "That Old Black Magic," and "Blues in the Night," the last two with lyricist Johnny MERCER. See also THE WIZARD OF OZ.

Arlington National Cemetery   Established in 1864 in Arlington, Virginia, this 500-acre site is the burial place for Americans killed in the service of their country. In addition to the graves of military personnel, it also contains the TOMB OF THE UNKNOWN SOLDIER and a memorial to assassinated President John F. KENNEDY.

armadillo   A small, shell-encased mammal found from the southern United States to South America. To Spanish explorers, it was a symbol of the New World. In the 1960s, its placidity made it an emblem of the Southwest COUNTERCULTURE. Today, because of its alleged dull-wittedness, it is affectionately known as the Texas turkey.

Armory Show   A painting exhibition held at New York City's 69th Regiment Armory in 1913. American painters of the ASHCAN SCHOOL were prominent, but the show also included hundreds of European modernists, affording Americans their first views of Picasso, Braque, Kandinsky, Cézanne, and Matisse. The show-stopper was Marcel Duchamp's *Nude Descending a Staircase*, which provoked vigorous debate over the virtues of abstract art.

armpit of the nation Any disagreeable or unattractive place, as perceived by outsiders. Because of its high pollution level, the term is often applied to New Jersey.

Armstrong, Jack See JACK ARMSTRONG, THE ALL-AMERICAN BOY.

Armstrong, Louis "Satchmo" (1900–71) Trumpeter, singer. Probably the most widely recognized jazz musician of all time, Armstrong studied music in a New Orleans boys' home and then under Dixieland trumpeter King Oliver. After playing briefly with Oliver's band in Chicago, he moved to New York, where he developed a "hot," inventive style that made his name. He scored a 1929 hit with Fats WALLER's tune "Ain't Misbehavin'," then acquired a new continent of fans and the nickname Satchmo (from his satchel-size mouth) on the first of many European tours. As well known for his raspy vocals and ebullient personality as for his playing, he was already universally loved by jazz musicians when he became a mainstream star at the age of sixty-four with a distinctive version of the Broadway show tune "Hello, Dolly!" In addition to his frequent television and movie appearances, he was also an official goodwill ambassador for the State Department. Fellow jazzman Teddy Wilson spoke for many when he called Armstrong "the greatest jazz musician that's ever been."

Armstrong, Neil (1930–) Astronaut. Armstrong made history on July 20, 1969, when he became the first human to set foot on the moon. The *Apollo 11* flight commander, he performed this feat at 10:56 P.M. (eastern daylight time), while uttering the static-garbled comment "That's one small step for [a] man, one giant leap for mankind." Much journalistic ink has been spent debating the significance, if any, of the questionable article.

Arnaz, Desi See I LOVE LUCY.

Arnold, Benedict (1741–1801) The nation's most famous turncoat, with his very name long a byword for treason. Arnold's military career before his defection was exceptional. He helped Ethan ALLEN in the capture of FORT TICONDEROGA, served brilliantly in the Saratoga campaign, and was twice wounded in the patriot cause. But debt and disappointment over what he considered slow promotion embittered him, and in 1780, as commander of a strategically important American fort at West Point, he conspired to turn it over to British forces. The plot was discovered; Arnold's accomplice, Major John ANDRÉ, was hanged; and Arnold, then a major general, fled to the British. After a year fighting his former comrades, he moved to England, where he remained until he died.

Arnold, Eddy (1918–) Singer. Country music's first crossover star, the "Tennessee Plowboy" sang briefly for the GRAND OLE OPRY in the 1940s, then took his polished, urbane style to radio and television, bringing country songs to many who had never heard them before. He dominated the country charts in the 1950s with such number-one hits as "Bouquet of Roses" and "Cattle Call."

Arrow shirt (or Arrow collar) man   An early 1900s advertising symbol for Arrow shirts. Cleanly virile, he was instrumental in dramatically boosting company sales.

Arrowsmith   A Pulitzer Prize novel (1925) by Sinclair LEWIS about a doctor torn between idealism and profit. John FORD directed a 1931 movie version with Ronald Colman in the title role.

arsenal of democracy   Calling for "lend-lease" assistance to the Allies in a 1940 speech, President Franklin D. ROOSEVELT used this phrase to describe the United States in what he proposed would be a noncombat role. In passing the arms supply act the following year, Congress readied the nation for entry into the war.

Arsenic and Old Lace   A 1941 comedy by Joseph Kesselring (1902–67). Produced by LINDSAY AND CROUSE, it ran for over fourteen hundred performances on Broadway. It concerns the hilariously venomous activities of two elderly women, Abbie and Martha Brewster, who make a habit of poisoning guests and burying them in the cellar. The one sane member of the Brewster family, their nephew, Mortimer, was played with rattled brilliance by Cary GRANT in Frank CAPRA's 1944 film.

Articles of Confederation   The nation's first constitution, in effect from 1781 to 1789. It left most power in the hands of the individual states, causing George Washington to call the Confederation "little more than the shadow without the substance." The document was superseded by the CONSTITUTION.

As the World Turns   See SOAP OPERAS.

"As Time Goes By"   See CASABLANCA.

Ashcan School   A group of artists whose fascination with urban life introduced realism into American painting. When they exhibited together in New York in 1908, they were known as the Eight. The "ashcan" label reflected member John Sloan's particular interest in alleys and slums. Other members included unofficial leader Robert Henri and George BELLOWS. See also ARMORY SHOW.

Ashe, Arthur   (1943–93) Tennis player. In 1968 Ashe became the first black male to win a major tennis tournament when he took the singles titles at both the U.S. National Amateur and U.S. Open tournaments. Six years after turning professional, he beat Jimmy CONNORS for the 1975 men's title at Wimbledon.

"Ask not what your country can do for you. Ask what you can do for your country"   The most famous line in John F. KENNEDY's inaugural address, entreating his countrymen to dedicate their energies to the national good. Probably the most visible response to his call was the flocking of idealistic youngsters to the PEACE CORPS.

Asta   See DOGS.

Astaire and Rogers   The most famous dance team in Hollywood history. Fred Astaire (1899–1987) and Ginger Rogers (1911–   ) brought a charm and effortless grace to singing and dancing that remain the standards against which contemporary musicals are still measured. Astaire had danced in vaudeville and on Broadway with his sister, Adele, before being paired in 1933 with the younger Rogers. Movie audiences already knew her as a chipper comedienne, and as Astaire's partner, she proved as quick on her feet as she was with a gag. Their ten films together included the choreographic sparklers *Flying Down to Rio* (1933), *The Gay Divorcee* (1934), *Top Hat* (1935), *Swing Time* (1936), and *The Story of Vernon and Irene Castle* (1939), in which they played the elegant dance duo of the previous generation. Both Astaire and Rogers were skillful actors as well, he winning an Oscar nomination for the 1974 *Towering Inferno,* she the Oscar itself for the 1940 *Kitty Foyle.*

Astor family A wealthy dynasty whose patriarch, German immigrant John Jacob Astor (1763–1848), became the richest man in the country through the sale of furs. By exploiting the skills of MOUNTAIN MEN, his firm, the American Fur Company, for decades controlled much of the Far West BEAVER trade; Astoria, Oregon, is the site of its Pacific shoreline trading post. John Jacob's son, William Backhouse Astor (1792–1875), became known as the landlord of New York because of his real estate holdings there, while a daughter-in-law, the former Caroline Schermerhorn, was the redoubtable "Mrs. Astor" of society legend. In his will, John Jacob provided for the funding of the Astor Library, later incorporated into the New York Public Library; the city's Waldorf-Astoria Hotel was also built with family money. Once called "a self-invented money making machine" by a New York newsman, the elder Astor was a legendary embodiment of the American dream. By the 1840s, "rich as Astor" was a byword for wealth. See also THE 400.

Astor Place Riot See Edwin FORREST.

astronaut The National Aeronautics and Space Administration's term for the pilots and crew of its space launches. The original seven astronauts—lionized as extravagantly as movie stars—worked for NASA's 1959–63 Mercury program. They were Scott Carpenter, Gordon Cooper, John GLENN (first American to orbit the earth), Gus Grissom, Wally Schirra, Alan Shepard (first American in space), and Donald Slayton.

Atkins, Chet (1924–) Guitarist, music executive. Once called the most influential man in Nashville, Atkins served in the 1960s as head of RCA records' country music division. Both in his executive capacity and as a revered studio guitarist, he honed the commercial, polished music that became the NASHVILLE sound. The popularity of solo guitar owes much to his influence.

Atlanta The capital of Georgia. Famous as a railroad hub from the 1830s, the city was burned by General William T. SHERMAN during the Civil War, an event immortalized in the book and movie GONE WITH THE WIND. It is the home base of several sports franchises and a myriad of businesses. COCA-COLA was invented there in the 1880s.

Atlantic City New Jersey shore community that has been a popular resort since the 1850s. Its attractions include the country's first BOARDWALK (1870), the annual MISS AMERICA PAGEANT, and, since the 1970s, legalized casino gambling.

Atlantic Monthly, The   Literary magazine founded in Boston in 1857. Named by Oliver Wendell HOLMES and first edited by James Russell Lowell, it has featured the work of many of the nation's canonical writers, including Emerson, Stowe, Longfellow, Whittier, and Twain. It survives today as a distinguished forum for public affairs writing.

Atlas, Charles   (1894–1972) Professional name of strongman and fitness promoter Angelo Siciliano. A self-proclaimed "97-pound weakling" as a child, Atlas built himself up so dramatically with isometric exercises that in 1922 a magazine called him "the world's most perfectly developed man." The title helped him start a mail-order business that sold millions of hopefuls on his "dynamic tension" bodybuilding method. The method was known as much for its comic-strip-style advertisements as for its results. In the typical Atlas ad, a bully kicks sand in a spindly beachgoer's face; the victim writes off for the dynamic tension course; and, reborn as a he-man Adonis, he routs the bully.

Attucks, Crispus   First and most famous victim of the BOSTON MASSACRE (1770), in which British redcoats killed five tax protesters. An escaped slave and former sailor, the mulatto Attucks became one of the first martyrs of the Revolutionary cause. Black companies before the Civil War often styled themselves Attucks Guards, and a monument on Boston Common reveres his memory.

Audubon, John James   (1785–1851) Naturalist, painter. Born in Haiti, Audubon studied in Paris with Jacques-Louis David, then moved to Pennsylvania and later New Orleans, where he earned an income doing portraits and teaching drawing. His great work, a portfolio of over four hundred color engravings called *Birds of America* (1827–38), remains an unsurpassed model of nature study; complete sets now fetch hundreds of thousand of dollars. The conservationist Audubon Society (1905) is named for him.

Aunt Jemima   (1) The trademark face on a pancake mix first marketed by the Davis Milling Company in the 1890s. The model for the rotund MAMMY figure was Nancy Green, a cook who advertised the product at the 1893 Chicago world's fair. (2) In black parlance, an "Aunt Jemima" often means a complacent black woman, a female equivalent to "Uncle Tom." See UNCLE TOM'S CABIN.

"Aunt Rhody"   A traditional children's folk song, often seen as "Go Tell Aunt Rhody" (or Aunt Nancy). "Go tell Aunt Rhody, the old gray goose is dead."

Austin, Stephen F.   (1793–1836) Settler and founder of the Republic of Texas. Born in Virginia, Austin began to bring settlers into Texas in the 1820s and became a Mexican citizen as a sign of loyalty to the newly independent government. After two years in a Mexican jail under false charges of subversion, his attitude changed, and he joined with Sam HOUSTON in the Anglo revolt against SANTA ANNA. Once Texas autonomy was secured, he served briefly as the new republic's secretary of state. The current capital of Texas is named for him.

Automat   A self-service restaurant in which cooked dishes are dispensed from behind coin-operated glass doors. The first Automats, run by the Horn and Hardart Company, opened at the turn of the century. They remained popular, inexpensive eating places until the rise of FAST FOOD in the 1960s.

Autry, Gene (1907–) The best-known SINGING COWBOY, Autry was a major star for Republic Pictures in the 1930s and 1940s. With his horse, Champion, and his sidekick, Smiley Burnette, he appeared in dozens of formula westerns as a straight-shooting hero. When he joined the service during World War II, a young Roy ROGERS assumed his King of the Cowboys title, and Autry turned his attention to various businesses. Of his many song hits, the most successful were the Christmas ditties ''Here Comes Santa Claus,'' ''FROSTY THE SNOWMAN,'' and ''RUDOLPH THE RED-NOSED REINDEER.''

Avon lady A saleswoman who sells cosmetics door-to-door. The Avon company grew out of the California Perfume Company, founded in 1886 by David McConnell. It now employs roughly a million Avon ladies around the world.

Avondale A Pennsylvania coal site where, on September 6, 1869, over one hundred miners were asphyxiated underground after a gas fire cut off their escape. The disaster inspired the best known of American mining ballads, ''The Mines of Avondale.''

AWOL Absent without official leave or absent without leave. The military usage connotes an offense graver than mere tardiness, but less serious than desertion. Pronounced as individual letters or as *ay-wall*.

Axis Sally The airwave name of American actress Mildred Gillars, who broadcast pro-Nazi propaganda to U.S. troops during World War II. See TOKYO ROSE.

Aztec two-step Southwestern slang for diarrhea or turista. Probably from the sufferer's constant ''stepping'' to the toilet. See also MONTEZUMA.

Aztecs The last Indian rulers of central Mexico. Known for their military prowess, elaborate religion, and human sacrifices, they were conquered in 1521 by Hernando CORTÉS.

Aztlan The legendary homeland of the ancient Aztecs, believed to have been located in the American Southwest. In the CHICANO activist movement of the 1970s, it became a potent symbol of romantic nationalism.

B

B&O The Baltimore & Ohio Railroad, chartered in 1827 as the country's first passenger rail line. The fame of its steam locomotive, the Tom Thumb (1), stimulated the infant rail industry. During the Civil War, it was a major supply line for Union troops.

B movie Or "B picture." A second rate, low budget film. From their prevalence as second features on double bills in movie houses of the 1930s and 1940s. See Foy family.

Babbitt Someone mindlessly conformist in tastes and standards. From George Babbitt, the self-satisfied civic booster of Sinclair Lewis's 1922 novel *Babbitt*. Middle-class complacency is sometimes called Babbitry.

Babe (1) Paul Bunyan's fabulous bovine companion. (2) For *the* Babe, see Babe Ruth.

baby boom A U.S. population rate increase that followed World War II. People born between roughly 1945 and 1960 are referred to as the baby boom generation, baby boomers, or simply boomers.

Baby LeRoy (1932–) Stage name of LeRoy Winebrenner. He was W. C. Fields's dimpled antagonist in four films, including notably *It's a Gift* (1934). He retired from pictures at the age of four.

Baby Ruth A candy bar first produced in 1920 and sold by the Curtiss Candy Company. Its namesake is uncertain. Often erroneously associated with Babe Ruth, it was actually named for either President Grover Cleveland's daughter or the granddaughter of its manufacturer's president.

Baby Snooks See Fanny Brice.

Bacall, Lauren (1924–) Actress. Born Betty Joan Perske, Bacall starred with her husband Humphrey Bogart in four films, including her debut, at the age of nineteen, in To Have and Have Not. Bacall also appeared in The Big Sleep, *Key Largo* (1948), and John Wayne's last film, *The Shootist* (1976). She won a Tony Award in 1970 for her stage work in the Broadway show *Applause*.

Bacharach, Burt (1929–) Songwriter. Bacharach got his break as an arranger for Marlene Dietrich's 1950s concert tours. He wrote effectively for pop singer Dionne Warwick in the 1960s and won an Oscar for the score of *Butch Cassidy and the Sundance Kid* (1969). His hits—written with Hal David for

Warwick—included "What the World Needs Now," "I'll Never Fall in Love Again," and "Alfie."

"Back to Normalcy" The 1920 Republican campaign slogan. Playing on Americans' growing apprehension about Woodrow WILSON's internationalism, it helped send dull, eminently "normal" Warren G. Harding to the White House.

Baez, Joan (1941–) Singer, songwriter. The premier female performer of the 1960s FOLK REVIVAL, Baez was as well known for political activism as for her bel canto sound. She popularized the civil rights anthem "WE SHALL OVERCOME" and was a prominent opponent of the Vietnam War. Her 1975 hit "Diamonds and Rust" poignantly reflects on her youthful romance with Bob DYLAN.

Balboa, Rocky See ROCKY.

Balboa, Vasco Núñez de (1475–1519) The first European to see the America's Pacific Coast. In 1510, at Darién on the east coast of Panama, CONQUISTADOR Balboa overthrew the colony's leader and made himself governor. Late in 1513, relying on Indian reports, he led an expedition through the isthmus's jungles to the "South Sea." After his return, he enjoyed his fame for only five years, when a new governor had him executed for alleged treason.

bald eagle The national emblem of the United States since 1782. The imputed baldness is actually white head feathers. Benjamin FRANKLIN ridiculed the choice, citing the eagle's habit of stealing other birds' dinner as evidence of its "bad moral character." See also TURKEY.

Baldwin, James (1924–87) Writer. The major black writer of his generation, Baldwin scored a triumph with his first novel, *Go Tell It on the Mountain* (1953), a richly textured multiple portrait of Harlem churchgoers. His passionate engagement with racial and sexual turmoil also generated the novel *Another Country* (1964) and several volumes of searing essays. Of these, *Notes of a Native Son* (1955) reassesses Richard WRIGHT; *Nobody Knows My Name* (1961) and *The Fire Next Time* (1963) reflect on the contemporary CIVIL RIGHTS MOVEMENT.

Ball, Lucille See I LOVE LUCY.

ballad A term designating three types of song. (1) The traditional or "oral" ballad, imported from the British Isles, is a story told in song, often on a tragic theme, such as the mendacity or misfortune of star-crossed lovers. Many of these late medieval songs became as popular in North America as in their homelands; "Barbara Allen," for example, is found in hundreds of American versions. (2) The modern or "print" ballad, produced in both the Old and the New Worlds, applies a similar sensibility to contemporary events. Many eighteenth-century British "broadside" ballads recorded the exploits of faithless lovers and romantic highwaymen; American counterparts did the same with a regional bias. The best-known native American ballads tell the tales of failed romance ("FRANKIE AND JOHNNY," "TOM DOOLEY") or "good bad men" (Sam BASS, Jesse JAMES); others immortalize the tragedies of heroic workers ("THE JAM ON GERRY'S ROCK," Casey JONES, John HENRY). (3) In the post–TIN PAN ALLEY era, "ballad" also means any romantic song, especially one that is languorously sentimental. Thus in everyday parlance, the nonnarrative "As TIME GOES BY" would be classed as a ballad. See also CORRIDO.

Bambi (1942) A sentimental, perenially popular animated film by the Walt DISNEY studios. The protagonist is a young deer named Bambi whose woodland home is ravaged by hunters and a forest fire.

banana split See ICE CREAM.

Band, the Popular music group. First famous as Bob DYLAN's backup band, this group of four Canadians and one southerner wrote songs that rivaled his in complexity. The powerful lament "The Night They Drove Old Dixie Down," from their second album, became a hit for Joan BAEZ in 1971. Their farewell concert was filmed as *The Last Waltz* (1978) by Martin Scorsese.

Band-Aid An adhesive gauze strip used for surface wounds. The name is a trademark of the Johnson & Johnson company, although it is used generically for all such strips. Metaphorically, to place a Band-Aid on a problem means to provide merely a cosmetic solution.

"The Band Played On" (1895) Gay Nineties waltz in which an anonymous Casey dances with the "strawberry blonde" as the band plays on. The lyrics were by John Palmer, the music by vaudevillian Charles Ward.

banned in Boston See BOSTON.

Bara, Theda (1890–1955) Screen name of Theodosia Goodman, whose starring role as a femme fatale in *A Fool There Was* (1915) launched her on a decade of lucrative hoopla. The movie's most famous line, "Kiss me, my fool," became fashionable banter, while Hollywood flacks billed Bara as "the Vamp," invented a mysterious birth for her in the Sahara, and observed that her name unscrambled to "Arab Death." She milked the image gleefully, surrounding herself with snakes and "Nubian" slaves while vamping on-screen as Cleopatra and Salome. Her last film, *Madame Mystery* (1926), was a parody directed by Stan Laurel.

Baraka, Imamu Amiri (1934–) Writer. LeRoi Jones shocked audiences and charmed critics in the 1960s with the violently imaginative Off-Broadway plays *Dutchman* (1964), *The Slave* (1965), and *The Toilet* (1965). He became a BLACK MUSLIM at the same time, changing his name. His prose works include *Blues People* (1963) and *The Dead Lecturer (1964).*

"Barbara Frietchie" An 1863 poem by John Greenleaf WHITTIER relating a fictional meeting between Stonewall JACKSON and Barbara Frietchie, an aged Maryland Unionist. Besieged by Jackson's troops, she flies a Union flag out her window, admonishing the soldiers: " 'Shoot, if you must, this old gray head / But spare your country's flag,' she said." On Jackson's order they leave her unharmed.

Barbary Coast (1) In the eighteenth and nineteenth centuries, the North African coast, comprising the shoreline of the predatory states Morocco, Algiers, Tripoli, and Tunis. (2) From about 1850 to 1900, San Francisco's waterfront district, so called because its rough inhabitants resembled the pirates of the original Barbary Coast.

Barbary Pirates   State-supported pirates who exacted tribute from foreign vessels off the North African BARBARY COAST until 1815, when the system was stopped by naval commander Stephen DECATUR.

barbed wire   Fencing wire with regularly placed points, or "barbs," to discourage wandering cattle. Its introduction after the Civil War, which led to bitter conflicts between farmers and "free-range" cattlemen, hastened the end of the cowboy era. Cowboy attitudes toward the innovation are reflected in the Cole PORTER song "Don't Fence Me In." The preferred pronunciation west of the Mississippi is *bobwahr*.

barbershop quartet   A male foursome that sings sentimental favorites in close harmony. Such groups performed informally in barbershops in TIN PAN ALLEY days, and they have survived as nostalgia clubs with significant followings. In national competitions, female groups also perform; they are called SWEET ADELINES, after one of the quartets' favorite tunes.

Barbie doll   (1) A children's fashion doll introduced by the Mattell toy company in 1959. Barbie and similar "dress-up" dolls, complete with elaborate wardrobes, quickly replaced baby dolls in girls' affections; the appearance of Barbie's "brother" Ken, in 1961, consolidated the company's influence. Hence (2) a woman thought to be mindlessly appearance-conscious. "Ken doll" has the same connotation for a preening male.

"barefoot boy with cheek of tan"   The signature phrase from John Greenleaf WHITTIER's poem "The Barefoot Boy" (1855), evoking the lost innocence of his rural childhood.

Barker, Kate   (1871?–1935) Born in Missouri, Ma Barker was the mother of four ne'er-do-well sons whose gang, known as the Bloody Barkers, terrorized the Midwest in the 1920s and 1930s with robberies, kidnappings, and murders. One member recalled her as a doting matriarch, only vaguely aware of her brood's activities. The feds saw it differently, calling her the brains of the outfit, a "Bloody Mama," and—in J. Edgar HOOVER's words—"a veritable beast of prey." She died with her youngest son, Freddie, in a Florida shoot-out with the FBI. Shelley Winters played her in *Bloody Mama* (1970).

Barnburners   Antislavery Democrats who, in 1848, left their party to oppose its proslavery position. The name recalled the tale of a shortsighted farmer who burned his barn down to rid it of rats.

Barney Google   A comic strip created in 1919 by Chicago writer and artist Billy DeBeck (1890–1942). It began by following the fortunes of small-time operator Barney Google and his racehorse, Spark Plug, moving into more exotic themes—mystery, romance, adventure—in the 1930s. In that decade a subsidiary character, the grumpy hillbilly Snuffy Smith, gradually became more visible, and by the 1940s, he had become the central character. The feature's popularity made Spark Plug, in Ron Goulard's words, "the Snoopy of his day." It also inspired a pair of novelty tunes. Louis ARMSTRONG's hit, "Heebie Jeebies," was named for one of DeBeck's favorite phrases. Billy ROSE's song about the main character spoke humorously of his "goo-goo-googly eyes."

barnstorming Today, this means a political candidate's travels through rural areas in search of votes. In the 1910s and 1920s, it meant the air shows put on by daredevil pilots over farmlands. A century before that, it referred to the life of traveling dramatists—obliged to sleep and to perform in the same barns.

Barnum, P. T. (1810–91) Impresario. A self-proclaimed "Prince of Humbugs," Connecticut-born Phineas Taylor Barnum was the most successful and outrageous showman of his day. He began his career in the 1830s by passing off an aged black woman, Joice Heth, as the childhood nurse of George Washington. Over the next three decades, as owner of the American Museum in New York City, he made millions from equally improbable attractions, including a fish-tail and monkey-torso doll he brazenly labeled the Feejee Mermaid. His bona fide draws included the world's largest elephant, Jumbo; its smallest man, General Tom Thumb (see Tom Thumb [2]); the original Siamese twins; and the Swedish soprano Jenny Lind, for whom he arranged a sellout tour in the 1850s. Barnum's lasting legacy was a circus: the Barnum & Bailey "Greatest Show on Earth," which merged with the Ringling Brothers enterprise in 1907. The quintessential Connecticut Yankee, Barnum is also remembered for the self-revealing quip "There's a sucker born every minute."

Barrow, Clyde See Bonnie and Clyde.

Barrymore family The premier American acting family of this century. The patriarch and matriarch of the clan, Maurice Barrymore (1847–1905) and Georgiana Drew (1856–93), were accomplished theater people in their own right. Their children Lionel (1878–1954), Ethel (1879–1959), and John (1882–1942) captivated audiences for half a century on stage and screen. Lionel, a superb character actor, entered films under the wing of D. W. Griffith and became best known as Dr. Gillespie in the Dr. Kildare films. Ethel kept mostly to the stage, becoming known as the First Lady of the American Theater. Raffish, flamboyant John, whose features elicited the sobriquet Great Profile, was equally at home in the role of romantic lover and in character parts like Svengali and Captain Ahab; his tour de force was the dual role in *Dr. Jekyll and Mr. Hyde* (1920), in which he turned into Hyde without benefit of makeup. The trio played together in *Rasputin and the Empress* (1933); John and Lionel teamed with Greta Garbo in *Grand Hotel* (1932).

Bartholdi, Frederic See Statue of Liberty.

Bartlett's Quotations Or *Bartlett's Familiar Quotations*. A miscellany of literary and historical quotations first published in 1855 by Cambridge, Massachusetts, bookseller John Bartlett (1820–1905). The autodidact Bartlett was well known in the college town as a trivia authority, and "Ask John Bartlett" was a Harvard University catchphrase. Current *Bartlett's Quotations* are expanded versions of his original idea.

Barton, Clara (1821–1912). Founder of the American Red Cross. Barton's nursing of Civil War wounded earned her the name Angel of the Battlefield. Similar work in France during the Franco-Prussian War brought her into contact with the International Red Cross, and she established the United States's first chapter in 1881. Its first president, she served until 1904.

baseball Long considered the national sport, baseball derives from the English game of rounders, which was popular decades before Abner DOUBLEDAY was born. The game's real inventor—or more precisely, the person who roughed out the original rules—was New Yorker Alexander Cartwright, whose team, the Knickerbockers, was in need of standard regulations. In 1845, he diagrammed a ball field with ninety-foot baselines and a home plate batter's box; modern baseball rules are (extensive) modifications of his scheme. Cartwright's baseball was called the "New York game." It became the "national game" in the 1860s (from the recently formed National Association of Baseball Players) and the "national pastime" in the 1920s.

Basie, Count (1904–84) Pianist, bandleader. After studying with Fats WALLER, William "Count" Basie played Kansas City and New York City jazz clubs before starting his own group in 1935. One of the major big bands of the swing era, it was known for Basie's own elegant piano work and soloists like singer Jimmy Rushing and saxophonist Lester YOUNG. Basie himself wrote much of the music, including the popular "One o'Clock Jump." The group continued to tour extensively into the 1960s, recording with Sammy DAVIS, Jr., and Frank SINATRA.

Basin Street The main street of New Orleans's Storyville section, a red-light district that spawned New Orleans JAZZ.

basketball A court and ball game developed in 1891 by YMCA physical education instructor James NAISMITH. Now a multimillion-dollar sport, it began modestly in Springfield, Massachusetts, as a winter diversion for Naismith's students: They used a soccer ball and peach baskets hung on poles. Springfield is the home of the Basketball Hall of Fame.

Bass, Sam (1851–78). Outlaw. Born in Indiana, Bass left home as a teenager, worked as a cowhand, then turned to bank and train robbery, achieving in folklore a "beloved renegade" status rivaling those of BILLY THE KID and Jesse JAMES. Within months of his death at the hands of TEXAS RANGERS, he became a national legend. Partly because of his reputed generosity—he often "tipped" his victims with gold coins—and partly because of a posthumous ballad, "Sam Bass," he became known as the Robin Hood of the Southwest. Folklorist Frank Dobie, in *Tales of Old-time Texas,* called him "the best known of all Texas bad men, and the best liked." Legends persist of Bass's buried treasure.

bat a thousand To achieve perfection. From baseball, where batting percentages are quoted to the thousandth place, the average .346, for example, being read as "three forty-six," with the "thousandths" understood. A "thousand" average, therefore, would be 1.000—or one hit for every time at bat. In reality only a handful of players have ever batted over .400.

bathtub gin Any alcoholic beverage—not necessarily one approximating gin—made at home from raw alcohol, water, and flavoring. From the era of PROHIBITION, when real gin was illegal.

Batman Cartoon character. Created in 1939 by Bob Kane and Bill Finger, the "caped crusader" appeared first in *Detective Comics,* where he soon rivaled even SUPERMAN in popularity. Batman is the *nom de justice* of socialite Bruce Wayne, who dons a bat costume to do battle with the forces of evil. His young sidekick, Robin the Boy Wonder, is Dick Grayson, the orphaned, athletic son of circus performers. Much of the ''dynamic duos' '' appeal over half a century has had to do with appurtenances such as the Batcave and the Batmobile, and with a gallery of exotic villains like the Penguin and the Joker. A campy television series (1966–68) played the pair's adventures for laughs, while two blockbuster movies (1989 and 1992) restored the ominous feeling of the Bob Kane drawings.

Battle Creek, Michigan The home of the American BREAKFAST CEREAL industry.

"Battle Cry of Freedom, The" (1863) A Civil War song by George Frederick Root (1820–96). Its stirring chorus began,

> *Yes, we'll rally round the flag, boys,*
> *We'll rally once again,*
> *Shouting the Battle Cry of Freedom.*

In maintaining Union troop morale, the song did as much as, and possibly more than, ''THE BATTLE HYMN OF THE REPUBLIC.'' Root turned out dozens of other war songs and was told by President Lincoln in a letter, ''You have done more than a hundred generals and a thousand orators.''

"Battle Hymn of the Republic, The" A principal Union Army marching song during the Civil War and a patriotic favorite ever since. The melody, from an old religious song, had already been adapted for the antislavery anthem ''John Brown's Body'' when Boston poet Julia Ward HOWE gave it new words:

> *Mine eyes have seen the glory of the coming of the Lord;*
> *He is trampling out the vintage where the grapes of wrath are stored.*
> *He hath loos'd the fateful lightning of his terrible swift sword;*
> *His truth is marching on.*

This opening stanza gave John Steinbeck the title for his Pulitzer Prize novel THE GRAPES OF WRATH.

battle of the bulge Media slang for dieting. The reference is to the World War II battle. See ''NUTS!''

Baum, L. Frank See THE WIZARD OF OZ.

Bay Psalm Book A 1640 translation of the Psalms by a group of Massachusetts Bay Colony ministers. It is considered the first book printed in the English colonies.

bayou A swampy, slow-moving stream, common in southern Louisiana. The term is a corruption of Choctaw *bayuk* (creek). The region's CAJUNS have traditionally negotiated the waterways in shallow-draft boats called *bateaux*.

"Be Prepared" The official motto of the BOY SCOUTS OF AMERICA.

"Be sure you're right, then go ahead" A line from Davy CROCKETT's 1834 autobiography, often taken to be his personal motto.

Beach Boys Pop music group. Originators of an upbeat, harmonically complex vocal style known as the California sound, the Beach Boys also invented "surfer music," celebrating the jejune thrills of teen romance and endless summers. First peaking in the 1960s, they remained in demand for two decades as a nostalgia act. Their biggest hits were "Surfin' USA," "I Get Around," "Help Me Rhonda," and "Good Vibrations."

Beacon Hill Boston's most traditionally respectable and expensive neighborhood—the home of "society."

Beadle, Erastus and Irwin See DIME NOVELS.

Beale Street See MEMPHIS.

"Beam me up, Scotty" On the STAR TREK television series, this line is spoken frequently by Captain Kirk when, after exploring a newly discovered planet, he wants his engineer, Officer Scott, to return him to the *Enterprise* by activating the dematerialization/rematerialization "beam." A bumper sticker of the 1970s adapts the command: "Beam me up, Scotty. There's no intelligent life on this planet."

Bean, Roy (ca. 1825–1903) Frontier judge. Born in Kentucky, Bean moved to Texas after the Civil War, opening a saloon in the Pecos River settlement of Vinegaroon. Smitten by the Jersey-born actress Lily Langtry, he called his place of business the Jersey Lily and, after becoming justice of the peace, renamed the town itself Langtry. Using the saloon as his courthouse, Bean styled himself "the Law West of the Pecos" and for years dispensed an eccentric brand of justice. Reviewing the death of a man struck by a train, he exonerated the railroad but confiscated the victim's pistol and pocket money because he had broken a law against carrying a concealed weapon. He freed an Oriental's murderer because his legal Bible—an outdated California statute book—failed to mention that killing a Chinaman was a crime. When an eastern dude, charged a dollar for a beer, began to utter profanities, Bean fined him twenty dollars and quipped, "The beer's on me." The sagebrush Solon was played by Paul NEWMAN in 1972's *Life and Times of Judge Roy Bean.*

Beantown. Boston. From its traditional dish, baked beans.

bear Many American Indian peoples saw the bear as a symbol of vitality and power; native medicine was full of ursine charms and salves. Early settlers concurred with this estimation, although their relationship to bears was less reverential and more direct: Killing bears was a dominant metaphor for the mastery of wilderness. This was true in the East, where the legends of Davy CROCKETT and Daniel BOONE included scenes of their hand-to-hand combat with "riled" she-bears; it was true in the West, where the ferocious GRIZZLY BEAR shocked Lewis and Clark and subsequent explorers. When Teddy Roosevelt went bear-hunting around the turn of the century, he was following a long tradition of virility-testing against an emblem of the wild. See also SMOKEY BEAR; TEDDY BEAR.

Beat Generation   The Beats (reputedly from "beatific") were a loosely organized literary set of the 1950s that celebrated spontaneity and condemned the Babbitry of middle-class life. They included poets Lawrence FERLINGHETTI and Allen GINSBERG and novelists William S. BURROUGHS and Jack KEROUAC. Notable works included the "first" Beat novel, John Clellon Holmes's *Go* (1952); Ginsberg's "HOWL"; and Kerouac's ON THE ROAD. In 1958, San Francisco journalist Herb Caen dubbed the Beats' followers beatniks. The term remained a tag for principled opponents of the work ethic until it was superseded in the 1960s by FLOWER CHILDREN and HIPPIES.

beaver   (1) The main source of fashion fur in colonial America. With beaver hats the rage in Europe, hatters kept up the demand for furs for two centuries, providing an occupation for MOUNTAIN MEN and other trappers, stimulating a fur trade that made the ASTOR FAMILY fortune, and sparking the FRENCH AND INDIAN WAR between England and France over beaver-rich Canada. (2) *The* Beaver, aka. the Beeve, was the title character in the TV series LEAVE IT TO BEAVER.

bebop   Also called bop and rebop. A 1940s JAZZ style characterized by a lean rhythm section, innovative harmonies, and fast, improvisatory solo work. Its major inventors—all reacting in some degree to the conventional orchestration of the BIG BANDS—were guitarist Charlie Christian, pianist Thelonious Monk, trumpeter Dizzy Gillespie, and saxophonist Charlie "Bird" Parker.

Beckwourth, Jim   (1800?–?66) Mountain man. The son of a slave mother and white father, Beckwourth was the first black to achieve fame on the frontier. On a trapping expedition to the Rockies in the 1820s, he was adopted by the Crows and subsequently married several Indian women. His celebrity back East was established by the 1854 publication of Thomas Bonner's "as told to" biography, which made him, a little expansively, a Crow "chief." He guided fortune hunters to both the California and Pikes Peak gold fields.

bee   A gathering of people to perform a collective task, as in "husking bee" or "quilting bee." The American "spelling bee," less collective than competitive, was first suggested in the eighteenth century by Benjamin FRANKLIN.

Beecher's Bibles   A nickname in the 1850s for Sharps rifles, after Brooklyn preacher Henry Ward Beecher had encouraged shipping them to abolitionist settlers in "BLEEDING KANSAS."

"Beer That Made Milwaukee Famous, The"   Slogan for Schlitz beer, founded in 1874 by Joseph Schlitz. With its large German population, Milwaukee was indeed known for its lager. But it wasn't all Schlitz's doing: By 1874, the Valentine Blatz and Frederick Miller breweries were twenty years old.

Belafonte, Harry   (1927–   ) Singer. The major pop interpreter of CALYPSO MUSIC, Belafonte was the West Indian representative of the GREENWICH VILLAGE folk music scene in the 1950s and 1960s. He went on to act in films and television shows.

Belasco, David (1853–1931) Dramatist and producer. The nation's first major theatrical impresario, Belasco mounted lavish productions, encouraged American playwrights, and wrote numerous melodramas, two of which—*Madame Butterfly* (1900) and *The Girl of the Golden West* (1905)—inspired Puccini operas. In New York City, where he influenced popular theater from the 1880s until World War I, his severe wardrobe earned him the nickname Bishop of Broadway. A famous Broadway theater carries his name.

Believe It or Not! See RIPLEY'S BELIEVE IT OR NOT!

Bell, Alexander Graham (1847–1922) Inventor of the telephone. Born in Scotland, Bell was, like his father and grandfather, a teacher of the deaf. Years of research on acoustics bore fruit on March 10, 1876, when he spilled acid on himself in his Boston laboratory and called his assistant with the words "Mr. Watson, come here, I want you." Watson, in an adjoining room, heard Bell over the apparatus they had been working on—and the age of telecommunications was born. Bell's invention won a gold medal at that year's Centennial Exposition in Philadelphia, and in 1877 he formed the company that bore his name.

Bellamy, Edward See LOOKING BACKWARD.

Bellows, George (1882–1925) Realist painter. A student of ASHCAN SCHOOL leader Robert Henri, Bellows helped to mount the 1913 ARMORY SHOW. A lifelong resident of New York, he painted gritty urban tableaus such as *The Cliff Dwellers* (1913) and *River Front* (1925) but is more generally known for his prizefight scenes. Among these were *Stag at Sharkey's* (1907) and *Dempsey Through the Ropes* (1924).

Ben-Hur (1880). Novel by Lew Wallace (1827–1905) about the conversion of a young Jew to Christianity. Set in Roman times, it includes scenes of slave galleys and chariot racing. Enormously popular and widely translated, it led to equally successful films in 1926 and 1959.

Benét, Stephen Vincent (1898–1943) Writer. Benét, who specialized in historical themes, was best known for two Pulitzer Prize creations: his 1937 story THE DEVIL AND DANIEL WEBSTER and the narrative poem JOHN BROWN'S BODY (2).

Benny, Jack (1894–1974) Comedian. Master of the pregnant pause, deadpan delivery, and self-parody, Benny (born Benjamin Kubelsky) starred on radio in the 1930s, made movies in the 1940s, and then on TV became a national institution. With his longtime foil, black valet Eddie "Rochester" Anderson, he created skits relying heavily on the triple fiction that he was miserly, vain, and musically inept. Few Benny shows were complete without a reference to his basement vault, a joke about his age (always thirty-nine) or a risible attempt to torture a melody from his violin. *The Jack Benny Show* stayed on the air for fifteen years (1950–65).

Benton, Thomas Hart (1889–1975) Painter. The grandnephew of Missouri Senator Thomas Hart Benton (1782–1858), he painted dramatic scenes of working people and rural life. Like his stylistic influences the Mexican muralists Orozco,

Rivera, and Siqueiros, Benton celebrated the robust life in public places. His most famous mural adorns the Missouri State Capitol.

Bergen, Edgar   (1903–78) Ventriloquist. Beginning in vaudeville, Bergen became a national star on radio in the 1930s before going on to appear in films and on television. His most famous dummy, wisecracking Charlie McCarthy, was often accompanied by a charming dull-wit, Mortimer Snerd. Bergen's daughter, Candice, is a film and TV star. Charlie McCarthy is in the Smithsonian Institution.

Bergman, Ingrid   (1915–82) Actress. Swedish-born Bergman became a major Hollywood star in the 1940s on the strength of performances in CASABLANCA, FOR WHOM THE BELL TOLLS, *Gaslight* (1944), *Joan of Arc* (1948), and the HITCHCOCK thrillers *Spellbound* (1945) and *Notorious* (1946). She temporarily derailed her career in 1950 by leaving her husband for Italian director Roberto Rossellini, but she was back on track in 1956 with *Anastasia,* for which she received the second of three Oscars. She also won for *Gaslight* and *Murder on the Orient Express* (1974).

Berkeley, Busby   (1895–1976) Choreographer, director. The master of the "all singing, all dancing" musical, Berkeley enchanted Depression-era audiences with elaborately staged, ingeniously shot choral numbers in such films as 42ND STREET and *Gold Diggers of 1933.* His exotic, often erotic showgirl extravaganzas set a pattern for much subsequent theatrical glitz. Berkeley's star performer was dancer Ruby KEELER.

Berle, Milton   (1908–   ) Entertainer. Born Milton Berlinger, Berle was a radio and nightclub comedian before becoming the host of a TV variety show, *The Texaco Star Theater,* in 1948. His comic patter and skits delighted the new medium's first audience, and he became known, by the mid-1950s, as Mr. Television. The show was canceled by the end of the decade, but Berle retains his status as an entertainment legend.

Berlin, Irving   (1888–1989). Songwriter. Born Israel Baline in Russia, Berlin came to the United States as a child, grew up on New York's Lower East Side, and had his first hit with "ALEXANDER'S RAGTIME BAND." Over the next forty years he dominated American popular music, writing prolifically for the parlor piano, the stage, and films. In addition to writing the music for the movie TOP HAT and the Broadway musical *Annie Get Your Gun* (1946), Berlin produced several songs that have become American classics, including "EASTER PARADE," "Blue Skies," the Kate Smith tear-jerker "GOD BLESS AMERICA," and—his most successful number—"WHITE CHRISTMAS."

Bernstein, Carl   See WOODWARD AND BERNSTEIN.

Bernstein, Leonard   (1918–90) Composer, conductor. The best-known American conductor of his time, Bernstein was the New York Philharmonic's musical director from 1958 to 1969. Internationally known for his classical compositions, he provided an arresting score for ON THE WATERFRONT and became a household name in 1957 with the success of the Broadway show WEST SIDE STORY. Bernstein was a beloved television fixture in the 1960s for his dynamic presentation of Young People's Concerts.

Berra, Yogi (1925–) Baseball player. A New York Yankee catcher from 1946 to 1963, Berra was known for three things: expert fielding, powerhouse hitting, and a unique way with words. At a gala in his honor, he thanked the audience for "making this night necessary." On the game of baseball, he commented, "It ain't over 'til it's over." Such bons mots became known as Yogi-isms. See also Casey STENGEL.

Berry, Chuck (1926–) Singer, songwriter. Born in St. Louis, the former autoworker and beautician Charles Edward Berry had a greater influence on the development of ROCK MUSIC than anyone other than LITTLE RICHARD and Elvis PRESLEY. Known as much for his rollicking guitar style and stage "duck walk" as for his wittily rebellious lyrics, he wrote dozens of songs that became cover staples. The best known are "Maybelline," "Carol," "Roll over Beethoven," "Sweet Little Sixteen," "No Particular Place to Go," and "Johnny B. Goode." Most of these were recorded before 1959, when Berry began a two-year prison term for violating the Mann Act: He had brought a teenage prostitute across state lines to check hats in his nightclub.

Best Years of Our Lives, The   Director William WYLER's 1946 film about the readjustment problems of returning World War II veterans. It won eight Academy Awards, including those for best picture, best direction, best actor (Fredric MARCH), best supporting actor (Harold Russell), and best screenplay (Robert SHERWOOD). Amateur Russell, who had lost his arm in the war, also got a special award for "bringing hope and courage to his fellow veterans."

Betsy-Wetsy   A realistic "wetting" doll. Children can "feed" her from a tiny bottle, then "change" her as the liquid runs through.

Better Homes and Gardens   A consumer magazine founded in 1922 and sold, chiefly at newsstands, to over 8 million readers a month. It is—after READER'S DIGEST, TV GUIDE, and NATIONAL GEOGRAPHIC—the fourth largest-selling magazine in the country.

Betty Boop   Cartoon character. Created by the FLEISCHER BROTHERS in 1930, Betty was a miniskirted, squeaky-voiced young woman whose signature phrase was "boop boop a doop." The phrase was borrowed from singer Helen Kane's scatted version of the 1920s hit "I Wanna Be Loved by You." Originally a movie novelty, Betty soon moved into the comic pages as well and was responsible for a raft of merchandising tie-ins.

Betty Crocker   Corporate symbol. Created in 1921 by a flour company and since 1928 a General Mills trademark. Although her picture has been frequently updated, she retains the "happy homemaker" image with which she began. The *Betty Crocker Cooking School of the Air* drew a million listeners in the 1930s and 1940s, and over 50 million people have bought Betty Crocker cookbooks. General Mills employs a staff of twenty to answer her mail and phone calls—some from people who still believe she is a real person.

Beulah   The title character of a radio series that spun off from FIBBER MCGEE AND MOLLY in 1945. Beulah was a black maid whose savvy was the frequent salvation of her white employers, the crisis-prone Hendersons. The character was created by a white male actor, Marlin Hurt, who popularized the phrase "Somebody bawl fo' Beulah?" In the 1950s, she was played on television by Ethel WATERS and Louise Beavers.

"Beulah, peel me a grape"   See Mae WEST.

Beverly Hillbillies, The   A 1960s television sitcom. It gently mocked the American dream of wealth by pitting a Beverly Hills banker against the hillbilly Clampetts, whose discovery of oil on their Ozark property had made them millionaires.

Beverly Hills   An expensive residential area of Los Angeles. Since the 1900s, it has been the home of many movie stars.

Bible Belt   The South, because of its fundamentalism. From the 1920s, and sometimes attributed to H. L. Mencken.

"Bicycle Built for Two, A"   (1892) The popular title for a song by Henry Dacre. Along with the Central Park bicycle excursions of Diamond Jim BRADY and Lillian RUSSELL, it helped to promote the vogue of tandem bicycles. Dacre's actual title was "Daisy Bell."

big   Since the 1820s a synonym for "excellent" or "preeminent." In numerous combinations it indicates an important (or self-important) person: big cheese, big chief, big enchilada, big gun, big guy, big man on campus (BMOC), big shot, big spender, big talker, big-time operator, big wheel, and Mr. Big. "Big deal" means both an important person and a significant undertaking or situation. "No big deal," sometimes abbreviated "No biggie," is slang for "It doesn't matter." See also the following specialized uses.

Big Apple   New York City. Sometimes simply "the Apple." From the jazz musician's "apple," for a city—possibly suggesting its "ripeness" with possibilities.

big bands   The large dance bands of the SWING MUSIC era, when jazz enjoyed its widest popularity. Among the major big band leaders were Count BASIE, Jimmy and Tommy DORSEY, Duke ELLINGTON, Benny GOODMAN, and Glenn MILLER.

Big Bird   See MUPPETS.

Big C   Cancer. After John Wayne's first operation for the disease, he proclaimed, "I licked the Big C."

Big D   (1) Dallas, Texas. (2) Detroit, Michigan.

big daddy   An assertive, powerful male. From Tennessee Williams's CAT ON A HOT TIN ROOF, in which the domineering patriarch was "Big Daddy" Pollit.

Big Ditch   (1) The ERIE CANAL. (2) The PANAMA CANAL.

Big Easy   New Orleans. From the alleged availability of "easy money" and "easy women."

Big Foot   See Wounded Knee.

big house   A federal penitentiary. From around 1900, when it was applied particularly to Sing Sing.

big leagues   Baseball's major leagues, as opposed to the minor or "bush" leagues. Hence "playing in the big leagues" for any undertaking of great competitiveness and great rewards.

big mama   An assertive, sexually attractive, and (usually) large woman. Black slang from the 1950s.

Big Muddy   The Missouri River. In the seventeenth century, Indians living near the confluence of the Missouri and Mississippi rivers called the former Pekitanoui, or "muddy water."

Big Pretzel   Philadelphia.

"Big Rock Candy Mountains"   Hobo chantey of the 1930s, reflecting the yearning for security of the decade's homeless. The mountains are a jobless tramp's fantasyland, where "the handouts grow on bushes" and "the hens lay softboiled eggs," where "the sleet don't fall and the wind don't blow" and "the railroad bulls are blind."

Big Sleep, The   Mystery novel written (1939) by Raymond Chandler and featuring his private detective Philip Marlowe. It was filmed in ominous film noir style in 1946, with Howard Hawks as director, William Faulkner as one of the screenwriters, and Humphrey Bogart as the cynical private eye. See also hard-boiled fiction.

big stick   Popular description of Theodore Roosevelt's foreign policy, from his personal motto, "Speak softly and carry a big stick." Among the fruits of his interventionism were the acquisition of land for the Panama Canal, the establishment of a U.S. naval base at Cuba's Guantánamo Bay, and the 1904 announcement of the Roosevelt Corollary, which consolidated American hegemony in the Western Hemisphere.

big top   Since the 1890s the main, thus tallest, tent in a circus. Often used metonymically to mean "circus" itself.

bigfoot   See Sasquatch.

Bill of Rights   The first ten amendments to the U.S. Constitution, ratified by the states and approved by Congress in 1791. Reflecting popular suspicion of strong government, they itemize personal liberties that the government may not abridge (such as the right to free speech, free assembly, and a speedy trial) as well as prohibit offenses like "unreasonable searches and seizures" and "cruel and unusual punishments." The Federalists, then in power, claimed that such a document was unnecessary, but as Supreme Court Justice Earl Warren later put it, "Our people wanted explicit assurances. The Bill of Rights was the result."

Billings, Josh   (1818–85) The pen name of Henry Wheeler Shaw. One of the nineteenth century's best-loved cracker-barrel philosophers, Shaw learned humorous misspelling from Artemus WARD and made his first splash with the 1864 "Essa on the Muel." His homespun musings, collected posthumously, filled four volumes. In a series of "Allminax," he wryly lampooned THE OLD FARMER'S ALMANAC. The verb "josh" possibly comes from his name.

Billings, William   (1746–1800) Composer. By trade a tanner, Billings pursued his sideline so intensely that he wrote the country's first single-author songbook, *The New England Psalm Singer,* in 1770. Its most famous composition was the patriotic "CHESTER."

Billy Budd   A short novel by Herman MELVILLE. It concerns the conflict between a sailor naïf and the evil officer Claggart, who plots to destroy him. In a dumb rage Billy kills him and is hanged for the offense. The work was not published until 1924.

Billy the Kid   (1859–81) Outlaw. Born William H. Bonney in New York City, the Old West's most famous desperado moved West with his family as a child and is said to have killed a man (for insulting his mother) when he was twelve. As a rustler and hired gun in the Lincoln County, New Mexico, range wars, he cultivated his deadly potential, reputedly killing one person for every year of his life, "not counting Indians and Mexicans." To this trigger-happy sociopath, border legends counterposed a softer Kid—a ladies' man beloved of the common people. His character remains conjectural. The record shows that he was offered amnesty by the territorial governor, Lew Wallace (author of BEN-HUR), that he was jailed and in the process of escaping killed two guards, and that he met his end at the hand of a friend, Sheriff Pat GARRETT.

To counter the fabrications of dime novelists (see DIME NOVELS), Garrett collaborated with journalist Ash Upson on the Kid's first biography (1882). Aaron Copland scored his story for ballet (1938). Of endless movie treatments, the best known, although not necessarily the most reliable, are those starring Johnny Mack BROWN (*Billy the Kid,* 1930), Jack Beutel (*The Outlaw,* 1943), and Paul NEWMAN (*The Left-handed Gun,* 1958). See also OUTLAWS.

Bingo   A game of chance in which players win prizes for covering with markers a straight line of numbers on a printed card. A fund-raising activity at many Roman Catholic churches, it was first manufactured in 1929 by toymaker Edwin Lowe, who modeled it on the European game variously known as beano, lotto, and keno. "Bingo!"—by which players indicate that they have covered a row—has also become a generic signal of success, equivalent to "Eureka!" or "I've got it!"

"Birches"   A reflective lyric on his boyhood by Robert FROST. Appearing in the 1916 volume *Mountain Interval,* it helped to establish the poet's reputation.

Bird   See Charlie PARKER.

Bird, Larry   (1956–   ) Basketball player. Bird was one of the sparks of the Boston Celtics in the 1970s and 1980s. He won the NBA most valuable player award three years running (1984–86) and scored an average of over twenty-four points a game. In a total of over twenty thousand games, he also hit with almost 90 percent of his free-throw tries.

"Bird in a Gilded Cage, A"   (1900) A ballad by Arthur Lamb and Harry Von Tilzer. Although the unhappy woman of the title was supposed to be a rich man's wife, popular opinion has often taken her as his mistress.

Bird Woman   See Sacajawea.

Birdman of Alcatraz   Nickname of murderer Robert Stroud (1887–1963), who during roughly half a century behind bars became a world renowned authority on canary diseases. Although most of his life was spent in other prisons, he acquired the Alcatraz tag because of its fame. Burt Lancaster played him in a 1962 film.

Birds, The   (1962) One of Alfred Hitchcock's most popular controversial films, it explores the fragility of human relationships against a horror-show motif: the growing aggressiveness of a small town's feathered population.

Birdseye, Clarence   (1886–1956) Inventor. Birdseye started the frozen-food industry in the 1920s when he developed a method for quick-freezing fish. The company to which he sold his patent became General Foods. Its freezer line still carries Birdseye's name.

"Birmingham Jail"   See "Down in the Valley."

"Birth of a Nation, The"   (1915) A silent film directed by D. W. Griffith. Griffith built his story of the Old South's decline on Thomas Dixon's best-selling novel *The Clansman* (1905). In both novel and film, the Ku Klux Klan appears as the savior of "white womanhood" against the Reconstruction Era licentiousness of freed slaves. Narratively compelling, the film was once considered the American screen's greatest epic; it is generally scorned now for its racist sentiments.

"Birth of the Blues, The"   (1926) Song written by Buddy De Sylva, Lew Brown, and Ray Henderson. A club standard frequently heard in films, it was introduced in the same Broadway show that produced the black bottom: George White's Scandals of 1926.

Black Bart   (1830–?1917) Bandit. A road agent with a literary bent, Charles Boles, alias Black Bart, held up Wells, Fargo stagecoaches in California in the 1870s, leaving doggerel verses in the empty strongboxes as poetic recompense. A typical effort went like this:

> *I'll start out tomorrow*
> *With another empty sack.*
> *From Wells Fargo I will borrow*
> *But I'll never pay it back.*

Signing himself "Black Bart, Po8," the rhyming bandit prospered for several years until being caught and spending six years in San Quentin Prison. Upon his release, according to legend, the Wells, Fargo company put him on a pension in exchange for his promise not to rob them again.

black bottom   A social dance of the 1920s, basically the CHARLESTON augmented by a slap on the bottom. It was popularized by GEORGE WHITE'S SCANDALS of 1926.

Black Friday   September 24, 1869, when government sales of U.S. gold reserves caused a price collapse and panic in the metals market. Financiers Jay GOULD and James FISK in effect engineered the crash by a near corner on gold, and since they escaped its ill effects, the incident came to symbolize the unscrupulous profiteering of the Gilded Age.

Black Hawk War   (1832) The last episode of native American resistance east of the Mississippi. The Sauk leader Black Hawk (1767–1838) attempted to regain land that had been ceded to the whites in Illinois until his band was driven north into the woods of Wisconsin. Its remnants—including women and children—were slaughtered by the Army.

Black Hills   A region in South Dakota and Wyoming granted by treaty (1868) to the Sioux. When white prospectors, entering the area illegally, claimed they had discovered gold, the federal government pressured the Indians to sell; they refused and left the reservation. When George Armstrong CUSTER was sent to retrieve them, the results were Custer's Last Stand and the subsequent cession of the land (1876). The Black Hills are now the site of Mount RUSHMORE.

"Black is beautiful"   Slogan of the 1960s BLACK POWER movement. It was first used in the 1920s by Marcus GARVEY.

Black Jack   See (1) John J. PERSHING and (2) CHEWING GUM.

Black Maria   (1) Slang term for a police van, or PADDY wagon. Hence (2) the name given to Thomas EDISON's West Orange movie studio by employees who felt the black building resembled such a vehicle.

Black Mask   The premier pulp magazine of the interwar years, founded in 1920 by H. L. MENCKEN and George Jean Nathan. Specializing in HARD-BOILED FICTION, it launched the careers of Raymond CHANDLER and Dashiell HAMMETT.

Black Muslims   A black separatist movement that urges adherence to the Koran and identifies itself as the Nation of Islam. Founded in Detroit in the 1930s by Wali Farad, it gained prominence in the 1960s under Elijah Muhammad (1897–1975), who attracted followers like Muhammad ALI and MALCOLM X. Muhammad's vitriol against "white devils" was muted by his son Wallace Muhammad, who assumed the leadership at his father's death.

black national anthem   See "LIFT EVERY VOICE AND SING."

Black Panthers   A militant black organization founded in Oakland, California, in 1969. Its leaders, including Huey Newton and Bobby Seale, preached economic independence and armed self-defense. Before being obliterated by arrests and police attacks, the Panthers also operated clinics and free meal programs for ghetto children. Arguably the group's most articulate member, Minister of Information Eldridge Cleaver (1935–   ), wrote a searing book of essays, *Soul on Ice* (1968). See also CHICAGO EIGHT.

Black Power   First a rallying cry, then an unofficial title, for the black activist movement of the 1960s. The phrase was coined by SNCC chairman Stokely Carmichael and was gradually adopted by the BLACK PANTHERS and other radicals. The gravely serious movement also had its theatrical edge, as expressed in the title of Julius Lester's book *Look Out, Whitey, Black Power's Gon' Get Your Mama* (1968).

Black Sox scandal   In 1919, eight members of the Chicago White Sox baseball team conspired with gambler Arnold Rothstein to throw the World Series to the obvious underdog, the Cincinnati Reds. The players were paid several thousand dollars each, the fraud was discovered, and even though a jury found them not guilty, the eight were barred from baseball for life by the game's newly created commissioner, Kenesaw Mountain Landis. The incident led to the epithet "Black Sox" and to a well-publicized expression of disbelief. Leaving the courtroom, star fielder "Shoeless Joe" Jackson was accosted by a young fan who demanded tearfully, "Say it ain't so, Joe." The ingenuous remark continues to epitomize lost innocence.

Black Tuesday   October 29, 1929, when over 16 million shares were traded in panic selling on the New York Stock Exchange. The attendant market crash preceded the Great Depression.

Blackbeard   (d. 1718) Pirate. Originally an English privateer, Edward Teach for several years terrorized ships and coastal settlements from Virginia to the Caribbean. His nickname came from a long beard worn in beribboned pigtails; to make himself even more fearsome-looking, he stuck slow-burning cannon fuses in his cap, giving him the demeanor, and the aroma, of a walking smudge pot. Teach was killed by Virginia naval officer Robert Maynard after a prolonged battle on the James River. Rumors persist of an oaken treasure chest that he is supposed to have abandoned near the coast of Maryland.

Blanc, Mel   (1908–89) Vocal specialist. Originally a musician, Blanc joined the Warner Brothers studio in 1937 and for decades did the voices for its cartoon characters. Among his best-known creations are the voices of BUGS BUNNY, DAFFY DUCK, and PORKY PIG.

"Bleeding Kansas"   The Kansas-Nebraska Act of 1854 established those two territories and called for their residents to decide by popular sovereignty where they would stand on the divisive issue of slavery. Nebraska was clearly antislavery, but both proslavery and antislavery settlers flocked into Kansas, and the ensuing conflicts were violent enough to spark this catchphrase. Among the pro-slavers were so-called Border Ruffians from Missouri, who burned the town of Lawrence in 1856; their chief antagonists were Henry Ward Beecher (see BEECHER'S BIBLES) and John BROWN. Kansas became a free state in 1861.

Blizzard of '88   An extreme snowstorm that hit the northern states in March of 1888, killing hundreds. Old-timers in the 1950s still recalled that year as the bitterest winter of their lives.

Blondie   One of the most durable American comic strips, *Blondie* was created in 1930 by Chic Young (1901–73) and continued by other artists after his death.

The heroine, originally a FLAPPER, evolved into a sensible housewife while her bungling husband, Dagwood Bumstead, took center stage. His hapless attempts to change Baby Dumpling's diapers, his petty fights with neighbor Herb Woodley, his abuse by his employer, Mr. Dithers, his affection for huge sandwiches, and his midday catnaps provided the basis for six decades of domestic comedy. The movie *Blondie* (1938), starring Penny Singleton and Arthur Lake, was the first of a series that ended with *Beware of Blondie* (1950).

bloomers   Turkish-style pantaloons for women, worn with a short skirt. Named for feminist editor Amelia Jenks Bloomer (1818–94), who promoted the style in her magazine *The Lily* as an alternative to the cumbersome hoopskirt. A symbolic expression of women's freedom, the fad peaked in the early 1850s, although the term was later applied to girls' long underwear.

"Blow the Man Down"   Sea chantey. Popular among American sailors in CLIPPER SHIP days.

"Blowin' in the Wind"   A 1963 "protest" song written by Bob DYLAN and popularized by PETER, PAUL, AND MARY. Its plaintive pacifism made it a favorite among Vietnam War protesters.

blue and the gray, the   Shorthand for the opposing armies in the Civil War. From the colors of their uniforms, Union blue and Confederate gray.

blue bellies   In the Civil War and Reconstruction, a contemptuous southern term for Union soldiers. From their uniform color.

Blue Eagle   The symbol of the NEW DEAL's National Recovery Administration, which established codes of fair business practice. Merchants who displayed it, along with the slogan "We do our part," were announcing their compliance with NRA policy.

blue jeans   Blue-dyed denim trousers popularized during the California GOLD RUSH by immigrant Levi Strauss (1829–1902), who designed them and sold them to miners. The company he founded, which manufactures the brand name Levi's, retains a major share of the worldwide jeans market, and Levi's themselves are so widely identified as an American national costume, especially for young people, that the Smithsonian Institution has a pair in its collection. The term "jean" is from a Genoese cloth, *geane fustian*.

blue laws   Laws against various offenses to the Sabbath, printed on blue paper in colonial New England. Once so numerous in Connecticut that it was called the Blue Law State, they survive vestigially in local restrictions on Sunday retailing.

"Blue Moon"   (1934) A nightclub standard composed by Richard RODGERS and Lorenz HART. It was the first of their hits to become known through sheet-music sales rather than stage performance.

"Blue Suede Shoes"   Song. Written and recorded in 1956 by Carl PERKINS, it was covered later that year by Elvis PRESLEY. A rockabilly classic, it was the first song simultaneously to top the rhythm and blues, pop, and country charts. See also Sam PHILLIPS, ROCK MUSIC.

"Blue Tail Fly" See Dan EMMETT.

bluegrass (1) Any grass with a peculiar bluish tint, especially the strain known as Kentucky bluegrass. Hence (2) a type of country music characterized by plaintive high harmonies, a driving rhythm, and virtuoso string work. It was pioneered by Kentucky musician Bill MONROE, whose band the Blue Grass Boys gave it a name.

blues An African-American song type characterized by three-line stanzas, an eight- or twelve-bar structure, flatted, or "bent," notes, and usually (although not always) a "hard luck" message. Growing out of the field hollers and work songs of slavery days, the blues evolved both rural and urban styles. In Mississippi in the early 1900s, W. C. HANDY collected and scored traditional blues. In the 1920s, guitarist singers like Robert JOHNSON and Lightnin' HOPKINS developed a melancholic, sparsely instrumented "country blues." In Memphis and Chicago a generation later, John Lee HOOKER, B. B. KING, and Muddy WATERS produced amplified blues that featured guitar and harmonica solos. The diverse strains fused in the 1960s, influencing nearly all American popular music, from RHYTHM AND BLUES and SOUL to ROCK MUSIC.

Bly, Nellie (1867–1922) Journalist. Born Elizabeth Cochran, she became famous in 1887 when, feigning insanity to be admitted to an asylum, she exposed conditions there in *Ten Days in a Mad House*. The following year, *New York World* publisher Joseph PULITZER sent her on a circulation-boosting around-the-world journey. She beat the time of Jules Verne's hero Phileas Fogg by over a week, and told the story in *Around the World in 72 Days* (1890).

boardwalk A wooden promenade. The term dates from the 1870s, when Atlantic City, New Jersey, opened a famous, four-mile-long prototype; other resort towns followed suit. "Under the Boardwalk" was a 1964 hit for the Drifters.

Bobbsey Twins The protagonists in a series of juvenile stories by "Laura Lee Hope," first collected in *Bobbsey Twins, or Merry Days Indoor and Out* (1904). Actually, there were two sets of twins: Bert and Nan, who were eight, and Freddie and Flossie, who were four. See Edward STRATEMEYER.

Bodmer, Karl (1809–93) Artist. Swiss painter Bodmer accompanied German Prince Alexander Philip Maximilian on an 1833–34 journey up the Missouri. The watercolors he did there, reproduced as engravings in the prince's *Travels in the Interior of North America* (1839–41), included strikingly realistic views of the northern Plains Indians. Known only to Europeans in his lifetime, Bodmer is now considered the artistic equal of his better-known contemporary George CATLIN.

Bogart, Humphrey (1899–1957) Actor. Crusty, tight-lipped "Bogie" began his film career as gangster Duke Mantee in THE PETRIFIED FOREST (2). In the 1940s, he became a major star, playing hard-boiled detectives in THE MALTESE FALCON and THE BIG SLEEP while creating movie history as disenchanted Rick Blaine in CASABLANCA. The crisp, wisecracking TO HAVE AND HAVE NOT was the first of four films with his wife Lauren BACALL. His most imaginative work came in his later years, with the superb character portraits of THE TREASURE OF THE SIERRA MADRE, THE AFRICAN QUEEN, and THE CAINE MUTINY.

Bojangles   See Bill ROBINSON.

bomb, the   Cold war expression for the atomic bomb, or A-bomb, developed by the MANHATTAN PROJECT and used on Hiroshima in 1945. Later also the hydrogen bomb, or H-bomb.

"Bomb them back into the Stone Age"   Air Force General Curtis LeMay's proposed solution to the drawn-out Vietnam War. He was no stranger to such tactics. In March 1945, he had ordered the use of napalm against Tokyo—the first major deployment of that incendiary. In 1968, he was George WALLACE's vice presidential running mate.

Bonanza   (1959–73) After GUNSMOKE, the most popular TV western of all time. Set on the Ponderosa Ranch near Virginia City, Nevada, it related the adventures of the wealthy Cartwright clan: father Ben and sons Adam, Hoss, and Little Joe. The show's theme song, by Jay Livingston and Ray Evans, made the HIT PARADE.

Bonhomme Richard   John Paul JONES's flagship in his famous fight with the *Serapis*. Jones chose the name, which means roughly "poor Richard," in honor of Benjamin FRANKLIN.

Bonnie and Clyde   Bonnie Parker (1909–34) and Clyde Barrow (1910–34), Depression-era holdup artists who harassed southwestern banks and small businesses for four years before being killed in a police ambush in Louisiana. They enhanced their reputation by leaving snapshots and doggerel poetry in their wake, and that reputation was secured in 1967, with the release of director Arthur Penn's romanticized movie *Bonnie and Clyde*. Fitting solidly in the Hollywood tradition of "good bad men" films, it presented the duo as carefree youngsters victimized by circumstance.

"Bonnie Blue Flag, The"   (1862) Song by Annie Chambers-Ketchum and Henry Macarthy. It was a favorite of Confederate soldiers in the Civil War.

Bonus Army   Impoverished World War I veterans who set up a shack city in Washington, D.C., in 1932 while petitioning Congress for early payment of their military bonuses. Congress said no, and President Hoover sent in troops to clear them out. Ignoring Hoover's order to use restraint, Army Chief of Staff Douglas MACARTHUR routed the squatters with the help of tanks, tear gas, and fire.

boob tube   Television. Sometimes just "the tube." See IDIOT BOX.

booboisie   H. L. Mencken's acerbic coin for the complacent, easily gulled American bourgeoisie. From the early-twentieth-century "boob," for a simpleton.

boogie-woogie   A JAZZ piano style utilizing an eight-beat-to-the-bar rolling bass. It reached its greatest popularity in the 1930s.

Book-of-the-Month Club   Established in 1926, the BOMC is the country's oldest club offering members discounted books through the mail. Its chief competitor, the Literary Guild, was founded in 1927.

boomtown   A municipality whose population expands rapidly, the "boom" usually the result of local opportunities. In the first two years of the California GOLD

RUSH, for example, the population of San Francisco went from several hundred to over thirty thousand. See also GHOST TOWNS.

Boone, Daniel   (1734–1820) Frontiersman. Before Davy CROCKETT started stealing his thunder, ''Old Dan'l'' was the nation's premier pioneer. Born in what is now Pennsylvania, he survived BRADDOCK'S DEFEAT in 1755 and began exploring the Kentucky mountains in the 1760s. When he cut the WILDERNESS ROAD through the CUMBERLAND GAP in 1775, he opened the trans-Appalachian west to white expansion; his own Boonesboro was settled by families he shepherded through. He himself was never satisfied with the sedentary life. An Indian fighter who also lived among the Shawnee (and was adopted by them during the Revolution), Boone spent his last years in frontier Missouri, after the Kentucky he had helped to settle became too crowded.

As early as 1784, Boone's woodland exploits were known to easterners through John Filson's adulatory *Discovery, Settlement, and Present State of Kentucky*. James Fenimore Cooper used him as a model for his hero Leatherstocking (see LEATHERSTOCKING TALES), Lord Byron mentioned him in *Don Juan,* and sensational novelists helped to make him a national icon. He remained at his death the most celebrated of the LONG HUNTERS.

Boone, Pat   (1934–) Singer. A clean-cut, all-around boy from Nashville, Boone was seen as the parent's answer to Elvis PRESLEY. At the height of the rock 'n' roll frenzy of the 1950s, he topped the charts with sweet ballads like ''April Love'' and ''Love Letters in the Sand.'' His daughter Debby's 1977 recording of the equally saccharine ''You Light up My Life'' became the longest-running hit single of all time.

Boot Hill   A frontier cemetery, from cowboys' and gunfighters' supposed desire to die—and be buried—with their boots on. One of the most famous, in TOMBSTONE, Arizona, is now a tourist attraction.

Booth, Edwin   (1833–93) Actor. The most famous American tragedian of his day, Booth continued a tradition begun by his grandfather of bringing Shakespeare to culture-conscious American audiences. Celebrated especially for his subtle, brooding Hamlet, he also managed New York's Winter Garden Theater and, when it burned down, built the Booth Theater to replace it. After his brother John Wilkes BOOTH killed President Lincoln, Edwin retired briefly from the stage, but he returned triumphantly in the 1870s and did not fully retire until two years before his death.

Booth, John Wilkes   (1838–65) The assassin of President Abraham Lincoln. Like his brother Edwin BOOTH, John was a distinguished actor; unlike Edwin, he was a southern sympathizer who blamed Lincoln for the Confederacy's defeat. Two days after the surrender at APPOMATTOX COURTHOUSE, he shot the president in the head while he and Mrs. Lincoln were watching a play at Ford's Theatre. After the attack, he jumped from the presidential box to the stage, crying, ''*Sic semper tyrannis!* The South is avenged.'' The jump broke his leg, but he managed to get it treated by Dr. Samuel MUDD and escaped to Virginia, where twelve days later he was cornered in a barn by Union soldiers. The barn was fired, and in an ensuing gun battle Booth was mortally wounded. Soldier Boston Corbett claimed to have fired the shot that killed him, although some believe that the assassin shot himself.

bootlegging The illegal manufacture, transportation, or sale of alcoholic beverages. From the custom of hiding such wares in the upper part, or leg, of a boot. By the 1920s, bootleggers had been circumventing local dry laws for decades, but it was PROHIBITION that gave the term—and the practice—national appeal.

Borden, Lizzie (1860–1927) A Massachusetts schoolteacher charged in 1892 with murdering her parents with an ax. Although she was acquitted, her reputation was irretrievably tarnished by this jingle:

> *Lizzie Borden took an ax*
> *And gave her mother forty whacks.*
> *When she saw what she had done*
> *She gave her father forty-one.*

Borglum, Gutzon See Mount RUSHMORE.

Borscht Belt A resort area in New York State's Catskill Mountains frequented especially by Jewish vacationers. From "borscht," an eastern European beet soup popular with Jewish immigrants. Performers in the area's many clubs and theaters sometimes call it the Borscht Circuit. The Catskills are also known as the Jewish Alps.

Boss, the See CONNECTICUT YANKEE; Bruce SPRINGSTEEN.

Boston The capital of Massachusetts and the largest city in New England (1990 population 2.9 million). A hotbed of Puritanism in the seventeenth century and of patriot activism in the eighteenth, it was home to the Cotton MATHER and John ADAMS clans as well as to John HANCOCK and Paul REVERE. It is rich in colonial sites, including those of the BOSTON MASSACRE and BOSTON TEA PARTY. A pioneer in education, Boston opened the colonies' first public school, the Boston Public Latin School, in 1635, and its first university, HARVARD, a year later; contemporary Boston is home to many colleges. The city's Puritan heritage, coupled with heavy Irish Catholic immigration in the nineteenth century, gave it a reputation for moral rigidity, and "banned in Boston" described books and plays that were censored there. The social elite of fashionable Beacon Hill were commonly and snappishly known as Boston Brahmins, while the accent of the Boston area was long a comic target, especially during the administration of John F. KENNEDY. In the nineteenth century, the city was also known for TRANSCENDENTALISM and its ABOLITIONISTS' politics. See also CABOT (2); FANEUIL HALL; PURITANS.

Boston Blackie A fictional criminal-turned-detective created in the early 1900s by Jack Boyle. Boyle's pulp magazine stories and novel *Boston Blackie* (1919) led to a string of B movies starring Chester Morris as well as a radio and a TV series. Blackie's antagonist is dull Inspector Faraday.

Boston Brahmin A member of that city's "cultivated" gentry; someone with standing in polite, educated society. Oliver Wendell HOLMES called New England's Brahmin caste "the harmless, inoffensive, untitled Aristocracy." See CABOT (2).

Boston Massacre   (March 5, 1770) A skirmish between Boston-based British redcoats and tax-protesting citizens that resulted in the troops firing on a crowd, killing five—among them the mulatto freedman Crispus ATTUCKS. Paul REVERE recorded the incident in an engraving, and Samuel ADAMS used it to feed anti-British sentiment.

Boston Strangler   Murderer. Albert DeSalvo (1933–73) killed thirteen elderly women between 1962 and 1964 before being captured by Boston police and confessing to the crimes. While serving a life sentence, he was stabbed to death by a fellow inmate.

Boston Tea Party   (December 16, 1773) The most famous act of tax resistance in the pre-Revolutionary period. Faced with Parliament's grant of a monopoly to the British East India Company for the importation of tea, American radicals disguised themselves as Indians, boarded British vessels, and dumped hundreds of tea chests into Boston Harbor. There is no truth to the pleasant legend that Americans switched en masse to coffee on December 17.

bourbon   A whiskey made of corn, malt, and rye. Its French name notwithstanding, bourbon is an American invention, having originated in Bourbon County, Kentucky—itself named for the French royal family. True bourbon mash is no less than 51 percent corn. Connoisseurs take it neat, as "sippin' whiskey," or slightly diluted, as in "bourbon and branch," that is, river water.

Bow, Clara   (1905–65) Actress. After starring as a FLAPPER in the 1927 film *It*, Bow became known as the It Girl, and "it" itself became a euphemism for sex appeal. She capitalized on the image briefly before retiring from the screen in 1933.

Bowery   A New York City street that led originally to the Dutch governor's farm, or *bouwerie*. Once in the heart of Manhattan's theater district, it has for over a century been the city's most famous skid row. "Bowery bum" is a catchphrase for any derelict.

Bowery Boys   (1) See MOSE THE BOWERY B'HOY. (2) Heroes of a series of B movies deriving from, and starring, the DEAD END KIDS.

Bowie, James   (1796–1836) Adventurer. Slave trader, land speculator, and all-purpose roughneck, Bowie killed a pistol-wielding rival in a Natchez, Mississippi, "Sandbar Duel" on September 19, 1827, whereupon the victorious weapon, dubbed the Bowie knife, was widely copied. Probably designed by James's brother Rezin, it became the most popular nonballistics sidearm on the frontier. Bowie himself went west, seeking gold, in the 1830s. Texas legend says that when he died a hero's death at the ALAMO, he defended himself to the last moment with his "Arkansas toothpick." His name is pronounced *boo-ee*.

Bowleg Bill   Tall-tale hero. A cowboy-turned-sailor, Bowleg Bill brings phenomenal range skills to the open waters, amazing his mates by roping whales and riding tunas. A cross between PECOS BILL and OLD STORMALONG, he made his debut in *Bowleg Bill, the Sea-Going Cowboy,* a 1938 spoof by Jeremiah Digges.

Boy Orator of the Platte   Nickname for William Jennings BRYAN, through whose state of Nebraska the Platte River runs.

Boy Scouts of America   The American branch of the international scouting movement started in 1907 by British army officer Lord Baden-Powell. Formed in 1910, BSA supervises outdoor camping, community service projects, and other activities for troops of boys from eleven to seventeen years old. Scouts progress through a hierarchy of ranks while gaining "merit badges" for mastering various skills. Younger boys may join the Cub Scouts, organized in dens; older ones may join the Explorers, who meet in posts. See also GIRL SCOUTS OF AMERICA.

Boys Town   A community for homeless or delinquent boys established by a Catholic priest, Edward Flanagan (1886–1948), in 1917. The Omaha, Nebraska, institution, supported by charity, was the subject of a 1938 movie, *Boys Town,* in which Spencer Tracy earned an Oscar as Father Flanagan. Its promotional literature often cites the founder's belief that "there is no such thing as a bad boy." Girls have been admitted since 1979.

Braddock's Defeat   The first major battle of the FRENCH AND INDIAN WAR. British General Edward Braddock (1695–1755), marching to attack Fort Duquesne on the Ohio River, was surprised by French forces and overwhelmed; his command was routed and he himself was killed. In addition to serving as an object lesson in wilderness fighting, the incident had one other important consequence: Young George Washington so distinguished himself as a volunteer under Braddock that Virginia made him commander of its militia.

Brady, Diamond Jim   (1865–1917) Financier, bon vivant. A colorful creature of the Gilded Age, Brady made a fortune in railroads and spent much of it extravagantly on Lucullan feasts, Broadway shows, horses, and women—including his longtime companion Lillian RUSSELL. The diamond collection that gave him his nickname was said to be worth $2 million. Johns Hopkins and New York hospitals both profited from his philanthrophic bequests. See THE GILDED AGE.

Brady, Mathew   (ca. 1823–96) Photographer. In 1844—only four years after the invention of the daguerreotype—Brady opened a New York portrait studio. His works there and in Washington appeared in the 1850 *Gallery of Illustrious Americans.* He took dozens of the surviving portraits of Abraham Lincoln and virtually invented combat photography during the Civil War. His coverage of that conflict, now a national treasure, so depleted his fortune that he died in poverty.

Brain Trust   The press corps' term for the inner circle of advisers who helped Franklin D. Roosevelt draft the NEW DEAL. Chief among them were former Columbia University professors Adolf Berle and Rexford Guy Tugwell.

brainwashing   See KOREAN WAR.

Brand, Max   (1892–1944) Pen name of writer Frederick Faust, who produced hundreds of potboiler adventure stories, mostly westerns, in the 1920s and 1930s. His most famous western was the frequently filmed *Destry Rides Again* (1930). He also created the character of DR. KILDARE.

Brand X   A hypothetical nondescript brand. Used in brand-name advertisements to suggest the inferiority of the competition.

Brando, Marlon   (1924–   ) Actor. The perennial bad boy of American films, Brando achieved instant stardom in 1947 for a brilliantly vulgar portrayal of Stanley Kowalski, the tough-guy lead in A STREETCAR NAMED DESIRE. Nominated four years in a row for Oscars, he finally won as Terry Malloy in ON THE WATERFRONT. A second Oscar came almost twenty years later, for his emphysemic, lumbering mafioso in Coppola's THE GODFATHER; he refused this award to protest the mistreatment of the American Indian. A favorite target for nightclub impressionists, Brando uttered much-parodied lines in each of these films. In *Streetcar*, it was the animal shriek "Stellaah!" In *Waterfront*, it was Terry's anguished complaint to his brother, "I coulda been a contender." In *The Godfather*, it was "Make him an offer he can't refuse."

Breakfast at Tiffany's   See TIFFANY'S.

breakfast cereal   The American contribution to breakfast, dry cereal, was developed in Battle Creek, Michigan, at the turn of the century. The town had been home since the 1860s to a "sanitarium" of Seventh-Day Adventists; its director, Dr. John Harvey Kellogg, promoted first GRANOLA and then, in 1907, KELLOGG'S CORN FLAKES. His fellow religionist and business rival C. W. Post followed suit, developing granolalike Grape-Nuts in 1898 and Post Toasties (originally called "Elijah's Manna") ten years later. The companies they helped to found still dominate the American cereal market.

"Breakfast of Champions, The"   Advertising slogan for WHEATIES, a BREAKFAST CEREAL first produced in 1922. The manufacturer favors professional-athlete spokespersons.

Breed's Hill   See BUNKER HILL.

Brer Rabbit and Brer Fox   See UNCLE REMUS.

Brice, Fanny   (1891–1951) Comedienne. Born Fanny Borach, she started as a chorus girl in the ZIEGFELD FOLLIES, where she earned an enormous following not only for singing and dancing but for her comic sketches with a Brooklyn accent. Among her creations were the "Yiddish Squaw" and, on radio, the voice of "Baby Snooks." A Broadway musical (1964) based on her life became the film *Funny Girl* (1968); in both of them, Brice was played by Barbra STREISAND.

Bridge of San Luis Rey, The   (1927) A Pulitzer Prize novel by Thornton WILDER, it explores the philosophical implications of a bridge collapse. It was twice filmed (1929 and 1944).

Bridger, Jim   (1804–81) The most famous of the MOUNTAIN MEN, Bridger went West in the 1820s in search of furs, married three Indian women, is believed to have been the first white man to see the Great Salt Lake, and blazed numerous trails that facilitated westward expansion. Because his accounts of Yellowstone's geysers seemed unbelievable, he also figured in easterners' writings as a taleteller. "Bridger's Lies" included reports of invisible mountains, petrified air, and his own invincibility. According to legend, when he was asked why an arrowhead lodged for years in his back had not festered, he replied, "Meat don't spoil in the Rockies."

"British are coming, the British are coming, The" Sometimes "The red-coats are coming, the redcoats are coming." A warning line often associated with Paul REVERE's famous ride through the Massachusetts countryside. Evidently a folk attribution, as it appears nowhere in "PAUL REVERE'S RIDE." It is in any event an unlikely phrasing; more idiomatic would have been "The Regulars are out!" Its familiarity was parodied by the title of a 1966 film, *The Russians Are Coming, the Russians Are Coming.*

Broadway A New York City street that has long been a thoroughfare of the theater district—hence a code term for the city's theater industry. For a stock or regional production to "go to Broadway" means to hit the big time. True Broadway shows are put on in midtown Manhattan; those done in other sections of the city are called OFF-BROADWAY (or even Off-Off-Broadway) productions.

Brodie, Steve A New Yorker who claimed in 1886 that he had survived a jump from the BROOKLYN BRIDGE. Since the feat was not verified, his celebrity was tainted with incredulity. "To do a Brodie" came to mean (1) to fail extravagantly, (2) to perform a dangerous stunt, and (3) to commit suicide by jumping. See Sam PATCH.

Broken Arrow (1950) A western directed by Delmer Daves, one of the first to portray the American Indian in a positive light. James STEWART played Indian agent Tom Jeffords smitten with unlikely Apache "princess" Debra Paget. The story generated a short-lived (1956–58) TV series.

Bronson, Charles (1921–) Actor. Born Charles Bunchinsky, Bronson had a minor career in television and in crime movies (including the lead in the 1958 *Machine Gun Kelly*) before his work in SPAGHETTI WESTERNS and other action films made him virtually the best-known actor in the world. The French, who especially adored him, called him the "holy monster." His persona was roughly similar to that of another engaging tough guy, Clint EASTWOOD, and in 1974 he capitalized on that image by playing an urban vigilante in *Death Wish.* Its success further boosted his appeal and generated several sequels.

Bronx cheer An insulting sound made by protruding the tongue and blowing hard through pursed lips. Possibly from Yankee Stadium, which is in the New York City borough of the Bronx. The equivalent term "raspberry" (from which "razz") is English rhyming slang: "raspberry tart" for "fart."

Brook Farm A utopian community in West Roxbury, Massachusetts, which lasted from 1841 to 1847. Founded by Transcendentalist writer George Ripley and dedicated to Charles Fourier's principles of cooperation, it attracted such literary lights as Charles Dana and Nathaniel HAWTHORNE; Hawthorne's novel *The Blithedale Romance* (1852) is based on his sojourn there. Lukewarm sympathizer Ralph Waldo EMERSON characterized the experiment as an "Age of Reason in a patty-pan."

Brooklyn Bridge   A suspension bridge linking the New York City boroughs of Brooklyn and Manhattan. Its construction cost the lives of several workers and its designer, John Roebling (1837–1926), giving it a reputation for misfortune; but when it opened in 1883 as the longest suspension bridge in the world, it was hailed as the eighth wonder of the world. It remains a symbol of American ingenuity and a noted landmark. "Selling the Brooklyn Bridge" is a legendary hoax and con game.

Brooklyn Bums   The Brooklyn Dodgers, a colorful New York baseball team that acquired its unsavory nickname during a 1920s slump. Frequent pennant winners in the 1940s and 1950s, the Bums made history in 1939 by hosting the first telecast game at Ebbets Field, and in 1947 by hiring Jackie ROBINSON. The team's departure for Los Angeles in 1958 is still considered an act of treason by former fans.

Brooklynese   The dialect of Brooklyn, New York, often stereotyped in popular culture as the New York accent. Its peculiarities include *oi* for *er, d* for *th,* and dropped *r.* Thus, "My grandmother got this skirt in New Jersey" becomes, in stock Brooklynese, "My granmudda got dis skoit in New Joisey."

brother   A term of address and informal title for the male members of various groups. In usages that are now largely defunct, it indicated a native American's affection for either white or red friends; and solidarity within a "brotherhood" of trade unionists. It remains common within religious communities, college fraternities, and—since the 1960s—groups of (especially young) black Americans, who often shorten the term of address to "Bro." See SISTER.

"Brother, Can You Spare a Dime?"   The unofficial theme song of the Great Depression. Written by E. Y. "Yip" Harburg and Jay Gorney, it was originally a show tune from the Broadway play *Americana* (1932).

Brother Jonathan   (or simply **Jonathan**) In colonial times, the symbolic personification of the rustic Yankee, and hence of the country at large. By turns cagy and guileless, provincial and intensely patriotic, the figure was the colonies' answer to John Bull. Jonathan appeared in the first homegrown comedy, Royall Tyler's *The Contrast* (1787), and remained a symbol of the nation until being supplanted by UNCLE SAM. See also Sam SLICK; "YANKEE DOODLE."

Brown, Charles Brockden   See WIELAND.

Brown, Henry "Box"   One of the more inventive beneficiaries of the UNDERGROUND RAILROAD, Brown was an escaped slave who in 1856 had himself shipped North in a packing crate. His emergence in Philadelphia, bruised but grinning, brought him brief celebrity as a lecturer, and songs were written in honor of his deliverance.

Brown, James   (1933?–) Variously styled Soul Brother Number One, the Godfather of Soul, and the Hardest Working Man in Show Business, Brown was the most successful black singer of the 1960s. As well known for his footwork as for his screeching vocals, he ended his stage shows by feigning collapse, then being "revived" to thunderous applause for multiple encores. Brown's melodically sparse but rhythmically driving hits included "I Got You," "Say It Loud, I'm Black and Proud," and "Papa's Got a Brand New Bag."

Brown, Jim   (1936–   ) Football player. Considered by many to be the finest running back in the history of football, Brown had a dazzling career at Syracuse University before joining the Cleveland Browns in 1956. In a relatively short career (nine seasons), he set records for yards gained rushing (12,312), touchdowns scored (126), and most yards gained in a single season, (1,863). He retired in 1965 to pursue a movie career. Although his films were hardly memorable, Ephraim Katz calls him "the first bona-fide black male 'sex symbol' of the American screen."

Brown, John   (1800–59). Abolitionist martyr. A deeply religious Ohio farmer, Brown had been working on the UNDERGROUND RAILROAD for several years when, in 1856, he came to public prominence by killing five proslavery settlers near the Pottawatomie River in "BLEEDING KANSAS"; the incident was labeled the Pottawatomie Massacre. Three years later, Brown and a score of followers seized a federal arsenal at Harpers Ferry, Virginia, planning to use its arms to foment a slave rebellion. Thwarted by troops under Robert E. LEE, Brown was hanged for treason on December 2. His memory was enshrined in the Civil War song "JOHN BROWN'S BODY" and in Stephen Vincent BENÉT's poem of the same name.

Brown, Johnny Mack   (1904–74) Movie cowboy. An All-American football player, Brown played BILLY THE KID in a 1930 movie of that name and went on to play in hundreds of B westerns. In the 1940s, he rivaled Gene AUTRY and Roy ROGERS in popularity.

Brown Bomber   Nickname for boxer Joe LOUIS.

Brown v. Board of Education   A landmark Supreme Court case (1954) that struck down segregation in the public schools of Topeka, Kansas. "Brown" was Linda Brown, a black child whose exclusion from an all-white school was challenged by the NAACP. In reversing the "separate but equal" ruling of PLESSY v. FERGUSON, it opened a door for desegregation in general.

Brownies   See GIRL SCOUTS OF AMERICA.

Bruce, Lenny   (1926–66) Comedian. Stage name of Leonard Schneider, who introduced the colloquial vulgarity that subsequently became de rigueur on the stand-up circuit. He was convicted of obscenity in 1964 and spent the rest of his life contesting the decision. A year before dying of a drug overdose, he wrote an autobiography, *How to Talk Dirty and Influence People* (1965).

Bryan, William Jennings   (1860–1925) Politician. Three times an unsuccessful candidate for president, Bryan got closest to the office in 1896, condemning the probusiness Republicans' gold standard and championing the populist Democrats' "FREE SILVER." A brilliant orator, he secured the nomination in a ringing "cross of gold" speech, intoning, "You shall not crucify mankind upon a cross of gold." The religious sensibility evident in that line carried through his life, and especially in his last great hurrah—an impassioned defense of fundamentalism in the SCOPES TRIAL. He was successful in prosecuting Scopes for teaching Darwin, but Clarence DARROW's attack on him took a heavy toll; he died a week after his paper victory.

Bryant, William Cullen (1794–1878) Poet. Like his friends the HUDSON RIVER SCHOOL painters, Bryant was a popular exponent of Romantic nature worship. He is known for two poems: the lyric "To a Waterfowl" and the long, meditative "Thanatopsis." In the latter, a salvific, encompassing nature resolves the poet's anxiety about death.

Bubba. Southern male nickname, typically suggesting good-natured backwardness. Possibly from black dialect for "brother." See BROTHER; GOOD OLD BOY.

bubble gum See CHEWING GUM.

buck (1) A young male Indian or, later, black slave. From the original meaning, male deer or goat—the implication being that nonwhites were sexually potent. (2) A dollar. From the frontier practice of reckoning value in terms of buckskins.

Buck Rogers Comic strip. Created in 1929 by writer Phil Nowlan and artist Dick Calkins, this was the first major science fiction adventure strip, and it made the superhero Buck a role model for millions of youngsters. Popular both in the newspapers and in movie serials, it established futuristic terms like "ray gun" and "rocket ship" and made "Buck Rogers" itself a byword for fanciful science. See also CAPTAIN VIDEO; FLASH GORDON.

"buck stops here, The" President Harry S TRUMAN's comment on the responsibilities of command. The saying was engraved on a plaque that he kept on his White House desk.

Buckley, William F. (1925–) Writer. Buckley founded the journal *National Review* in 1955 and made it a principal forum for American conservatism. He has written a newspaper column, "On the Right," since 1962 and hosted a television interview show, *Firing Line,* since 1966. His books include studies of politics and culture as well as spy novels about the agent Blackford Oakes. His whimsical run for mayor of New York City was recorded in *The Unmaking of a Mayor* (1966). When he was asked, before his loss, what he would do if he won, he replied with characteristic wit, "Demand a recount."

buffalo The common, although technically incorrect, name for the American bison, a species of large, shaggy-coated cattle that roamed the Great Plains in the tens of millions before white settlement. The beasts were the foundation of the Plains Indian economy, providing food, clothing, shelter, tools, and even fuel (from the animals' dried dung, commonly known as buffalo chips). Decimation of the herds began casually in the 1860s at the hands of hunters for the Union armies and the TRANSCONTINENTAL RAILROAD. Reckless sport shooting intensified the process, and by the end of the century, when conservationists moved for restoration, fewer than a thousand head of buffalo remained. With the giant herds went the Plains Indian way of life; the return of the buffalo was a significant promise of GHOST DANCE revivalists.

Buffalo Bill (1846–1917) Frontiersman, showman. As a young man, William Frederick Cody rode for the PONY EXPRESS, lavishly shot buffalo for the Kansas Pacific Railroad (hence his nickname), and served as a U.S. cavalry scout in the SIOUX Indian wars. He might have died just one more anonymous plainsman had he not been discovered around 1870 by Ned BUNTLINE. In a series of hair-raising DIME NOVELS, Buntline transformed him into the "Scout of the Plains," giving him adventures to match Davy CROCKETT's and Daniel BOONE's. Cody capitalized on the notoriety in 1883 by organizing a world-renowned WILD WEST SHOW. Drink and naïveté bankrupted him, but he still died as the most famous westerner of his generation.

"Buffalo Gals"   A popular play-party song in the nineteenth century, adapted from the minstrel tune "Lubly Fan," which began, "Lubly Fan, won't you come out tonight?" John LOMAX, noting a plethora of other adaptations, commented that it could be (and was) "sung about or to any gals you're courting." Or men, too: The Andrews Sisters made a SWING MUSIC version in the 1940s. The title varied to fit performance venues: Buffalo refers to Buffalo, New York.

"Buffalo Skinners"   A ballad about the hardships of the white hunter's life "on the range of the buffalo." A folk-song standard, it reflects the massive destruction of buffalo herds in the 1870s.

bug juice   See KOOL-AID.

Bugs Bunny   Cartoon character. The most famous rabbit in the world, wisecracking Bugs first appeared in a Warner Brothers movie in 1938; within a few years, he was equally visible in comic books. The star of scores of animated shorts, he is frequently pitted against dim-witted hunter ELMER FUDD, whose attempts to bag the "wascally wabbit" are always in vain. Like Brer Rabbit (see UNCLE REMUS) and like his Warner Brothers colleague DAFFY DUCK, Bugs is a mass-media version of the traditional trickster, who ridicules conventional behavior by applauding the anarchic. His signature line is the inquisitive greeting "What's up, doc?" See also Mel BLANC.

Bulfinch, Charles   (1763–1844) Architect. Strongly influenced by English neoclassicism, Bulfinch developed an American variant, the FEDERAL STYLE. His major projects included designs for the Connecticut and Massachusetts statehouses, the restoration of FANEUIL HALL, and the completion, after the departure of Benjamin LATROBE, of the U.S. Capitol. His son Thomas (1796–1867) wrote *The Age of Fable* (1855) and *The Age of Chivalry* (1858), often printed together as *Bulfinch's Mythology*.

Bull Durham   Trade name of a popular chewing tobacco. Durham, North Carolina, is in the heart of tobacco country.

Bull Moose party   The Progressive party of 1912, organized by presidential aspirant Theodore ROOSEVELT after he lost the GOP nomination to William Howard Taft. The name reflected Roosevelt's response to queries about his health; he was, he said, as fit as a bull moose. The Progressives pushed for women's suffrage, labor legislation, and an expansion of what SDS later called "participatory democracy." Both TR and Taft lost to Woodrow WILSON.

Bull Run   The site of two Civil War battles, both victories for the Confederacy. In the first (July 21, 1861), the tenacity of Thomas Jackson's troops earned him the nickname Stonewall. In the second (August 29–30, 1862), Federal troops were driven from Virginia. South of the MASON-DIXON LINE, Bull Run is known as Manassas. See also Stonewall JACKSON.

"Bully!" Synonym for "excellent" popularized by Theodore ROOSEVELT. He referred to the U.S. presidency as "a bully pulpit."

Bumppo, Natty The principal character in James Fenimore Cooper's LEATH-ERSTOCKING TALES. A "natural man" modeled on Daniel BOONE, Bumppo chooses wilderness over civilization and is often accompanied by an Indian comrade, CHINGACHGOOK. Bumppo is also called Leatherstocking, Hawkeye, the Deerslayer, and the Pathfinder.

buncombe Foolish talk, nonsense. From a Buncombe County, North Carolina, congressman who, when asked why he had made an aimless speech, admitted he was talking just "for Buncombe." Abbreviated "bunk," it gives us "That's the bunk," "debunk," and Henry FORD's quip "History is mostly bunk."

bundling An English courting custom popular in Puritan New England: Engaged couples slept in the same bed, usually clothed and sometimes separated by a "bundling board." Despite such precautions, the custom not infrequently led to pregnancy and the birth of a "six-month child" after the couple's marriage.

Bunker, Archie Television character. Racist, opinionated Archie Bunker, played by Carroll O'Connor, was the star of the 1970s sitcom *All in the Family* (1971–83). Produced by liberal writer Norman Lear, the show parodied working-class conservative prejudices by making them blatant: Archie blithely condemned "spics and spades," railed against "welfare chiselers," and denounced his "bleeding heart" son-in-law as "the Polack" and "Meathead." The appearance of sympathetic blacks as cast regulars defused criticism that the show promoted racism, but it remained as controversial as it was popular throughout its run.

Bunker Hill The site of the first major battle of the Revolutionary War, fought June 17, 1775, on a slope outside of Boston actually called Breed's Hill. Colonial forces twice repulsed a British attack before being forced to retreat because of lack of powder. The redcoats' Pyrrhic victory cost them over one thousand casualties. The Americans' success may be credited partly to Israel Putnam (1718–90), who supervised their fortifications and instructed the sharpshooters, "Don't fire until you see the whites of their eyes." The line has also been attributed to Colonel William Prescott.

Buntline, Ned (1823–86). Writer. The author of hundreds of DIME NOVELS, Edward Z. C. Judson is remembered principally for having "created" BUFFALO BILL. In several novels and in an 1872 play, *The Scouts of the Plains,* Buntline transformed the obscure scout William F. Cody into a national hero; he did the same, on a generic scale, for the hard-riding COWBOY. As suspicious of foreigners as he was adulatory of westerners, Buntline went to jail for his part in the anti-British Astor Place Riot (see Edwin FORREST), and was a founding member of the xenophobic KNOW-NOTHING PARTY. Long-barreled revolvers that he gave to Wyatt EARP and Bat MASTERSON became known as Buntline Specials.

Bunyan, Paul Tall-tale hero. Bunyan is a giant lumberjack who, accompanied by an equally massive blue ox named Babe, displays prodigious feats of invention, strength, and endurance. Rolling in his sleep as an infant, he knocks down four square miles of forest. He drags his ax behind him—and leaves the Great Lakes in his wake. He has mighty Babe pull the kinks out of a crooked road. You cannot see across his pancake griddle. Even his bedbugs are so large he calls them bedcats. Commonly referred to as a "folklore" hero, Paul is actually an example of what Richard Dorson labeled "fakelore"—a literary (and in this case) commercial invention. His chief creator was a Red River Lumber Company copywriter, William Laughead, who developed him in the 1920s as an advertising symbol. Numerous juvenile books added to his appeal, so that he is among the best known, if not the best pedigreed, of national heroes.

Burgess, Gelett   See "THE PURPLE COW."

Burma Shave   A shaving cream whose roadside ad campaigns, beginning in the 1920s, made doggerel couplets part of the American landscape. Set at intervals along the highway, Burma Shave signs exhorted the motorist to drive carefully and shave frequently in such jingles as this 1936 offering:

Cooties love bewhiskered places
Cuties love the smoothest faces

And this 1940 admonition:

Don't stick your elbow out so far
It might go home in another car

Still seen occasionally on back roads, the signs had largely vanished by the 1960s, victims of the electric razor and the interstate highway system.

Burns and Allen   Comedy team. George Burns, né Nathan Birnbaum (1896–   ), and Gracie Allen (1906–64) were a husband-and-wife act successful in vaudeville, radio, and films before moving to television situation comedy in the 1950s. The stage patter of their early days fit seamlessly into the TV format, with Allen's deliciously skewed logic eliciting twinkling resignation from Burns to create a perfect fusion of verbal gags and domestic humor. In 1975, Burns returned to films, winning an Oscar as an aging comedian in *The Sunshine Boys*.

burnsides   See SIDEBURNS.

Burr, Aaron   (1756–1836) Politician. An ambitious New York senator who served four years as Thomas JEFFERSON's vice president, Burr is chiefly remembered for his fatal duel with Alexander HAMILTON. The fruit of long enmity between the two men, it led to the latter's death in 1804. Burr beat an ensuing murder charge, but in 1807 added another black mark to his record, when President Jefferson ordered him arrested for mounting an expedition into the Louisiana Territory with the aim of seizing it from the United States as his own fief. Luckily for Burr, Chief Justice John MARSHALL, presiding over his trial, defined treason to the jury so narrowly that they took less than half an hour to acquit him. The people at large did not, and Burr escaped their wrath by fleeing to Europe. His traitorous reputation matches Benedict ARNOLD's. See also DUELING; LOUISIANA PURCHASE.

Burroughs, Edgar Rice (1875–1950) Writer. Although Chicago-born Burroughs wrote in various pulp genres—including crime novels, westerns, and science fiction—he is remembered principally as the man who created TARZAN.

Burroughs, William S. (1914–) Writer. The heir to an adding-machine fortune, Burroughs is the elder statesman of the BEAT GENERATION. His heroin addiction formed the basis for his first novel, *Junkie* (1953), and his most famous work, the ingeniously experimental *Naked Lunch*. Published in Paris in 1959, it was released in the United States in 1962, establishing its author as a cult hero.

Burton, Richard (1925–84) Actor. Welshman Burton excited Broadway audiences in the 1960s with portrayals of King Arthur (in *Camelot*, 1960) and Hamlet (1964). His romance with Elizabeth TAYLOR flowered on the set of their joint venture *Cleopatra* (1963), and they reappeared together in *Who's Afraid of Virginia Woolf?* (1966) and *The Taming of the Shrew* (1967). Their tempestuous relationship—including his gift to her of a mammoth diamond—was a TABLOID favorite into the 1970s. Burton's roles in the costume dramas *Becket* (1964) and *Anne of the Thousand Days* (1969) earned him two of his six Oscar nominations.

"Bury Me Not on the Lone Prairie"   Cowboy-style parlor song, also called "The Dying Cowboy," in which the singer pleads not to be buried in the great wide-open. His request is to no avail.

> *Yes, we buried him there on the lone prairie,*
> *Where the owl all night hoots mournfully,*
> *And the blizzard beats and the wind blows free*
> *O'er his lonely grave on the lone prairie.*

"business of America is business, The"   A comment attributed to President Calvin COOLIDGE, summarizing his administration's probusiness stance.

Buster Brown   Trademark. Now the mark of a children's shoe brand, Buster Brown, with his dog, Tige, once advertised a wide range of items, including soap, harmonicas, apples, coffee, and clothing. A winking urchin in a smock and tam, he was created in 1902 by R. F. Outcault, who six years earlier had invented the YELLOW KID.

Butler, Rhett   See GONE WITH THE WIND.

"Bye Bye Blackbird"   A sentimental ballad (1926) by Ray Henderson and Mort Dixon.

> *No one here can love and understand me;*
> *On what hard luck stories they all hand me.*
> *Make my bed and light the light;*
> *I'll arrive late tonight.*
> *Blackbird, bye bye.*

Byrds, the   1960s pop music group. The Byrds made only two albums before personnel changes spelled their demise, but the first, featuring Bob DYLAN's "Mr. Tambourine Man," virtually created the genre of folk rock. The showpiece of the second album, "Turn, Turn, Turn," was a passage from Ecclesiastes set to music by Pete SEEGER.

C note   A $100 bill. From the Roman numeral C, for *centum* (100). More rarely called a century.

Cabeza de Vaca, Álvar Núñez   (ca. 1490–1557) Explorer. Leader of the first Spanish expedition into the American Southwest (1528–36), he brought back tales of the fabulous cities of CÍBOLA that inspired Coronado's search in the following decade.

cable car   A public transport vehicle moved by motor-driven cables along city streets. San Francisco's cable car system, dating from the 1870s, is one of the Bay Area's distinctive attractions.

Cabot   (1) Italian explorer John Cabot (ca. 1450–ca. 1499), born Giovanni Caboto, was the first European to reach North America after the Vikings. In 1497, sailing for England's Henry VII, he landed on Newfoundland and claimed it for his sponsor. (2) The Cabots were a BOSTON BRAHMIN family whose social airs elicited a famous skewer from John Collins Bossidy:

> *And this is good old Boston,*
> *Home of the bean and the cod,*
> *Where the Lowells talk to the Cabots*
> *And the Cabots talk only to God.*

Cadillac   (1) A luxury automobile first manufactured in 1902 and named for the founder of Detroit, French explorer Antoine Cadillac (ca. 1656–1730). Hence (2) a byword for excellence, wealth, or social arrival.

Caesar, Sid   (1922–   ) Entertainer. The star of early TV's best-written variety show, *Your Show of Shows* (1950–54), Caesar excelled at dialect humor, broad characterizations, and general zaniness. His skits with costar Imogene Coca ("The Hickenloopers") prefigured the domestic SITCOMS of the 1950s. The show gave starts to writers Woody ALLEN, Mel Brooks, and Neil SIMON.

Cagney, James   (1899–1986) Actor. A versatile performer, Cagney won the 1942 Oscar for portraying song-and-dance man George M. COHAN in YANKEE DOODLE DANDY, but he was better known as a tightly wound bad guy. He became a star in 1931, after pushing a grapefruit into girlfriend Mae Clark's face in that year's gangster classic *The Public Enemy.* He also starred in THE ROARING TWENTIES and WHITE HEAT. His crisp, staccato delivery made him a favorite with nightclub impersonators, especially for the line "YOU DIRTY RAT."

Cahn, Sammy   (1913–93) Lyricist. A prolific creator of movie show tunes, Cahn worked particularly well with composers Jule STYNE and Jimmy VAN HEUSEN. With Styne he wrote the words for the SWING MUSIC favorite "I've Heard That Song Before" (1942) and the Academy Award winner "Three Coins in the Fountain" (1954). With Van Heusen he produced three songs that became associated with Frank SINATRA: "All the Way" (1957), "High Hopes" (1959), and "My Kind of Town" (1964).

Cain, James M.   (1892–1977) Novelist. Fascinated by characters obsessed with sex, danger, and money, Cain produced three suspense novels that became FILM NOIR classics: *The Postman Always Rings Twice* (1934, film 1946), *Mildred Pierce* (1941, film 1945), and *Three of a Kind* (1943, filmed as *Double Indemnity,* 1944).

Caine Mutiny, The   (1951) A Pulitzer Prize novel by Herman Wouk (1915–   ) about a mutiny against an unbalanced naval officer. A 1954 movie version of the story starred Humphrey BOGART as the troubled Captain Queeg.

"Caissons Go Rolling Along, The"   (1908) Written by West Pointer Edward Gruber and popularized by John Philip SOUSA, this is the official song of the U.S. Artillery.

Cajuns   Residents of Louisiana descended from French colonists who, in 1755, were deported from Nova Scotia by the British. Stories of their expulsion and exodus form part of a regional folklore including distinctive foods such as crayfish and gumbo and dance music featuring accordion and violin. Cajuns, many of whom remain bilingual today, trapped and fished in the BAYOU country and were thus distinguished from the more cosmopolitan New Orleans CREOLES; modernity has expanded their range of occupations. The name "Cajun" is a corruption of "Acadian," from "Acadia," an old French term for the Canadian maritime provinces. See also "EVANGELINE."

cakewalk   (1) A high-stepping dance performed by American blacks at the turn of the century. Originally a competitive dance with a cake as a prize (hence "take the cake"), it spread to the stage and the ballroom. (2) Anything easily done. A later, illogical derivation.

Calamity Jane   (1852–1903) Frontierswoman. Born Martha Jane Canary, Calamity Jane was reputedly a PONY EXPRESS rider and Army scout before ending up in Deadwood, South Dakota, in the 1870s. There, dressing and shooting like a man, she became Wild Bill HICKOK's lover, although her claims that they had been secretly married were never verified. She nursed the sick in the town's 1878 smallpox epidemic, spent some time with the WILD WEST SHOWS, and was buried next to Hickok in the Deadwood cemetery.

Caldwell, Erskine   (1903–87) Writer. Georgia-born Caldwell shocked middle-class readers in the 1930s with two earthy portraits of the southern poor: TOBACCO ROAD and GOD'S LITTLE ACRE. With his wife, photographer Margaret Bourke-White, he produced an illustrated volume on the same subject, *You Have Seen Their Faces* (1937).

Calhoun, John C.   (1782–1850) Politician. The "Golden Voice of Slavery," Calhoun defended the South's "peculiar institution" for half a century. Vice president under Andrew JACKSON, he was as strong a states' rights champion as his boss was not, and he resigned his post over the issue of federal power. He died shortly after opposing the Compromise of 1850, muttering a doleful prediction, "The South, the poor South."

"Call for Philip Morris" Slogan introduced in 1933 by the Philip Morris cigarette company. Their ads featured a midget bellboy, the well-known Johnny, calling for Philip Morris in a hotel lobby.

"Call me Ishmael" See ISHMAEL.

Call of the Wild, The A 1903 novel by Jack LONDON. Counterposing the brutality of humans against the relative purity, however bloody, of the wild, it relates the adventures of a kidnapped dog among a pack of wolves.

Calloway, Cab (1907–) Bandleader. Calloway's rendition of a novelty tune, "Minnie the Moocher," in 1931, helped to popularize SCAT SINGING among Depression audiences and tagged him forever as the "hi-de-ho" man. He also played the colorful rogue Sportin' Life in a 1950s revival of PORGY AND BESS.

calypso music A West Indian dance music that enjoyed a brief vogue in the 1950s FOLK REVIVAL. Its principal exponent was Jamaican-born Harry BELAFONTE.

Camel A blended-tobacco cigarette brand introduced by the R. J. Reynolds company in 1913. Before the advent of the MARLBORO MAN, nonfiltered Camels were the macho teenager's COFFIN NAILS of choice. The brand's symbol, Old Joe, was modeled on a camel owned by the Barnum & Bailey Circus (see P. T. BARNUM). A famous advertising slogan was "I'd walk a mile for a Camel."

Camelot Nickname for the John F. KENNEDY White House. *Camelot* was a 1960 Broadway musical about King Arthur's court, and the usage reflected the popular view that "Jack" and "Jackie" were American royalty. After his death it came to suggest a vanished age of grace.

Camp, Walter (1859–1925) Yale football player and coach considered the Father of American Football. In addition to establishing the team size of eleven, the downs system, and standardized scoring, he also selected the first All-American team.

Camp Fire Girls A recreation organization for girls founded in 1910 by a Maine couple, Luther and Charlotte Gulick. Its watchword, Wohelo, stands for "Work, Health, Love." Boys have been admitted since the 1970s under the revised name Camp Fire Inc.

camp meetings Open-air religious gatherings of the early 1800s which were the main venues of the GREAT REVIVAL. The prototype was an 1800 event in Logan County, Kentucky, where revivalists such as James McGready preached for days. Camp meetings, which took the place of regular churchgoing, spread evangelical Christianity and its music along the frontier.

Campbell's Soup A Camden, New Jersey, company that has produced canned soup since the 1890s. Its red-and-white label, inspired by the colors of the Cornell

College football team, became a national icon in the 1960s, when it was mass-silk-screened by pop artist Andy WARHOL. The rosy-cheeked, trademarked Campbell Kids first appeared in 1904, the work of Philadelphia illustrator Grace Wiederseim.

"Camptown Races" A MINSTREL SHOW song written by Stephen FOSTER.

Candid Camera A hidden-camera television show that opened in 1948 and ran for twenty years. Hosted by Allen Funt, it filmed the humorous reactions of innocent "victims" to implausible setups—like an empty fish tank labeled "Invisible Fish" and a stalled car that turned out to have no motor. The show's signature line was "Smile. You're on *Candid Camera.*"

Cantor, Eddie (1892–1964) Entertainer. Born Edward Iskowitz, the genial, versatile Cantor did song, dance, and comedy work in settings from vaudeville to television. Known for a manic stage presence and protruding "banjo" eyes, he was identified with the song "IF YOU KNEW SUSIE LIKE I KNOW SUSIE."

Canuck A French Canadian.

Cape Canaveral The Florida launch site for U.S. space flights. For a decade after President Kennedy's death, it was called Cape Kennedy in his honor.

Cape Cod A curving spit of Massachusetts land reaching away from Boston into the Atlantic Ocean. A resort area, it was the 1620 landfall of the MAYFLOWER. "Cape Cod turkey" was a nineteenth-century sailor's term for salted fish.

Capitol The U.S. Capitol building, in Washington, D.C., houses the legislative branch of the federal government—the Senate in one wing and the House of Representatives in another. The original building plan (1792) was by William Thornton. It was later supplemented by James Hoban, Benjamin LATROBE, and Charles BULFINCH, with its most imposing feature, a central dome, being added in 1855–65 by Thomas Walter. The building sits on the city's Capitol Hill; hence "the Hill" as a metaphor for the federal legislature.

Capone, Al (1899–1947) Brooklyn-born Alphonse Capone, known as Scarface because of a razor wound, was the Roaring Twenties' most notorious mobster. As head of the Chicago bootleg and protection rackets, he made millions, directed an army of "enforcers," and orchestrated the ST. VALENTINE'S DAY MASSACRE. When he was sent to federal prison in 1931 for income tax evasion, he moaned, "All I ever did was to sell whiskey to our best people." He was portrayed in films by Paul Muni (1932), Rod STEIGER (1959), and Al Pacino (1983).

Capp, Al (1909–79) Cartoonist. Born Alfred Caplin, Capp worked on the *Joe Palooka* comic strip with Ham Fisher before launching his legacy, LI'L ABNER, in 1934.

Capra, Frank (1897–1991) Film director. A master of carefully crafted sentimentality, Capra began as a gag writer for Mack SENNETT, then dominated Hollywood in the 1930s with films about regular Joes doing battle with an oppressive system. Gary COOPER played the type in *Mr. Deeds Goes to Town* (1936) and

Meet John Doe (1941), James Stewart in *Mr. Smith Goes to Washington* (1939) and IT's A WONDERFUL LIFE. Capra won Oscars for the first and last of these as well as for IT HAPPENED ONE NIGHT. His style is sometimes called Capra-corn. See also ARSENIC AND OLD LACE; YOU CAN'T TAKE IT WITH YOU.

Captain Kangaroo   A children's television show that ran daily from 1955 to 1975. Long on conversation and short on cheap thrills, it was hosted by the low-key "Captain," Bob Keeshan.

Captain Kidd   (ca. 1645–1701) Pirate. Scottish-born William Kidd served the British crown as a privateer before turning to piracy in the 1690s. He plied mostly the New England coastal waters, and after he was hanged on London's Execution Dock, a legend said he had buried his treasure just off Connecticut, at an unmarked spot on tiny Gardiners Island. The legend influenced Edgar Allan POE's story "The Gold Bug" and Robert Louis Stevenson's *Treasure Island.*

Captain Marvel   Comic book hero. Invented in 1940 by C. C. Beck and Bill Parker, Captain Marvel was a caped crusader against evil who briefly outstripped even SUPERMAN in popularity. The "Cap" tag covered the identity of orphaned newsboy Billy Batson, who transformed himself into the muscular hero by saying "Shazam"—an acronym for Solomon, Hercules, Atlas, Zeus, Achilles, and Mercury. The character's success led to the founding of Marvel Comics.

Captain Video   TV hero. An early television space opera *Captain Video and His Video Rangers* captivated American children in the early 1950s with tales of its hero "saving the world" with futuristic gadgetry. A young sidekick, the Ranger, and a mechanical villain, Tobor, were as well known as the Captain himself. Thousands of viewers wrote the network for free "decoder rings."

Cardiff Giant   Archaeological hoax. A huge stone figure of a man unearthed on a Cardiff, New York, farm in 1869 and advertised as the fossilized evidence of a giant race. The man responsible, George Hull, had it carved by a stonecutter, artificially aged with sulfuric acid and darning needles (to create "pores"), and buried it for a year before having well-diggers "discover" it. Before the hoax was exposed, thousands of tourists paid fifty cents for a glimpse of the "prehistoric" marvel. P. T. BARNUM's copy, displayed in New York City, pulled in even more gawkers than the original.

CARE package   A package of food, clothing, or other goods sent to one in need. Now used to describe parental gifts to college students, it referred originally to post–World War II charity donations through the Cooperative for American Relief in Europe.

Carmichael, Hoagy   (1899–1981) Songwriter, pianist. Known principally as the composer of the romantic standard "STAR DUST," Carmichael also appeared frequently in films, notably as Lauren BACALL's accompanist in TO HAVE AND HAVE NOT.

Carnegie, Andrew   (1835–1919) Industrialist, philanthropist. The quintessential "rags to riches" hero, Carnegie left his native Scotland almost penniless, made a fortune in railroads and steel, and spent the last twenty years of his life giving it away. The author of the influential essay "The Gospel of Wealth" (1900), he considered his money a "sacred trust," and disbursed about $350 million before he died. Among the beneficiaries of this largess were 2,500 public libraries, various foundations, and New York City's Carnegie Hall. The latter, founded in 1891, has been a Mecca for classical musicians ever since.

Carnegie, Dale (1888–1955) Self-help promoter. A farm boy turned super-salesman, Carnegie wrote *How to Win Friends and Influence People* in 1936. Based on the idea that success comes from understanding the other person's point of view, it became one of the biggest self-help guides of all time. Self-improvement courses modeled on its philosophy still blanket the country. See also Norman Vincent PEALE.

carpetbaggers Northern agents of the federal RECONSTRUCTION policy who streamed into the South carrying their belongings in carpet-covered bags. They acquired an often-deserved reputation for venality. See also SCALAWAG.

"Carry Me Back to Ol' Virginny" (1878) MINSTREL SHOW song by the black composer James Bland, who also wrote "OH DEM GOLDEN SLIPPERS." It became Virginia's state song in 1940.

Carson, Johnny (1925–) Comedian, TV host. Unflappable, wry Carson hosted the nightly TONIGHT SHOW for so long (1962–92) that it was commonly known as the Carson show; to "do Carson" became an essential step in an entertainer's career. Carson's second-banana cohost, Ed McMahon, introduced him in words that became a household phrase: "Heeere's Johnny."

Carson, Kit (1809–68) Frontiersman. Even if his exploits had not been embellished by dime novelists (see DIME NOVELS), the historical Christopher Carson would have been an important figure in the opening of the West. Born in Missouri, he trapped furs in the Rockies in the 1830s and then, between 1842 and 1846, guided the FRÉMONT expeditions to Wyoming and California. He served as an Indian agent in the 1850s in New Mexico and earned a brevet generalship from the Union during the Civil War.

Carter, Nick A detective hero introduced by writer John R. Coryell (1848–1924) in an 1886 story for *New York Weekly*. He starred in countless pulp-magazine stories and DIME NOVELS, with over one thousand of them written by Frederick Van Rensselaer Dey (1861–1922). The character inspired the MGM mystery *Nick Carter, Master Detective* (1939), two sequels, and a radio series (1943–55).

Carter family A major influence on country music, the original Carters were Virginians Alvin Pleasant (1891–1960), his wife Sara (1898–1979), and sister-in-law Maybelle (1909–78). Their recordings of traditional songs in the 1920s and 1930s, including their biggest hit, "Wildwood Flower," made them the first family of "hillbilly" music. "Mother" Maybelle, whose "Carter lick" guitar style was also influential, sang with her daughters beginning in the 1940s. One of them, June, married Johnny CASH.

Carver, George Washington (1861–1943) Scientist. Born a slave, Carver worked his way through a master's degree at an Iowa agricultural college and in

1896 became head of the agricultural department at Booker T. WASHINGTON's Tuskegee Institute. There he spent half a century researching crops and sharing his discoveries with farmers in a "school on wheels." Known principally for his work on PEANUTS and sweet potatoes, he found hundreds of uses for these and other plants.

Casablanca   (1942) The winner of Academy Awards for best picture, best director (Michael Curtiz), and best screenplay (Julius and Philip Epstein and Howard Koch), *Casablanca* is one of the best-loved movies in Hollywood history. The story of an American café owner who chooses honor over romance, it starred Humphrey BOGART as the embittered Rick Blaine and Ingrid BERGMAN as Ilsa Lund, his never-to-be true love. The film survives as a cultural icon largely on the basis of its quotable lines. These include Ilsa's request for the song "As Time Goes By," "Play it, Sam" (often misquoted as "Play it again, Sam"); Rick's toast "Here's looking at you, kid"; and the film's exit line, "Louis, I think this is the beginning of a beautiful friendship."

"Casey at the Bat"   (1888) A poem by Ernest Lawrence Thayer first published in the *San Francisco Examiner* and recited thousands of times to theater crowds by William Hopper. The story of a baseball slugger's fall, it ends with this lament:

> *Oh somewhere in this favored land the sun is shining bright;*
> *The band is playing somewhere, and somewhere hearts are light.*
> *And somewhere men are laughing, and somewhere children shout;*
> *But there is no joy in Mudville—mighty Casey has struck out.*

"Casey Jones"   See Casey JONES.

Cash, Johnny   (1932–   ) Singer, songwriter. Arkansas-born Cash, known as the Man in Black because of his dress, was among the first country stars to be recognized by a general audience. His star rose in the 1950s with the hits "Folsom Prison Blues" and his signature tune, "I Walk the Line." After overcoming drug problems in the 1960s, he married June Carter of the CARTER FAMILY, recorded "Jackson" with her in 1967, and appeared the following year on a Bob DYLAN album. He sang at the White House in 1970, and by the 1980s had become a patriarch of crossover country.

Caspar Milquetoast   (or simply **Milquetoast**) A timid or ineffectual person. A character in a 1930s comic strip by H. T. Webster. See also Walter MITTY.

Cassidy, Butch   (1867–1908?) Outlaw. Born Robert Leroy Parker, Cassidy formed a gang called the Wild Bunch or Hole-in-the-Wall Gang (from their Wyoming hideout) in the 1890s and robbed western banks until around the turn of the century. Then he and Harry Longbaugh, the so-called Sundance Kid (1861–?1908), left for South America to escape Pinkerton agents. They are thought to have been killed by Bolivian police following a robbery. Their fame, modest in their own lifetimes, was enhanced by a romanticized film, *Butch Cassidy and the Sundance Kid* (1969), in which they were played by Paul NEWMAN and Robert REDFORD.

Cassidy, Hopalong See HOPALONG CASSIDY.

Castle, Vernon and Irene Dancers. British-born Vernon Blythe (1887–1918) and American Irene Foote (1893–1969) transformed social dancing just before World War I. Their performances helped to popularize the tango and waltz, while Irene's bobbed hair became a Roaring Twenties fad. The couple was played by ASTAIRE AND ROGERS in a 1939 movie.

Cat in the Hat, The See DR. SEUSS.

Cat on a Hot Tin Roof (1955) A Pulitzer Prize play by Tennessee WILLIAMS about maneuvering over a family inheritance in the Mississippi Delta. A 1958 film version furthered the careers of Paul NEWMAN, Elizabeth TAYLOR, and Burl IVES.

catbird seat An enviable position. From the title of a 1942 James THURBER story.

Catch-22 An unwinnable situation, especially one in which the solution is logically precluded. The title of Joseph Heller's 1961 military novel, where the character Yossarion, needing to demonstrate insanity to get out of flying missions, proves his sanity by the very act of fearing them.

Catcher in the Rye, The (1951) J. D. SALINGER's novel about an ingratiatingly unconventional adolescent, Holden Caulfield, on a search for self and meaning in New York City. Considered sexually daring for its time, it is now required reading in many high schools.

Cather, Willa (1876–1947) Writer. Born in Virginia, Cather was raised in Nebraska and frequently set her work in the Midwest's prairies. Settlers' lives form the focus of her novels *O Pioneers!* (1913) and *My Antonia* (1918). The equally respected *Death Comes for the Archbishop* (1927) concerns the work of missionaries in frontier New Mexico.

Catlin, George (1796–1872) Painter. Originally a lawyer, Catlin turned in the 1820s to recording the vanishing lives of North American Indians. His work, based on extensive western travels, included hundreds of paintings, an engraving-rich ethnography (1841), and a portrait gallery that toured for almost a decade. Easterners' images of the noble savage owed much to his efforts.

Cats A musical based on T. S. ELIOT's *Old Possum's Book of Practical Cats.* It opened in 1982 and became the third longest-running Broadway play, after A CHORUS LINE and *Oh! Calcutta!*

Catskills A scenic, mountainous region of New York State. Discovered by Henry HUDSON and often painted by members of the HUDSON RIVER SCHOOL, the Catskills were also the setting for "RIP VAN WINKLE." See also BORSCHT BELT.

catsup See KETCHUP.

Caulfield, Holden See THE CATCHER IN THE RYE.

Cave-in-Rock An outlaw stronghold near the juncture of the Ohio and Mississippi rivers. In the 1800s, it sheltered hordes of river pirates.

CB Citizens band. A radio frequency used by private citizens and popular since the 1970s among motorists, especially truck drivers. Many CB operators have their own nicknames (''handles''), and they have evolved an elaborate jargon for en route chatter. See, for example, SMOKEY BEAR (2).

CCC Civilian Conservation Corps. A NEW DEAL program that put young men to work on conservation-related projects such as road and dam construction and reforestation. Between 1933 and 1941, the CCC employed over 2 million. Many motorist rest stops and picnic areas were CCC projects.

"Celebrated Jumping Frog of Calaveras County, The" (1865) A short story that established Mark TWAIN's reputation. It tells in humorous dialect how a champion jumping frog, Daniel Webster, loses a contest after being force-fed birdshot.

chain gangs Groups of convicts, chained together to prevent escape, who performed hard labor, often on roadways throughout the South. The gang system was used to intimidate ''uppity'' blacks after the Civil War and was only eliminated through prison reform in the 1940s. It inspired Oscar-nomination performances in three movies: for Paul Muni in *I Am a Fugitive from a Chain Gang* (1932), Tony Curtis in *The Defiant Ones* (1958), and Paul NEWMAN in *Cool Hand Luke* (1967). ''Chain Gang'' was a Top 40 hit (1960) for Sam Cooke.

chain letter A moneymaking scheme that arose in the Great Depression and that surfaces periodically in spite of its illegality. Would-be participants are sent lists of names and asked to send money to the person at the top of the list, add their own names to the bottom, and circulate copies of the letter. Logically, the scheme should enrich everyone; in reality, this fails when the chain is broken.

chair, the See ELECTRIC CHAIR.

Chairman of the Board See Frank SINATRA.

Chamberlain, Wilt (1936–) Basketball player. Nicknamed Wilt the Stilt because of his height (7'3"), Chamberlain dominated professional basketball in the 1960s. In a fourteen-year career, he was named most valuable player four times, led the NBA in scoring seven years straight, and scored a record one hundred points in one game.

Chan, Charlie See CHARLIE CHAN.

Chandler, Raymond (1888–1959) Writer. A charter member of the HARD-BOILED FICTION detective school, Chandler created the private eye Philip MARLOWE, who became as well known on the screen as in the author's novels. The best of these were THE BIG SLEEP, *Farewell, My Lovely* (1940, films 1944 and 1975), and *The Long Goodbye* (1953, film 1973).

Chaney, Lon (1883–1930) Actor. The ''Man of a Thousand Faces,'' Chaney was a master of makeup who astonished Hollywood in the silent era with his character roles. Of his more than one hundred parts, the most famous were Quasimodo in *The Hunchback of Notre Dame* (1923) and the title role in *The Phantom* *of the Opera* (1925). His son Lon Chaney, Jr. (1906–73), also an actor, specialized in horror roles such as Frankenstein's monster and the Wolfman.

Chaplin, Charlie   (1889–1977) Filmmaker. London-born Charles Chaplin first went onstage as a child, toured with Fred Karno's company as a teenager, and in 1913 joined Mack SENNETT's Keystone company. There he made over thirty films, gradually developing the persona that brought him fame: the baggy-trousered, cane-twirling "Little Tramp." After the character came to full flower in *The Tramp* (1915), Chaplin worked with various studios producing shorts and, in 1921, his first feature: *The Kid*'s revenues that year were second only to THE BIRTH OF A NATION's. From then on, having formed the United Artists Corporation in 1919 (in partnership with Mary PICKFORD, Douglas FAIRBANKS, and D. W. GRIFFITH), Chaplin produced a string of independent features that made him the first superstar of American cinema. The highlights of his career were *The Gold Rush* (1925); *City Lights* (1931); *Modern Times* (1936); his first talkie, *The Great Dictator* (1940); and *Limelight* (1952).

As popular as his movies were, Chaplin took constant criticism for his personal and political lives. His marriages to a series of teenagers, coupled with his apparent sympathy for left-wing causes and his refusal to take American citizenship, made him the frequent target of conservative attacks, and his 1947 pacifist film, *Monsieur Verdoux*, was effectively boycotted by the AMERICAN LEGION. From 1952, when he was denied reentry into the country after a trip abroad, until 1972, when he returned to receive a special Academy Award, Chaplin lived in Switzerland with his fourth wife, Oona, the daughter of playwright Eugene O'NEILL. His former boss Sennett once called him the "greatest artist who ever lived."

Charles, Nick and Nora   Fictional detectives. The dapper, sybaritic hero and heroine of Dashiell HAMMETT's novel THE THIN MAN, the couple was portrayed in sparkling screen adaptations by William Powell and Myrna Loy.

Charles, Ray   (1930–   ) Singer, pianist. One of the inventors of SOUL music, blind "Genius" Ray Charles (born Ray Charles Robinson) became nationally known in 1955 with "I Got a Woman." His subsequent number-one records included "What'd I Say?" (1959), "Georgia on My Mind" (1960), "Hit the Road, Jack" (1961), and "I Can't Stop Loving You" (1962).

Charleston   The major dance craze of the 1920s. It involved kicking out the heels while swinging the arms. Named for Charleston, South Carolina, it was introduced to the New York public in a 1923 all-black revue.

Charlie   Vietnam War slang for the Vietcong. From the code designation for "VC": "Victor Charlie."

Charlie Brown   See PEANUTS (2).

Charlie Chan   Fictional detective. Created in 1925 by novelist Earl Derr Biggers (1884–1933), Charlie Chan was a philosophical Chinese gentleman who was expert at solving crimes that baffled the police. In the 1920s to the 1940s, the character was portrayed dozens of times on the radio and in B movies, most notably by Warner Oland and Sidney Toler. Frequently assisted by his "Number One son," Chan was much given to hokey Confucianisms, such as "Bad alibi like dead fish. Cannot stand test of time."

Charlie McCarthy See Edgar BERGEN.

"Charlotte's Web" A juvenile story (1952) by E. B. WHITE. It concerns the spider Charlotte's rescue of a doomed pig, Wilbur, and his reconciliation to her inevitable death. It became an animated film in 1973.

Charter Oak A Hartford, Connecticut, landmark where colonists in 1687 were said to have hidden a colonial charter from a royal minister authorized to suspend it.

Chautauqua Movement A combination education and entertainment movement that swept the country between the 1870s and the 1920s, providing public lectures, correspondence courses, and traveling tent shows in an atmosphere reminiscent of CAMP MEETINGS. It grew out of an institute for Sunday school teachers founded in 1874 in Chautauqua, New York; this organization—*the* Chautauqua—was soon copied by dozens of unaffiliated, smaller "chautauquas." It has been estimated that, at its peak, the Chautauqua Movement reached one-third of the U.S. population.

Chávez, César (1927–93) Labor leader. The son of CHICANO migrants, Chávez founded the United Farm Workers union in the mid-1960s to fight the exploitation of fellow workers by Anglo growers. UFW strikes against grape and lettuce producers were a major element in an emerging Chicano consciousness.

Checker, Chubby See The TWIST.

Checkers speech Richard Nixon's televised answer, during his 1952 vice presidential run, to charges that he had accepted campaign gifts. Checkers was a cocker spaniel that had been given to his children; with much hand-wringing, Nixon "confessed" that they were "going to keep it."

cheesebox on a raft A mocking nickname for the Union ship *Monitor*, which fought the Confederate *Merrimack* on March 9, 1862, in history's first engagement of ironclad vessels. Although inconclusive in itself, the battle demonstrated the obsolescence of wooden warships. See MONITOR AND MERRIMACK.

Cherokee Of the FIVE CIVILIZED TRIBES, the Cherokee of Georgia lived most like whites. Farmers and traders, they had a written language devised by SEQUOYAH and used it in 1827 to write a constitution. Evicted from their lands by Georgia and the federal government, they were force-marched to Oklahoma in the 1830s, on the devastating trek known as the TRAIL OF TEARS. A northern section of Oklahoma where they were settled became known as the Cherokee strip. In 1893 that, too, was opened to white encroachment.

Chesnutt, Charles W. (1858–1932) Writer. The nation's first black novelist, Chesnutt made history in 1887 when his story "The Goophered Grapevine" became the first work by a black writer to appear in THE ATLANTIC MONTHLY. His story collections *The Conjure Woman* and *The Wife of His Youth* (both 1899), like his novels *The House Behind the Cedars* (1900) and *The Colonel's Dream* (1905), all deal to some degree with racial prejudice.

"Chester" (1770) A patriotic song by William BILLINGS, boasting of how British generals yield to "beardless Boys." Extremely popular in its day, it has been called "The Marseillaise" of the American Revolution.

Chevy A Chevrolet automobile. First produced in 1911 and named for a Swiss racing driver, Louis Chevrolet, who was the partner of company founder William Durant. Since the 1920s, the Chevy has rivaled the Ford as a "people's" car. The 1957 Chevy is a classic car buff's favorite.

chewing gum According to legend, Mexican dictator SANTA ANNA brought the chicle-chewing habit to the United States when he was exiled in New York City in the 1870s. Thomas Adams popularized it with his Adams' New York chewing gum and followed up with the oldest-flavored gum still in existence, Black Jack. Frank Fleer's rival company came up with Chiclets in 1899 and the first bubble gum, Dubble Bubble, in 1928. The Topps company's Bazooka bubble gum was introduced ten years after that. See also William WRIGLEY, Jr.

Cheyenne An Indian people, encountered by the LEWIS AND CLARK EXPEDITION in the BLACK HILLS, who by the mid-nineteenth century were Great Plains buffalo hunters. Their hostility to whites was encouraged by the SAND CREEK MASSACRE, and they were critical to the defeat of George Armstrong CUSTER at the LITTLE BIGHORN. Wyoming adopted their name for its state capital.

Chicago The third largest city in the United States (with a 1990 population of 6 million), a Midwest metropolis on the southern shore of Lake Michigan. It was founded in 1804 as Fort Dearborn, grew rapidly in the nineteenth century, and was largely rebuilt after the CHICAGO FIRE of 1871. A center of the meatpacking and railroad industries, it experienced severe labor troubles in the 1880s (see HAYMARKET RIOT) and gang warfare (see Al CAPONE) in the 1920s. Important in the development of SKYSCRAPER technology, Chicago is home to the world's tallest building, the SEARS TOWER, and to the world-renowned University of Chicago (founded 1890). Black immigration after World War II helped to create a distinctive electrified music called Chicago blues. In *Chicago Poems* (1916), Carl SANDBURG described the city ecstatically as "Hog Butcher, Tool Maker, Stacker of Wheat, Player with Railroad and Freight Handler to the Nation."

Chicago Eight A group of anti–Vietnam War protesters who were tried in 1969–70 for inciting a riot near the 1968 Democratic party convention in Chicago. The trial became a media event thanks to the courtroom shenanigans of YIPPIE defendants Jerry Rubin and Abbie Hoffman as well as the legal antics of the judge, Julius Hoffman, who had a third defendant, BLACK PANTHER Bobby Seale, bound and gagged. The "riot" in question was later traced to the police, and most of the defendants' convictions were reversed on appeal.

Chicago Fire A three-day fire (October 8–10, 1871) that destroyed four square miles of Chicago, including the business district. It began in the barn of one Patrick O'Leary, and legend says that Mrs. O'Leary's cow, kicking over a lantern, started the blaze. It left ninety thousand people homeless, killed three hundred, and so nearly leveled the city that rebuilding had to begin virtually from scratch. Steel-and-concrete Chicago rose from the ruins.

Chicano The politically preferred label since the 1970s for members of the Mexican-American community. With its feminine form, "Chicana," it derives from Spanish *mexicano*. See also César CHÁVEZ.

"chicken in every pot, a car in every garage, A" A Republican party slogan in the 1928 election campaign. The "chicken" part was copied from French King Henry IV, the "car" attributed to the "Republican prosperity" of sitting President Calvin COOLIDGE. The idea was to vote for Coolidge's man, Herbert Hoover.

chili A spicy dish made of beef and chili peppers; hence the full name, *chili con carne,* or "chili with meat." From the Nahuatl *chilli,* for the plant. A staple of Mexican-American and TEX-MEX cooking, chili sparks feverish debates and competitive cook-offs in the Southwest. Purists scoff at the addition of beans, a common practice now even in Texas. The presence of tomatoes gives the slang term "a bowl of red."

Chinatown (1) The Chinese section of a large city, specifically New York and San Francisco. (2) *Chinatown,* a 1974 film directed by Roman Polanski about corruption in the Chinatown district of Los Angeles. Set in the 1930s, it is a brilliant, bleak homage to FILM NOIR.

Chinese fire drill (1) An adolescent game played at a stoplight. The occupants of a car jump out and run around it as many times as they can before the light turns green. (2) Anything confused or confusing.

Chingachgook The Mohawk companion of Natty Bumppo in James Fenimore Cooper's LEATHERSTOCKING TALES. He is the father of Uncas, the title character of the series' second novel, *The Last of the Mohicans* (1826).

Chiquita Banana A trademark developed in 1944 by the United Fruit Company and still affixed to the company's bananas. Chiquita wears a fruit-filled sombrero. She became widely known thanks to a 1944 song that was recorded by both Xavier CUGAT and Carmen MIRANDA.

Chisholm Trail The major cattle trail from Texas to ABILENE, Kansas, in the 1860s and 1870s. Named for Indian trader Jesse Chisholm, it carried millions of Texas LONGHORNS to market before the railhead moved farther west to DODGE CITY. Cowboys memorialized the trail in a song, "The Old Chisholm Trail," which was said to have one thousand verses.

chitlins Hogs' intestines. Often considered quintessential SOUL food, "chitterlings" were actually known in England a century before Chaucer's time.

chop suey A Chinese-American dish invented in the mid-nineteenth century by Chinese cooks working on the western railroads. A mélange of bean sprouts, water chestnuts, bamboo shoots, and slivered meat, it is unknown in China, where its name would mean something like "bits and pieces."

Chorus Line, A The longest-running Broadway play of all time. A dance musical choreographed by Bob Fosse, it opened in 1975 and closed in 1990 after 6,137 performances.

chowder A thick seafood soup. The name comes from the French *chaudière,* for "cooking kettle." The American version, which features clams, has two varieties. New England (formerly Cape Cod) clam chowder is a milky broth seasoned with herbs and salt pork. Manhattan (formerly Rhode Island) clam chowder is a thinner soup using tomatoes as well as clams. Partisanship abounds. John Mariani quotes one New England cook: "Tomatoes and clams have no more affinity than ice cream and horseradish." A vegetarian variant is corn chowder.

Christian Science See Mary Baker EDDY.

Christmas, Annie "Fakelore" heroine. Six feet eight, 250 pounds, and the owner of a magnificent mustache, Annie Christmas could carry three barrels of flour at a time and once towed a keelboat from New Orleans to Natchez without stopping for breath. For every eye she gouged out or ear she chewed off in a fight, she added one bead to a long trophy necklace. At her death it measured thirty feet, and Mike FINK himself gave her a wide berth. Invented by two New Orleans newsmen as a spoof on Mississippi River legends, the character appeared in *Times-Picayune* features in the 1920s.

Christmas, Joe The tortured hero of William Faulkner's *Light in August* (1932). A light-skinned mulatto, he is castrated and murdered by a racist mob because of his involvement with, and killing of, a white woman.

Christy Minstrels A MINSTREL SHOW started in the 1840s by Philadelphia showman Edwin P. Christy (1815–62). It introduced such conventions as the comics Mr. Tambo and Mr. Bones, toured successfully for years, and popularized many of the songs of Stephen FOSTER.

chuck wagon A kitchen plus commissary on wheels that accompanied cowboys on their trail drives. "Chuck" was an old British term for "food."

Cíbola Region containing the Seven Cities of Cíbola, rumored to be incalculably wealthy, that Spanish CONQUISTADORS sought in vain in the sixteenth century. According to CABEZA DE VACA, they were located in today's Arizona and New Mexico. Francisco Coronado (1510–54) traveled there from Mexico in 1540–42, but all he found were Hopi and Zuñi pueblos—the adobe walls of which were hardly gold. Undaunted, and inspired by reports of another golden city, Quivira, he pressed on into what is now Kansas and discovered other Indian villages, just as poor. His journeys increased Spanish knowledge of the Southwest, but their goal proved to be a phantom.

cigar store Indian A wooden Indian used as an advertising symbol by tobacconists. From the association of native Americans with smoking. The figures first became popular in the late 1800s.

cinco de mayo Spanish for "the fifth of May." On May 5, 1862, Mexican soldiers achieved a momentous victory over an invading French force at the city of Puebla. The event is celebrated not only in Mexico but throughout the Spanish-speaking Southwest.

Cisco Kid Fictional western hero. The name Cisco Kid first appeared in the O. HENRY story "The Caballero's Way" (1907), but the character itself—a Mexican version of the cowboy fighting for justice—was a creation of the movies. Warner Baxter gave an Oscar-winning performance as the Southwest Robin Hood in the 1929 film *In Old Arizona.* Duncan Renaldo picked up the role in the 1940s and, with Leo Carrillo as his sidekick, Pancho, brought the Kid's adventures to children's television in the 1950s. Episodes of the TV series ended invariably with the two friends' trading laughter and the formula exchange "Oh Ceesco" . . . "Oh Pancho." Jimmy Smits starred as the Kid in a 1994 movie, with Chicano comic Cheech Marin as his companion.

Citizen Kane (1941) Often called the greatest American movie ever made, *Citizen Kane* was all the more remarkable for being the product of a Hollywood newcomer—the brashly inventive, indefatigable Orson WELLES, who directed, did much of the script, and played the lead. A biography in flashbacks of millionaire Charles Foster Kane, the film explores the problematic relationship between self and persona, suggesting that the "key" to a person's life—like the meaning of Kane's last mysterious word, "Rosebud"—can never be known. Widely praised for its cinematography (Gregg Toland) and acting, the film won best screenplay awards for Welles and cowriter Herman Mankiewicz. Its celebrity was enhanced by the open secret that it was a veiled biography of William Randolph HEARST.

City of Brotherly Love Philadelphia. From the early QUAKER influence of William PENN. The name itself, in Greek, means "city of love."

City of the Angels See LOS ANGELES.

"city upon a hill" See UTOPIAN COMMUNITIES.

"Civil Disobedience" See Henry David THOREAU.

civil rights movement The existence of slave rebellions (see Nat TURNER, Denmark VESEY) and the UNDERGROUND RAILROAD shows that movements for the liberation of black Americans antedated the Civil War by decades. The term "civil rights movement," however, usually refers to the activism of the 1950s and 1960s, when blacks pushed to abolish segregation in the South and achieve a fuller participation in national life. The groundwork for this movement had been laid by the NAACP and other groups; it came to fruition after the Supreme Court decision in BROWN v. BOARD OF EDUCATION opened the way for the desegregation of schools. Rosa PARKS is often considered the modern movement's "mother"; its most articulate spokesman was Martin Luther KING, Jr. His example inspired younger activists like the FREEDOM RIDERS and members of SNCC, but when he was assassinated in 1968, many of them rejected his nonviolent stance and adopted a less conciliatory BLACK POWER philosophy. See BLACK MUSLIMS; BLACK PANTHERS; MALCOLM X.

Civil War (1861–65) The most costly conflict in American history, the Civil War is often remembered as a war over slavery. Disagreement over slavery, to be sure, was an important feature in the dissension, but the underlying reasons were grounded as much in economics as in the moral outrage of the ABOLITIONISTS: For decades before the war, the slaveholding South, eager to protect its agricultural livelihood, had invoked the Jeffersonian doctrine of STATES' RIGHTS to resist protectionist tariffs that favored northern factory owners. Tariff debates inflamed sectional passions as early as the 1820s, when advocates of NULLIFICA-TION proposed that the states should be able to void any federal law they disliked and defenders of centralized power like Daniel WEBSTER countered with a thunderous "Union forever!"

The question came to a head in 1860, with the elevation of Abraham LINCOLN to the presidency. Fearing that even such a mildly antislavery leader would threaten the plantation economy, eleven states immediately withdrew from the Union and elected Jefferson DAVIS president of the Confederacy. However moderate his slavery position, Lincoln was adamant about the preservation of the Union, and on April 6, 1861, he ordered a relief ship to be sent to FORT SUMTER, a federal installation in Charleston Harbor which the new, secessionist government had claimed as its own. Six days later, Confederate batteries fired on the fort, and Lincoln called for volunteers to quell the insurrection.

The North's expectation that the rebellion would be over shortly met a rude awakening at the Battle of BULL RUN, and both sides settled in for a long ordeal. With the South under the command of Robert E. LEE and the North successively under George McClellan, Ambrose Burnside, George Meade, and Ulysses S. GRANT, brother fought brother in bloody encounters from the Deep South to western Tennessee and north to Pennsylvania. The North was generally on the defensive until its victory at Antietam (September 17, 1862) encouraged Lincoln to issue the EMANCIPATION PROCLAMATION; this instantly transformed the sectional conflict into a moral crusade that killed all southern hopes for European aid.

In 1863, the momentum shifted, as a Confederate surge into Pennsylvania was stopped at GETTYSBURG and Grant captured strategically critical Vicksburg, Mississippi. He then directed a two-year eastward onslaught. He took the Confederate capital, Richmond, himself in 1865, months after William T. SHERMAN had devastated the Dixie heartland by burning ATLANTA and everything between it and the sea. The war ended in 1865 at APPOMATTOX COURTHOUSE, with the surrender of "Lee's ragamuffins" on April 9.

The Union's celebration was short-lived, for five days after the surrender Lincoln was shot. His death had serious repercussions in the South, as his anticipated policy of "malice toward none" was undone by the more vindictive forces of RECONSTRUCTION. Not only because of the defeat of the LOST CAUSE itself but because of Reconstruction, the wounds of the Civil War took decades to mend, while the attitudinal differences that caused the conflict—differences regarding the nature of government and the nature of human beings—were still a matter of debate in the 1950s.

No war in American history—not even the Revolution—was so celebrated in story and song as this fratricidal episode. Known in the South as the War Between the States and in the North as the War of the Rebellion, the clash between Union blue and Confederate gray prompted Stephen CRANE's RED BADGE OF COURAGE, Stephen Vincent BENÉT's "JOHN BROWN'S BODY," Walt WHITMAN's *Drum Taps* (1865), and John Greenleaf WHITTIER's "BARBARA FRIETCHIE" as well as the novel-inspired film classics THE BIRTH OF A NATION and GONE WITH THE WIND. Its most stirring musical legacies are "DIXIE" and "THE BATTLE HYMN OF THE REPUBLIC."

See also Mathew BRADY; George Armstrong CUSTER; HOOKER; Stonewall JACKSON; PICKETT'S CHARGE; Jeb STUART.

Civilized Tribes   See FIVE CIVILIZED TRIBES.

Claghorn, Senator   The stereotypical incarnation of regional buffoonery, Beauregard Claghorn, the "Dixie foghorn," was a fixture on the Fred ALLEN radio program in the 1940s. Raucous, bombastic, and intensely "southron," the senator specialized in punning self-congratulations, as in this estimation of his undergraduate career: "Ah was voted the member of the senior class most likely to secede and ah was graduated magnolia cum laude." His vocal mannerisms were copied for the WARNER BROTHERS' animated rooster Foghorn Leghorn.

Clanton gang   See O.K. CORRAL.

Clark, Dick   See AMERICAN BANDSTAND.

Clark Kent   See SUPERMAN.

Clay, Cassius   (1) Abolitionist. As a member of the state legislature and editor of the newspaper *True American,* Clay (1810–1903) fought bitterly against slavery in his native Kentucky, killing at least one opponent in a duel and having to guard his office from mobs with a set of cannon. (2) The birth name of Muhammad ALI.

Clay, Henry   (1777–1852) Congressman. The most famous member of the GREAT TRIUMVIRATE, Clay was also known as the Great Pacificator for his deal-making skills: Passages of the Missouri Compromise and the Compromise of 1850 were due to his efforts. Three times an unsuccessful presidential candidate, he remarked, "I would rather be right than be President." Throwing his support to John Quincy Adams in the 1824 election, he was made secretary of state at Adams's victory. Accused of having made a "corrupt bargain," he fought an uneventful duel with fellow senator John Randolph. When Randolph died, he asked to be buried facing west, so he could keep an eye on his Kentucky rival.

Cleaver, Eldridge   See BLACK POWER.

Clemens, Samuel Langhorn   See Mark TWAIN.

Clemente, Roberto   (1934–72) Baseball player. Born in Puerto Rico, Clemente was a fielder for the Pittsburgh Pirates who won four National League batting titles in the 1960s. The league's most valuable player in 1966, he amassed a career total of three thousand base hits. He acquired a legendary status, especially among Puerto Ricans, after he died in a plane crash while on a Nicaraguan earthquake relief mission.

Clementine   See "MY DARLING CLEMENTINE."

Clermont   The nation's first commercially successful steamboat. Built by engineer Robert FULTON, it was widely derided as "Fulton's Folly," yet its maiden voyage from New York to Albany in 1807 transformed river traffic. Within a decade dozens of steamboats plied the Mississippi.

cliff-hanger   A suspenseful story or situation. From the adventure serials of the silent screen, in which episodes often ended with the heroine hanging from a cliff (literally or figuratively), with the story "To Be Continued" the following week. Pearl White was called Queen of the Cliff-hangers. See PERILS OF PAULINE.

Cline, Patsy   (1932–63) Singer. A country star of the early 1960s, Virginia Patterson Hensley got national attention in 1957, when she won first place on Arthur GODFREY's *Talent Scout Show*. An emotionally powerful singer, she had hits with "Walking After Midnight," "Crazy," and "I Fall to Pieces" before dying in a plane crash at the age of thirty.

Clinton's Big Ditch   The ERIE CANAL. New York Governor DeWitt Clinton (1769–1828) was its major supporter.

clipper ships   Extremely fast sailing ships developed in the 1840s, clippers were used to fetch Chinese tea and to bring prospectors to the California and Australian gold fields. Sleek, high-masted square-riggers that visually defined the "Age of Sail," they dramatically cut sailing times and boosted profits. The most famous builder, Boston's Donald McKay (1810–80), designed the record-breaking *Flying Cloud* (east coast to west coast in eighty-nine days) as well as the largest clipper ever built, the *Great Republic*. The ships were obsolete by the 1870s, thanks to steam and railroads.

Cobb, Ty   (1886–1961) Baseball player. Often called the game's greatest player, Detroit Tiger outfielder Tyrus Cobb, known as the Georgia Peach, batted over .300 for his entire 23-season career, had a lifetime average of .367, and set a long-standing stolen-base record of 892. He was the first member of the Baseball Hall of Fame.

Coca-Cola   The most popular soft drink in the world. It was invented in 1886 by Atlanta pharmacist John S. Pemberton, who used, as the name indicates, extracts of the coca leaf (the source of cocaine) and the cola nut. Originally touted as a health tonic, "Coke" is now as symbolic of America as baseball or Old Glory. The fluted bottle, designed to suggest a cola nut, came in around 1915. Company slogans have included "The pause that refreshes" (1929), "It's the real thing" (1941), and "Coke is it" (1982). There is no truth to the rumors that vestigial cocaine makes the drink addictive and that a nail left in it overnight will be eaten away.

Cochise   (ca. 1823–74) Chiricahua Apache war chief. Unjustly accused of kidnapping in 1861, Cochise led his people on a decade-long war against the whites from strongholds in the Arizona mountains. He surrendered to the U.S. Army in 1872 with the understanding that his friend Tom Jeffords would become Indian agent. The story of their friendship is told in BROKEN ARROW.

codfish aristocracy   A New England slur for the nouveau riche, especially those who earned their money in maritime commerce.

Cody, William Frederick   See BUFFALO BILL.

coffin nails   Cigarettes. The term became popular in the late 1800s, and in the 1890s a waggish manufacturer, Leslie & Welsh, sold cigarettes under the brand name Coffin Nail. Since the 1840s "coffin varnish" has meant cheap alcohol.

Cohan, George M.   (1878–1942) A theatrical jack-of-all-trades and master of many, Cohan dominated the American stage in the first part of this century.

Beginning as a child vaudevillian with his family the "Four Cohans," he became famous in 1904 by starring in *Little Johnny Jones*. The Broadway musical, which he also wrote, introduced two of his most famous songs, "GIVE MY REGARDS TO BROADWAY" and "I'm a Yankee Doodle Dandy." Cohan's subsequent hits included "YOU'RE A GRAND OLD FLAG," "Mary's a Grand Old Name," and the World War I smash "OVER THERE." His life inspired the 1942 film *Yankee Doodle Dandy*, starring James CAGNEY, and the 1968 play *George M.*

Cohn, Harry (1891–1958) Hollywood executive. The head of COLUMBIA PICTURES from the 1920s until his death, Cohn was a vulgar, suspicious tyrant known as Harry the Horror and—in Ben HECHT's famous quip—White Fang. He was closely associated with the careers of Frank CAPRA and Rita HAYWORTH. The huge crowds at his funeral elicited an acerbic explanation from Billy WILDER: "Well, give the people what they want . . ."

coke (1) A slang term for cocaine. (2) First a slang term, then, as Coke, a trademark for COCA-COLA. The Coca-Cola Company resisted the usage for half a century before capitulating in the 1940s and having it trademarked.

cold war Common term for the period immediately following WORLD WAR II and extending through the 1980s, during which competition between the United States and the Soviet Union, the two atomic "superpowers," was the driving force of international politics. Espionage and fear of espionage were endemic features, generating the James Bond novels of Ian Fleming and the ROSENBERG CASE. U.S. foreign policy followed Harry S TRUMAN's principle of "containment," leading to numerous minor brushes around the world and to major stands in the KOREAN WAR and the VIETNAM WAR. In Asia particularly, containment reflected acceptance of the "domino theory," which said that once one nation fell to communism, its neighbors would inevitably topple in its wake. A particularly fearsome moment occurred in 1962, when cold warrior John F. KENNEDY risked a nuclear confrontation in successfully blocking a Soviet missile shipment to communist Cuba. See also Alger HISS; HOUSE UN-AMERICAN ACTIVITIES COMMITTEE; "ICH BIN EIN BERLINER"; Joseph MCCARTHY.

Cole, Nat "King" (1919–65) Singer. Nathaniel Coles made television history in 1956 by becoming the first black to have his own variety show. In the year it lasted, he hosted such performers as Count BASIE, Harry BELAFONTE, and Ella FITZGERALD. A master of the languorous ballad, Cole had his biggest hits with "Unforgettable" and "Mona Lisa." His daughter Natalie is also a popular singer.

Cole, Thomas (1801–48) Painter. The founder of the HUDSON RIVER SCHOOL, English-born Cole was among the first to translate American landscapes into "acceptable" art. His romantic views stress the grandeur of wild nature. In the 1830s, he turned to vast pictorial allegories like *The Course of Empire* (1835–36) and *The Voyage of Life* (1840).

Colonel Sanders See KENTUCKY COLONEL.

Colt, Samuel (1814–62) Firearms manufacturer. New Englander Samuel Colt invented the most widely carried handgun in the American West. Especially popular with TEXAS RANGERS and with Union soldiers in the Civil War, the Colt "six-shooter'' was called the Peacemaker and, after the fact, as the Gun That Won the West. Colt .45 is the brand name of a malt liquor that reputedly has the ''kick'' of a Colt handgun.

Colter, John   (1775–1813) Mountain man. A member of the LEWIS AND CLARK EXPEDITION, Colter later trapped and explored in what is now YELLOWSTONE PARK. Around 1808, he was captured by a group of Blackfoot Indians who gave him a chance to run for his life with them in pursuit. His escape, naked and bleeding from prickly-pear cuts, became the set piece ''Colter's Run'' in frontier folklore. See also MOUNTAIN MEN.

Coltrane, John   (1926–67) Jazz saxophonist. Coltrane began his work in big bands, joined Miles DAVIS in the 1950s, and formed his own quartet in 1960. His detailed improvisations are a typical feature of the jazz style known as new wave.

''Columbia, the Gem of the Ocean''   (1843) A patriotic song written in Philadelphia by Thomas Becket. Recasting the line ''Three cheers for the red, white and blue,'' English tunesmiths soon adapted it as ''Britannia, the Gem of the Ocean.''

Columbia Pictures   A Hollywood studio founded in 1924. With Harry COHN at the helm and Frank CAPRA in the principal director's chair, it became a major studio by the 1940s, furthering the careers of Rita HAYWORTH and William HOLDEN. Among Columbia films that won best picture Oscars were ALL THE KING'S MEN, FROM HERE TO ETERNITY, and ON THE WATERFRONT.

Columbus, Christopher   (1451–1506) Sailor. Born into a weaver's family in Genoa, Cristoforo Colombo went to sea as a teenager and had already made several voyages along the African coast when, in 1484, he proposed a novel idea to Portugal's King John. If the king would fund the voyage, Columbus proposed to sail west, around the globe, to the fabulous Indies. Refused by John, he went to Spain, and after years of lobbying convinced the monarchs, Ferdinand and Isabella, to back his venture. Setting out in August 1492 with a tiny fleet—the *Pinta*, the *Niña,* and the *Santa María*—Columbus reached San Salvador, in the Bahamas, on October 12. Mistakenly believing that he had found the Indies, Columbus named the peaceful Arawaks he met ''Indians'' and began the first of many fruitless searches for gold.

A fine sailor but an incompetent administrator, Columbus returned to Spain, leaving a settlement, Navidad, with rapacious underlings; on a second voyage, he found both them and it destroyed. His final two voyages also ended in disappointment. On the third, he was arrested for malfeasance and sent back to his royal sponsors in chains; on the fourth, he was marooned for a year on the island of Jamaica. He died ignorant of his accidental achievement, vainly pressing his claims for a larger share of the new lands' treasures.

Because Columbus was no more respectful of native peoples than others of his day, and because his voyages eventually resulted in their decimation, he is often castigated as an imperialist monster who blundered into fame. That assessment is as one-sided as the traditional picture: the ''Admiral of the Ocean Seas'' as the spotless servant of God and country. His obvious failings and current fashion notwithstanding, it is perfectly reasonable, from a European viewpoint, to see his accomplishment as the discovery of America.

Comanche (1) A Plains Indian people known for expert horsemanship and unremitting hostility to white settlement. They kept the French and Spanish out of the Plains in the eighteenth century, and in the nineteenth were at constant war with expansionist Texans. Of the many white captives they took, the most famous was Cynthia Parker, the mother of QUANAH. (2) The sole U.S. Army survivor of Custer's Last Stand, a gray horse owned by Captain Myles Keogh. See LITTLE BIGHORN.

"Come up and see me some time" One of Mae WEST's most quoted lines. She delivered it to Cary GRANT in *She Done Him Wrong* (1933).

comics An American invention, the comic strip emerged from a New York City newspaper circulation war. In 1896, Joseph PULITZER's *World* ran a series of cartoons depicting life in an urban slum. Drawn by Richard Outcault, *Hogan's Alley* starred a youngster known first as the Kid and, when he adopted a yellow nightshirt, as the Yellow Kid. When *New York Journal* publisher William Randolph HEARST hired Outcault away and Pulitzer assigned the feature to another artist, the Yellow Kid became a fixture of both papers—sparking the twin birth of the American "comic" and YELLOW JOURNALISM.

In 1897, Hearst added the KATZENJAMMER KIDS, and by World War I, the American people were following the adventures of MUTT AND JEFF, KRAZY KAT, and MAGGIE AND JIGGS. The interwar period saw a vogue for crime and adventure comics, with the appearance first of TARZAN and BUCK ROGERS (both 1929), then in rapid succession DICK TRACY, TERRY AND THE PIRATES, and FLASH GORDON. The 1930s also saw the first comic books and the rise of superheroes such as BATMAN, SUPERMAN, and WONDER WOMAN. After World War II, the violence gradually subsided, as *Peanuts* (see PEANUTS [2]) brought a kids'-eye view to everyday problems and POGO fed a "funny papers" tone into political satire. The rebellious 1960s saw the rise of underground comics, although old standbys such as L'IL ABNER and BLONDIE retained their appeal.

"Common Sense" (1776) An antiroyalist pamphlet by Thomas PAINE which presented the case for independence as "common sense." Phenomenally popular in the colonies, it both prefigured and hastened the DECLARATION OF INDEPENDENCE.

communes See UTOPIAN COMMUNITIES.

company store A company-owned store where employees may purchase supplies on credit against their salaries. Legal gouging at such a store in the "company town" of Pullman, Illinois, led to the PULLMAN STRIKE of 1894. In Merle TRAVIS's mining ballad "Sixteen Tons," the singer moans,

> *Saint Peter, don't you call me cause I can't go;*
> *I owe my soul to the company store.*

Comstock Lode The largest silver deposit ever found in the United States, the Comstock Lode was located in the Nevada mountains by prospector Henry Comstock in 1859. Until it played out in the 1890s, it yielded $400 million worth of silver and gold. Not realizing its potential, Comstock sold his claim for $10,000.

comstockery Legislation or other activism against obscenity. The term was coined by George Bernard Shaw after U.S. postal inspector Anthony Comstock (1844–1915) began a crusade against smutty mail in the 1870s. Comstock was simultaneously secretary of the New York Society for Suppression of Vice.

Concord A village west of Boston, Massachusetts, that was the home of the nineteenth-century "American Renaissance." Among the literary lights who took up residence there were THOREAU, EMERSON, HAWTHORNE, and Louisa May AL-COTT. Thoreau's WALDEN Pond is within the village limits, as is the North Bridge, at which the Battle of Concord was fought on April 19, 1775. Emerson immortalized that engagement in his 1837 poem "Concord Hymn." It contains the famous lines

> *By the rude bridge that arched the flood,*
> *Their flag to April's breeze unfurled,*
> *Here once the embattled farmers stood*
> *And fired the shot heard round the world.*

Conestoga A Pennsylvania town that in the eighteenth century was a principal building site for COVERED WAGONS; hence "Conestoga wagon" as an equivalent term. Conestoga cigars were called Conestogas, then stogies.

Coney Island A Brooklyn, New York, beachfront popular with tourists since the nineteenth century. It is known for its amusement park, BOARDWALK, and spicy HOT DOGS. The original Nathan's stand opened there in 1913.

Confederacy Common name for the Confederate States of America, the secessionist South during the CIVIL WAR. Led by President Jefferson DAVIS, it was formed in February 1861 by Alabama, Florida, Georgia, Louisiana, Mississippi, and South Carolina. Texas joined in March, and after the capture of FORT SUMTER in April, the CSA ranks swelled to eleven with the addition of Arkansas, North Carolina, Tennessee, and Virginia. The Confederate government dissolved with the surrender at APPOMATTOX COURTHOUSE.

Congress The legislative branch of the federal government. It evolved from the CONTINENTAL CONGRESS of the revolutionary period, and was established by Article I of the CONSTITUTION. A bicameral body, Congress is composed of an "upper" house, the Senate, and a "lower" one, the House of Representatives, whose elected members serve for, respectively, six-year and two-year terms. Each state sends two senators to Washington; the number of representatives varies according to state population. See also CAPITOL.

Congressional Medal of Honor See MEDAL OF HONOR.

Connecticut Yankee Like Yankees in general, the Connecticut Yankee has been stereotyped since colonial times as a unique blend of craftiness, ingenuity, and droll humor. In literature, the most famous example is probably the Hartford, Connecticut, factory foreman who becomes "the Boss" in Mark TWAIN's 1889 novel, *A Connecticut Yankee in King Arthur's Court.* In the flesh, the hands-down winner was P. T. BARNUM. See also Sam SLICK.

Connors, Jimmy (1952–) Tennis player. The best American men's singles player of the 1970s, Connors won his first U.S. Open in 1974 and in the following decade took the title four more times. Often a Wimbledon finalist in the same period, he took the British championship in 1974 and 1982. His frequent rival was the equally powerful, and equally temperamental, John McENROE.

conquistadors Spanish military adventurers who explored both Americas in the sixteenth century. As befit their name (which means "conquerors"), they often brutally repressed the native peoples. They included the conquerors of Mexico and Peru, CORTÉS and Pizarro, as well as BALBOA, CABEZA DE VACA, DE SOTO, and PONCE DE LEÓN. See also CÍBOLA.

"conspicuous consumption" See Thorstein VEBLEN.

Constitution The U.S. Constitution, or "supreme law of the land," was written by the Constitutional Convention in 1787 and ratified by the original states in 1787–90. Its broad goals were stated in a preamble:

We the people of the United States, in Order to form a more perfect Union, establish Justice, insure domestic Tranquillity, provide for the common defense, promote the general Welfare, and secure the Blessings of Liberty to ourselves and our Posterity, do ordain and establish this Constitution for the United States of America.

Designed to replace the ARTICLES OF CONFEDERATION with something more substantial, the Constitution defined the basics of American government: the federal system, the electoral process, and the three branches. The document gratified the Federalists, who had fought for its adoption; opponents who felt it slighted individual liberties were mollified the following year with the BILL OF RIGHTS.

Constitution, U.S.S. See OLD IRONSIDES.

continental (1) Paper money issued by the Continental Congress during the Revolution. Practically worthless, it gave rise to the smirking expression "not worth a continental." (2) A ballroom dance tune popularized by ASTAIRE AND ROGERS in the 1933 film *The Gay Divorcee*. It won the 1934 best song award.

Continental Congress An assembly of representatives from the original colonies which first met in Philadelphia in 1774 to debate and coordinate resistance to British taxation. This brief initial meeting was followed by the Second Continental Congress, which convened in 1775. Its accomplishments included the adoption of the DECLARATION OF INDEPENDENCE, the drafting of the ARTICLES OF CONFEDERATION, ratification of the Peace of Paris (1783), and the adoption of the federal CONSTITUTION. From 1781 the body was known as the United States in Congress Assembled, and it was from that description that "United States" derived. See also CONGRESS.

Continental Op A private detective created by Dashiell HAMMETT. One of the earliest examples of the hard-boiled type, "the Op" (short for "operative") worked for San Francisco's Continental Detective Agency. He made his first appearance in BLACK MASK. See also HARD-BOILED FICTION.

Contrast, The   (1787) A play by jurist Royall Tyler (1757–1826). A romantic comedy, it was the first drama written in the United States by an American. It introduced the character of Jonathan, the stereotypical rustic Yankee.

Conwell, Russell   See ACRES OF DIAMONDS.

cookbooks   Aside from family recipe collections, the first native cookbook was Amelia Simmons's *American Cookery* (1796), which contained instructions for cranberry sauce and pumpkin pie. Following its success came numerous "housewifery" guides such as Lydia Maria Child's 1829 *Frugal Housewife* and the 1841 *Treatise on Domestic Economy for the Use of Young Ladies at Home and at School,* by Harriet Beecher STOWE's older sister Catherine Beecher. Fannie FARMER revolutionized the field in 1896 by writing the first cookbook to use accurate measurements, and this was followed by a twentieth-century explosion of kitchen guides. Cookbooks remain, pardon the pun, publishers' bread and butter. The overall sales leaders are, in order, the BETTER HOMES AND GARDENS *Cook Book* (first published in 1930), BETTY CROCKER'S COOKBOOK (1950), and Irma Rombauer and Marion Rombauer Becker's JOY OF COOKING (1931).

Coolidge, Calvin   (1872–1933) President. "Silent Cal" lives in popular memory not for any great state accomplishments, but for his "typically Yankee" wit. Biographers have debunked the myth of his laconic style, yet curt gems still enrich the legend. On being asked what a preacher had just said about sin: "He's agin it." To a woman who told him she had bet a friend that she could get more than two words out of him: "You lose." To a man who asked how it felt to be president: "You got to be mighty careful." And his comment on the possibility of a second term: "I do not choose to run for president in 1928"—truncated, in support of the myth, to "I do not choose to run."

coon   (1) Short for "raccoon." A "coon's age" means a long time, from the belief that the animals are long-lived. (2) Nickname for a frontiersman, from his preference for eating (and wearing) raccoons. (3) By the mid-nineteenth century, a generally derogatory term for a black person. "Coon songs," by the turn of the century, meant MINSTREL SHOW numbers.

coonskin   The skin of a raccoon. Coonskin caps, popular among frontiersmen in the early 1800s, were revived as a children's fad during the 1950s Davy CROCKETT craze. Coonskin coats were worn by 1920s college students.

Cooper, Gary   (1901–61) Actor. The ultimate strong, silent type, Frank James Cooper won Academy Awards for his portrayals of Alvin YORK in *Sergeant York* (1941) and the abandoned western sheriff in HIGH NOON. He played Wild Bill HICKOK in *The Plainsman* (1937), Lou GEHRIG in *The Pride of the Yankees* (1942), and the leads in two HEMINGWAY adaptations, *A Farewell to Arms* (1933) and FOR WHOM THE BELL TOLLS. He also delivered one of Hollywood's most quoted lines. As the lead in 1929's *The Virginian,* he answers an insult by saying, "When you call me that, smile."

Cooper, James Fenimore   (1789–1851) Writer. One of the first Americans to achieve international literary fame, Cooper grew up in Cooperstown, New York, which had been developed by his father, and had his first success with a Revolutionary War tale, *The Spy* (1821). His great work was the five-volume LEATHER-STOCKING TALES, which tells the story of Natty Bumppo from youth to death. *The Pilot* (1823), whose central figure is modeled on John Paul JONES, is credited with having started the novel of mariners. Filled with vivid portrayals of the American landscape, Cooper's novels are nonetheless marred by a stiff style that elicited a classic lampoon from the dialect master Mark TWAIN. "Fenimore Cooper's Literary Sins" has a frontier hero lifting a river out of its bed and trekking the wild with an Indian ally named Chicago (see CHINGACHGOOK).

Cooperstown A small resort village in upstate New York. The childhood home of James Fenimore COOPER, it is also the mythical birthplace of American BASE-BALL and the site of the National Baseball Hall of Fame. See Abner DOUBLEDAY.

Copley, John Singleton (1738–1815) Painter. America's first great portraitist, Copley earned a wide reputation in the colonies and exploited it, after 1774, in London. His national importance rests on his realistic Boston studies of the 1760s, especially portraits of John HANCOCK and Paul REVERE.

copperhead (1) One of the four poisonous snakes indigenous to North America. Hence (2) a northerner sympathetic to the South during the Civil War, thought capable of striking at the war effort without warning.

Coppola, Francis Ford See The GODFATHER.

Corbett, Gentleman Jim (1866–1933) Boxer. The first star of the padded-glove era, James J. Corbett took the heavyweight crown from John L. SULLIVAN in 1892, knocking him out after twenty-one rounds in New Orleans. Known for quick jabs and his own innovation, the left hook, he kept his title until 1897, when he lost it to "Battling Bob" Fitzsimmons. Errol FLYNN played him in a 1942 film.

Corey, Giles The sole male victim of the 1692 SALEM WITCH TRIALS. Refusing to plead in his own defense, he was put to death by being crushed beneath stones.

Corman, Roger (1926–) Hollywood's most prolific director of low-budget genre films. Equally adept at teen movies, gangster films, science fiction, and "biker" films, he achieved cult status as the director of an Edgar Allan POE cycle that begins with *The House of Usher* (1960) and ended with *The Masque of the Red Death* (1964); his principal star in this series was Vincent PRICE. His fascination with crime led to biographies of Machine Gun KELLY (*Machine Gun Kelly* 1958), Ma BARKER (*Bloody Mama* 1970), and Al CAPONE (*Capone* 1975).

corn Probably the Indians' greatest gift to the early settlers. Unknown in Europe before 1492, it was brought back by Columbus as "Turkey corn" and later helped to ensure the survival of the New England colonists (see SQUANTO). Economically essential to many tribes, it was the focus of ritual dances among peoples as widely separated as the southwest Pueblo, southeastern Shawnee, and northern Iroquois. Corn maidens and corn mothers figure widely in North American Indian belief systems.

  Corn soon became as central to the newcomers' cooking as it had been to that of the natives. American dishes based on it include cornmeal mush (originally

"Indian pudding"); various baked and fried breads including HUSH PUPPIES, corn fritters, and corn pone; and the side dishes succotash, hominy grits, and corn on the cob. This is not counting its major use: feed for livestock. By the 1880s, the Indians' "maize" was a major crop, and the fertile Midwest had become known as the Corn Belt.

corn liquor (or likker)   Whiskey made of no less than 80 percent corn mash. Popular especially in the southern mountains, it is also known as corn whiskey, corn, moonshine, white lightning, and mountain dew—the last also being the trade name of a popular soft drink. See also MOONSHINE.

cornball   An unsophisticated, countrified person. From an early-nineteenth-century term for a piece of corn pone. Hence of or like this kind of person, as in "cornball humor." An equivalent term is "corny." "Corn" in this sense refers to humor that is broad, sentimental, or old-fashioned. Kentucky was once called a place

> *Where the corn is full of kernels*
> *And the colonels are full of corn.*

The reference may be to the grandiosity of "southern colonels" or to their supposed liking for CORN LIQUOR.

Cornwallis, Lord   See YORKTOWN.

Coronado, Francisco   See CÍBOLA.

corrido   A Mexican border BALLAD. Typically about love, tragedy, or adventure, *corridos* are often responses to contemporary events. The form developed along the Rio Grande in the last century and is still being exploited today.

Corrigan, Wrong Way   (fl. 1930s) Pilot. Douglas Corrigan became an instant, if unusual, celebrity in July 1938 when he flew a single-engine plane from New York to Dublin. He planned to fly to California, but he became turned around after takeoff in a fog. Whether his feat was a mistake or moxie, it got him a New York City ticker tape parade.

Cortés, Hernando   (1485–1547) Conquistador. In 1519, the Spanish adventurer Cortés marched five hundred men from Tabasco to Tenochtitlán, the AZTEC capital. At first received warmly, Cortés soon alienated the ruler, MONTEZUMA, by his demands for gold and other tribute. After two years of diplomatic maneuvering and bloody fighting, the king was killed and Cortés claimed Mexico for Spain.

Cortéz, Gregorio   (1875–1916) Outlaw. Mexican-born Cortéz was farming in Texas when, in 1901, he was unjustly accused of stealing a horse. Resisting arrest, he killed a sheriff; in the ensuing chase, more posse members fell to his guns. Captured, he spent over a dozen years in prison before public support—from both Mexicans and Texans—led to a pardon. His bravery made him a hero along the Rio Grande. His story was told in numerous CORRIDOS and a film, *The Ballad of Gregorio Cortéz* (1982).

Corvette   A sports car introduced in 1953 by Chevrolet. Still the ultimate American sportster, "the Vette" was driven by the adventurers Tod and Buz in the 1960s TV series ROUTE 66.

Cosa Nostra   See MAFIA.

Cosby, Bill   (1937–   ) Comedian, actor. One of the most highly paid performers of the century, Cosby began as a stand-up comic, creating classic characters like Fat Albert and a befuddled Noah ("An ark? What's an ark?"). As Robert Culp's sidekick in television's *I Spy* (1965–68), he was the first black to star in a weekly series. His own sitcom, *The Cosby Show* (1984–92), depicted an upwardly mobile professional family; Cosby himself played physician Heathcliff Huxtable.

Cosmopolitan   A periodical founded in 1886 which, under the editorship of Helen Gurley Brown (1922–   ) became a slick, "adventurous" woman's magazine. Brown, author of the popular working woman's guide *Sex and the Single Girl* (1962), set the magazine's new tone by urging its readers to emulate the "Cosmo Girl"—a modern combination of sense and sensuality. See also GIBSON GIRL.

cotton   A minor crop in the eighteenth century, cotton became the basis of the southern economy after 1793, when Eli WHITNEY invented a cotton gin (short for "engine") to remove its seeds. By 1860, nearly two-thirds of the nation's exports came from cotton, making the South a "cottonocracy." The crop's importance is reflected in the opening line of "DIXIE," "I wish I was in the land of cotton," and in the catchphrase "King Cotton," from David Christy's 1855 study, *Cotton Is King, or The Economical Relations of Slavery*.

cotton candy   (1) A frothy, spun-sugar candy first sold in amusement parks in the 1920s. Hence (2) any insubstantial, facilely satisfying entertainment.

Cotton Club   A HARLEM nightclub that between the two world wars showcased major jazz performers, including Duke ELLINGTON, Count BASIE, and Louis ARMSTRONG. It was patronized enthusiastically by integrated audiences.

"Cotton-eyed Joe"   A MINSTREL SHOW song that Bob Wills made a novelty standard in WESTERN SWING. The accompanying dance—done in a shoulder-to-shoulder, floor-circling pattern—includes intermittent, obligatory shouts of the word "Bullshit!"

cotton gin   See Eli WHITNEY.

cottonmouth   See WATER MOCCASIN.

couch potato   A lazy person, specifically one who spends an inordinate amount of time watching television.

Coughlin, Charles   (1891–1979) Political commentator. A Roman Catholic priest who spoke weekly from a Detroit radio station, Father Coughlin amassed a huge following in the 1930s by inveighing against the NEW DEAL, foreign entanglements, and Jewish bankers, whom he blamed for U.S. entry into World

War II. After PEARL HARBOR, his appeal faded, and his superiors ordered him to cease his inflammatory broadcasts.

counterculture   A 1960s catchall phrase indicating a wide array of anti-ESTABLISHMENT and "alternate" lifestyles. Pitted against the common enemy of mainstream culture (and its creature, the Vietnam War) were people as stylistically distinct as NEW LEFT theorists, "back to the land" communards, HIPPIES, environmentalists, and the BLACK PANTHERS. The range of "counter" sensibilities was examined in Theodore Roszak's *The Making of a Counterculture* (1969) and Charles Reich's *The Greening of America* (1970).

country music   American country music evolved out of the fiddle tunes and traditional BALLADS of the nineteenth century, many of which had been imported from the British Isles and which gave "hillbilly" music its common themes: failed romance, death, and a paradoxical blend of homesickness and wanderlust. The "mountain music" sound, however, was also influenced by the religious music of the GREAT REVIVAL, by BLUES, and by the cowboy and folk tunes of the Southwest. The last factor was once so dominant that the common term for this eclectic music was "country and western."

Until the 1920s, country music was largely a local phenomenon, particularly strong in the southern Appalachians and in Texas. At that time, radio helped to create the first country stars, Jimmie RODGERS and the CARTER FAMILY. By the 1930s, NASHVILLE, Tennessee, had become a center of country music production because of its GRAND OLE OPRY broadcasts and its local talent; Roy ACUFF started the first "all country" publishing business there. At the same time, Bill MONROE developed BLUEGRASS, Bob Wills and his Texas Playboys invented WESTERN SWING, and Gene AUTRY became the best-known "singing cowboy."

"Traditional" country music relied on acoustic instruments and high-pitched, often nasal singing. Country stars of the 1940s and 1950s, beginning with the influential songwriter Hank WILLIAMS, added electrical instruments and even drums (banned from the Grand Ole Opry stage) to create the even more eclectic sounds of rockabilly, country rock, and—most recently—the pop-inspired "new country." By the 1960s, country music had reached far beyond its original southern audiences. City dwellers as far afield as Detroit and Vancouver had become fans of country stars George JONES and Loretta LYNN, while the writing of "outlaw" singers Willie NELSON and Waylon Jennings had made Austin, Texas, an alternative site for music production.

See also the names of individual performers.

coureurs de bois   French-Canadian "woods runners" who, beginning in the seventeenth century, lived as trappers and hunters in the northern forests.

"Courtship of Miles Standish, The"   (1858) A poetic romance by Henry Wadsworth LONGFELLOW set in the PLYMOUTH COLONY of New England. Colony leader Miles Standish entrusts the wooing of Priscilla Mullins to his friend John Alden, but she, preferring the messenger to the message, utters the famous line "Why don't you speak for yourself, John?" After much mental travail, Priscilla and John are married, with the avuncular blessings of the older Standish. The three principals were all real people, but the love triangle was Longfellow's own concoction.

Cousy, Bob (1928–   ) Basketball player. Playing for the Boston Celtics in the 1950s and 1960s, Cousy was known for his superb passing ability, which earned him a most valuable player award in 1957 and a career total, then a record, of 6,955 assists. He made the All-Pro team in ten out of his thirteen Celtic seasons.

covered wagon A wagon drawn by horses, mules, or oxen and covered with a tentlike canvas tarp. Covered wagons, originally made in CONESTOGA, Pennsylvania, carried freight and families west in the nineteenth century. Called prairie schooners from their quasi-nautical appearance, they often traveled in strings, or "wagon trains." The pulling of these trains into circles against Indian attacks is a familiar image in the Hollywood western.

Cowardly Lion One of the fearful foursome in L. Frank Baum's THE WIZARD OF OZ. The character was immortalized by Bert Lahr in the 1939 movie.

cowboy (1) During the Revolution, a cowboy was a Tory guerrilla who lured patriot soldiers into ambush with the sound of cowbells. (2) In the nineteenth century, the term came to mean, like the Mexican *vaquero,* one who earned his living by rounding up and herding cows. The great era of the American cowboy lasted roughly twenty-five years, from the late 1860s, when the first Texas-bred cattle were driven north to Kansas railheads, to about 1890, when BARBED WIRE and railroad expansion made such long drives redundant. The actual lives of the cowboys—filled with tedium and economic exploitation—were romanticized by Owen Wister (see THE VIRGINIAN) and dime novelists (see DIME NOVELS) almost before the last dust had settled, and Hollywood picked up where they left off. Hence the image of the cowboy as a rugged free spirit—and of the Old West as endless spaces and endless gunfights.

cowboys and Indians A term dating from about the 1880s for the children's game of make-believe frontier fighting.

"Cowboy's Lament, The" A typical "warning" ballad of unknown authorship in which a dying cowboy tells how wild living has done him in. The most frequently printed (and parodied) of cowboy tunes, it is also known as "The Streets of Laredo," from its first line: "As I walked out in the streets of Laredo." The singer's repentance appears in the final line: "I'm a young cowboy and I know I've done wrong."

Coxey's Army A group of unemployed workmen who in 1894 marched from Ohio to Washington, D.C., to petition Congress for cheap money and government jobs. Their leader, Jacob Coxey (1854–1951), proposed social reforms that prefigured the NEW DEAL. He was arrested for trespassing and his "army" disbanded. See also BONUS ARMY.

coyote A wild dog indigenous to the western states, the coyote often symbolizes the "wide open spaces." A famous cowboy song, for example, begins, "Bury me not on the lone prairie / Where the coyote howls and the wind blows free." In the lore of many Indian peoples, the animal is at once a culture hero and an obscene "trickster" figure who subverts cultural values. As a dangerous but humorous embodiment of contradictions, he appears in legends told from the Great Plains to California.

Crabbe, Buster   (1907–83) Actor. Following a pattern set by Johnny WEIS-MULLER, Larry "Buster" Crabbe turned an Olympic gold medal in swimming (1932) into Hollywood roles as a muscular TARZAN. He then branched out into other adventure films, playing FLASH GORDON and BUCK ROGERS in 1930s serials, then BILLY THE KID in a string of low-budget westerns.

cracker   A poor, backward white southerner, especially one from Florida or Georgia—the latter of which was once called the Cracker State. Folk etymology sometimes traces the term to the sound of a country drover's cracking bullwhip; Stuart Berg Flexner relates it to the cracking of dry corn by folks who were too poor to buy cornmeal.

cracker-barrel philosopher   One who dispenses homespun wisdom from the rostrum of a country-store cracker barrel. Sometimes seen as "cracker-box philosopher."

Cracker Jack   The brand name of a caramel-covered popcorn and peanut mixture developed in the 1870s by Chicago vendor F. W. Rueckheim. It was a hit at the 1893 Chicago world's fair and took its name from a slang expression meaning "excellent." The 1908 song "TAKE ME OUT TO THE BALL GAME" reflected its popularity in the lines

> *Buy me some peanuts and Cracker Jack.*
> *I don't care if I never get back.*

Sales were further boosted in 1912, when tiny toy "surprises" were first placed inside the packages.

Cradle of Liberty   See FANEUIL HALL.

Crane, Ichabod   The spindly, timid protagonist of Washington Irving's "THE LEGEND OF SLEEPY HOLLOW."

Crane, Stephen   (1871–1900) Writer. The author of THE RED BADGE OF COURAGE, Crane first achieved critical notice with a realistic novel about slum life, *Maggie: A Girl of the Streets* (1893). Of his many stories, the most famous are "The Open Boat," "The Bride Comes to Yellow Sky" (both 1898), and "The Blue Hotel" (1899).

Crater, Judge   One of the most famous missing persons in American history, Joseph Crater was a state supreme court justice who entered a New York City cab on August 6, 1930, and was never seen again. A secret romance and fear of exposure for graft have been suggested as possible causes, but his disappearance, like Jimmy HOFFA's, remains a mystery.

Crawford, Joan   (1904–77) Actress. Lucille Fay Le Sueur became Joan Crawford after MGM ran a nationwide publicity contest to find her a stage name. A major star for over forty years, she was known for her portrayals of strong women, and won an Oscar in 1945 for MILDRED PIERCE. She joined her rival Bette DAVIS in the 1962 horror film *What Ever Happened to Baby Jane?* After her death, her daughter Christina exposed her parental failings in a best-selling book, *Mommie Dearest* (1978).

Crazy Horse (ca. 1849–77). Sioux war chief. In 1875, after gold was discovered in the BLACK HILLS, the federal government ordered all Sioux onto a reservation to prevent them from harassing invading prospectors. Crazy Horse refused. With a band of warriors, he eluded Army troopers for half a year, beating them at the Rosebud River and the LITTLE BIGHORN. Fleeing retaliatory U.S. forces, he endured a bitter winter in Canada and then surrendered to General Nelson Miles. While in custody, he was stabbed to death by a guard. He is still revered as the Oglala Sioux's greatest war chief. A monumental sculpture to his memory has been in progress for over forty years in the face of Thunderhead Mountain, South Dakota.

"Cremation of Sam McGee, The" (1907) A narrative poem by Robert W. SERVICE. It tells of the death by freezing of an Arctic adventurer born in Tennessee. A friend tries to cremate his remains, but when he checks on the fire, a smiling Sam asks him to close the door.

> *It's fine in here, but I greatly fear*
> *you'll let in the cold and storm.*
> *Since I left Plumtree, down in Tennessee,*
> *it's the first time I've been warm.*

Creole In old Louisiana, (1) someone of French or Spanish descent born in the New World. French-speaking Creoles acquired a reputation for aristocratic ways—including a fondness for DUELING—which set them apart from the more rustic CAJUNS. Among the surviving elements of Creole culture are culinary specialties such as gumbo and French coffee as well as the New Orleans version of MARDI GRAS. (2) Someone of mixed French or Spanish and black heritage. "Creole balls," held in the early 1800s, were dances for white men and their Creole mistresses. (3) The French dialect spoken by Louisiana Creoles—a patois rich in proverbs and animal tales.

Cripple Creek A tiny Colorado town near Pike's Peak. A gold strike there in the 1890s made it a lodestone for prospectors, inspiring the fiddle tune "Cripple Creek."

Croatan See ROANOKE COLONY.

Crocker, Betty See BETTY CROCKER.

Crockett, Davy (1786–1836) Frontiersman. Three factors made Tennessee "Colonel" David Crockett the most talked-about backwoods hero of the nineteenth century. First, he displayed a genius for self-promotion that made him appear not just another bear-killing, Indian-fighting hick, but the embodiment of the famed western ROARER, "half horse and half alligator," boasting that he owned "the roughest rocking horse, the prettiest sister, the surest rifle, and the ugliest dog" in the country. Second, backed by Whig politicians who ran him against his former field commander, Andrew JACKSON, he served three terms as a U.S. congressman, using the House floor to further embellish his reputation. His opposition to Jackson's Indian removal policy (see TRAIL OF TEARS) rang his defeat in 1835, but not before the capital had been entertained for six years by a congressman who could "grin the bark off a tree." Finally, a series of Crockett

Almanacs, published from 1835 to 1856, gave him international adventures as well as domestic ones, parodying the TALL TALE tradition with brilliant excess. In one almanac legend, wrote Richard Dorson in *American Folklore,* Davy rescued the planet itself when it had "frozen" in its axis. "He climbed up the peak of Daybreak Hill, squeezed bear's oil on the axis, and returned with a piece of sunrise in his pocket." By the time Crockett died at the ALAMO defending Texas independence, he had become a "swashbuckling demigod of American hue."

Davy was outstripped at the turn of the century by the gun-toting COWBOY, but he enjoyed a revival, thanks to Walt DISNEY, in the 1950s. When Disney's *Mickey Mouse Club* ran a three-part film biography of the famous Tennesseean starring Fess Parker, the country was swept again by Crockett mania. The show's theme song, "The Ballad of Davy Crockett," became a Top 10 hit, toy stores did a thriving business in coonskin caps, and many baseball card collectors switched to Davy Crockett cards. Capitalizing on this fad, John WAYNE in 1960 produced and directed *The Alamo,* in which he himself played the frontier hero.

Cronkite, Walter   (1916–) Newsman. As anchorman of the *CBS Evening News* for a quarter of a century (1954–81), Cronkite was frequently called the most trusted figure in the United States. He brought his air of calm, avuncular authority to two TV series as well: *You Are There* (1953–57) and *The Twentieth Century* (1957–66). He ended each episode of the former show—which dramatized historical events—with a formula farewell: "What kind of a day was it? A day like all days, filled with those events that alter and illuminate our times. And you were there."

Crosby, Bing   (1904–77) Entertainer. Harry Lillis Crosby's liquidly sonorous voice made him the most popular, and widely copied, crooner of the 1930s. Equally well known from his recordings, radio show, and films, Crosby embarked on a series of comic "Road" pictures in the 1940s which were extremely successful for him and his costars Bob HOPE and Dorothy Lamour. In a more serious vein, he won an Oscar in 1944 for his portrayal of an Irish priest in *Going My Way.* His "White Christmas" (1942) is the biggest-selling recording ever made.

cross of gold speech   See William Jennings BRYAN.

cruel and unusual punishments   Along with excessive bail and fines, these are specifically prohibited by the Eighth Amendment. The phrase is often invoked by constitutional opponents of capital punishment.

Cub Scouts   See BOY SCOUTS OF AMERICA.

Cugat, Xavier   (1900–90) Bandleader. Born in Spain and raised in Cuba, Cugat helped to introduce Latin rhythms to ballroom dancing. Known as the Rhumba King, he led his orchestra in MGM musicals of the 1940s.

Cukor, George   (1899–1983) Director. Known as a woman's director, Cukor elicited memorable performances from Greta GARBO (*Camille,* 1937), Ingrid BERGMAN (*Gaslight,* 1944), Judy Holliday (*Born Yesterday,* 1950), Judy GARLAND (A STAR IS BORN), and Audrey Hepburn (MY FAIR LADY), for the last of which he won an Academy Award. He worked particularly well with Katharine HEPBURN, directing her in THE PHILADELPHIA STORY, *Adam's Rib* (1949), and *Pat and Mike* (1952).

Cumberland Gap A natural pass in the Appalachian Mountains near the juncture of Kentucky, Virginia, and Tennessee. Daniel BOONE cut the Wilderness Road through it in 1775.

cummings, e. e. (1894–1962) Poet. Known to generations of high school students as the poet who didn't use capital letters, Edward Estlin Cummings became "e. e." in 1917, when a printer's error in *Eight Harvard Poets* gave him a new identity. He was known for the inventiveness of his language as well as typography and for a unique blend of childlike wonder and disillusionment.

Currier & Ives A printmaking firm whose hand-colored lithographs provide a panorama of nineteenth-century daily life. Nathaniel Currier (1813–88), who founded the firm in the 1830s, was joined in 1857 by James Merritt Ives (1824–95). Jointly, they produced thousands of individual scenes which were sold for prices ranging from twenty-five cents to a few dollars. Favorite subjects were rural and frontier life, sports events, ships and trains, political figures, and current disasters. The company survived until 1907.

Custer, George Armstrong (1839–76). Soldier. No American military leader has been more lionized or more vilified than the "Boy General" Autie Custer. After graduating last in his West Point class, Custer became the youngest general in Army history for his daring (some said recklessness) during the Civil War. Posted to the frontier, he survived a suspension for insubordination and was given command of the 7th Cavalry in 1868. Fighting the CHEYENNE and SIOUX, he earned the nicknames Yellowhair, for his unshorn locks, and Son of the Morning Star, for attacking a Cheyenne village at dawn. It was Custer who scouted the BLACK HILLS in 1874 to confirm rumors that gold had been discovered there; who was sent against the Sioux in 1876 to return renegade warriors to the reservation; and who, on June 25 of that year, lost his entire command in an Indian ambush at the LITTLE BIGHORN. That defeat, which made him an instant martyr, has been the subject of countless novels and Hollywood films.

Custer's Last Stand See LITTLE BIGHORN.

Czolgosz, Leon (1873–1901) The assassin of President William MCKINLEY. An unemployed factory worker with an interest in anarchism, Czolgosz shot McKinley on September 6, 1901, at the Buffalo, New York, Pan-American Exposition. Before he was sent to the ELECTRIC CHAIR on October 29, he said he had killed the president because he was "the enemy of the people."

DA (1) District attorney. (2) Duck's ass, a 1950s teenage hairstyle suggesting the bird's swept-back tail feathers.

Daddy Warbucks (1) The millionaire who rescues Annie from poverty in the comic strip LITTLE ORPHAN ANNIE. Hence (2) any wealthy benefactor.

Daffy Duck Cartoon character. One of the oldest members (1937) of the Warner Brothers animated animal stable, Daffy Duck is a frenetic, fast-talking schemesman who, with his sometime companion BUGS BUNNY, makes life miserable for the dim-witted hunters PORKY PIG and ELMER FUDD. To express his frustration with adversaries, he spits, "You're despicable!"

dago An insulting term for an Italian. Originally applied to Spaniards, it is a corruption of "Diego." "Dago red" is cheap Italian wine. See also WOP.

Dagwood sandwich An overstuffed sandwich, especially one made with unusual or incompatible ingredients. From Dagwood Bumstead's yen for such creations. See BLONDIE.

Daisy Mae LI'L ABNER's voluptuous wife in Al Capp's comic strip.

Dakota (1) The Indian people more commonly called SIOUX. They gave their name to North and South Dakota. (2) A luxury apartment hotel on New York City's Upper West Side. It was the home of former Beatle John Lennon when he was killed in front of it in 1981.

Dallas (1) The second largest city in Texas, named for George Mifflin Dallas, vice president under James Polk. President John F. KENNEDY was assassinated there in 1963. (2) *Dallas,* a television series (1978–91) depicting the lives of the city's rich, famous, and corruptible. It made the name of its hero/villain, J. R. Ewing, a byword for oily ambition.

Dallas, Stella See STELLA DALLAS.

Dalton gang Outlaws. The Dalton brothers Grattan (1865–92), Robert (1870–92), and Emmett (1871–1937) robbed banks and trains in Kansas and Oklahoma until trying two banks at once in Coffeyville, Kansas, in 1892. In an ambush there, the gang was wiped out. Grat and Bob were killed. Emmett went to jail for fifteen years and when he came out became an advocate for prison reform.

"Damn the torpedoes! Full speed ahead!" Command given by Union naval commander David G. Farragut (1801–70) at the battle of Mobile Bay in the Civil

War. "Torpedoes" were Confederate mines, one of which had already claimed a Union ship. He won the battle and became the nation's first admiral.

Damn Yankees See YANKEES.

Dana, Richard Henry See TWO YEARS BEFORE THE MAST.

DAR See DAUGHTERS OF THE AMERICAN REVOLUTION.

Dare, Virginia The first English child born in the New World. Daughter of Eleanor Dare and granddaughter of the ROANOKE COLONY's governor, John White, she was born in 1587 and, like the rest of that "Lost Colony," vanished by 1591. A local legend said that she returned in the early 1600s as an elusive white doe.

"Dark as a Dungeon" See Merle TRAVIS.

"Darktown Strutters' Ball" (1917) Ragtime dance tune written by Shelton Brooks and popularized by Sophie TUCKER. "Darktown" was an 1880s term for the black ghetto.

darky Since the eighteenth century, a condescending term for a black person.

Darrow, Clarence (1857–1938) Attorney. The most famous defense lawyer of his day, Darrow made his reputation in 1894 by defending PULLMAN STRIKE leader Eugene V. DEBS. He lost that case, but in 1907 got another labor leader, Big Bill HAYWOOD, acquitted on a murder charge. In a celebrated use of the insanity defense, he defended "thrill" murderers LEOPOLD AND LOEB in 1924, getting them life imprisonment instead of the electric chair. The following year, he spoke for evolution in the SCOPES TRIAL; his performance there was interpreted by Spencer TRACY in the 1960 film *Inherit the Wind*.

"date which will live in infamy, A" December 7, 1941, the date on which Japan attacked PEARL HARBOR. Franklin D. ROOSEVELT used the phrase the following day, in asking Congress for a declaration of war.

Daughters of the American Revolution Founded in 1890, the DAR is a conservative, patriotic organization whose members trace their lineage to the Revolutionary period. Its dumbest hour came in 1939, when it barred black opera singer Marian Anderson from its Washington, D.C., concert hall.

Davis, Bette (1908–89) Actress. A tough, ambitious New Englander, Davis broke new ground for women in Hollywood by portraying spunky independence both on- and offscreen. She won Oscars for *Dangerous* (1935) and *Jezebel* (1938) and delivered her most memorable performance as Margo Channing in ALL ABOUT EVE. Another triumph, which capitalized on her harridan brilliance, was her title role in *Whatever Happened to Baby Jane?* (1962). A favorite target of impersonators, Davis also parodied herself to great effect. On talk shows she delighted in playing with a cigarette-holder prop and in snapping out the imperious line "What a dump!"

Davis, Jefferson (1808–89) President of the Confederacy. After a distinguished career in the U.S. Army, the Senate, and Franklin Pierce's cabinet (as secretary of war), Mississippian Davis became head of the Confederate States of America in 1861 and led them, not very effectively, through the Civil War. After the Union victory, he was imprisoned on charges of treason, but was released in 1867 without going to trial. He wrote a history of his government in 1881 and died eight years later in New Orleans.

Davis, Jimmie (1902–) Politician, country singer. Louisiana-born Davis sang blues and hillbilly music in the 1930s, frequently working with black musicians and copying the yodeling style of Jimmie RODGERS. His legacy is the country classic "You Are My Sunshine," a song he wrote and used as the theme of his 1944 campaign for the Louisiana governorship. He won the election then and again in 1960.

Davis, Miles (1926–91) Jazz musician. A mainspring of 1950s "cool" jazz, trumpeter Davis studied at Juilliard, worked with Charlie PARKER in the 1940s, and formed his own group in 1949. He influenced many younger players, in rock music as well as in jazz. His 1968 album *Bitches Brew* was a best-seller.

Davis, Sammy, Jr. (1925–90) Entertainer. A vaudeville performer at the age of three, Davis had one of the longest careers in show business history. A top-billed singer on the nightclub circuit, he became a member of Frank SINATRA's "Rat Pack" in the 1960s, following their debut film, *Ocean's Eleven* (1960). Undaunted by the loss of an eye in an automobile accident, Davis remained active until a year before his death, when a television special celebrated his sixty years as a singer, actor, and dancer.

Day, Clarence See LIFE WITH FATHER.

"Day of Doom, The" (1662) An eschatological poem by Congregational minister Michael Wigglesworth (1631–1705), subtitled "A Poetical Description of the Great and Last Judgment." Its vast circulation, both in Wigglesworth's Massachusetts and farther south, made it the English colonies' first best-seller.

"Days of '49, The" A nostalgic song about mining life in the California GOLD RUSH. It was written after the glory days were past, probably by one C. Rhoades.

D.C. See WASHINGTON, D.C.

"De Colores" A traditional Mexican folk song adopted as an anthem by migrant farmworkers. The "colors" are those of the Mexican landscape.

De Mille, Cecil B. (1881–1959). Film director, producer. Hollywood's master of spectacle, De Mille was the creative power behind Paramount Pictures, the virtual inventor of the feature film, and some say the inventor of "Hollywood" itself—certainly of its image as the home of creative glitz. After helping to produce and direct the industry's first feature, *The Squaw Man* (1913), he became known for other westerns, such as *The Virginian* (1914) and *The Plainsman* (1937), and for his biblical and historical epics. Among these were *Cleopatra* (1934), *Samson and Delilah* (1949), and two versions of *The Ten Commandments* (1923 and 1956). De Mille won a best picture Oscar for *The Greatest Show on Earth* (1952).

de Soto, Hernando (ca. 1500–42) Explorer. One of the most violent of the CONQUISTADORS, de Soto marched an army from Florida to the Mississippi River in 1539–41, brutalizing Indians as he pressed westward seeking gold. He called the Mississippi, which he "discovered," the Río del Espiritu Santo. The De Soto automobile (1913) was named in his honor.

"Deacon's Masterpiece, The" (1858) A poem by Oliver Wendell HOLMES, subtitled "The Wonderful One-Hoss Shay." It describes a minister's carriage, built to last forever, that remains solid for a century, then abruptly falls apart all at once. It is interpreted as a satire on Calvinist theology.

Dead End Kids *Dead End* was a 1935 play by Sidney Kingsley about an engaging gang of New York juvenile delinquents. William WYLER's 1937 movie starred Humphrey BOGART as a gangster and, as the chief urchins, Leo Gorcey (1915–69) and Huntz Hall (1920–). The youngsters appeared in derivative crime dramas first as the Dead End Kids, then the East Side Kids, and finally the Bowery Boys.

dead man's hand See ACES AND EIGHTS.

Deadheads See GRATEFUL DEAD.

Deadwood Now in South Dakota, Deadwood was settled in the 1870s after the BLACK HILLS gold strike. It was the home of CALAMITY JANE, Wild Bill HICKOK, and DEADWOOD DICK.

Deadwood Dick (1) The masked bandit hero of the DIME NOVEL *Deadwood Dick: The Prince of the Road* (1877) and over 125 sequels. The Deadwood Dick series, brought out by Beadle and Adams, lasted until 1897. Dick took his name from the town of Deadwood, where he was supposed to have fitfully wooed CALAMITY JANE. (2) A Tennessee-born black cowboy, Nat Love (1854–1921), who assumed or acquired the nickname Deadwood Dick in 1876 after winning the town's shooting and rodeo contests. The title appears in his 1907 autobiography, *The Life and Adventures of Nat Love, Better Known in the Cattle Country as "Deadwood Dick."* He did not claim, nor is there likely, a connection between the novelistic exploits and his real ones.

Dean, Dizzy (1911–74) Baseball player. One of the finest pitchers of the 1930s, Jay Hanna Dean played for the St. Louis Cardinals' "Gas House Gang," winning thirty games for them in 1934. That year he and his brother Paul "Daffy" Dean, also a pitcher, won two games each to earn the Cardinals the World Series championship. Dean was noted for amusing malapropisms, such as the comment "He slud into third."

Dean, James (1931–55) Actor. The epitome of moody adolescence, Dean was a sophisticated film performer who gathered a huge audience on the basis of three films before dying in a car crash at age twenty-four. Still cult favorites, they were REBEL WITHOUT A CAUSE, EAST OF EDEN, and *Giant* (1956).

"Dear Abby" A syndicated personal advice column, written from 1956 by Abigail van Buren (1918–). Her twin sister, writing as "Ann Landers," produced a similar, and equally popular, feature beginning in 1955. The sisters' given names are Pauline ("Abby") and Esther ("Ann") Friedman.

Dear John letter A letter announcing the writer's intention to end a romantic relationship. World War II military slang.

Death of a Salesman (1949) Arthur MILLER's Pulitzer Prize play about the disillusionment and eventual suicide of Willy Loman, a traveling salesman who reflects the failure of middle-class values. The role was created on Broadway by Lee J. Cobb and subsequently performed on film by Fredric MARCH (1951) and on stage by Dustin HOFFMAN (1984).

Death Valley A desert basin in Southern California that contains the point of lowest elevation in the Western Hemisphere (282 feet below sea level). Barren and hot (with a 1913 record temperature of 134 degrees), it was named by Sacramento-bound FORTY-NINERS, many of whom perished trying to cross it. The area's bleakness generated stories of characters like Death Valley Scotty, whose secret mine netted him enough to hire a private train for a 1905 jaunt to Chicago. A television drama series based on its lore, *Death Valley Days,* ran regularly from 1952 to 1972. Its longtime host was Stanley Andrews, the "Old Ranger"; its most famous one, the pregubernatorial Ronald REAGAN.

Debs, Eugene V. (1855–1926) Social activist. For thirty years Debs was the voice of socialism in the United States. He organized the American Railway Union in 1893 and led it in the PULLMAN STRIKE the following year—an action that cost him six months in prison. Also active in the founding of the Socialist Party (1901) and INDUSTRIAL WORKERS OF THE WORLD, he ran for president five times on the Socialist ticket, the last time from jail, where he was serving a sentence for opposing World War I. "While there is a lower class," he once said, "I am in it."

Decatur, Stephen (1779–1820) Naval officer. Decatur became a national hero during the wars against the BARBARY PIRATES, when he boarded and scuttled a captured American frigate. His reputation for bravery grew in the War of 1812 and in a subsequent mission to North Africa, when he put an end to the pirates' depradations. At a dinner in his honor in 1815, he offered a famous toast: "Our country—right or wrong." Five years later, he was killed in a duel by a fellow officer.

Declaration of Independence The document that transformed the hostilities begun at LEXINGTON AND CONCORD into the Revolutionary War. It was approved (not signed) by Congress on July 4, 1776; the formal signing began one month later. Written chiefly by Thomas JEFFERSON, it followed the natural-rights theory of John Locke in proclaiming the equality of "all men" and their "unalienable Rights" to "Life, Liberty, and the pursuit of Happiness." Governments were established, Jefferson wrote, to secure these rights; when they failed to do so, the people could "abolish" them. Such "self-evident" truths were anathema to the British crown, and they made the colonial revolt, overnight, a matter of treason. The FOUNDING FATHERS understood this. At the signing, John HANCOCK said, "Now we must all hang together." "Or," grinned Benjamin FRANKLIN, "most assuredly we will all hang separately."

Decoration Day See MEMORIAL DAY.

"Deep in the Heart of Texas" (1941) A novelty tune by June Hershey and Don Swander, involving hand-clapping at the end of various phrases. Frequently recorded in the 1940s, it also appears in such movies as *Thirty Seconds over Tokyo* (1944) and *How to Marry a Millionaire* (1952).

deep shit Serious trouble. Presidential aspirant George Bush put a patrician spin on the phrase in 1988, when he observed that his election campaign was in "deep doo-doo."

Deep South A 1920s term for Georgia, Alabama, Mississippi, and Louisiana.

Deere, John (1804–86) Inventor, manufacturer. Vermont blacksmith Deere designed a steel plow in 1937 that was ideal for breaking the thick earth of the prairies. It proved essential to the domestication of the west and established the Deere farm-implements company that survives today.

Deerslayer See Natty BUMPPO.

Deganawidah A sixteenth-century Indian statesman who, according to legend, founded the IROQUOIS LEAGUE. See also HIAWATHA.

Delaware (1) An Indian people, also known as the Lenni Lenape, who in the eighteenth century lived in New Jersey. (2) The river separating New Jersey from Pennsylvania. George Washington crossed it December 25, 1776, for a surprise attack on Trenton during the Revolutionary War. (3) The first state to adopt the Constitution (December 7, 1787). The name was that of Virginia's first colonial governor, Baron De La Warr.

Delmonico's A New York City restaurant founded by Swiss brothers John and Peter Delmonico in 1837. After several moves to accommodate its increasing popularity, it settled on 44th Street and Fifth Avenue in 1897, becoming one of the Gilded Age's most fashionable eateries. Famous for its steaks, it also set vogues for chicken à la king, lobster Newburg, and pie à la mode. See THE GILDED AGE.

Democracy in America See Alexis de TOCQUEVILLE.

Democratic party See POLITICAL PARTIES.

Democratic-Republican party See POLITICAL PARTIES.

Dempsey, Jack (1895–1983) Boxer. Born in Manassa, Colorado, Dempsey was known as the Manassa Mauler because of his devastating punches. He held the heavyweight title for seven years (1919–26), defending it in 1921 in the sport's first million-dollar gate. His 1926 loss to Gene Tunney led the following year to a controversial "long count" rematch. Knocked down, Tunney earned a few extra seconds on the canvas while the referee waited for Dempsey to go to a neutral corner; Tunney won on points after ten rounds.

Dennis the Menace A comic strip begun in 1951 by cartoonist Hank Ketchum. The towheaded hero is a five-year-old, less "menacing" than irrepressibly high-spirited. The frequent butt of his well-intentioned mischief is a long-suffering neighbor, Mr. Wilson. See also KATZENJAMMER KIDS.

depth charge   (1) An explosive charge developed during World War I for use against submarines. (2) A beer containing a submerged shot glass of whiskey. When the two drinks are served separately—with the beer as a chaser—the combination is known as a boilermaker.

derringer   A precursor of the SATURDAY NIGHT SPECIAL, the derringer was a palm-size pistol sold widely in the 1850s and named for its inventor, Philadelphia gunsmith Henry Deringer. John Wilkes BOOTH used one to kill President Lincoln.

Desert Storm   See GULF WAR.

Destry Rides Again   A western novel (1930) by Max BRAND. It formed the basis of three Hollywood films, with the stalwart hero played by Tom MIX (1932), James STEWART (1939), and Audie MURPHY (1954).

"Devil and Daniel Webster, The"   (1937) A story by Stephen Vincent BENÉT adapted for both the stage and the screen. The orator redeems the soul of a New England farmer, Jabez Stone, by pleading his case to a jury of reprobates including Benedict ARNOLD, Aaron BURR, and Simon GIRTY.

Dewey, George   (1837–1917) Naval officer. Civil War veteran Dewey became an admiral—and later the nation's first five-star admiral—based on his victory over the Spanish fleet in Manila Bay on May 1, 1898. His order to attack, given to flagship captain Charles Gridley, was "You may fire when you are ready, Gridley"—often seen in the short version "Fire when ready, Gridley." Touted briefly for president in 1900, Dewey also received encomia such as the following newspaper verse:

> *Oh, dewy was the morning upon the first of May,*
> *And Dewey was the admiral down in Manila Bay.*
> *And dewy were the Spaniards' eyes, them orbs of black and blue,*
> *And dew we feel discouraged? I dew not think we dew!*

Dewey decimal system   Until the advent of the Library of Congress classification system, this was the standard system for all American libraries. Based on a division of knowledge into ten broad categories, each of them further subdivided, it was devised by librarian Melvil Dewey (1851–1931).

"Dewey Defeats Truman!"   A famous headline blooper. It was run on the front page of the *Chicago Tribune* for November 3, 1948, anticipating the "sure" victory of New York Governor Thomas Dewey over the incumbent President, Harry S TRUMAN. After Truman's surprise win, he was photographed flashing the paper and an enormous smile.

Dick and Jane   The protagonists of a series of children's readers widely used in U.S. grammar schools from the 1940s to the 1970s. Often mocked for their simplistic style ("Look, Jane, look. See Spot run"), they nonetheless taught the BABY BOOM generation to read. They were produced under the direction of Zerna Sharp and illustrated by Eleanor Campbell.

Dick Tracy   Comic strip created in 1931 by Chester Gould (1900–85). A square-jawed detective who entered crime work to avenge the murder of his girlfriend Tess Trueheart's father, Tracy fought Prohibition-style ganglords in the 1930s, then in the 1940s turned to surrealistic villains such as the faceless Blank and the ghoulish Mrs. Pruneface. Gould drew the strip until his retirement in 1977. Filmed in the 1930s with Ralph Byrd as Tracy, the story was redone in 1990 in a glossy version starring Warren Beatty and MADONNA.

Diddy-Wah-Diddy   A mythical promised land in black folklore. Its principal attraction is the availability of food. As Zora Neale HURSTON described it for the Federal Writers' Project in 1938, it was a place where the hungry traveler need only sit and wait. "Soon he will hear something hollering 'Eat me! Eat me! Eat me!' and a big baked chicken will come along with a knife and fork stuck in its sides." See BIG ROCK CANDY MOUNTAINS.

Dietrich, Marlene   (1901–92) Actress, singer. With a husky voice and an air of smouldering sensuality, Maria Magdalene Dietrich was the essential femme fatale—an edgier version of the ethereal Greta GARBO. She was a rising stage and screen star in her native Germany when director Josef von STERNBERG discovered her in 1930. Her work as cabaret singer Lola Lola in his *The Blue Angel* (1930) led to a Paramount contract and six more collaborations, including *Morocco* (1930, *Blonde Venus* (1932), and *The Devil Is a Woman* (1935). Their relationship delighted the peeping press, who hinted that it went beyond the professional, and Dietrich was sued unsuccessfully by the director's wife for alienation of her husband's affections.

Under other directors after 1935, Dietrich rang endless changes on the Lola character, but never quite captured the panache of the von Sternberg years. She was convincing, however, as a dance hall hostess in the western DESTRY RIDES AGAIN (1939) and riveting as Tyrone Power's lover in *Witness for the Prosecution* (1958). She turned to nightclub performing in the 1950s and had a successful singing career into her seventies.

diez y seis   Spanish "sixteen," pronounced *dee-ess ee sace.* September 16, 1810, marked the beginning of a popular revolt in central Mexico that led to the overthrow of Spanish rule. *Diez y seis de septiembre,* the Mexican day of independence, is celebrated in Mexican-American communities.

Dillinger, John   (1903–34) Bank robber. Dillinger became the FBI's first PUBLIC ENEMY number one in 1933 while on a Midwest rampage during which his gang hit numerous banks and killed several people. Betrayed by a girlfriend whom the press called the "woman in red," he was killed by federal agents in Chicago after leaving a show at the Biograph Theater.

DiMaggio, Joe   (1914–   ) Baseball player. Expert fielding combined with consistent hitting made the "Yankee Clipper" one of the game's all-time greats. He helped bring the New York Yankees nine World Series titles, twice led the American League in batting, and was voted its most valuable player in 1939, 1941, and 1947. In 1941, he set a still-untouched major league record by getting a hit in fifty-six consecutive games. He was married for nine months to Marilyn MONROE.

dime novels Paper-covered adventure novels that sold for ten cents each in the second half of the nineteenth century. The pioneers of the form were the Beadle brothers, Erastus (1821–94) and Irwin (1828–82), whose publication of Ann St. Stephens's *Malaeska: The Indian Wife of the White Hunter* (1860) started the cheap-thrills craze. Competitors abounded, although the Beadles, in various partnerships, retained their leadership. Dime novels, which often celebrated the American past, jump-started what would become the "mythic West" with richly embroidered biographies of frontier heroes. Among the figures established, if not actually created, by the Beadle potboilers were BUFFALO BILL, DEADWOOD DICK, and CALAMITY JANE. The books also popularized detectives like Nick CARTER, and the All-American hero Frank MERRIWELL.

Dionne quintuplets Five daughters born in 1934 to an Ontario farm couple, Elzire and Oliva Dionne. To prevent their parents from exploiting them, the Canadian government made them wards of the state and set about exploiting them itself. Kept in a special "living museum" on the Dionne farm, they were gawked at by tourists for seven years, earning Ottawa and private promoters considerable money, before their parents were able to regain custody. Their fishbowl childhood has been called "North America's number-one peep show."

Dirty Harry (1971) An action movie directed by Don Siegel and starring Clint EASTWOOD as Detective Harry Callahan. A tough, laconic "enforcer" hamstrung by criminal-coddling liberals, Dirty Harry is the fantasy revenge of respectable citizens who, in the 1960s and 1970s, felt threatened by violent crime and permissive laws. The movie generated several sequels, also starring Eastwood. In *Sudden Impact* (1983), he utters the series's most famous line. With his gun trained on a cowering suspect, he dares the man to reach for his own weapon. "Go ahead," he growls smugly. "Make my day."

disc jockey One who plays records for a living, either on radio or for public dancing. Usually associated with the early days of ROCK MUSIC, DJs actually surfaced in the 1930s as radio promoters for the BIG BAND sound.

disco See ROCK MUSIC.

Disney, Walt (1901–66) Showman. More than any other single individual, Walter Elias Disney defined family entertainment in this century. He was a Hollywood cartoon animator when, in 1928, he and fellow artist Ub Iwerks created a perky rodent they called Mortimer Mouse. Renamed MICKEY MOUSE, the character starred in dozens of sound shorts beginning with that year's STEAMBOAT WILLIE; generated a menagerie of friends including Minnie Mouse, DONALD DUCK, and Pluto; and became the basis of an entertainment empire. By the 1930s, Disney ran a virtual animation factory, producing not only Mickey films but also "Silly Symphony" shorts such as THREE LITTLE PIGS (1933). In 1938, he challenged Hollywood convention by releasing the first animated feature, SNOW WHITE AND THE SEVEN DWARFS. Its success led in the next two decades to an extraordinary body of full-length cartoons, among them PINOCCHIO, FANTASIA, DUMBO, BAMBI, SONG OF THE SOUTH, *Cinderella* (1950), *Alice in Wonderland* (1951), PETER PAN, *Lady and the Tramp* (1955), *Sleeping Beauty* (1959), and *101 Dalmatians* (1961).

In the 1950s, Disney moved into live-action films, producing a series of nature films that began with the acclaimed *Living Desert* (1953); adventure tales such as *Treasure Island* (1950), *20,000 Leagues Under the Sea* (1954), and *The Sign of Zorro* (1960); and light comedies such as *The Absent-minded Professor* (1961), *The Parent Trap* (1961), and *Mary Poppins* (1964). The 1950s also saw a move into television, with the introduction first of *Disneyland* and then of the afternoon variety show *The Mickey Mouse Club*. The former, which under various names became the medium's longest-running prime-time series (1954–90), presented a rotating fare keyed to the four theme areas of Disney's California amusement park, DISNEYLAND.

At his death Disney had garnered over two dozen Academy Awards. The studio he founded, now called Walt Disney Enterprises, remains a potent force world-wide in entertainment.

Disneyland   An Anaheim, California, amusement complex. Created by and named for Walt DISNEY, it opened in 1955. It includes four theme sections—Fantasyland, Adventureland, Frontierland, and Tomorrowland—as well as an entrance area, Main Street U.S.A., depicting the quiet charm of a turn-of-the-century small town. An Orlando, Florida, version of the park, Walt Disney World, opened in 1971. Euro Disney, near Paris, opened in 1992.

Divine, Father   See FATHER DIVINE.

Dix, Dorothy   (1861–1951) Pen name of Elizabeth Meriwether Gilmer, who wrote a syndicated MISS LONELYHEARTS column, "Dorothy Dix Talks," in the early 1900s. Editors at William Randolph HEARST's *New York Journal,* which carried the column, also had her cover murder trials.

"Dixie"   (1859) A "plantation number" composed by Dan EMMETT for the Dan Bryant minstrel show. It was an instant hit in both the North and the South. When the Confederacy made it a regional anthem, Ohioan Emmett added some "Union" verses, now as forgotten as his "old times" are not. The opening lines of "Dixieland" (Emmett's actual title) can still bring tears to southern eyes:

> *I wish I was in the land of cotton;*
> *Old times there are not forgotten.*
> *Look away, look away, look away, Dixieland.*

The term "Dixie" had meant the South before Emmett's day, and probably derived from the MASON-DIXON LINE; another reasonable explanation is that it echoes the *dix* (French for "ten") on Louisiana banknotes.

Dixie cup   A paper cup, like those dispensed at the start of this century by vending machines of the American Water Supply Company. Stuart Berg Flexner traces the name to the financial flimsiness of Louisiana paper money (see "DIXIE").

Dixieland   See JAZZ.

"Do a good turn daily"   The official slogan of the BOY SCOUTS OF AMERICA. Its charge underlies the touching, if clichéd, picture of Scouts helping old ladies across the street.

"Do your own thing" Catchphrase of the 1960s COUNTERCULTURE, reflecting its members' antipathy to ESTABLISHMENT values.

Dr. J. See Julius ERVING.

Dr. Kildare The protagonist in a series of 1930s and 1940s movies about the adventures of a young intern in a city hospital. The character, created by Max BRAND in the story "Interns Can't Take Money" (1937), was popularized by actor Lew Ayres in *Young Dr. Kildare* (1938); Lionel Barrymore played his mentor, Dr. Gillespie. In a 1960s television series, the roles were taken by Richard Chamberlain and Raymond Massey.

Dr. Pepper A soft drink created in 1885 in Wade Morrison's Waco, Texas, drugstore. It was named for another pharmacist, back in Virginia, who had run Wade out of town for romancing his daughter. The "10, 2, 4" slogan is a vestige of the original "Drink a bite to eat at 10, 2, and 4 o'clock."

Dr. Seuss The pen name of Theodor Seuss Geisel (1904–91), who wrote and illustrated dozens of children's books distinguished by a gentle humor and inventive wordplay. Designed to be read aloud, they became popular in the 1960s, when they were found to be effective in teaching reading. They included *The Cat in the Hat* and *How the Grinch Stole Christmas* (both 1957), *Hop on Pop* (1963), and *Green Eggs and Ham* (1960).

Dr. Strangelove (1964) A "nightmare comedy" about the end of the world in a nuclear exchange. Adapted by film director Stanley Kubrick from the Peter George novel *Red Alert,* it broadly satirizes COLD WAR military posturing in figures like General Jack D. Ripper (Sterling Hayden), Colonel Bat Guano (Keenan Wynn), and the neofascist Dr. Strangelove (Peter Sellers). Its subtitle was "How I Learned to Stop Worrying and Love the Bomb."

Dodge, Mary Mapes (1831–1905) Writer, editor. Best remembered as the author of the children's classic HANS BRINKER, OR THE SILVER SKATES, Dodge also edited the influential juvenile magazine *St. Nicholas* from 1873 until her death.

Dodge City A Kansas railhead that, in the 1880s, was known as the wickedest little city in America. Like nearby ABILENE, it gave just-off-the-trail cowboys a smorgasbord of gambling, drinking, dancing, whoring, and gunfights—all on the town's much ballyhooed Front Street. Its reputation for violence spurred Andy ADAMS to call it a town where "the average bad man finds himself badly handicapped. . . . Dodge's officers are as game a set of men as ever faced danger." Among those officers were Wyatt EARP and the fictional Marshal Dillon (see GUNSMOKE).

"Does she or doesn't she?" A Clairol slogan from the 1950s, pitching the natural look of the company's hair dyes. The surface meaning was "Does she color her hair?" but the double entendre didn't hamper sales.

dogs Those famous in American story and popular culture include the following:

Asta The pet terrier of Nick and Nora CHARLES.

Buck The protagonist of THE CALL OF THE WILD and WHITE FANG.

Checkers See CHECKERS SPEECH.

Deputy Dawg A Terrytoon cartoon figure from the 1970s. He is a dull-witted Mississippi lawman.

Fala The pet of the Franklin D. Roosevelt family.

Goofy A DISNEY character from 1932. Gangling and endearingly slow, he was originally called Dippy Dawg.

Huckleberry Hound An amiable animated bloodhound created by HANNA AND BARBARA. He had his own television show from 1958 to 1962.

Lady and the Tramp The title couple of a 1955 DISNEY movie. She is a refined cocker spaniel, he a mutt.

Lassie See LASSIE.

Mighty Manfred The "Wonder Dog." The companion of Tom Terrific in the CAPTAIN KANGAROO show's regular cartoon.

Old Yeller The title hound in a 1957 DISNEY tearjerker set in the rural South.

Pluto MICKEY MOUSE'S friend in numerous DISNEY films. He made his first appearance in 1930.

Rin Tin Tin See RIN TIN TIN.

Sandy Little Orphan Annie's sandy-colored mutt. See "LITTLE ORPHAN ANNIE."

Snoopy See PEANUTS (2).

Tige BUSTER BROWN'S bulldog.

Toto Dorothy Gale's pet in THE WIZARD OF OZ. She addresses him in a famous line: "Toto, something tells me we're not in Kansas anymore."

Yukon King See SERGEANT PRESTON OF THE YUKON.

dollar-a-year-man A business executive who offered his services to the government during World War I. Some were paid a dollar a year token salary plus expenses.

Domino, Fats (1929–) Singer, pianist. Rock 'n' roll pioneer Antoine "Fats" Domino perfected a boogie-woogie piano style in his native New Orleans, played rhythm and blues in the 1940s, and sold more records in the 1950s than anyone but Elvis PRESLEY. His hits included "Ain't That a Shame" (1955), "Blueberry Hill" (1956), and "I'm Walkin' " (1957).

domino theory See COLD WAR.

Donald Duck Cartoon character. Irascible, scratchy-voiced Donald Duck, who debuted in a 1934 film, *The Wise Little Hen,* is the best-recognized DISNEY creation after MICKEY MOUSE. Regulars in his many cartoons and comic books are his girlfriend, Daisy, his nephews Huey, Dewey, and Louie, and his miserly millionaire uncle, Scrooge McDuck. His distinctive voice was first done by Clarence Nash.

donkey The symbol of the Democratic party. It was introduced in this sense by Thomas NAST.

Donner party California-bound pioneers who were trapped by snow in the Sierra Nevadas in November 1846. They built cabins and sent out a rescue crew, but before help came nearly half of the original eighty-seven had died, and some survivors had resorted to cannibalism to save themselves. The spot that claimed them is now called Donner Pass.

"Don't fire until you see the whites of their eyes"   Order given to the entrenched colonial sharpshooters at the Battle of BUNKER HILL.

"Don't give up the ship"   The last order of fatally wounded naval officer James Lawrence (1781–1813), whose ship the *Chesapeake* was about to be captured in the WAR OF 1812. The British boarded in spite of his command.

"Don't look back"   See Satchel PAIGE.

"Don't take any wooden nickels"   See WOODEN NICKELS.

"Don't Tread on Me"   Revolutionary War slogan. It appeared on the Navy Jack of 1775 with the image of a RATTLESNAKE about to strike.

"Don't trust anyone over thirty"   A 1960s COUNTERCULTURE slogan, indicating a puerile, if fervent, distrust of established authority. It was first spoken in 1964 by Berkeley Free Speech movement member Jack Weinberg.

doo-wop   A type of singing first used by black street musicians and assimilated into 1950s ROCK MUSIC. Repeated nonsense phrases like "doo-wop" and "sha-boom" provided rhythm behind the style's a capella harmonies.

Dooley, Mr.   See Finley Peter DUNNE.

Dooley, Tom   See TOM DOOLEY.

Doonesbury   See Garry TRUDEAU.

doozy   Anything wonderful or exceptional. From the Duesenberg automobile, a luxury model of the 1930s.

Dorgan, T.A.D.   (1877–1929) Cartoonist. In his prime, Thomas Aloysius Dorgan, or "Tad," was the best-paid sports cartoonist in the country. He worked first in his native California, then for William Randolph HEARST's *New York Journal*. His alternating series, "Outdoor Sports/Indoor Sports," ricocheted from boxing to craps and back again, while his social commentary gave his work a satirical edge. Dorgan invented the terms HOT DOG, DUMB DORA (a character in one of his cartoons), and "yes-man."

Dorsey, Jimmy and Tommy   Bandleaders. Brothers James (1904–57) and Thomas (1905–56) led two of the most popular dance bands of the SWING MUSIC era. With Jimmy on clarinet and Tommy on trombone, they ran a joint orchestra from 1933 to 1935.

Dorsey, Thomas A.   (1899–1993) The "Father of Gospel Song," Dorsey began his career as "Georgia Tom," a writer and performer of ribald blues. Based in Chicago from the 1920s, he formed the National Convention of Gospel Choirs and Choruses (1932) and made that city a center of gospel music. His most famous compositions were "Take My Hand, Precious Lord" and "Peace in the Valley"—the latter a hit for Elvis PRESLEY and Red FOLEY.

Dos Passos, John (1896–1970) Novelist. Simultaneously infatuated with and disillusioned by American society, Dos Passos attacked the delusions of both left and right in a series of novels known for their verbal inventiveness. His "U.S.A." trilogy comprised *The 42nd Parallel* (1930), *1919* (1932), and *The Big Money* (1936); sometimes touted as the GREAT AMERICAN NOVEL, it sparkled with "camera eye" impressions, "newsreel" reporting, and crisp biographies.

double Various meanings play on the core sense of "twice" and "alike." In filmmaking, a double performs the "real" actor's dangerous stunts. In saloon slang, double is short for "double shot"—two shot glasses of whiskey. Teenagers began "double dating" in the 1920s, watching "double features" and eating "double dip" (or "double scoop") ice cream cones a decade later. Baseball gives us "doubleheader" for two games in one meeting and "double play" for two outs on one play. Two of the most popular chewing gum brands are Doublemint (introduced in 1914) and Double Bubble (1928). A "double SAWBUCK" has been a twenty-dollar bill since the 1850s. The "double nickel" is CB slang for the 55-mile-per-hour speed limit. "Double Dutch" is a schoolgirls' jump rope game using two revolving ropes instead of one. "Double jeopardy," or being tried twice for the same crime, is illegal under the FIFTH AMENDMENT.

Doubleday, Abner (1819–93) Army officer. Legend says that he invented baseball at COOPERSTOWN, New York, in 1839. The story was discredited long ago, but Cooperstown remains the shrine of the "national game." Among Doubleday's actual accomplishments: He directed the first Union fire at Fort Sumter and secured the charter for San Francisco's first CABLE CAR.

doughboys American soldiers in World War I. The term actually dates from the 1860s; its etymology is uncertain.

Douglas, Kirk (1916–) Actor. Born Issur Danielovitch, Douglas was a ruggedly intense star of 1950s and 1960s action films. His most famous "sword and sandal" role was the lead in *Spartacus* (1960), the best of many western parts that of Doc HOLLIDAY in *Gunfight at the O.K. Corral* (1957). He also played Vincent Van Gogh in *Lust for Life* (1956), based on a 1934 novel by Irving STONE. His actor son Michael (1944–), similarly intense, is best known for the erotic thriller *Fatal Attraction* (1987).

Douglas, Stephen A. (1813–61) Politician. An Illinois senator known as the Little Giant, Douglas stumped widely for westward expansion and proposed that "popular sovereignty" decide the nettlesome slavery issue. Abraham LINCOLN challenged his seat in 1858; their campaign debates made the newcomer a national figure.

Douglass, Frederick (ca. 1817–95) Abolitionist. Born a slave in Maryland, Douglass fled North in 1838 and soon became an eloquent speaker for the anti-slavery movement. His weekly *North Star* (later *Frederick Douglass's Paper*) reached a large black audience, and his autobiography, *Life and Times,* became a narrative classic. It was thanks in part to his urging that black troops served with distinction in the Civil War.

Dow, Lorenzo   (1777–1834) Preacher. In the early 1900s, "Crazy Lorenzo Dow" spread the Methodist gospel, with eccentric embellishments, along the East Coast. Speaking at CAMP MEETINGS and, failing that, from farmers' woodpiles, he earned a reputation for studied oddity and down-home glibness. A good psychologist, he once exposed a thief hiding in a crowd by threatening to stone him: When Dow drew back his arm, the culprit ducked, giving himself away.

"Down by the Old Mill Stream"   (1910) A novelty song by Tell Taylor which sold millions of sheet-music copies in the 1910s. Its gimmick is facetious call-and-response, as in the opening lines:

> *Down by the old (not the new but the old)*
> *Mill stream (not the river but the stream)*
> *Where I first (not second but first)*
> *Met you (not me but you)*

Down East   Sometimes New England in general, but more commonly Maine. A vessel bound from Boston to Maine would sail east "down" the prevailing winds.

"Down in the Valley"   A traditional folk song from the 1840s. It opens mournfully with the lines

> *Down in the valley, the valley so low*
> *Hang your head over, hear the wind blow.*

Originating in the southern mountains, it was appropriated widely and adapted to regional tastes. The best-known adaptation, from Alabama, gave it the alternate title "Birmingham Jail."

Downing, Jack   See Seba SMITH.

dozens, playing the   A speech game of black urban youths. Players compete in "topping" each other's insults, with special attention to rhymes and erotic bragging. Also called sounding and the dirty dozens.

Dragnet   On radio (1949–56) and then on television (1952–59, 1967–70), *Dragnet* was the first major real-life police drama series. A gritty procedural set in Los Angeles, it starred Jack Webb as Sergeant Joe Friday. The character's legacies are the lines "My name's Friday—I'm a cop" and (to rambling witnesses) "Just the facts, ma'am." The show's stories were culled from police files. Each episode began with the announcement "The story you are about to see is true; only the names have been changed to protect the innocent" and ended with the somber intoning of the criminal's sentence.

Dred Scott decision   (1857) Dred Scott was a Missouri slave who, after visiting the North with his owner, sued for emancipation on the grounds that his presence in free territory had made him free. In rejecting his claim, the U.S. Supreme Court reaffirmed property rights over personal ones, indirectly hastening the Civil War.

Dreiser, Theodore (1871–1945) Writer. Bitterly critical of the American dream of success, Dreiser is best known for two "socially conscious" novels. *Sister Carrie* (1900), portraying the rise of a country girl to unhappy prosperity, scandalized his generation because of its "immorality." *An American Tragedy* (1925) traced the equally bleak career of Clyde Griffiths, a poor boy who seduces and murders a factory girl. Based on an actual case, it was filmed as *A Place in the Sun* in 1951, with Montgomery Clift as the young killer. Songwriter Paul DRESSER was the novelist's brother.

Dresser, Paul (1857–1906) Composer, lyricist. Paul Dreiser was the older brother of novelist Theodore DREISER. He was well known as a TIN PAN ALLEY balladeer. His songs about his native state include "Way Down in Old Indiana" and "On the Banks of the Wabash." His most successful tune, "My Gal Sal," was also the title of a 1942 movie about his life.

Drew, Nancy The plucky heroine of a series of juvenile mysteries that began with *The Secret of the Old Clock* (1930). Created by "Carolyn Keene," Nancy Drew starred in over fifty books and several movies and a TV show. The daughter of a criminal lawyer, she was an ingenious and intrepid female counterpart to the contemporary HARDY BOYS. Both series were produced by the Edward STRATEMEYER syndicate.

drive-in Originally, this meant a filling station's drive-through bay, but by the 1940s, it was applied to restaurant take-out windows and then outdoor theaters where patrons watched movies from their cars. Drive-in movies reflected the growing mobility of postwar America as well as the liberalization of moral attitudes that went with it: By the 1960s, a drive-in date had sexual connotations.

drop a dime To inform on someone. From the use of a pay telephone to call the police.

drop out To shun conventional behavior and societal patterns; or one who does so. In the 1960s, HIPPIES and other disaffected youth "dropped out" of school and the workforce to live "authentically." The ESTABLISHMENT press generally reviled them as shiftless "dropouts." Acid guru Timothy LEARY was more accommodating. His advice to the young was "Tune in, turn on, drop out."

drugstore In the early 1800s, a pharmacy. The modern drugstore evolved gradually, adding soda fountain and snack areas first, then the merchandise that makes today's drugstore a miniature department store. A "drugstore cowboy," beginning in the 1920s, was a make-believe wrangler who made a drugstore his open range.

dry Said of an area that prohibits the sale of alcohol, such as a dry county or dry state. From the TEMPERANCE MOVEMENT of the nineteenth century.

Du Bois, Blanche The delusionary heroine of Tennessee Williams's A STREETCAR NAMED DESIRE. Intimidated and raped by Stanley Kowalski, she goes to a mental home uttering the famous words "I have always depended on the kindness of strangers."

Du Bois, W.E.B. (1868–1963) Writer, activist. The articulate, elegant champion of an educated black elite, William Edward Burghardt Du Bois earned a doctorate from Harvard and became widely admired for the lyrical essays in *The Souls of Black Folks* (1903). He opposed Booker T. WASHINGTON's "go slow" approach and in 1905 organized the Niagara Movement, the forerunner of today's National Association for the Advancement of Colored People. After leaving the NAACP and the country, he died in Ghana.

dude   In the 1880s, a dude was (1) a "duded up" individual, a dandy, and (2) an easterner. Dude ranches, beginning around the turn of the century, catered to dudes' penchants for playing cowboy. Recently, "dude" has become (3) an adolescent term of address, like "man" or "guy." The rarer female equivalent is "dudette."

due process   A guarantee established in the Fifth and Fourteenth amendments. No one may be deprived of life, liberty, or property without "due process of law"—meaning the arrest, indictment, and trial procedures of the legal system.

dueling   The settlement of an "affair of honor" by force of arms. Dueling was a well-established European tradition by the seventeenth century. In America, it was widespread in the South, where "cavalier" pretensions were strongest, and especially around New Orleans, whose Dueling Oaks field of honor was a popular meeting place. Southerners who killed opponents in duels included Andrew JACKSON and (in the noted Sandbar Duel) James BOWIE. Other celebrated duels were fought between Alexander HAMILTON and Aaron BURR; Henry CLAY and John Randolph; and James Barron and Stephen DECATUR.

Duke   A nickname for (1) jazz composer Edward Kennedy ELLINGTON, (2) actor John WAYNE, and (3) Michael Dukakis, the Massachusetts governor who ran unsuccessfully for the presidency in 1988.

Dumb Dora   An insulting term for a slow-witted or scatterbrained woman. The original, who was less dim than she made out, appeared in a comic strip drawn by Tad DORGAN.

Dumbo   An ugly-duckling story starring a baby elephant whose huge ears make him the object first of ridicule, then of wonder when they enable him to fly. Walt Disney's animated film *Dumbo* was made in 1941. Because Dumbo initially credits his flying ability to a magic feather, a "Dumbo's feather" is any sugar-pill-type talisman.

Duncan, Isadora   (1877–1927) Dancer. Rejecting the formal constraints of classical ballet, San Francisco–born Duncan performed barefoot in loose-flowing garments. The toast of the European avant-garde by the 1890s, she was taken up by American audiences in the 1900s. As well known for her love affairs as for her influence on modern dance, she suffered the loss of her two children in 1913 and lost her own life in a freak auto accident at the age of fifty. Vanessa Redgrave played her in the film *Isadora* (1968).

Dunne, Finley Peter   (1867–1936) Satirist. Chicago journalist Dunne created the Irish barkeeper-philosopher Martin Dooley as a mouthpiece for his commentary on politics and society. "Mr. Dooley" first pontificated in the *Chicago Evening Post* in 1893; over the next three decades, he appeared in hundreds of sketches, sharing his views with his constant customer, Malachi Hennessey. Beginning with *Mr. Dooley in Peace and War* (1898), Dunne filled several books with the Irishman's witticisms. They included the characterization of justice as not only blind but also "deaf and dumb, and has a wooden leg"; and this caustic view of judicial impartiality: "Whether th' Constitution follows th' flag or not, th' Supreme Court follows th' illiction retarns."

Durand, Asher B. (1796–1886) Painter. The leader of the HUDSON RIVER SCHOOL after the death of Thomas COLE, Durand combined an engraver's attention to detail with his predecessor's religious feel for natural sublimity. His most famous picture, *Kindred Spirits* (1849), shows Cole and William Cullen BRYANT in a Catskill glen.

Durant, Will and Ariel Historians. William James Durant (1885–1981) and his wife, Ariel (1898–1981) collaborated on the eleven-volume *Story of Civilization* (1935–75), which became a staple introductory offering of the BOOK-OF-THE-MONTH CLUB. Volume 10, *Rousseau and Revolution* (1967), won the Pulitzer Prize. Will's own book, *The Story of Philosophy* (1926), presented the subject to millions of readers in popular language.

Durante, Jimmy (1893–1980) Entertainer. First successful as a teenager in vaudeville, singer/comic Durante was still going strong in his eighties as a guest star in television specials and Las Vegas nightclubs. Known as Schnozzola because of his large nose, he specialized in malapropisms, heavy-handed piano, and gravelly singing. His trademark sign-off line was "Good night, Mrs. Calabash, wherever you are."

Durocher, Leo (1905–91) Baseball manager. Durocher, whose ready mouth earned him the nickname the Lip, managed the Brooklyn Dodgers in the 1940s, then their traditional rivals, the New York Giants, in the 1950s. His Giants swept the World Series from the Cleveland Indians in 1954, making Durocher (for the third time) manager of the year. He is best known, outside of baseball, for a misquoted line. In 1947, he observed of the Giants, "All nice guys. They'll finish last." This quickly shrank to the version in BARTLETT'S QUOTATIONS: "Nice guys finish last."

Dust Bowl The Great Plains roughly from Texas to the Dakotas, hit in the 1930s with a crippling drought. Overfarming had eliminated the prairie grasses, leaving the topsoil exposed to winds that created giant dust storms. These "black blizzards" drove thousands of families from their homes in the famous OKIE migrations of the GREAT DEPRESSION. Woody GUTHRIE described their plight in "Talking Dust Bowl Blues," as did John STEINBECK in THE GRAPES OF WRATH.

Dylan, Bob (1941–) Singer, songwriter. The most influential songwriter of his generation, Robert Zimmerman was born in Minnesota, took the legal name Dylan from the Welsh poet Dylan Thomas, and made his first impact in the Greenwich Village coffeehouse scene during the FOLK REVIVAL of the 1960s. Influenced by fellow midwesterner Woody GUTHRIE, he wrote "protest songs" that were widely adopted by the antiwar movement—"Masters of War," "A Hard Rain's A-Gonna Fall," "BLOWIN' IN THE WIND"—as well as more personal songs with highly inventive lyrics. Among the many singers who helped to popularize his early work were PETER, PAUL, AND MARY; his lover Joan BAEZ; and THE BYRDS.

Dylan alienated traditional folk-song enthusiasts when he sang with an electric band at the 1965 Newport Folk Festival, but his album of that year, *Bringing It All Back Home,* created a wide audience for his enigmatic lyrics; its best song, "Like a Rolling Stone," became a rock standard. A motorcycle accident in 1966 nearly cost Dylan his life, but he came back to write two country-style albums, *John Wesley Harding* (1968) and *Nashville Skyline* (1969), that further broadened his appeal. By the 1970s, he had become a pop icon, with a vast audience treating his albums as holy writ. The best of these were *Blood on the Tracks* (1974), *The Basement Tapes* (a 1975 release of songs he had done years before), and *Slow Train Coming* (1980), which marked his conversion to Christianity and included the Grammy-winning gospel tune "You Gotta Serve Somebody."

Dylan's forays into film have been less polished but nonetheless fascinating. He played a cameo in and wrote the score (including "Knockin' on Heaven's Door") for *Pat Garrett and Billy the Kid* (1973); appeared in his former backup group THE BAND's concert film *The Last Waltz* (1978); and filmed his own Rolling Thunder tour as *Renaldo and Clara* (1978).

e pluribus unum Latin: "Out of many, one." Since 1782, the motto on the Great Seal of the United States. It was proposed in 1776 by John ADAMS, Benjamin FRANKLIN, and Thomas JEFFERSON, who knew it as the legend of a popular magazine. It stands for federal unity out of state diversity.

eagle, bald See BALD EAGLE.

Eagle Scout The highest rank in the BOY SCOUTS OF AMERICA. Because attaining it requires discipline and community service, the term casually connotes "model student" or "goody-goody," as does "Boy Scout" itself.

Eakins, Thomas (1844–1916) Painter. A pioneering realist, Eakins died without seeing the impact of his example, especially on the painters of the ASHCAN SCHOOL. He shocked polite audiences first with his *Gross Clinic* (1875), an explicit study of an operating theater, and then by the use of nude models in his drawing classes. The latter gaffe forced him to resign in 1886 from the Pennsylvania Academy of Fine Arts. Notable also for his photographic studies of body motion, Eakins is now considered as significant a realist as Winslow HOMER.

Earhart, Amelia (1898–?1937) Aviator. Earhart set numerous flying records—she was the first woman to solo across the Atlantic (1932) and the first person to make it from Hawaii to California alone—yet she is most remembered for a spectacular failure. In the summer of 1937, she and navigator Frederick Noonan left New Guinea intending to fly around the world. They disappeared somewhere in the Pacific, and "Lady Lindy" was never seen again. She is often lionized as a model of the independent woman.

"Early to bed early to rise / makes a man healthy, wealthy, and wise" A maxim from POOR RICHARD'S ALMANACK.

Earp, Wyatt (1848–1929) Lawman, gunfighter. The best known of the four Earp brothers (the others were Virgil, Morgan, and James), Illinois-born Wyatt did police work in Wichita and DODGE CITY in the 1870s before reaching his destiny in TOMBSTONE, Arizona. There the Earp clan went up against the Clanton boys in a famous gunfight at the O.K. CORRAL. Cleared of resulting murder charges, Wyatt then killed two men he blamed for Morgan's murder and fled Arizona for Colorado ahead of a posse. He died half a century later in Los Angeles. A television series starring Hugh O'Brian ran from 1955 to 1961.

earthquake   See SAN FRANCISCO EARTHQUAKE.

East of Eden   (1952) An allegorical story by John STEINBECK resetting the Cain and Abel story in modern times. In Elia KAZAN's arresting film (1955), the part of Cal (Cain) was played by James DEAN.

"Easter Parade"   A seasonal song by Irving BERLIN. It was the title tune of the 1948 musical *Easter Parade,* starring Fred ASTAIRE and Judy GARLAND.

> *In your Easter bonnet, with all the frills upon it,*
> *You'll be the grandest lady in the Easter parade.*

The reference is to Easter Sunday promenades that are held in various cities, notably New York.

Eastman, George   (1854–1932) Inventor, businessman. Eastman revolutionized photography in the 1880s first with flexible roll film and then with the KODAK box camera. The company he founded, Eastman Kodak, became the world's largest maker of photographic supplies.

Eastwood, Clint   (1930–   ) Actor. After enjoying some success as the character Rowdy in the TV western RAWHIDE, Eastwood became an international star in the 1960s as the "Man with No Name" of Sergio Leone's SPAGHETTI WESTERNS. He created a second pop-culture icon in 1971, when he played the tight-lipped detective DIRTY HARRY. His directorial career began with *Play Misty for Me* (1971) and peaked with the 1992 western *Unforgiven*, which earned him best picture and best direction Oscars.

"Easy Rider"   (1) A country blues song from the early part of this century. Also known as "C. C. Rider." (2) *Easy Rider,* a 1969 film starring Peter Fonda and Dennis Hopper as drug-infatuated bikers "looking for America." With a sound track featuring Steppenwolf and Jimi HENDRIX, the film capitalized to great effect on the vogue of the COUNTERCULTURE.

Eddy, Mary Baker   (1821–1910) The founder of Christian Science, a religious philosophy endorsing prayer, rather than medicine, as the key to health. Eddy happened on its basic principle in 1866 as she read the Bible while confined to bed as the result of a fall. Her recovery led her to found the Christian Science Association in 1877 and, in 1879, its church counterpart. Eddy's philosophy was best expressed in *Science and Health* (1875). She founded the *Christian Science Monitor,* a respected newspaper, in 1908.

Eddy, Nelson, and Jeanette MacDonald   Billed as "America's Sweethearts," Nelson Eddy (1901–67) and Jeanette MacDonald (1901–65) were Hollywood's most popular singing duo in the 1930s. Their light, cloying operettas included *Naughty Marietta* (1935), *Rose Marie* (1936), *Maytime* (1937), and *The Girl of the Golden West* (1938). They were identified with the romantic duet "Indian Love Call."

Edison, Thomas   (1847–1931) Inventor. The "Wizard of Menlo Park" (so called from his New Jersey laboratory), Edison is remembered chiefly as the inventor of the electric light. In fact the "lamp" he perfected in 1879 was not the first, although it was the first commercially practical, incandescent lightbulb. The phonograph, however, was solely his invention, as were the mimeograph machine, the movie projector, and over one thousand other devices. The power station he installed in lower Manhattan in 1882 was the foundation of the electrical utilities system; his Black Maria film complex in West Orange, New Jersey, was the world's first movie studio; and his 1896 projection of Vitascope shorts in a New York City vaudeville theater was in effect the world's first "picture show."

Probably the nation's most successful dropout, Edison left school at twelve, began to lose his hearing shortly afterward (probably from scarlet fever), and patented his first major invention, a stock ticker, in 1869. MGM produced twin films about him in 1940, with Mickey ROONEY in *Young Tom Edison* and Spencer TRACY in *Edison the Man*. Albert EINSTEIN called him "the greatest inventor of all time." His own comment on his genius was disarmingly candid; he called it "1 percent inspiration and 99 percent perspiration."

Edsel A Ford automobile introduced with great fanfare in 1957. Named for Henry FORD's son Edsel (1893–1943), it sported a garish, vertical oval grille design that made it one of the greatest flops in automobile history.

Edwards, Jonathan (1703–58) Preacher. The fire-breathing leader of the GREAT AWAKENING, Edwards was a pastor in Northampton, Massachusetts, for twenty years, then a missionary to local Indians and, for a few months, president of the College of New Jersey (which later became Princeton University). An unbending Calvinist, Edwards explored human insignificance in the treatise *Freedom of the Will* (1754) and the sermon "Sinners in the Hands of an Angry God" (1741). The latter work contains the striking metaphor of human beings as helpless spiders, being dangled over a flame by an omnipotent God.

Eggleston, Edward See THE HOOSIER SCHOOLMASTER.

eight ball, behind the In the variant of pool called eight ball, a player who sinks that ball before sinking all his other balls automatically loses the game. Thus to act from "behind the eight ball" is to be in a difficult, inhibiting situation.

eight-hour day A principal goal of American labor from the 1860s. Demands for it peaked in the 1880s, and Chicago rallies formed in its behalf led to the police attacks that culminated in the HAYMARKET RIOT. Ten-hour workdays remained common, however, until Henry FORD in 1926 implemented an eight-hour, five-day week in his automobile plants.

eighteen-wheeler A semitrailer truck with eighteen wheels. Drivers of these large "rigs" are considered the top guns of the trucking fraternity, and the phrase appears intermittently in country music.

eighty-six To cancel or kill something. From lunch counter cook's slang meaning "nix," that is, "We're out of it" or "Don't serve that person."

Einstein, Albert (1879–1955) Physicist. German-born Einstein revolutionized modern physics with his theory of relativity and earned a reputation not only as an apostle of brotherhood but as the "smartest man who ever lived": "an Einstein'' in the 1950s meant anyone brilliant. Ironically, it was this pacifist's 1939 letter to President Roosevelt, warning of Nazi Germany's nuclear research, that launched the MANHATTAN PROJECT and thus the atom bomb. A Jewish refugee from the Third Reich, Einstein did research at Princeton University from 1933 until his death.

Eisenhower, Dwight D.   (1880–1969) President. After serving as Allied supreme commander in World War II, "Ike" became the Republican president in 1953. His administration was hardly devoid of incident—it included the start of the CIVIL RIGHTS MOVEMENT, the end of the KOREAN WAR, and the U-2 incident—yet he was widely seen as a do-nothing leader, the perfect figurehead for the SILENT GENERATION. "What's an Eisenhower doll?" went a riddle of the time. "You wind it up and it sits around for four years" (reelected in 1956, he actually sat for eight years). Alert to the Pentagon's impact on the economy, he warned in his farewell address against the influence of the MILITARY-INDUSTRIAL COMPLEX.

electric chair   Invented in the 1880s by Dr. Alphonse Rockwell, "the chair" was first used in 1890, in the new "death chamber" of the Auburn, New York, state prison. The victim was murderer William Kemmler, and the operation was such a success that eventually about half the states adopted the procedure. Early slang terms included "hot seat" and "Old Sparky."

elephant   (1) The symbol of the Republican party, as devised in the 1870s by Thomas NAST. (2) In the nineteenth century, "seeing the elephant" meant seeing (or doing) all that you had wanted to. Probably from circus slang, it was also adopted as a code term for being fed up. Benjamin Botkin notes in his *Treasury of American Folklore* that one party of disappointed prospectors returned from the gold fields with an elephant sketched on its wagon. The legend read, "What we saw at Pikes Peak" (see "PIKES PEAK OR BUST").

Eliot, Charles W.   (1834–1926) Educator. President of his alma mater, HARVARD UNIVERSITY, from 1869 to 1909, Eliot introduced the elective system, raised entrance requirements, and laid the groundwork for the school's current eminence. When he retired from the Crimson presidency, he developed the great-books collection known as the Harvard Classics—popularly known as Dr. Eliot's Five-Foot Shelf.

Eliot, John   (1604–90) Preacher. English-born Eliot reached the New World in 1631 and, after fifteen years in a Massachusetts pastorship, went to the wilderness to preach to the Indians in their own languages. He established several "praying Indian" communities and translated the Bible into Algonquian—the first Bible published in North America.

Eliot, T. S.   (1888–1965) Poet. Born in St. Louis, Thomas Stearns Eliot shook the literary world in 1915 with a searing glimpse of social paralysis, "The Love Song of J. Alfred Prufrock." Seven years later, he deepened his exploration of spiritual aridity in the heavily allusive, stylistically revolutionary "THE WASTE LAND." These two works continue to provide many schoolchildren with their first introduction to modern (and "modernistic") poetry. Eliot won the Nobel Prize in 1948. Years after his death, an uncharacteristically light work, *Old Possum's Book of Practical Cats* (1939), inspired the Broadway musical CATS.

Eliza   The mulatto heroine of UNCLE TOM'S CABIN. One of the novel's most famous scenes is her flight across the Ohio River clutching her baby.

Elks   A social organization founded in 1868 for "white male citizens of the United States." Under their full aegis, the Benevolent and Protective Order of Elks, member "lodges" raise money for hospitals, college scholarships, and other beneficiaries. The race requirement was dropped in 1973.

Ellington, Duke   (1899–1974) Pianist, composer, bandleader. Edward Kennedy Ellington, called Duke for his elegant attire, became a celebrity in the 1920s through radio broadcasts of his band's performance at the COTTON CLUB. His reputation as jazz music's most prolific composer rests on a repertoire of concertos, movie scores, and religious works as well as a string of popular dance numbers. The best known of the latter—all from the 1930s—were "Mood Indigo," "Satin Doll," and "Sophisticated Lady." His arranger Billy Strayhorn collaborated with him on "TAKE THE A TRAIN."

Ellis Island   A small island in New York Bay which in the 1890s became a major entry point for foreign immigrants. Now a national museum, the Ellis Island processing facility admitted 12 million newcomers between 1895 and 1924.

Ellison, Ralph   See INVISIBLE MAN (2).

Elmer Fudd   A Warner Brothers animated cartoon character who first appeared in *Elmer's Candid Camera* (1939). Earnest and befuddled, he is the principal antagonist of BUGS BUNNY.

Elmer Gantry   (1927) A novel by Sinclair LEWIS about the machinations of a hypocritical preacher. He was played by Burt LANCASTER in an Oscar-winning movie role (1960).

Emancipation Proclamation   Abraham LINCOLN's executive order, issued on January 1, 1863, freeing the slaves in all states then fighting the Union. It actually freed no one (true emancipation came in 1865, with the Thirteenth Amendment), but it did isolate the rebellious South from potential allies and transform the Civil War into a moral crusade. It also earned Lincoln the title of Great Emancipator.

embalmed beef   A short-lived scandal of the SPANISH-AMERICAN WAR, involving rumors that chemically treated beef had been sent, as a sub-rosa experiment, to troops in Cuba. An investigating commission turned up no proof, although the secretary of war, Russell Alger, was forced to resign.

Emerson, Ralph Waldo   (1803–82). Writer. The most famous member of the CONCORD, Massachusetts, literary fraternity, the "Sage of Concord" was best known for his stirring essays: His "American Scholar" address to Harvard University (1837) was called the country's "intellectual declaration of independence," while "Self-Reliance" remains a gem of transcendentalist pluck. His faith in organic order is best expressed in *Nature* (1936). Of his many poems, the best known, although not the most characteristic, is "Concord Hymn."

Emmett, Dan   (1815–1904) Songwriter. Founder of an early MINSTREL SHOW troupe, the Virginia Minstrels, Ohioan Emmett later joined Dan Bryant's company.

For Bryant he wrote his famous song, "DIXIE," which he was still performing to teary applause when he was nearly eighty. "Uncle Dan" also wrote "Old Dan Tucker" and "Blue-Tail Fly."

Emmy Awards   Awards for outstanding television performances given annually since 1949 by the National Academy of Television Arts and Sciences. The actual Emmy is a statuette. The name is a variant of "Immy," for image orthicon tube.

Empire State Building   From 1931, when it was completed, to 1973, when the WORLD TRADE CENTER topped it, the Empire State Building, in New York City, was the world's tallest building. The structure itself is 1,250 feet high, with TV antennas (added in 1950) increasing the height to 1,472 feet. The building's two observation decks, 86 and 102 stories up, made it a major tourist attraction. KING KONG climbed it in the 1933 movie.

Enola Gay   The B-29 Superfortress bomber that, on August 6, 1945, dropped the atomic bomb on Hiroshima, Japan. See WORLD WAR II.

"entangling alliances with none"   A phrase from Thomas JEFFERSON's inaugural address (1801) defining his cautiously neutral foreign policy. It echoed George WASHINGTON's warning, in his farewell address, against "permanent alliances with any portion of the foreign world." An isolationist watchword ever since, it is often misquoted as "no entangling alliances."

"envelope, please, The"   See ACADEMY AWARDS.

Equal Rights Amendment   A proposed amendment to the U.S. CONSTITUTION that would outlaw discrimination based on gender. First introduced in Congress in 1923, it was fiercely debated in the 1970s, and although various states have their own ERAs, the national version still has not been ratified.

ERA   See EQUAL RIGHTS AMENDMENT.

Ericsson, Leif   See LEIF ERICSSON.

Erie Canal   A 363-mile-long inland waterway dug between 1817 and 1825 from Albany to Buffalo. Because it was promoted by New York Governor DeWitt Clinton, it was referred to as Clinton's Big Ditch (or simply *the* Big Ditch). It connected Lake Erie, via the Hudson River, to New York City, and was enormously important to the settlement of the Great Lakes region. By the 1840s, thousands of barges used the ditch, while song and story celebrated the brawling, whiskey-loving Irishmen who lived and worked on it. One mock ballad told of a "terrible storm" that suspends the "canawlers' " principal amusement:

> *Oh the E-ri-e was a-risin'*
> *And the gin was gettin' low.*
> *And I scarcely think we'll get a drink*
> *Till we get to Buffalo.*

Erving, Julius   (1950–   ) Basketball player. "Dr. J" dazzled fans in the 1970s with his acrobatic skills and adroit team playing. With the Philadelphia 76ers from 1976, he was the NBA's most valuable player in 1981. He retired with a career record of over fifteen hundred steals.

Establishment, the   From the 1960s. The complex of industrial, political, and military power that radicals blamed for the injustices of society. An American version of Europe's "ruling class," the Establishment comprised both liberal and conservative leaders and was identified as chiefly interested in its own aggrandizement.

E.T.: The Extra-Terrestrial   (1982) For a decade the biggest moneymaking movie in Hollywood history (over $225 million in North America alone). Directed by Steven SPIELBERG, it explores the friendship between a shipwrecked extraterrestrial and a little boy. The movie spawned an explosion of commercial spin-offs—T-shirts, trading cards, dolls—that dwarfed everything since the Davy CROCKETT craze.

"Evangeline"   (1847) A verse romance by Henry Wadsworth LONGFELLOW. It tells of an Acadian couple, Gabriel Lajeunesse and Evangeline Bellefontaine, who are separated when the British, in 1755, deport the Acadians (see CAJUNS) to Louisiana. Reunited as elderly people, they are buried together. A statue to Evangeline (whose prototype has not been identified) stands in Grand Pré, Nova Scotia. The poem opens with a famous description of that area: "This is the forest primeval."

Evans, Dale   See Roy ROGERS.

Evans, Walker   (1903–75) Photographer. One of the Farm Security Administration's most accomplished photographers, Evans is best known for illustrating James Agee's book about tenant farming, *Let Us Now Praise Famous Men* (1941). He also worked for *Fortune* magazine for twenty years and taught photography at Yale University.

Everett, Edward   (1794–1865) Orator. Everett was the principal speaker at Gettysburg National Cemetery on the day that President Lincoln delivered the GETTYSBURG ADDRESS. He spoke expansively, as was the custom, and humbly wrote Lincoln the following day: "I should be glad, if I could flatter myself that I came as near the central idea of the occasion, in two hours, as you did in two minutes." He also served as president of Harvard, governor of Massachusetts, United States congressman, and secretary of state.

Everglades   A southern Florida swampland covering about four thousand square miles and containing Everglades National Park, which protects a wide variety of plant and animal life. Of the original SEMINOLE inhabitants, a couple of hundred descendants still reside there.

Everly Brothers   The sons of country singers Ike and Margaret Everly, Don (1937–) and Phil (1939–) Everly brought a spirited beat and rich harmonies to their performances that made them a major country influence on ROCK MUSIC. Their late 1950s hits included "Bye Bye Love," "Wake Up Little Susie," "Bird Dog," and "All I Have to Do Is Dream"—all written by Felice and Boudleaux Bryant. The brothers themselves wrote "When Will I Be Loved?" and "Cathy's Clown."

Evert, Chris   See Chris Evert LLOYD.

"Every Man a King"   The campaign slogan that made Huey LONG governor of Louisiana in 1928. An egalitarian appeal to hard-pressed farmers, it read in full, "Every man a king, but no man wears a crown."

Exorcist, The   (1971) A horror novel by William Blatty about the demonic possession of a young girl. The best-selling book was made into a blockbuster movie (1973), which won Linda Blair an Oscar nomination for her role as the tortured heroine.

"Extremism in the defense of liberty"   A phrase from Barry GOLDWATER's nomination acceptance speech at the 1964 Republican Party convention. Countering critics who saw his small government/big military posture as extremist, he announced in full, "Moderation in the pursuit of justice is no virtue, and extremism in the defense of liberty is no vice." He lost the election to "Landslide Lyndon" JOHNSON.

"Face on the Barroom Floor, The" A poem (1887) by Hugh Antoine D'Arcy. A balladlike lament, it recalls the narrator's loss of the "lovely Madeleine," whose likeness he scrawls in chalk on the floor of a saloon.

Fain, Sammy (1902–89) Songwriter. Fain, who began as a pianist in radio and nightclubs, wrote romantic songs for Hollywood films. He won Academy Awards for "Secret Love" (from the 1953 *Calamity Jane*) and for the title song of *Love Is a Many-Splendored Thing* (1955). Other hits included the title songs of I'LL BE SEEING YOU, *Young at Heart* (1955), and *April Love* (1957).

Fairbanks, Douglas (1883–1939) Actor. Born Douglas Ulman, Fairbanks became the silent screen's best-loved swashbuckler in films showcasing his carefree grace and physical prowess. Among them were *The Mark of Zorro* (1920), *The Three Musketeers* (1921), *Robin Hood* (1922), *The Thief of Bagdad* (1924), and *The Black Pirate* (1926). In 1919, with Mary PICKFORD, Charlie CHAPLIN, and D. W. GRIFFITH, he founded United Artists. The following year he and Pickford married, becoming Hollywood's dream couple in their estate, Pickfair; the one film they made together was *The Taming of the Shrew* (1929). Fairbanks's son by his first marriage, Douglas Fairbanks, Jr. (1909–), had a less spectacular but solid film career, highlighted by *Dawn Patrol* (1930), *The Prisoner of Zenda* (1937), and *Sinbad the Sailor* (1947).

Fairfax, Sally A Virginia woman to whom George WASHINGTON wrote the year before he died that none of his achievements had been able to "eradicate from my mind those happy moments, the happiest of my life, which I have enjoyed in your company." Some historians cite the comment as evidence that she had been his one true love.

fais do-do A CAJUN term for a country dance. Literally "go to sleep," it refers to the children who were obliged to retire while the adults caroused.

"Fall of the House of Usher, The" (1839) A gothic story by Edgar Allan POE. It relates the consequences of physical and spiritual morbidity among the last members of the gloomy Usher line. It was filmed in 1960 as *The House of Usher,* with Vincent PRICE as the protagonist, Roderick Usher.

false faces Carved wooden masks worn in various Iroquois religious ceremonies. Members of false-face societies donned the masks in house-to-house processions designed to purify the village and command respect from impressionable youngsters.

Faneuil Hall   A Boston market and meeting hall called the Cradle of Liberty because of its pre-Revolutionary anti-British gatherings. Given to the city in 1742 by merchant Peter Faneuil, it was restored by Charles BULFINCH after a 1761 fire. It is still a market and, since 1967, a national landmark.

Fantasia   (1940) An animated film by the DISNEY studio which set cartoon sketches to classical music scores. In one sequence, dinosaurs are overcome by a massive earthquake to Stravinsky's *Rite of Spring.* In another, tutu-clad hippopotamuses dance to Tchaikovsky's *Nutcracker Suite.* In a third, Mickey Mouse battles an army of disobedient brooms to the frenzied strains of Dukas's *Sorcerer's Apprentice.* Reviled by some as inanely pretentious, the film has also been lauded as a creative milestone in the history of animation.

Farewell to Arms, A   (1929) Ernest HEMINGWAY's partially autobiographical third novel, the story of a doomed romance between an ambulance driver and a British nurse. The vivid World War I tale was filmed in 1932 with Gary COOPER playing the lead.

Farm Security Administration   An ALPHABET AGENCY created in 1937, the FSA helped impoverished tenants buy their own farms by offering them government-backed, low-interest loans. It also hired photographers—among them Walker EVANS and Dorothea LANGE—to record its work. Their job assignments constitute a vivid catalog of Depression America.

Farmer, Fannie   (1857–1915) Cooking authority. The first cookbook writer to indicate precise measurements in her recipes, Farmer graduated from the Boston Cooking School in 1889, became its director two years later, and in 1896 published the *Boston Cooking School Cook Book,* popularly known as *Fannie Farmer's Cookbook.* It eliminated the guesswork of "pinch and dash" cooking and brought quality control into the American kitchen.

"Farmer in the Dell, The"   A children's song, often sung with an accompanying game, popular since about the 1880s. Wedding parties sometimes adapt it humorously as "The Bride Cuts the Cake."

Farmer's Almanac   See THE OLD FARMER'S ALMANAC.

Farrell, James T.   See STUDS LONIGAN.

fast food   Restaurant food that is easy to prepare, inexpensive, consumed by customers "on the go," and—since it is typically sold by nationwide chains—uniform in taste and quality around the country. The prototypical fast food was the McDONALD's hamburger, first produced in the 1950s; it spawned a wide array of sandwich-and-shake rivals.

Father Abraham   A nickname for Abraham LINCOLN. From his "paternal" guardianship of the slaves.

Father Divine   (1864?–1965) Religious leader. Born George Baker in Georgia, the African-American preacher whom many saw as God settled in HARLEM in 1915 and by the 1930s had attracted a large following. Some of them came for the inexpensive food and lodging he offered in his nationwide system of boardinghouses, known as Heavens. Others found the asceticism he preached— but seldom practiced—the chief allure of his "Kingdom of Peace." Under the slogan "Father Will Provide," he eventually spoke to millions worldwide, weathering frequent suits from outraged husbands whose wives he had seduced. When he died, the movement was passed to Mother Divine, a white Canadian woman eighty years his junior whom he had taken as his "virgin bride" in the 1940s.

Father Knows Best   Television show. A domestic comedy set in fictional Springfield, it rivaled OZZIE AND HARRIET as a popular depiction of an ideal family. The Andersons were warm, sensible Jim and Margaret and their three children, Betty, Bud, and Kathy. The show ran from 1954 to 1963.

Father of His Country   George WASHINGTON. Among national leaders who had carried the sobriquet before him were Julius and Augustus Caesar and Cosimo de' Medici.

Father of the Constitution   See James MADISON.

Father of Waters   The MISSISSIPPI RIVER. The term has also been applied to the Irrawaddy and the Nile.

Father's Day   Now celebrated on the third Sunday in June, it became a national holiday in 1927. By that time, it had been observed on an ad hoc basis for over sixty years. The idea came from a Mrs. John Bruce, who proposed it in memory of her own father.

Faulkner, William   (1897–1962) Novelist. The winner of the 1949 Nobel Prize for literature, Faulkner combined a keen eye for the social dramas of his native Mississippi with an inventive passion for multiple perspectives and interior monologues. As a result, his novels, the best of them set in mythical Yoknapatawpha County, were as revolutionary in their way as the work of James Joyce. Now widely read in high schools, they include *The Sound and the Fury* (1929), *As I Lay Dying* (1930), *Light in August* (1932), and *Absalom, Absalom!* (1936). The sexually shocking *Sanctuary* (1931) brought Faulkner his biggest commercial success; "The Bear" (1942) is considered his most accomplished story. For film director Howard HAWKS, he also worked on the scripts for TO HAVE AND HAVE NOT and THE BIG SLEEP.

favorite son   A person nominated for president by his own state's party delegation. Such nominations, seldom serious bids in their own right, can still be useful as bargaining chips in deadlocked conventions, when the favorite son, in releasing his delegates, can influence the outcome.

FBI   See FEDERAL BUREAU OF INVESTIGATION.

FDR   See Franklin D. ROOSEVELT.

Feboldson, Febold   One of several manufactured folk heroes who followed the success of Paul BUNYAN, Feboldson was the mythic embodiment of Great Plains hardihood, battling the rigors of Midwest life, especially the weather. In one tale he ties a tornado into knots. In another he brings sand from DEATH VALLEY to melt a "petrified snow." In a third he becomes the inadvertent inventor of popcorn balls when the Great Heat goes to work on his corn and the Big Rain washes the syrup from his sugarcane. The character was popularized in stories written by Paul Beath for the *Gothenburg* (Nebraska) *Times*. Often credited with inventing him, Beath claimed that Feboldson was part of oral tradition by the 1920s and that his and others' tales elaborated on the legend.

Fed, the   (1) Shorthand for the Federal Reserve System, the central bank of the United States. (2) The plural "Feds" refers to the federal government in general, and in particular to its law enforcement (FBI) or tax-collection (IRS) officers.

Federal Bureau of Investigation   The FBI, as it is commonly known, is an enforcement division of the U.S. Department of Justice. Established in 1907, it was frequently used to harass political dissidents until J. Edgar HOOVER became its reform director in 1924. Hoover's long tenure (he served until his death in 1972) saw both the Bureau's glory days as the nation's front line against 1930s gangsterism and its less savory involvement in the infiltration and wiretapping of 1960s radicals. With its extensive criminal files, including the world's largest fingerprint file, and its periodic publication of "most wanted" lists, it remains the closest thing the country has (or wants) to a national police force. Cases from its files provided the basis for the television series *The FBI* (1965–74).

federal style   An architectural style popular at the turn of the eighteenth century. It stressed neoclassical forms, white columns against red brick backgrounds, and Greek pediments or "fanlight" windows surmounting doorways. Its chief proponent was Boston architect Charles BULFINCH.

Federalist, The   A collection of essays (1787–88) by Alexander HAMILTON, James MADISON, and John JAY urging ratification of the U.S. CONSTITUTION. Signed "Publius," they remain the chief philosophical defense of that document. The collective title is sometimes given as *The Federalist Papers*. The affection for strong government that they embodied was also evident in the Federalist party, which brought George WASHINGTON and John ADAMS to the presidency.

Federalist party   See POLITICAL PARTIES.

Feds   See FED (2).

Felix the Cat   Cartoon character. A spunky feline prone to JAZZ AGE high jinks, Felix was the creation of animator Otto Messmer and producers Pat Sullivan and Margaret Winkler, who made him a star in dozens of silent shorts. Irrepressible, wide-eyed, and ever ready for action, he remained the best-known animal figure in American film until being eclipsed by the less obstreperous MICKY MOUSE in the 1930s.

Feminine Mystique, The   See WOMEN'S LIBERATION.

Ferber, Edna   (1887–1968) Writer. Chiefly a novelist, Ferber wrote with such dramatic cogency that her works were often adapted for the stage or screen. Her family saga *Show Boat* (see SHOWBOAT [2]) became a Broadway smash in the hands of Jerome KERN and Oscar HAMMERSTEIN II. Her western novels *Cimarron* (1930) and *Giant* (1952) became successful films. With George Kaufman—a fellow member of the ALGONQUIN ROUND TABLE—she wrote the sparkling plays *The Royal Family* (1927) and *Dinner at Eight* (1932). She won the Pulitzer Prize for a 1924 novel, *So Big*. See also KAUFMAN AND HART.

Ferlinghetti, Lawrence (1919–) Poet. The most entrepreneurial of the writers of the BEAT GENERATION, Ferlinghetti founded San Francisco's City Lights Bookstore, which became a salon for the poetic rebels of the 1950s, and under the City Lights imprint published much of their work. His own poems appeared in *Pictures of the Gone World* (1955) and *A Coney Island of the Mind* (1958).

Ferris wheel An amusement park ride consisting of a large, vertically rotating wheel supporting a series of evenly spaced passenger cars. The prototype, designed by engineer George Washington Gale Ferris, was the pièce de résistance of the 1893 Chicago World's Columbian Exposition. A 250-foot giant with thirty-six cars, it carried hundreds of passengers at a time over the White City.

Fetchit, Stepin (1902–85) Actor. Florida-born Lincoln Perry rechristened himself Stepin Fetchit after a horse that had won him some money. In films of the 1920s and 1930s, he played a string of Negro stereotypes, timid and shiftless, that made his name a racist byword for the "comic darky." He made millions as the movies' first African-American star.

Fibber McGee and Molly One of the longest-running shows of radio's Golden Age, this domestic SITCOM pitted hyperbolic hubby "Fibber" against his long-suffering, sensible spouse Molly. Set pieces included appearances by the McGees' windbag neighbor, Throckmorton P. Gildersleeve, and the sound of crashing items whenever Fibber opened his closet door. On radio the series ran for two decades (1935–57); it lasted on television (1959) only four months. In 1941, it spawned the first sitcom spin-off, *The Great Gildersleeve,* which featured further adventures of the blustery womanizer. The Gildersleeve show lasted until 1958.

Fiddler on the Roof A stage show (1964), then a Hollywood musical (1971), about a Jewish father fighting for tradition in a changing world. Based on stories by Sholem Aleichem, it starred Zero Mostel in a run that set a Broadway record (3,242 performances) which survived until the long run of GREASE. Its best-known songs, written by Jerry Bock and Sheldon Harnick, were "If I Were a Rich Man" and "Sunrise, Sunset."

Field, Eugene (1850–95) Poet. Because of poems like "Little Boy Blue" and "Wynken, Blynken, and Nod," Field is chiefly remembered as the "poet of childhood." In his lifetime he was also known as a newspaper columnist. His "Sharps and Flats" was a humorous fixture of the *Chicago News.*

Field, Marshall (1834–1906) Businessman. Born in Massachusetts, Field moved to Chicago in his twenties, worked his way up from clerk to general manager of a dry-goods store, and founded the firm that became Marshall Field and Company—Chicago's premier department store. Field revolutionized retailing by clearly pricing his wares, increasing advertising, keeping large inventories, and producing many of the goods that reached his shelves. He made sizable gifts to the city and to the University of Chicago.

Fields, Dorothy   (1904–74) Lyricist. The daughter of Lew Fields (of Weber and Fields), she wrote songs for plays and films, often collaborating with Jimmy McHugh (1894–1969); their biggest hit was "I'm in the Mood for Love" (1935). She won an Academy Award for "The Way You Look Tonight" (1936), wrote the book for *Annie Get Your Gun* (1946), and played herself in the 1943 film *Stage Door Canteen*.

Fields, Lew   See Weber and Fields.

Fields, W. C.   (1879–1946) Actor. Bulbous-nosed, raspy-voiced William Claude Dukenfield started as a vaudeville juggler in the 1890s, then spent decades on the musical stage before entering films. In his first short, *Pool Sharks* (1915), he handled a pool cue with studied, hilarious incompetence; his skill at transforming "bumbling" into sight gags was further demonstrated in a string of silent features. With sound his jaundiced humor reached full potential, and he became the bibulous, bombastic curmudgeon of Hollywood legend. The image pervaded his private life as thoroughly as it did his performances in the comedy classics My Little Chickadee, *The Bank Dick* (1940), and *Never Give a Sucker an Even Break* (1941).

Fields is a perennial favorite with nightclub impersonators, who delight in regaling audiences with his famous lines. To his on-screen nemesis, the child actor Baby LeRoy; "Go away, kid, you bother me." To a party hostess who offered him a glass of water: "Never touch the stuff; fish fuck in it." And the aperçu he allegedly wanted for his headstone: "All things considered, I'd rather be in Philadelphia."

Fife, Barney   Character in the *Andy Griffith Show* (see Mayberry). Played hilariously by Don Knotts, Fife was Sheriff Andy Taylor's good-hearted but perpetually rattled deputy, forever on the lookout for crime in a crime-free town. Because of his tendency to overreact, Taylor issued him only one bullet, which he was obliged to keep secure in his uniform pocket. Knotts had been a regular on the Steve Allen variety show (1956–1960), and he played in the 1980s on the sitcom *Three's Company*.

Fifth Amendment   A constitutional amendment, part of the Bill of Rights, which protects the rights of American citizens accused of a crime. Guaranteed under its provisions are grand jury indictments in federal cases; prohibited are punishment without due process, double jeopardy proceedings, and enforced self-incrimination. The right of an accused person not to incriminate himself or herself has led to the phrase "taking the Fifth" for refusing to testify.

Fifth Avenue   A New York street symbolizing wealth and privilege. The connotation derives from its Gilded Age popularity as a residence for millionaires and, more recently, from the proliferation of elegant shops.

"Fifty-four Forty or Fight"   An expansionist slogan of the 1840s, used by the Democrats in the 1844 election. The reference was to the 54° 40' parallel, which proponents of Manifest destiny wanted as Oregon's northern border. Their candidate, James Polk, won the election, but agreed to a compromise with the British at the forty-ninth parallel. Had his backers won, British Columbia and the Yukon would be U.S. territory.

"Fifty million Frenchmen can't be wrong"   See Texas GUINAN.

"57 Varieties"   An advertising slogan of the Heinz food company, extolling a range of products that included pickles, relishes, and KETCHUP. It was introduced in 1896 by company founder Henry J. Heinz.

Fighting Irish   Nickname for the Notre Dame football team, from the school's once heavily Irish student body. Stuart Berg Flexner, relaying a 1930s joke, comments that the more heterogeneous enrollment of the era made the "Irish" roster read "like a page out of the Warsaw phone book."

film noir   A film style of the 1940s and 1950s pervaded by narrative cynicism and shadowy, expressionist lighting. The story lines of many films noirs (the term is French for "black film") emphasize the ominousness and venality of urban life. Notable examples include *The Maltese Falcon* (1941), *This Gun for Hire* (1942), *Double Indemnity* (1944), *The Big Sleep* (1946), *The Naked City* (1948), *Force of Evil* (1948), *Sunset Boulevard* (1950), *The Big Heat* (1953), and *Touch of Evil* (1958). The genre sparked the careers of Humphrey BOGART and Alan Ladd.

fink   (1) An informer. Probably from the slang term "to finger," meaning to point to someone in accusation. (2) A strikebreaker. The etymology for this sense is uncertain. H. L. Mencken speculated reasonably that it arose during the 1892 HOMESTEAD STRIKE, when PINKERTON agents, known as Pinks, were employed as scabs.

Fink, Mike   (1770–?1822) Frontiersman. The most famous of Ohio and Mississippi rivermen, Fink earned nicknames ranging from Snag and Snapping Turtle to King of the Keelboatmen. His fame as a boasting western ROARER was exceeded only by that of Davy CROCKETT, while tall tales of his marksmanship and rowdiness were the equal of any told of the Tennesseean. A prodigious fighter and drinker, Fink was also known for a sadistic streak. He enjoyed shooting tin cups, William Tell style, from comrades' heads; crippled a black man from a hundred yards to demonstrate his accuracy ("I'll jest trim that feller's heel so he can wear a decent boot"); and set his own wife on fire to discourage her flirting. Fink's prowess was often exploited in the Crockett Almanacs, and he appeared as the Colonel's rival in the *Disneyland* series. In 1822, as STEAMBOATS began to drive the KEELBOATS out, Fink joined a trapping expedition to the Rocky Mountains, where shortly afterward he was shot to death.

"Fire when ready, Gridley"   See George DEWEY.

fireside chats   Radio addresses to the American people given by Franklin D. ROOSEVELT beginning in 1933. In the 1930s, they provided reassurance about the NEW DEAL; after PEARL HARBOR the focus shifted toward the war.

First Amendment   The first item in the BILL OF RIGHTS. An honored, though often contested, touchstone of liberalism, it prohibits Congress from interfering with freedom of speech, freedom of assembly, or freedom of religion. The freedom of speech and assembly clauses have brought the American Civil Liberties Union to the defense of Nazi marchers; the freedom of religion clause—read as enjoining a gulf between church and state—got morning prayers expelled from the schools in 1963.

"First in war, first in peace, and first in the hearts of his countrymen" A tribute given to George WASHINGTON at his death by his former Army friend, "Light-Horse Harry" Lee. A cavalry colonel, Lee was the father of Robert E. LEE.

First Lady An informal title given to the wife of the U.S. president. "First Family" is sometimes seen when the couple has children, and a canine pet may be referred to as the First Dog. Jimmy Carter's colorful sibling Billy occasionally appeared in the sniping press as the "First Brother."

Fisk, James (1834–72) Financier. As unscrupulous as he was inventive, Fisk specialized in stock watering and in the market finagling that resulted in the BLACK FRIDAY panic of 1869. Three years after that debacle, he was shot to death by a rival suitor for his mistress's favors.

Fisk Jubilee Singers A chorus of African-American students from Fisk University, formed in 1872 to raise funds for the nearly bankrupt school. Their United States and European tours popularized the "Negro spiritual" and brought in $150,000 for their alma mater. Choirs from other black colleges—Hampton Institute, Howard, and Tuskegee—followed the pattern, and the success, set by Fisk.

Fitzgerald, Ella (1918–) Jazz singer. The grand old lady of American jazz, Fitzgerald began singing with big bands in the 1930s, had her first hit with a spirited "A-Tisket, A-Tasket" (1938), and has performed with Count BASIE, Duke ELLINGTON, and numerous symphonies. She is as well known for her sensitive treatment of romantic ballads as for her rapid-fire, witty SCAT SINGING.

Fitzgerald, F. Scott (1896–1940) The premier novelist of the JAZZ AGE, Minnesota-born and Princeton-educated Francis Scott Fitzgerald was nearly as well known for his elegantly dissipated lifestyle as for the novels and short stories that reflected it. He was part of the international social set, whose sense of unease, glitteringly disguised by endless partying, he captured in *The Beautiful and Damned* (1921) and THE GREAT GATSBY. Even more directly autobiographical was *Tender Is the Night* (1934), which reflected his marriage to mentally unbalanced Zelda Sayre. Always a heavy drinker, he experienced a mental collapse himself in 1935—an episode he searingly described in the essay "The Crack Up" (1936). A novel about Hollywood, *The Last Tycoon,* was never finished.

five-and-dime A department store featuring inexpensive goods, priced at a nickel and a dime in the 1880s, when the term arose. Also called five-and-ten. See also F. W. WOOLWORTH.

Five Civilized Tribes The relatively Europeanized tribes of the southeastern United States: the CHEROKEE, Chickasaw, Choctaw, Creek, and SEMINOLE. Their adoption of white ways (including farming, Christianity, and Western dress) did not prevent the U.S. government from stealing their land in the 1830s. Their descendants live in Oklahoma, where the tribes were force-marched in that decade's TRAIL OF TEARS.

Five-Foot Shelf A nickname for the Harvard Classics, the great-books set edited by Charles W. ELIOT. The tag referred to the educator's comment "One could get a first-class education from a shelf of books five feet long."

Five Nations   The IROQUOIS LEAGUE, after its five original members: the Cayuga, Mohawk, Oneida, Onondaga, and Seneca.

Flag Day   June 14. Designated as such in 1949 but still not an official national holiday. It commemorates the Continental Congress's adoption of the STARS AND STRIPES on June 14, 1777.

Flagg, James Montgomery   (1877–1960) Artist. Trained in Europe, Flagg was New York State's official military artist when he came up with the recruiting poster that secured his fame: the picture of a white-goateed UNCLE SAM exhorting the viewer with an admonishing finger, "I Want YOU." Flagg himself was the model for the figure.

flak   (1) Antiaircraft fire. From German *FLiegerAbwehrKanonen,* meaning, straightforwardly enough, "guns providing defense against flyers." Hence (2) criticism or opposition to one's designs.

Flanagan, Father   See BOYS TOWN.

flapper   A young woman of unconventional behavior in the 1920s. The term connoted short skirts, long necklaces, and longer parties replete with all-night CHARLESTONS, smoke-filled SPEAKEASIES, and sexual license.

Flash Gordon   A successful BUCK ROGERS clone, Flash Gordon was a spaceship superhero who debuted in a comic strip in 1934 and expanded into radio and movie serials by the end of the decade. In the serials, the title player was Buster CRABBE, who had also starred in Buck Rogers serials. Along with girlfriend Dale and scientist ally Dr. Zharkov, Flash defended the universe against the megalomania of Ming the Merciless—a sinister emperor whose Oriental appearance pandered to the period's sinophobia.

Flatt and Scruggs   Musicians. Guitarist Lester Flatt (1914–79) and banjo-picker Earl Scruggs (1924–) were the most widely heard BLUEGRASS players of the 1950s and 1960s. Veterans of Bill MONROE's Blue Grass Boys, they formed their own group, the Foggy Mountain Boys, in 1948, reaching national audiences with "Roll in My Sweet Baby's Arms" and their signature tune, "Foggy Mountain Breakdown," which became the theme for the 1967 movie BONNIE AND CLYDE. The duo also provided the theme for THE BEVERLY HILLBILLIES. The partnership broke up in 1969.

Fleischer brothers   Animators. In the 1930s Max (1889–1972) and Dave (1894–1979) Fleischer were second to no one but DISNEY as movie cartoonists. Their most enduring creations were BETTY BOOP and POPEYE the Sailor.

Fletcherism   An eating fad of the 1900s, prompted by a 1903 book, *The ABC of Nutrition.* Its author, Horace Fletcher (1849–1919), advocated chewing each mouthful of food thirty-two times—one chomp for each adult tooth. Hence "fletcherize," for to masticate into mush. True believers included John D. ROCKEFELLER and Thomas EDISON.

flicks   The movies. Short for "flickers," from the jumpy projection of silent films. In the 1960s, "to flick out" meant to go to a movie.

Flintstones, The   The most successful cartoon series in prime-time history (1960–66), *The Flintstones* was an animated comedy set in prehistoric Bedrock. The main characters, Fred and Wilma Flintstone, lived in a split-level cave with a pet dinosaur (Dino) and a "Stoneway" piano. The show gently parodied both the domestic SITCOM and media stars like Ed SULLIVAN (Ed Sullystone) and PERRY Mason (Perry Masonry). The characters continue to appear on children's lunch boxes and other merchandise.

"Float like a butterfly, sting like a bee"   See Muhammad ALI.

flower children   The pacifist, HIPPIE element of the 1960s COUNTERCULTURE. From their fondness for flowers as adornment and peace symbols. Scott McKenzie's 1967 anthem to the "love-in" capital, "San Francisco" began:

> *If you're going to San Francisco*
> *Be sure to wear some flowers in your hair.*
> *'Cause when you go to San Francisco*
> *You're sure to meet some gentle people there.*

Floyd, Pretty Boy   (1901–34) Bank robber. Charles Arthur Floyd, nicknamed Pretty Boy because of his looks, hit midwestern banks in the 1930s, becoming PUBLIC ENEMY number one before the FBI killed him. He was credited with having murdered ten people, but hatred of bankers during the GREAT DEPRESSION made him an Oklahoma folk hero. Woody GUTHRIE wrote a song in his honor.

Flying Cloud   See CLIPPER SHIPS.

Flying Fortress   The B-17 bomber of World War II, developed for long-range bombing runs over Nazi Europe. The largest bomber of its day, it carried a payload of 4,800 pounds. It was superseded by the B-29 Superfortress, the "hemisphere defense weapon" that dropped the atomic bombs on Japan.

Flying Tigers   U.S. civilian fighter pilots, officially called the American Volunteer Group, who defended China against Japanese bombers during WORLD WAR II. Led by Air Force General Claire Chennault (1890–1958), they shot down nearly three hundred enemy planes.

Flynn, Elizabeth Gurley   (1890–1964) Labor organizer. Known to her admirers as the Rebel Girl, Flynn joined the INDUSTRIAL WORKERS OF THE WORLD in 1906; led textile strikes in Lawrence, Massachusetts (1912), and Paterson, New Jersey (1913); and helped to found the American Civil Liberties Union. A member of the Communist Party from the 1930s, she spent two years in prison (1955–57) for "subversion." When she got out, she led the party until her death.

Flynn, Errol   (1909–59) Actor. Tasmanian-born Flynn came to Hollywood in 1935 and became an overnight success as a pirate in *Captain Blood*. The romantic leads that WARNER BROTHERS then threw his way made him the quintessential adventure hero of his time. He was Miles Hendon in *The Prince and the Pauper* (1937), the Sherwood archer in *The Adventures of Robin Hood* (1938), an English privateer in *The Sea Hawk* (1940), George CUSTER in *They Died with Their Boots on* (1942), James CORBETT in *Gentleman Jim* (1942), and the legendary lover in

The Adventures of Don Juan (1949). His offscreen life was as outsize as his roles, with drinking, drug use, and wenching his standard fare. A 1942 trial for statutory rape left him acquitted but with his marriage in ruins, and it made "in like Flynn" a prurient synonym for "OK" and "lucky." He played charming drunks in *The Sun Also Rises* (1957) and *Too Much, Too Soon* (1958), then succumbed to a life of indulgence at the age of fifty. His chief problem, he once observed, was in "reconciling my net income with my gross habits."

"Foggy Mountain Breakdown" See FLATT AND SCRUGGS.

Foley, Red (1910–68) Country singer. In the late 1940s and early 1950s, Clyde Julian Foley hosted the NBC broadcasts of the GRAND OLE OPRY. Introducing the acts, playing straight man for comedienne Minnie PEARL, and rendering his own versions of blues, gospel, and swing tunes, he did much to bring the show a national following. Country music historian Bill Malone called him perhaps the "most versatile singer of the 1950s."

folk music The traditional, nonelite "music of the people" as distinct from "classical" music on the one hand and commercial "pop" music on the other. In North America, folk music comprises an array of European and indigenous styles, including the orally disseminated BALLADS of the British Isles, native ballads such as COWBOY and prison tunes, fiddle-based dance tunes such as the Virginia reel, children's play songs, and the SPIRITUALS and country BLUES of the slave tradition. Some folklorists insist that "true" folk music is rural, anonymous, and orally transmitted. Others believe that the border between folk and pop is indistinct, and that a comprehensive definition of the "folks' " music should include the radio productions of the GRAND OLE OPRY as well as the songs of urban professionals like Stephen FOSTER. See also COUNTRY MUSIC; John and Alan LOMAX.

folk revival A resurgence of interest in traditional acoustic performance that developed in tandem with rock 'n' roll in the late 1950s. The largely urban "folkie" movement looked back fondly to rural singers like Woody GUTHRIE and LEADBELLY while augmenting the ballad repertoire with political "protest" songs. The most commercially successful folk revivalists were, in roughly chronological order, THE WEAVERS, Pete SEEGER, Burl IVES, Harry BELAFONTE, the KINGSTON TRIO, PETER, PAUL, AND MARY, Joan BAEZ, and Bob DYLAN.

folk rock A popular mesh of folk lyrics and a rocking beat. Two early examples of the style, both released in 1965, were THE BYRDS' rendition of Bob DYLAN's "Mr. Tambourine Man" and SIMON AND GARFUNKEL's "The Sounds of Silence." Dylan's own amplified music of that year, recorded on the album *Bringing It All Back Home*, brought the haunting energy of the eclectic form to full fruition.

"Follow the Drinking Gourd" A folk song from antebellum times about the work of the UNDERGROUND RAILROAD "conductor" Pegleg Joe. The song describes the foot trail he leaves ("Left foot, peg foot, going on") while advising escaped slaves to keep their eyes on the "drinking gourd"—the Big Dipper, whose prominent stars point to the north.

For the old man is waiting for to carry you to freedom
If you follow the drinking gourd.

Fonda family Film stars. Henry (1905–82), who began his career on the stage, became a Hollywood leading man in the 1930s, showing his engaging personality and versatility in features that made him one of the most beloved of screen stars. For director John FORD, he made the American historical dramas *Young Mr. Lincoln* (1939), *Drums Along the Mohawk* (1939), THE GRAPES OF WRATH, *My Darling Clementine* (see "MY DARLING CLEMENTINE" [2]), and FORT APACHE. His title role in the World War II drama MISTER ROBERTS brought him back to Broadway in 1948 and back to Hollywood in the 1955 film version. Other major roles came in *The Lady Eve* (1941), *Twelve Angry Men* (1957), and *On Golden Pond* (1981), for which he won an Academy Award.

Henry's daughter Jane (1937–), after studying in New York with Lee STRASBERG, did comedy in *Cat Ballou* (1965) and *Barefoot in the Park* (1967), then turned increasingly to political activism during the Vietnam War: She was known as Hanoi Jane for her visit to that city. Frequently nominated for Oscars, she won for *Klute* (1971) and the returning-veteran drama *Coming Home* (1978). Her brother Peter (1939–) produced, coscripted, and starred in *Easy Rider* (see "EASY RIDER"[2]).

Fonz, the TV character. Originally a supporting character in the series *Happy Days* (1974–84), Arthur "Fonzie" Fonzarelli, as played by Henry Winkler, soon became the show's romantic and comedic star. A leather-jacketed high school dropout with magical power over women, the Fonz contrasted sharply with Richie Cunningham (Ron Howard) in the nostalgic look at 1950s teendom. Largely because of Winkler's ingratiating bravado, the show became a major hit of the 1970s; the rebel's jacket was given to the Smithsonian Institution.

Foolish John See JEAN SOT.

football An American version of English rugby, football was first played on the college level in 1869, in a six-goal-to-four victory of Rutgers over Princeton. The form of play remained erratic until the 1880s, when the "father of American football," Walter CAMP, trimmed the team size and standardized the scoring system. The game's brutality at the turn of the century was offset by the introduction of the forward pass (1906), an innovation brought to perfection by Knute ROCKNE. Professional football started in embryo in 1895 and took off with the National Football League in the 1920s. Televised pro ball is now a major spectator sport, with interest peaking at the end-of-season SUPER BOWL.

For Whom the Bell Tolls (1940) Ernest HEMINGWAY's novel about an American teacher who finds love and death in the Spanish Civil War. It includes a famous love scene in which "the earth moves" beneath the lovers, and a nihilistic parody of the Lord's Prayer: "Our *nada,* who art in *nada,* hallowed be thy *nada.*" Filmed in 1943, it starred Gary COOPER and Ingrid BERGMAN. The title refers to John Donne's *Devotions:* "No man is an island . . . and therefore never send to know for whom the bell tolls; it tolls for thee."

Ford, Henry (1863–1947) Industrialist. Contrary to popular opinion, Henry Ford neither invented the automobile nor started the U.S. car industry. His innovations were in developing the MODEL T, in revolutionizing manufacturing by his use of the assembly line, and in paying his workers a then unheard-of five dollars a day wage. Before long, Ford's methods—the Germans called them *Fordismus—*

were being copied by manufacturers on two continents, and he was so firmly identified with modern science that Aldous Huxley set his dystopian novel *Brave New World* (1932) in the futuristic year 632 AF (After Ford). He would have been appalled to hear the joke, told years after his death, that FORD stood for "Fix or Repair Daily."

Ford, John   (1895–1973) Movie director. Legend says that John Ford (born Sean O'Feeney) once introduced himself, "My name is John Ford. I make westerns." His westerns, which featured John WAYNE, James STEWART, and Henry Fonda (see FONDA FAMILY), included Wayne's breakthrough film *Stagecoach* as well as a famous "cavalry trilogy" (FORT APACHE, SHE WORE A YELLOW RIBBON, and the 1950 *Rio Grande*), *My Darling Clementine* (see "MY DARLING CLEMENTINE" [2]), *The Searchers* (1956), and *The Man Who Shot Liberty Valance* (1962). The cavalry films involved so many battles with hostile Indians that Ford's pro-Indian *Cheyenne Autumn* (1964) was seen as an "apology." But Ford also made distinguished nonwesterns. He earned Oscars for two World War II documentaries and for the features *The Informer* (1935), THE GRAPES OF WRATH, *How Green Was My Valley* (1941), and *The Quiet Man* (1952). The most populist and narratively rich of American directors, he was as respected by his peers as by the public. When Orson WELLES was asked who had influenced him, he replied, "The old masters: John Ford, John Ford, and John Ford."

Ford, Robert   The young man who killed Jesse JAMES. A member of the outlaw's gang, he shot him in the back of the head while he was dusting a picture. He is immortalized in the last lines of the famous ballad:

> *The dirty little coward who shot Mister Howard*
> *Has laid Jesse James in his grave.*

Ford's Theatre   The Washington, D.C., theater where John Wilkes BOOTH assassinated President LINCOLN. Its builder, John T. Ford (1829–94), was accused of complicity and briefly imprisoned after the tragedy; after his acquittal, the place was sold and shut down. Since 1968 it has been a Lincoln museum.

Forest Lawn   A showy, "celebrity" cemetery in Glendale, California. Built in 1917 as Forest Lawn Memorial Park and visited by a million and a half tourists a year, it was the prototype for funerary excess in Evelyn Waugh's satirical novel *The Loved One* (1947).

forgotten man   The average, mind-your-own-business American who pays his taxes yet is always falling behind. This term for the underprivileged classes was coined by social Darwinist William Graham Sumner in his 1883 book, *What the Social Classes Owe to Each Other*. Franklin D. ROOSEVELT picked it up in his first presidential campaign, making the forgotten man the intended recipient of his NEW DEAL.

Forrest, Edwin   (1806–72) Actor. The most popular American tragedian of his day, Forrest specialized in expansive renderings of Shakespeare's Othello. His rivalry with British actor William Macready caused a riot among opposing fans in 1849, when the latter played New York's Astor Place Opera House. Quelled by militia at the cost of twenty-two lives, the Astor Place riot damaged Forrest's reputation, although there was no proof he had encouraged it.

Fort Apache (1948) A western movie directed by John FORD, the first in a trilogy about the U.S. cavalry. It starred Henry Fonda (See FONDA FAMILY) as an overconfident commander whose disastrous last stand is modeled roughly on George CUSTER's.

Fort Knox An army post near Louisville, Kentucky, and the site of a Treasury Department depository of U.S. gold reserves: hence "all the gold in Fort Knox" for great wealth. The site was named for Revolutionary War artillery officer Henry Knox (1750–1806), who later headed both WEST POINT and the War Department.

Fort McHenry A fort on an island in Baltimore Harbor. Its bombardment by the British during the WAR OF 1812 inspired Francis Scott KEY to write "THE STAR-SPANGLED BANNER."

Fort Sumter A fort in Charleston Harbor, South Carolina. After the formation of the Confederacy in the spring of 1861, southern batteries ringed the Union emplacement and CSA President Jefferson DAVIS ordered it evacuated. Instead, President Abraham LINCOLN sent additional supplies, and on April 12, the South attacked in a dawn bombardment. Union artillery under Abner DOUBLEDAY responded, marking the first engagement of the Civil War. Surrendered on April 13, Sumter was held by the Confederacy until 1865.

Fort Ticonderoga A fort on Lake Champlain in upstate New York, erected as "Carillon" by the French in 1755. The French lost it to the British in the FRENCH AND INDIAN WAR, and the British to Ethan ALLEN in 1775.

Fortune 500 A list of the five hundred largest U.S. corporations published annually by *Fortune* magazine. Complete with sales, profit, and other figures, the list is a snapshot of American business's most influential firms.

"forty acres and a mule" A catchphrase for agricultural self-sufficiency, popular first among freed slaves after the Civil War. During the war, William T. SHERMAN had "liberated" plantation land from fleeing slaveowners and promised it to the slaves on his own authority. The U.S. government did not back the promise.

forty-niners The prospectors who trooped to California in 1849 hoping to strike it rich in the gold fields. See GOLD RUSHES.

42nd Parallel, The The first book in John DOS PASSOS's "U.S.A." trilogy.

42nd Street A street in midtown Manhattan, New York City. Known for its many porno shops, it lies at the heart of the city's theater district. George M. COHAN saluted it in his song "Give My Regards to Broadway": "Tell all the gang at 42nd Street / That I will soon be there." It also gave titles to the film that made Ruby KEELER a star and to a Broadway musical that had almost 3,500 performances in the 1980s.

Foster, Stephen (1926–64) Songwriter. Producer of the country's best-loved minstrel songs, Stephen Collins Foster was born in Pennsylvania and visited the South, with which he was identified, only once. Of his hundreds of songs, most were intended for home performance, although some of the best were done on contract for the CHRISTY MINSTRELS. His enduring works are "Oh Susanna" (1848), "Camptown Races" (1850), "Old Folks at Home" (1851), "My Old Kentucky Home" (1853), "Jeanie with the Light Brown Hair" (1854), and "Old Black Joe" (1860). Since he wrote for hire rather than royalties, he enjoyed minimal profit from his work, and he died virtually destitute in New York City. See also MINSTREL SHOWS.

Founding Fathers   The members of the Constitutional Convention of 1787, which drafted and adopted the U.S. CONSTITUTION. Sometimes seen as simply "the Founders" or "the Framers."

fountain of youth   See Juan PONCE DE LEÓN.

Fountainhead, The   (1943) A novel by "objectivist" writer Ayn RAND. The story of an architect, Howard Roark, who chooses the integrity of his vision over money, it is thought to reflect the career of Frank Lloyd WRIGHT. Gary COOPER played Roark in King VIDOR's 1949 film.

4-F   A Selective Service classification meaning the potential draftee is physically unfit to serve. (Suitable candidates are classified 1-A.) Cinema warriors Errol FLYNN and John WAYNE were both 4-F.

Four Freedoms   In his 1941 State of the Union message, Franklin D. ROOSEVELT called for a world founded on "four essential human freedoms: freedom of speech and expression, freedom of worship, freedom from want and freedom from fear." The first two spoke to the promises of the FIRST AMENDMENT; the second two suggested the traumas of the European war. The four were enshrined in that year's Atlantic Charter and inspired a quartet of paintings by Norman ROCKWELL.

4-H clubs   A youth organization founded in 1900 that promotes citizenship, home economics, and scientific farming. Started in Illinois, the system came under Department of Agriculture auspices in 1914 and now includes over 5 million members. 4-H club projects are designed to improve the four Hs: head, hands, heart, and health.

Four Horsemen   In his Book of Revelation (chapter 6), the evangelist John mentions four dread riders, usually taken to represent famine, war, pestilence, and death. Three years after Rudolph VALENTINO became a star in 1921's *Four Horsemen of the Apocalypse,* sportswriter Grantland Rice applied the term to the Notre Dame football team's backfield: Jim Crowley, Elmer Layden, Don Miller, and Harry Stuhldreher. The tag's popularity evoked a taunt from center Adam Walsh: "We are just the seven mules. We do all the work so that these four fellows can gallop into fame." Hence the "Seven Mules" for the Notre Dame line.

400, the   New York high society at the turn of the century. The term, which was coined by socialite Ward McAllister, is generally thought to indicate the number of "fashionable" people who could crowd comfortably into Mrs. William Astor's ballroom. See ASTOR FAMILY.

Four Million, The   A 1906 story collection by O. HENRY, including his most famous tale, "THE GIFT OF THE MAGI." Four million was the approximate population of New York City, and the title of the book—filled with tales of "little people"—was a conscious snap at Ward McAllister's snooty 400.

Four Seasons   A 1960s pop vocal group featuring falsetto lead Frankie Valli. Their number-one hits included "Sherry," "Walk like a Man," "Rag Doll," and "Big Girls Don't Cry."

Four Tops   One of the MOTOWN label's strongest acts in the 1960s. Their hits included "Same Old Song," "I Can't Help Myself," "Reach Out, I'll Be There," and "Standing in the Shadows of Love."

"Fourscore and seven years ago"   The opening phrase of the GETTYSBURG ADDRESS.

Fourteen Points   Woodrow WILSON's plan for postwar peace, announced to Congress in January of 1918. The fourteen points included "open covenants of peace, openly arrived at," the removal of economic barriers, arms reduction, freedom of the seas, adjustment of land claims, and—most important—the establishment of a "general association of nations" that could guarantee "political independence and territorial integrity." This last point led to the founding of the League of Nations.

Fourth of July   A holiday celebrating American independence; hence the alternate designation Independence Day. It commemorates July 4, 1776, when the Continental Congress adopted the DECLARATION OF INDEPENDENCE. The date is observed with picnics and community fireworks.

Foy family   Comic and dancer Edwin Fitzgerald "Eddie" Foy (1856–1928) spent over four decades on the vaudeville and musical stage. His children appeared with him as the Seven Little Foys, and two of them went on to show business careers. Eddie, Jr. (1905–83), played his famous father in several movies, including the 1942 YANKEE DOODLE DANDY. Bryan (1896–1977) directed the first all-talking movie, *Lights of New York* (1928), then produced so many B movies that his colleagues called him Keeper of the Bs.

Foyt, A. J.   (1935–   ) Race car driver. Anthony Joseph Foyt was the first driver to win one hundred U.S. Auto Club–sponsored races. In the 1960s and 1970s, he excelled in all racing divisions, winning the INDIANAPOLIS 500 a record five times. After his 1967 Indy win, he shared the Le Mans victory spot with codriver Dan Gurney.

Frankenstein   (1931) A movie rendition of Mary Shelley's novel made in Hollywood by English director James Whale. It started the horror career of Boris KARLOFF and created a cottage industry in lesser sequels. In two of these—*The Bride of Frankenstein* (1935) and *Son of Frankenstein* (1939)—Karloff himself reprised his monster role.

"Frankie and Johnny"   A nineteenth-century murder ballad about a prostitute, Frankie, who is executed for murdering her lover, faithless Johnny. The commonest of its many variant titles is "Frankie and Albert." Each verse ends with the rueful comment: "He was her man / But he done her wrong."

Franklin, Aretha   (1942–   ) Singer. The daughter of a Baptist minister, Franklin sang GOSPEL MUSIC in his Detroit church as a child, moved to New York and RHYTHM AND BLUES in her twenties, and became the queen of SOUL ("Lady Soul") in the 1960s. Of her many million-selling songs, the best known were "Since You've Been Gone," "Think," "Chain of Fools," and "Respect."

Franklin, Benjamin   (1706–90) An Enlightenment-era "universal man," Franklin shone in everything he touched—and he touched everything. A master of business, literature, science, politics, and not least of all conversation, he so charmed the not easily impressed French that they called him the "wisest American."

Born in Boston, Franklin apprenticed in his brother's bookshop, reading voraciously, until running away to Philadelphia at the age of sixteen. There he started a newspaper, became a printer, published POOR RICHARD'S ALMANACK, and so prospered that he was able to retire at forty-two. The industry to which he attributed his success was vividly described in his *Autobiography,* one of the great self-help books of all time; it was first published in full in 1868. In his leisure time, Franklin established Philadelphia's first fire company, street lighting, night watchmen, insurance company, and college—the institution that became the University of Pennsylvania. He also developed a prototype of the so-called Franklin stove; invented bifocals; and—after flying a kite in a storm to show that lightning was electricity—developed lightning rods to capitalize on the discovery.

In the 1750s and 1760s, he turned to politics, promoting a "Plan of Union" to consolidate the colonies against the French and arguing the colonial cause in two visits to the mother country. As a member of the Continental Congress (1775), he gave editing tips to Thomas JEFFERSON on the DECLARATION OF INDEPENDENCE, signed that document, and uttered a famous quip at the signing ceremony. When John HANCOCK observed that the signers—de facto traitors—must "hang together," Old Ben added, "Or most assuredly we will all hang separately." In 1776, he went to Paris, almost single-handedly securing French aid for the "embattled farmers." Seven years later, he was a signatory of the Treaty of Paris.

Practical and witty, "wealthy and wise," Franklin was the eighteenth century's essential American. John Paul JONES named a flagship in his honor, the U.S. government put his face on the $100 bill, and when he died, twenty thousand mourners paid him homage.

"Frankly, my dear, I don't give a damn"   Rhett Butler's famous kiss-off line, uttered to Scarlett O'Hara at the end of GONE WITH THE WIND. When the book was filmed in 1939, the HAYS OFFICE was still firmly in the saddle, and the use of "damn" cost the film's producers a $5,000 fine.

fraternities and sororities   Boarding organizations for male and female college students respectively which stress fellowship, community service, social connections, and, last but not least, wild partying. PHI BETA KAPPA, the honorary fraternity, was established in 1776, but the first social "frat" was Union College's Kappa Alpha (1825), the first sorority Adelphean, founded at Georgia's Wesleyan College in 1851. The "Greek" system—so-called because the organizations take

Greek-letter names—grew rapidly in the nineteenth century, declined in the activist 1960s (when houses were seen as discriminatory and conventional), and is still a subject of widespread college debate. Humiliating and sometimes dangerous initiation rites, collectively called hazing, have gotten the system barred from several campuses, while on others it continues to dominate social life. Outsiders call members Greeks or frat rats.

Fredonia (1) A short-lived republic (1826) set up by Americans living in Texas who wanted independence from Mexico. Promising the local Indians half of the territory in exchange for their support, they held the town of Nacogdoches briefly until Mexican troops, helped by Stephen F. AUSTIN, drove them out. (2) A mythical kingdom comically mismanaged by the MARX BROTHERS in their 1933 romp *Duck Soup.*

free lunch Counter lunches available in saloons from about the middle of the nineteenth century. The expression "no free lunch" came to mean "You can't get something for nothing."

"Free Silver" A Populist and later Democratic campaign cry in presidential politics of the 1890s. The "free," or unlimited, coinage of silver was seen as an economic panacea for debtors and farmers, who had suffered for over two decades from tight money policies. See William Jennings BRYAN.

Free-Soilers Nineteenth-century opponents of the extension of slavery. Specifically, members of the Free-Soil party (established 1848), which ran Martin Van Buren for president in that year's election. Most Free-Soilers were later absorbed into the Republican party. See also BARNBURNERS.

Freed, Alan (1922–65) Disc jockey. Although his claim to having invented the term "rock 'n' roll" is debatable, Freed was undeniably influential in the music's popularity. As the host of integrated concerts and a promoter of RHYTHM AND BLUES, he made "race" music a familiar sound for white audiences. Although frequently denounced as a "nigger lover," he made his New York radio station, WINS, the city's top music station of the 1950s before being ruined in the 1962 payola scandals.

freedom of the press, freedom of religion, freedom of speech See FIRST AMENDMENT.

freedom riders CIVIL RIGHTS MOVEMENT activists who, in 1961, challenged the "SEPARATE BUT EQUAL" customs of the Deep South by sitting together, black and white, on segregated buses. The initiative was sponsored by the Congress of Racial Equality. Its participants were violently attacked and many were jailed.

Frémont, John C. (1813–90) Explorer, politician. Frémont's survey of the OREGON TRAIL and his treks on to California in the 1840s earned him the nickname the Pathfinder. He served briefly as the California territory's governor, then as one of the state's first U.S. senators, before being drafted by the Republican Party in 1856 as its first presidential candidate. During the Civil War he supervised the Western Department, and when he proclaimed Missouri slaves free was relieved of command.

French, Daniel C.   (1850–1931) Sculptor. French is known for two patriotic statues. His heroic *Minute Man* (1873–75) stands at CONCORD Bridge in Massachusetts, where the first MINUTEMEN started the Revolutionary War. His massive, noble *Abraham Lincoln* (1911–22) sits in the LINCOLN MEMORIAL in Washington, D.C.

French and Indian War   (1755–63) The American theater of the Seven Years War, fought between England and France for the control of colonial territory. It began with BRADDOCK'S DEFEAT and ended with the surrender of Quebec (1759) and Montreal (1760). In the Treaty of Paris, signed in 1763, France surrendered its claims on Canada to the British. The war strained the British budget so severely, though, that Parliament levied new taxes to redeem the loss—including the STAMP ACT tax, which hastened the Revolution.

French Quarter   From the 1860s, the French-speaking quarter of New Orleans, formerly called the Vieux Carré.

Freneau, Philip   (1752–1832) Poet. Freneau's patriotic verse and an account of his Revolutionary War imprisonment, "The British Prison Ship" (1781), made him the "poet of the Revolution." He was also known for the lyrics "The Wild Honeysuckle" and "The Indian Burying Ground" and for editing a Jeffersonian paper, the *National Gazette*.

Friday, Joe   See DRAGNET.

Friday the 13th   An extremely unlucky day, according to superstitions that are common in European folklore. Hence the title of a series of horror movies of the 1980s about a madman, Jason, who stalks his victims on that day.

Frietchie, Barbara   See "BARBARA FRIETCHIE."

Frisbee   A platelike plastic disc that can be made to sail, when properly thrown, like a flying saucer. Marketed since the 1950s by the Whamo-O toy company, it was named for the Bridgeport, Connecticut, Frisbie pie company, whose plates college students had been tossing in fun since the turn of the century.

Frisco   San Francisco. A term not universally admired by the city's residents. Herb Caen's history of the place (1935) was entitled *Don't Call It Frisco*.

From Here to Eternity   A sprawling, sexy novel (1951) by James Jones (1921–77) about army life in PEARL HARBOR before the Japanese attack. A 1953 movie won Oscars for best picture, best director (Fred ZINNEMANN), best supporting actress (Donna Reed), and best supporting actor (Frank SINATRA). In its most famous scene, Deborah Kerr and Burt LANCASTER make love in the surf.

Front Page, The   (1928) A comic drama about newspaper life by Ben HECHT and Charles MacArthur (1895–1956), the husband of Helen HAYES. A hit on Broadway, it was filmed three times, twice (1931 and 1974) with the original title and once (1940) as *His Girl Friday*; the 1940 version starred Cary GRANT.

frontier thesis See TURNER THESIS.

Frost, Robert (1874–1963) Poet. Almost as much as Carl SANDBURG, Robert Frost was known as a people's poet. Born in San Francisco but raised mostly in New England, he was identified strongly with that region, and his work evokes the rugged dignity of its people. The success of his first volumes of poetry, *A Boy's Will* (1913) and *North of Boston* (1914), enabled him to buy a farm in New Hampshire, which he used as a constant resource in his writing. The winner of four Pulitzer Prizes, Frost gradually became a national institution. In one of his last public appearances, he read "The Gift Outright" at John F. KENNEDY's inauguration. The lyrical highlights of the preceding half-century had included "BIRCHES," "MENDING WALL," and "Stopping by Woods on a Snowy Evening."

"Frosty the Snowman" A children's song written by Steve Nelson and Jack Rollins. A Christmas season classic, it tells the story of a snowman who comes to life with the aid of a magic silk hat. It was a 1950 hit for Gene AUTRY, following his previous year's success with "RUDOLPH, THE RED-NOSED REINDEER."

Fruitlands See UTOPIAN COMMUNITIES.

Fu Manchu, Dr. The hero in a series of novels by the British crime writer Sax Rohmer (ca. 1883–1959). An evil oriental genius, the doctor figured in a number of 1930s films, of which the most notable, *The Mask of Fu Manchu* (1932), starred Boris KARLOFF. A "Fu Manchu mustache," modeled on the character's, turns down at the ends toward the chin.

Fudd, Elmer See ELMER FUDD.

"Full Dinner Pail" A Republican party promise that helped put William McKINLEY in the White House in 1896. Their slogan in full went "McKinley and the Full Dinner Pail"—a pocketbook pitch that the Democrats' "FREE SILVER" failed to overcome.

Fuller, Margaret See TRANSCENDENTALISM.

Fuller, R. Buckminster (1895–1983) Designer. The inventor of various energy- and materials-efficient devices, including a three-wheeled car and a portable house, "Bucky" Fuller was best known for his geodesic dome (1947), which has been called the "most revolutionary advance in architecture since the arch." The hemispheric structure, which encloses maximum space with minimum materials, was used by the military beginning in the 1950s and became a favored domicile for youthful dropouts in the 1960s. Fuller himself became a COUNTERCULTURE guru for that invention and his visionary projections for "spaceship Earth."

Fulton, Robert (1765–1815) Engineer, inventor. Best known for his design of the steamboat CLERMONT, Fulton also produced a submarine, or "diving boat," called the *Nautilus* (1800) and a floating fort to defend New York harbor in the WAR OF 1812. Although he did not invent the steamboat—prototypes had been around since the 1780s—he did prove its commercial viability.

Fulton's Folly   See CLERMONT.

fundamentalism   A belief in the literal inerrancy of the Christian Bible; hence the stereotyped perception of fundamentalists as "Bible thumpers." A reform movement in the Protestant churches, it reached its greatest influence in the South in the 1920s. Stung by the ridicule of William Jennings BRYAN in the SCOPES TRIAL, the literalist faith became less prominent in following decades, although it was reborn with the MORAL MAJORITY in the 1980s.

funnies (or funny pages)   The COMICS; the comic strip section of a newspaper.

fur trade   The popularity of BEAVER hats in seventeenth-century Europe, and the scarcity of fur-bearing animals in the Old World, made the fur-thick forests of North America a desirable prize, and in that century the COUREURS DE BOIS made good use of it. Competition from the HUDSON'S BAY COMPANY in the following century led ultimately to the FRENCH AND INDIAN WAR, in which Canada—and her furs—passed to the British. Fur was also an economic lure farther west, leading to the foundation of John Jacob Astor's American Fur Company (see ASTOR FAMILY) and the employment of many MOUNTAIN MEN as trappers. By the 1840s, their lucrative business had largely evaporated, as even isolated wilderness areas became trapped out and the silk hat, replacing the beaver, dried up demand.

G

G (1) One thousand dollars. Short for GRAND. (2) In the Motion Picture Association of America's rating system, the abbreviation for "General"—for films with no restrictions on admission.

G-men A 1920s abbreviation for "government men," meaning Department of Justice investigators. Machine Gun KELLY helped to popularize the term by telling the agents who captured him, "OK, G-men, you got me." Previous terms had included "DJs" (for Department of Justice) and "Feds."

Gable, Clark (1901–60) Actor. Ohio-born William Clark Gable brought a breezy macho authority to his roles that made him the undisputed King of Hollywood in the 1930s. When he arrived there, Darryl ZANUCK sized him up thus: "His ears are too big. He looks like an ape." But within three years, the "big ape" had made twenty films, playing opposite such stars as Joan CRAWFORD, Greta GARBO, and Jean HARLOW. In 1934, he won an Oscar for IT HAPPENED ONE NIGHT; according to legend, when he unbuttoned his shirt in that film, revealing a bare chest, undershirt sales plummeted overnight. Among a string of rough-and-ready roles, the two highlights of the decade were his Fletcher Christian in MUTINY ON THE BOUNTY and the part for which he is most remembered, Rhett Butler in GONE WITH THE WIND. Gable's storybook marriage (1939–42) to actress Carole Lombard ended tragically when she died in a plane crash. The King joined the Air Force, came back from the war decorated, and made a number of films lacking the punch of his earlier work. He made *The Misfits* (1961) with Marilyn MONROE just before he died.

Gadsden Purchase A strip of land along the Mexican border of New Mexico and Arizona. The United States bought it from Mexico as a railroad right-of-way in 1853. It was named for railroad Baron James Gadsden.

Galloping Ghost A nickname for Red GRANGE. It was coined by sportswriter Grantland Rice, who also provided the nickname FOUR HORSEMEN.

Gallup polls Public opinion polls run since 1958 by the Gallup Organization, the best-known polling group in the United States. Named for journalist George Gallup (1901–84), who made his reputation in 1935 when his newly formed American Institute of Public Opinion predicted Franklin D. ROOSEVELT's victory over Alf Landon.

Gangbusters A cops-and-robbers action show that ran for twenty-one years (1936–57) on radio, then for one season (1952) on television. The radio version opened with a frenzied clatter of gunfire and sirens; hence the expressions "like gangbusters'' and ''coming on like gangbusters'' to describe anything showy, successful, or aggressive.

Gantry, Elmer   See ELMER GANTRY.

GAR   See GRAND ARMY OF THE REPUBLIC.

Garbo, Greta   (1905–90) Actress. Swedish-born actress Greta Louisa Gustafsson, brought to America in 1925 by her mentor Mauritz Stiller, captivated audiences with her alluring remoteness and was soon known by a host of sobriquets: the Swedish Sphinx, the Sarah Bernhardt of films, and the Face. Her most famous silent film, *Flesh and the Devil* (1927), costarred her real-life lover, John Gilbert. Her first sound film, *Anna Christie* (1930), was trumpeted with giant ads proclaiming "Garbo Talks!" Among her other tragic, subtly sensual roles were the leads in *Grand Hotel* (1932), *Anna Karenina* (1935), and *Camille* (1937), while an uncharacteristic film, the sparkling *Ninotchka* (1939), showed an underdeveloped flair for comic invention. Garbo retired from the screen in 1941. Her subsequent reclusiveness only added to her air of mystery, perfectly reflected in her famous line "I WANT TO BE ALONE."

Gardner, Ava   (1922–90) Actress. A Hollywood "love goddess" of the 1940s and 1950s, Gardner was better known for her stardom than her performances. Her films included *One Touch of Venus* (1948), *Show Boat* (1951), *The Sun Also Rises* (1957), *On the Beach* (1959), and *The Life and Times of Judge Roy Bean* (1972), in which she played the actress Lily LANGTRY. Gardner was married, each time briefly, to Mickey ROONEY, band leader Artie Shaw, and Frank SINATRA.

Gardner, Erle Stanley   See PERRY MASON.

Garfield, James A.   (1831–81) U.S. president chiefly remembered for the beginning and the end of his life. He was the last president to be born in a LOG CABIN, and he was assassinated after only a few months in office. Because his killer, Charles GUITEAU, was a disappointed office seeker, the tragedy led to a reassessment of the SPOILS SYSTEM and the establishment of civil service exams for government jobs.

Garfunkel, Art   See SIMON AND GARFUNKEL.

Garland, Judy   (1922–69) Singer, actress. Introduced to the vaudeville stage at the age of four, Garland (née Frances Gumm) became a child star opposite Mickey ROONEY in the "Andy Hardy" series, then captivated the world as Dorothy Gale in THE WIZARD OF OZ. She made an apparently smooth transition to adult singing roles in *Meet Me in St. Louis* (1944) and *Easter Parade* (1948), although she was becoming increasingly dependent on pills. Alcohol and depression compounded her problems, and by 1954, when she gave an Oscar-nominated performance in A STAR IS BORN, she had already made at least one suicide attempt. A disastrous London club engagement (1968) preceded her death from an overdose of sleeping pills. A brilliant torch singer (see TORCH SONG) as well as an actress, she was married to director Vincente MINNELLI for seven years; their daughter is entertainer Liza Minnelli.

Garrett, Pat   (1850–1908) Lawman. Garrett was the New Mexico sheriff who, in 1881, ambushed and killed his former friend BILLY THE KID. Before coming to New Mexico, he had been a buffalo hunter, cowboy, and Texas Ranger. With Ash Upson he wrote the Kid's first biography (1882).

Garrison, William Lloyd   (1805–79) Abolitionist. Known chiefly as the editor of the weekly *Liberator* (1831–65), Garrison also helped to found the American Anti-Slavery Society (1833), denounced the slavery-condoning CONSTITUTION as "a covenant with death and an agreement with Hell," and publicly cheered John BROWN's raid on Harpers Ferry.

Garvey, Marcus   (1887–1940) Black nationalist. Born in Jamaica, Garvey moved to HARLEM in 1916, where through his Universal Negro Improvement Association he preached a "Back to Africa" message to African Americans. Millions applauded his separatist plan, and at a 1920 Convention of the Negro People of the World, he was elected provisional president of Africa. The Black Star shipping line he founded to implement his plan, however, was funded by unconventional selling of stock, and the "Black Moses" was convicted of mail fraud in 1923. Pardoned after three years in prison, he was deported to Jamaica. His emphasis on racial pride and self-sufficiency prefigured the BLACK POWER movement.

gas chamber   A sealed room for executing prisoners with poison gas. First used in 1924 in Nevada. See also ELECTRIC CHAIR; LYNCHING.

Gasoline Alley   A comic strip developed in 1918 by Frank King. A spin-off of King's "Rectangle" gag page for the *Chicago Tribune,* it focused—as the "Yellow Kid" had focused years before—on the colorful denizens of an urban neighborhood. King himself drew the strip for over forty years.

Gatling gun   A crank-operated, rotating-barrel machine gun invented in 1862 by North Carolinian Richard Gatling (1818–1903). The U.S. Army used it from 1866 to 1911, and it figures often in "twilight" westerns like THE WILD BUNCH (2). "Gat," for a pistol, also comes from Gatling's name.

gay   Homosexual. Used both as an adjective and as a noun, and referring usually, although not always, to males. Associated with the gay activism of the 1970s, this meaning of the word dates from the 1940s.

Gay Nineties   The 1890s. From the Depression-torn 1930s, when the turn of the century seemed carefree by comparison. The Gay Nineties stereotype, ignoring the period's labor troubles and the Spanish-American War, emphasizes nickel beers, bicycles built for two, the GIBSON GIRL, John Philip SOUSA, and TIN PAN ALLEY.

Gehrig, Lou   (1903–41) Baseball player. The "Iron Horse," although overshadowed by his famous teammate Babe RUTH, was one of the best hitters, and most reliable players, in baseball history. With the New York Yankees from 1925 to 1939, he played a record 2,130 consecutive games, earning a lifetime batting average of .341 (with 493 home runs) and participating in seven World Series. The disease that killed him, amyotrophic lateral sclerosis, is often called Lou Gehrig's disease.

Gentleman Jim   See Gentleman Jim CORBETT.

Gentlemen Prefer Blondes   A 1925 novel by screenwriter Anita LOOS (1893–1981) satirizing JAZZ AGE GOLD DIGGERS. Her dramatization of the story ran twice on Broadway. The second run (1949–50) included songs by Jule STYNE and Leo Robin, the most famous of which, "Diamonds Are a Girl's Best Friend," was sung by Marilyn MONROE in a 1953 film directed by Howard HAWKS. Monroe played Lorelei Lee, a part that had been a success on the stage for Carol Channing.

George III   (1738–1820) The longest-reigning king in English history (1760–1820), the Hanoverian George III presided over the loss of the American colonies, whose loyalty he had helped to alienate by unwise taxes. A disorder known as porphyria destroyed his sanity, bringing his son to a regency rule in 1811. The familiar canard that he spoke no English is the result of guilt by association with his great-grandfather, George I.

George, Henry   (1839–97) Reformer. Shocked by the inequities of industrial capitalism, George proposed a "single tax" on land, which, he claimed, would abolish other taxes as well as poverty. His theories, which influenced tax reform in the West and in Europe, were articulated in his best-selling book *Progress and Poverty* (1879). He ran for mayor of New York twice without success.

George Washington Bridge   (1931) A suspension bridge across the Hudson River linking New York City with Fort Lee, New Jersey. Until the construction of the GOLDEN GATE BRIDGE in 1937, it was the longest bridge in the world. The lower of its two traffic decks is informally known as Martha.

George Washington Crossing the Delaware   (1851) Historical painting by German-born artist Emanuel Leutze (1816–68). It shows the Continental general standing in a boat on Christmas Night, 1776, crossing the icy river to surprise the Hessians at the Battle of Trenton.

George White's Scandals   A series of musical revues, modeled on the ZIEG-FELD FOLLIES, staged by actor/producer George White from 1919 to 1932. They gave songwriting experience to George GERSHWIN and Sammy FAIN while further-ing the careers of Ethel MERMAN and Rudy VALLEE. A number of film versions appeared in the 1930s.

Georgia cracker   See CRACKER.

"Georgia on My Mind"   A popular ballad written in 1930 by Hoagy CARMI-CHAEL and Stuart Gorrell. It was a number-one hit for Ray CHARLES in 1959.

Georgia Peach   See Ty COBB.

Gerber baby   Trademark of the Gerber baby food company, the face of an infant sketched around 1928 by artist Dorothy Hope Smith. Contrary to a long-standing rumor, it was a child named Ann Cook, not Humphrey BOGART, who was the model.

Geronimo   (1829–1909) Apache leader. Born Goyathlay ("He who yawns"), Geronimo was a Chiricahua war chief who, as his people were being moved onto reservations in the 1880s, led a band of "hostiles" on frequent raids throughout the Southwest. A symbol then and now of the irredeemable "bad Indian," he eluded the U.S. Army until 1886, when he surrendered and was immediately deported to a Florida prison. Later settled at Fort Sill, Oklahoma, he sold pictures of himself at the 1904 St. Louis World's Fair and rode the following year in Teddy ROOSEVELT's inaugural parade.

gerrymander   (noun) A politically motivated redrawing of a voting district. (verb) To draw up such a district. The prototype was a Massachusetts district that was tortuously restructured in 1812 to give an advantage to Governor Elbridge Gerry's (1744–1814) Democratic-Republican party. The district's new shape was said to resemble a salamander and then, as a snap at the governor, a "gerrymander." Gerry, who had represented the United States in the XYZ AFFAIR, went on to serve as James MADISON's vice president.

Gershwin, George   (1898–1937) Composer. Like Duke ELLINGTON, Gershwin bridged the gap between "serious" and popular to create a uniquely American musical style. After working on TIN PAN ALLEY as a teenager, he had his first hit with "Swanee" (1919), which became Al JOLSON's most famous number, and soon began to write for the stage and screen. His famous concert pieces were RHAPSODY IN BLUE and AN AMERICAN IN PARIS, his most successful musicals *Of Thee I Sing* (1931) and PORGY AND BESS. His brother, Ira (1896–1983), wrote the lyrics for many of his songs.

"Get there first with the most men"   Confederate General Nathan Bedford Forrest's (1821–77) rule of battle, uttered after one of his many coups against Union supply lines. It was "colorized" over time by repetition, so that it usually appears in the fake-folk form "Get thar fustest with the mostest men." William T. SHERMAN called Forrest the "most remarkable man" on either side in the Civil War. Certainly, he didn't dawdle once he "got there." He had countless horses shot from under him and was wounded four times. After the war he became the KU KLUX KLAN's first grand wizard.

Getty, J. Paul   (1892–1976) Businessman, art collector. Jean Paul Getty followed his father into the oil business, made his first million before he was twenty-four, took out long-term leases on unproven Middle Eastern real estate, and—when it began gushing in the 1950s—amassed a fortune that made him the world's richest man. He left behind the Getty Oil Company and the Malibu, California, J. Paul Getty Museum.

Gettysburg   A small town in southeastern Pennsylvania. The Battle of Gettysburg, fought there on July 1–3, 1863, was a turning point of the Civil War. At heavy cost to both sides, Union General George G. Meade effectively repulsed a Confederate invasion of the North. The battle's most daring episode was the fruitless PICKETT'S CHARGE.

Gettysburg Address   A brief speech delivered by Abraham LINCOLN at the dedication of a battlefield cemetery for the dead of GETTYSBURG. The ceremony, which took place on November 19, 1863, featured a prior, two-hour address by Edward EVERETT, a former congressman and one of the nation's premier orators. Thinking himself overwhelmed by Everett's brilliance, Lincoln muttered glumly,

"That speech went sour." But many journalists, and Everett himself, did not agree, recognizing in the presidential effort an oratorical classic. It is remembered best for its stirring opening and close. Lincoln began: "Four score and seven years ago, our fathers brought forth on this continent a new nation, conceived in liberty and dedicated to the proposition that all men are created equal." He ended by calling for a rededication to the work of freedom, so that "government of the people, by the people, and for the people shall not perish from the earth." The Gettysburg Address remains the most famous of American speeches. There is no truth to the tale that Lincoln drafted it on the back of an envelope.

ghost dance   A millenarian revival among the Plains Indians begun in the 1880s by the Paiute prophet Wovoka. Ghost dancers believed that personal purification accompanied by ritual dancing would cleanse the earth, bring back the BUFFALO, and drive out the whites. But the revival only hastened the end of Indian resistance. In the U.S. Army's push to quell the fervor, SITTING BULL was killed, as were scores of Sioux women and children at WOUNDED KNEE.

ghost towns   Towns abandoned, or largely abandoned, by their inhabitants. In the American West these are the residue of nineteenth-century GOLD RUSHES (and silver rushes), silent reminders of the "boom and bust" nature of speculative mining. Some ghost towns, revitalized by tourism, serve as "living museums" of the vanished West.

Ghostbusters   (1984) A comic horror film about a quartet of "spirit exterminators." Impressive special effects and a bouncy sound track made it one of the major successes in Hollywood history.

G.I.   Originally an abbreviation for "galvanized iron" (as in garbage cans), by the 1930s this had come to stand for "government issue." Stenciled on soldiers' uniforms and supplies, it was applied in World War II to the men themselves, after the comic strip *G.I. Joe* in the service weekly *Yank*. The G.I. Bill of Rights, or Servicemen's Readjustment Act (1944), provided financial aid for homes and education to returning veterans; millions went to college on the G.I. Bill.

Gibson, Josh   (1911–47) Baseball player. The "Black Babe Ruth," Gibson was the greatest hitter of the Negro National League, making about eight hundred home runs in his seventeen-year career, seventy-five of them in a single season (1931). He died in the same year Jackie ROBINSON integrated the game.

Gibson girl   A fashion ideal of the 1890s. Athletic, serene, and decidedly gentry, she was created by illustrator Charles Dana Gibson (1867–1944), whose name also gave us the Gibson cocktail. Modeled on Gibson's own stylish wife, Irene Langhorne, the Gibson girl typified the "new American woman" until the advent of the 1920s FLAPPER.

"Gift of the Magi, The"   O. HENRY's most famous story, part of the 1906 collection THE FOUR MILLION. It is the tale of a young couple, Jim and Della, who sell prized possessions to buy each other Christmas presents. Their sacrifices, which make the presents ironically unusable, reaffirm their love for one other.

Gilded Age, The   (1873) A novel by Mark TWAIN and Charles Dudley Warner (1829–1900) depicting the venality and rampant greed of the post–Civil War years. The character William Weed is modeled on BOSS TWEED. The book's title became a tag for the scandalous era.

Gillespie, Dizzy (1917–93) Jazz trumpeter. John Birks Gillespie was a principal force in the creation of the BEBOP sound. He played in a wide range of groups, from small combos to big bands, and was influential in bringing the style to general audiences.

Gilligan's Island Television series of the 1960s and 1970s. It involved the comic misadventures on a desert island of seven shipwreck victims; a charter boat captain and one of his crew, a millionaire and his wife, a movie star, a naïve country girl, and an egghead professor. The crew member, endearingly inept Gilligan, was played by Bob Denver.

Ginsberg, Allen (1926–   ) Poet. A leading voice of the BEAT GENERATION, Ginsberg combines the prophetic sense of Blake and Whitman with Eastern mysticism. He is best known for "HOWL," *Kaddish* (1961), and *The Fall of America* (1974). As an opponent of the Vietnam War, he called for fellow protesters to "levitate" the Pentagon by surrounding it and chanting.

Gipper, the See "WIN ONE FOR THE GIPPER."

girl Friday A reliable right-hand woman, as, for example, an office assistant. The female equivalent of "man Friday," from Defoe's *Robinson Crusoe*. The Hecht-MacArthur newspaper comedy THE FRONT PAGE was filmed in 1940 as *His Girl Friday*.

girl in the red velvet swing See Stanford WHITE.

Girl Scouts of America A scouting organization for girls founded in 1912 by Juliette Low (1860–1927). Originally called Girl Guides, it became the Girl Scouts in 1915, with Mrs. Low as its first president. Troops' activities are as diverse as those of the BOY SCOUTS OF AMERICA, although the most visible one is the door-to-door selling of Girl Scout cookies. The FIRST LADY serves as the organization's honorary president. Girl Scouts under nine are called Brownies; those in kindergarten are Daisies.

Girty, Simon (1741–1818) Frontiersman. The "Great Renegade" Simon Girty deserted the American army in 1778 to join the Shawnee in their battles against the whites. The most famous of adopted "white Indians," he was feared for his alleged cruelty to captives and appears in "THE DEVIL AND DANIEL WEBSTER" on the "demonic" jury.

Gish, Lillian (1896–1993) Actress. The "First Lady of the Silent Screen," Gish rose to stardom under the wing of D. W. GRIFFITH, for whom she turned in melodramatic gems in THE BIRTH OF A NATION, *Broken Blossoms* (1919), *Way Down East* (1920), and *Orphans of the Storm* (1922). In *Orphans* she was joined by her sister, Dorothy (1898–1968), who also had a stellar silent career. With the coming of sound, both careers faded, although Lillian continued to do guest shots in movies and TV.

"Git Along, Little Dogies" A cowboy ballad from the 1880s. A dogie (sometimes "doggie") is an orphaned calf, and the song was used to quiet them on the long drives north. The song, which is mentioned in Andy ADAMS's *Log of a Cowboy* (1903), is sometimes called, from its opening line, "Whoopee Ti Yi Yo":

> *Whoopee ti yi yo, git along, little dogies*
> *For you know Wyoming will be your new home.*

"Give 'em hell, Harry"   An unofficial slogan of Harry S TRUMAN's 1948 reelection campaign. Supposedly first shouted from a crowd while the campaigner was skewering the Republicans. Truman later joked: "I didn't give 'em hell. I just told the truth and they thought it was hell."

"Give me liberty or give me death"   The final line of Patrick HENRY's most famous speech, given on the eve of the Revolution (March 1775) in the Continental Congress. Demanding an end to conciliation, it asked the colonies to adopt a "posture of defense":

> *Is life so dear, or peace so sweet, as to be purchased at the price of chains and slavery? Forbid it, Almighty God! I know not what course others may take. But as for me—give me liberty or give me death!*

"Give me your tired, your poor"   See Emma LAZARUS.

"Give My Regards to Broadway"   A 1904 song by George M. COHAN. An unofficial theme song of the New York theater world.

> *Give my regards to Broadway, remember me to Herald Square.*
> *Tell all the gang at 42nd Street that I will soon be there.*

Glass Menagerie, The   (1944) Tennessee WILLIAMS's first successful play. It turns on the isolation of a disabled girl, Laura Wingfield, who comforts herself with a collection of glass animals. A "gentleman caller" breaks her briefly out of her shell, and the play's success gave that phrase a popular currency.

Gleason, Jackie   (1916–87) Entertainer. A portly, expressive comic, the "Great One" started on television as Chester Riley (see LIFE OF RILEY [2]), then emceed a weekly variety show throughout the 1950s and 1960s. Among the characters he invented for the show's skits were the timid Poor Soul, understanding Joe the Bartender, stuffy Reggie Van Gleason III—and boisterous Ralph Kramden, star of THE HONEYMOONERS. Gleason's introductory monologues often included his signature phrase "How sweet it is" and ended with the barker's segue "And awaaaay we go!" He played pool shark Minnesota Fats in *The Hustler* (1961).

Glenn, John   (1921–   ) Astronaut, politician. On February 20, 1962, Marine Corps test pilot John Glenn, one of the original seven ASTRONAUTS, became the first American to orbit the earth. After business ventures in the 1960s, he joined the U.S. Congress as an Ohio Democrat in 1974.

Globetrotters   See HARLEM GLOBETROTTERS.

"Go Down, Moses"   (1) A Negro spiritual, probably of the 1860s, first published in 1872. A perfect example of the double meaning of many spirituals, it conflates the biblical and antebellum bondages in a plaintive cry:

Go down, Moses, way down in Egypt land.
Tell old Pharaoh to let my people go.

The contemporary relevance was further enhanced by the fact that "Moses" was a common nickname for Harriet TUBMAN. (2) *Go Down, Moses,* a collection of stories by William FAULKNER. It contains his most famous short work, "The Bear."

"Go West, young man"   Advice often attributed to Horace GREELEY because of his consistent encouragement of westward expansion and because he used the phrase in his *New York Tribune* editorials. It was first used by Indiana newspaperman John Lane Soule (1815–91) in an 1851 article in the *Terre Haute Express.* See also MANIFEST DESTINY.

"God Bless America"   (1939) A patriotic song written by Irving BERLIN and made famous by singer Kate SMITH. In the 1960s, the title became a conservative catchphrase; it was the closing line of Ronald REAGAN's presidential speeches.

Godey's Lady's Book   The largest women's magazine of the nineteenth century, known for its fashion plates, advice columns, sentimental fiction, and women's rights advocacy. Founded in 1830 by Louis Antoine Godey (1804–78), it prospered under the editorship of Sarah Josepha HALE, reaching a peak circulation in the 1850s of 150,000.

Godfather, The   A 1969 novel by Mario Puzo about the lives of an Italian-American Mafia family. After becoming the biggest-selling work of fiction in American history, it was brought to the screen, with similar success, by director Francis Ford Coppola (1939–   ). The 1972 film won Oscars for best picture and best actor (Marlon BRANDO as Don Corleone), while popularizing the veiled-threat chestnut "We'll make him an offer he can't refuse." A 1974 sequel, *The Godfather, Part II,* again took the best picture award—and one for Coppola.

Godfrey, Arthur   (1903–83) Entertainer. A major radio emcee in the 1940s, Godfrey brought his low-key, down-home style—and his ukulele—to TV in 1949, and for a decade rivaled Ed SULLIVAN as a variety host. His "talent scouts" discovered Pat BOONE and Patsy CLINE; they passed up shots at Elvis PRESLEY and Buddy HOLLY.

God's country   Broadly, any beloved spot or territory conceived of as a heaven on earth. Specifically, the "wide open spaces" of the American West, as glowingly described by nineteenth-century boosters. The vision of a land specially favored of God was as old as the Puritans' "city upon a hill" and Daniel BOONE's recollection of Kentucky as "a spot of earth where nature seems to have concentrated all her bounties." Martha Smith, whose memoir *Going to God's Country* (1941), recalled her 1890 trek west in search of this paradise, came to understand better than most its interior nature:

We learned that God's Country isn't in the country. It is in the mind.
As we looked back we knew that all the time we was hunting for
God's Country we had it. We worked hard. We was loyal. Honest. We
was happy. For forty-eight years we lived together in God's Country.

God's Little Acre (1933) A racy novel by Erskine CALDWELL about a shiftless family of Georgia mountaineers. The main character, Ty Ty Walden, promises the income from an acre of ground to the church, then keeps "moving" the acre to escape the obligation. Until the appearance of GONE WITH THE WIND three years later, it was the biggest-selling novel in American publishing history.

Goethals, George Washington (1858–1928) Engineer. The chief engineer on the PANAMA CANAL, Goethals supervised not only the construction but also the housing, feeding, and care of thirty thousand workers. After the project was completed, he became the Canal Zone's first governor (1914–16), then retired to run his own engineering firm.

"Going Down the Road Feeling Bad" A blueslike ballad written by Woody GUTHRIE about the hard times of DUST BOWL farmers in the 1930s.

Going down the road feeling bad, Lord, Lord;
I ain't going to be treated thisaway.

"Gold Bug, The" (1843) A short story by Edgar Allen POE about the recovery of a buried fortune. It is thought to reflect the legend of CAPTAIN KIDD'S treasure.

gold digger A woman who seeks wealthy men to support her, with or without benefit of clergy. Gold diggers had already been the subject of two films when Mervyn Leroy directed *Gold Diggers of 1933,* in which Ginger Rogers (as Fay Fortune) sings "We're in the Money." Busby BERKELEY's version, *Gold Diggers of 1935,* featured the song-and-dance classic "Lullaby of Broadway."

gold rushes Three major gold strikes invited "rushes" of prospectors in nineteenth-century America. The first and most famous, at John Sutter's sawmill trace near Sacramento (1848), brought thousands of FORTY-NINERS the next year to California. The second, on Cherry Creek near Denver (1858), attracted enough fortune hunters sailing under "PIKES PEAK OR BUST" banners to make Colorado a U.S. territory within three years. The third, in Canada's barren Klondike (1897), provided grist for the mills of Robert W. SERVICE and Jack LONDON. The most widely seen, and personal favorite, of Charlie CHAPLIN's films, *The Gold Rush* (1925), was filmed on site in Northern California.

Goldberg, Rube (1883–1970) Cartoonist. As a cartoonist for the New York *Evening Mail* in the 1910s, Reuben Lucius Goldberg developed the characters LaLa Palooza, Boob McNutt, and Lucifer Gorgonzola Butts. To Butts he attributed the invention of various machines meant to perform tasks that could be done more easily without them. After these devices appeared in his cartoons, "Rube Goldberg contraption" came to mean any elaborate but unnecessary solution.

Goldbergs, The Radio and television series. A radio staple in the 1930s and 1940s, *The Goldbergs* starred Gertrude Berg as Molly Goldberg, the matriarch of a Jewish family. One of the early "ethnic" shows on network television (see also AMOS 'N' ANDY, MAMA), it ran from 1949 to 1954, with Berg still in the central role.

Golden Arches See MCDONALD'S.

Golden Gate Bridge A 4,200-foot-long bridge spanning the entrance to San Francisco Bay. When it was completed in 1937, it was the longest suspension bridge in the world. It remains a principal tourist attraction of the Bay Area.

Golden Gloves Amateur boxing's highest award. The Golden Gloves Association (1927), sponsored by the *Chicago Tribune* and the *New York Daily News,* promotes tournaments whose winners represent the United States at the Olympic Games.

golden spike ceremony On May 10, 1869, the TRANSCONTINENTAL RAILROAD was declared officially completed as Central Pacific President Leland Stanford drove a silver-headed maul toward a final golden spike, joining the CP and Union Pacific rails at Promontory, Utah. His swing actually missed the spike, as did that of UP Vice President Thomas Durant, but telegraph operators got the news out sans the double glitch. The actual spike, removed after the ceremony and replaced with iron, is now at the president's namesake, Stanford University.

Goldman, Emma (1869–1940) Anarchist. Born in Lithuania, "Red Emma" emigrated to America as a teenager and, after a few years of factory work, fell in love with philosophical anarchism and Alexander Berkman. When Berkman was imprisoned (1892) for the attempted murder of industrialist Henry Clay Frick, Goldman became the movement's principal speaker, advocating the abolition of all forms of tyranny, including wage slavery, marriage, and private property. After impeding the World War I draft, she was jailed and then deported to the Soviet Union.

Goldwater, Barry (1909–) Arizona Republican Senator Barry Goldwater was a major conservative voice of the 1950s and 1960s. See "EXTREMISM IN THE DEFENSE OF LIBERTY."

Goldwyn, Samuel (1882–1974) Film producer. "Mr. Sam," born Samuel Goldfisch, was the Goldwyn in Metro-Goldwyn-Mayer (MGM), a company he left in 1924 to become the film colony's best-known independent producer. Movies that showed the celebrated "Goldwyn touch" included *Wuthering Heights* (1939), THE BEST YEARS OF OUR LIVES, and PORGY AND BESS. A Polish immigrant, Goldwyn was also famous for his unique English. Short of extras for a western, he is said to have mused, "We can get all the Indians we want at the reservoir." Other famous slips were "I can tell you in two words: im possible" and the classic kiss-off line "Include me out."

Gompers, Samuel (1850–1924) Labor leader. When the HAYMARKET RIOT broke the back of American socialism, cigar maker Gompers moved into the gap, making the American Federation of Labor, which he founded in 1886, the country's largest worker's organization. A champion of bread-and-butter issues, he eschewed alliances with more radical laborites, claiming that "the way out of wage slavery is higher wages."

Gone with the Wind (1936) The sole novel of Georgia writer Margaret Mitchell (1900–49). A sweeping historical romance set in the South during the Civil

War and Reconstruction, it won the Pulitzer Prize in 1937 and was for twenty years (until PEYTON PLACE) the most widely read of all American novels. The protagonist, headstrong and spoiled Scarlett O'Hara, loves her cousin Melanie's husband, Ashley Wilkes, a genteel cavalier who represents a society "gone with the wind." Scarlett is in turn loved by the charming rascal Rhett Butler, whose pragmatic daring prefigures the new, "reconstructed" South. The chief minor players include Scarlett's father, the irascible Gerald O'Hara; and the de facto mistress of his Georgia plantation, the redoubtable Mammy.

However successful the novel, the 1939 movie, produced by David Selznick and directed by Victor Fleming, brought Mitchell's story to a vastly larger audience. Fan letters practically forced Selznick to cast Clark GABLE as Rhett Butler, and the casting of unknown Vivian Leigh as Scarlett O'Hara followed a widely touted two-year search through fourteen hundred hopefuls. The filming included the luxuriant use of Technicolor, the employment of thousands of extras, and the torching of an entire studio back lot to simulate General SHERMAN's burning of Atlanta. The money involved, which was phenomenal, proved well spent. Fleming, Selznick, Leigh, and Hattie McDANIEL (as Mammy) all won Academy Awards. Gable lost the nod to Robert Donat (for *Goodbye, Mr. Chips*), while Thomas Mitchell (Gerald O'Hara) won for another film, John Ford's STAGECOACH. In addition, *GWTW* broke box-office records everywhere. It remains unarguably the most famous of American films.

See also "FRANKLY, MY DEAR, I DON'T GIVE A DAMN"; TARA.

goober peas (1) PEANUTS. From a central African word for peanut, *nguba*. Southern rustics used to be known as goobers or goober grabbers, and Georgia was the Goober State in the 1870s. (2) "Goober Peas," or "Eating Goober Peas," was a Confederate camp song in the Civil War:

> *Peas, peas, peas, peas, Eating goober peas;*
> *Goodness, how delicious, eating goober peas.*

Good fences make good neighbors   See "MENDING WALL."

Good Humor man   See ICE CREAM.

good neighbor policy   Franklin D. ROOSEVELT's term for his accommodating policy toward Latin America, as compared to his cousin's BIG STICK interventionism. FDR withdrew Marines from Haiti, raised the annual payment for the Panama Canal, and abolished the U.S. protectorate over Cuba.

"Good Night Irene"   A LEADBELLY song, written probably in the 1930s. A pop hit in 1950 for THE WEAVERS, it is a traditional closing song in folk-song gatherings.

"Good Night, Mrs. Calabash, wherever you are"   See Jimmy DURANTE.

good old boy   A white male southerner who exhibits the region's stereotypical traits: charm, suspicion of Yankees, and racial prejudice. The term arose in the 1960s to refer to the Texas friends of President Lyndon JOHNSON.

"Good to the Last Drop"   An advertising slogan associated with Maxwell House coffee. The company claims the line was originally uttered by President

Theodore ROOSEVELT on a 1907 visit to its founder's home. If that is so, Roosevelt was quoting a slogan then being used by COCA-COLA.

Goodman, Benny (1909–86) Clarinetist, bandleader. Goodman led one of the most popular dance bands of the 1930s as well as a quartet featuring drummer Gene Krupa, vibraphonist Lionel Hampton, and pianist Teddy Wilson—the first black player to be featured in a white group. The Goodman band gave the first jazz concert ever in Carnegie Hall (1938) and brought him worldwide fame as the "King of Swing."

Goodnight, Charles (1836–1929) Cattleman. The grand old man of the Texas cattle country, Goodnight established ranches throughout the Southwest, including one that covered a million acres. The Goodnight-Loving Trail, from Texas to Wyoming, was named for him and his partner, Oliver Loving. He is credited with the invention of the CHUCK WAGON.

Goodyear, Charles (1800–60) Inventor. Goodyear discovered a process for vulcanizing rubber—treating it for added strength and elasticity—in 1839, but failed to patent it until 1844. By that time, more enterprising souls had stolen the idea, and Goodyear spent the remainder of his life in lawsuits and debt. The rubber-based Goodyear company honors his name.

Goodyear blimp A familiar sight overhead during large sporting events—such as the SUPER BOWL—the television-equipped Goodyear blimp is actually a fleet of four dirigibles, named *America, Columbia, Enterprise,* and *Europa.* They are reminders of the company's early dominance of the U.S. dirigible market. Its plans to provide transatlantic passenger service were dashed by the HINDENBURG disaster.

Goofy See DOGS.

Google, Barney See BARNEY GOOGLE.

GOP An abbreviation for "Grand Old Party," a nickname for the Republican party.

Gordon, Flash See FLASH GORDON.

gospel music "Gospel" refers to two separate strains of American religious song, one stemming from the hymns of white revivalist Ira D. SANKEY, the other a blend of Negro SPIRITUALS and BLUES brought to fruition by Georgia composer Thomas A. DORSEY. White hymn-singing had a profound influence on COUNTRY MUSIC, while Dorsey's work laid the foundation for a more strictly defined "gospel music" industry that promoted the work of artists as varied as sister Rosetta Tharpe, Mahalia JACKSON, and Aretha FRANKLIN.

Gotham (1) In Washington IRVING's *Salmagundi Papers* (1807), a nickname for New York City. (2) Gotham City, the fictional locale of the BATMAN adventures.

Gould, Jay (1836–92) Railroad owner, speculator. The most nefarious of the ROBBER BARONS, Gould conspired with James FISK, causing the BLACK FRIDAY panic of 1869. He acquired control of numerous railroads through stock manipulation, eventually owning about 10 percent of U.S. rail lines. A fellow speculator who had been ruined in a Gould scheme called him the "worst man on earth since the beginning of the Christian era."

Grable, Betty   (1916–73) Actress. The star of Fox Studio musicals in the 1940s, Grable was known especially for her legs, which were highlighted in the 1939 film *Million Dollar Legs,* insured by Lloyds of London, and largely responsible for her selection, during World War II, as the American soldier's favorite PINUP girl. Once Hollywood's highest-paid performer, she faded in the 1950s with the decline of the musical.

Graceland   (1) Elvis PRESLEY's mansion in Memphis, Tennessee. Since his death it has become a tourist shrine. (2) See SIMON AND GARFUNKEL.

Graham, Billy   (1918–   ) Evangelist. The grand master of "born again" Christianity, Baptist minister William F. Graham preached the first of his conversion "crusades" in 1949 to a Los Angeles audience of 350,000. A skillful user of both radio and television, he has been responsible for "commitments to Christ" around the world. A personal adviser to President Richard NIXON, he has written several books, including *How to Be Born Again* (1977).

graham cracker   A sweet cracker made of whole-wheat flour. It was named for health promoter Sylvester Graham (1794–1851), who saw meat, alcohol, sex, and white flour as a quadruple threat to the human body. "Grahamism" was a fad in the 1830s. A graham cracker topped with melted marshmallow and a Hershey bar is called a s'more—a campfire invention generally credited to the Girl Scouts.

Grammy Awards   Established in 1958, these are annual awards acknowledging excellence in music recording. The Grammies (from "gramophone") are given to performers and producers by the National Academy of Recording Arts and Sciences.

grand   A thousand dollars. Often abbreviated, especially in gangster movies, as "G."

Grand Army of the Republic   The GAR was an organization of Civil War veterans, established in 1866, that had considerable national impact toward the turn of the century. It helped to block Grover Cleveland's reelection in 1888 after he had vetoed a pension bill, and it lobbied successfully for the establishment of soldiers' homes. A GAR-sponsored "Decoration Day" (1868) was the forerunner of today's MEMORIAL DAY.

Grand Canyon   A spectacular river gorge in northern Arizona. It measures eighteen miles across, over two hundred miles long, and a mile from its rim to the Colorado River below. First sighted by whites on the Coronado expedition of 1540, it is a major tourist attraction, bringing 2 million viewers a year to Grand Canyon National Park.

Grand Central Station   A railroad terminal in midtown New York City. Designed by architect Whitney Warren (1864–1943), it features a vast hall completed in 1913. The daily crush of travelers has made "Grand Central Station" a metaphor for hectic activity.

Grand Coulee Dam   The largest concrete dam in the world. Eight-tenths of a mile long and 550 feet high, it spans the Columbia River in Washington State. It was completed in 1941 to provide irrigation control and hydroelectricity.

Grand Old Flag   See "YOU'RE A GRAND OLD FLAG."

Grand Old Party   See GOP.

Grand Ole Opry   A weekly radio program, originally called *WSM Barn Dance,* which has broadcast COUNTRY MUSIC from Nashville, Tennessee, since 1925. Its first star was Uncle Dave MACON, who brought it national acclaim in the 1930s. He was followed in the 1940s by Roy ACUFF, and since then by all major performers, for whom the Opry remains the home of country music. From 1941 until 1974, the show was broadcast from Ryman Auditorium; since then it has come from the larger Opryland, an entertainment and tourist complex outside of Nashville.

grand slam   In baseball, a home run with three runners already on base, that is, with the "bases loaded." Such a hit scores four runs and has thus become a metaphor for any outstanding accomplishment.

"Grandfather's Clock"   (1876) A popular sentimental song by Henry Clay WORK, playing on the sympathetic link between a clock and its aged owner. "The clock stopped, never to go again, when the old man died."

Grandma Moses   See Grandma MOSES.

Grange, Red   (1903–91) Football player. University of Illinois running back Harold Edward Grange earned the nickname the Galloping Ghost after scoring five touchdowns in a 1924 victory over Michigan. in his three years with Illinois (1923–25), he ran for 3,637 yards, making All-American every year he played. Leaving before graduating to join the Chicago Bears, he helped to popularize the emerging sport of professional football.

Grange, National   An organization founded in 1867 to further the collective interests of impoverished farmers. Members formed cooperatives, fought for lower railroad and grain elevator rates, and were influential in the establishment of rural free delivery (see RFD).

granola   A cold cereal composed chiefly of nuts and grains. The likely prototype was Granula, sold in the 1830s by followers of Sylvester Graham (see GRAHAM CRACKER), but the marketing possibilities were realized by John Harvey Kellogg, who made Granola required eating at his Battle Creek spa. The product took off in the 1970s health food craze. See BREAKFAST CEREAL.

Grant, Cary   (1904–86) Actor. British-born Archibald Leach was a Hollywood heartthrob for over thirty years in roles that displayed a slyly effortless charm. He starred with Mae WEST in the 1933 *She Done Him Wrong,* then sparkled in a series of SCREWBALL COMEDIES, including *Bringing Up Baby* (1938), HIS GIRL FRIDAY, THE PHILADELPHIA STORY, and ARSENIC AND OLD LACE. He was also a reliable lead for Alfred HITCHCOCK, who starred him in *Notorious* (1946), *To Catch a Thief* (1955), and *North by Northwest* (1959). Responding to comments that his acting range was limited, he once shrugged, "I play myself to perfection."

Grant, Ulysses S. (1822–85) Soldier, U.S. president. An 1843 graduate of West Point, Grant pursued a desultory, drink-shadowed army career until the Civil War provided him a destiny. Early victories convinced President Lincoln of his value, and he stuck by him in spite of later losses. On one occasion when he was asked to cashier the "drunkard," Lincoln replied, "I can't spare this man. He fights." On another, according to legend, he told a temperance committee, "Would you tell me what brand of whiskey Grant drinks? I would like to send a barrel of it to my other generals." Placed in command of the Union Army in March of 1864, Grant conducted the war so skillfully that the Confederacy was forced to surrender eleven months later.

Elected president in 1869, the "Hero of Appomattox" proved less efficient as a civic leader. His administration was riddled by financial scheming, and his enemies acidly spoke of "U.S. Graft." Among the lowlights of his White House tenure were the scandals of BLACK FRIDAY and the WHISKEY RING. He was interred in a stately tomb in New York City; his wife, Julia, was buried beside him in 1902. Hence the correct answer to Groucho Marx's throwaway question "Who is buried in Grant's Tomb?" (see YOU BET YOUR LIFE) is actually not just "Grant" but "Grant and his wife."

Grapes of Wrath, The (1939) A Pulitzer Prize novel by John STEINBECK about the hardships of migrant laborers in the 1930s. The hero, Tom Joad, becomes a labor organizer after realizing that "a feller ain't got a soul of his own, but only a piece of a big soul." As played by Henry FONDA in John FORD's 1940 movie, Joad becomes a mythic embodiment of the American "people," survivors who defeat all attempts of "the system" to crush them. Oscars went to Ford for best direction and to Jane Darwell for her portrayal of Ma Joad.

Grateful Dead Rock band. Pioneers of ACID rock in the 1960s, "the Dead" evolved gradually into a social phenomenon, attracting hordes of passionate "Deadheads" to their concerts and inspiring a cottage industry in bootleg tapes. Defiantly leaderless, the group has revolved for twenty years around a five-man core: guitarists Jerry Garcia and Bob Weir, bassist Phil Lesh, and drummers Bill Kreutzmann and Mickey Hart. Among their blues-, folk-, and country-flavored songs—many with words by lyricist Robert Hunter—are "Ripple," "Truckin," "Dark Star," and "Uncle John's Band."

Grauman's Chinese Theater A Hollywood movie theater, named for the original owner, Sid "Pop" Grauman. For decades newly minted film stars have placed their foot- (or hand-) prints in wet cement near the showplace's entrance as a public certification of their arrival.

Grease A musical about the romantic trials of 1950s teenagers. Immensely successful on Broadway (1972–80), it also became a major hit on film (1978). The "nice hoodlum" lead was played by John Travolta.

greasy spoon   A 1920s term for an inexpensive restaurant or diner, whether or not it deserves the "unsanitary" slur. Previous terms for such establishments had included "hash house," "lunch counter," and "snack bar."

Great American Desert   A nineteenth-century misnomer for the Great Plains, deriving from Zebulon Pike's description of them as treeless and arid; another explorer, Stephen Long, coined the term on an 1820 expedition. The image discouraged settlement for decades. Modern farming made the Plains bloom, although they have continued to be subject to periodic drought. See Dust Bowl.

great American novel   The "definitive" novel of the American experience, as *Don Quixote* is the definitive novel of imperial Spain. Many scholars see this novel as a will-o'-the-wisp—an imaginative ideal that has not yet been achieved. Others confer the title on Moby-Dick, Dos Passos's "U.S.A." trilogy, or Gone with the Wind.

Great Awakening   A religious revival of the early eighteenth century, enlivening the period's staid Christianity with frenzied evangelism. Leaders included Theodorus Frelinghuysen in New Jersey and Jonathan Edwards in Massachusetts. Aside from its spiritual effects, the Awakening also led to the founding of denominational colleges, notably New Jersey's Princeton (1746) and Rutgers (1766).

Great Books   A reading program established at the University of Chicago by Robert Maynard Hutchins and Mortimer Adler. Their edition of *Great Books of the Western World* (1945–52) became a canon of Western classics from Homer to Freud, superseding Charles Eliot's Harvard Classics.

"Great Caesar's ghost!"   See Superman.

Great Depression   The worldwide economic depression of the 1930s, which put millions out of work in the United States and elicited the massive recovery program known as the New Deal. The period had a major impact on the arts and letters; see, for example, Woody Guthrie; Clifford Odets; John Steinbeck.

Great Divide   The Continental Divide or, more roughly, the Rocky Mountains. To "cross the great divide" means to die.

Great Emancipator   Abraham Lincoln, because of the Emancipation Proclamation.

Great Gatsby, The   (1925) F. Scott Fitzgerald's third and most famous novel. The story of millionaire Jay Gatsby's hopeless affection for his married ex-lover Daisy Buchanan, it explores the interplay of dream and reality in Roaring Twenties high life. The book's popularity with curriculum committees has made it the best-selling of all American "literary" novels. It was filmed to modest success in 1974, with Robert Redford in the title role.

Great Gildersleeve, The   See Fibber McGee and Molly.

Great Lakes   Five glacial lakes separating the American Midwest from Canada's Ontario. Collectively the largest body of fresh water in the world, the five are (east to west) Ontario, Erie, Huron, Michigan, and Superior. First explored extensively by the French, they were an important artery of the FUR TRADE and westward expansion. They remain significant in U.S. and Canadian shipping.

Great Pacificator   Henry CLAY, for his conciliatory expertise in the U.S. Congress.

Great Plains   The vast central region of North America, a generally flat grasslands running from Texas to the Canadian provinces of Albert, Saskatchewan, and Manitoba; and from the Mississippi River Valley to the Rocky Mountains. The Plains supported a wide variety of Indian cultures, especially BUFFALO hunters, and were initially shunned by prospective farmers as the GREAT AMERICAN DESERT. The RAILROADS opened them to settlement in the late nineteenth century, and they support intensive grain and livestock production.

Great Profile   Nickname of John Barrymore. See BARRYMORE FAMILY.

Great Revival   A religious revival of the early nineteenth century, beginning in Kentucky around 1797. Sometimes called the Kentucky Revival or the Second Awakening (see GREAT AWAKENING), it was sparked by the fiery sermons of James McGready (1758–1815), who preached at its first CAMP MEETING in 1800.

Great Salt Lake   A large lake in northwestern Utah, one of the planet's most saline bodies of water. Discovered in 1824 by Jim BRIDGER, it is the site of MORMON-founded Salt Lake City.

"Great Scott!"   An expression of surprise. The reference is to General Winfield Scott, also known as OLD FUSS AND FEATHERS.

Great Seal of the United States   A two-sided national emblem adopted by the Continental Congress in 1782 and seven years later by the U.S. Congress. The front side shows a spread eagle holding an olive branch and a sheaf of arrows, its beak clutching a banner announcing E PLURIBUS UNUM. The reverse shows a pyramid surmounted by an eye, with the Latin expressions *Annuit coeptis* ("He [God] has approved our beginnings") and *Novus ordo seclorum* ("A new order of the ages"). Both designs appear on the dollar bill.

Great Society   President Lyndon B. JOHNSON's domestic agenda, comprising an extensive package of social reforms. Great Society programs focused especially on civil rights, poverty, and medical care.

"Great Speckled Bird"   A religious song associated with Roy ACUFF, whose career it helped to start in the 1930s. It dates from the Pentacostal revival at the turn of the century and describes the isolation—and eventual triumph—of the persecuted church. Jeremiah 12:9 reads "Mine heritage is unto me as a speckled bird, the birds round about are against her."

Great Spirit   The supposed "central god" of North American Indians. An Anglo invention of the nineteenth century, it figures prominently in depictions of Indian religion and is often conflated with the Algonquian Manitou.

Great Stone Face   See Buster KEATON.

Great Train Robbery, The   (1903) A twelve-minute film directed by Edwin Porter, it was the first major American film to tell a story, and it dramatically increased the appeal of the new medium. A "western" complete with a posse chase and gunfight, it was actually shot in New Jersey.

Great Triumvirate   The three most famous orators of the U.S. Senate in the 1840s: John C. CALHOUN, Henry CLAY, and Daniel WEBSTER. Also called the immortal trio.

Great White Father   An alleged Indian title for the U.S. president, popularized in pulp novels at the turn of the century.

Great White Fleet   A naval fleet that Theodore ROOSEVELT sent on a world tour in 1907 to demonstrate U.S. military might.

great white hope   (or simply **white hope**) In the 1910s, a tag for any promising white boxer. See Jack JOHNSON.

Great White Way   New York City's BROADWAY. From the many lights of the theater district.

Greatest, the   See Muhammad ALI.

Greatest Show on Earth   See P. T. BARNUM.

Greeley, Horace   (1811–72) Newspaperman. The most influential publisher of the nineteenth century, "Uncle Horace" founded (1841) and edited the *New York Tribune,* which became a forum for his expansionist and abolitionist views. It was in its pages that "GO WEST, YOUNG MAN" became well known. Greeley helped to found the Republican party and supported Lincoln in spite of what he considered his tepidness on the slavery issue. He ran for president in 1872 and died after being beaten by incumbent U. S. GRANT.

Green, Hetty   (1834–1916) Financier. The heiress of a New England shipping family, Henrietta Green, née Robinson, became the wealthiest woman in the world through savvy investing. Notoriously stingy, she carried GRAHAM CRACKERS into restaurants to reduce her bill and commuted to her New York office from a New Jersey apartment. The "Witch of Wall Street," as her rivals called her, was worth $100 million at her death.

Green Berets   An elite U.S. Army unit, named for its dress headgear, that became famous for jungle combat in the VIETNAM WAR. Their exploits inspired Robin Moore's best-selling novel *The Green Berets* (1965), John WAYNE's film *The Green Berets* (1968), and Sergeant Barry Sadler's hit record "The Ballad of the Green Berets" (1966).

Green Giant   Trademark of the Green Giant food company. Developed by the Minnesota Valley Canning Company in 1925, the original figure was a fur-clad creature holding a giant pea; his leafy cloak and green skin came in the 1930s.

Company promotion now places him in the Valley of the Jolly Green Giant with a protégé, Sprout.

"Green Grow the Lilacs" A traditional love song of the nineteenth century. According to an often repeated although erroneous story, Mexicans overhearing U.S. soldiers sing it during the MEXICAN WAR mispronounced the opening words "Green Go," thus creating the ethnic epithet GRINGO.

Green Hornet, The A radio adventure series of the 1930s and 1940s that capitalized on the SUPERMAN and BATMAN fads. Hero Britt Reid was a crusading newspaperman by day, the masked crime-fighter Green Hornet by night. In a brief television series (1966–67), Reid's right-hand man, Kato, was played by future karate star Bruce LEE.

Green Mountain Boys A group of Vermont irregulars commanded by Ethan ALLEN in the Revolutionary War. They captured FORT TICONDEROGA in 1775. They were also known, among their detractors, as the Bennington Mob.

Green Pastures, The (1930) A Pulitzer Prize play by Marc Connelly (1890–1981). It presents biblical stories in southern black dialect, as a preacher links them to the lives of his congregation. It was filmed in 1936.

greenbacks Paper currency first issued during the Civil War and continued, in response to debtor pressure, into the 1880s. The Greenback party elected several congressmen in the 1876 through 1880 elections, but within a few years its members' attention had turned to "FREE SILVER."

Greenough, Horatio (1805–52) Sculptor. The United States's first professional sculptor, he expressed the basic idea behind the aesthetic known as functionalism in his 1851 book *Form and Function*. His most famous statue, a seated George Washington (1833), caused a scandal by presenting its subject only partially clothed.

Greenwich Village (or the Village) A New York City neighborhood identified with the "creative" lifestyles of writers and artists. The home of New York University and Washington Square Park, it was a center of the BEAT GENERATION and the FOLK REVIVAL.

Gretzky, Wayne (1961–) Hockey player. First in goals and first in assists, Ontario-born Gretzky has scored more points than anyone else in the history of hockey. He dominated the ice in the 1980s, winning the National Hockey League most valuable player award in all but one year and the Lady Byng sportsmanship trophy twice (1980 and 1991). "The Great One" skated for the Edmonton Oilers and now plays for the Los Angeles Kings. At the close of the 1993/94 season, his career total was 2,458 points.

Grey, Zane (1875–1939) Writer. Beginning with *The Spirit of the Border* (1905), Grey produced dozens of western novels that were widely adapted for the large and small screens. His other books included *The Last of the Plainsmen* (1908) and *Riders of the Purple Sage* (1912).

Griffith, Andy   See MAYBERRY.

Griffith, D. W.   (1875–1948) Film director. Often called the greatest single figure in American film, if not all film, David Wark Griffith began as an actor in his native Kentucky, made hundreds of one- and two-reelers in the early 1900s, and in 1915 scored a triumph with THE BIRTH OF A NATION. Stung by justifiable charges that it was racist, he followed it with an even lengthier epic, *Intolerance* (1916), which broke him financially but made him a hero in international art circles: Sergei Eisenstein, among others, saw him as a master. In 1919, Griffith joined Mary PICKFORD, Douglas FAIRBANKS, and Charlie CHAPLIN to create the independent production company United Artists. His first UA film, *Broken Blossoms* (1919), starred Lillian GISH, the most famous of many stars whose careers he shaped. Fascinated by historical epic, he tackled the French Revolution in *Orphans of the Storm* (1922), the American Revolution in *America* (1924), and postwar Europe in *Isn't Life Wonderful* (1924).

gringo   A disparaging Mexican term for a North American. From Spanish *griego,* for "stranger" or "Greek" (as in "It's Greek to me").

grits   Ground hominy. Served as a side dish, like rice or potatoes, throughout the South, and as strongly identified with that region as okra or BOURBON.

grizzly bear   A large, aggressive bear of the western mountains. Its sour reputation was reflected in its early names: *Ursus horribilis* and *Ursus ferox,* for "terrifying" and "fierce." Teddy ROOSEVELT suggested the spelling be "grisly."

Groundhog Day   February 2. According to folklore, the groundhog serves as a weather vane on this day. If it sees its shadow upon emerging from its den, it goes underground for another six weeks of winter; the absence of a shadow betokens an early spring. The superstition reflects European prototypes in which badgers, bears, and hedgehogs are the forecasters.

Grover's Corners   The setting of Thornton Wilder's play OUR TOWN.

Grover's Mills   See THE WAR OF THE WORLDS.

Guadalupe Hidalgo   See MEXICAN WAR.

Guinan, Texas   (1884–1933) Speakeasy hostess. The "Queen of Whoopee," Mary Louise Cecilia Guinan became "Texas" during a brief bronco-riding career, entertained American troops during World War I, and under Prohibition became New York's most famous saloon manager. Her customers included politicians and society types as well as gangsters, and her stage shows introduced Ruby KEELER and Rudolph VALENTINO. Guinan's waggish charm survives in the maxim "A guy who would cheat on his wife would cheat at cards"; her standard greeting to customers, "Hello, sucker"; and the alleged puff for one of her shows that had captivated Paris: "Fifty million Frenchmen can't be wrong."

Guiteau, Charles   (1941–82) The assassin of President James A. GARFIELD. A member of a rival faction in Garfield's divided Republican party, Guiteau had failed to find preferment there. He shot the president in a Washington, D.C., railroad station and was hanged a year later for the crime.

Gulf of Tonkin Resolution   See VIETNAM WAR.

Gulf War   (1991) The briefest war in American history, also known by its code name, Desert Storm. After the dictatorial president of Iraq, Saddam Hussein, invaded his neighbor Kuwait in 1990, the U.S. president, George Bush, issued an official warning that such aggression would not go unchallenged. When Saddam refused to leave, Bush sent half a million U.S. troops to the Persian Gulf region, backed by more modest numbers from an international coalition. This U.N. alliance forced the Iraqis back to Baghdad in a technologically sophisticated blitzkrieg that lasted two months and that was aired, virtually hour by hour, on U.S. television.

With his approval rating high and the country awash in yellow ribbons—a symbolic expression of support for the troops—Bush proclaimed the victory the birth of a "new world order." Cynical observers saw the cause of the war as the Western nations' reliance on Mideast oil, the availability of which Saddam had threatened to curtail. Indeed, in a bizarre scorched-earth fillip, he had ignited Kuwaiti wells before his retreat from the country, and they continued to burn uncontrollably long after the cease-fire. Nevertheless, Desert Storm made a nine days' hero of the president and of his field commander, "Stormin' Norman" Schwarzkopf.

Gullah   The African-American population of the sea islands (and some coastal areas) of North Carolina, Georgia, and northern Florida. The Gullahs' isolation has fostered a unique culture and a dialect that is more deeply African than standard black English. Gullah folklore is rich in proverbial sayings. Examples; "Cut finger 'faid ax" and "Ef you ent hab hoss to ride, ride cow."

gumbo   A seafood (sometimes meat) soup, often spicy and always including okra. From the Bantu *ngombo*, meaning okra. Derived from African stews, it is traditional in both CREOLE and CAJUN cooking.

Gun that Won the West   A nickname variously applied to the Colt .44 revolver and the Winchester .73 repeating rifle. See Samuel COLT; WINCHESTER RIFLE.

gung ho   Enthusiastic, eager to get a job done. World War II Marine slang, probably from a Chinese term meaning "fiery."

Gunsmoke   The most popular TV western of all time. It starred James Arness as Matt Dillon, marshal of DODGE CITY, with Amanda Blake as Long Branch Saloon owner Kitty Russell and Milburn Stone as grizzly Doc Adams. The first "adult" western, it was introduced in a 1955 pilot by John WAYNE (who had been offered the lead but declined). TV's top program for four years (1957–61), the show precipitated dozens of other "socially conscious" westerns, and outlasted them all, until 1975.

Guthrie, Arlo   (1947–) Folksinger. The son of Woody GUTHRIE, Arlo achieved prominence in his own right with his antiwar talking balled "Alice's Restaurant." The highlight of his first album (1967), it was made into a popular film (1969) in which he starred. His other major hit, "The City of New Orleans" (1972), was a train song written by Steven Goodman.

Guthrie, Woody   (1912–67) One of American history's most prolific songwriters, Woodrow Wilson Guthrie produced an estimated one thousand songs while becoming the quintessential folk poet of the twentieth century. Born in Oklahoma, he left home when his father's business failed and spent the Depression years wandering around the country, recording the hardships of working-class life and flirting with communism: A sticker on his guitar proclaimed, "This Machine Kills Fascists." In New York toward the end of the 1930s he met Pete SEEGER, with whom he subsequently toured, and Alan Lomax (see John and Alan LOMAX), who recorded his songs for the Library of Congress in a twelve-record set entitled *Dust Bowl Ballads*.

The "Dust Bowl" songs fused indignation at the plight of working people with an abiding love of the physical landscape that gave them birth. The collection included several "instant classics": "UNION MAID," "Pastures of Plenty," "GOING DOWN THE ROAD FEELING BAD," "So Long, It's Been Good to Know You," and Guthrie's most enduring legacy, "THIS LAND IS YOUR LAND." He also wrote three albums of children's songs and an autobiography, *Bound for Glory* (1943). When he died of Huntington's chorea at the age of fifty-five, he had become the éminence grise behind the FOLK REVIVAL.

Guys and Dolls   A 1932 story collection by Damon RUNYON that inspired a hit musical (1950) and a film (1955). The male leads, New York City gamblers, were played in the film by Marlon BRANDO and Frank SINATRA.

Gypsy Rose Lee   See Gypsy Rose LEE.

Haggard, Merle (1937–) Singer, songwriter, A country singer of the 1960s, Haggard caused a national stir in 1969 with his song "Okie from Muskogee," which defended traditional patriotism against HIPPIE attacks during the VIETNAM WAR. An ex-convict, Haggard wrote poignant prison songs such as "I'm a Lonesome Fugitive" and "Branded Man" as well as exploring the common country music themes of poverty ("Hungry Eyes"), drinking ("I Threw Away the Rose"), trucking ("Movin' On"), and romance ("Today I Started Loving You Again)."

Haight-Ashbury A residential section of San Francisco that became a HIPPIE haven in the 1960s. Home to the GRATEFUL DEAD and JEFFERSON AIRPLANE, it was also called simply the Haight and—because of its drug subculture—Hashbury.

"Hail Columbia" A patriotic song by Joseph Hopkinson to music by Philip Phile. It was written in 1798 on a wave of anti-French feeling following the XYZ AFFAIR, and for half a century it was the nation's unofficial anthem. The object of the song, Hopkinson later said, was to "get up an American spirit which should be independent of . . . passion and policy."

Hail Mary pass In football, a long, last-second touchdown pass that wins the game. Hence any desperate measure that brings success. From the idea that such a pass is the equivalent of (or should be accompanied by) the recitation of the Catholic prayer Hail Mary.

"Hail to the Chief" (1812) A march with words by Sir Walter Scott to music probably by James Sanderson. Since at least James Polk's inauguration (1845), it has been played to announce the arrival of the U.S. president.

Hair A musical about the COUNTERCULTURE written by Galt MacDermot, Gerome Ragni, and James Rado. The title referred to the long hair favored by young rebels. Successful on Broadway for four years (1968–72), it fostered a road show and a movie.

Hair Buyer A Revolutionary War nickname for the British governor of Detroit, Henry Hamilton, who gave his Indian allies bounties for American scalps.

Hale, Edward Everett See "THE MAN WITHOUT A COUNTRY."

Hale, Nathan (1755–76) Revolutionary War hero. A schoolteacher turned soldier, Hale volunteered to go behind British enemy lines in 1776 to scout out their defenses for General Washington. Captured, he was tried as a spy and hanged.

According to legend (and a British officer who witnessed the execution), his last words were "I only regret that I have but one life to lose for my country." Hale was quoting, in a rough adaptation, a line from Joseph Addison's drama *Cato*.

Hale, Sarah Josepha (1788–1879) As editor of GODEY'S LADY'S BOOK, Hale published works by Longfellow, Hawthorne, and Poe. She also used the magazine to mount a long campaign for a national Thanksgiving holiday; it bore fruit in 1863. Under her editorship, the magazine combined women's rights politics, sentimental literature, and fashion advice in a format that made it the first successful women's magazine in America. Hale also wrote novels, numerous magazine pieces, and the children's poem "Mary Had a Little Lamb."

Haley, Alex See ROOTS.

Haley, Bill (1925–81) Singer. Haley's 1954 cover of Sunny Dae's "Rock Around the Clock" is often considered to have started ROCK MUSIC. It was the number-one record of 1955 and the theme song of that year's *Blackboard Jungle,* a movie about contemporary teen rebellion. With a cover of Joe Turner's "Shake, Rattle, and Roll" (1955), Haley and his band, the Comets, became the most sought-after rock 'n' roll act in the world. Their other hits included "Crazy, Man, Crazy" (1953) and "Skinny Minnie" (1958).

Half Moon See Henry HUDSON.

Hall-Mills case A sensational murder case of the 1920s. On September 16, 1922, the bodies of Episcopal minister Edward Hall and a choir singer in his church, Eleanor Mills, were found together in a lovers' lane near New Brunswick, New Jersey. Letters showed that the two had been lovers, and suspicion fell on the preacher's widow, Frances Hall, but it took four years for state prosecutors to get an indictment. The trial of Mrs. Hall and her two brothers, alleged accomplices, took place in the fall of 1926, with the reporters' gallery including Damon RUNYON and Dorothy DIX. The prosecution's star witness was a bedridden hog farmer, Jane Gibson, whom the press gleefully dubbed the Pig Woman, but whose supposedly eyewitness account of the crime the jury rejected. Hall and her siblings were acquitted, and the case remains unsolved to this day.

"Hallelujah, I'm a Bum" A song about HOBO life written by Mac McClintock as a parody on the camp meeting hymn "Revive Us Again." Composed around 1928, it became, according to protest song scholar John Greenway, the "unofficial anthem" of the INDUSTRIAL WORKERS OF THE WORLD.

Halley's Comet The comet, which is named for English astronomer Edmund Halley (1656–1742), appeared to the JAMESTOWN colonists in 1607, supposedly presaging an extremely cold winter. In American literature, it is the sign of Mark TWAIN's birth in 1835 and his death, at the comet's next pass, in 1910.

"Halls of Montezuma" See "THE MARINE HYMN."

hamburgers The quintessential American light meal, named for the city of Hamburg in Germany, where residents pounded their beef soft in the nineteenth century. Around the turn of the century such "hamburg" meat was further pulverized in a meat grinder, and by 1912, "hamburger" patties were served on buns. The current ubiquity of hamburgers derives from the success in the 1920s of the White Castle chain, then in the 1950s of McDONALD'S.

Hamilton, Alexander (1755–1804). The most "fiscally responsible" of the FOUNDING FATHERS, Hamilton represented New York at the Constitutional Convention, contributed to THE FEDERALIST, and served as the nation's first secretary of the treasury. In the latter capacity he established credit for the new nation and fought for a strong, probusiness central government. In 1801, when Thomas JEFFERSON and Aaron BURR were tied in electoral college voting for the presidency, Hamilton helped to elect Jefferson, thus securing the enmity of his fellow New Yorker, who killed him in a duel three years later. See also ZENGER TRIAL.

Hammer, Mike   See Mickey SPILLANE.

Hammerstein, Oscar, II   (1895–1960) The Broadway musical's most distinguished lyricist, Hammerstein scored an early hit with the words for *Show Boat* (see SHOWBOAT [2]), then formed a partnership with Richard RODGERS in the 1940s that produced several classics of the American theater: *Carousel* (1945), OKLAHOMA!, SOUTH PACIFIC, *The King and I* (1951), and THE SOUND OF MUSIC.

Hammett, Dashiell   (1894–1961) Writer. A founder of the HARD-BOILED FICTION school, Hammett was a former PINKERTON agent who introduced his first successful detective, the Continental Op, in BLACK MASK. His second winner, Sam Spade, was the no-nonsense hero of THE MALTESE FALCON. His third, the team of Nick and Nora CHARLES, reparteed their way through THE THIN MAN. Hammett was the longtime lover of Lillian HELLMAN. He served six months in jail in 1951 for refusing to cooperate during a federal government court trial of fellow leftists.

Hancock, John   (1737–93) The first signer of the Declaration of Independence—an honor accorded him as president of the Continental Congress. He made his mark with a huge flourish so that, according to legend, George III would be able to read it "without his spectacles." Hence the term "John Hancock" for a signature. Hancock, reputedly the richest man in Boston, served two terms in the 1780s as Massachusetts's governor.

Handy, W. C.   (1873–1958) "Father of the Blues." The cornetist and composer William Christopher Handy played with MINSTREL SHOWS as a teenager, then devoted himself to collecting and popularizing traditional blues. His first successful original blues, "Mr. Crump," was written as a 1909 campaign song for a Memphis politician; retitled "Memphis Blues," it made Handy's name. He is most closely identified today with "ST. LOUIS BLUES."

hang ten   See SURFING.

Hanna, Mark   (1837–1904) Politician. Republican kingmaker Marcus Alonzo Hanna stage-managed the election of William McKINLEY in 1896. Strongly probusiness, he resisted McKinley's choice of Teddy ROOSEVELT as a running mate in 1900, and at the president's assassination moaned, "Now look, that damned cowboy is President of the United States." He served for seven years as a senator from Ohio.

Hanna and Barbera   Cartoonists. William Hanna (1910–) and Joseph Barbera (1911–) worked for MGM in the 1940s and 1950s, then established their own television production company in 1957. For MGM they did TOM AND JERRY, for television THE FLINTSTONES, *Huckleberry Hound* (see DOGS), and YOGI BEAR.

Hans Brinker, or The Silver Skates   (1865) A juvenile novel by Mary Mapes DODGE. Set in Holland, it contains the famous tale of a little boy who saves his country by plugging a leak in a dike with his finger. The book made the story so well known that the Dutch erected a statue in the fictional child's honor.

happenings   Improvisational, multimedia art events staged in avant-garde circles in the 1960s. Similar to performance art in their preference for theatrical collage, they were often staged in New York artists' studios.

"Happy Birthday"   (1893) A song by sisters Patty and Mildred Hill, traditionally sung to a child at the presentation of a birthday cake. The original title was "Good Morning to You." A common children's parody runs:

Happy birthday to you, you belong in a zoo.
You look like a monkey and you act like one too.

Happy Days   Television comedy series (1974–84). A nostalgic look at the 1950s, the show revolved around the friendship of a "nice" teenager, Richie Cunningham (Ron Howard), and his good-hearted but wild mentor, THE FONZ. In 1976–77 it was the medium's top show. Its sound track featured Bill HALEY's "Rock Around the Clock."

"Happy Days Are Here Again"   Democratic campaign song in the 1932 election, composed in 1929 by Milton Ager and Jack Yellen. With FDR in the White House, it was a NEW DEAL theme song.

happy hunting ground   The supposed reward after death of the American Indian. It was an invention of Washington IRVING in his history *Astoria* (1836): "They will see the happy hunting grounds, with the souls of the brave and the good living in tents in green meadows."

Harburg, E. Y. "Yip"   (1898–1981) Lyricist. Harburg's most enduring work was for THE WIZARD OF OZ: He did the lyrics to "The Witch Is Dead," "We're Off to See the Wizard," and "Over the Rainbow." He also wrote "BROTHER, CAN YOU SPARE A DIME?"

hard-boiled fiction   Detective fiction of the 1920s and 1930s characterized by brutal realism and terse writing. First introduced in the pulp magazine BLACK MASK, it was brought to grim perfection by Dashiell HAMMETT and Raymond CHANDLER. By the 1940s, the genre had evolved—some say degenerated—into the laconic sadism of Mickey SPILLANE.

hard-shell Baptists   Uncompromising, conservative Baptists. See also FUNDAMENTALISM.

Hardy, Andy   See Mickey ROONEY.

Hardy, Oliver   See LAUREL AND HARDY.

Hardy Boys   The heroes of a series of boys' adventure books beginning with *The Tower Treasure* (1927). Frank and Joe Hardy are the adolescent sons of detective Fenton Hardy. With the help of their friend Chet Morton, they solve crimes with ingenuity and grit. The nominal author of the series was Franklin W. Dixon; it remained popular with juvenile readers into the 1950s. See Edward STRATEMEYER.

Harlem   The largest African-American section of New York City. Originally a Dutch enclave called Nieuw Haarlem, it was by turns a farm community, a summer resort area, and an urban ghetto. See also APOLLO THEATER; HARLEM RENAISSANCE.

Harlem Globetrotters   Basketball team. Founded in Chicago (1926) as a barnstorming team, the Globetrotters use trick passes and other razzle-dazzle techniques in staged shows and exhibition games for international audiences. Their presentations, although played for laughs, rely on world-class ball-handling; among their alumni is NBA superstar Wilt CHAMBERLAIN.

Harlem Renaissance   An efflorescence of literary effort that came out of the HARLEM community in the 1920s and 1930s. Among the figures involved were Countee Cullen (1903–46), Langston Hughes (1902–67), and Zora Neale HURSTON.

Harley   Short for Harley-Davidson, a motorcycle manufacturer. Harleys are the Cadillacs of the biker world; anything *but* a Harley (among the HELL'S ANGELS, for example) is virtually unthinkable.

Harlow, Jean   (1911–37) Actress. The platinum-blonde bombshell of the 1930s, Jean Harlow (born Harlean Carpenter) played brassy, sensuous women who could hold their own, verbally and mentally, with their male counterparts. Her most memorable films were *Platinum Blonde* (1931), *Red Dust* (1932), *Bombshell* (1933), *Dinner at Eight* (1934), *China Seas* (1935), and *Libeled Lady* (1936).

Harper's   Two important periodicals were published under this name in the nineteenth century. *Harper's* magazine, begun in 1850 and still in existence, has long concentrated on current affairs and quality fiction. *Harper's Weekly,* which ran from 1857 to 1916, rivaled Frank LESLIE's *Illustrated Newspaper* for pictorial news. Its most famous staff members were Winslow HOMER and Thomas NAST.

Harpers Ferry   See John BROWN.

Harrigan and Hart   Theatrical partners Edward "Ned' Harrigan (1844–1911) and Tony Hart (1855–91). In the 1870s and 1880s they delighted New York theatergoers with their "Mulligan's Guards" sketches—song-and-dance comedies about German, Irish, and other immigrant groups. Their vogue elicited George M. COHAN's song "Harrigan."

Harris, Joel Chandler   (1848–1908) Author of the UNCLE REMUS stories. The first of these appeared in the *Atlanta Constitution,* on whose staff Harris worked from 1876. He also wrote a novel, *Gabriel Tolliver* (1902), and a memoir of his Georgia boyhood, *On the Plantation* (1892).

Harrison, William Henry (1773–1841) Soldier, president. Elected president on the basis of his military career (see "TIPPECANOE AND TYLER TOO"), Harrison gave a lengthy address at his inauguration, caught pneumonia, and died exactly one month later.

Hart, Lorenz (1895–1943) Lyricist. Hart was best known for his collaboration with Richard RODGERS, which began while they were Columbia University undergraduates and peaked with the Broadway smash PAL JOEY. Hart's credits include the sentimental standards "Blue Moon," "This Can't Be Love," and "My Funny Valentine."

Hart, Moss   See KAUFMAN AND HART.

Hart, William S. (1872–1946) Actor. The silent screen's first major western star, Hart translated memories of his Dakota boyhood into gritty, realistic dramas of life on the plains—often writing and directing as well as playing the leads. The dour original of the genre's "good bad man," Hart was at his best in *Hell's Hinges* (1916), *The Toll Gate* (1920), *Wild Bill Hickok* (1923), and *Tumbleweeds* (1925).

Harte, Bret (1836–1902) Writer. New York–born Francis Brett Harte moved to California in 1854, where he wrote his first collection of western stories, *The Luck of Roaring Camp and Other Sketches* (1870). None of his nineteen other volumes equaled its success. Hart's most famous tale is "THE OUTCASTS OF POKER FLAT."

Harvard Classics   A fifty-volume set of famous authors (from Homer to John Stuart Mill) edited by retired Harvard President Charles William ELIOT. Until the Chicago GREAT BOOKS appeared, it was the nation's definitive collection of classic literature.

Harvard University   The English-speaking colonies' first university, established in 1636 with a single teacher and named after John Harvard, its financial angel. In the seventeenth century, it trained clergymen like the Cotton MATHER family, in the eighteenth several leaders of the American Revolution. It was the alma mater of five presidents: John ADAMS, John Quincy Adams, Theodore and Franklin D. ROOSEVELT, and John F. KENNEDY. The richest university in the country, it is also one of the IVY LEAGUE's "Big Three." See also Charles W. ELIOT.

Harvey (1944) A Pulitzer Prize comedy by Mary C. Chase (1907–81) about a genial alcoholic, Elwood P. Dowd, and his friend Harvey, an invisible rabbit. After a five-year run on Broadway, it was filmed (1950) with James STEWART playing Dowd.

hasty pudding   A cornmeal mush common in old New England. It inspired Connecticut poet Joel Barlow's mock epic "The Hasty Pudding" (1796); served as a metaphor for "thickness" in "YANKEE DOODLE"; and gave a name to the Hasty Pudding Club, HARVARD UNIVERSITY's undergraduate drama group.

Hatfield-McCoy feud   A long-running feud between two Appalachian Mountain clans: the Kentucky McCoys and the West Virginia Hatfields. It began in the 1860s as an afterthought to the Civil War (the McCoys had been Unionists, the Hatfields Confederates) and reached a peak of violence in the 1880s. Personal grudges and MOONSHINE fed the war, which claimed at least sixty-five and possibly as many as two hundred lives.

Hauptmann, Bruno   (1899–1936) A German-born carpenter, Hauptmann went to the electric chair in 1936 for the kidnapping and subsequent murder of the Charles LINDBERGH baby. He maintained his innocence to the end, and recent studies have cast doubt on the guilty verdict.

Have Gun, Will Travel   Television series. In the great age of the TV western, this show was the medium's third most popular series—bested only by GUNSMOKE and *Wagon Train* (See WAGON TRAIN). It starred Richard Boone as a dapper gunslinger, Paladin, whose business card read, "Have Gun, Will Travel." It ran from 1957 to 1963.

Hawkeye   See Natty BUMPPO.

Hawkins, Sadie   See SADIE HAWKINS DAY.

Hawks, Howard   (1896–1977) Film director. The consummate genre director, Hawks did solid, craftsmanlike work for forty years, with memorable results in the gangster movie (SCARFACE), SCREWBALL COMEDY (*Bringing Up Baby,* 1938; HIS GIRL FRIDAY), the action film (*Sergeant York,* 1941; TO HAVE AND HAVE NOT), the private-eye film (THE BIG SLEEP), westerns (*Red River,* 1948; *Rio Bravo,* 1959), and even the musical (GENTLEMEN PREFER BLONDES). Hawks's fondness for strongly silent, "can-do" males showed in his direction of Humphrey BOGART and John WAYNE.

hawks and doves   Shorthand for the holders of "prowar" and "antiwar" sentiments during the VIETNAM WAR. "Hawk" recalled the WAR HAWKS of 1812, while "dove" was a traditional symbol of peace.

Hawthorne, Nathaniel   (1804–64) Writer. Of the CONCORD crowd, the most pessimistic and captivated by the past. Hawthorne is best known for his second novel, THE SCARLET LETTER. His fascination with New England's PURITAN heritage also appears in THE HOUSE OF THE SEVEN GABLES and in his stories. A brief stay at BROOK FARM in the 1840s provided material for *The Blithedale Romance* (1852), while a stay in Italy led to the expatriate novel *The Marble Faun* (1860). Henry JAMES was one of many who called Hawthorne the "father of the American psychological novel." Herman Melville dedicated MOBY-DICK to him.

Hawthorne effect   In studies done at Western Electric's Hawthorne, Illinois, factory in 1927, researchers found that worker productivity went up when assembly line lighting was improved—and also when it was deliberately made worse. They concluded that the fact of being studied itself had a positive effect on worker morale. This so-called Hawthorne effect became a central premise of industrial psychology.

Hayes, Gabby   (1885–1969) Actor. The ultimate sidekick, George "Gabby" Hayes started in vaudeville, played villains in the silent era, then found his métier in the 1930s as a grizzled old-timer, providing the comic relief in Hopalong Cassidy and Roy Rogers westerns.

Hayes, Helen   (1900–93) Actress. The "First Lady of the American Theater," Hayes began acting as a child, making her first Broadway appearance at the age of nine. She excelled in both the traditional and the modern classics—Shakespeare to Shaw—and scored her greatest triumph in Laurence Housman's *Victoria Regina* (1936). Her film appearances were intermittent, although she won an Academy Award for her first effort, in *The Sin of Madelon Claudet* (1931), and another for a minor role in *Airport* (1970). In 1959, a New York theater was named for her in honor of her first fifty years on Broadway.

Haymarket Riot   At a labor rally held in Chicago's Haymarket Square on May 4, 1886, an unidentified person threw a bomb, killing seven policemen. Because the rally had been held under anarchist auspices, the city's anarchist leaders were promptly rounded up; convicted as accessories to murder, four were hanged. Thanks to guilt by association, the incident virtually dismantled the socialist movement as well, and labor's demands quickly became less political. See Samuel Gompers.

Hays, Jack Coffee   See Texas Rangers.

Hays Office   The common name for Motion Picture Producers and Distributors of America, Inc., an organization formed in 1922 to improve Hollywood's scandalous image by censoring its films. Its head, Will Hays (1879–1954), was a former chair of the Republican National Committee and U.S. postmaster general. He took his job seriously, drafting a Production Code that stayed in effect for three decades (1934–66). The Hays Code prohibited, among other things, the depiction of "illegal drug traffic," "pointed profanity," and "lustful embracing." Two years after it fell, the current RATING system admitted all of the above, if properly labeled.

Haywood, Big Bill   (1869–1928) Labor leader. William Dudley Haywood was a Utah miner who, in 1905, founded the Industrial Workers of the World (IWW). The following year, indicted for the murder of a former Idaho governor, he was acquitted after a defense by Clarence Darrow. In 1921, awaiting a retrial on a conviction for sedition, he jumped bail and went to the Soviet Union, where he died.

Hayworth, Rita   (1918–87) Actress. Hollywood's "Love Goddess" of the 1940s, Margarita Cansino began as a dancer, like her parents. Dancing in Mexican border towns in her teens, she was noticed by movie scouts. She smoldered appealingly as the mysterious *Gilda* (1946) and the deadly *Lady from Shanghai* (1948)—the latter film directed by her onetime husband Orson Welles. When servicemen tested an atomic bomb on Bikini Atoll in 1946, they pinned a *Life* magazine photograph of Hayworth on the casing.

"He kept us out of war"   Woodrow Wilson's 1916 reelection slogan, referring to his patience in the face of German provocation during his first term. Reelected in March 1917, he asked for a declaration of war the following month.

"He that will not work shall not eat" Captain John SMITH's radical domestic policy after he became council president of JAMESTOWN in 1609. It discouraged reckless gold-hunting and put the colonists' eyes where they belonged, on the fertile ground.

Headless Horseman See "THE LEGEND OF SLEEPY HOLLOW."

Hearst, William Randolph (1863–1951) Newspaper publisher. Given the *San Francisco Examiner* as a birthday present from his industrialist father, Hearst dramatically boosted its sales through YELLOW JOURNALISM, then bought the *New York Morning Journal* to widen his reach. Circulation rivalry between the *Journal* and Joseph PULITZER's *World* led directly to the establishment of COMIC strips and encouraged the American appetite for the SPANISH-AMERICAN WAR. At the height of his influence in the 1920s, Hearst directed an empire of twenty papers from his California estate, San Simeon, where he lived with his mistress, actress Marion Davies. His most famous, if not most accurate, biography was CITIZEN KANE. His granddaughter Patricia was the notorious "Tania" of the SYMBIONESE LIBERATION ARMY.

"Heartbreak Hotel" A 1956 record by Elvis PRESLEY. His first number-one hit on the popular charts, it transformed him from a country phenomenon into a national star.

Hecht, Ben (1893–1964) Writer. A playwright and novelist, Hecht was best known for the plays he wrote with Charles MacArthur (1895–1956): THE FRONT PAGE and *Twentieth Century* (1932). The duo also worked on various screenplays. Hecht won a best original story Oscar for the 1927 film *Underworld*.

Hee Haw Television variety show hosted by Roy Clark and Buck OWENS and featuring guest appearances by dozens of other country music stars. A genially addled blend of fast picking, rustic stereotypes, and cornball humor, it lasted for only two years (1969–71) on network TV, but secured a faithful following in syndication.

Hefner, Hugh See PLAYBOY.

Heinz ketchup See KETCHUP.

Heisman Trophy An annual award for the college football player judged the season's finest by a panel of writers and sportscasters. It was established in 1935 by the New York City Downtown Athletic Club and named in honor of club director John W. Heisman (1869–1936). Heisman had been a spectacular coach at Georgia Tech.

Hellman, Lillian (1907–84) Writer. As a playwright, Hellman scored successes with *The Children's Hour* (1934), *The Little Foxes* (1939), and *Watch on the Rhine* (1941). Her memoirs are included in *An Unfinished Woman* (1969), *Pentimento* (1973), and *Scoundrel Time* (1976), the final volume of which records her experiences during the Joseph McCARTHY era with her lifelong friend and fellow writer Dashiell HAMMETT.

Hello, Dolly! A musical (1964) based on Thornton WILDER's play *The Matchmaker* (1954), about a turn-of-the-century marriage broker, Dolly Levi. It ran for seven years on Broadway, with Carol Channing starting in the title role, and was filmed in 1969 with Barbra STREISAND. The title song was a hit for Louis ARMSTRONG.

Hell's Angels   Motorcycle gang. The most famous of several California-based biker clubs, "the Angels" have a history of intimidating "citizens" that has inspired numerous "outlaw" movies, including a Marlon BRANDO vehicle, *The Wild One* (1954), and Roger CORMAN's *The Wild Angels* (1966), starring Peter Fonda. Their jacket logo is a winged skull.

Hemingway, Ernest   (1899–1961) Writer. Among the most admired, and certainly the most frequently parodied, of American writers, Hemingway combined a keen sense of human interaction with a crisply crafted, spare style now called Hemingwayesque. He became a spokesman for the so-called LOST GENERATION with his novel THE SUN ALSO RISES and solidified his fame with A FAREWELL TO ARMS and *Death in the Afternoon* (1932), a study of a lifelong obsession, the Spanish bullfight. Other major novels were TO HAVE AND HAVE NOT, FOR WHOM THE BELL TOLLS, and THE OLD MAN AND THE SEA. He was also critically praised for his short stories.

"Papa's" life, which was as adventurous as his prose, gave him a reputation as a fearless romantic. He was wounded as an ambulance driver in World War I, joined the expatriate colony in Paris in the 1920s, hunted big game in Africa, covered the Spanish Civil War for a newspaper syndicate, and hunted German submarines from his yacht in the 1940s. Seven years after receiving the Nobel Prize for literature, he killed himself with a shotgun in his Idaho home.

Hendrix, Jimi   (1942–70) Rock musician. Widely praised as rock 'n' roll's most accomplished guitarist, Hendrix also specialized in extravagant stage business, such as playing a guitar with his teeth or behind his back. After achieving fame in England, he became an American superstar at the Monterey Pop Festival (1967). The three albums recorded by his trio, the Jimi Hendrix Experience, included the original songs "Foxy Lady," "Are you Experienced?," and "Purple Haze" as well as covers of the old blues "Hey Joe" and the Bob DYLAN song "All Along the Watchtower." The highlight of Hendrix's WOODSTOCK performance was an avant-garde, virtuoso performance of "THE STAR-SPANGLED BANNER." His death in London was attributed to an accidental drug overdose.

Henry, John   (d. 1873?) Folk hero. A black laborer of phenomenal strength and endurance, John Henry was a "steel driving man" for the C&O Railroad, which in 1873 was cutting the Big Bend Tunnel in West Virginia. The job depended on the recently invented steam drill, which inevitably threatened the livelihood of manual laborers; the Henry story encapsulates the resulting tension. Challenged to pit himself against the machine, he replies with what John and Alan LOMAX call "the noblest lines in American folklore":

> *John Henry said to the captain,*
> *A man ain't nothing but a man.*
> *But before I let that steam drill beat me down*
> *I'll die with my hammer in my hand, Lord Lord,*
> *I'll die with my hammer in my hand.*

These lines are from the anonymous ballad "John Henry," which celebrates the big man's Pyrrhic victory. He beats the drill but in the process bursts a blood vessel, so that he

> ... laid down his hammer and he died, Lord Lord,
> Laid down his hammer and he died.

The ballad, found in numerous variants since the 1870s, transformed the hapless worker into a legend, and he soon acquired the trappings of TALL-TALE characters, such as the ability to lift a railroad car singlehandedly. The LOMAXES call it the best-loved of southern ballads, celebrating "the common man beating a raw country into shape." Its subject became the ultimate working class hero, the model for such later fabrications as Paul BUNYAN, PECOS BILL, and OLD STORMALONG.

Henry, O.   See O. HENRY.

Henry, Patrick   (1736–99) Orator, statesman. One of the golden voices of the American Revolution, the Virginian Henry is remembered for two speeches. In the first, given to the House of Burgesses in 1765, he attacked the STAMP ACT in words that many took as treasonous: "Caesar had his Brutus, Charles I his Cromwell, and George III may profit from their example. If this be treason, make the most of it!" The second ended with the famous challenge "GIVE ME LIBERTY OR GIVE ME DEATH."

Henson, Jim   See MUPPETS.

Hepburn, Katharine   (1909–   ) Actress. Probably the most respected film actress of her generation, Hepburn was equally at home in soul-searching and comedic roles. Her dramatic skills won her three Academy Awards, for *Morning Glory* (1933), *Guess Who's Coming to Dinner* (1968), and *The Lion in Winter* (1969). Her comic edge was best shown in the roles she played opposite Cary GRANT— *Bringing Up Baby* (1938) and THE PHILADELPHIA STORY—and opposite her lover of almost thirty years, Spencer TRACY. Their best comedies together were *Woman of the Year* (1942), *Adam's Rib* (1949), and *Pat and Mike* (1952). Hepburn also turned in memorable performances in THE AFRICAN QUEEN and *Long Day's Journey into Night* (1962).

Ironically, the "First Lady of the American Screen" also elicited a trio of famous insults. After finishing her first film, *A Bill of Divorcement* (1932), she told her costar, the notoriously lecherous John Barrymore (see BARRYMORE FAMILY), that she would never act with him again. "Really, my dear?" he said. "I didn't know you ever had." A year later, reviewing her performance in a Broadway play, Dorothy PARKER wrote that Hepburn had run "the gamut of emotions from A to B." And as late as 1938, she was labeled "box-office poison."

Herbert, Victor   (1859–1924) Composer. Born in Ireland, Herbert came to America as a cellist, conducted the Pittsburgh Symphony for five years, and earned acclaim for his romantic tunes and operettas. His most famous operettas were *Babes in Toyland* (1903) and *Naughty Marietta* (1910), his best-known song, "Ah, Sweet Mystery of Life (At Last I've Found You)."

Herblock   The pen name of Herbert Lawrence Block (1909–   ), a syndicated editorial cartoonist with the *Washington Post*. The winner of two Pulitzer Prizes, he is known for his wittily jaundiced liberalism.

"Here's Johnny"   See Johnny CARSON.

"Here's looking at you, kid"   See CASABLANCA.

Hermitage   Andrew JACKSON's plantation home near Nashville, Tennessee.

Hershey bar   A chocolate candy bar developed in the 1890s by Milton S. Hershey (1857–1945). The "Great American Chocolate Bar" became the foundation of his fortune and his company, which is still based in Hershey, Pennsylvania.

Hessians   German mercenaries used by Great Britain during the American Revolution. From their place of origin, the principality of Hesse-Kassel.

Heston, Charlton   (1923–   ) Actor. Tall, handsome leading man who became, in the words of Ephraim Katz, "Hollywood's resident epic hero." He won an Academy Award for the title role in BEN-HUR (1959) and played Moses in *The Ten Commandments* (1956), John the Baptist in *The Greatest Story Ever Told* (1965), and Michelangelo in *The Agony and the Ecstasy* (1965).

hex signs   Circular, symbolic designs on PENNSYLVANIA DUTCH barns. Although some discount the figures as merely decorative, they are commonly viewed as talismans against evil. "Hex" is from the German *Hexe,* for "witch."

"Hi-Yo, Silver"   See THE LONE RANGER.

Hiawatha   (1) The founder of the IROQUOIS LEAGUE. (2) The hero of "The Song of Hiawatha" (1855), a romantic poem by Henry Wadsworth LONGFELLOW about an Ojibwa hero living near Lake Superior. Aside from the name, the two figures bear no relation to each other.

Hickok, Wild Bill   (1837–76) Gunfighter, lawman. Born James Butler Hickok in Illinois, he spied for the union during the Civil War, scouted for George Armstrong CUSTER in the late 1860s, and in 1871 became marshal of hell-raising ABILENE, Kansas. A long-haired, flamboyant gambler, a crack shot with a pistol, and the reputed lover of CALAMITY JANE, he was said to have killed twenty-seven men before dying at the hand of Jack McCall, a publicity seeker who shot him from behind while he was playing poker. Gary Cooper played Hickok in the 1937 movie *The Plainsman*; Guy Madison portrayed him in the 1950s TV series *Wild Bill Hickok.*

Hicks, Edward   See THE PEACEABLE KINGDOM.

High Noon   (1952) A Hollywood western directed by Fred ZINNEMANN. It starred Gary COOPER as an embattled sheriff, Will Kane, who is deserted by the frightened townspeople he is hired to protect. In a "high noon" gunfight on the town's main street, Kane's life is saved by his Quaker wife (Grace Kelly), who shoots his attacker from behind. Cooper won the best actor Oscar.

Hill, Joe   (ca. 1879–1915) Labor organizer. As a member of the INDUSTRIAL WORKERS OF THE WORLD, Swedish-born Joseph Hillstrom organized California dockers and wrote workers' songs such as "The Rebel Girl" and "The Preacher and the Slave" (see PIE IN THE SKY). Convicted of murder in 1914, he became the focus of an international rescue movement convinced that he had been railroaded for his radicalism. When he was executed by a Utah firing squad, he became, in the words of John Greenway, "the first saint in the martyrology of labor." Before he died, he telegraphed IWW leader Big Bill HAYWOOD, "Don't waste any time mourning. Organize!" The message is often called his last words. In fact, they were "Let her go! Fire!"

Hill, the   See CAPITOL.

hillbilly   A backwoods mountaineer. Applied since about 1900 to residents of both the Appalachians and the Ozarks. In caricature he appears (in the words of a 1941 Arkansas state guide) as "a seven-foot combination of malnutrition and hookworm, asleep on his front porch with the dogs." The term "hillbilly music" came from the 1920s, when at least two southern mountain groups called themselves the Hill Billies. See also THE BEVERLY HILLBILLIES; L'IL ABNER.

Hindenburg   A German dirigible built in 1936 for luxury transatlantic passenger service. In its first year it carried over thirteen hundred people between Frankfurt am Main and Lakehurst, New Jersey. While landing at Lakehurst on May 6, 1937, it caught fire, killing thirty-six people. The tragedy closed the brief age of airship travel.

hippies   Young people who rejected ESTABLISHMENT values in the 1960s to adopt a less goal-oriented, more pleasure-loving lifestyle. They affected Indian dress (both the North American and the Eastern variety); experimented with ACID, marijuana, and "liberated" sex; and opposed their parents' "uptight" work ethic with a philosophy of love. They were the most colorful, if self-indulgent, part of the COUNTERCULTURE.

His Girl Friday   (1940) A SCREWBALL COMEDY directed by Howard HAWKS. A stylish remake of THE FRONT PAGE, it delighted audiences with its fast-paced dialogue. Cary GRANT played newspaper editor Walter Burns, Rosalind RUSSELL his star reporter, Hildy Johnson.

His Master's Voice   A painting done in 1894 by Francis Barraud. It depicts Barraud's dog, a mutt named Nipper, peering curiously into the horn of an old-style record player. The image, and the legend, were adopted in 1901 as the trademark of the Victor Talking Machine Company (makers of the Victrola). When RCA bought out Victor in 1929, the ad slogan was part of the deal.

Hiss, Alger   (1904–   ) A U.S. State Department employee who, in 1948, was accused of spying for the Soviet Union. His conviction for perjury got him five years in prison, while the sensational investigation furthered the career of Richard NIXON.

Hit Parade   A weekly entertainment show that presented live performances of top-selling songs. It started on radio in 1935, moved to television as *Your Hit*

Parade in 1950, and folded in 1959. Sponsored by Lucky Strike cigarettes, it featured a house band and a quartet of resident singers whose gifts proved incapable of adjusting to rock 'n' roll.

Hitchcock, Alfred   (1899–1980) Film director. By exploring the psychological, rather than merely sensational, aspects of the thriller, Hitchcock earned the title Master of Suspense. By the time he came to the United States in 1939, he had already established himself in his native England with classics such as *The Thirty-nine Steps* (1935). Highlights of his Hollywood period—all critical as well as financial successes—included *Rebecca* (1940; best picture), *Suspicion* (1941), *Notorious* (1946), *Strangers on a Train* (1951), *Rear Window* (1954), *Vertigo* (1958), *North by Northwest* (1959), PSYCHO, and THE BIRDS. Hitchcock also hosted two mystery series for television (1955–65). The possessor of a puckish humor and untrammeled ego, he made brief appearances in all of his films, and was known for treating actors like speaking props. When one of them bristled at his reputed comment that actors were "cattle," he drily explained, "I didn't say they were cattle. I said they should be *treated* like cattle."

Ho Chi Minh   (1890–1969) The first president of independent Vietnam and the president of North Vietnam from 1954 to 1969, Ho Chi Minh led his people first against the French and then, in the 1960s, against U.S.-backed South Vietnam. The major North-South supply route during the Vietnam War was known as the Ho Chi Minh Trail. When Saigon fell, it was renamed Ho Chi Minh City.

Hoban, James   See WHITE HOUSE.

hobo   An 1890s term for an itinerant laborer, or at least someone actively looking for work, as opposed to the less ambitious "tramp" or "bum." Stuart Berg Flexner suggests as possible sources of the term the greeting "Ho, Beau," the expression "homeward bound," and the view of hoboes as farm runaways, or wayward "hoe boys."

Hoffa, James   (1913–75?) Labor leader. Hoffa led the powerful Teamsters Union from 1957 to 1967, when he was convicted of having mismanaged union funds. Four years after being released from prison in 1971, he vanished, the supposed victim of a gangland execution. He thus became the most famous missing American since Judge CRATER.

Hoffman, Abbie   See YIPPIES.

Hoffman, Dustin   (1937–   ) Actor. The versatile Hoffman was an OBIE AWARD winning stage player when, in 1967, he achieved stardom as a confused college student in Mike Nichols's comedy *The Graduate*. He was a street bum in *Midnight Cowboy* (1969), a "white Indian" in *Little Big Man* (1970), Lenny BRUCE in *Lenny* (1974), reporter Carl Bernstein in *All the President's Men* (1976), a distraught father in *Kramer vs. Kramer* (1979), a hilarious cross-dresser in *Tootsie* (1982), and an idiot savant in *Rain Man* (1989). Five times nominated for the best actor Oscar, he won for *Kramer vs. Kramer* and *Rain Man*. He played Willy Loman in a 1984 Broadway version of DEATH OF A SALESMAN.

Hogan, Ben   (1912–   ) Golfer. The greatest player of the 1940s and 1950s, Hogan was the sport's leading moneymaker in 1940–42, 1946, and 1948. He won four U.S. Open titles and two Masters titles, and was PGA player of the year four times. The story of his comeback from a disastrous automobile accident was told in the 1951 movie *Follow the Sun*.

Holden, William (1918–81) Actor. A versatile leading man, Holden (born William Beedle) made his mark as a boxer in *Golden Boy* (1939), then played George Gibbs in the film version of OUR TOWN (1940). His best roles were in SUNSET BOULEVARD, *Stalag 17* (1953; Academy Award), *The Bridge on the River Kwai* (1957), and *The Wild Bunch* (see WILD BUNCH [2]).

Hole-in-the-Wall Gang See Butch CASSIDY.

Holiday, Billie (1915–59) Singer. Born Eleanor Fagan in Baltimore, "Lady Day" was the most distinctive jazz/blues singer of her time. Influenced by Louis ARMSTRONG and Bessie SMITH, she made her first recording with Benny GOODMAN in 1933, achieved fame with Goodman's pianist Teddy Wilson, and later sang with Count BASIE and Artie Shaw. Her unique improvisatory style made her a legend, and it was enhanced by the tragic facts of her life, including a childhood rape and a lifelong drug addiction. One of her most poignant songs, "Strange Fruit" (1939), was a protest against southern LYNCHING. Diana Ross of the SUPREMES portrayed her in the 1972 film *Lady Sings the Blues*.

Holliday, Doc (1851–87) Gunman. The tubercular dentist John Henry Holliday achieved legendary status in 1881, when he assisted Wyatt EARP in the famous gunfight at the O.K. CORRAL. Born in Georgia, he had practiced dentistry in Atlanta before coming west in the 1870s for his health. He met Earp in Dodge City, followed him to Tombstone in 1880, and acquired a reputation as a gambler, drunk, and rowdy. Earp himself once arrested him for murder and attempted robbery, and the charges (later dropped) were verified by Holliday's own wife. After leaving Tombstone in 1882, he became a drifter before dying of TB in California.

Holly, Buddy (1938–59) Singer, songwriter. Texan Charles "Buddy" Holly was rock 'n' roll's first major songwriter. With his band the Crickets he helped to define an early rock canon with the songs "Peggy Sue," "Every Day," "That'll be the Day," "Maybe Baby," "Not Fade Away," and "Rave On." When he died at the age of twenty in a plane crash, the new music entered a period of decline that lasted until the "British invasion" of the mid-1960s.

Hollywood A section of Los Angeles, California, which in the 1900s was a sleepy town surrounded by orange groves. Cecil B. DE MILLE's decision to shoot *The Squaw Man* there in 1913 opened filmmakers' eyes to its possibilities, and within a decade it had replaced New York as the movie capital. Even though production is now less centralized than it was in the major studios' Golden Age (1930–50), the term "Hollywood" still stands symbolically for American movies.

Hollywood Ten A group of movie professionals, chiefly writers, who in 1947 were asked to testify before the HOUSE UN-AMERICAN ACTIVITIES COMMITTEE about communist influence in the movie industry. Their refusal to implicate either themselves or others got them fined, jailed, and blacklisted. The ten were Alvah Bessie, Herbert Biberman, Lester Cole, Edward Dmytryk, Ring Lardner, Jr., John Howard Lawson, Albert Maltz, Samuel Ornitz, Adrian Scott, and Dalton Trumbo.

Holmes, Oliver Wendell   (1809–94) Writer. Most widely known for his poem "Old Ironsides" (see OLD IRONSIDES), Holmes helped to establish both American literature and THE ATLANTIC MONTHLY with the chatty essays collected in *The Autocrat of the Breakfast Table* (1858). A member of the Harvard medical faculty, he was also a forceful teacher who considered his greatest achievement a pioneering study of childbirth fever.

Holmes, Oliver Wendell, Jr.   (1841–1935) Jurist. Known as the Great Dissenter, the younger Holmes was a Supreme Court justice appointed by Theodore ROOSEVELT. In his most famous ruling (1919), he upheld the conviction of a socialist war protester by insisting that "circumstances" can properly limit free speech. The FIRST AMENDMENT, he wrote, "does not protect a man in falsely shouting fire in a crowded theater.... The question in every case is whether words used are of such a nature as to create a clear and present danger" of "substantive evils."

Holy Experiment   See William PENN.

Holy Rollers   Evangelical Christians whose services include such expressions of ecstasy as rolling on the floor. A derogatory term from the 1840s.

"Home on the Range"   The most famous of all cowboy songs and the state song of Kansas. Its authorship has been contested, but the words appeared in a Kansas newspaper in 1874 as the poem "Western Home" by a Dr. Brewster Higley. Their setting to music is credited to Daniel Kelley, who moved from Rhode Island to Kansas in 1872.

> *Oh give me a home where the buffalo roam*
> *And the deer and the antelope play.*
> *Where seldom is heard a discouraging word*
> *And the skies are not cloudy all day.*

home run   Or simply "homer." A hit in baseball that allows the batter to round the bases and "come home." Hence "hit a home run" and "make a home run" as metaphors for success.

"Home, Sweet Home"   A sentimental song written by the actor and playwright John Howard Payne (1791–1852) to a folk tune generally credited to Henry Bishop. Raised in New York, Payne wrote the words while in Paris in 1823.

> *'Mid pleasures and palaces though we may roam,*
> *Be it ever so humble, there's no place like home.*

Homer, Winslow   (1836–1910) Painter. After covering the Civil War as a pictorial reporter for HARPER'S magazine, Homer concentrated on rural scenes and seascapes. Two of his best-known paintings, *The Life Line* (1884) and *The Gulf Stream* (1899), realistically depict the hazards of life at sea. He is also known for sensitive studies of children at play.

Homestead Act   (1862) An act that granted 160 acres of western land free to any potential "homesteader" who would agree to live on it for five years. Designed to encourage family farms, it was subverted systematically by greedy speculators, yet still contributed significantly to western settlement. The act's detractors included the Plains Indians and free-range cattlemen (see BARBED WIRE).

Homestead strike   (1892) A strike at the Homestead, Pennsylvania, plant of the Carnegie Steel Company brought about by a company wage cut. After clashes between workers and PINKERTON agents killed ten men, the militia was called in, the strike was broken, and union activism in the steel industry virtually died.

Honest Abe   See Abraham LINCOLN.

Honest Injun   An oath of veracity from the 1890s. Used ironically, reflecting Indians' supposed duplicity.

Honeymooners, The   Television sitcom. A spin-off of *The Jackie* GLEASON *Show, The Honeymooners* ran for less than a year as an independent series (1955), yet became a legendary feature of television's Golden Age. It starred Gleason as Ralph Kramden, a blustery bus driver given to grandiose plans; Audrey Meadows as his wittily incredulous wife, Alice; Art Carney as the guileless, slightly rattled sewer-worker, Ed Norton; and Joyce Randolph as Norton's wife, Trixie. A recurrent theme was Ralph's frustration with Alice's common sense ("One of these days, Alice . . . POW! Right in the kisser!") followed by his chastened realization that she was right ("Alice . . . you're the greatest").

honky-tonk   Since the 1890s, a cheap saloon and/or dance hall. The term spread in the 1930s, after the repeal of Prohibition created legal nightspots filled with the combination of drinking and dancing that became known as honky-tonking. As a musical description, "honky-tonk" is applied both to heavy-handed piano BLUES and to amplified COUNTRY MUSIC.

hooker   A prostitute. An 1840s term referring to "the Hook," a red-light section of New York City. It was later applied to the camp followers of "Fighting Joe" Hooker, commander of the Army of the Potomac in 1863.

Hooker, John Lee   (1917–   ) Blues musician. Mississippi-born Hooker played in Memphis and Cincinnati in the 1930s, then settled in 1943 in Detroit. His two-sided record "Boogie Chillun/Sally Mae" was a blues hit in 1949, and he also scored big with "I'm in the Mood" and "Boom Boom." Although basically a Delta-style acoustic player, he strongly affected the development of electric blues and by the 1960s was a father figure to English rockers. Both the Animals and the Rolling Stones acknowledged his influence.

hoop snake   A mythical beast which, by grasping its tail in its mouth, forms a hoop that rolls threateningly after its prey. The creature figures occasionally in Paul BUNYAN stories.

Hoosier   A person from Indiana. The etymology is uncertain. It has been derived from a slang term for mountaineer, tramp, or ruffian; from "husher" (one who "hushes" an argument with his fists); from "Whose ear?" (as in "Whose ear have I just bitten off in this fight?"); and from the isolated cabin-dweller's greeting "Who's there?"

Hoosier Schoolmaster, The   (1871) A widely read novel by Edward Eggleston (1837–1902). It deals with Indiana frontier life before the Civil War. Its lesser known sequel was *The Hoosier Schoolboy* (1883).

hootenanny   An informal folk music gathering, usually with audience participation adding to the performances. The term dates from the 1920s and became generally known in the urban FOLK REVIVAL.

Hoover, J. Edgar   (1895–1972) Director of the FEDERAL BUREAU OF INVESTIGATION for almost half a century (1924–72), Hoover turned the hitherto politicized agency into an effective anticrime unit which ended the careers of John DILLINGER, Pretty Boy FLOYD, and Baby Face NELSON. Then, in the 1950s, he turned it to his own political aims, preaching anticommunism and investigating political "subversives." He wrote an exposé of communist tactics called *Masters of Deceit* (1958).

Hoover Dam   A dam across the Colorado River in Arizona and Nevada. When it was completed in 1936, it was the tallest dam in the world. The original name, changed in 1947 to honor ex-President Herbert Hoover, was Boulder Dam.

Hoovervilles   Shack cities constructed by homeless people during the presidential administration of Herbert Hoover (1929–33), whose conservative policies were blamed for exacerbating the Great Depression.

Hopalong Cassidy   Originally a rather unsavory character in stories by Clarence E. Mulford, Cassidy became a straight-thinking, straight-shooting cowboy hero in the 1935 movie *Hopalong Cassidy*. William Boyd (1898–1972) portrayed him there and in sixty other films before turning with equal success to television in the 1950s. Astride his white horse, Topper, and accompanied by his sidekick, Gabby HAYES, "Hoppy" was a matinee favorite for twenty years.

Hope, Bob   (1903–   ) Entertainer. Born Leslie Townes Hope in England, Bob Hope appeared in comedy shorts in the 1930s, then hit it big with the first of many "road" pictures, *The Road to Singapore* (1940), costarring his lifelong rival Bing CROSBY and Dorothy Lamour. His comic timing brought him dozens of other film roles, TV specials, and a nightclub career spanning five decades. At one time the richest comic in the world, he was known for his humanitarian work and his USO tours, on which he entertained U.S. troops in three wars. His theme song is "Thanks for the Memories."

Hopedale   See UTOPIAN COMMUNITIES.

Hopi   An Indian people of northeast Arizona. Encroached upon by the NAVAJO beginning in the 1820s, they are now encircled by a Navajo reservation. Their religious ceremonies include snake dances and KACHINA dolls.

Hopkins, Lightnin'   (1912–82) Blues musician. After playing for decades in Texas bars and on Houston street corners, Sam "Lightnin' " Hopkins recorded "Baby Please Don't Go" and other songs in the late 1940s, then was discovered by musicologists in the FOLK REVIVAL. He joined Pete SEEGER and Joan BAEZ in a 1960 Carnegie Hall concert and wrote part of the sound track for the 1972 film *Sounder*.

Hopper, Hedda   (1890–1966) Gossip columnist. Along with her longtime rival Louella PARSONS, Hopper provided tidbits on the rich and famous in syndicated columns from 1938 until her death. Known for her hats, she also appeared in over fifty forgettable films, as well as SUNSET BOULEVARD, where she played herself.

hopping John   Black-eyed peas (cowpeas) and rice cooked with bacon. It is a traditional New Year dish throughout the South, thought to bring good luck. The name may derive from the invitation "Hop in, John" or from the French *pois de pigeon,* for "pigeon peas."

Horatio Alger story   See Horatio ALGER.

Horn & Hardart   See AUTOMAT.

Horne, Lena   (1917–   ) Singer, actress. Horne started as a teenage dancer in the COTTON CLUB, sang with big bands in the 1930s, and then became the first African-American performer to sign a long-term contract with a Hollywood studio (MGM). She was acclaimed for her acting in *Panama Hattie* (1942), *Cabin in the Sky* (1943), and *Stormy Weather* (1943)—the title song of which became her signature tune. Blacklisted in the McCarthy period, she rebounded in the 1960s, and in 1978 played the good witch Glinda in *The Wiz* (see THE WIZARD OF OZ).

horse opera   Slang for a film or TV WESTERN. Also called an oater, from the horses' feed.

horses   Introduced to North America by the Spanish, horses became economically essential to the Plains Indians, who used them in buffalo hunting and in warfare. Horses, or "cow ponies," were also critical to the COWBOY, and by extension to his incarnations on the screen. Hollywood and television cowboys have frequently been closely identified with their mounts. Famous examples, with their riders, include Champion (Gene AUTRY), Diablo (the CISCO KID), Fritz (William S. HART), Scout (TONTO), Silver (THE LONE RANGER), Tony (Tom MIX), Topper (HOPALONG CASSIDY), Trigger (Roy ROGERS), and Widowmaker (PECOS BILL).

hot dog   A sausage, originally beef but now increasingly an amalgam of meats and grains, served on a soft roll (or "hot dog bun") and garnished with mustard, sauerkraut, or chili (in which case it is called a chili dog). Hot dogs are standard fare at baseball games. First called frankfurters and wieners from their places of origin in Frankfurt and Vienna, they became "dachshund sausages" around 1900. "Hot dog" came from a sketch by Tad DORGAN of a dachshund nestled firmly in a roll. The nation's leading producer is Oscar Mayer.

"Hot Time in the Old Town Tonight, A"   (1896) A song written for the minstrel stage by Joseph Hayden and Theodore Metz. It was popular during the SPANISH-AMERICAN WAR and said to have been played during the ROUGH RIDERS' attack on San Juan Hill.

Houdini, Harry   (1874–1926) Magician. The greatest escape artist in history, the "Great Houdini" was born Erich Weiss, probably in Hungary, and changed his name in honor of French magician Robert-Houdin. He thrilled audiences by picking and wriggling his way out of handcuffs, straitjackets, padlocked crates, and jail cells—including one at Scotland Yard—as well as walking through walls and making elephants disappear. In his most famous trick, the Water Torture Cell, he survived being suspended head-down in a tank of water with his ankles locked above him in a set of stocks. He spent much time exposing supposed "spiritualists" by showing how their "otherworldly" contacts were stage-managed. Proud of his physical fitness, he invited audience members to hit him in the stomach after he had tensed his muscles; a punch thrown at him before he had prepared himself caused an internal rupture from which he died. Tony Curtis played him in a 1953 film.

"Hound Dog"   (1956) A blues song written by Jerry Leiber and Mike Stoller. First recorded by Big Mama THORNTON, it was covered by Elvis PRESLEY and became one of his four number-one hits that year. It boosted the sale of hound dogs both real and stuffed, and eventually became the singer's signature tune.

"house divided against itself cannot stand, A"   A line from an 1858 speech by Abraham LINCOLN, noting the divisiveness of the slavery issue. Lincoln continued, "I believe this government cannot endure, permanently half slave and half free." The origin of his thought was in Mark 3:25.

House of Representatives   See CONGRESS.

House of the Seven Gables, The   (1851) A novel by Nathaniel HAWTHORNE exploring the consequences of "inherited guilt" in a New England family. Matthew Maule's house is obtained illegally by Colonel Pyncheon, who has Maule charged with witchcraft and condemned to death. Maule's curse on the colonel's descendants animates the story. In a 1940 movie version, Vincent PRICE played his first gothic role, as Clifford Pyncheon.

House That Ruth Built   Yankee Stadium (see YANKEES). From Babe RUTH's salutary influence on Yankee gate receipts in the three years preceding its construction.

House Un-American Activities Committee (HUAC)   A House of Representatives investigating committee formed in 1938 to ferret out Nazi sympathizers. After World War II it turned its attention to suspected communists, among them Alger HISS and the HOLLYWOOD TEN.

Houston, Sam   (1793–1863) Soldier, statesman. Houston was raised in Tennessee, where he built close friendships as a young man with the Cherokee people. He fought with Andrew JACKSON in the Creek Wars (1813–14), served in Congress and as governor of Tennessee, and in the 1830s lived with the Cherokee in INDIAN TERRITORY. He commanded the Texans in their war for independence (1836), becoming the "Hero of San Jacinto" after beating SANTA ANNA there. After the war he became the new republic's first president, and after statehood its senator and finally governor. He was forced from office in 1861 when he resisted popular sentiment for secession. Texas's largest city is named for him.

How the Other Half Lives   (1890) A report by journalist Jacob Riis (1849–1914) on slum conditions in New York City's Lower East Side. The book, complete with shocking photographs, led to the razing of some slums and to laws regarding housing and child labor. The Danish-born Riis, whom Theodore ROOSEVELT called "the best American I ever knew," was a forerunner of the MUCKRAKERS.

How to Make Friends and Influence People See Dale CARNEGIE.

Howard Johnson's A restaurant chain established in the 1920s by Massachusetts businessman Howard D. Johnson. With their Simple Simon logo, highly visible orange-and-turquoise color scheme, and predictable family fare, "Ho-Jo" restaurants became the first nationwide roadside chain. The first turnpike unit opened in 1940 on the Pennsylvania Turnpike, then known as America's dream road.

Howard University The country's leading black university, founded in 1867 largely through the efforts of Freedmen's Bureau commissioner Oliver Otis Howard (1830–1909), who also served as its first president. Now increasingly cosmopolitan and integrated, Howard University was long known as the Black Harvard.

Howdy A common western greeting. Short for "How do ye?" or "How do you do?"

Howdy Doody The puppet star of a children's television show, first broadcast in 1943 and extremely successful through the 1950s. Howdy—an ingratiating hayseed type—was joined by Clarabell the Clown, the Indian Princess Summer-Fall-Winter-Spring, and the show's host, buckskin-clad Buffalo Bob. The young studio audiences sat in the Peanut Gallery.

Howe, Elias (1819–67) Usually identified as the inventor of the sewing machine, Howe actually patented a lock-stitching device that had already been invented by Walter Hunt—Hunt had declined to patent it fearing it would eliminate seamstresses' jobs. After years of wrangling with infringers like Isaac SINGER, Howe was awarded his patent rights, and he earned $2 million in royalties before he died.

Howe, Gordie (1928–) Hockey player. Canadian Gordon Howe played twenty-five years for the Detroit Red Wings before retiring in 1971; he returned to the ice in the 1970s, with the Aeros and Whalers. At his second retirement in 1980, he was the highest-scoring player in professional hockey history, with a lifetime record of 1,850 points, accumulated in a record 1,767 games.

Howe, Julia Ward (1819–1910) The author of "THE BATTLE HYMN OF THE REPUBLIC," Howe was active in both the abolitionist and women's suffrage movements. She edited an antislavery paper, *Commonwealth,* with her husband, Samuel Howe, and helped to found the American Woman Suffrage Association.

Howells, William Dean (1837–1920) Writer. Little read today, Howells was immensely influential in the nineteenth century, both as editor in chief of THE ATLANTIC MONTHLY (1871–80) and as a novelist. As editor he published the work of Henry JAMES and Mark TWAIN. His best novels—which demonstrate his championship of literary realism—were *A Modern Instance* (1882), *The Rise of*

Silas Lapham (1885), and *A Hazard of New Fortunes* (1890). Howells's liberalism showed in his defense of the HAYMARKET RIOT anarchists and in his support for the 1910 founding of the NAACP.

"Howl"   (1955) The title piece of *Howl and Other Poems,* which brought Allen GINSBERG national notoriety. An often coarse, often mystical meditation on society's outcasts, it begins:

> *I saw the best minds of my generation destroyed by*
>   *madness, starving hysterical naked,*
> *dragging themselves through the negro streets at dawn*
>   *looking for an angry fix,*
> *angelheaded hipsters burning for the ancient heavenly*
>   *connection to the starry dynamo in the machinery of*
>   *night . . .*

HUAC   See HOUSE UN-AMERICAN ACTIVITIES COMMITTEE.

Hubbard, Elbert   (1856–1915) Writer. Best known for "A MESSAGE TO GARCIA," "Fra Elbertus" also wrote a series of "Little Journeys" to the homes of famous people, countless epigrams, and inspirational essays in his magazines, *The Philistine* and *The Fra.* Much of this work was published at his Roycroft Press, part of his upstate New York crafts compound. A unique blend of the pragmatist and the aesthete, Hubbard lost his life in the sinking of the LUSITANIA.

Hubbard, L. Ron   See SCIENTOLOGY.

Huckleberry Finn   (1884) Mark TWAIN's most highly regarded novel. A sequel to TOM SAWYER, *The Adventures of Huckleberry Finn* tells the story of Tom's friend Huck and an escaped slave, Jim, traveling down the Mississippi River on a raft. Couched in the form of a juvenile adventure yarn, it pointedly counterposes the constraints of society to natural freedom. At the end Huck, like Daniel BOONE, intends to "light out for the territory" (the West) to avoid being "sivilized."

Hudson, Henry   (d. 1611?) Explorer. An English navigator, Hudson sailed under both the English and Dutch flags in a vain search for the NORTHWEST PASSAGE. On a 1609 voyage for the Dutch East India Company, he sailed the *Half Moon* up the Hudson River as far as Albany; the next year, in the English ship *Discovery,* he reached Hudson's Bay. In the spring of 1611, he was set adrift there by a mutinous crew and not seen again. The river and bay that bear his name were not his discoveries; Portuguese and Italian sailors had found them decades before.

Hudson River School   A group of painters who produced luminous, mystically charged views of the American landscape from the New England woodlands to the Rocky Mountains. Their particular fondness for the Hudson Valley gave them their name. Principal "members" of the loose-knit group were Frederick Edwin Church, Thomas COLE, and Asher DURAND.

Hudson's Bay Company   A joint-stock company chartered in 1670 to conduct the "sole trade and commerce" of English Canada. It established a network of trading posts and forts that gave it dominance over the upper Canadian FUR TRADE and led to trade wars, and eventually actual war, with the rival French. Now under Canadian control, the company is still the world's largest fur trader.

Hughes, Howard (1905–76) Businessman, pilot, moviemaker. Beginning with a tool company he had inherited from his father, Hughes built a multibillion-dollar industrial empire while fascinating celebrity-watchers with his colorful exploits. As a film producer he started Jean HARLOW's career with *Hell's Angels* (1930), backed THE FRONT PAGE and SCARFACE, and created an uproar with his "sexy" western, 1943's *The Outlaw*. As an aviation buff he broke speed records in the 1930s and contributed to war research in the following decade with the "Spruce Goose," a giant seaplane which was retired after its maiden flight. Frequently paired with starlets in Hollywood's Golden Age, Hughes turned increasingly reclusive after a 1946 plane crash, living the last twenty years of his life in virtual isolation in the penthouse of the Desert Inn in Las Vegas. A faked 1971 biography by Clifford Irving added to the legend of the "mystery man," and his death precipitated a cascade of spurious wills.

hula hoops Plastic hoops sold as toys in the 1950s. During the brief hula hoop craze, children (and many adults) placed the hoops around their waists, then rotated them by means of hip gyrations that were said to resemble the motions of the Hawaiian hula dance.

Hulk, the See INCREDIBLE HULK.

Hull, Bobby (1939–) Hockey player. The Canadian-born "Golden Jet" Bobby Hull played in the 1960s for the Chicago Black Hawks, twice winning the National Hockey League's most valuable player award and in 1965 its Lady Byng trophy for good sportsmanship. That same year he became the first player in history to score fifty goals in a season. He retired in 1979, with an NHL career total of 610 goals and 1,170 points.

Hull House A settlement house founded in 1889 by Jane ADDAMS to promote the assimilation and protection of immigrant families. Now a museum, it was named for Charles Hull, who constructed (1856) the original building.

Hundred Days See NEW DEAL.

"Hunters of Kentucky" (1826) A ballad by Samuel Woodworth celebrating the American victory at the Battle of NEW ORLEANS (1815). It contains the familiar image of the Kentucky backwoodsman as an "alligator horse" and was enlisted as an Andrew JACKSON campaign song in 1828.

Hurston, Zora Neale (1901–60) Writer. A student of Franz Boas, Hurston used her anthropological training in producing important records of folklore as well as fiction. Among the works that displayed her knowledge of southern black folkways were the collection *Mules and Men* (1935) and the novels *Jonah's Gourd Vine* (1934) and *Their Eyes Were Watching God* (1937).

Hurt, Mississippi John (1892–1966) Blues musician. Like Lightnin' HOPKINS, Hurt spent much of his life in obscurity before being discovered during the 1960s

FOLK REVIVAL. Strongly influenced by Jimmie RODGERS, he played folk blues around his home base of Avalon, Mississippi, composing "Chicken" and "Coffee Blues" in the 1920s. His appearance at the 1963 Newport Folk Festival helped to popularize not only these originals but such older blues as "Stagger Lee" (see STAGOLEE) and "Candy Man."

hush puppies   (1) Balls of cornmeal dough fried in deep fat. A common side dish in southern cooking. From the expression "Hush, puppy," when throwing them to a barking dog. (2) The brand name of a casual shoe, from the 1950s. The company logo is a sitting hound dog.

Huston, John   (1906–87) Film director. Huston's first directing job, THE MALTESE FALCON, established him early as a force in American film. His uneven career following that success was highlighted by three triumphs of genre work: the modern western THE TREASURE OF THE SIERRA MADRE, the crime drama *Asphalt Jungle* (1950), and the romantic adventure THE AFRICAN QUEEN. He tackled literary classics in THE RED BADGE OF COURAGE and MOBY DICK, and played a believable villain in the modern FILM NOIR *Chinatown* (1974).

Hutchins, Robert M.   (1899–1977) Educator. The "boy wonder of American education," Hutchins became dean of the Yale Law School at twenty-nine and president of the University of Chicago the following year. At Chicago he banned football, liberalized entrance requirements, and implemented the GREAT BOOKS program, which is his enduring legacy outside the university.

Hutterite Brethren   See UTOPIAN COMMUNITIES.

Hyannis Port   A small community on the southern shore of CAPE COD. The KENNEDY family maintains a compound there.

Hyde Park   A small town on the banks of the Hudson River. It was the birthplace and lifelong home of Franklin D. ROOSEVELT, who is buried there with his wife, Eleanor. The Roosevelt estate is a national historic site.

"I am not a crook" Richard NIXON's assurance, in a public message during the WATERGATE crisis, that he had not been personally involved in illegal activity.

"I cannot tell a lie" A comment attributed to young George WASHINGTON after his father had discovered a chopped-down cherry tree. The famous moral anecdote ends with George confessing that he has destroyed the tree, and with his father exulting over his honesty. The tale was invented by Parson Mason Locke WEEMS. Mark TWAIN surmised that he was more moral than young George because he *could* lie if he wanted, but chose not to.

"I coulda been a contender" See ON THE WATERFRONT.

"I do not choose to run" See Calvin COOLIDGE.

"I Get a Kick out of You" A song written by Cole PORTER for the musical *Anything Goes* (1934) and introduced there by Ethel MERMAN and William Gaxton. The daring line "I get no kick from cocaine" was often changed thereafter to "Some like the perfume from Spain."

> *I get no kick from champagne;*
> *Mere alcohol doesn't thrill me at all.*
> *Then why should it be true*
> *I get a kick out of you.*

"I Got Rhythm" A song written by George and Ira GERSHWIN for the musical *Girl Crazy* (1930). Ethel MERMAN, in her Broadway debut, belted it out with such verve that it became, in the estimation of one scholar, "the single most important factor in making her a star."

> *I got rhythm, I got music,*
> *I got my man . . . Who could ask for anything more?*

"I have a dream" The rhetorical hook of Martin Luther KING, Jr.'s most famous speech, given to a huge civil rights march on Washington in August 1963.

"I have always depended on the kindness of strangers" See Blanche DU BOIS.

"I have not yet begun to fight" John Paul JONES's response to the British surrender demand during the battle between the BONHOMME RICHARD and the *Serapis* on September 23, 1779. Jones's flagship was lost, but he won the fight.

"I Left My Heart in San Francisco"   A popular song by Douglass Cross and George Cory. It became Tony Bennett's theme song in 1962, when it sold 3 million copies and won two Grammies.

"I Like Ike"   The Republican campaign slogan in the election of 1952. "Ike" was presidential candidate Dwight D. EISENHOWER.

I Love Lucy   (1951–61) Television sitcom. The most popular comedy of the 1950s and among the first to be filmed for future syndication, *I Love Lucy* starred Lucille Ball (1911–89) as Lucy Ricardo, the scatterbrained, endearingly ambitious wife of bandleader Ricky Ricardo, played by Ball's real-life husband, Cuban musician Desi Arnaz (1917–86). The Ricardos' best friends were Fred Mertz (William Frawley) and his wife Ethel (Vivian Vance), who supported respectively Ricky's practicality and Lucy's zaniness. "Little Ricky" came on board in 1953, in a birth that coincided with that of the stars' own child and whose incorporation into the story line broke rating records. The "crazy redhead" later had her own series, *The Lucy Show,* which ran from 1962 to 1974.

"I only regret that I have but one life to lose for my country"   See Nathan HALE.

"I pledge allegiance to the flag"   See PLEDGE OF ALLEGIANCE.

I Remember Mama   See MAMA.

"I shall return"   Douglas MACARTHUR's public promise, made in the spring of 1942, that he would regain control of the Philippine Islands, from which the Japanese were then driving him. He made good on it in October of 1944.

"I should of stood in bed"   See "WE WAS ROBBED."

"I taut I taw a puddy tat"   See SYLVESTER AND TWEETY.

"I Want a Girl Just like the Girl"   A 1911 song with music by TIN PAN ALLEY king Harry VON TILZER and words by William Dillon. "I want a girl just like the girl that married dear old Dad."

"I want to be alone"   A line attributed to Greta GARBO because of her reclusiveness. She approximates the phrasing in *Grand Hotel* (1932), where, as a Russian ballerina, she tells her maid, "I want to be left alone." In a 1950s joke, Garbo sprinkles grass seed on her head, muttering in her Swedish accent, "I vant to be a lawn."

"I will fight no more forever"   See Chief JOSEPH.

"I wish I was in the land of cotton"   See "DIXIE."

"I would rather be right than be President"   Henry CLAY's observation on his lack of success in running for the presidency. A political rival, probably John Randolph, is said to have quipped in response, "He will never be either."

Icaria See UTOPIAN COMMUNITIES.

ice cream Known in America from the 1770s, ice cream was popular with the first presidents (WASHINGTON and JEFFERSON both owned ice-cream machines) and received a boost in James MADISON's administration when his wife Dolley made it common at the White House (Dolley Madison is a contemporary ice-cream brand). Americans added many refinements to the treat. Ice cream with syrup and other toppings was called a Sunday in the 1890s, when it was introduced as a morally safe alternative to the scandalous imbibing of soda water on the Sabbath; the spelling "sundae" was a later variation. Scoops of ice cream first appeared in a pastry cone at the 1904 St. Louis WORLD'S FAIR. Marvels introduced around 1920 included the Eskimo Pie ice-cream bar; the fruit ice Popsicle, developed by Californian Frank Epperson and first known less euphoniously as the Eppsicle; and the Good Humor company's ice cream on a stick. The white trucks that hawked this last creation made the bell-jingling Good Humor man a summertime icon. Last but not least was the banana split, which attained its popularity in the 1930s. The name may have reflected either the lengthwise-sliced fruit that served as its base or the dessert's size, which let one split it with a friend.

"Ich bin ein Berliner" To counter Soviet pressure in Eastern Europe, John F. KENNEDY went to the Berlin Wall in 1963 and announced that "Ich bin ein Berliner" was the modern equivalent of the ancient Romans' boast *"Civis Romanus sum."* He meant "I am a citizen of Berlin." The German actually translates "I am a jelly doughnut."

Ichabod Crane See "THE LEGEND OF SLEEPY HOLLOW."

"I'd walk a mile for a Camel" See CAMEL.

idiot box A slang term for television. Also called the boob tube. Inveterate watchers are called vidiots and couch potatoes.

"If I Had a Hammer" A song, written in 1958 by WEAVERS Lee Hays and Pete SEEGER, about the ongoing struggle for freedom, justice, and love. Among the most widely heard songs of the FOLK REVIVAL, it was PETER, PAUL, and MARY's first success.

> If I had a hammer, I'd hammer in the morning;
> I'd hammer in the evening, all over this land.
> I'd hammer out danger, I'd hammer out a warning;
> I'd hammer out love between my brothers and my sisters
> All over this land.

A cynical lapel button of the 1980s ridiculed the song's fraternal optimism: "If I had a hammer ... there'd be no more folksingers."

"If nominated I will not run. If elected I will not serve" William Tecumseh SHERMAN's comment on attempts to draft him for the presidency in 1883. See also Calvin COOLIDGE; SMOTHERS BROTHERS.

"If this be treason, make the most of it"   See Patrick HENRY.

"If you can't stand the heat, get out of the kitchen"   A line attributed to Harry S TRUMAN regarding the press "heat" that came with the presidential territory.

"If You Knew Susie like I Know Susie"   (1925) A song written by Bud De Sylva and Joseph Meyer for Al JOLSON. Jolson, having little success with it, offered it to Eddie CANTOR, who made it his special number. At Cantor's initial performance, which brought the audience to its feet, Jolson commented drily, "Eddie, if I'd known the song was that good, you dirty dog, you'd never have gotten it."

Ike   Dwight D. EISENHOWER's nickname.

"I'll Be Seeing You"   A popular ballad by Irving Kahal and Sammy FAIN. Written in 1938, it became enormously popular five years later in recordings by Hildegarde and Frank SINATRA. In 1944 it spent half a year on the HIT PARADE, and it remains one of the great nostalgia tunes of World War II.

> *I'll see you in the morning sun*
> *And when the day is through.*
> *I'll be looking at the moon*
> *But I'll be seeing you.*

"I'm from Missouri"   Slang for "I'm skeptical; prove it." Missourians' reputation for incredulity goes back at least to the turn of the century, when Missouri Congressman Willard Vandiver, speaking at a state banquet, claimed, "Frothy eloquence neither convinces nor satisfies me. I am from Missouri. You have got to show me." Hence Missouri's nickname, the Show Me State.

impeachment   The bringing of charges against a public official by the lower house of a legislature. Under the CONSTITUTION, the House of Representatives may impeach a federal official, try him before the Senate, and if successful remove him from office. President Andrew JOHNSON was so charged in 1868 after he had offended the Radical Republicans by his moderation; the Senate narrowly failed to convict him. Richard NIXON was almost charged over the WATERGATE scandal, but he left office before the impeachment vote.

In God We Trust   The national motto since 1956, it first appeared on U.S. currency in 1864, on a two-cent piece, and was gradually added to other coins and bills. A novelty amendment of the slogan, from the 1960s, was "In God We Trust. All Others Pay Cash."

In His Steps   (1897) A novel by Congregationalist minister Charles Monroe Sheldon (1857–1946). It told the stories of people who pledged to fashion their lives after the question "What Would Jesus Do?" It had a great impact on the social gospel and was said to have sold more copies in its day than any book other than the Bible and the works of Shakespeare. Until the publication of GOD'S LITTLE ACRE, it was the most widely read of all American novels.

"in like Flynn" See Errol FLYNN.

In the Heat of the Night A 1967 movie, based on a novel by John Ball, about the relationship between a small-town southern police chief and a black detective, Virgil Tibbs, who works beside him. Sidney POITIER's Tibbs was an important portrayal of an assertive black professional. The film itself, and Rod STEIGER as the chief, won Academy Awards.

"Include me out" See Samuel GOLDWYN.

Incredible Hulk A comic strip character created in 1962 by Stan Lee. He was the powerful, green-skinned alter ego of research scientist David Banner, who had acquired the second self in a laboratory accident and who turned into the Hulk whenever he became enraged. In a television series (1978–82), Banner was played by Bill Bixby, the Hulk by bodybuilder Lou Ferrigno.

Independence Day See FOURTH OF JULY.

Independence Hall A Georgian-style building in Philadelphia, the meeting site for the Continental Congress that adopted the DECLARATION OF INDEPENDENCE and the 1787 convention that drafted the CONSTITUTION. It was begun in 1732 under the supervision of Edmund Wooley; the central tower, which once housed the LIBERTY BELL, was completed in 1753.

Indian corn Commonly used to mean any dried corn, especially the bunches of ears that decorate doors in the autumn season. See CORN.

Indian giver One who offers a gift and then demands its return. Possibly from the native American custom of reciprocal gift-giving—or from whites' stereotype of Indians as unreliable.

Indian pudding Cornmeal mush made with molasses. The New England colonists got the dish from the local peoples.

Indian summer A brief period of warm weather at the end of fall, corresponding to the European St. Martin's summer. Eastern Indians burned grass, hunted, and moved camps in this period, and their visibility may have given it a name.

Indian Territory Originally a vague term for the vast unsettled West. After the Indian Removal Act of 1830, it was applied more narrowly to reservations in Oklahoma, Kansas, Nebraska, and the Dakotas. By midcentury the term's compass, like the tribes' land itself, had shrunk even further, to correspond roughly to the current state of Oklahoma. In 1889 it, too, was opened to settlement.

Indian wars Conflict between red and white over land, race, and cultural differences was a virtually constant element of European expansion. For highlights of this doleful history, see (in chronological order) KING PHILIP'S WAR; FRENCH AND INDIAN WAR; PONTIAC; TECUMSEH; "TIPPECANOE AND TYLER TOO"; BLACK HAWK WAR; TRAIL OF TEARS; SAND CREEK MASSACRE; LITTLE BIGHORN; Chief JOSEPH; GERONIMO; and WOUNDED KNEE.

Indian wrestling   Three types of one-on-one competition popular since the turn of the century among young males. In the first, the two competitors lie on their backs, side by side and facing different directions, then raise their inside legs and try to hook the opponent over onto his side. In the second, the two grasp hands, as in a handshake, and try to force each other off balance. In the third, usually called arm wrestling, they sit across from each other with their elbows on a table, grasp each other's upright hand, and attempt to force it down onto the table. Arm wrestling is a test of strength in barracks and bars.

Indiana Jones   The hero of a series of adventure films directed by Steven SPIELBERG. An archaeologist with a taste for danger, he was introduced in *Raiders of the Lost Ark* (1981) and returned in *Indiana Jones and the Temple of Doom* (1984) and *Indiana Jones and the Last Crusade* (1989)—all massive box-office successes. The character is played by actor Harrison Ford (1942–).

Indianapolis 500   A 500-mile automobile race held in the Indiana capital each Memorial Day. First run in 1911, the "Indy 500" draws the largest attendance of any spectator sport—generally three or four times that of the SUPER BOWL.

Indians   Christopher COLUMBUS's misnomer for the original inhabitants of the New World, which he took to be his desired destination, the East Indies. The aboriginal inhabitants of North America had no concept of themselves as "one people," although some native Americans began to develop such a sense in the 1970s, putting away tribal differences for a united front. The descendants of Asian nomads who crossed the frozen Bering Strait in Pleistocene times, native Americans numbered in the millions before 1492 but were decimated, largely by European diseases, within a century. White encroachment continued what measles had begun. See also individual tribal names.

Industrial Workers of the World   A revolutionary union formed in 1905 by Big Bill HAYWOOD, Eugene V. DEBS, and socialist leader Daniel De Leon. Its leaders, who intended to unite all workers into "one big union," preached class warfare and called repeatedly for a general strike. The Wobblies, as the IWW was called, led major textile strikes in Massachusetts and New Jersey, but the organization was effectively shattered during World War I, when most of its leaders were imprisoned for resisting the war effort. See also Joe HILL.

Inge, William   (1913–73) Playwright. Born in Kansas, Inge specialized in carefully crafted, sensitive treatments of average midwesterners. His best plays were *Come Back, Little Sheba* (1950), the Pulitzer Prize *Picnic* (1953), and *Bus Stop* (1955), all three of which became successful films.

Inherit the Wind   See SCOPES TRIAL.

Internal Revenue Service   The federal government's tax-collection agency. Precursors were established in 1789 and 1862, but the current IRS dates from 1913, when the Sixteenth Amendment authorized an income tax. Payment of income tax is now governed by a complex code. Employers withhold part of each year's tax from workers' paychecks, and the balance, if any, must be mailed to the IRS each April 15—commonly, and grumblingly, known as tax day.

Intolerable Acts   Restrictions placed on the American colonies in 1774 as a punitive reaction to the BOSTON TEA PARTY. The British Parliament closed Boston harbor, limited town meetings, and provided for the quartering of troops in private homes. The colonial reaction was the formation of a Continental Congress, which intensified resistance and led to the DECLARATION OF INDEPENDENCE.

Invasion of the Body Snatchers   (1956) A horror film about mysterious "pod" creatures who infiltrate a small community and take over its residents' bodies. Directed by Don Siegel, it reflected common tropes of the vampire genre as well as hinting metaphorically at the insidious nature of "creeping communism." Leslie Halliwell called it "the most subtle film in the science-fiction cycle, with no visual horror whatever." It was remade in 1978.

Invisible Man   (1) As *The Invisible Man:* a 1933 film about a scientist going mad from the side effects of an "invisibility serum." Directed by James Whale from a story by H. G. Wells, it starred Claude Rains in his first movie role. (2) A 1952 novel by Ralph Ellison (1914–94) about the disillusionment of a naïve black southerner who comes to understand that he is "invisible" to white society. Winner of the National Book Award, it remains a landmark of African-American literature.

IOU   A promissory note. Short for "I owe you."

iron horse   (1) A Plains Indian term for the railroad, which was destroying their way of life by scattering the buffalo. (2) As *The Iron Horse:* the title of a John FORD motion picture (1924) about the building of the TRANSCONTINENTAL RAILROAD. (3) As Iron Horse: a nickname for Lou GEHRIG.

ironclads   See MONITOR AND MERRIMACK.

Iroquois League   Also called the Iroquois Confederacy, the Five Nations Confederacy, and (in the 1700s) the Six Nations Confederacy. It was a political alliance of related Indian peoples formed in the sixteenth century by the holy man Deganawidah with the assistance of the prophet Hiawatha. The original five members—the Cayuga, Oneida, Onondaga, Mohawk, and Seneca—were joined in 1722 by the Tuscarora, making the union a power as far west as the Mississippi River until its division, and subsequent decline, in the Revolutionary War. The democratic nature of the league's proceedings is said to have influenced the structure of the U.S. government.

IRS   See INTERNAL REVENUE SERVICE.

Irving, Washington   (1783–1859) Writer. The United States' first professional writer, Irving published a satirical *History of New York* (1809) under the name "Diedrich Knickerbocker" and achieved international fame a decade later as "Geoffrey Crayon." Crayon's *Sketch Book* (1819–20) contained essays and stories of the Hudson Valley, including Irving's best-known tales, "RIP VAN WINKLE" and "THE LEGEND OF SLEEPY HOLLOW." He also wrote lives of Christopher COLUMBUS and George WASHINGTON.

Ishmael   The hero-narrator of Melville's MOBY-DICK. The book's famous opening line is "Call me Ishmael."

It Girl   See Clara Bow.

It Happened One Night   (1934) One of the first and most famous SCREWBALL COMEDIES. The story of an unconventional romance between a flighty heiress and a poor reporter, it swept the Academy Awards, winning Oscars for best picture, best direction (Frank CAPRA), best screenplay (Robert Riskin), best actress (Claudette Colbert), and best actor (Clark GABLE). Forced to share a room together before they realize their affection for each other, the couple divides it with a blanket dubbed "the walls of Jericho"; at the end of the film, the makeshift wall comes tumbling down.

It's a Wonderful Life   (1946) A film directed by Frank CAPRA. It is the story of a small-town banker, George Bailey (James STEWART), who is about to kill himself when he is stopped by an angel. When the angel shows him how bleak the world would have been without him, he reconsiders and embraces his "wonderful life." The film's Christmas setting has made it a television favorite in that season.

"I've Been Working on the Railroad"   A traditional song from about the 1880s. The tune was adapted in 1903 for "The Eyes of Texas Are upon You."

I've Got a Secret   Television quiz show. Panelists interrogated guests in an attempt to guess secrets of which the audience was already aware. Moderated by Garry Moore and Steve Allen, it was among the longest-running quiz shows in TV history (1952–67).

Ives, Burl   (1909–   ) Folksinger, actor. Raised in rural Illinois, the "Wayfaring Stranger" learned traditional ballads from his grandmother and supplemented his folk-song repertoire by hitching around the country in the 1930s, listening to cowboys, lumbermen, and camp meeting singers. In New York from the 1940s, he developed his own radio show and performed on Broadway in the musical *Sing Out, Sweet Land*. His *Burl Ives Song Book* (1953) became a standard anthology during the FOLK REVIVAL. Ives's acting career, while less extensive, was equally distinguished. He created the part of domineering Big Daddy in the stage and screen versions of CAT ON A HOT TIN ROOF and won an Academy Award for his work in *The Big Country* (1958).

Ivory soap   A hand and bath soap produced by the Procter & Gamble Company since 1879. It is known for marketing slogans that successfully capitalized on its buoyancy and its purity: "It floats" and "99 and 44/100 percent pure."

Ivy League   A group of prestigious eastern schools linked by athletic competition and similar, sometimes cooperative, admissions procedures. The name refers to the ivy-covered buildings of older campuses. Members are Dartmouth College and the universities of Brown, Columbia, Cornell, HARVARD, Pennsylvania, PRINCETON, and YALE. See also SEVEN SISTERS.

Iwo Jima   A Japanese island dominated by a volcanic peak, Mount Suribachi. It was the site of a bloody battle in World War II, in which U.S. Marines suffered heavy losses before their victory. A photograph of Marines raising the American flag on Mount Suribachi inspired a statue now in Arlington National Cemetery.

IWW   See INDUSTRIAL WORKERS OF THE WORLD.

Jack Armstrong, the All-American Boy   An adventure series that dominated juvenile radio from 1933 to the end of the 1940s. Jack Armstrong, a student at Hudson High, picked up where Frank MERRIWELL had left off, tearing up the playing fields on his home turf and, increasingly, the forces of villainy in exotic locales. His frequent companions were Billy and Betty Fairchild and their uncle, industrialist Jim Fairfield, who provided a yacht and hydroplane in many of the episodes. Jim Harmon, author of *The Great Radio Heroes,* captures the hero's squeaky-clean enthusiasm in an excerpt from an early script. "When I think of this country of ours," Jack tells Billy, "with millions of homes stretching from sea to sea, and with everybody working and pulling together to have a nation where people can be free, and do big, fine things—why, it makes me realize what a terribly important job we've got ahead!" The series was the creation of Robert Hardy Andrews.

jackalope   A horned rabbit depicted on novelty postcards, especially in the West. A fanciful hybrid of jackrabbit and antelope.

Jackson, Andrew   (1767–1845) Soldier, president. Born in the Carolinas and trained in the law there, Jackson moved to Tennessee as a young man, served briefly as its first U.S. congressman, and was about to adopt the life of a gentleman planter when the WAR OF 1812 intervened. In that conflict he defeated the British-backed Creek Indians at Horseshoe Bend (1814) and became a national hero in the Battle of New Orleans (1815) by thwarting a British invasion of that city. Elected president in 1828, "Old Hickory" soon proved as tough in office as he had been in the field, resisting his fellow southerners' attempts to nullify tariff laws, destroying the Bank of the United States (a Philadelphia-based "moneyed monster"), and backing the removal of the FIVE CIVILIZED TRIBES to INDIAN TERRI-TORY. In support of the "common man," Jackson became so defiant of Congress (using the hitherto dormant veto twelve times) that his enemies dubbed him King Andrew I. He left office one of the most influential, if not universally loved, of American presidents. See JACKSONIAN DEMOCRACY; SPOILS SYSTEM.

Jackson, Helen Hunt   (1830–85) Writer. Jackson wrote two books highlighting the mistreatment of the American Indian. The first, the documentary *A Century of Dishonor* (1881), earned her a federal appointment to study the native peoples of California. Out of that study came *Ramona* (1884), a widely read romance of Indian life.

Jackson, Mahalia   (1911–72) Singer. The most famous GOSPEL MUSIC singer of her day, Jackson, a protégée of Thomas A. DORSEY, achieved international fame through her 1940s recordings. A traditionalist in approach to music that was becoming increasingly pop-oriented in the 1960s, she nevertheless made frequent television appearances in that decade.

Jackson, Michael   (1958–) Pop singer. Jackson performed as a child with his brothers (they were known as the Jackson Five), then began a solo career in the 1970s. His dance steps, including a signature "moon walk," and spirited vocals won him a huge following. His 1982 album *Thriller,* featuring "Beat It" and "Billie Jean," became the largest-selling record in music history. After plastic surgery and skin lightening altered his features, he drew considerable snickering and even larger audiences. Jackson's career slowed in the 1990s after child abuse allegations.

Jackson, Reggie   (1946–) Baseball player. One of the game's great power hitters, Reginald Martinez Jackson was known as Mr. October for his end-of-season performances. He helped the Oakland Athletics win three straight World Series (1972–74) and the New York Yankees two (1977–78). He retired in 1987 with a lifetime record of 563 home runs.

Jackson, Shirley   (1919–56) Writer. A master of "civilized horror," Jackson published her most famous story, "The Lottery," in *The New Yorker* in 1948. Her neo-gothic novels include *The Haunting of Hill House* (1959) and *We Have Always Lived in the Castle* (1962).

Jackson, Shoeless Joe   See BLACK SOX SCANDAL.

Jackson, Stonewall   (1824–63) Confederate General Thomas Jackson earned his nickname Stonewall at the first battle of BULL RUN, when his fellow general Barnard Bee, noting the solidity of his line, remarked, "There stands Jackson like a stone wall." Probably the South's most effective tactician, Jackson devastated Union troops for two years until, at the Battle of Chancellorsville (1863), he was accidentally killed by his own men. A deeply religious man, he was also known as Deacon Jackson.

Jacksonian democracy   A catchphrase for a broadening of the electorate that preceded and was associated with Andrew JACKSON's presidency. Detractors characterized this expansion—which benefited farmers and the middle class—as the debilitating rule of "King Mob." Its champions saw it as perfected democracy, that is, as the rule of all the people, not just the privileged. The "Age of Jackson" built the modern Democratic party, with its mass appeal and reliance on party loyalty. See also SPOILS SYSTEM.

"Jam on Gerry's Rock, The"   A Maine logger's ballad of the late nineteenth century. It tells of the death of several loggers, led by the young foreman Jack Monroe, in their attempt to break loose a massive logjam. Richard Dorson calls it "the lumberman's classic."

> *Come all of you bold shanty boys and hear as I relate*
> *Concerning a young riverman and his untimely fate;*
> *Concerning a young riverman so manly, true, and brave.*
> *'Twas on the jam at Gerry's Rock he met a watery grave*

jambalaya   (1) A dish of rice cooked with ham, sausage, or shellfish. Common in Louisiana, it was probably named after the French (*jambon*) or Spanish (*jamón*) for ham. John Mariani suggests a less cogent but more interesting etymology: A cook, Jean, is asked to "mix some things together." Since *balayer* means "to sweep" (or "sweep together"), what resulted was a "Jean Balayer." (2) "Jambalaya," the title of a 1952 song by Hank WILLIAMS, celebrating the conviviality of Cajun life.

James, Frank   See Jesse JAMES.

James, Henry   (1843–1916) Writer. James wrote meticulously crafted, psychologically penetrating stories and novels which made him revered by academics. Living in London for most of his life, he explored the inner life of Americans abroad in *The American* (1877), *Daisy Miller* (1879), *The Portrait of a Lady* (1881), and *The Ambassadors* (1903). His older brother was the psychologist William JAMES.

James, Jesse   (1847–82) Outlaw. After riding with QUANTRILL'S RAIDERS during the Civil War, Jesse Woodson James and his brother Frank (1843–1915) struck out on their own, robbing banks and trains in their native Missouri and bordering states. Joined by their cousins Cole and Bob Younger, the James gang became the country's most talked-about outlaws, pursued fiercely by railroad police and PINKERTON agents even as folklore turned them into Robin Hoods. Richard Dorson quotes a Missouri farmer in a typically romanticized assessment of the band's activities. "They didn't ever cause farmers any trouble. Mostly they robbed banks and railroads and express companies that had plenty of money."

Active throughout the early 1870s, the James boys endured an 1875 Pinkerton attack on their family home that left their half brother dead and their mother maimed. The following year, the gang was decimated in a robbery of a Northfield, Minnesota, bank, and the brothers, who eluded a posse, went into hiding. In 1882, Jesse was shot from behind by a turncoat gang member, Robert Ford, while living in St. Louis under the alias Howard. Frank survived him to be acquitted of his wrongdoing and to live a life that the *Dictionary of American Biography* called "in all respects honorable." Ford became the frontier's ultimate Judas figure, his deed vilified in a famous ballad that followed Jesse's death:

> *Jesse had a wife who mourned for his life;*
> *Three children, they were brave.*
> *But the dirty little coward who shot Mr. Howard*
> *Has laid Jesse James in his grave.*

The ballad was only the beginning. The figure of the ingenious, good-hearted bandit, forced into crime by bad luck and "society," also emerged in DIME NOVELS and Hollywood films. Of the many movies celebrating the James boys' exploits, the best were the 1939 *Jesse James,* with Tyrone POWER and Henry FONDA, and the 1957 *True Story of Jesse James,* with Robert Wagner and Jeffrey Hunter.

James, William   (1842–1910) Philosopher, psychologist. James was a Harvard University professor whose writings on the practical, functional nature of mental constructs contributed to the American "pragmatic" school. Rejecting the absolutist view of truth, he called the "ultimate test" of a given truth's meaning "the conduct it dictates or inspires.'' James wrote his generation's standard psychology text, *The Principles of Psychology* (1890), and explored religious sentiments in *The Varieties of Religious Experience* (1902). He also introduced the terms ''stream of consciousness'' and ''the bitch goddess success.''

Jamestown   The first permanent English settlement in North America. Founded in 1607 and named for King James I, it experienced severe hardships in its early years, especially during the ''starving time'' of 1609–10, but prospered under the leadership of Captain John SMITH. The English colonies' first representative assembly, the Virginia House of Burgesses, met there in 1619—the same year Jamestown received its first African slaves, brought in to harvest the TOBACCO crop. It was the capital of Virginia until 1699. See also POCAHONTAS; POWHATAN; John ROLFE.

Jane Doe   In law, a female party whose identity is unknown. The male equivalent is ''John Doe.''

Jap   (1) Since the 1890s, a disparaging contraction for ''Japanese.'' (2) For ''JAP,'' see JEWISH AMERICAN PRINCESS.

Jaws   (1974) A novel by Peter Benchley about a giant shark that ravages a vacation spot. After becoming a best-seller, it was made into a movie (1975) by Steven SPIELBERG. The movie generated three sequels, fostered a ''blockbuster'' mentality among Hollywood filmmakers, and has taken in over $125 million.

Jay, John   (1745–1829) The first chief justice of the United States (1789–95), Jay had been a reluctant revolutionary—believing that ''those who own the country ought to govern it''—but he warmed to the idea after the Declaration of Independence, and even presided over the Continental Congress for a year. As chief justice he negotiated a treaty with Great Britain (1794) that led to the evacuation of British forts in U.S. territory. Since it failed to protect U.S. ships from British inspection, however, it struck many Americans as conciliatory, and Jay was burned in effigy by several mobs.

Jaycees   A business and civic organization founded in St. Louis in 1915. The original title, of which ''Jaycees'' is a contraction, was the Junior Chamber of Commerce. Members must be under thirty-six years old and male.

Jayhawker   (1) Any of the antislavery irregulars who flocked to ''BLEEDING KANSAS'' in the 1850s. From the name of a mythical bird of prey. Hence (2) a resident of Kansas, whose nickname is the Jayhawk State.

Jay's Treaty   See John JAY.

jazz   An indigenous American music that emerged at the turn of the century from a mixture of African rhythms, BLUES structure, RAGTIME syncopation, and an unusually heavy reliance on improvisation. Its original home was New Orleans, and in particular the brothels and dance halls of the Storyville district, where pianist Jelly Roll MORTON and trumpeter King Oliver (Louis ARMSTRONG's mentor) got their starts. New Orleans jazzmen adapted the brass accompaniment patterns of black funeral bands to create a style that became known as Dixieland jazz. Picked up by white musicians, it became a universal dance music of the 1920s, with bandleaders Paul WHITEMAN and Fletcher Henderson laying the groundwork for the big band sound of the 1930s SWING MUSIC era.

The 1930s was the high-water mark of jazz's popularity, with Benny GOODMAN and Duke ELLINGTON in particular bringing sophisticated blends of solo and orchestra work to international audiences. The 1940s saw a retrenchment to smaller combos and more esoteric forms of expression by members of the innovative BEBOP and "progressive" schools. The loss of audience that this entailed was further aggravated by the ROCK MUSIC revolution. Since the 1960s, although it remains a musically rich and constantly evolving idiom, jazz has been increasingly a coterie passion.

Jazz Age   The 1920s. From the popularity of JAZZ music and its attendant attractions, drinking and dancing. F. Scott FITZGERALD's second collection of stories (1922) was entitled *Tales of the Jazz Age.*

Jazz Singer, The   (1927) A moving picture starring Al JOLSON as a cantor's son, Jakie Rabinowitz, who rejects his orthodox past to become a popular singer. Often called the first talking picture, it was actually the first to integrate sound (including snippets of dialogue) effectively into a story—and the first to command a sizable audience. Its success was due largely to Jolson himself, who was already a major star before its release and who amazed viewers (and listeners) with a sensitive performance. In paving the way for the first "all-talking" film, *Lights of New York* (1928), *The Jazz Singer* wrote an epitaph for the silent era. Its musical highlights were "Toot Toot Tootsie," Irving BERLIN's "Blue Skies," and Jolson's most famous song, "Mammy." It also included the actor's legendary phrase, "You ain't heard nothing yet."

Jean Sot (or Sotte)   A Louisiana version of the worldwide numbskull character, Jean Sot (French for "Foolish John") is a figure of fun in many CAJUN folktales. In one, he dives into a bayou to avoid getting wet in the rain. In another, told by his mother to *tire la vache,* he reads the wrong meaning into the ambivalent verb *tirer* and ends up shooting, rather than milking, the family cow.

"Jeanie with the Light Brown Hair"   A love song written (1854) by Stephen FOSTER.

jeans   See BLUE JEANS.

jeep   A four-wheel-drive, all-terrain vehicle designed for the U.S. Army in 1941. Small and versatile, it is used widely in the military and has gradually become more accepted in everyday use.

Jefferson, Blind Lemon   (ca. 1897–1930) Blues singer. Born in rural Texas, Jefferson was a successful country blues stylist in the 1920s, with his recordings extremely popular in the "race" market. His best-known song was probably "See That My Grave Is Kept Clean." He had a significant influence on other blues performers, including fellow Texan Lightnin' HOPKINS and B. B. KING.

Jefferson, Joseph   (1829–1905) Actor. The major comic actor of the nineteenth century, Jefferson began acting as a child and kept at it for over seventy years. Beginning in 1865, he became identified with one role, playing Rip Van Winkle for nearly forty years (see "RIP VAN WINKLE"). His annual tours elicited enormous affection nationwide. In the late nineteenth century, the *Dictionary of National Biography* says with understandable hyperbole, "Every child in America was taken to see *Rip* as part of its education."

Jefferson, Thomas (1743–1826) Writer, planter, president. Even if he had never served as president, the Virginian Jefferson would still be remembered as a major influence on the theory of STATES' RIGHTS and as the principal author of the DECLARATION OF INDEPENDENCE. That document he considered one of his three greatest achievements. The other two were Virginia's statute of religious freedom, which he wrote, and the University of Virginia, which he founded. He wanted these on his tombstone, and "not a word more."

The "more" was considerable. Jefferson was a member of the Continental Congress, minister to France, George WASHINGTON's secretary of state, author of the Kentucky Resolutions seeking to restrain federal power, a founder of the Democratic-Republican party (forerunner of the Democratic party), and—as that party's first president (1801–9)—initiator of the LOUISIANA PURCHASE. This is not counting such bagatelles as the designing of his family home, MONTICELLO, or the introduction into the country of French ice cream. The "Sage of Monticello" died on July 4, 1826—the fiftieth anniversary of the Declaration. See JEFFERSONIAN DEMOCRACY.

Jefferson Airplane   Rock band. The principal exponent of ACID rock, Jefferson Airplane was a San Francisco band that featured inventive, frequently jazzlike arrangements backing the searing, crystalline vocals of Grace Slick. Their major 1960s hits were "Somebody to Love" and "White Rabbit"—the latter banned by some radio stations as a "druggie" anthem. The band broke up shortly after performing at WOODSTOCK, although some of the members later re-formed as Jefferson Starship.

Jeffersonian democracy   The idea that American democracy would be best served by promoting the interests of small, yeoman farmers. The agricultural bias was named for Virginia planter Thomas JEFFERSON, who observed, "Those who labor in the earth are the chosen people of God."

Jeffries, James (1875–1953) Boxer. Heavyweight champion from 1899 to 1905, Jeffries popularized the defensive crouch and twice defeated Gentleman Jim CORBETT. Touted as the GREAT WHITE HOPE during a 1910 comeback, he was knocked out by Jack JOHNSON after fifteen rounds.

Jehovah's Witnesses   A Christian millenarian sect started in the 1870s by Charles T. RUSSELL. Witnesses believe in a fundamentalist reading of the Bible and the imminence of Armageddon and the Second Coming. Legal battles have been fought over their rejection of blood transfusion, flag saluting, and military service. To the general public they are best known as peripatetic evangelists, handing out Bible tracts and inspirational messages door-to-door.

Jell-O   A trade name for a gelatin dessert developed in the 1920s for what is now the General Foods company. A traditional "fun" dessert for children, it is also used in aspics and cubed in fruit cocktails.

Jemima See AUNT JEMIMA.

Jeopardy! A television QUIZ SHOW popular since 1974 in both daytime and prime-time versions. Contestants compete with each other for money prizes by guessing the question that goes with a given answer. For example, given the answer "He shot Lincoln," the correct question would be "Who was John Wilkes Booth?"

Jersey Devil Also called the Leeds Devil. A monster appearing in New Jersey legend and popular culture. Although historical "sightings" give it various forms, it is most often described as a demon, sporting leathery skin, claws, wings, and horns. The legend dates to 1735, when a woman known as Mother Leeds, already burdened with a large family, expressed the reckless wish that her next child be born a devil; it was, and immediately flew up the chimney. New Jersey history has been punctuated by recurrent Devil scares, the most extended being in 1909. The New Jersey Devils are a professional hockey team.

Jersey lightning Applejack brandy. From its distillation in the 1800s in New Jersey.

Jersey Lily See Judge Roy BEAN.

Jersey Shore The New Jersey coastline, known since the early nineteenth century as a beach resort area. Its major vacation draws were ATLANTIC CITY and Long Branch.

Jesus freak An insulting term for a religious Christian, especially one of fundamentalist views recently converted from a HIPPIE lifestyle. From the 1960s, when "Jesus people" were a counterculture splinter group.

Jewish Alps See BORSCHT BELT.

Jewish American Princess Abbreviated JAP. A wealthy young Jewish woman, used to being pampered and attended to. The term is used, with light disparagement, by Jews themselves as well as Gentiles. Leo Rosten relates a typical JAP joke. "What do JAPs usually make for dinner?" "Reservations."

Jewish penicillin Chicken soup. From its allegedly curative properties.

JFK John F. KENNEDY.

Jim Crow (1) The stage name of "Daddy" Thomas RICE, from his theme song, "Jump Jim Crow." Hence (2) a name for African Americans in general. (3) As "Jim Crow laws"; restrictive statues passed in the 1890s that established a six-decade pattern of southern segregation. See PLESSY V. FERGUSON.

Jiminy Cricket A cricket who serves as PINOCCHIO's conscience in the Walt DISNEY movie about the puppet.

"Jingle Bells" (1857) A winter season song by J. S. Pierpont. It was popularized in the 1940s by Bing CROSBY and the Andrews Sisters.

Jingle bells, jingle bells, jingle all the way.
Oh what fun it is to ride in a one-horse open sleigh.

jitterbug A ballroom dance involving fast footwork, turns, and acrobatics. A product of the 1930s SWING MUSIC craze, it bridged the generations into the era of ROCK MUSIC.

Joad, Tom The hero of THE GRAPES OF WRATH. Woody GUTHRIE wrote a ballad in his honor.

Joe An average person, nobody special. The name appears in numerous expressions indicating ordinariness: Joe Blow, Joe Doakes, Joe Schmo, Joe Six-pack, Joe Zilch, a good Joe, an ordinary Joe, and—in World War II—G.I. Joe. "Joe College" has a somewhat different flavor, suggesting the ostensibly more distinguished manner of the undergraduate. See also Joe CHRISTMAS; Joe MAGARAC; PALOOKA.

John Like JOE, "John" often serves as a code word for averageness, as in John Q. Public, John Q. Citizen, and John Doe. Frank CAPRA had the latter sense in mind in his study of the "average guy," *Meet John Doe.* But it also has more specific senses. In law, a John Doe is a party whose name is unknown; Jane Doe is the female equivalent. A John Hancock or a John Henry is a signature. John Law is an old term for a policeman. Johnny-come-lately indicates a recent arrival—a social upstart or parvenu. A stage-door Johnny is one who frequents the stage entrance of a theater hoping to secure an actress's attention.

John, Old See OLD JOHN AND OLD MASTER.

"John Brown's Body" (1) A folk song on the martyrdom of abolitionist John BROWN. Taken up as a marching song by Union troops in the Civil War, it was gradually supplanted by "THE BATTLE HYMN OF THE REPUBLIC," which was set to the same old religious melody. (2) A narrative poem (1928) on the Civil War by Stephen Vincent BENÉT. It depicts the conflict in a series of vivid tableaus.

John Brown's body lies amouldering in the grave;
His truth goes marching on.

John Henry See John HENRY.

"John Jacob Jingleheimer Schmidt" A traditional nonsense song popular especially in children's summer camps.

John Jacob Jingleheimer Schmidt,
That's my name too.
Whenever we go out, the people always shout,
"There goes John Jacob Jingleheimer Schmidt!"

Johnny Appleseed See Johnny APPLESEED.

johnny cake A flat cornmeal bread eaten widely, especially in New England, from the early eighteenth century. A precursor of the pancake, it was probably named originally "journey" cake from its ease of preparation on the trail.

Johnny-come-lately   See JOHN.

Johnny Reb   A Confederate soldier. From REBEL.

Johnson, Jack   (1878–1946) Boxer. The first black heavyweight champion, Johnson outraged racist society not only by his skill in the ring but by his flashy lifestyle and marriages to white women. Among the GREAT WHITE HOPES put forward to humiliate him were Jim JEFFRIES, whom he defeated in 1910, and Jess Willard, who knocked him out five years later. In a Broadway play (1966) and a film (1970) entitled *The Great White Hope,* Johnson was portrayed by actor James Earl Jones.

Johnson, James Weldon   (1871–1938) Writer, civil rights leader. The first black admitted to the Florida bar, Johnson served the Theodore ROOSEVELT administration in Latin American consular posts before moving to HARLEM to work with the NAACP; he was its executive secretary throughout the 1920s. Johnson edited a pioneering anthology of black writers' work (1922), published several volumes of verse including *God's Trombones* (1927), and produced lyrics for popular songs. The best known of these was "LIFT EVERY VOICE AND SING."

Johnson, Lyndon Baines   (1908–73) Senate majority leader from 1955 to 1961 and vice president from 1961 to 1963, the brash, politically astute Texan LBJ became president on the death of John F. KENNEDY. As president he pushed forward a landmark package of social legislation as part of his promise to implement a "GREAT SOCIETY." The VIETNAM WAR, however, destroyed his popularity, and he withdrew from the reelection race in 1968.

Johnson, Magic   (1959–   ) Basketball player. Second in career steals (1,698) and first in assists (9,921), Earvin Johnson was the spectacular mainspring of the Los Angeles Lakers in the 1980s. Discovery that he had contracted the HIV virus forced him into early retirement in 1993. He was three times the NBA's most valuable player.

Johnson, Robert   (1911–38) Blues singer, songwriter. A strong influence on both blues and rock 'n' roll singers, Delta-born Johnson wrote "Crossroads," "Terraplane Blues," "Dust My Broom," "Hellhound on My Trail," "Come on in My Kitchen," and "Love in Vain." His short life was restless and violent. Rumor said he had learned to play guitar through a pact with the devil and that he had died after being poisoned by a jealous lover.

Johnson, Walter   (1887–1946) Baseball player. As a pitcher for the Washington Senators, Johnson earned the nickname Big Train for a fastball many consider the best in baseball history. His career tally of 416 games won is second behind Cy YOUNG's, and his 113 shutouts are a major league record. In a twenty-year career (1907–27), he struck out 3,509 batters.

Johnstown flood   A devastating flood caused by the rupture of a dam at Johnstown, Pennsylvania, on May 31, 1889. One of North America's worst disasters, it caused the loss of 2,200 lives—four times the toll of the SAN FRANCISCO EARTHQUAKE.

Joker, the BATMAN's principal adversary. So named because of his "fiendishly clever" criminal tricks.

"Jolie Blon' " An old CAJUN tune brought to the wider country music market in the 1940s by Louisiana-born musician Harry Choates. The title means "Pretty Blonde." It is a standard among contemporary Cajun bands.

Jolliet, Louis See MARQUETTE AND JOLLIET.

Jolson, Al (1886–1950) Singer. Born in Russia, Asa Yoelson came to the United States around 1895, worked in minstrel shows and vaudeville, and won major acclaim in the Broadway revue *La Belle Paree* (1911), where he used the minstrel-style blackface that became his trademark. Aside from the songs popularized in his most famous film, THE JAZZ SINGER, he was also associated with "California, Here I Come" and "April Showers." He dubbed the singing for *The Jolson Story,* a 1946 film starring Larry Parks.

Jonathan See BROTHER JONATHAN.

Jonathan Livingston Seagull (1970) A short work of inspirational fiction by Richard Bach, expressing the lessons of a seagull seeking happiness. It was one of the major best-sellers of the 1970s.

Jones, Bobby (1902–71) Golfer. A world-class golfer who never surrendered his amateur status, Jones had a relatively short (fourteen years) but spectacular career, winning nearly half of the major tournaments he entered. He retired in 1930 after achieving golf's first and only "grand slam," winning that year's Amateur and Open contests in the United States and Great Britain. He helped to design the Augusta, Georgia, golf course that since 1934 has hosted the Masters Tournament.

Jones, Casey (d. 1900) Irish-American railroading legend, immortalized for recklessness. Born John Luther Jones, he took the nickname Casey from his hometown of Cayce, Kentucky, and as an engineer on the Illinois Central distinguished himself for resourcefulness, bravado, and a signature whistle moan. Driving his Cannonball Express into Vaughn, Mississippi, one April night, he miscalculated a sidetrack clearing distance, saw a wreck coming, ordered his fireman to jump, and died at the controls—one hand on the brake, the other on the whistle cord. A memorial ballad written by his friend Wallace Saunders, a black engine wiper, quickly entered the folksong canon; the GRATEFUL DEAD's "Casey Jones" (1973) refracted the legend.

Jones, George (1931–) Country singer, songwriter. Known both as a single performer and as the sometime husband and singing partner of Tammy WYNETTE, Jones worked in the 1950s out of his native Texas, touring frequently with his band, the Jones Boys. In 1962, he had two Top 10 songs, "Aching, Breaking Heart" and "She Thinks I Still Care." In Nashville after 1970, he battled alcoholism and financial setbacks to emerge as one of country music's most durable stars. His "He Stopped Loving Her Today" (1980) was the Grammy and Country Music Association song of the year.

Jones, Grandpa (1913–) Country performer. Kentucky-born Louis Marshall Jones became "Grandpa" as part of his act when he was twenty-three. He was then performing, chiefly as a banjo player, on Chicago's NATIONAL BARN DANCE radio show. He graduated to the GRAND OLE OPRY in 1946 and remained one of its most colorful figures for over forty years. With his whiskers, high boots, and driving banjo, he was also a staple on the television show HEE HAW. He became affectionately known as Everybody's Grandpa.

Jones, Indiana See INDIANA JONES.

Jones, James See FROM HERE TO ETERNITY.

Jones, John Paul (1747–92) Naval hero of the American Revolution. Scottish-born John Paul adopted the name Jones in 1773 after fleeing the British navy for having killed a mutinous sailor. Successful as a privateer in the Continental Navy, he was given command of a converted merchant vessel he called the BONHOMME RICHARD; on September 23, 1779, he sailed it against the heavily armed British *Serapis* to the most famous American naval victory of the war (see "I HAVE NOT YET BEGUN TO FIGHT"). After the war Jones served in the Russian navy, then retired to Paris from 1790 until his death.

Jones, LeRoi See Imamu Amiri BARAKA.

Jones, Mother (1830–1930) Labor activist. Born in Ireland, Mary Harris came to the United States as a child, married an ironworker, George Jones, lost her entire family in an 1867 yellow fever epidemic, and in the 1870s turned her attention to labor work. First as a member of the KNIGHTS OF LABOR and then as a wandering organizer, she galvanized workers for fifty years with her eloquent speeches. The radical magazine *Mother Jones* was named for her.

Jones, Spike (1911–64) Bandleader. Jones, originally a drummer, headed the City Slickers, a novelty orchestra of the 1940s and 1950s. Their ingenious cacophony was displayed in such spoofs as the wartime hit "Der Führer's Face."

Joneses See KEEPING UP WITH THE JONESES.

Jonestown A religious commune based briefly in Guyana which became the site of a tragic mass suicide. Commune members were followers of revivalist preacher Jim Jones (1931–78), who had established the San Francisco–based People's Temple in 1971 and become increasingly involved in city politics as well as religion. Claiming persecution at the hands of the press, Jones left for Guyana in 1977 to establish "Jonestown" with several hundred followers. When a California congressman flew to the commune to investigate charges that Temple members were being held prisoner, he and accompanying reporters were killed. Afterward, Jones himself committed suicide, demanding that his flock do the same. Some willingly and some under pressure drank poison. The final death toll was over nine hundred.

Joplin, Janis (1942–69) Texas-born white blues singer whose impassioned performances and Dionysian lifestyle galvanized her generation even as they anticipated her early death from an overdose of heroin. Her hits included "Piece of

My Heart,'' "Try (Just a Little Bit Harder),'' and a soulful cover of writer Kris Kristofferson's "Me and Bobby McGee.''

Joplin, Scott   (1868–1917) The most famous exponent of RAGTIME music, black composer Joplin was born in Texas, made a modest fortune from "Maple Leaf Rag'' (1899) and other hits, produced a rag opera, *Tremonisha,* and died two years later in a New York mental hospital. His complex, jaunty piano pieces enjoyed a revival in the 1970s after they provided a score for the Hollywood movie *The Sting* (1973).

Jordan, Michael   (1963–   ) Basketball player. Averaging over 32 points per game, Jordan was the most consistently high scorer in the history of professional basketball. His graceful, soaring baskets made "Air Jordan'' a familiar catchphrase to fans of the Chicago Bulls. Following a seven-year streak (1986–93) as NBA scoring champion, he retired in 1993, shortly after the murder of his father.

Joseph, Chief   (ca. 1840–1904) Nez Percé leader. In June of 1877, after decades of accepting white encroachment on their lands, the Nez Percé Indians of Oregon and Idaho finally ran out of patience, and a group of young men killed several settlers. For the next three months Chief Joseph led his band—150 warriors and about 550 women and children—on a 1,600-mile retreat across the Bitterroot Mountains, besting the Army in several battles along the way. When he was finally caught just a few miles from the Canadian border, his people had dwindled to just over 400, and he gave up with an eloquent surrender speech:

My people ask me for food, and I have none to give. It is cold, and we have no blankets, no wood. My people are starving to death. Where is my little daughter? I do not know. Perhaps, even now, she is freezing to death. Hear me, my chiefs. I have fought. But from where the sun now stands, I will fight no more forever.

Joseph's surrender in effect ended Indian resistance in the Northwest, and he and his people were sent to reservations. A soldier who witnessed the event wrote later, "I think that, in his long career, Joseph cannot accuse the government of the United States of one single act of justice.''

josh   See Josh BILLINGS.

Joy of Cooking   A cookbook written in 1931 by Irma Rombauer and Marion Rombauer Becker. A steady seller for over sixty years, it has elicited a number of nonculinary, copycat titles, notably an erotic manual, *The Joy of Sex,* and a study of language, *The Joy of Lex.*

Judson, Edward Z. C.   See Ned BUNTLINE.

jug band   A band that plays traditional blues or folk music with inexpensive or makeshift instruments such as washboards, washtub basses, spoons, harmonicas, and jugs: The latter serve to resonate the voice and provide a bass line.

juke   "Juke,'' from a West African word meaning "wicked,'' originally meant to make the rounds of brothels and bars. "Jukeboxes,'' for playing records, appeared in the 1930s; among the first places to install them were bars called juke joints. See HONKY-TONK.

Jukes family   A cover name for a family of evidently "congenital" criminals discovered by prison investigator Richard Dugdale in 1874. Dugdale's findings, published in *The Jukes: A Study in Crime, Pauperism, and Heredity* (1884), were alleged to prove the genetic base of "criminal traits." Later research has questioned the validity of his conclusions. See also KALLIKAKS.

Jumbo   A six-and-a-half-ton elephant bought from the London Zoo in 1881 to be a featured attraction of the Barnum & Bailey Circus. Hence "jumbo" for anything exceptionally large. See P. T. BARNUM.

Juneteenth   June 19. A Texas holiday celebrating the emancipation of the state's slaves. Traditionally observed with barbecues and parades, it commemorates June 19, 1865, when a Union general told Galveston slaves that they were free. See also EMANCIPATION PROCLAMATION.

Jungle, The   A 1906 novel by Upton SINCLAIR exposing the abuse of immigrant laborers in the Chicago stockyards. Sinclair's exposé of working conditions also called attention to meatpacking practices that were so unsanitary as to call for immediate reform; this came in the form of the Pure Food and Drug Act (1906). "I aimed at the public's heart," the author said of his best-seller, "and hit it in the stomach."

Jungle Jim   The "white hunter" hero of a series of African adventure films beginning with *Jungle Jim* (1948). Basically vehicles for Johnny WEISMULLER to recapture his fading TARZAN image, they led to a television series in the 1950s.

junk   (1) Anything worthless or trashy. Hence (2) narcotics, especially heroin. "Junkie" is a slang term for a drug addict, although it is applied by extension to other "addictions": One may speak of a "TV junkie" or "chocolate junkie."

junk food   Food that is high in calories but low in nutrition. Usually used to refer to snacks popular with the young: potato chips, pizza, soda.

junk mail   Unsolicited third-class mail such as advertisements. Junk mail is typically addressed to "Resident" or "Occupant."

"Just the facts, ma'am"   See DRAGNET.

"Just whistle"   See TO HAVE AND HAVE NOT.

K rations   The uniform food packets issued to U.S. servicemen in World War II. The nutritionally balanced rations were named for their designer, physiologist Ancel Keys (1904–   ).

kachina   Among the Hopi and other Southwest Indians, kachinas are supernatural beings who visit the earth during the winter season and spend the rest of the year in the spirit realm. Identified with the ancestors of the Indian people, they are represented in various rituals by masked figures whose dances ensure rainfall and the growth of crops. Indian children are often presented with carved kachina dolls, and in many pueblos the spirits figure in initiation ceremonies.

Kallikaks   Pseudonym of a degenerate family described by psychologist Henry Goddard in two studies of feeblemindedness in the 1910s. Like earlier studies of the JUKES FAMILY, they stressed the genetic factor in such clusters of abnormality.

Kane, Charles Foster   See CITIZEN KANE.

Kangaroo, Captain   See CAPTAIN KANGAROO.

Kansas-Nebraska Act   (1854) A congressional act establishing the territories of Kansas and Nebraska and stipulating that the presence of slavery within them should be decided on the basis of "popular sovereignty," that is, the expressed wishes of their inhabitants. Proposed by Stephen A. DOUGLAS as a compromise between slaveholders and abolitionists, the act was expected to result in a free Nebraska and slave Kansas; the actual results included "BLEEDING KANSAS" and the exacerbation of the slavery issue.

Karloff, Boris   (1887–1969) Actor. British-born stage actor William Henry Pratt played in dozens of silent films before achieving success as the Monster in James Whale's classic horror film FRANKENSTEIN (1931). For the rest of his career, Karloff rang changes off that role, playing not only updated versions of the Frankenstein character but other horror creatures, including *The Mummy* (1932), *The Ghoul* (1933), *The Body Snatcher* (1945), and Jekyll/Hyde (in 1953's *Abbott and Costello Meet Dr. Jekyll and Mr. Hyde*). Karloff and Bela LUGOSI, with whom he was often paired, became what Ephraim Katz calls "the most formidable duo of the macabre in film history."

Karsh, Yousuf   (1908–   ) The Turkish-born Canadian photographer Yousuf Karsh used high-contrast lighting and stark backdrops to create memorable portraits of famous people. Among the notable Americans who posed for him were opera singer Marian Anderson, painter Georgia O'KEEFE, and Ernest HEMINGWAY.

Katzenjammer Kids A comic strip created by Rudolph Dirks in 1897. The protagonists were a pair of mischievous youngsters, Fritz and Hans Katzenjammer, whose shenanigans were the constant torment of their parents. The family name Katzenjammer means "hangover." The strip gave us the expression "on the fritz."

Kaufman and Hart Playwrights George S. Kaufman (1889–1961) and Moss Hart (1904–61) were the most distinguished writing team of the 1930s. The best known of their witty plays, both successfully filmed, were YOU CAN'T TAKE IT WITH YOU and THE MAN WHO CAME TO DINNER. Kaufman also collaborated with Edna FERBER and Ring LARDNER and contributed to the book for George and Ira GERSHWIN'S musical OF THEE I SING (1932). Hart won a Tony Award for his 1957 direction of MY FAIR LADY; his autobiography, *Act One* (1959), was a best-seller.

Kay Kyser's Kollege of Musical Knowledge A radio contest show (1938–49) that featured the comic and musical talents of the "Old Perfesser" Kay Kyser (1906–85), a bandleader who awarded cash prizes for the answers to "brainbuster" questions. The Kyser band toured widely in the 1940s and was especially popular with American G.I.s. Its sidemen included novelty singer Ish Kabibble and dialect expert Dean Forman.

Kazan, Elia (1909–) Director. A cofounder of the Actors' Studio (1947), which introduced "Method" acting to American theatergoers, Turkish-born Elia Kazan (originally Kazanjoglou) made his mark on Broadway with A STREETCAR NAMED DESIRE (1947) and DEATH OF A SALESMAN (1949) and in Hollywood with progressive dramas about discrimination: *Gentleman's Agreement* (1947), about anti-Semitism, and *Pinky* (1949), about racial intolerance. His lasting impact on American film, however, came in his discovery and development of two major stars. He introduced the Actors' Studio's most famous graduate, Marlon BRANDO, in *Streetcar* and later directed him in *Viva Zapata!* (1952) and ON THE WATERFRONT. In 1955, he shaped the Oscar-nominated performance of James DEAN in that actor's first starring role, in EAST OF EDEN.

kazoo A musical instrument consisting of a hollow tube containing a hole across which is stretched a resonating membrane. It gives a buzzing tone to the voice when sung into. A child's toy from the 1880s, it is also used by JUG BANDS and other informal groups.

Keaton, Buster (1895–66) Actor, writer, director. One of the giants of the silent screen, Joseph Francis Keaton began in vaudeville as a child, then entered films in 1917 as a bit player in Fatty ARBUCKLE shorts. His own first feature was *The Saphead* (1920). It was followed by a string of slapstick masterpieces in which Keaton, with a characteristic determined deadpan, fenced nimbly with a world of vengeful objects. Films that made him second only to Charlie CHAPLIN in popularity included the shorts *One Week* (1920) and *The Boat* (1921) and the features *The Navigator* (1924) and *The General* (1927). His comic impassivity earned him the nickname the Great Stone Face.

keelboats Shallow-draft riverboats, propelled by poling, rowing, or towing, used for freight-hauling in the Mississippi River region from the end of the eighteenth century to about 1820, when steamboat traffic made them obsolete. The lives of rowdy keelboatmen provided much grist for the mills of American legendry. The most famous of their number was Mike FINK.

Keeler, Ruby   (1909–93) Remembered as the star of Busby BERKELEY musicals, Keeler prepared for her "all singing, all dancing" fame by doing chorus work for George M. COHAN and Florenz Ziegfeld (see ZIEGFELD FOLLIES). She was married from 1928 to 1940 to Al JOLSON.

keeping up with the Joneses   Remaining competitively consumerist and middle-class. The phrase was originally the title of a comic strip drawn by "Pop" Momand from 1913 to 1931. He tried out, and rejected, the title "Keeping Up with the Smiths."

Keith circuit   See VAUDEVILLE.

Keller, Helen   (1880–1968) Although blind and deaf from early childhood, Keller graduated with honors from Radcliffe College and became an internationally known lecturer and author promoting better understanding of the disabled. Her indebtedness to an extraordinary teacher, Anne Sullivan, was recorded in William Gibson's Pulitzer Prize play *The Miracle Worker* (1959); the film version (1962) won Patty Duke, as young Helen, an Academy Award. Keller's autobiography, *The Story of My Life,* appeared in 1903.

Kellogg's Corn Flakes   The most successful BREAKFAST CEREAL in history. It was the invention of Will K. Kellogg (1860–1951), whose brother John directed the health-conscious Battle Creek Sanitarium. In 1906, Will founded the Battle Creek Toasted Corn Flake Company, which grew into today's giant Kellogg's.

Kelly, Emmett   (1898–1979) America's most famous circus clown, Kelly created the hobo character Weary Willie, whose sad-eyed countenance brought smiles to millions in the 1940s and 1950s. Kelly worked for the Ringling Brothers circus and was a frequent guest on television and in films.

Kelly, Gene   (1912–) Dancer, singer, actor. In the 1940s, Kelly's athletic, modernistic dance style gradually replaced the ballroom elegance of the previous decade, and he became Hollywood's heir apparent to Fred ASTAIRE. His dancing and choreography shone in *Anchors Aweigh* (1945), for which he received an Academy Award nomination; in *On the Town* (1949) and SINGIN' IN THE RAIN, both of which he codirected with Stanley Donen; and in AN AMERICAN IN PARIS.

Kelly, Grace   (1928–82) Actress. A serene, polished Philadelphian, Kelly became a star as Gary COOPER's wife in HIGH NOON, won an Oscar for her work in the following year's *The Country Girl*, and became Alfred HITCHCOCK's favorite ice queen of the 1950s in the thrillers *Dial M for Murder* (1954), *Rear Window* (1954), and *To Catch a Thief* (1955). After her last film, *High Society* (1956), she married Prince Rainier of Monaco in one of the most photographed weddings of the century, then left Hollywood for regal retirement as "Princess Grace." The jet-setting antics of her daughters Caroline and Stephanie kept her in the public eye, thanks to the tabloids, until her death. She was killed in an automobile accident on a Monaco roadway.

Kelly, Machine Gun (1895–1954) George Kelly gained national attention in the early 1930s through his use of a machine gun in a series of Midwest robberies. In the fall of 1933, after kidnapping an Oklahoma millionaire, he was captured by the FBI and imprisoned for life.

Kelly, Shanghai See SHANGHAI.

Kelly, Shipwreck (1893–1952) The most famous "flagpole sitter" of the Roaring Twenties, Alvin Kelly acquired his nickname from his sailing days and international fame from his flagpole stunts. His record for remaining aloft, forty-nine days, inspired a wave of less intrepid perchers.

Kelly, Walt See POGO.

Kemo Sabe TONTO's pet name for the Lone Ranger. It is supposed to be "Indian" for "faithful friend." The derivation is unknown, although it has been suggested that it is a Spanish pun, from *Quién sabe?*, for "Who knows?" See also THE LONE RANGER.

Ken doll See BARBIE DOLL.

Kennedy, John F. (1917–63) President. After sparking a patriotic awakening in the early 1960s with his bright personality and call to social commitment, young John F. Kennedy became a martyr in Dallas, Texas, where he was shot to death. During his presidency (1960–63), he established the PEACE CORPS, approved an invasion of Cuba (the Bay of Pigs fiasco), turned back Soviet missiles from that island in the harrowing Missile Crisis of 1962, and committed the first ground forces to Vietnam. The checkered success of his "New Frontier" administration, however, was more than offset in the popular mind by the "Kennedy style" and by the graciousness of his wife, Jacqueline Bouvier. "Jack and Jackie" became the unofficial monarchs of an American "Camelot."

JFK's assassination generated almost as much print as his presidency itself. The government's WARREN COMMISSION determined that the lone assassin had been a Cuban and Soviet sympathizer, Lee Harvey OSWALD, but numerous investigators questioned that conclusion, and a virtual cottage industry developed in conspiracy theories. Almost thirty years after his death, filmmaker Oliver Stone earned a best picture Oscar nomination for *JFK* (1991), a docudrama attack on the Warren report—prompting renewed musings that the truth of Dallas had yet to be revealed.

A Massachusetts Democrat, JFK was the son of financier Joseph P. Kennedy, head of the Securities and Exchange Commission under Franklin D. ROOSEVELT. He and his wife, Rose, produced not only John but also Robert and Edward "Teddy" Kennedy. Bobby served as Jack's attorney general and was, like his brother, assassinated—during a 1968 run for the presidency. Teddy became a liberal power in the U.S. Senate.

Kensington runestone A 200-pound slab of inscribed rock discovered near Kensington, Minnesota, in 1898. The inscription, carved in runes, describes a Norse expedition to the area in 1362. Its authenticity as a Norse artifact is uncertain.

Kent, Clark See SUPERMAN.

Kentucky and Virginia Resolutions (1798–99) State legislative resolutions written respectively by Thomas JEFFERSON and James MADISON to counter the Alien and Sedition Acts (1798), which the Federalist government had passed to inhibit political opposition. A major expression of STATES' RIGHTS theory, they called for the NULLIFICATION by state governments of the federal law.

Kentucky colonel One afforded an honorary colonel's rank by the state of Kentucky. Such "commissions" were common enough by the late 1800s to make the phrase connote a façade of prestige; the broader "Southern colonel" has the same implication. The Kentucky colonel has been widely adopted as a trademark, notably by whiskey companies (see BOURBON) and by the Kentucky Fried Chicken restaurant chain, whose driving force was "Colonel" Harlan Sanders (1890–1980).

Kentucky Derby The most prestigious, and lucrative, horse race in the United States. The so-called run for the roses is held on the first Saturday of May at Churchill Downs racetrack in Louisville, Kentucky. It was first run in 1875.

Kermit the Frog See MUPPETS.

Kern, Jerome (1885–1945) Songwriter. One of the creators of the musical play, as distinct from the plotless revue, Kern started as a song plugger in a New York department store, so successfully plugged his own work that by 1915 he had songs in seven Broadway shows, and reached the peak of his creative energy in 1927, with the landmark musical *Show Boat* (see SHOWBOAT [2]). From that show came the standards "Bill" and "Ol' Man River." Kern also wrote "The Way You Look Tonight" and "Smoke Gets in Your Eyes."

Kerouac, Jack (1922–69) Writer. The main BEAT GENERATION novelist, Kerouac helped to define that movement with *On the Road* (1957), a celebration of picaresque freedom. Less famous novels were *Dharma Bums* (1958) and *Big Sur* (1962). His unedited, "spontaneous" prose style elicited a famous barb from fellow novelist Truman Capote: "That's not writing; that's typing." Kerouac claimed he had invented "Beat" as a contraction of "beatific."

Kesey, Ken (1935–) Novelist. Kesey became famous for his first work, *One Flew Over the Cuckoo's Nest* (1962), a novel about a psychiatric ward which was made into a 1975 film. He was also known for *Sometimes a Great Notion* (1964) and for touring the country with a gaggle of LSD devotees, the Merry Pranksters, whose antics were memorialized in Tom WOLFE's 1968 book *The Electric Kool-Aid Acid Test*.

ketchup Also spelled "catsup." A thick tomato sauce used as a dressing, especially for beef. The name comes from the Chinese *ke tsiap*, for pickled fish, and the original ketchups, made at home in the nineteenth century, were marinades of various fruits and vegetables. In 1876 "pickle king" Henry J. Heinz introduced a sugar-sweetened, tomato-based ketchup that overtook all others as the American standard.

Kettle, Ma and Pa   See Ma and Pa Kettle.

Kewpie doll   A child's doll manufactured since 1913 and modeled on figures created by Rose O'Neill (1874–1944). She accompanied a 1909 poem in *Ladies Home Journal* with a drawing of a "Cupidlike" creature, explaining "Kewpie means a small Cupid, just as puppy means a small dog." Inexpensive Kewpies appear as carnival prizes.

Key, Francis Scott   See "Star-Spangled Banner."

Keystone Kops   Bungling, pratfall-prone policemen who starred in a series of silent comedies of the Keystone Company. Their fruitless chases and general incompetence were recurrent themes in the film company's antic productions. See also Mack Sennett.

Kidd, Captain   See Captain Kidd.

Killers, The   (1927) One of Ernest Hemingway's "Nick Adams" stories. It deals with the effects on young Nick of his overhearing the violent plans of a pair of gangsters. The story was filmed twice. Robert Siodmak's 1946 version was actor Burt Lancaster's first film; Don Siegel's 1964 remake was Ronald Reagan's last.

Kilmer, Joyce   (1886–1918) Poet. The author of several gripping war poems, Kilmer was better known as the creator of "Trees." Aside from *Trees and Other Poems* (1914), he published two other poetry collections before dying on a French battlefield in World War I.

"Kilroy was here"   A slogan, usually accompanied by a drawing of a face looking over a wall, which became a ubiquitous graffito during World War II: it was spotted on surfaces as ostensibly inaccessible as the Statue of Liberty's torch. The originator is not certain, but the most likely candidate was Massachusetts ship inspector James J. Kilroy, who made his signature the equivalent of an inspection sticker.

King, the   Popular nickname for (1) Clark Gable (2) Elvis Presley, and (3) Richard Petty. See also Nat "King" Cole.

King, B. B.   (1925–) Blues musician. The most influential of living blues guitarists, Riley B. King was a disc jockey on a Memphis radio station in the 1950s, billing himself as the "Beale Street Blues Boy." As Blues Boy and then B. B., King built a following through local club performances and in 1951 had a national R&B hit, "Three O'Clock Blues." In the 1960s he had a major impact on both black and white blues bands, and he hit the pop charts with his 1970 single "The Thrill Is Gone."

King, Billie Jean   (1943–) Tennis player. The leading female player of the late 1960s and early 1970s, King captured a record twenty Wimbledon titles, was ranked first in the world four times, and was twice voted female athlete of the year. A vocal spokesperson for women's sports, she was the first woman athlete to earn more than $100,000 a year. In 1971, in a hoopla-rich grudge match, she beat former champion Bobby Riggs in a "Battle of the Sexes."

King, Martin Luther, Jr. (1929–68) Civil rights leader. A Baptist minister and dynamic orator, King led the southern desegregation movement from the mid-1950s until his death. Beginning with a boycott of the Montgomery, Alabama, segregated bus lines, he gradually widened his scope to encompass voter registration, attacks on institutionalized (rather than merely legal) discrimination, and resistance to the VIETNAM WAR. His influence peaked in the summer of 1963, when he organized a massive march on Washington to "subpoena the conscience of the nation"; there he delivered his "I HAVE A DREAM" address. The following year he won the Nobel Peace Prize. In 1968, while in Memphis to support a sanitation workers' strike, King was shot to death on a motel balcony by James Earl Ray. Ghetto riots erupted almost immediately, and the nonviolent movement he had led quickly splintered. His birthday, January 15, is an official holiday in most states.

King, Stephen (1947–) Novelist. King's first successful book, *Carrie* (1974), described an unpopular student's gruesome revenge on her high school tormentors. It introduced his interest in the macabre and a narrative skill that has made him the contemporary equivalent of Edgar Allen POE: an undisputed master of psychological horror. Among his other best-sellers—all successfully filmed—are *The Shining* (1977), *The Stand* (1978), *The Dead Zone* (1979), *Firestarter* (1980), and *Misery* (1987).

King Cotton   See COTTON.

King Kong (1933) A classic monster film by Merian C. Cooper. Kong is a giant ape who is brought from his jungle habitat to New York City, where his attraction to a young woman (Fay Wray) sends him on a rampage and eventually to his death. The "Beauty and the Beast" plot was enhanced by special effects that were startling in their day, including Kong's holding the wriggling girl in his palm, his battle with a giant serpent, and his scaling of the Empire State Building—then the tallest building in the world. In an extravagant 1976 remake, Jessica Lange played the beast's inamorata, and in his fateful ascent, he climbed the World Trade Center.

King of the Cowboys   See (1) Gene AUTRY and (2) Roy ROGERS.

King Philip's War (1675–76) A brief but bloody war between the New England colonists and Wampanoag Indians under the leadership of Metacomet, or "King Philip." The son of Massasoit, who had made peace with the Pilgrims in 1621, Metacomet envisioned a vast Indian alliance that would drive the English into the sea. His warriors wreaked havoc throughout the settlements until he was killed in 1676 and the vision died.

King Ranch   A huge cattle spread in southern Texas founded by livestock baron Richard King (1825–85). At its peak in the late nineteenth century, the ranch contained 100,000 head of cattle and covered a half million acres over five counties.

> *The sun's done riz and the sun's done set*
> *And I ain't offen the King Ranch yet.*

See also XIT RANCH.

Kingfish See (1) AMOS 'N' ANDY and (2) Huey LONG.

King's College The original name (1754) of Columbia University. Named for the grantor of its royal charter, George II, it was renamed Columbia College in 1784. See also QUEEN'S COLLEGE.

Kingston Trio A perky singing group of the 1950s and 1960s that rode the FOLK REVIVAL to fame with the traditional murder ballad "TOM DOOLEY" (1958) and the war protest song "Where Have All the Flowers Gone?" (1962). They named themselves after Kingston, Jamaica, a center of CALYPSO MUSIC.

Kinsey reports Pioneering "sexology" reports that generated widespread discussion of sexual practices—and attendant controversy—in the 1950s. Indiana zoologist Alfred C. Kinsey (1894–1956) headed the research teams that published *Sexual Behavior in the Human Male* (1948) and *Sexual Behavior in the Human Female* (1953)—the latter volume appearing in the same year as the inaugural issue of PLAYBOY magazine. The reports were an early sign of a "sexual revolution."

Kiss Me Kate (1948) A musical comedy based on Shakespeare's *The Taming of the Shrew*. Cole PORTER's most successful musical, it contained his songs "Wunderbar," "So in Love," and "Always True to You in My Fashion." It was filmed in 1953 by director George Sidney.

"Kiss me, my fool" See Theda BARA.

kitchen cabinet A group of unofficial advisers to President Andrew JACKSON. His legal cabinet did not enjoy his confidence, and he relied heavily on the counsel of "kitchen" friends.

Kitty Hawk A North Carolina beach that was the site of the first powered airplane flight. See WRIGHT BROTHERS.

Kiwanis A business and community service organization founded in Detroit in 1914. Membership is now worldwide. The name is allegedly an "Indian" word translated variously as "We trade," "We make ourselves known," or "We make noise."

KKK See KU KLUX KLAN.

Kleenex A brand name of the Kimberly-Clark Corporation for its "disposable handkerchiefs," sold since the 1920s. Originally called Celluwipes and pushed as makeup removers, they were remarketed with their current slant in the 1930s. Like COKE and BAND-AID, the name has come to be used generically.

Klondike A barren region in Canada's Yukon territory, site of the last great GOLD RUSH of the nineteenth century. After gold was discovered near the Yukon River in 1896, roughly thirty thousand fortune hunters trooped into the area. The boom lasted until just after the turn of the century. The flurry of fortune-hunting activity provided material for Jack LONDON and Robert W. SERVICE.

Knickerbocker Diedrich Knickerbocker was the pseudonym taken by Washington IRVING in his 1809 *History of New York*. The association of the Dutch name with the state led to "Knickerbocker" as a synonym for "New Yorker." It also became the name of the ball club that gave us the modern form of BASEBALL, a New York City professional basketball team (the Knicks), a New York State-brewed beer, and the short, gathered pants better known as knickers.

Knievel, Evel   (1938–   ) Motorcycle trick rider. Originally a ski jumper and hockey player, Robert Craig Knievel gained fame in the 1960s by performing ramp-launched motorcycle jumps over rows of cars. His most extravagant stunt, which was unsuccessful, was an attempted leap in a rocket-powered cycle over Idaho's Snake River Canyon.

Knights of Columbus   A Roman Catholic fraternal organization founded in New Haven, Connecticut, in 1882. Now international, the group provides financial support for members' families as well as furthering charitable, educational, and patriotic endeavors.

Knights of Labor   A labor union founded in 1869. Open to workers regardless of race or level of skill, it grew rapidly under the leadership of Terence Powderly (1849–1924), and by 1886 had 700,000 members. In that year, the HAYMARKET RIOT dealt a severe blow to all employee activists, especially the Knights, who had led the movement for an eight-hour day. They were gradually overshadowed by Samuel GOMPERS's AFL.

knock knock jokes   Children's riddle-style jokes that follow a five-line question-and-answer formula, with the final answer often a pun on a preliminary hint.

> *"Knock knock."*
> *"Who's there?"*
> *"Madam."*
> *"Madam who?"*
> *"My damn foot's caught in the door."*

Knots Landing   A nighttime SOAP OPERA of the 1980s. A spin-off of *Dallas* (see DALLAS [2]), it premiered in 1979 and concerned the public and private lives of middle-class couples in the Southern California town of Knots Landing.

Know-Nothing party   A popular term for the nativist American party, which reviled immigrants, especially Catholics, in the 1850s. The name Know Nothing was a reflection of members' secrecy. Their greatest influence came in the 1856 election, when their presidential candidate, Millard Fillmore, received one-fifth of the vote.

Knox, George   (ca. 1862–92) A legendary lumberjack of the Maine woods, credited locally with prodigious feats of strength. Although he was a real person (unlike Paul BUNYAN), his stories were often imbued with a sense of the magical. In some, he is a giant with two sets of teeth. In others, he moves boulders by putting them in his mouth and spitting them out of the way. By folk consensus, he was in league with the devil—the ultimate source of his extraordinary powers.

Knox, Fort   See FORT KNOX.

Kodak   A brand name of the Eastman Kodak Company, based in Rochester, New York, and founded in 1892 by George EASTMAN. He coined the term "Kodak" for marketing purposes, believing (correctly, as it turned out) that it would be easy to pronounce and spell in any language. The original Kodak box camera (1888) transformed leisure, and the aesthetic sense, for millions of Americans. Sold for $25, it came complete with enough film for one hundred pictures. Customers shipped the film, box and all, for developing in Rochester, and the company shipped it back, with a new roll ready, for an additional fee. The process exemplified Eastman's winning slogan: "You press the button. We do the rest."

Kojak   Television series. A realistic police drama set in New York City and starring Telly Savalas as Lieutenant Theo Kojak. The show was a prime-time favorite in the 1970s for its realistic stories and Savalas's trademark shticks: a lollipop and the rhetorical smirk "Who loves ya, baby?"

Kool-Aid   A brand name for a noncarbonated soft drink invented in 1927 and sold since 1953 by General Foods. Sold in powder form and mixed with water, it is produced in a variety of fruit flavors. A 1960s vogue for LSD-laced Kool-Aid is reflected in the title of Tom WOLFE's book *The Electric Kool-Aid Acid Test* (1968). The drink was also reputedly used at JONESTOWN to mask the poison administered to Jim Jones's followers. In summer camp slang, Kool-Aid or similar fruit drinks are known as bug juice.

Korean War   (1950–53) A United Nations "police action" fought predominantly by U.S. troops. In 1948, Korea was divided at the 38th parallel into a communist North and a pro-Western South. Two years later, when the North invaded the South, the U.N. put General Douglas MACARTHUR in charge of a multinational defense force. MacArthur pushed the Soviet-backed North Koreans across the 38th parallel and toward the Yalu River, the border between Korea and China. Chinese threats of retaliation raised the specter of nuclear war, and President TRUMAN ordered MacArthur to hold his ground. With his customary disregard for chain of command, he pushed ever closer to the Yalu until, in November of 1950, the Chinese sent 200,000 troops to check his advance. In the spring of 1951, after MacArthur voiced his criticism of presidential policy, Truman finally removed him from command, and Matthew Ridgway assumed the U.N. leadership.

The war ended in a deadlock two years later, with the North-South boundary set at almost exactly the same place it had been before the outbreak of hostilities. This first real firestorm of the COLD WAR devastated the Korean countryside, cost millions of civilian lives, and resulted in roughly 23,000 American deaths. It also gave us "brainwashing," for intimidating indoctrination—a technique that the communists had used on U.S. prisoners.

Kosciuszko, Tadeusz   (1746–1817) A Polish army officer and engineer, Kosciuszko fought on the American side in the Revolutionary War, providing fortifications at West Point and Saratoga. He later led his own country in a failed revolt against Russian domination. His will, executed by Thomas JEFFERSON, provided money to free and educate American slaves.

Koufax, Sandy (1935–   ) Baseball player. The most effective pitcher of the 1960s, Koufax won the Cy Young Award three times and helped win two World Series for the Los Angeles Dodgers. Before arthritis cut short his career, he led the National League five years straight in earned-run averages. In 1971, he became the Baseball Hall of Fame's youngest inductee.

Kowalski, Stanley   See A STREETCAR NAMED DESIRE.

Krazy Kat   A cartoon character created in 1911 by George Herriman (1880–1944) as part of his *New York Journal* feature *The Dingbat Family*. The protagonist of his own strip by 1913, Krazy Kat was a lovesick feline whose inamorata, Ignatz Mouse, returned his affections by pelting him with bricks; Officer Pupp was a perenially frustrated mediator. The trio appeared in strips and films for thirty years.

kryptonite   A green, rocklike substance whose radiation is the only thing that can kill SUPERMAN. The name comes from his home planet Krypton, which exploded into pieces of kryptonite just after he escaped from it. He can be protected from the lethal rays by barriers of lead.

Ku Klux Klan   The Ku Klux Klan is a white supremacist organization that was founded in Tennessee in 1866 with the express intention of intimidating southern blacks. Fearful of black power under Reconstruction, Klan members in ghostlike robes and hoods rode down on "uppity" blacks in the dead of night, beating and lynching many for imagined crimes. The Klan's "Invisible Empire" spread throughout the South until an 1871 civil rights act outlawed its activities. Dormant for a generation, it was reborn after the turn of the century, with an expanded charter that denounced Catholics and Jews as well as blacks. At its peak in the 1920s, this second Klan had over 4 million members. A third incarnation accompanied a national swing to the right in the 1980s; this "new Klan" played down the KKK's violent past, arguing that separation of the races was part of God's plan.

The Klan has always been as well known for its pseudomystical folklore as for its politics. The organization's name itself came from the Greek word *kyklos*, for circle, and this esotericism was heavily overlaid with other "mysteries," such as the admonitory burning of giant crosses and the use of various idiolect coinages. A Grand Dragon leader, for example, is also called a Kleagle (for "Klan" plus "eagle"), while a local chapter is called a Klavern (for "Klan" plus "cavern").

Kubrick, Stanley (1928–   ) A film director known for social cynicism and a meticulous attention to detail. His first major film, *Paths of Glory* (1957), explored the incompetence of the military hierarchy in World War I. He was equally successful—and controversial—with the Roman epic *Spartacus* (1960), an adaptation of Vladimir Nabokov's novel *Lolita* (1962), DR. STRANGELOVE, 2001, and the nightmarish *A Clockwork Orange* (1971).

Kukla, Fran, and Ollie   A children's television show of the 1950s. It starred the hand puppets Kukla (Russian for "doll") and Ollie (short for Oliver J. Dragon) as well as their human companion, actress Fran Allison. Burr Tillstrom designed the puppets and provided their voices.

Kwakiutl   A group of related Indian peoples who lived as gatherers and coastal fishermen in British Columbia. Studied in depth by Franz Boas (1858–1942) and other anthropologists, they were known for skillful wood carvings (including TOTEM POLES), secret societies, and the periodic destruction of private wealth in the potlatch ceremony.

Kyser, Kay   See KAY KYSER'S KOLLEGE OF MUSICAL KNOWLEDGE.

L.A. See Los Angeles.

Labor Day The first Monday in September, since 1894 a national holiday honoring workers. Congressional approval followed a decade of lobbying by the Knights of Labor, who in 1882 had sponsored a parade in New York City that took ten thousand workers off their jobs for a day. Labor Day signals the unofficial end of summer and the beginning of the school year.

lacrosse A soccerlike game in which teams maneuver a ball toward their respective goals by passing it from player to player with netted sticks. Invented by native peoples of the Northeast, it was originally called baggataway; French settlers called it lacrosse from the resemblance of the playing stick to a bishop's crosier (*la crosse*). Its inventors played with hundreds of men on a side; today's collegiate teams are set at ten.

Lady and the Tramp See Dogs.

Lady Day See Billie Holiday.

Lafayette, Marquis de (1757–1834) A French army captain who became a Continental general and a hero of the American Revolution. A close friend of George Washington, he earned the nickname the Soldier's Friend by sharing the troops' privations at Valley Forge; was instrumental in securing French support for the American cause; and commanded ably at Brandywine and Yorktown. Made a U.S. citizen in 1784, he participated as a moderate in the French Revolution and made a successful tour of the United States in 1824. His Paris grave was covered with earth from Bunker Hill.

"Lafayette, we are here" The most famous line of a speech delivered on July 4, 1917, at the Paris tomb of the Marquis de Lafayette. It signified U.S. entry into World War I and the symbolic repayment of a debt to France. Usually attributed to American Expeditionary Force commander John J. Pershing, the words were actually spoken by a junior officer, Charles E. Stanton.

Lafayette Escadrille A group of American pilots who flew volunteer fighter missions for France between April 1916 and February 1918, when they were absorbed by the U.S. military. Many members of the squadron were socially prominent, and their service was followed raptly by the American press.

Lafitte, Jean (ca. 1780–1826) Known as the Pirate of the Gulf, Lafitte was actually less a buccaneer than a middleman. In the early 1800s he ran a smuggling operation from a stronghold on Grand Terre Island, fencing the wares of seagoing bandits in nearby New Orleans. Holding letters of marque from the port of Cartagena, he styled himself a privateer rather than a pirate, and once killed a man for denying the distinction. In Frank Dobie's summation, Lafitte was "an energetic and efficient business man" with a "gift for making phrases" and "a conscience as elastic as any politician could wish for."

That elasticity—combined with a hatred of the British navy, which was impeding his business—made him offer his services to Andrew JACKSON at the Battle of New Orleans (1815). Jackson, who had no respect for Lafitte's "hellish banditti," accepted out of necessity; the battle was won; and President Madison pardoned the banditti as a reward. Soon afterward, Lafitte returned to his predations, working out of Galveston Island, until the American navy ran him out in 1821. As "Lord of Galveston Island," he owned a red house, the Maison Rouge, which legend said had been built with the help of the devil. Other legends place his buried treasure at numerous spots along the Gulf Coast. In Louisiana until quite recently, a paunchy man might be greeted with the gibe "What you hiding there, *mon ami*, Lafitte's treasure?"

La Follette, Robert   (1855–1925) Politician. A liberal Republican, "Fighting Bob" La Follette served three terms as governor of Wisconsin (1901–6), breaking with party bosses to push for the direct primary, tax reform, and regulation of railroads. After leaving the governorship, he spent almost twenty years in the U.S. Senate, where his eloquence on behalf of farmers and labor made him the Progressive party presidential candidate in 1924. He received 5 million votes in that election.

La Guardia, Fiorello   (1882–1947) Politician. Affectionately known as the Little Flower, La Guardia served several terms in the U.S. Congress before being elected mayor of New York City in 1933. In his long tenure there (he served until 1945), he pushed through a diverse reform package that addressed problems of health, housing, transportation, corruption, and crime. During a 1937 newspaper strike, he charmed the city's children by reading them the Sunday COMICS over the radio. New York's La Guardia Airport is named for him.

La Salle, Sieur de   (1643–87) Explorer. Between 1679 and 1682, Robert Cavelier, Sieur de La Salle, explored the Great Lakes and the entire length of the Mississippi River from its headwaters near Lake Michigan to its mouth in the Gulf. Claiming the river valley for France, he named it Louisiana in honor of Louis XIV, who authorized a second expedition in 1685. On this second journey, La Salle was murdered by his crew.

lame duck   A public official who has lost a reelection bid (or who is legally prevented from running again) and whose remaining time in office is thus seen as ineffectual. Before passage of the Twentieth Amendment (1933), presidential lame ducks faced four months of such "lame" time; the amendment shortened the period by about six weeks.

L'Amour, Louis   (1908–88) Writer. Born in rural North Dakota, L'Amour spent his youth drifting through the West, picking up frontier and Indian lore from old-timers and supporting himself briefly as a boxer. Between the 1940s and his death, he wrote hundreds of stories and nearly ninety novels, surpassing even

Zane GREY as a master of western fiction. His books featured rugged, faintly romantic heroes and a wealth of well-researched historical detail. Among the best known of his books—many of which sold over a million copies—were *Hondo* (1953), *The Silver Canyon* (1956), and *Shakalo* (1963).

Lancaster, Burt   (1913–) Actor. A former acrobat, Lancaster played robust leading men in a variety of roles beginning with the 1946 THE KILLERS. He was Jim THORPE in *Jim Thorpe—All-American* (1951), Wyatt EARP in *Gunfight at the O.K. Corral* (1957), and prisoner Robert Stroud in *The Birdman of Alcatraz* (1962). He won an Oscar for the title role in ELMER GANTRY and the New York Film Critics' best actor award for FROM HERE TO ETERNITY.

Land of Enchantment   State nickname of New Mexico.

Land of Lincoln   An unofficial nickname for Illinois, from which Abraham LINCOLN launched his political career.

Land of Opportunity   State nickname of Arkansas.

Landers, Ann   See "DEAR ABBY."

Lane, Lois   See SUPERMAN.

Lange, Dorothea   (1895–1965) One of several photographers hired by the FARM SECURITY ADMINISTRATION to document the bleak 1930s, Lange concentrated on California's migrant workers. Her portrait of a gaunt, impoverished housewife, *The Migrant Mother,* is among the best known of all Depression images. With her husband, Paul Taylor, she also produced the 1939 report *An American Exodus.*

Langtry, Lily   See Roy BEAN.

Lantz, Walter   See WOODY WOODPECKER.

Lardner, Ring   (1885–1933) Writer. Originally a Chicago sportswriter, Ring-gold Wilmer Lardner achieved fame in 1916 with *You Know Me, Al,* a volume of stories written in the form of letters from a bush league baseball player. Lardner's affection for common people, his ear for vernacular speech, and his cynicism are also evident in *Gullible's Travels* (1917) and *The Love Nest* (1926).

Las Casas, Bartolomé de   (1474–1566) Missionary. The "Apostle of the Indies," Las Casas was a Dominican priest who defended the rights of native Americans under Spanish rule. Working in Central America and Venezuela, he convinced the crown to outlaw forced Indian labor and wrote influential, graphic histories of the Spanish conquest. He was probably the first priest to be ordained in the New World.

Las Vegas   The largest city in Nevada and the United States's most popular gambling resort. Since the rise of casino hotels in the 1940s, "Vegas" has been a byword for extravagant entertainment, with a Vegas booking the epitome of popular success. Neon-laced nightclub strips, celebrities, showgirls, and the availability of instant marriages all contribute to the garish site's appeal. The name *Las Vegas* is Spanish for "the meadows."

Lassie The canine star of a long-running television series suggested by Eric Knight's best-selling novel *Lassie Come Home* (1940). A friendly, intelligent collie, Lassie rescued her human owners from weekly predicaments from 1954 to 1971. A juvenile synonym for collie is "Lassie dog."

Last of the Mohicans, The (1826) The second volume of the LEATHERSTOCKING TALES.

Latrobe, Benjamin Henry (1764–1820) The United State's first professional architect, Latrobe popularized the Greek Revival style. He was best known for the Baltimore Cathedral (1804–18) and for his rebuilding of the U.S. Capitol after it had been burned by the British during the WAR OF 1812.

Latter-Day Saints See MORMONS.

Laurel and Hardy The most successful comedy team in Hollywood history, Stan Laurel (1890–1965) and Oliver Hardy (1892–1957) starred in dozens of shorts and features for the Hal ROACH studios between 1926 and 1940. Masters of slapstick, they typically played a pair of endearing bunglers, with the lanky, lachrymose Laurel the ideal foil to the obese Hardy, spluttering in exasperation as he lamented, "That's another fine mess you've gotten us into." The team's features included *Babes in Toyland* (1934), *Way out West* (1937), and *A Chump at Oxford* (1940).

Law West of the Pecos See Roy BEAN.

Lazarus, Emma (1849–87) A New York-born translator, essayist, and poet, Lazarus is remembered for her sonnet "The New Colossus" (1883), which is inscribed on the base of the STATUE OF LIBERTY. It ends with this famous welcome:

Give me your tired, your poor,
Your huddled masses yearning to breathe free,
The wretched refuse of your teeming shore.
Send these, the homeless, tempest-tossed, to me.
I lift my lamp beside the golden door!

LBJ See Lyndon Baines JOHNSON.

Leadbelly (1888–1949) Folksinger. Born Huddie Ledbetter in Louisiana, Leadbelly spent his youth drifting along the Gulf Coast, singing folk blues to the accompaniment of twelve-string guitar. Jailed intermittently for violent crimes, he sang himself out of prison twice, from Texas and Louisiana penitentiaries. His release the second time, in 1934, was arranged by folk-song scholar John LOMAX, who transformed him into a national celebrity by recording his songs and setting up concert tours. A tall, powerful man, he earned his nickname as a tireless worker on black prison gangs, whose hollers and work songs strongly affected his style.

Leadbelly's repertoire included much traditional material, such as "JOHN HENRY," "Take This Hammer," and "EASY RIDER," but he also wrote a number of original tunes that made him a hero during the FOLK REVIVAL. These included the antisegregationist "Bourgeois Blues," the prison lament "Midnight Special," and his signature tune, "GOOD NIGHT IRENE." He died in New York of Lou GEHRIG's disease.

Leary, Timothy   (1920–   ) A Harvard University psychologist, Leary lost his job in 1963 after conducting experiments with psychotropic drugs. Soon thereafter he became a COUNTERCULTURE hero for his promotion of LSD as a "cerebral vitamin." In 1966 he founded the League for Spiritual Discovery, dedicated to "the ancient sacred sequence of turning on, tuning in, and dropping out." Among his books were *The Politics of Ecstasy* and *High Priest* (both 1968).

leatherneck   Nickname for a U.S. Marine. From the leather collars of enlisted men's uniforms, first seen in the WAR OF 1812.

Leatherstocking Tales   The magnum opus of writer James Fenimore COOPER, a quintet of novels that follows frontiersman Natty BUMPPO from his youth in the eastern forests to his death on the Plains. In order of publication, the novels were *The Pioneers* (1823), *The Last of the Mohicans* (1826), *The Prairie* (1827), *The Pathfinder* (1840), and *The Deerslayer* (1841).

Leave It to Beaver   A television sitcom (1957–63) starring Jerry Mathers as Theodore "Beaver" Cleaver, the young son of suburban couple Ward and June. To a cynical later generation, their pleasantly humdrum lives made them, like OZZIE AND HARRIET, the epitome of bourgeois conventionality. See BABBITT.

Leaves of Grass   Walt WHITMAN's first and most famous book of poems. Originally published as a slim volume in 1855, it was expanded continuously by the poet throughout his lifetime, the final (1892) version containing hundreds of poems. Among the most famous are "SONG OF MYSELF," "I Hear America Singing," and a tribute to Abraham LINCOLN, "O CAPTAIN! MY CAPTAIN!"

Lee, Ann   See SHAKERS.

Lee, Bruce   (1941–73) Actor, martial artist. After playing sidekick Kato in the 1960s television series THE GREEN HORNET, Lee achieved international cult stardom in a string of Hong Kong action movies that highlighted his idiosyncratic, pyrotechnical fighting style. The best of these, *Enter the Dragon,* was finished in 1973, the same year that the young Chinese-American star suddenly died. Death only enhanced his reputation, and low-budget karate movies of the 1970s were filled with Bruce Lee look-alikes called Li and Le. His career helped to make oriental martial arts an increasingly common feature of action films.

Lee, Gypsy Rose   (1914–70) Stripper. Rose Louise Hovick was born in Seattle, toured on vaudeville with her mother and sister at the age of four, and learned her titillating art in Kansas City from veteran performer Tessie the Tassel Twirler. Blending erotic suggestiveness with a studied refinement, she became the most famous stripper in U.S. history, playing bawdy clubs as well as the ZIEGFELD FOLLIES. Her 1957 autobiography, *Gypsy,* was the basis for a Broadway musical (1959) and a feature film (1962). See also LITTLE EGYPT, Sally RAND.

Lee, Harper   See TO KILL A MOCKINGBIRD.

Lee, Robert E.   (1807–70) Confederate general during the Civil War. Lee remains as revered in the South as any figure in history, as much for the dignity with which he bore defeat as for his expertise in battle. Born into a famous Virginia family (his father was a cavalry commander in the Revolution), Lee graduated second in his class at West Point (1829), served three years as his alma mater's superintendent (1852–55), and led the U.S. Marines who captured abolitionist John BROWN. At the outbreak of the Civil War, he was offered command of the Union Army, but in spite of his opposition to both slavery and secession, he refused, assuming instead command of his fellow Virginians.

As head of the Army of Northern Virginia, Lee led his troops ably against the North for two years, until the Confederacy's disastrous reversal at the Battle of GETTYSBURG. The South fought on for two more years, until Lee—by then the symbolic leader of the cause—surrendered to U.S. GRANT at APPOMATTOX COURTHOUSE. Worshipped by his men for his gentle dignity, Lee was also widely admired as a military commander. Winston Churchill was not alone in judging him ''one of the greatest captains known to the annals of war.''

"Legend of Sleepy Hollow, The"   (1819) A Halloween tale by Washington IRVING, set in the Hudson River Valley near Tarrytown, New York. Spindly, shy schoolteacher Ichabod Crane courts the beautiful Katrina Van Tassel until a rival, posing as a headless horseman, frightens him out of town. A cartoon version, narrated by Bing CROSBY, was a seasonal staple on the Walt DISNEY television shows.

Legree, Simon   The villain of UNCLE TOM'S CABIN. A northern-born plantation overseer, he flogs Uncle Tom so fiercely that he dies. The name has become a byword for brutal authority.

Leif Ericsson   (fl. 1000) Viking explorer. The son of Norse chieftain Eric the Red, Leif the Lucky grew up in Greenland, was converted to Christianity in Norway, and around 1000 made an ocean voyage to VINLAND. This is generally acknowledged to have been in the vicinity of Newfoundland, making Leif the first European discoverer of North America.

Lemonade Lucy   Nickname for Lucy Hayes, Rutherford B. Hayes's first lady. From her ban on alcoholic beverages in the White House.

Lenni Lenape   See DELAWARE.

Leopold and Loeb   Self-styled geniuses who were infatuated with the philosophy of Frederick Nietzsche, Chicago teenagers Nathan Leopold and Richard Loeb kidnapped and murdered their neighbor Bobby Franks in May 1924 as grisly proof of their status as ''supermen.'' Circumstantial evidence led to their confessions, and they were tried for having committed the ''crime of the century.'' Defender Clarence DARROW's eloquence got them life imprisonment.

Lerner and Loewe   Lyricist Alan Jay Lerner (1918–86) and composer Frederick Loewe (1904–88) were a musical comedy writing team. Their major theater successes were *Brigadoon* (1947), MY FAIR LADY, and *Camelot* (1960). Lerner also wrote the screenplays for two best picture films, AN AMERICAN IN PARIS and *Gigi* (1958). The title song of the latter film earned the writing team a separate Oscar.

LeRoy, Baby   See BABY LEROY.

Leslie, Frank   (1821–80) Publisher. Born Henry Carter in England, he took ''Frank Leslie'' as an illustrator's pen name while working for newspapers in London. In New York he started *Frank Leslie's Illustrated Newspaper* (1855), which featured lavish engravings of news events and was extremely successful during the Civil War. See also HARPER'S.

Leutze, Emanuel   (1816–68) A German-born artist known for the historical painting GEORGE WASHINGTON CROSSING THE DELAWARE. The U.S. Capitol contains his vast mural *Westward the Course of Empire Takes Its Way* (1862).

Levi's   See BLUE JEANS.

Levittown   A low-income tract housing development built on Long Island, near New York City, in 1947–51. Designed by contractor William Levitt, it became a prototype for the postwar building boom, which featured sprawling neighborhoods of virtually indistinguishable homes. Levitt himself built two other suburban towns (Levittown, New Jersey, and Levittown, Pennsylvania), and thousands of other developers followed suit.

Lewis, Jerry   See MARTIN AND LEWIS.

Lewis, Jerry Lee   (1935–   ) Singer, pianist. With a raw, screeching vocal style and stage antics that rivaled Elvis PRESLEY's, Louisiana-born Lewis, known as the Killer, became a top star of early rock 'n' roll. The unconventionality that characterized his performances (he was given to leaping on his piano and playing it with his feet) also found its way into his personal life, causing him trouble with drink and with his several wives. The most famous of these was his thirteen-year-old cousin Myra Gale Brown. Before their 1957 marriage, Lewis had topped the charts with ''Whole Lotta Shaking Goin' On,'' ''Great Balls of Fire,'' and ''Breathless.'' The child bride scandal derailed his career for a decade, but he made a comeback as a country singer in the 1970s.

Lewis, Sinclair   (1885–1951) Novelist. Minnesota-born Lewis skewered the complacency and materialism of American life in a series of best-selling novels in the 1920s. *Main Street* (1920), which made his reputation, portrayed the sterility of a small midwestern town. BABBITT was a pessimistic biography of a middle-class booster. *Arrowsmith* (1925), which charted the personal and professional trials of an idealistic doctor, earned Lewis a Pulitzer Prize, which he refused. ELMER GANTRY was a disillusioned study of 1920s revivalism. Lewis was the first American to win the Nobel Prize (1930) for literature.

Lewis and Clark Expedition   In 1803, President Thomas JEFFERSON commissioned his private secretary, Meriwether Lewis (1774–1809), to explore the recently acquired LOUISIANA PURCHASE. With army officer William Clark (1770–1838) as co-commander, Lewis led a party on a two-year journey (1804–6) from St. Louis to the Pacific Ocean and back again. Although they failed to find the NORTHWEST PASSAGE that Jefferson had hoped for, Lewis and Clark gathered enormous amounts of information about the new territory and helped to foster a romantic vision of the American West. The epic journey was filmed as *The Far Horizons* (1955), with Fred MacMurray as Lewis and Charlton HESTON as Clark. See also SACAJAWEA.

Lexington and Concord   Massachusetts towns where American colonists, facing British troops on April 19, 1775, fired the first shots of the Revolution. Ordered to seize munitions from a Concord supply depot, the redcoats advanced on the spot but were resisted first at Lexington, where the MINUTEMEN lost eight dead, and then at Concord's North Bridge, where they drove the British regulars back to Boston. The dual skirmishes marshaled support for the colonial cause; that June the Continental Congress authorized an army. The fighting also had an impact on popular literature. Longfellow's poem ''PAUL REVERE'S RIDE'' celebrates the April 18 warning of the Massachusetts countryside, while Emerson's ''Concord Hymn'' celebrates the battle (see CONCORD).

Liberace   (1919–87) Pianist. ''Lee'' Liberace, born Wladziu Valentino Liberace, was a flamboyant television personality whose musical skills were overshadowed, or rather oversparkled, by his appearance. With a hundred-watt smile, a bouffant hairdo, garishly expensive suits, and an ever-present candelabra on his piano, he made the classical repertoire an object of campy delight. With an orchestra led by his violinist brother, George, he headlined on several television shows in the 1950s and 1960s, then turned to the Las Vegas circuit and personal appearances.

Liberty Bell   A one-ton iron bell, cast in London in 1752, which hung originally in the tower of INDEPENDENCE HALL and is now kept in a special pavilion on that site. Inscribed with the biblical quotation ''Proclaim Liberty throughout all the Land,'' it is said to have been rung to announce, among other things, the battles of LEXINGTON AND CONCORD, the DECLARATION OF INDEPENDENCE, and the YORKTOWN surrender. The bell's distinguishing feature, a massive crack acquired in 1835, when it tolled out the death of John MARSHALL, makes it musically dysfunctional, although this defect has hardly marred its symbolic appeal.

Liberty Bonds   Government bonds sold during World War I to finance the military effort. Silent film stars were heavily involved in promoting them, and John Philip SOUSA wrote a ''Liberty Bond March.''

liberty cabbage   Sauerkraut. An anti-German euphemism during World War I. Stuart Berg Flexner notes that in the same period German measles became ''liberty measles'' and German shepherds became ''Alsatians.''

Liberty Enlightening the World   The official name of the STATUE OF LIBERTY.

Liberty Line   See UNDERGROUND RAILROAD.

Library of Congress   The national library of the United States. Created in 1800, it was originally housed in the Capitol, moving to its own building in 1897. It contains, at least in theory, a copy of every book printed in the United States.

Lichtenstein, Roy   (1923–) Painter. One of the most famous pop artists of the 1960s, Lichtenstein specialized in boldly colored enlargements of comic strip panels. Like Andy WARHOL'S soup cans, they were taken as ironic comments on popular culture. See also POP ART.

Life   The nation's premier photo journal from the 1930s through the 1960s. Originally a satirical magazine, it acquired its photographic eminence under publisher Henry LUCE, who purchased it in 1935 and whose staff photographers included Robert Capa and Margaret Bourke-White. *Life* went out of business in 1972 and was reborn, under new editors, six years later.

life of Riley   (1) A life of ease and material comfort. From entertainer Pat Rooney's 1883 hit "Is That Mr. Reilly?" The narrator, Terrence O'Reilly, imagines himself as a wealthy hotel owner. (2) As *The Life of Riley:* a 1950s television sitcom starring William Bendix as an amiable incompetent, Chester Riley, whose stock response to misfortune was "What a revolting development this is!" Bendix had created the character on radio.

Life Savers   A hard candy first sold in 1912. The original varieties, round white peppermints with a hole in the middle, resembled life preservers. Other flavors, in other colors, were added later. Life Savers are packaged in stacked "rolls," of which more than 30 billion have been sold.

Life with Father   A memoir (1935) by writer Clarence Day (1874–1935) about his childhood with a tyrannical but loving father. Dramatized by LINDSAY AND CROUSE, it had a stage run of 3,224 performances (1930–47), which held the Broadway record for over twenty years. William Powell played the father in a 1947 movie, Leon Ames in a television series (1953–55).

"Lift Every Voice and Sing"   A song whose lyrics were written by James Weldon JOHNSON for a 1900 Lincoln's Birthday celebration in his native Florida. With music by Johnson's brother, it is often called the black national anthem.

> *Lift every voice and sing*
> *Till earth and heaven ring*
> *Ring with the harmonies of Liberty.*

Lights of New York   See FOY FAMILY, THE JAZZ SINGER.

Li'l Abner   A comic strip created in 1934 by Al CAPP and drawn by him until his retirement in 1977. Set in the mythical hillbilly community of Dogpatch, U.S.A., it took a wry, often politically satirical, look at the Yokum family: Mammy, Pappy, their son Li'l Abner, and his wife Daisy Mae. The strip also introduced the bumbling, lovable Schmoo, a parody on DICK TRACY called Fearless Fosdick, and the invented tradition of SADIE HAWKINS DAY.

Liliuokalani   (1838–1917) Queen of Hawaii. She ruled from 1891 to 1895, when she was forced from power in a revolt that had begun two years earlier, with the backing of U.S. sugar interests. She was the author of the song "Aloha Oe."

Lincoln, Abraham   (1809–65) U.S. president. If the patrician Washington was the most respected of American leaders, the gangly "Rail-Splitter" Lincoln was the most beloved. His presidency saw the Civil War, the preservation of the Union, and the freeing of the slaves, yet he is remembered as much for his humanity and homespun wit as for these politically momentous events. His shooting by John Wilkes BOOTH in Washington's FORD'S THEATRE transformed him overnight into an American Christ figure, and the subsequent national mourning was not rivaled until the death of John F. KENNEDY a century later.

Born in Kentucky, Lincoln grew up in frontier farm communities, settled in Illinois in 1830, read law, and served several terms in the state legislature. Settling in Springfield, he married socialite Mary Todd (1842) and sat for two years (1847–49) in the House of Representatives, where he was an opponent of the MEXICAN WAR. Passage of the KANSAS-NEBRASKA ACT made slavery the dominant national issue, and throughout the 1850s the moderate Lincoln opposed extension of the "peculiar institution." Although he lost two bids for the Senate in this period, he became nationally known as an effective orator, especially after his 1858 debates with Stephen DOUGLAS, where he warned prophetically, "A house divided against itself cannot stand."

Lincoln's 1860 election as the nation's first Republican president precipitated the secession of the South and the Civil War. For Lincoln, the issue of that war was only secondarily slavery; he bent his energies primarily to saving the Union. This explains why the political act for which he is best remembered—the EMANCI-PATION PROCLAMATION—was not issued until the fall of 1862. Hoping to retain the loyalty of the border states, he postponed a deed that was sure to offend them, and once wrote to publisher Horace GREELEY, "If I could save the Union without freeing *any* slave, I would do it." The action, in the end, transformed the war into what many saw as a moral crusade; it made Lincoln, in the eyes of posterity, the "Great Emancipator."

As commander in chief, the country lawyer from Illinois outraged many with his arrogation of authority—blockading southern ports and abolishing the right of habeas corpus—while his comments on the Union's military leadership swelled the stock of his one-liners. To the cautious George McClellan he attributed "the slows," while to those who clucked their tongues at hard-drinking Ulysses GRANT, he replied, "Would you tell me what brand of whiskey Grant drinks? I would like to send a barrel of it to my other generals." The anecdote was one of many exhibiting the blend of pith and pragmatism that was the Lincoln style. The rhetorical beauty of his more carefully crafted observations is evident in the GETTYSBURG ADDRESS.

The folklore built around Lincoln was intrinsic to his appeal. Well before he went to Washington, his admirers knew that he had been born in a log cabin, that he split rails, that he devoured books by firelight, and that, while working in a country store, "Honest Abe" had walked for miles to return some change to a customer whom he had inadvertently overcharged. His appearance as presi-dent—in newly grown whiskers and stovepipe hat—added to the impression of rustic charm. He was even able to turn his physical defects (his secretary of war called him a "long-armed ape") into a visible metaphor of popular appeal. "God must love the common people," he was credited with saying. "He has made so many of them."

In spite of his conciliatory policy toward the South—he called for a peace "with malice toward none, with charity toward all"—Lincoln was roundly hated south of the MASON-DIXON LINE, and also reviled by northern editors who feared his "tyranny." The negativity generally stopped at his death, as he became the ultimate patriot martyr. His killer was cast as the American Judas, and thousands of mourners lined the railroad route that brought his body to rest in Illinois. Investigation of his death revealed a multiple assassination plot designed to incapacitate the U.S. government. Four conspirators, including a woman, Mary Surratt, were hanged; Samuel MUDD was sentenced to life in prison.

Like Washington, Lincoln earned durable places of honor in the nation's capital (see LINCOLN MEMORIAL), on Mount RUSHMORE, and on U.S. currency (the five-dollar bill and the penny). In popular culture, he has long outstripped the first president. Two of Walt WHITMAN's most poignant lyrics—"O Captain! My Captain" and "When Lilacs Last in the Dooryard Bloom'd"—were composed in his honor. Robert SHERWOOD and Carl SANDBURG won Pulitzer Prizes for their treatments, respectively, of the youthful and the wartime Lincoln. On film, Walter Huston shone in D. W. GRIFFITH's 1930 *Abraham Lincoln;* John FORD's *Young Mr. Lincoln* (1939) was an early triumph for Henry Fonda (see FONDA FAMILY).

Lincoln Brigade   See ABRAHAM LINCOLN BRIGADE.

Lincoln County wars   See BILLY THE KID.

Lincoln Logs   See LOG CABIN.

Lincoln Memorial   A shrine to the memory of Abraham LINCOLN that sits across from the WASHINGTON MONUMENT in the nation's capital. The building is in the style of a Doric temple. It contains a huge statue of the seated president by Daniel C. FRENCH.

Lind, Jenny   (1820–87) The "Swedish Nightingale," opera soprano Lind was the most famous singer of her time. She was already a star in Europe when P. T. BARNUM sponsored an American tour (1850–52) that made her, and him, a fortune. She donated much of it to charity, married her accompanist, and settled in England.

Lindbergh, Charles A.   (1902–74) Pilot. "Lucky Lindy" made aviation history when he became the first person to fly nonstop and solo across the Atlantic. After his landing at Paris on May 21, 1927, he was touted as a hero on two continents, promoted to colonel in the U.S. Army, and awarded the Congressional MEDAL OF HONOR. Five years after his triumph, he and his wife, Anne Morrow, lost their infant son in a kidnapping and murder. The sensational crime led to the execution of Bruno HAUPTMANN, the passage of a federal antikidnapping law (the "Lindbergh law"), and Mrs. Lindbergh's memoir *Hour of Gold, Hour of Lead* (1973).

On the eve of World War II, Lindbergh was an outspoken (many said anti-Semitic) isolationist, but he joined the American war effort after 1941, flying a number of missions against the Japanese. The plane he flew from New York to Paris, THE SPIRIT OF ST. LOUIS, was donated to the Smithsonian Institution. He recalled the flight in two memoirs, *We* (1927) And *The Spirit of St. Louis* (1953). The latter book inspired a 1957 film starring James STEWART.

Lindsay, Vachel   (1879–1931) Poet. Known for his dramatic sound effects and impassioned readings, Lindsay walked around the country in 1912, performing for meals the poems in *Rhymes to Be Traded for Bread* (1912). "General William Booth Enters into Heaven" (1913), a tribute to the founder of the SALVATION ARMY, was set to music by composer Charles Ives. "The Congo" (1914) was an affectionate though patronizing "study of the Negro race." "In Praise of Johnny Appleseed" (1923) celebrated the adventures of another creative tramp.

Lindsay and Crouse A theatrical writing and production team whose most famous collaboration was the play LIFE WITH FATHER. Howard Lindsay (1889–1968) and Russel Crouse (1893–1966) also worked together on the comedy ARSENIC AND OLD LACE, the Pulitzer Prize satire *State of the Union* (1945), and Rodgers and Hammerstein's THE SOUND OF MUSIC.

lindy A jitterbug dance of the 1930s. Probably named for flyer Charles A. LINDBERGH.

Lions A businessmen's service organization similar to the ELKS and ROTARY clubs. Founded in 1917, Lions International now has over a million members worldwide. The name is an acronym for "Liberty, Intelligence, Our Nation's Safety."

Lip, the See Leo DUROCHER.

Lippmann, Walter (1889–1974) Writer. Founder of the *New Republic* (1914) and longtime columnist for the *New York Herald Tribune* (1931–63), Lippmann was among the best-known political writers of his generation. Twice winner of the Pulitzer Prize in journalism, he also published several books, including *A Preface to Politics* (1913), *Public Opinion* (1922), and *The Public Philosophy* (1955).

Little, Malcolm See MALCOLM X.

Little Abner See LI'L ABNER.

Little Audrey The heroine of a 1930s joke cycle. A combination of POLLYANNA and the LITTLE MORON, Little Audrey "just laughed and laughed" in response to tragedy. About to be boiled by cannibals, she laughs, realizing she is not big enough to feed them all. Seeing her mother fall out of a car, she laughs, knowing that she is wearing a "light fall" suit. The jokes were popular especially in high schools and colleges.

Little Bighorn A river in Montana where, on June 25, 1876, George Armstrong CUSTER lost his life, and those of his entire command, to Sioux and Cheyenne warriors led by CRAZY HORSE. The battle, popularly known as Custer's Last Stand, sparked massive retaliation against the Indians and hastened the end of Plains resistance. Custer's death, celebrated in newspaper accounts, photogravures, and dime novels, obscured the faultiness of his strategy and made him a national martyr—the "American Roland"—in a matter of months. Of several movies made about the battle, the best known are *They Died with Their Boots On* (1942) and *Little Big Man* (1970). See also SITTING BULL; FORT APACHE.

Little Black Sambo See SAMBO.

"Little Brown Jug" A traditional novelty song, praising the virtues of home-made drink.

Ha ha ha, you and me;
Little brown jug, don't I love thee?

Little Caesar   (1930) A gangster film directed by Mervyn LeRoy and starring Edward G. Robinson as Rico Bandello. Its success started the urban mobster genre and made Robinson an overnight star. An unregenerate hoodlum, Rico dies uttering the curtain line, "Mother of mercy, is this the end of Rico?"

Little Egypt   (d. 1908) Dancer. Catherine Devine, billed as "Little Egypt," scandalized the 1893 Chicago world's fair by performing the exotic "coochee coochee" dance in flimsy attire (rumors abounded that she did it nude). For the next decade she was in demand for private stag parties, and she died leaving an estate of $250,000.

Little Engine That Could, The   A 1926 children's book by Watty Piper about a tiny locomotive's struggle to climb a mountain. Its inspirational message, embodied in the engine's chugging chant "I think I can, I think I can," has made it a juvenile classic for three generations.

Little Eva   The child heroine of Uncle Tom's Cabin. Her death, in one of the book's most famous scenes, was a favorite subject of sentimental engravings.

Little Flower   Fiorello La Guardia's nickname, a translation of the Italian *fiorello*.

Little Giant   A nickname for Stephen A. Douglas. From his short stature and giant rhetorical skills.

Little House on the Prairie   An autobiographical novel (1935) by Laura Ingalls Wilder (1867–1957) about her girlhood on the American frontier. It was one of a series of "Little House" books—the first was *Little House in the Big Woods* (1932)—that became children's classics and inspired a television series (1974–83).

Little Italy   The Italian section of a large city. The most famous one, in New York, is next to Chinatown.

Little League   An international children's baseball program. It was started in 1939 in Williamsport, Pennsylvania, which is still the site of the annual Little League World Series. Originally designed for boys from eight to twelve, the program began admitting girls in 1974.

Little Lord Fauntleroy   A foppish or spoiled young boy. From the title character of an 1886 novel by Frances Hodgson Burnett (1849–1924), filmed in 1936 with Freddie Bartholomew in the role.

Little Magician   See Martin Van Buren.

little moron (or simply **moron**)   The hero of a cycle of numskull jokes that were first popular in the 1940s and that often took a question-and-answer form. "Why did the little moron throw the clock out the window?" "He wanted to see time fly." More elaborate setups featured two numbskulls. Planning an escape from jail, one moron says to the other, "I'll shine this flashlight up to that window. You crawl up the beam and open it up." "Nothing doing," says his friend. "I'd get halfway up the beam and you'd turn the light off."

Little Orphan Annie   (1) As "Little Orphant Annie": a poem (1885) by James Whitcomb RILEY in which a servant girl, Orphant Annie, tells goblin tales until she eventually becomes the victim of her own creations. (2) As *Little Orphan Annie*: a comic strip begun in 1924 by Harold Gray. It features a poor girl, Annie, her dog Sandy, and their benefactor, millionaire Daddy Warbucks. The strip inspired a Broadway play, *Annie* (1977–83), and a 1982 movie of the same name.

Little Rascals   See OUR GANG COMEDIES.

Little Richard   (1932?—   ) Singer, pianist. With a whooping falsetto and a studiously outrageous stage presence, Georgia-born Richard Penniman became one of the flashiest stars of early rock 'n' roll. His first gold record, the exquisitely inane "Tutti Frutti," came out in 1955. In the next three years he also hit big with "Long Tall Sally," "Jenny, Jenny," "Keep a Knockin'," and "Good Golly Miss Molly." He retired at the height of his fame to become a preacher, but made frequent appearances thereafter on "oldies" shows.

Little Rock   The capital of Arkansas. It made international headlines in 1957 when Governor Orval Faubus, defying the Supreme Court's recent desegregation decision BROWN V. BOARD OF EDUCATION, ordered the National Guard to keep the high school white. The school was integrated, amid great violence, by federal paratroopers.

Little Sure Shot   A nickname for Annie OAKLEY, allegedly given to her by SITTING BULL.

Little Tramp   Charles CHAPLIN's most famous character, a baggy-trousered, waddling down-and-outer who first appeared in full form in *The Tramp* (1915).

Little Women   (1868) Louisa May ALCOTT's most famous novel. It is the story of the four March sisters: headstrong, literary Jo; sensible Meg; frail, artistic Beth; and fashionable Amy. The book, which brought Alcott national fame, was filmed in 1933, with Katharine HEPBURN as the spirited Jo.

Llorona, La   (Spanish "the weeping woman") La Llorona (pronounced *yo-ro-nah*) is a Mexican specter who wanders endlessly, inquiring after or lamenting her lost children. In one common variant of the legend, she has killed them herself and cries for penance.

Lloyd, Chris Evert   (1954–   ) Tennis player. Famous for a distinctive two-handed backhand, Chris Evert dominated American women's play in the mid-1970s by winning two Wimbledon singles titles (1974 and 1976) and four consecutive U.S. Open championships (1975 to 1978). After marrying fellow tennis pro John Lloyd in 1979, she went on to win another Wimbledon (1981) and two more Opens (1980 and 1982).

Lloyd, Harold   (1893–1971) Film actor. An athletic master of the improbable situation, Lloyd is best remembered as the star of *Safety Last* (1923), in which he dangles precariously, and hilariously, from a tower clock. Under the direction of Hal ROACH he became one of the highest-paid comedy stars of the silent era. His typical character—a bespectacled average Joe with a genius for pratfalls— rivaled CHAPLIN's Little Tramp in popularity.

Lloyd, Henry Demarest   (1847–1903). One of the earliest MUCKRAKERS, Lloyd attacked monopolies as financial writer of the *Chicago Tribune* and denounced business abuses in a famous book, *Wealth and Commonwealth* (1894).

lobsterbacks   An insulting equivalent for REDCOATS.

log cabin   A domestic dwelling made of rough-hewn, notched logs with earthen caulking. A Swedish import, the log cabin first appeared in New Jersey in the seventeenth century; the abundance of eastern forests soon made it a standard design on the frontier. In the 1840 presidential election campaign, supporters of Whig candidate William Henry Harrison (see "TIPPECANOE AND TYLER TOO") made the false claim that he had been born in a log cabin. The lie not only helped to win him the White House but entrenched the cabin as a symbol of American ruggedness. The presidents actually born in log cabins were Andrew JACKSON, James Polk, James Buchanan, Abraham LINCOLN, and James GARFIELD. The building's symbolic value is reflected in the brand names Log Cabin MAPLE SYRUP and Lincoln Logs—the latter a popular construction toy.

Log of a Cowboy   See Andy ADAMS.

Logan, Josh   (1908–88) Director. A major force in American theater of the 1940s, Joshua Logan organized a Cape Cod acting group that started the careers of James STEWART and Henry FONDA, studied METHOD ACTING under Stanislavsky in Moscow, and directed the initial Broadway productions of *Annie Get Your Gun* (see Annie OAKLEY), MISTER ROBERTS, and SOUTH PACIFIC. He also had success with film musicals.

Lolita   A novel (1958) by the Russian-born writer Vladimir Nabokov. The story of a middle-aged college professor's infatuation with an adolescent "nymphet," it scandalized audiences and made Nabokov's reputation. Stanley KUBRICK directed a 1962 movie version.

Loman, Willy   See DEATH OF A SALESMAN.

Lomax, John and Alan   Pioneers in the study of American FOLK MUSIC. Beginning in the 1900s, John (1875–1948) collected frontier ballads that he published in *Cowboy Songs* (1910), one of the earliest collections of such material. In the 1930s he and his son Alan (1915–   ) drove through rural America, recording works that appeared in *American Ballads and Folk Songs* (1934) and discovering, in a southern prison, the folksinger LEADBELLY. The Lomaxes contributed their work to the Library of Congress's Archive of American Folk Song, and they both served in turn as its curator. Alan's *The Folk Songs of North America in the English Language* (1960) remains a standard reference source for traditional music.

Lombardi, Vince   (1913–70) Football coach. As coach of the Green Bay Packers from 1959 to 1967, Lombardi brought them to five National Football League titles as well as victory in the first two SUPER BOWLS. A hard-driving, motivational leader, he was often credited—in spite of his disavowals—with the line "Winning isn't everything. It's the only thing."

London, Jack (1876–1916) Writer. Espousing a paradoxical blend of Marxism and machismo, San Francisco–born London became the best known American writer of the 1900s. His hatred of the capitalist system that had scarred his impoverished childhood is evident in *The Iron Heel* (1908) and *Martin Eden* (1909). His ambivalent attraction to robust individualism is best developed in his tragic, Nietzschean study *The Sea Wolf* (1904) and in his two Arctic novels, THE CALL OF THE WILD and WHITE FANG. The last two books built on London's experience of the Klondike GOLD RUSH of 1897–98.

Lone Eagle Nickname for Charles A. LINDBERGH, from his solo flight across the Atlantic.

Lone Ranger, The Beginning on radio in 1933, *The Lone Ranger* was a hit television western from 1949 to 1957. The title character, Texas Ranger John Reid, was the sole survivor of an outlaw ambush. Rescued from death by the Indian TONTO, he adopts a new, masked identity as the Lone Ranger and dedicates himself to frontier justice. Elements of the series that entered American folklore include the hero's unique calling card, a silver bullet; his encouraging yell to his horse, "Hi-yo, Silver"; Tonto's pet name for him, KEMO SABE; and the musical theme, Rossini's *William Tell* Overture. The television series star, Clayton Moore, also played him in a 1956 movie.

Lone Star State Texas. From 1836 to 1845, Texas was an independent nation, the Lone Star Republic, with a single star on its flag. The current Texas flag retains the design.

lonelyhearts columns See "DEAR ABBY"; Dorothy DIX; MISS LONELYHEARTS.

Long, Huey P. (1893–1935) Populist politician who, as governor of Louisiana (1928–32), exercised virtually complete control over state government. Backed by impoverished farmers, he entered office on the campaign slogan "Every Man a King," used patronage liberally while promoting social welfare, and attacked big business while enriching himself at public expense. In 1932, as a U.S. senator, he pushed a transfer-payment scheme called Share the Wealth, including a guaranteed income and a "millionaire's cap," which made him a national figure and a presidential hopeful. In 1935, the flamboyant "Kingfish" was beginning to challenge President Roosevelt's reelection when he was assassinated in the statehouse at Baton Rouge. Robert Penn Warren's 1946 novel, ALL THE KING'S MEN, was based loosely on his career.

long count See Jack DEMPSEY; Gene TUNNEY.

long hunters An eighteenth-century term for Appalachian frontiersmen like Simon Kenton and Daniel BOONE. From their wanderings far from home on hunts and travels.

long knives American Indian term first for Virginia settlers (ca. 1750), then for the U.S. cavalry (1870s). A reference to the whites' swords, it appears less frequently as "big knives."

Longfellow, Henry Wadsworth (1807–82) The most popular American poet of the nineteenth century. A professor of modern languages at Harvard for almost twenty years, Longfellow produced poems that were widely memorized, and almost as widely parodied, by American schoolchildren. "The Village Blacksmith" (1839) is a lyric to country life, beginning with the famous lines "Under the spreading chestnut tree / The village smithy stands." "The Wreck of the Hesperus" (1841) describes a celebrated ocean calamity. "EVANGELINE" became the first widely read long poem in the country's history; an Indian romance, "*The Song of* HIAWATHA" (1855), was almost as popular. In "THE COURTSHIP OF MILES STANDISH" and "PAUL REVERE'S RIDE," Longfellow established the mythic reputations of those heroes. As beloved in England as he was in America, he received honorary degrees from Oxford and Cambridge and is remembered with a bust in Westminster Abbey.

longhorn The cattle breed most common in Texas during the great trail drives of the 1800s. Sometimes called the Texas longhorn, it is the mascot of the University of Texas.

Lonigan, Studs See STUDS LONIGAN.

Looking Backward (1888) A utopian novel by Massachusetts reformer Edward Bellamy (1850–98). It describes Boston in the year 2000, when a benign collectivism has overcome the evils of capitalism. Published when those evils were particularly blatant, the book sold phenomenally, inspiring the formation of a short-lived Nationalist party to promote its message.

Looney Tunes A series of Warner Brothers cartoon shorts produced from the 1930s through the 1960s. The principal stars were BUGS BUNNY, PORKY PIG, and DAFFY DUCK. The films typically ended with Porky spluttering the formula farewell, "That's all, folks."

Loos, Anita (1893–1981) Writer. Primarily a screenwriter, she is remembered for a novel, GENTLEMEN PREFER BLONDES. It was followed by *But Gentlemen Marry Brunettes* (1928) and several volumes of autobiography, including *A Girl Like I* (1966).

Los Alamos A small town in northern New Mexico selected in 1943 as the location of the U.S. Atomic Research Laboratory, which made the world's first atomic and hydrogen bombs. The facility, renamed the Los Alamos Scientific Laboratory, now pursues a broader spectrum of research.

Los Angeles A sprawling urban area in Southern California. As of 1990, the combined population of L.A and adjoining Long Beach was 8.9 million, making it slightly larger than New York City proper. Founded by the Spanish in 1781, the "City of the Angels" prospered commercially during the 1848 GOLD RUSH and then expanded steadily, thanks to the citrus, oil, motion picture, and aircraft industries. Housing the second largest Mexican-born population in the world (after

Mexico City), it also has a sizable black population, concentrated in impoverished Watts. Racial tension has bloodied L.A.'s history, with the city being ravaged by fire in 1965 and 1992 riots, and the control of many neighborhoods today contested by gangs. Tourism continues to prosper, however. Millions come each year to visit HOLLYWOOD, BEVERLY HILLS, and nearby DISNEYLAND.

Lost Cause   The cause of the Confederacy in the Civil War. A common romantic tag after the South's defeat.

Lost Colony   See ROANOKE COLONY.

lost generation   The generation born in the 1890s, whose World War I experience left them bitterly disillusioned. The comment ''You are all a lost generation'' is often attributed to Gertrude STEIN, notably by Ernest HEMINGWAY in THE SUN ALSO RISES. Stein herself attributed it to a French garage owner. See also BEAT GENERATION.

Lost Weekend, The   (1945) A disturbing study of alcoholism directed by Billy WILDER. It won four Oscars, including those for best picture, best direction, and best actor (Ray Milland).

Louis, Joe   (1914–81) Often called the greatest boxer in history, black heavyweight Joseph Louis Barrow, known as the Brown Bomber, became champion in 1937. A year later, he knocked out German champion Max Schmeling in a fight that was widely touted as a racial contest and that severely embarrassed Schmeling's ''Aryan'' promoters. Louis held the crown until 1949, defending it a record twenty-five times. In a brief comeback, he was beaten by Ezzard Charles (1950) and Rocky MARCIANO (1951). His lifetime record was 68–3.

Louisiana Purchase   (1803) The United States's purchase from France of land between the Mississippi River and the Rocky Mountains. The acquisition, which cost about $15 million, doubled U.S. territory overnight, making it the single largest expansion in American history. See LEWIS AND CLARK EXPEDITION.

loup-garou   French for ''werewolf.'' Used in Canada and Louisiana for a person who has assumed an animal shape—often, but not always, that of a wolf. In French-speaking areas, there is a modest, gory folklore about their predations.

Love, Nat   See DEADWOOD DICK (2).

Love Story   A novel (1970) by Erich Segal. A bittersweet story of doomed love, it has sold roughly 10 million copies. The movie version (1970) further popularized the cloying definition ''Love is never having to say you're sorry.''

lover's leap   A cliff or rock from which a lover or lovers are alleged to have jumped to their deaths, typically because their love ''can never be.'' Such legendary spots are scattered throughout the country. Their ubiquity was parodied by humorist Frank Sullivan (1892–1976) in his story ''Quigley 873'' (1951), about a lover's leap at Wassamattawichez Notch, New Hampshire.

Loyalists   American colonists who opposed the war for independence. Estimates of their number range from one-fifth to one-third of the population; they were most numerous in the South and among large landowners. Some swore allegiance to the United States in spite of their convictions, while others forfeited their property and fled the country. The anti-British majority called them Tories.

LSD Lysergic acid diethylamide. A psychotropic substance popular, especially among college students, in the 1960s. Ingested even in minute quantities, it induces altered perceptions that have been identified as both mystical and psychotic. See also ACID; COUNTERCULTURE; Timothy LEARY.

Lucas, George (1945–) The creator of STAR WARS. Lucas began his directorial career with *American Graffiti* (1973), a nostalgic look at the 1960s that sparked the careers of several 1980s actors, including *Star Wars* hero Harrison Ford.

Luce, Henry R. (1898–1967) The most successful publisher of the twentieth century. Born in China to a missionary couple, he founded TIME (1923), *Fortune* (1930), LIFE (1936), and *Sports Illustrated* (1954). His wife was the Republican congresswoman and successful playwright Clare Boothe Luce (1903–87).

"Luck of Roaring Camp, The" (1868) A sentimental tale by Bret HARTE about the fundamental decency of gold rush miners. It established the writer's reputation.

Lucky Lindy Nickname for Charles A. LINDBERGH.

Lucy See I LOVE LUCY.

Lugosi, Bela (1882–1956) Actor. Hungarian-born Béla Blasko created a sensation first on stage (1927) and then on film (1931) as the title character in the vampire classic *Dracula*. He played macabre villains in dozens of other films and returned as Dracula in the 1948 spoof *Abbott and Costello Meet Frankenstein*. The Tod Browning–directed film in which he created the character made him as famous as Boris KARLOFF to horror fans. He was buried wearing his Count Dracula cape.

"Lullaby of Broadway" A 1935 song by Al Dubin and Harry Warren. In *Gold Diggers of 1935*, Busby BERKELEY used it to choreograph a fifteen-minute-long production number. It won the Academy Award for best song.

Lusitania A British liner sunk by a German U-boat on May 7, 1915, with the loss of over one hundred American lives. The incident fueled anti-German sentiment, temporarily discredited President Wilson's neutrality, and prepared Americans for entering the Great War two years later.

lynching The extralegal punishment, often including execution, of an alleged criminal, generally at the hands of a mob. Such vigilante justice was visited on suspects frequently on the colonial frontier, and one eighteenth-century "regulator," William Lynch of Virginia, not only drew up the first official Lynch law but also gave the practice his name. Although it was responsible for the deaths of many suspected horse thieves in the Old West, lynching did not reach its grim apogee until the turn of the century. Between the 1880s and the 1930s, thousands of southern blacks were dispatched by white mobs, typically by hanging, for supposed offenses against the regime of JIM CROW. See also KU KLUX KLAN; THE OX-BOW INCIDENT.

Lynn, Loretta   (1935–   ) Singer, songwriter. The first woman to win the Country Music Association's entertainer of the year award (1972), Kentucky-born Lynn sings gritty ballads about the hard work and personal troubles of simple people. Her hits include "Don't Come Home Drinkin' with Lovin' on Your Mind," "You Ain't Woman Enough," and the self-reflective "Coal Miner's Daughter." *Coal Miner's Daughter* was also the title of her autobiography (1976) and of a movie about her life (1980) starring Sissy Spacek. Lynn's younger sister is the pop country singer Crystal Gayle.

M

M&Ms A chocolate candy first sold in 1941 and named for its developers, Forrest Mars and Bruce Murries. Since the small chocolate wafers are protected by a sugar coating, they are resistant to heat. Hence the slogan "The milk chocolate melts in your mouth, not in your hand." M&Ms are also made with peanut and almond centers. Combined production exceeds 50 billion a year.

Ma and Pa Kettle A hillbilly couple introduced in the 1947 film *The Egg and I*. Their cutesy/folksy ways made them the stars of *Ma and Pa Kettle* (1949) and eight sequels. They were played by Marjorie Main and Percy Kilbride.

Ma Barker See Kate BARKER.

Ma Bell A nickname for Bell Telephone, the company founded by Alexander Graham BELL which became one of the world's largest monopolies, American Telephone and Telegraph (AT&T).

Ma Joad See THE GRAPES OF WRATH.

"Ma, Ma, Where's My Pa?" A song written by H. R. Monroe as an 1884 Republican campaign jingle. It taunted Democratic presidential candidate Grover Cleveland, who had admitted to fathering a child out of wedlock. When Cleveland won, his supporters smirked, "Gone to the White House, ha, ha, ha."

Ma Perkins A radio series that ran from 1933 to 1960. The title character, played by Virginia Payne, was a "tough but tender" widow who dispensed advice to the residents of Rushville Center. She has been described as one of the "great homespun philosophers of old-time radio."

Ma Rainey See Gertrude RAINEY.

MacArthur, Charles (1895–1956) Writer. MacArthur was best known for two plays he wrote with Ben HECHT, THE FRONT PAGE and *Twentieth Century* (1932). He contributed to the screen versions of both those works as well as to those of *Gunga Din* and *Wuthering Heights* (both 1939).

MacArthur, Douglas (1880–1964) The most controversial American general of the twentieth century, West Pointer MacArthur came to public prominence in 1932 when, against the orders of President Herbert Hoover, he evacuated the BONUS ARMY by burning their shacks. As commander of U.S. Far East forces in World War II, he was driven from the Philippines by the Japanese, announced imperiously, "I shall return," and did so in 1944, amid a horde of *Life* reporters and cameramen. MacArthur accepted the Japanese surrender in 1945 on the deck of the battleship U.S.S. *Missouri,* and five years later commanded U.N. troops in Korea. His aggressiveness during the Korean conflict—he urged the bombing and blockading of China—got him removed from command by President TRUMAN, and he instantly capitalized on the "disgrace" by imploring Congress for a hard line against aggression. The speech in which he made the plea contained his most famous comment, "Old soldiers never die. They just fade away." The spirit of MacArthur's ambition was aptly caught in the title of William Manchester's biography, *American Caesar.*

McCall, Jack See Wild Bill HICKOK.

McCarthy, Charlie See Edgar BERGEN.

McCarthy, Joseph (1908–57) Politician. The junior senator from Wisconsin, McCarthy entered the U.S. Senate in 1946 and soon began a campaign to eradicate communists from what he said was their bailiwick in the federal government. Between 1950 and 1954, he chaired congressional hearings on the hidden Red menace, creating a climate of fear that cost many their jobs. When he turned his attention to the army, the Senate rebuked him, and "McCarthyism" gradually came to an end. Arthur MILLER's 1953 play *The Crucible* drew a parallel between the senator's "witch-hunts" and the SALEM WITCH TRIALS. See also HOUSE UN-AMERICAN ACTIVITIES COMMITTEE.

McClure's See MUCKRAKERS.

McCormick, Cyrus (1809–84) Inventor, businessman. McCormick's invention of the reaper in 1831 not only revolutionized American agriculture but, through the company he formed to market it in 1847, made him one of the country's richest men.

McCoy, the real Slang term for anything genuine, excellent, or original. Probably, although not certainly, from boxer "Kid" McCoy (1873–1940), whose success led to a cadre of Kid McCoy imitators. This "real" McCoy, actually named Norman Selby, lost his last fight to Gentleman Jim CORBETT in 1900.

McCoy-Hatfield feud See HATFIELD-McCOY FEUD.

McDaniel, Hattie (1895–1952) Actress. Buxom, matronly McDaniel played a series of maids in 1930s movies, then won an Oscar for her portrayal of Mammy in GONE WITH THE WIND. Originally a band vocalist, she was the first black woman to sing on American radio.

MacDonald, Jeanette See Nelson EDDY.

McDonald's A fast-food restaurant founded in California in the 1950s and transformed by entrepreneur Ray Kroc (1902–84) into the biggest restaurant chain in the nation's history. The original fare—hamburgers, soft drinks, and french fries—has been expanded over the years to include fish, chicken, breakfast, and even salad items, but the company's central philosophy remains unchanged: provide uniform quality, in a matter of minutes, to a hurried population. With the nationwide spread of the chain in the 1960s, McDonald's became as well known for its marketing symbols as for its menu. These include the company logo, a pair of golden arches; a peppy mascot clown called Ronald McDonald; the posting of national sales figures at every store (''Over 2 Billion Sold''); and the advertising jingle ''You Deserve a Break Today.'' Of the fast-food franchises that followed McDonald's lead, the most prominent include Wendy's, Kentucky Fried Chicken, and Burger King.

McDuck, Scrooge See DONALD DUCK.

McEnroe, John (1959–) Tennis player. Irascible and intense, McEnroe was a court phenomenon in the 1980s, winning the mens' U.S. Open three times straight (1979–81) and a fourth time in 1984. He also took the British title at Wimbledon in 1981, 1983, and 1984.

McFarland, Spanky See OUR GANG COMEDIES.

McGhee, Brownie See Sonny TERRY.

McGuffey Readers A series of grade school texts (1836–57) edited by William Holmes McGuffey (1800–73). Compilations of verse, proverbs, and uplifting stories, they were the universal curriculum of the nineteenth century and were often reprinted up to the 1920s. McGuffey helped to found the Ohio school system and served as president of Ohio University.

MacGuffin ''The MacGuffin'' was Alfred HITCHCOCK's term for an item or other story element that, although seemingly minor, actually drives the plot. In his film *Strangers on a Train* (1951), it is a cigarette lighter that proves the hero's innocence. In CITIZEN KANE, it is the deathbed utterance ''Rosebud.''

McHenry, Fort See FORT MCHENRY.

Mack, Connie (1862–1956) Baseball manager. Cornelius Alexander McGillicuddy was the first manager (later owner) of the Philadelphia Athletics. Between 1910 and 1930 he brought them to five World Series. Beginning as a player in the 1890s, he spent over sixty years in professional baseball.

Mack, Ted (1904–76) Emcee of *The Original Amateur Hour,* a weekly talent show that began on radio in the 1930s and lasted for over twenty years (1948–70) on television. Among its finds were Frank SINATRA (on radio) and Pat BOONE.

Mack truck A byword for formidable size or sturdiness, as in ''built like a Mack truck'' and ''You look like you've been hit by a Mack truck.'' The brothers John and Augustus Mack started producing heavy trucks in the 1900s. Their company's products today may be identified by a bulldog hood ornament.

McKay, Donald See CLIPPER SHIPS.

McKinley, William (1843–1901) U.S. president. An Ohio Republican, McKinley championed high tariffs as a U.S. congressman, then served two terms as his state's governor before defeating William Jennings BRYAN for the presidency in

1896. The chief business of his first term was the SPANISH-AMERICAN WAR, although he also succeeded in passing a Gold Standard Act. Reelected in 1900 with Theodore ROOSEVELT as his running mate, he was assassinated by Leon CZOLGOSZ in 1901. See also Mark HANNA.

McKinley, Mount   At 20,320 feet, this is the highest mountain in North America. Located in southern Alaska, it was named in 1896 for William MCKINLEY.

McKuen, Rod   (1933–) Poet. Mocked by the literati for his sentimentalism, McKuen's self-described "love words for music" made him the household poet of the 1960s. His poetry made the best-seller lists consistently from 1967 to 1971, and in 1968 he broke an industry record by having three best-sellers in the same year. These were *Stanyan Street and Other Sorrows, Lonesome Cities,* and *Listen to the Warm.*

Macon, Uncle Dave   (1870–1953) The first major star of the GRAND OLE OPRY. An accomplished banjo picker, singer, and homespun comic, Macon was approaching sixty when he joined the Opry (1926), but he was a polished performer from years of amateur playing, and he charmed audiences with both topical and traditional songs. He appeared in radio and tent shows up until his death.

McPherson, Aimee Semple   (1890–1944) Revivalist. Canadian born "Sister Aimee" amassed a huge following in the 1920s with theatrical preaching that prefigured Billy GRAHAM. Promoting her Foursquare Gospel from a home base in Los Angeles's Angelus Temple, she also founded a radio station and a Bible college. Her popularity fell in 1926 when she evidently engineered a phony kidnapping so that she could spend time unobserved with her married lover. Still preaching in the 1940s, she died from an overdose of sleeping pills.

Macy's   A department store in New York City, known as the R. H. Macy drygoods company in the 1880s, when its ownership was assumed by the brothers Isidor and Nathan Straus. They turned it into a world-famous shopping emporium. Since the beginning of this century, the store has sponsored a Thanksgiving Day parade, now known for its huge balloons.

Mad   An adolescent humor magazine, founded in 1952, which features irreverant, elaborate spoofs of popular icons. Its figurehead, Alfred E. Neuman, is known for a goofy smile and the expression "What, me worry?"

"Mademoiselle from Armentières"   A song popular with American and British soldiers in World War I. Its authorship, and the identity of the Frenchwoman it ribaldly commemorates, are uncertain.

> *Mademoiselle from Armentières, parlay-voo;*
> *Mademoiselle from Armentières, parlay-voo.*
> *Mademoiselle from Armentières never heard of underwear;*
> *Hinky dinky parlay-voo.*

Madison, Dolley   (1768–1849) The wife of James MADISON, Dolley Madison became Washington's premier party-giver even before his accession to the presidency, when she served as the widowed Thomas JEFFERSON's official hostess. She is said to have popularized ICE CREAM in the White House, and a major brand of the dessert carries her name.

Madison, James (1751–1836) The fourth U.S. president (1809–17), Madison held office during the WAR OF 1812. He is better known for his activities thirty years earlier, when as a member of the Continental Congress, he vigorously championed the creation of a strong central government. A prime mover behind the 1787 Constitutional Convention, he was so central to its planning sessions that he is often called the Father of the Constitution. He fought for that document in THE FEDERALIST and as a congressman (1789–97) advocated the BILL OF RIGHTS.

Madison Avenue The advertising industry. From the prominence of ad agencies on that New York City street.

Madison Square Garden (or simply **the Garden**) An entertainment complex in New York City, housing a 20,000-seat main arena, the 5,000-seat Felt Forum, and other facilities. The current building, erected in 1968, is the fourth building to be called Madison Square Garden. The architect of the second one, Stanford WHITE, was shot to death in its theater in 1906.

Madoc A Welsh prince who, according to legend, made a journey in the twelfth century to North America. The search for his progeny of "Welsh-speaking Indians" was an antiquarian obsession of the nineteenth century.

Madonna (1958–) Pop singer. Campy suggestiveness, peppy tunes, and a voice that was once described as "Minnie Mouse on helium" made Madonna Ciccone a 1980s pop star. She set fashion trends with flashy, not to mention fleshy, stage costumes and had the first of several hits with the album *Like a Virgin* (1984). She also appeared in movies and exploited her pseudo–Marilyn MONROE image by posing for a book of nude photographs entitled *Sex* (1992).

Mafia A secret organization that started in Sicily and is said to control organized crime in the United States. Also known as Cosa Nostra ("our thing") and "the mob," the Mafia came to public attention in the 1950s during U.S. congressional hearings on organized crime. Its alleged influence has been the subject of novels, "insider" confessions, and several movies, including THE GODFATHER.

Magarac, Joe Tall-tale hero. An industrial, urban equivalent of Paul BUNYAN, Magarac appeared in stories written by Owen Francis for *Scribner's Magazine* in 1931. Allegedly a folk creation of Slavic millworkers, the giant Magarac, made of steel, had phenomenal strength. He could lift hundreds of pounds of steel with one hand and squeeze molten steel from between his fingers into the shape of rails. In a final story, he has himself melted down to improve the grade of steel in a new mill.

Maggie and Jiggs The central characters in the comic strip *Bringing Up Father*, which was created in 1912 by illustrator George McManus. The humorous pretensions of the nouveau-riche couple, along with Jiggs's attempts to evade his wife's wrath, made the feature a kind of newspaper SITCOM. It was enormously popular for over half a century.

mah-jongg   A parlor game similar to rummy but using decorated tiles instead of playing cards. Adapted by Joseph Babcock from the Chinese game *ma chiang*, it enjoyed a vogue in the 1920s.

Mailer, Norman   (1923–) Writer. Mailer scored an instant success with his first novel, THE NAKED AND THE DEAD, based on his experiences as a World War II soldier. With the exception of the darkly comedic *An American Dream* (1965), his subsequent novels have been only modest successes, although his personal, quirky journalism is well respected. Books that display it include *The Armies of the Night* (1968), a Pulitzer Prize record of a peace march to the PENTAGON; *Miami and the Siege of Chicago* (1968), on that year's presidential nominating conventions; and *The Executioner's Song* (1977), about the execution of a Utah murderer.

Main Street   (1) Sinclair LEWIS's first major novel, a sobering portrait of a dull Minnesota town. (2) A synonym for "mainstream" or "conventional." Taken, like Lewis's title, from the prevalence of so-named streets in small-town America.

Maine, U.S.S.   An American battleship that, on February 15, 1898, exploded in Havana Harbor, killing 260 crewmen. The ship had been sent to Cuba to protect American interests amid increasing resentment against Spanish rule, and the responsibility for the tragedy was placed on Spain. The William Randolph HEARST and Joseph PULITZER newspapers soon outdid themselves in calling for revenge ("Remember the Maine" became a jingoist slogan); the result, less than two months later, was the SPANISH-AMERICAN WAR. Modern research tends to confirm an original Spanish investigation's finding that the blasts had been caused by a fire in the battleship's coal stores.

"Mairzy Doats"   A nonsense song written in 1943 by Milton Drake, Al Hoffman, and Jerry Livingston. The lyrics reflect the slurred pronunciation that Drake had heard from his four-year-old daughter. Hence "Mairzy doats and dozey doats and little lamsy divey" is the song's version of "Mares eat oats and does eat oats and little lambs eat ivy."

"Make love, not war"   A 1960s slogan, reflecting both the pacifist and the erotic proclivities of the COUNTERCULTURE.

"Make my day"   See DIRTY HARRY.

"Making Whoopee"   A song by Gus Kahn and Walter Donaldson, introduced by Eddie CANTOR in the movie *Whoopee* (1928). "Whoopee" once meant general exuberance, but now refers chiefly to sexual activity.

Malcolm X   (1925–65) Black revolutionary leader. Born Malcolm Little in Nebraska, he moved east as a teenager and became a pimp and confidence man in New York. While serving a prison term for burglary in the 1940s, he was converted to the BLACK MUSLIM movement through the writings of its leader, Elijah Muhammad, and upon his release changed his name to Malcolm X. An impassioned, articulate speaker, Malcolm spread the Muslim faith until 1964, when his hope for an interracial socialist revolution drove a wedge between his followers and those of his mentor. That wedge led to his assassination at a New York rally.

His posthumously published *Autobiography,* dictated to Alex Haley (see ROOTS), is a thoughtful, shocking bildungsroman.

male chauvinist pig   A 1970s feminist term for a gender-biased, "phallocentric" male. Sometimes abbreviated "MCP."

Maltese Falcon, The   A HARD-BOILED FICTION crime novel (1930) by Dashiell HAMMETT about a treacherous circle's search for a jeweled statue. Filmed by John HUSTON in his directorial debut (1941), it starred Humphrey BOGART as embittered sleuth Sam Spade.

Mama   A television series (1949–56) about a Norwegian-American family in turn-of-the-century San Francisco. One of the first successful family dramas, it was based on the story collection *Mama's Bank Account* (1943), by Katherine Forbes. A hit play (1944) and a movie (1948) made from the book were both entitled *I Remember Mama.*

Mamas and the Papas, the   Singing group. Among the most successful exponents of the "California sound," they had a string of soft-rock hits in the mid-1960s, including "California Dreamin'," "Words of Love," and "Monday, Monday." Leader and writer John Phillips also wrote the Summer of Love anthem "San Francisco," recorded in 1967 by Scott McKenzie.

Mammy   (1) A black woman who acts as a nurse to white children. Common in the plantation South before the Civil War, and depicted with inimitable élan by Hattie McDANIEL in the 1939 film of GONE WITH THE WIND. (2) One of Al JOLSON's biggest hits, introduced in the 1927 film THE JAZZ SINGER.

Man of a Thousand Faces   Lon CHANEY.

Man of La Mancha   A Broadway musical based on *Don Quixote* that played over 2,300 performances in the late 1960s. Its best known song was "The Impossible Dream."

"Man on the Flying Trapeze, The"   A song originally performed by singing clowns in nineteenth-century circuses and revived as a novelty tune in the 1890s. The author is unknown.

> *He floats through the air with the greatest of ease,*
> *The daring young man on the flying trapeze.*

For *The Daring Young Man on the Flying Trapeze,* see William SAROYAN.

Man Who Came to Dinner, The   A 1939 comedy by KAUFMAN AND HART. The guest, whose broken leg prevents him from leaving his hosts, is a witty egotist modeled on Alexander WOOLLCOTT. Monty Woolley played him on stage and in a 1942 movie version.

"Man with the Hoe, The"   A poem (1899) by Edwin Markham (1852–1940) expressing sympathy for society's downtrodden. Inspired by Jean-François Millet's painting of a toiling peasant, it was widely translated and made Markham famous.

Bowed by the weight of centuries he leans
Upon his hoe and gazes on the ground,
The emptiness of ages in his face,
And on his back the burden of the world.

"Man Without a Country, The" A short story (1863) by Boston minister Edward Everett Hale (1822–1909). Protagonist Philip Nolan, a treasonous naval officer, says he never wishes to hear of his country again. The court obliges him with lifetime imprisonment on ships at sea. The story is said to have been inspired by Clement VALLANDIGHAM's caustic remark that he "did not want to belong to the United States."

Manassa Mauler Nickname of Jack DEMPSEY.

Mancini, Henry (1924–) Composer, songwriter. A prolific writer of television and movie scores, Mancini made his mark with the theme song for the TV detective show *Peter Gunn* (1958–61). He went on to score almost forty movies, winning Oscars for "MOON RIVER" and "Days of Wine and Roses" (from the 1963 movie of that name). He also contributed the theme for the THE PINK PANTHER series.

Manhattan The most densely populated borough of New York City, and what non–New Yorkers mean when they say "New York." It sits on Manhattan Island, named for the original Indian inhabitants, from whom Peter MINUIT is said to have bought it for twenty-four dollars worth of trinkets.

Manhattan Project A secret federal project of the early 1940s that produced the atomic bomb in 1945. Chief designer for the bomb was J. Robert Oppenheimer (1904–67). Its first test came at ALAMOGORDO, New Mexico, on July 16, 1945.

manifest destiny The nineteenth-century philosophy of American expansion. The phrase came from an 1845 editorial in the *Democratic Review.* Calling for the annexation of Texas, editor John O'Sullivan (1813–95) claimed that the country had a "manifest destiny to overspread the continent allotted by Providence for the free development of our yearly multiplying millions." Texas statehood late that year precipitated the MEXICAN WAR.

Manilow, Barry (1946–) Pop singer. Manilow parlayed a mellow vocal style and unabashedly romantic lyrics into one of the major careers of the 1970s. His recordings of "Mandy," "Looks Like We Made It," and "I Write the Songs" were number-one hits, while virtually every album he made went platinum. In 1977, he equaled a record previously set by Frank SINATRA and Johnny MATHIS in having five albums on the charts simultaneously.

Manitou See GREAT SPIRIT.

Mann, Horace (1796–1859) Founder of the U.S. public school system. As secretary of Massachusetts's first board of education (1837–48), Mann established public high schools and teacher training colleges, championed compulsory schooling, and influenced boards around the country with his annual reports. He also served two terms in the U.S. Congress and became the first president of Ohio's Antioch College.

Mann Act   (1910) The so-called White Slave Traffic Act, this federal law prohibits the interstate transport of females for "immoral purposes." Named for its Illinois sponsor, Congressman James Mann, it was chiefly used to curtail prostitution. See Chuck BERRY.

Manson, Charles   (1934–) Architect of the most sensational murders of the 1960s, Manson headed a "family" of drifters and dropouts devoted indiscriminately to God, the devil, and Manson himself. In August 1969, a group of his followers, acting on his command, stabbed seven people to death near Los Angeles. Among the victims were pregnant starlet Sharon Tate and a middle-aged couple, Leno and Rosemary LaBianca. The ensuing "Tate-LaBianca" murder trial, filled with sensational accounts of the killings and stories of "Charlie's" hold on his female disciples, ended in the conviction of Manson and four of the band. Their death sentences were later commuted to life imprisonment.

Mantle, Mickey   (1931–) Baseball player. A center fielder for the New York Yankees, Mantle was one of the great power hitters of the 1950s. The American League's most valuable player in 1956, 1957, and 1962, he hit 536 home runs in an eighteen-year career.

Mantovani   (1905–80) Orchestra conductor. Annunzio Paolo Mantovani, born in Venice, was the king of symphonic "mood music." His violin-heavy arrangements of light classical and popular melodies made him an album favorite in the 1950s and 1960s. He was the first artist to sell a million stereo albums.

"Maple Leaf Rag"   See Scott JOPLIN.

maple syrup   A thick, sweet syrup used principally on PANCAKES. It is produced by boiling down the sap of the sugar maple, a process that New England colonists learned from the Indians and that remains associated with that region. Vermont produces the bulk of the nation's true maple syrup, while artificially flavored syrups exist in profusion.

March, Fredric   (1897–1975) Actor. A distinguished stage actor who often appeared with his wife, Florence Eldridge (1901–88), March was born Ernest Bickel in Wisconsin. His stage parody of John Barrymore (see BARRYMORE FAMILY) in *The Royal Family* (1926) got him a movie contract, which he turned to distinguished account in 1932, with an Academy Award for *Dr. Jekyll and Mr. Hyde*. He earned a second Oscar for THE BEST YEARS OF OUR LIVES and also turned in subtle, emotionally compelling performances as Mark TWAIN in *The Adventures of Mark Twain* (1944), Willy Loman in DEATH OF A SALESMAN, and William Jennings BRYAN in *Inherit the Wind* (1960).

March King   Nickname of John Philip SOUSA.

March of Time, The   A weekly newsreel series shown in movie theaters from 1935 to 1951. Produced by TIME magazine's parent company, Time, Inc., it copied the format of a similarly named radio feature and was a main source of visual news until the advent of television. Orson WELLES parodied its brashly upbeat style in CITIZEN KANE.

"Marching Through Georgia" A Civil War ballad (1865) by Henry Clay Work, celebrating William T. Sherman's ravaging of Georgia. It incensed southerners and evidently irritated the general too. Hearing it at a Grand Army of the Republic convention, he is said to have remarked that if he knew his feat was going to inspire a song, he "would have marched around the state."

Marciano, Rocky (1923–69) Boxer. Massachusetts brawler Rocco Marchegiano was the only professional heavyweight never defeated. He took the crown from Jersey Joe Walcott in 1952, after a string of forty-two professional victories, and retired after six defenses four years later. In a 1969 computer-simulated "Super Fight," "the Rock" knocked out Muhammad Ali in thirteen rounds. Less than one month later he died in a plane crash.

Mardi Gras Shrove Tuesday or, more generally, the pre-Lenten carnival celebration that precedes it. The term, which is French for "Fat Tuesday," refers to the last indulgence in meat before the Lenten fast. North America's most famous Mardi Gras is held in New Orleans.

mariachi A type of Mexican band featuring guitars, violins, and more recently brass instruments. Probably they were originally wedding bands, as reflected in the term, from French *mariage*. They are popular in Chicano communities as well as in Mexico.

"The Marine Hymn" The official song of the U.S. Marine Corps. The words, by an uncertain author, follow a melody by the French composer Jacques Offenbach. References in the opening line, "From the halls of Montezuma to the shores of Tripoli," are to the Marines' involvement in, respectively, the Mexican War and the war against the Barbary pirates.

Marlboro Man A cowboy who serves as symbol for Marlboro cigarettes. Introduced to reframe the former "woman's" cigarette for a male market, he is often shown in a rugged mountain landscape ("Marlboro country").

Marlowe, Philip A hard-bitten, wise-cracking private eye who stars in three Raymond Chandler novels: *The Big Sleep* (1939), *Farewell My Lovely* (1940), and *The Long Goodbye* (1953). He has been portrayed on-screen by Humphrey Bogart and Robert Mitchum.

Marquette and Jolliet Explorers. Jacques Marquette (1637–75) was a Jesuit missionary, Louis Jolliet (1645–1700) a trapper and trader. In 1673, under orders from the governor of New France, the two canoed from the Great Lakes region down the Mississippi to the mouth of the Arkansas. Their conviction that the river flowed to the Gulf of Mexico was confirmed by Sieur de La Salle in 1682.

Marquis, Don See Archie and Mehitabel.

Marshall, John (1755–1835) The nation's first great chief justice. During his long tenure (1801–35), Marshall dominated the Supreme Court, personally writing hundreds of majority opinions and setting the basic tone of American justice. His opinion in *Marbury v. Madison* (1803) established the high court's right of judicial review; his view on *McCulloch v. Maryland* (1819) gave broadly defined "implied powers" to the federal government.

Marshall Field   See FIELD, Marshall.

Marshall Plan   A massive aid program aimed at restoring the European econo-
mies—and protecting them from communist influence—after World War II. Between 1948 and 1952, the United States sent Europe $13.5 million in funds,
goods, and trade benefits. The plan was named for former Army Chief of Staff
and then Secretary of State George Marshall (1880–1959), who had proposed it
in a 1947 speech.

Martha and the Vandellas   A popular MOTOWN "girl group" starring a Detroit native, lead singer Martha Reeves. Their major 1960s hits were "Quick-
sand," "Heat Wave," and "Dancin' in the Streets."

Martin, Mary   (1913–90) Singer, actress. A major star of the musical comedy
stage. With a sparkling personality and a clear, powerful voice, she scored triumphs in SOUTH PACIFIC, PETER PAN, and THE SOUND OF MUSIC. Her son, Larry
Hagman, became the starring villain of the TV series *Dallas* (see DALLAS [2]).

Martin and Lewis   The most popular comedy team of the 1950s. Singer Dean
Martin (1917–) played the suave, romantic straight man, and Jerry Lewis
(1926–) his goofy, unpredictable partner, in performances that began in nightclubs in 1946 and inspired seventeen movies over the following decade. The
films, such as *That's My Boy* (1951) and *The Caddy* (1953), capitalized on Lewis's
mugging skills, making him an unlikely cult hero, *"Le Roi du Crazy,"* to French
intellectuals. After 1956, Lewis carried his wacky persona into a solo career
highlighted by *The Sad Sack* (1957), *Cinderfella* (1960), and *The Nutty Professor*
(1963). Martin's insouciant charm earned him his own TV variety show (1965–74)
as well as movie roles.

martini   A cocktail made with gin and dry vermouth, with the proportions a
matter of feverish debate. It has been popular since the 1890s and was probably
named for the Martini and Rossi vermouth firm. Middle-class folklore abounds
with secrets for mixing the perfect martini; by consensus it is served well chilled
and dry (that is, with much more gin than vermouth). Acceptable garnishes are
green olives, lemon twists, and pearl onions—the latter of which makes the drink
a Gibson (see GIBSON GIRL).

Marty   A television play (1953) written by Paddy Chayevsky about the romantic
yearnings of a bashful butcher. Carried by the *Goodyear TV Playhouse* with Rod
STEIGER in the title role, it became in the words of Tim Brooks and Earle Marsh
"the single most acclaimed live drama in the history of television." The movie
version (1955) garnered a best actor Oscar for Ernest Borgnine.

Marx Brothers   Comedy team whose vaudeville skits and movie plots built on
zany situations, nonstop action, and ingenious patter. The sons of a New York
tailor and an enterprising stage mother, the Marxes were Chico (Leonard,
1886–1961), Harpo (Adolph, 1888–1964), Groucho (Julius, 1890–1977), Gummo
(Milton, 1893–1977), and Zeppo (Herbert, 1901–79). Gummo left the act in
vaudeville days and Zeppo served mainly as a straight man, but the elder trio
took Broadway by storm in the 1920s, with *I'll Say She Is* (1924), *The Cocoanuts*
(1925), and *Animal Crackers* (1928). Films of the latter two (1929 and 1930)

started their movie careers, and in the 1930s, they filmed a string of madcap masterpieces, notably *Monkey Business* (1931), *Duck Soup* (1933), and *A Night at the Opera* (1935). The improbable plots were excuses for classic characterizations: Groucho as the leering, mustachioed schemer; Chico as a master of Italian dialect; and silent Harpo as the genius of visual humor. Margaret Dumont was the frequent butt of their gags.

After the brothers' last appearance as a team in *Love Happy* (1950), Chico and Harpo retired from public life. Groucho did a handful of indifferent films and hosted the TV quiz show YOU BET YOUR LIFE (1950–61).

"Mary Had a Little Lamb" (1830) A short poem by Sarah Josepha HALE. A lamb follows Mary to school, which is "against the rules" but makes Mary's classmates "laugh and play." Sung to a simple ditty, the poem's cheery repetitiveness and veiled rebelliousness have made it a childhood favorite for generations.

"Maryland, My Maryland" A patriotic song with verses by James Ryder Randall, set to the tune of the German Christmas song "O Tannenbaum." Written in 1861, it became a rallying cry for the Confederate cause until the state, divided over slavery, was restrained from leaving the Union by martial law. It became Maryland's state song in 1939.

M*A*S*H A television comedy series (1972–83) based on a hit movie (1970) of the same name. Set during the KOREAN WAR, it portrayed the daily life of a medical staff in a Mobile Army Surgical Hospital, confronting the carnage around them with bleak humor. With the setting suggesting parallels to the VIETNAM WAR, the series became enormously popular; its final episode, screened in February 1983, drew the largest audience in television history.

Mason, Perry See PERRY MASON.

Mason-Dixon line The state line shared by Pennsylvania and Maryland, laid out in the 1760s by British surveyors Charles Mason and Jeremiah Dixon to settle a boundary dispute. It is the symbolic border between North and South.

Masters, Edgar Lee See SPOON RIVER ANTHOLOGY.

Masters and Johnson Sexuality researchers. Physician William Masters (1915–) and his assistant (later his wife) Virginia Johnson (1925–) studied human reactions to sexual stimuli. Their findings appeared in several books, the first of which, the best-selling *Human Sexual Response* (1966), became the KINSEY REPORT of its generation. The couple's work spawned a "sex therapy" industry devoted to the treatment of sexual dysfunction.

Masterson, Bat (1853–1921) Lawman, gambler, journalist. Canadian-born Masterson, nicknamed Bat either because he carried a cane or because his given name was Bartholomew, served as peace officer (1877–79) of notorious DODGE CITY, gambled with Wyatt EARP in TOMBSTONE (and with others practically everywhere else), and earned an inflated reputation as a gunfighter. After 1902, he wrote colorful, opinionated sports copy for a New York City newspaper. The dapper Masterson of legend was depicted, with his signature cane and bowler hat, by Gene Barry in a brief television series (1959–61). The real one, just before he died of a heart attack, left a philosophical note on his writing desk: "There are many in this old world of ours who hold that things break about even for us. I have observed, for example, that we all get about the same amount of ice. The rich get it in the summertime and the poor get it in the winter."

Mather, Cotton (1663–1728) Puritan clergyman, writer. The most famous member of an illustrious New England family, Mather wrote prolifically on both religion and science. His pronouncements on witchcraft helped to spark the SALEM WITCH TRIALS of 1692—events that Mather himself roundly denounced. His *Magnalia Christi Americana* (1702) remains a standard source on New England church history, while *The Angel of Bethesda* (1721) was the first American treatise on medicine. Pompous, erudite, and intellectually adventurous, Mather was a founder of Yale College (see YALE UNIVERSITY) and a defender, against heavy scorn, of smallpox vaccination.

Mathewson, Christy (1880–1925) Baseball player. A pitcher for the New York Giants, Christopher Mathewson won twenty or more games a year for twelve years straight (1903–14). In a seventeen-year career (1900–16), he retired 2,505 batters and won an astonishing two-thirds of the games he pitched. His lifetime win figure, 374, is third behind those of Cy YOUNG and Walter JOHNSON.

Mathis, Johnny (1935–) Singer. In the heyday of early rock 'n' roll, Mathis became, atavistically, a major star with his mellifluous delivery of ballads like "It's Not for Me to Say," "The Twelfth of Never," "Chances Are," and "MISTY." His romantic albums continued to sell for decades; *Johnny's Greatest Hits* (1958) was in the charts for ten years.

"Maud Miller" (1845) A poetic tale of thwarted romance by John Greenleaf WHITTIER. It contains the familiar couplet "For all sad words of tongue or pen / The saddest are these: It might have been."

Maui The second largest of the Hawaiian Islands. Renowned in the 1970s for a potent marijuana strain called Maui Wowie.

Mauldin, Bill (1921–) During World War II, as cartoonist for the service paper *Stars and Stripes,* Mauldin chided the brass and lionized the common soldier in work that made his long-suffering infantrymen, Willie and Joe, household names. His war pieces were collected in *Up Front* in the same year (1945) he won his first Pulitzer Prize. The second, for editorial cartooning on the *St. Louis Post-Dispatch,* came in 1959. Mauldin also published books on the troops of Korea (1952) and the American Revolution (1978).

Mauna Loa An active volcano on the island of Hawaii. Its frequent eruptions (about twice a decade) make it the most newsworthy of Hawaii's peaks. Local legend makes it the home of the fire-goddess Pele.

maverick (1) In cowboy terminology, a stray, unbranded cow or calf. From Texas cattleman Samuel Maverick (1803–70), whose huge herds lost such animals to neighboring ranchers. Hence (2) someone of a headstrong or independent nature. (3) The title of a television western series (1957–62) about the adventures of drifter Bret Maverick (James Garner) and his brother Bart (Jack Kelly). The show affectionately parodied the "shoot 'em up" genre.

Mayberry   A fictional North Carolina town that was the setting for two television sitcoms about the modest daily trials of rural America. *The Andy Griffith Show* (1960–68) starred Griffith as Sheriff Andy Taylor, Frances Bavier as his aunt Bee, Ron Howard as his son Opie, and Don Knotts as his perpetually rattled deputy, Barney Fife. *Mayberry R.F.D.* (1968–71) starred Ken Berry as Taylor's successor, Sheriff Sam Jones. The shows' hominess made them so popular that a 1986 TV "reunion" film, *Return to Mayberry,* was the highest-rated movie of the year.

Mayer, Louis B.   (1885–1957) Movie executive. Born in Russia, Eliezer Mayer started in films as a New England theater owner and, as vice president and general manager of MGM (1924–51), became the highest-paid individual in the United States. Under his tyrannical, intensely personal leadership, the studio became the world's greatest purveyor of "wholesome" entertainment. His flamboyant management style is suggested by the title of Bosley Crowther's biography, *Hollywood Rajah* (1960).

Mayflower   The ship that carried the first permanent settlers of New England from the Old World to America. About equally divided between religious dissenters and entrepreneurs, they sailed from Plymouth, England, in September of 1620, reached Massachusetts in November, and established PLYMOUTH COLONY the following month. To say that one's ancestors came over on the Mayflower is to boast of a staunchly English colonial pedigree.

Mayflower Compact   A document signed by the forty-one male passengers of the MAYFLOWER, agreeing to establish a "civil body politick" to be governed by "due submission and obedience" to commonly drafted laws. The Compact was a model for many other "plantation covenants," and is considered the New England colonists' first step toward self-government.

Mays, Willie   (1931–   ) Baseball player. As well known for his spectacular catches as for his power hitting, center fielder "Say Hey Willie" Mays played for the National League Giants for over twenty years (1951–72). Four times his league's home run leader and twice its most valuable player, he retired in 1973 with a career record of 660 home runs—third behind Hank AARON and Babe RUTH.

"Me Tarzan, you Jane"   See TARZAN.

Mead, Margaret   (1901–78) Anthropologist. After studying at Columbia under the "father of American anthropology," Franz Boas, Mead did fieldwork in the Pacific that resulted in her first book, *Coming of Age in Samoa* (1928). It disputed the given wisdom that adolescence was necessarily a time of strife, encouraged a romantic view of the South Seas as an erotic paradise, and did much to establish anthropology as a public discipline. Her later books, notably *Male and Female* (1949), reinforced her relativist reading of gender behavior and made her among the most visible members of her profession. Long associated with New York's American Museum of Natural History, Mead was its curator of ethnology from 1964 to 1969 and curator emeritus from 1969 until her death.

Medal of Honor   Usually called the Congressional Medal of Honor, this is the United States military services' highest decoration. First given to Union sailors in the Civil War, it is typically awarded for valor shown in battle. Occasional awards have gone for noncombat deeds, such as Charles LINDBERGH's flying of the Atlantic.

Meet John Doe (1941) Frank CAPRA's tragicomic study of a penniless "common man" and his manipulation by political interests. The ingenuous hero was played by Gary COOPER.

Meet the Press A weekly television program in which a panel of journalists interviews current newsmakers. Although its time slot and hosts have shifted over the years, it has run continuously since 1947, making it the longest-running series on network TV.

melting pot A common expression for American society, from its ability to absorb, and homogenize, waves of immigrants. It comes from Israel Zangwill's play *The Melting Pot* (1908), about an interethnic romance. "America is God's crucible," says one character, "the great melting pot where all the races of Europe are melting and reforming."

"Melts in your mouth, not in your hand" See M&Ms.

Melville, Herman (1819–91) Writer. The author of MOBY-DICK, Melville was born in New York City, went to sea as a young man, and later settled in western Massachusetts. His early experiences in the South Seas formed the background for his novels *Typee* (1846) and *Omoo* (1847). His later, richly philosophical works include *Pierre* (1852), *The Confidence Man* (1857), and the novelette BILLY BUDD, which was not published until thirty years after his death. Melville, who enjoyed little recognition in his lifetime, is now seen as one of America's greatest novelists.

Memorial Day Celebrated on the last Monday in May, this is a national holiday honoring U.S. war dead. It was first observed in the 1860s as Decoration Day, a time for decorating the graves of Civil War soldiers. Graveyard speeches and parades are still part of its observance, although it has also acquired nonmilitary connotations. It marks the running of the INDIANAPOLIS 500 and the beginning of summer.

Memphis The largest city in the state of Tennessee. Its nightclub district on Beale Street was important in the development of the BLUES; W. C. HANDY wrote both "Beale Street Blues" and "Memphis Blues" in its honor. Elvis PRESLEY's recording career began here, and his home, GRACELAND, remains a tourist attraction.

Mencken, H. L. (1880–1956) Writer. Acerbic erudition made Baltimore journalist Henry Louis Mencken one of the nation's most amusingly trenchant writers. He coined the term "booboisie" to show his contempt for everyday Americans, yet his multivolume study *The American Language* (1919–48) is testimony to his fascination with their speech. As a *Baltimore Sun* columnist, editor of the influential *American Mercury,* and author of a series of books aptly titled *Prejudices,* he had a profound impact on the literary culture of his time, especially in promoting such newcomers as Theodore DREISER, Sinclair LEWIS, and Eugene O'NEILL.

"Mending Wall"   (1914) A poem by Robert FROST recounting the mutual repair of a wall by the poet and a neighbor. It is remembered chiefly for its opening line, "Something there is that doesn't love a wall," and the neighbor's paradoxical adage "Good fences make good neighbors."

Mennonites   See AMISH.

Mercer, Johnny   (1909–76) Lyricist. Mercer began in the 1930s as a singer, doing duets with among others Bing CROSBY, but he achieved fame with the words to hundreds of romantic ballads. With Harold ARLEN he wrote "Blues in the Night" and "That Old Black Magic"; with Henry MANCINI, "Moon River" and "Days of Wine and Roses"; and with Billy Strayhorn and Duke ELLINGTON "Satin Doll." His solo compositions included the parlor cowboy son "I'm an Old Cowhand" and the sprightly pep tune "Ac-Cent-Chu-Ate the Positive."

Mercury Theater   See THE WAR OF THE WORLDS.

Merman, Ethel   (1909–84) Singer, actress. With a voice as robust as her personality, Ethel Zimmerman was one of Broadway's great red-hot mamas. She got her break in *Girl Crazy* (1930) and was thenceforth forever linked to its big number, George GERSHWIN's "I GOT RHYTHM." Her other hit shows included Cole PORTER's musical ANYTHING GOES (1934), Irving BERLIN's *Annie Get Your Gun* (1946)—which gave her another trademark, "THERE'S NO BUSINESS LIKE SHOW BUSINESS"—and *Call Me Madam* (1950).

Merriwell, Frank   The hero of the Frank Merriwell series of juvenile novels, written between 1900 and 1933 by William G. Patten (1866–1945). A Yale athlete and scholar, Merriwell was the impeccable epitome of the All-American boy. His adventures filled over two hundred volumes, selling in the vicinity of 25 million copies.

"Message to Garcia, A"   (1899) An inspirational tale by Elbert HUBBARD. Based on a real incident, it celebrates a young American who delivers a message to Cuban rebels in the days preceding the SPANISH-AMERICAN WAR. Read by business managers as a parable of pluck and industry, it sold roughly 40 million copies.

method acting   An acting technique that involves intense analysis and identification with the character. Developed by the Russian director Konstantin Stanislavsky, "the Method" was introduced to American audiences by the Group Theater in the 1930s. Method artists include Elia KAZAN, Marlon BRANDO, and Rod STEIGER.

Mexican War   (1846–48) Sometimes called Mr. Polk's War, the Mexican War put a military seal on President James Polk's MANIFEST DESTINY policy and ended in the transfer from Mexico to the United States of the region now typically called the American Southwest. Tension between the countries had been high since the annexation of Texas in 1845, and they developed into open conflict in 1846 after General Zachary Taylor (1784–1850) twice drove Mexican border forces across the Rio Grande. In interpreting the clashes, Congress conveniently begged the question of sovereignty, proclaiming "American blood has been shed on American soil.'' For the next two years, U.S. troops saw to it that that soil would be considerably increased in size, as Mexican troops under President SANTA ANNA lost literally every engagement they began.

U.S. victories in California and northern Mexico preceded General Winfield SCOTT's march from Vera Cruz to Mexico City late in 1847. His capture of the capital virtually ended the war, although the conflict did not officially end until 1848, with the signing of the Treaty of Guadalupe Hidalgo. It gave Mexico an indemnity of $15 million, in exchange for which the United States received over half a million square miles of new territory—including the current states of Arizona, New Mexico, and California. Mexicans, then as now, saw this as a land grab. Among the few Americans who agreed were Henry David THOREAU and Abraham LINCOLN. Most were delighted with the result, and in gratitude elected Taylor president.

MGM   Metro-Goldwyn-Mayer, the biggest and most successful Hollywood studio. It was formed in 1924 by a merger of Metro Pictures with companies run by Samuel GOLDWYN and Louis B. MAYER. With Mayer at the helm, MGM dominated moviemaking for three decades with glamorous, quality productions such as *Grand Hotel,* THE THIN MAN, *The Good Earth, T*HE WIZARD OF OZ, and GONE WITH THE WIND. With director Vincente MINNELLI and performers Fred ASTAIRE and Judy GARLAND on its payroll, the studio made ''MGM musical'' a watchword for style. Its trademark, a roaring lion, appeared before the credits of every film, while its hyperbolic slogan, ''More stars than there are in the heavens,'' accurately suggested the depth of its acting team. A mere glance at the MGM roster would reveal the names of the BARRYMORES, Clark GABLE, Joan CRAWFORD, Greta GARBO, Katharine HEPBURN, Spencer TRACY, and Elizabeth TAYLOR.

Miami Beach   An oceanfront in Miami, Florida, which has been a vacation and resort attraction since about 1900. The city itself has large Jewish and Cuban populations.

Michener, James   (1907–) Writer. Arguably the most durable author of the century, Michener published his first story collection, *Tales of the South Pacific* (1947), when he was nearly forty. Based on his World War II adventures in the U.S. Navy, it made his reputation and became the musical SOUTH PACIFIC. Many of his subsequent works have been massive, meticulously researched, and intensely personal studies of regional cultures. They have included books about Japan (*The Bridges at Toko-Ri,* 1953), the Hawaiian islands (*Hawaii,* 1959), Israel (*The Source,* 1965), Spain (*Iberia,* 1968), the American West (*Centennial,* 1974), and Mexico (*Mexico,* 1992).

Mickey Finn   A drink designed to render someone unconscious. Possibly from nineteenth-century San Francisco bartender Michael Finn, the inside member of a SHANGHAI ring. To ''slip someone a Mickey'' means to give him or her such a drink.

Mickey Mouse   The most famous rodent in the world. The cartoon character Mickey (originally called Mortimer) Mouse made his debut in Walt Disney's 1928 short *Plane Crazy* and acquired his squeaky voice (Disney's own) in that year's STEAMBOAT WILLIE. His irrepressible perkiness carried him through over a hundred subsequent cartoons, making him the linchpin of the Disney empire and a familiar face on scores of merchandising tie-ins, including the now collectible Mickey Mouse watch. *The Mickey Mouse Club,* a children's show starring young performers called the Mouseketeers, aired on afternoon television from 1955 to 1959.

middle passage   The transatlantic crossing for captured slaves, so named because it fell between a first passage from their African homes to the slavers' ships and a final journey from New World docksides to their owners' homes. Crowding below decks, lack of ventilation, poor food, and mistreatment made this passage the deadliest leg of their unwelcome journey: an estimated 20 percent of them died en route.

"Midnight Ride of Paul Revere"   See "PAUL REVERE'S RIDE."

Mighty Mouse   The hero first of a series of film shorts (from 1942) and then of a 1950s children's television series. A murine parody of SUPERMAN, the muscular, caped crusader was originally called Supermouse. He rescued innocents in distress from feline wiles.

Mildred Pierce   A novel (1941) by James M. CAIN about the relationship between a selfless mother and a thankless daughter. Joan CRAWFORD won an Academy Award for playing the mother in a 1945 movie.

military-industrial complex   A favorite phrase of social and political reformers who see the American economy bound too tightly to defense. It was first used by outgoing President Dwight D. EISENHOWER. In his 1961 farewell address, he warned against the growing combination of "an immense military establishment and a large arms industry."

Millay, Edna St. Vincent   (1892–1950) Poet. With a blend of lyricism and disillusionment, Millay became one of the best-read American poets of the 1920s. She won the Pulitzer Prize for *The Harp Weaver and Other Poems* (1923), but is more popularly remembered for her poetic account of a spiritual awakening, *Renascence* (1912). From *A Few Figs from Thistles* (1920) comes an often-cited quatrain:

> *My candle burns at both ends;*
> *It will not last the night;*
> *But, ah, my foes, and oh, my friends—*
> *It gives a lovely light.*

Miller, Arthur   (1915–) Playwright. The poet of the common man in the throes of uncertainty, Miller achieved his first wide success with the family tragedies *All My Sons* (1947) and DEATH OF A SALESMAN. *The Crucible* (1953), set in Salem during the 1690s, was a veiled critique of Joseph McCARTHY's witch-hunting. *After the Fall* (1964), about a troubled relationship, reflected the writer's own marriage to Marilyn MONROE. Miller also wrote the screenplay for her last film, *The Misfits* (1961). He has won numerous awards, including (for *Salesman*) the Pulitzer Prize.

Miller, Glenn   (1904–44) Bandleader. For five years before his death in a plane crash, Miller led the most popular dance band in the world. From 1940 to 1943, his group's expert section playing and lush arrangements gave them more than forty Top 10 records. Their hits included the novelty tunes "Little Brown Jug" and "Chattanooga Choo Choo" as well as the SWING MUSIC favorites "Moonlight Serenade," "In the Mood," and "String of Pearls."

Miller, Henry   (1891–1980) Novelist. Miller earned international notoriety when a novel about his philosophically misspent youth, *Tropic of Cancer* (1934), was banned in the United States for obscenity. In a sequel, *Tropic of Capricorn* (1938), and a later autobiographical trilogy, *The Rosy Crucifixion* (1949–60), he continued the erotic and verbal inventiveness that secured his reputation as an avant-garde master. When the American edition of *Cancer* finally appeared (1961), it became an instant best-seller.

"Millions for defense but not one cent for tribute"   See XYZ AFFAIR.

Milquetoast, Caspar   See CASPAR MILQUETOAST.

"Mines of Avondale, The"   See AVONDALE.

Minnelli, Vincente   (1910–86) Hollywood's most accomplished director of MU-SICAL COMEDIES. After an apprenticeship as a choreographer under Busby BERKELEY, he directed some of MGM's most sparkling vehicles, including the Oscar winners AN AMERICAN IN PARIS and *Gigi* (1958) and the box-office hit *Meet Me in St. Louis* (1944), starring his first wife, Judy GARLAND. Their daughter, Liza Minnelli (1946–   ), like her mother, is a riveting performer. She took the best actress Oscar for her work in *Cabaret* (1972).

minstrel shows   The dominant theater form of the mid-nineteenth century, featuring blackface whites performing skits and songs in Negro dialect. "Daddy" Thomas RICE initiated the genre in the 1820s, and within a decade it was supporting numerous troupes, one of the first being Dan EMMETT's Virginia Minstrels. The most successful troupe, run by Edwin Christy, publicized the songs of Stephen FOSTER. Minstrelsy's reliance on plantation motifs made it archaic by the end of the century, although isolated shows survived into the age of VAUDEVILLE, and Al JOLSON was still using its conventions in the 1920s. See also CHRISTY MINSTRELS.

Minuit, Peter   (1580–1638) The first director general of the New Netherland colony, whose capital, New Amsterdam, became New York City. Legend has him buying Manhattan Island from local Indians for the equivalent, in beads and baubles, of twenty-four dollars. He later served as governor of New Sweden, whose residents built the country's first LOG CABINS.

Minutemen   Colonial soldiers who, like volunteer firemen, could assemble ready to fight at a moment's notice. They fought in Maryland, New Hampshire, and Connecticut during the Revolutionary War, but are best remembered for their stand at Massachusetts's CONCORD Bridge, where a statue honors their bravery. The Minuteman symbol—a Continental with rifle at the ready—has been adopted by various organizations including the University of Massachusetts football team and the Connecticut-based Liberty Insurance Company.

Miranda, Carmen   (1909–55) Singer, dancer. The "Brazilian Bombshell," Miranda became widely known in the 1940s for her Latin-style dancing in Hollywood films. Her trademark, a huge hat filled with fruit, was noted in the 1943 song "The Lady with the Tutti Frutti Hat," and was adopted by the United Fruit Company for CHIQUITA BANANA. She was identified with the 1941 song *"Mama Eu Quero"* (Mama, I Love You).

Miranda decision   The Supreme Court decision in *Miranda v. Arizona* (1966), which held that a person suspected of a crime must, prior to questioning by the police, be fully informed of his or her FIFTH AMENDMENT rights, and that evidence obtained from a person who had not been so informed was inadmissible in court. The ruling freed convicted rapist Ernesto Miranda and made "reading him his rights" standard police procedure. Following Chief Justice Earl Warren's opinion in the case, law officers now are expected to recite to everyone they arrest, "You have the right to remain silent. If you choose not to remain silent, anything you say can be taken down and used against you in a court of law. You have the right to an attorney. If you cannot afford an attorney, one will be appointed for you by the court." This invocation is sometimes referred to as Mirandizing.

Miss America Pageant   A nationwide beauty contest held annually since 1921 in Atlantic City, New Jersey. Contestants represent their home states in swimsuit, talent, and evening gown competitions, with the judges' pick becoming "Miss America" for a year. Longtime host Bert Parks's crooning of the pageant theme song became a traditional kitsch finale in the 1960s.

Miss Lonelyhearts   (1) The most famous book (1933) of novelist Nathaniel WEST. It is the story of an advice columnist's tragic involvement in his correspondents' forlorn lives. Hence (2) "Miss Lonelyhearts column" or simply "lonelyhearts column" for a newspaper feature offering personal advice. See "DEAR ABBY"; Dorothy DIX.

Miss Piggy   See MUPPETS.

Mississippi River   North America's greatest river, known variously as the Father of Waters, Old Man River, and the Mighty Mississip. Discovered by the Spanish explorer Hernando DE SOTO in 1541, it drains ten states from the Great Lakes region to the Gulf of Mexico, and is the symbolic border between the East and the West. River traffic has been heavy since the seventeenth century, first with fur traders' canoes, then with KEELBOATS, and finally with STEAMBOATS. The spelling of the name is a traditional stumper for schoolchildren. See also Mike FINK; Mark TWAIN.

Missouri River   The Mississippi River's main tributary, the Missouri runs for over 2,300 miles from its headwaters in the Rocky Mountains to its mouth near present-day St. Louis. First explored by the LEWIS AND CLARK EXPEDITION, it became a major highway for the eighteenth-century fur trade. Its extreme turbidity gave it the nickname Big Muddy.

Mr. Big   See BIG.

Mr. Charlie   Black slang for a white person. Racial tension is the subject of James BALDWIN's 1964 play *Blues for Mister Charlie*.

Mr. Clean   Someone of impeccable character. The trademark personification of a household cleanser.

Mr. Magoo   Animated cartoon character. An elderly, nearsighted gentleman whose poor eyesight generates mayhem that he miraculously escapes. The figure was created in 1949 by John Hubley; Jim Backus provided his raspy voice.

Mr. October   See Reggie JACKSON.

Mr. Peanut   Trademark of the Planters Nut Company. The prize design in a promotional contest, he is a peanut adorned in a top hat, monocle, cane, spats, and white gloves.

Mister Roberts   (1955) A comedy directed by John FORD and Mervyn LeRoy about the clash between a bored naval crew and their tyrannical captain. Henry Fonda (see FONDA FAMILY) played the crew's officer spokesman, James CAGNEY the captain. It was based on Thomas Heggen's 1946 novel.

Mister Rogers' Neighborhood   A children's television show hosted since 1967 by soft-spoken, avuncular Fred Rogers. The gentle tone of each daytime episode was set by Rogers removing his street shoes and donning sneakers while singing, "It's a beautiful day in the neighborhood. Would you be mine? Won't you be my neighbor?"

Mr. Smith Goes to Washington   (1939) Frank CAPRA's schmaltzy populist movie about a flunky, sent to Washington by corrupt politicians, who dismays them and charms the public by exposing their venality. The portrayal of Senator Jefferson Smith won James STEWART an Oscar nomination.

"Mr. Watson, come here, I want you"   The cry for help uttered by Alexander Graham BELL on March 10, 1876, summoning his assistant, Thomas Watson, from the next room. It was the first clearly audible message ever received by telephone.

"Misty"   A romantic ballad (1954) with words by Johnny Burke and music by jazz pianist Errol Garner. A lounge favorite, it was a gold record in 1959 for Johnny MATHIS and the dramatic centerpiece of Clint EASTWOOD's 1971 thriller *Play Misty for Me*.

Mitchell, Margaret   Author of GONE WITH THE WIND.

Mitty, Walter   The protagonist of JAMES THURBER's 1942 story "The Secret Life of Walter Mitty." Timid, henpecked Mitty escapes from his humdrum life by imagining himself the hero of extravagant adventures. Danny Kaye played him in a 1947 movie.

Mix, Tom   (1880–1940) Actor. The biggest cowboy star of the 1920s, Mix was a former WILD WEST SHOW rider who entered films as a bit player in 1909. His physical daring and athletic skills served him well in over a hundred largely interchangeable films. He also had a brief circus career with his horse, Tony, and started a radio series that continued long after his death.

mob, the   See MAFIA.

Moby-Dick   (1851) Herman MELVILLE's intricate, mammoth novel about a sea captain's hunt for the white whale that has crippled him. On the surface, the book is a rousing sea story, filled with endless obiter dicta about nineteenth-century whaling. Its philosophical undercurrents, however, are so complex that it is often touted as the GREAT AMERICAN NOVEL. The sailor narrator begins the tale with one of the most famous opening lines in literature, ''Call me Ishmael.'' Other characters include his bunkmate, the Polynesian harpooner Queequeg; the single-minded, tortured Captain AHAB; and the white whale himself, Moby-Dick. Melville dedicated the book to Nathaniel HAWTHORNE. It was filmed in 1956 by John HUSTON.

moccasin   (1) The standard footwear of various Indian peoples from the eastern forests to the Great Plains. Moccasins were made of deerskin or other leather and were commonly decorated with elaborate quill- or beadwork. (2) See WATER MOCCASIN.

mockingbird   A gray-and-white songbird with the ability to mimic other species' calls. Native to the South, it is the state bird of Arkansas, Florida, Mississippi, Tennessee, and Texas. A popular lullaby, sometimes called ''The Mockingbird Song,'' begins ''Hush little baby, don't say a word / Mama's gonna buy you a mockingbird.'' See TO KILL A MOCKINGBIRD.

Model T   An automobile produced by the Ford Motor Company from 1908 to 1927. Designed as an inexpensive vehicle ''for the great multitude,'' the Tin Lizzie revolutionized manufacturing as well as personal transportation; Henry FORD's production system introduced the modern assembly line. Ten years after its introduction, half of all the motorcars in the world were Model Ts. A common joke of the era was Ford's supposed comment that a customer could have the car in any color, ''as long as it was black.''

Mohawk   An Indian people who were one of the five members of the IROQUOIS LEAGUE. The young men's distinctive hairdo—the head shaved except for a central ridge of hair—was adopted in the 1970s by American and English ''punks,'' who referred to the radical style as a mohawk.

Molly Maguires   An Irish-American secret society whose members practiced terrorism against Pennsylvania mine owners in the 1860s and 1870s. They sponsored an effective strike in 1874–75, but were soon thereafter infiltrated by a PINKERTON agent. Subsequent murder convictions and hangings of their leaders led to their collapse.

Molly Pitcher   See Molly PITCHER.

mom-and-pop store   A small business run by a married couple. The term dates from the 1950s, when such businesses first lost serious ground to chain stores and suburban shopping malls.

Monday-morning quarterback   An expert on how the previous weekend's football game should have been played. Hence anyone with twenty-twenty hindsight; an armchair general.

Monitor and Merrimack   Civil War ironclads. The Union's *Monitor,* a flat, single-turreted ship, was ridiculed as a "cheesebox on a raft." The *Merrimack,* a scuttled Union frigate, was raised by the Confederates, refitted with iron, and renamed the *Virginia.* Their inconclusive battle at Hampton Roads, Virginia, on March 9, 1862, was the world's first confrontation between armored vessels; it symbolically ended the age of military sail.

Monk, Maria   (1817–49) The alleged author of an anti-Catholic best-seller, *The Awful Disclosure of Maria Monk,* published in 1836 by the Society for the Diffusion of Christian Knowledge. The book claimed that, as a nun in a Montreal convent, Maria had witnessed routine seductions by priests, the physical abuse of novices who resisted, and the burial on nunnery grounds of aborted children. The scandalous tract was exposed as a fraud, but not before swelling the ranks of KNOW-NOTHING PARTY sympathizers.

Monk, Thelonious   (1917–82) Jazz musician. One of the originators of BEBOP, pianist Monk performed with Dizzy GILLESPIE and Charlie PARKER, and as a soloist. His composition "Round Midnight" became a jazz classic.

monkey trial   See SCOPES TRIAL.

Monopoly   A board game invented in 1933 by Charles Darrow and distributed since 1935 by Parker Brothers. The object is for one player to bankrupt the others—and thus secure a monopoly—by trading properties named for streets in ATLANTIC CITY. The internationally successful game (there are editions promoted in dozens of countries) has brought the company $100 million in sales.

Monroe, Bill   (1911–) The "Father of Bluegrass," Kentuckian Monroe played with his brother Charlie as the Monroe Brothers before founding the Blue Grass Boys in 1938. With Monroe providing a driving mandolin line and a plaintive, "high lonesome" singing style, the group introduced the music that bears its name. Of the many bluegrass stars who began as Monroe sidemen, the most famous were the duo FLATT AND SCRUGGS.

Monroe, Marilyn   (1926–62) Actress. Elevated by her early death to the status of a tragic heroine, Monroe was in her lifetime the epitome of the vulnerable starlet. Born Norma Jean Baker in Los Angeles, she endured an unhappy childhood, a brief teenage marriage, and several bit parts before finding her métier as a light comedienne in GENTLEMEN PREFER BLONDES. Similar parts, displaying a unique blend of sensuality and breathy innocence, followed in *How to Marry a Millionaire* (1953), *The Seven Year Itch* (1955), and SOME LIKE IT HOT. As the chorus-girl wiggle got more attention than her comedic talents, Monroe became an increasingly popular, and increasingly frustrated, sex symbol, yearning for the acceptance as a serious actress that was continually denied her. Critical praise for her work in *Bus Stop* (1956) and *The Misfits* (1961) did not alleviate her distress, and she died of an overdose of sleeping pills, a likely suicide, at thirty-six. Her second and third husbands were Joe DiMAGGIO and Arthur MILLER.

Monroe Doctrine   The most significant accomplishment of President James Monroe's administration (1817–25). Outlined in Monroe's annual message to Congress in 1823, it proposed that the Western Hemisphere, from that point on, should be considered an American, rather than a European, preserve. Speaking of the recently independent Latin American nations that were prime targets for "recolonization," Monroe proclaimed that they were henceforth "not to be considered as subjects for future colonization" and that any European attempt to do so would be considered "as dangerous to our peace and safety." In its day the doctrine was mostly bluster, but it became the basis of the United States' Latin American policy, making the Caribbean by the end of the century an "American lake."

Montana, Joe (1956–) Football player. Quarterback for the San Francisco 49ers throughout the 1980s, Montana is the most precise passer in the history of the game. He has passed for over 35,000 yards, with a career rating of 93.4 percent accuracy. He has led teams to four SUPER BOWL victories.

Montezuma (ca. 1480–1520) AZTEC ruler. Head of the Aztec nation when Hernando CORTÉS landed in Mexico, Montezuma took the invaders as returning gods, invited them into his capital, Tenochtitlán, and thus secured his own speedy downfall. It is unclear whether the Spaniards or his own people were responsible for his death in the revolt that followed his fateful error. "Montezuma's revenge" is slang for traveler's diarrhea, or turista.

Monticello Thomas JEFFERSON's home near Charlottesville, Virginia. Built between 1768 and 1809 to Jefferson's own design, it is a masterpiece of neoclassical architecture. It rests on a hill; hence the Italian name, "little mountain."

Moody, Dwight Lyman (1837–99) Evangelist. A nonordained minister, Moody called Christians to God (rather than to a specific denomination) in one of the nineteenth century's most durable revivals. Between his first English tour in 1873 and his retirement almost twenty years later, Moody preached to millions on two continents. His close associate was the GOSPEL MUSIC hymnist Ira SANKEY.

Moody, Helen Wills See Helen Newington WILLS.

"Moon River" A moody ballad that started the songwriting collaboration of Johnny MERCER and Henry MANCINI. It appeared first in the movie *Breakfast at Tiffany's* (1961), then became a major hit (and a theme song) for Andy Williams.

moonshine Illegally distilled whiskey. The term, dating from the eighteenth century in England, probably referred to the necessarily nocturnal activities of producers and smugglers. In the United States, it is associated most closely with the Appalachian backwoods, where tax-dodging "moonshiners" have plied their trade since colonial times.

Moore, Clement Clarke See "THE NIGHT BEFORE CHRISTMAS."

Moore, Mary Tyler (1937–) Television actress. Moore's perky, wholesome characterizations of housewife Laura Petrie on *The Dick Van Dyke Show* (1961–66) and news producer Mary Richards on *The Mary Tyler Moore Show* (1970–77) made her a model of the sensibly ambitious modern woman. The latter show—praised for having destigmatized the single woman—led to spin-off shows for three of the supporting characters.

Moral Majority   A conservative political action group founded in 1979 by fundamentalist preacher Jerry Falwell, who reached millions through his Virginia-based television ministry. Members were influential in electing Ronald REAGAN to the White House. See also SILENT MAJORITY.

Morgan, J. P.   (1837–1913) Financier. An enormously successful ROBBER BARON, John Pierpont Morgan founded the banking house that became J. P. Morgan & Company, bought out Andrew CARNEGIE in 1901 to form the U.S. Steel Corporation, and through his influence on a vast network of company managements, virtually ran the U.S. economy at the turn of the century. When President Teddy ROOSEVELT turned to trust-busting (see TRUSTS), it was Morgan's giant holding company, the Northern Securities Company, that he attacked first. J.P.'s reaction to the government threat was characteristically arrogant: "If we have done anything wrong, send your man to my man and they can fix it up." (Despite his blitheness, the firm was dissolved in 1904.) Morgan left much of his superb art collection to New York City's Metropolitan Museum of Art, his books and manuscripts to the Morgan Library.

Morgan, Sir Henry   (ca. 1635–88) Privateer. With a royal commission from the English government, Welsh-born Morgan raided Spanish shipping in the Caribbean between 1668 and 1672. He also hit ports in Cuba, Venezuela, and Panama, capturing the latter's capital in 1671. Tried in London for piracy, he was punished with a knighthood from King Charles II and, in 1674, with the governorship of Jamaica.

Mormons   Members of the Christian denomination known as the Church of Jesus Christ of Latter-Day Saints. It was founded in 1830 by Joseph Smith (1805–44), an upstate New York farmer who claimed that the angel Moroni had approached him in a vision and shown him golden tablets containing the "Book of Mormon." Using this prophetic document as a scripture, Smith established communities throughout the Midwest, with his major base at Nauvoo, Illinois. Local resentment at the newcomers—who were both prosperous and polygamous—led to Smith's murder in 1844 and the elevation of Brigham YOUNG to church leadership.

Under Young, the Latter-Day Saints in 1847 blazed a trail across the Plains to the Great Salt Lake, to found a community beyond the reach of "Gentiles." Their infant Salt Lake City grew rapidly, thanks to the discipline and cooperative efforts of church members, but the "promised land" was in constant conflict with the U.S. government, especially after passage of a federal antibigamy law (1862). Mormon elders finally abandoned "plural marriage" in 1890, and six years later Utah became a state. Mormon doctrine has broadened over the years (for example, black men were admitted to the priesthood in 1978) and the church remains a force in Utah politics.

moron joke   See LITTLE MORON.

Morse, Samuel F. B.   (1791–1872) Artist, inventor. Morse was respected in his day as a portrait painter, and he served sixteen years as president of the National Academy of Design. Today he is remembered as the inventor of the telegraph, a signaling device he designed in 1838 and whose first public message, sent in 1844 from Baltimore to Washington, was "What hath God wrought!"

Morse's transmission code, a system of electrically recorded dots and dashes, became universally known as Morse code.

Morton, Jelly Roll   (1885–1941) Jazz pianist. The Creole musician Ferdinand Joseph LaMenthe, after an apprenticeship playing piano in New Orleans's STORY-VILLE district, made influential jazz recordings in the 1920s and 1930s, both solo and with his Chicago group the Red Hot Peppers. He claimed, with more flair than logic, that he had "personally invented jazz in 1902."

Mosconi, Willie   (1913–93) Generally considered the greatest pool player of all time, Mosconi won the international pocket billiards crown thirteen times in the 1940s and 1950s. He once sank 526 balls without a miss.

Mose the Bowery B'hoy   Protagonist of Benjamin Baker's 1848 melodrama *A Glance at New York*. A dandified volunteer fireman who divided his time equally between strutting, brawling, and saving imperiled infants, Mose was played by Frank Chanfrau (1824–84) first in New York, then in a road show that hit two dozen cities. The character's brash appearance and slang-peppered conversation elicited imitators throughout the 1850s, making him in the words of Richard Dorson "America's first urban folk hero."

Moses   Nickname of Harriet TUBMAN.

Moses, Grandma   (1860–1961) Painter. The farmer's wife Anna Mary Robertson Moses took up painting in her sixties and had her first New York City show when she was eighty. Self-taught, she painted rural scenes in a nostalgic, primitivist style that made her a high-art counterpart to Norman ROCKWELL. Typical subjects were titled *The Old Oaken Bucket, Christmas at Home,* and *The Quilting Bee.*

Mother Ann Lee   See SHAKERS.

Mother Divine   See FATHER DIVINE.

Mother's Day   A national holiday celebrated since 1914 on the second Sunday in May. The first, unofficial observance was in 1908, when West Virginia schoolteacher Anna Jarvis, eager to honor her own mother, sold the idea to Philadelphia churches.

Motor City   See MOTOWN.

Motown   (1) Detroit, Michigan. Also known as "Motor City," from the dominance there of the auto industry. (2) A type of SOUL music developed there in the 1960s. Motown Records, founded by Berry Gordy, Jr. (1929–   ), specialized in a "Motown sound" featuring heavy bass lines, rich harmonies, and danceable beats. The company's stars included THE SUPREMES, THE TEMPTATIONS, and Stevie WONDER.

Mott, Lucretia   (1793–1880) Feminist reformer. Mott helped to found an early ABOLITIONIST group, the American Antislavery Society, in 1833, and opened her home in 1850 to runaway slaves. Refused seating at a London antislavery convention because of her gender, she organized the SENECA FALLS CONVENTION with Elizabeth Cady STANTON. She opposed, but acquiesced to, its WOMEN'S SUFFRAGE plank.

Mount McKinley   See Mount MCKINLEY.

Mount Rushmore   See Mount RUSHMORE.

Mount Vernon   The Alexandria, Virginia, estate of George WASHINGTON, a riverfront plantation with a Georgian-style mansion. Washington inherited it from his half brother when he was twenty and enlarged the building in stages over the years. The property became a national shrine in 1860.

mountain dew   See CORN LIQUOR.

mountain men   Fur trappers who, in pursuit of the riches available from the BEAVER trade, explored the Rocky Mountain region and beyond in the early 1800s. Some were the hardy *isolés* of western legend, although most of them worked for John Jacob Astor or other fur barons (see ASTOR FAMILY), and many were only part-time pioneers who enhanced their income by scouting and more bourgeois pursuits. Among the best-known mountain men were Jim BRIDGER, Kit CARSON, John COLTER, and Jed SMITH.

mountain oysters   Also "Rocky mountain oysters." The testicles of a sheep, pig, or bull. Breaded and fried, they are considered a delicacy in some western regions.

Mounties   See ROYAL CANADIAN MOUNTED POLICE.

Mouseketeers   See MICKEY MOUSE.

moxie   Courage, nerve. From the brand name Moxie, a once popular soft drink with a bitter "punch."

Ms.   A feminist all-purpose title, suggested in the 1970s as a replacement for the "Miss" and "Mrs." that would not reveal marital status. *Ms.* magazine, a feminist forum, was founded in 1972.

MTV   Music Television. A television channel that debuted in the 1970s with video presentations of popular songs. Since expanded to include comedy and interview formats, it is a principal venue for the promotion of music and as powerful a register of teenage taste as AMERICAN BANDSTAND was in the 1950s.

muckrakers   Crusading journalists who, in the first decade of this century, attacked abuses of government and private industry. They were given the name by President Theodore ROOSEVELT, who, although he approved generally of their critiques, likened them to the "man with the muck rake" in John Bunyan's allegory *Pilgrim's Progress*. Significant muckraking works included Lincoln STEFFENS's study of municipal graft *The Shame of the Cities* (1903), Ida TARBELL's *History of the Standard Oil Company* (1903), Ray Stannard Baker's *The Railroads on Trial* (1906), and Upton SINCLAIR's shocking novel THE JUNGLE. The principal forum for such exposés was *McClure's* magazine, which tripled its circulation with the radical reporting.

Mudd, Samuel (1833–83) A Maryland physician who treated John Wilkes BOOTH's broken leg after his escape from FORD's THEATRE. Convicted of complicity in the Lincoln assassination, he spent four years in prison before being pardoned. The expression "His name is mud" does not, as is often supposed, come from his name. It was current in England long before Booth was born.

Mudville See "CASEY AT THE BAT."

mugwumps Reform Republicans who left their party during the 1884 election to back Democratic presidential candidate Grover Cleveland. The name, from the Algonquin for "chief," had previously been applied to pompous politicos. There is no substance to the explanation that it meant the mugwumps had their mugs on one side of a fence and their "wumps" on the other.

Muhammad Ali See Muhammad ALI.

Mullins, Priscilla See "THE COURTSHIP OF MILES STANDISH."

munchkin A small, fetching child. From the Munchkins, small characters in THE WIZARD OF OZ film.

Muppets Puppets designed in the 1950s by Jim Henson (1936–90). Regular players on SESAME STREET from 1969, they soon acquired their own guest-studded *Muppet Show* (1976–81) and even a *Muppet Movie* (1979). Posters, dolls, and other merchandising tie-ins made them the best-marketed characters since MICKEY MOUSE. Chief among Henson's dozens of characters were wisecracking Kermit the Frog and vain Miss Piggy. The show's many spoofs included the STAR TREK–like adventure "Pigs in Space" and a pas de deux between Miss Piggy and Rudolf Nureyev from the porcine ballet *Swine Lake.*

Murder Inc. Nickname for a group of hired killers employed by a 1930s crime syndicate to eliminate its rivals. Syndicate bosses included "Lucky" Luciano, Louis "Lepke" Buchalter, Vito Genovese, Frank Costello, and the goon squad leader, "Bugsy" Siegel. The organization devised the code terms "contract" for a killing assignment and "hit" for the killing itself. Hence "hit man" for any hired assassin.

Murieta, Joaquín (ca. 1832–53) The Mexican-born "Robin Hood of the Southwest," Murieta attacked miners and other Anglos during the California GOLD RUSH, acquiring a reputation as a dashing, invincible ladies' man whose social banditry was a response to racist mistreatment. After he was killed by California Rangers, his head was cut off, preserved in alcohol, and widely exhibited.

Murphy, Audie (1924–71) The most decorated U.S. soldier of World War II, the recipient of the MEDAL OF HONOR and over two dozen other awards. He played himself in the 1955 movie of his war autobiography *To Hell and Back,* and also appeared in a string of forgettable westerns.

Murphy's Law The facetiously dyspeptic observation "If anything can go wrong, it will." The originator was a California engineer, Edward Murphy, who around 1949 used a similar phrase to ridicule an incompetent supervisor. Modern versions, of which there are hundreds, include "The minute you take a catnap is the minute the boss walks in" and "Nature always sides with the hidden flaw."

Murrow, Edward R. (1908–65) News broadcaster. The most famous TV journalist of his day, Murrow made his mark reporting the London blitz, then hosted two landmark television news shows. On *See It Now* (1952–55) he examined current events, attacking Joseph MCCARTHY in one famous episode. On *Person to Person* (1953–59) he took a more casual approach, prefiguring the modern celebrity interview with visits to the homes of people such as Marilyn MONROE, Fidel Castro, and John F. KENNEDY.

Musial, Stan (1920–) Baseball player. In a twenty-two-year career (1941–63), St. Louis Cardinals fielder "Stan the Man" Musial came to bat more times than anyone but Ty COBB. He won the National League batting championship seven times, set NL records for hits (3,630) and runs batted in (1,949), and was the league's most valuable player three times.

Music Television See MTV.

musical comedy Charles Barras's 1866 hit *The Black Crook* is generally considered the first American musical, but the genre really took shape in the early twentieth century, when theatrical producers blended elements of European light opera and the English music hall revue into a distinctively American form of entertainment. The loosest examples of the new form were showgirl extravaganzas like ZIEGFELD'S FOLLIES, while the narrative coherence that evolved after World War I was pioneered by Victor HERBERT and George M. COHAN. Between the wars the Broadway musical matured, with such composers as Jerome KERN, George GERSHWIN, Irving BERLIN, and Cole PORTER making "show tune" a synonym for sophisticated songwriting. The 1940s saw the emergence of the musical theater's two greatest writing teams, Richard RODGERS and Oscar HAMMERSTEIN II and LERNER AND LOEWE, the 1950s that of Leonard BERNSTEIN. In the past quarter century, as "serious" theater fell into the doldrums, musical comedy remained the industry's salvation. Of the ten longest-running Broadway shows of all time, seven were musicals introduced since 1960. These were *A Chorus Line* (1975–90), *Oh! Calcutta!* (1976–89), *Cats* (1982–), *42nd Street* (1980–89), *Grease* (1972–80), *Fiddler on the Roof* (1964–72), and *Hello, Dolly!* (1964–71).

Hollywood's equally profitable investment in the musical began with the advent of sound in the 1930s, when Busby BERKELEY's glitter and ASTAIRE AND ROGERS's elegance dominated the screen. The following decade saw the dazzling work of Vincente MINNELLI and Gene KELLY, while since the 1950s many successful Broadway shows have been filmed, often with the same leads, by California studios.

mustang (1) A small wild horse of the American West. The Spanish name *mestengo* means "stray." (2) As Mustang: a medium-size, sporty car produced by the Ford Company beginning in 1964.

Mutiny on the Bounty A 1932 historical novel by Charles Nordhoff (1887–1947) and James Hall (1887–1951) about a mutiny against an eighteenth-century British sea captain, William Bligh. The first book in a trilogy, it was filmed twice. The first version (1935), with Charles Laughton as Bligh and Clark GABLE as mutineer Fletcher Christian, won the Academy Award for best picture. The second version (1962) starred, respectively, Trevor Howard and Marlon BRANDO.

Mutt and Jeff Tall, gangly Mutt and pudgy Jeff were the principals in an animated cartoon series which in the 1920s was second only to FELIX THE CAT in popularity. Their appearance made "Mutt and Jeff" a shorthand for physical disparity.

Muzak Programmed, generally bland music that is piped into tens of thousands of businesses around the world. Invented in 1934, it has been sold since the 1940s as a productivity enhancer, on the theory that upbeat but soothing music can offset sluggishness. Variants on the trademark name Muzak are "supermarket music" and "elevator music."

"My Country, 'Tis of Thee" See AMERICA (2).

"My Darling Clementine" (1) A popular song about a miner's unfortunate daughter. Percy Montrose is said to have written it in 1884, although the GOLD RUSH theme suggests an earlier date, and Montrose may have adopted an older tune.

> *Oh my darling, oh my darling,*
> *Oh my darling Clementine,*
> *You are lost and gone forever,*
> *Dreadful sorrow, Clementine.*

(2) As *My Darling Clementine:* a western directed in 1946 by John FORD. The story of the gunfight at the O.K. CORRAL, it stars Henry Fonda (see FONDA FAMILY) as Marshal Wyatt EARP.

My Fair Lady A LERNER AND LOEWE musical comedy (1956) based on George Bernard Shaw's play *Pygmalion.* The story of the romance between a brash Cockney girl and her elocution coach, it contains the songs "I've Grown Accustomed to Her Face" and "I Could Have Danced All Night." The initial New York production, in which Julie Andrews played Eliza Doolittle, stayed on Broadway over six years. A 1964 movie, starring Audrey Hepburn, won Oscars for best picture, best director (George CUKOR), and best actor (Rex Harrison).

My Lai A Vietnamese hamlet where, in 1968, American soldiers searching for Vietcong sympathizers massacred hundreds of civilians, including women and children. Revelation of the incident in 1970 widened U.S. opposition to the VIETNAM WAR, and public outcry forced an army investigation. A subsequent court-martial laid the blame on William Calley, a young lieutenant who served ten years at hard labor. Since Calley was the only soldier convicted, the investigation was widely viewed as a cover-up.

My Little Chickadee (1939) A comic western starring Mae WEST and W. C. FIELDS. The title, which he delivers to her leeringly, became a common term of mock endearment.

"My Old Kentucky Home"　A MINSTREL SHOW tune written by Stephen FOSTER. Introduced in 1853, it became one of his best-loved melodies as well as the state song of Kentucky.

> *Oh the sun shines bright on my old Kentucky home,*
> *My old Kentucky home far away.*

NAACP National Association for the Advancement of Colored People, an organization formed in 1910 to promote social and economic justice for blacks. W. E. B. Du Bois edited its journal *The Crisis*. Before the radicalization of the movement in the 1960s, it was the leading activist group for civil rights.

Naismith, James (1861–1939) The Canadian-born inventor of basketball, Naismith was a physical education instructor at the YMCA training school in Springfield, Massachusetts, when in 1891 he devised basketball for his students. A shortage of boxes, which he had wanted to use for the goals, led to the substitution of peach baskets and the description "basket ball."

Naked and the Dead, The (1948) Norman Mailer's best-selling first novel, based on his experiences as a World War II infantryman. Raoul Walsh filmed it in 1958.

Naked Lunch See William S. Burroughs.

Nam U.S. military slang for Vietnam. From the period of the Vietnam War.

Namath, Joe (1943–) Football player. "Broadway Joe" Namath, one of professional football's first superstars, quarterbacked the University of Alabama team to three bowl games, signed with the New York Jets for an unprecedented $427,000 in 1965, and astonished football insiders four years later when he directed a Super Bowl victory over the much-favored Baltimore Colts. In a thirteen-season career, he passed for 218 touchdowns.

name is mud See Samuel Mudd.

Nancy Drew See Nancy Drew.

Nantucket sleigh ride A nineteenth-century whaling term. Nantucket Island, off the mainland of Massachusetts, was a whaling center. When whales were hunted from open boats, a harpoon hit often caused the quarry to drag the boat behind it as it sought to escape. The resulting wild ride was called a Nantucket sleigh ride.

Nasby, Petroleum V. The pen name of journalist David Locke (1833–88). During the Civil War, he published satirical letters in the *Findlay* (Ohio) *Jeffersonian*, putting proslavery arguments into the mouth of a drunken racist. *The Nasby Papers* (1864) was the first of several collections.

Nash, Ogden (1902–71) Poet. The undisputed American master of light verse, Nash wrote frequently for The New Yorker and published several collections of his pun-studded oeuvre, including *The Bad Parent's Garden of Verse* (1936) and *You Can't Get There from Here* (1957). Typical couplets are his *Reflection on Ice-Breaking,* "Candy is dandy/But liquor is quicker," and his observation on a dinnertime trial, "You shake and shake the ketchup bottle/Nothing comes, and then a lot'll."

Nashville   The capital of Tennessee. It is known chiefly as the home of COUNTRY MUSIC because of the presence there of the GRAND OLE OPRY. Other attractions include Vanderbilt and Fisk universities and Andrew Jackson's home, the HERMITAGE.

Nast, Thomas   (1840–1902) Born in Germany, Nast came to the United States as a child and, as the chief political cartoonist (1862–86) for *Harper's Weekly,* was instrumental in the downfall of Boss TWEED. A staunch Republican, he did pro-Union illustrations during the Civil War that caused President Lincoln to call him "our best recruiting sergeant." Nast's pen also produced the prototypes of the Republican party elephant, the Democratic donkey, and the American SANTA CLAUS.

Nat Turner's Rebellion   See Nat TURNER.

Nation, Carry   (1846–1911) Temperance reformer. Nation emerged from a brief marriage to an alcoholic to become, at the turn of the twentieth century, the country's most famous precursor of PROHIBITION. Originally endorsed by the Women's Christian Temperance Union, she was repudiated by them in the 1890s after she began direct action against liquor sellers. Armed with a hatchet, she destroyed numerous kegs and bottles of the demon rum in dedicated vandalism she called "hatchetation." Fines incurred from her numerous arrests were met by lecture fees and a brisk sale in souvenir hatchets.

Nation of Islam   See BLACK MUSLIMS.

National Barn Dance   A weekly radio show broadcast from Chicago (1924–68). Before the rise of the GRAND OLE OPRY, it was the nation's premier COUNTRY MUSIC show.

National Enquirer   See TABLOID.

national game   See BASEBALL.

National Geographic   A scientific and travel magazine founded in 1888 as the official journal of the National Geographic Society. Famous for its photographs of exotic locales and its maps, it reaches a circulation of over 10 million— exceeded only by READER'S DIGEST and TV GUIDE.

national pastime   See BASEBALL.

National Review   See William F. BUCKLEY, Jr.

Native Son   Richard WRIGHT's 1940 novel about a black youth, Bigger Thomas, who kills a white girl in a panic and is condemned to death. A powerful indictment of racism, it had a profound impact on younger writers.

Nautilus   Name of (1) a submarine, or "diving boat," designed by Robert FULTON in 1800 and (2) a U.S. Navy vessel, built in 1954, that was the world's first nuclear-powered submarine.

Navidad, La   The first European settlement in the New World. See also Christopher COLUMBUS.

Navajo   The most populous native American group in North America. Originally nomads, they have farmed and raised livestock, principally sheep, in the arid Southwest for the past three hundred years. Although their meager economy hardly suggests its importance, their artistic creativity is well known to the Anglo world through their woven blankets, sand paintings, and silver jewelry.

necktie party   A LYNCHING. Western slang from the 1830s.

Nelson, Baby Face   (1908–34) Bank robber. A onetime ally of both Al CAPONE and John DILLINGER, the Chicago-born gunman Lester Gillis became Public Enemy No. 1 in the 1930s before being killed in a shoot-out with the FEDERAL BUREAU OF INVESTIGATION.

Nelson, Ozzie and Harriet   See OZZIE AND HARRIET.

Nelson, Ricky   See OZZIE AND HARRIET.

Nelson, Willie   (1933–   ) Country singer, songwriter. The best known of the so-called outlaw singers of the 1970s, Nelson enjoys demigod status in his native Texas for his inventive writing, his annual Fourth of July picnics, and the exposure he brought to the city of Austin as a rival to NASHVILLE. His early success, however, came in Nashville, where he wrote the 1960s songs "Hello Walls," "Funny How Time Slips Away," and "Crazy"—the last one a major hit for Patsy CLINE. His biggest seller of the 1970s was the album *Red-headed Stranger*, while his pop country hits of the 1980s included "On the Road Again" and "Always on My Mind."

nerd   High school slang for a socially inept, usually "brainy" male. Pocket protectors for holding pens are referred to as nerd packs. A possible source of the term is Mortimer Snerd, a hayseed dummy friend of Charlie McCarthy (see Edgar BERGEN).

Nesbit, Evelyn   See Stanford WHITE.

Ness, Eliot   See THE UNTOUCHABLES.

Neuman, Alfred E.   See MAD.

New Colossus   See STATUE OF LIBERTY.

New Deal   Blanket term for the massive legislation passed in Franklin D. ROOSEVELT's first two administrations. Candidate Roosevelt had promised a "new deal for the American people" that would reverse the effects of the GREAT DEPRESSION. In his first three months in office—the famous Hundred Days—he pushed through laws on banking, manufacturing, and public works. Later New Deal measures created millions of government jobs; regulated agriculture, labor relations, and stock trading; and laid the groundwork for the Social Security system. Modern welfare capitalism may be traced directly to the New Deal.

New England Primer   First published around 1690 in Boston, this was New England's first widely adopted grammar school textbook. In addition to a morally illustrative alphabet ("In Adam's fall we sinned all"), it contained uplifting stories and the colonial child's standard bedtime prayer:

> *Now I lay me down to sleep;*
> *I pray the Lord my soul to keep.*
> *If I should die before I wake*
> *I pray the Lord my soul to take.*

New Frontier   See John F. KENNEDY.

New Harmony   See UTOPIAN COMMUNITIES.

New Left   Catchphrase for the student radicals of the 1960s, united loosely in their opposition to the VIETNAM WAR. The Marxist flavor of their social critique was eloquently in evidence in the Port Huron Statement, the founding document of the loose-knit movement's best-known organization, Students for a Democratic Society (SDS). The students were called new leftists to distinguish them from the older leftists of the 1930s.

New Orleans   Louisiana's largest city, famed as the birthplace of JAZZ and the home of MARDI GRAS. Founded by the French in 1718, it has a rich CREOLE heritage whose architectural component is vividly displayed in the Vieux Carré ("Old Square"), or French Quarter. On January 8, 1815, General Andrew JACKSON halted a British attack on the city in the widely celebrated Battle of New Orleans. Although the event took place two weeks after the official end of the WAR OF 1812, it was remembered as that war's greatest American victory, inspiring the 1826 ballad "HUNTERS OF KENTUCKY" and a 1959 pop song, "The Battle of New Orleans."

New Thought   A spiritualist movement begun in the nineteenth century that stressed the power of "divine" mind over matter. It grew from the teachings of Phineas P. QUIMBY, was dubbed New Thought by Quimby's disciple Julius Dresser (1838–93), and held its first convention in San Francisco in 1894.

New York   The largest city in the United States, called from its prominence both the City and the Big Apple. It consists of five boroughs: MANHATTAN, the Bronx, Brooklyn, Queens, and Richmond (Staten Island). One of the great cultural and economic capitals of the world, New York is known especially for its BROADWAY theater district, the WALL STREET financial district, and the elegant residential areas of FIFTH AVENUE and PARK AVENUE. Among its most famous tourist attractions are the Wildlife Conservation Society/Bronx Zoo, GREENWICH VILLAGE, the EMPIRE STATE BUILDING, the STATUE OF LIBERTY, TIMES SQUARE, and the WORLD TRADE CENTER.

New York Times   The United States's self-styled "paper of record," the *New York Times* was founded in 1851. In 1896, it was taken over by Adolph Ochs (1858–1935), who gave it its current aura of authoritativeness, established a tradition of Pulitzer Prize–winning reporting, and coined the slogan "All the News That's Fit to Print." Student radicals in the 1960s, irritated by the paper's centrist politics, twisted the slogan to read "All the News That Fits."

New Yorker, The A weekly magazine published in New York City. Under its founder (1925) and original editor, Harold Ross, it developed a posture of urbane wittiness that it still cherishes. The magazine popularized cartoons captioned with wry one-liners as well as the writings of Ogden NASH, Dorothy PARKER, J. D. SALINGER, James THURBER, and E. B. WHITE.

Newman, Paul (1925–) Film actor. Excellent roles and a fine emotional range made Newman one of the superstars of the 1960s. He received Oscar nominations for his work in *Cat on a Hot Tin Roof* (1958), *The Hustler* (1960), *Hud* (1963), and *Cool Hand Luke* (1967) and also starred in the financial block-busters *Butch Cassidy and the Sundance Kid* (1969) and *The Sting* (1973). He has also portrayed a trio of Old West heroes: BILLY THE KID (*The Left-handed Gun,* 1958), Roy BEAN (*The Life and Times of Judge Roy Bean,* 1972), and BUFFALO BILL (*Buffalo Bill and the Indians,* 1976).

Newport A small city on the Atlantic coast of Rhode Island. It contains several summer mansions erected during the Gilded Age—including the VANDERBILT FAMILY's lavish home the Breakers—and is the site of the AMERICA'S CUP races and the Newport Jazz Festival. See THE GILDED AGE.

Newsweek A weekly newsmagazine founded in 1933. Similar in format and coverage to its model, TIME, it reaches approximately 3.2 million readers.

Nez Percé (French "pierced nose") An Indian people of the Snake River region of the Northwest. Originally fishers and gatherers, they became expert horsemen in the 1700s, famous for huge herds of APPALOOSA. Their four-month flight from the U.S. Army in 1877 was led by the remarkable Chief JOSEPH.

Niagara Falls A waterfall of the Niagara River, separating Ontario province from New York State. Actually divided into two falls, the American and the Canadian (or Horseshoe) falls, by an island, Niagara Falls became a tourist at-traction in the early 1800s, and soon thereafter the "honeymoon capital of the world." It has also attracted significant numbers of daredevils who have attempted to cross it on wires or go over it in barrels. See Sam PATCH.

"Nice guys finish last" See Leo DUROCHER.

Nick Carter See Nick CARTER.

nickelodeon (1) In the 1880s, a "penny arcade" where, for a nickel, customers could view peep shows or listen to Gramophone recordings. (2) After the turn of the century, a small, storefront enterprise where the same nickel would gain one admittance to a silent film; these nickelodeons were the country's first movie theaters. (3) By the 1930s, a synonym for a jukebox (see JUKE).

> *Put another nickel in, in the nickelodeon;*
> *All I want is loving you and music, music, music.*

Nicklaus, Jack (1940–) Golfer. Financially the world's most successful golfer, Nicklaus dominated the sport in the 1960s and 1970s, winning more championships than anyone else in history. These included five Masters, four

PGA tournaments, three U.S. Opens, and three British Opens. A sportswriters' poll taken in 1979 selected him as the athlete of the decade.

nigger   The most common insulting term for an African or African American, from the Spanish and Portuguese *negro,* for "black." Although it is not American in origin ("neger" is a sixteenth-century British equivalent), it has been wildly elaborated in the race-conscious United States. Among the many expressions that play on the slur, the most common include "to work like a nigger," meaning to work hard; "nigger in the woodpile," for an unexplained source of trouble; "nigger heaven," for the segregated upper balcony in a movie theater; "nigger show," for a MINSTREL SHOW; and "nigger lover," for a white sympathetic with blacks—a term originally applied to ABOLITIONISTS in the 1830s. "Nigger babies" were dark candies popular from the 1890s, and Nigger Jim was the escaped slave in HUCKLEBERRY FINN.

"Night and Day"   (1932) A song by Cole PORTER inspired by the rhythms of a Moroccan folk tune. Introduced by Fred Astaire in the stage play *Gay Divorce,* it was also used in the screen adaptation, *The Gay Divorcee* (1934), which starred the just developing team of ASTAIRE AND ROGERS. *Night and Day* was also the title of a 1946 film about Porter, with Cary GRANT starring as the composer.

"Night Before Christmas, The"   A poem that first appeared two days before Christmas 1823 in the *Troy* (New York) *Sentinel.* The anonymous author, it was later revealed, was literature professor Clement Clarke Moore (1779–1863). Copied widely and reprinted in his 1844 collection *Poems,* it became the most familiar of all seasonal ditties and the literary springboard for the American SANTA CLAUS. "A Visit from St. Nicholas," as it was properly called, established the conventions of the jolly elf, the chimney stockings, and the "eight tiny reindeer."

> *'Twas the night before Christmas and all through the house*
> *Not a creature was stirring—not even a mouse.*

night riders   Common term for KU KLUX KLAN members who terrorized southern blacks under cover of darkness.

Nimrod Wildfire, Colonel   The prototype of the "ring-tailed roarer," or boastful frontiersman. Thought to be modeled on Davy CROCKETT, the figure appeared in James Paulding's 1831 play *The Lion of the West.* Portraying the character, "a raw Kentuckian recently elected to Congress," became a twenty-year career for actor James Hackett.

NINA   Acronym that appeared in nineteenth-century job announcements, meaning "No Irish Need Apply."

Niña   (Spanish "young girl") See Christopher COLUMBUS.

"Nine Old Men"   Franklin D. Roosevelt's slighting term for the members of the U.S. Supreme Court, which in the mid-1930s was rolling back NEW DEAL reforms. To counter this judicial attack, Roosevelt proposed appointing one extra justice to the court for each one over seventy who would not retire. Critics denounced this "packing the court" idea, and it died in senatorial committee.

"99 and 44/100 percent pure"   See IVORY SOAP.

"97-pound weakling"   See Charles ATLAS.

Nixon, Richard M.   (1913–94) One of the most respected and most reviled of American politicians, Nixon entered Congress in 1948 as an anticommunist Republican. He achieved national prominence for aggressively investigating Alger HISS, while his campaign tactics—such as labeling his opponents "soft on communism"—earned him the unsavory sobriquet Tricky Dick. As Dwight D. EISENHOWER's running mate in 1952, he deftly dodged charges that he had been supported by a secret "slush fund" (see CHECKERS SPEECH) and went on to serve two terms as vice president. His twin losses of the presidency (to John F. KENNEDY) and the California governorship elicited a notorious snap at the press— "You won't have Nixon to kick around any more"—but in 1968, he finally won the Oval Office. The foreign policy success of his two terms—including gradual disengagement from the VIETNAM WAR, the signing of an arms reduction treaty, and the easings of tensions with both China and the Soviet Union—were overshadowed by the WATERGATE scandal, and he left office in 1974 to avoid IMPEACHMENT.

"no entangling alliances"   See "ENTANGLING ALLIANCES WITH NONE."

"no taxation without representation"   A colonial slogan denouncing both the British tax system and Parliament, in which North Americans were represented "virtually" but not directly. Boston radical James Otis, in decrying the STAMP ACT, said in 1765, "The very act of taxing exercised over those who are not represented, appears to be depriving them of one of their most essential rights."

Nob Hill   Since the nineteenth century, an exclusive residential neighborhood of SAN FRANCISCO. "Nob" is English slang for a person of position.

noble experiment   PROHIBITION. In his 1928 run for the presidency, Herbert Hoover called it "an experiment noble in motive and far-reaching in purpose."

Nolan, Philip   The exiled hero of "THE MAN WITHOUT A COUNTRY."

Norris, Frank   (1870–1902) Novelist. One of the country's first naturalists, Norris is remembered for his proposed trilogy "The Epic of the Wheat," revealing the social forces controlling its growth and sale. The first volume, *The Octopus* (1901), depicts the struggle of California farmers against an engulfing railroad. The second volume, *The Pit* (1903), reveals the excesses of market speculation. The unwritten final volume, *The Wolf,* was to have focused on a European famine. In his credo *The Responsibilities of the Novelist* (1903), Norris claimed that the true artist must be able to say, "I never took off the hat to fashion and held it out for pennies. By God, I told them the truth."

North, Lord   (1732–92) British prime minister from 1770 to 1782, Lord Frederick North presided over the loss of the American colonies, an event that his own policies had helped to bring about. He introduced the INTOLERABLE ACTS in 1774 and resigned after the British defeat at YORKTOWN.

North, Oliver   (1943–) A U.S. Marine colonel who, in the mid-1980s, directed covert international operations that resulted in the transfer of funds to

Nicaraguan rebels, known as Contras. Investigated by Congress for violating a specific law against such aid, North defended his actions as patriotic while implying that President REAGAN himself had approved of the scheme. The affair saturated the airwaves for months and turned the minion of a "higher law" into a conservative folk hero. Legally he suffered a light suspended sentence.

North American Phalanx   See UTOPIAN COMMUNITIES.

North Star Line   See UNDERGROUND RAILROAD.

Northwest Ordinance   See NORTHWEST TERRITORY.

Northwest Passage   A water route through Canada from the Atlantic to the Pacific, a principal will-o'-the-wisp of early explorers. Among those who searched for it in vain were John CABOT, Henry HUDSON, and the English sailor Sir John Franklin, who led a major expedition (1845) to its doom in the Arctic wastes. The Norwegian Roald Amundsen finally made it through in 1906.

Northwest Territory   A vast territory between the Great Lakes and the Ohio River that became United States territory as a result of the Revolution. Also known as the Old Northwest, it was administered under the Northwest Ordinance of 1787, which provided for its division into states. The original inhabitants objecting to this expansion, the place became the scene of intermittent warfare, with decisive battles fought at Fallen Timbers (1794) and Tippecanoe (1811). After Indian resistance was quelled, the land was broken up into Ohio, Indiana, Illinois, Michigan, and Wisconsin.

novus ordo seclorum   A motto on the reverse side of the dollar bill. Latin for "a new order of the ages."

"Now I lay me down to sleep"   See NEW ENGLAND PRIMER.

Noyes, John Humphrey   See ONEIDA.

nullification   A political doctrine that held that states could nullify federal laws within their borders. It was championed in various forms by a long line of STATES' RIGHTS proponents, including Thomas JEFFERSON, James MADISON, and John C. CALHOUN. A hot topic in pre–Civil War debates over slavery, it was also invoked as recently as 1954, when southern states tried to void the Supreme Court ruling (BROWN V. BOARD OF EDUCATION) that had declared segregated schools unconstitutional.

"Nuts!"   During the Battle of the Bulge in December 1944, a German commander called on the U.S. 101st Airborne Division to surrender. Division commander Anthony C. McAuliffe (1898–1975) shot back this one-word reply. The American position held, and McAuliffe was promoted.

O

"O Captain! My Captain!"   Walt WHITMAN's famous elegy to Abraham Lincoln, written shortly after the president's assassination and included in the poet's 1867 LEAVES OF GRASS. It employs the conventional "ship of state" metaphor for the Union.

> *But O heart! heart! heart!*
> *O the bleeding drops of red,*
> *Where on the deck my Captain lies,*
> *Fallen cold and dead.*

O. Henry   (1862–1910) Pen name of William Sydney Porter, a prolific writer of sentimental short stories whose penchant for the ironic ending gave it the common tag "O. Henry ending." Born in North Carolina, he moved to Texas in 1882, where he worked as a ranch hand, journalist, and bank teller until being indicted for embezzlement in 1894. After a brief flight to Latin America, he returned for trial and spent three years in an Ohio federal prison. While there he published his first story, "Whistling Dick's Christmas Stocking," and collected anecdotes he later worked into his fiction. His move to New York City in 1902 gave him a vast new source of characters, and it is that city—his "Baghdad on the Subway"—with which he is most associated. The most famous of his story collections, THE FOUR MILLION, poignantly explored the lives of everyday New Yorkers; his best-known tales include "The Last Leaf," "The Cop and the Anthem," and "THE GIFT OF THE MAGI." The O. Henry Memorial Awards honor the best stories published each year in American magazines.

O Pioneers!   A novel (1913) by Willa CATHER. The first of her Nebraska novels, it concerns the trials and triumphs of a Swedish farm family.

Oakley, Annie   (1860–1926) Sharpshooter. As a teenager, tiny Phoebe Anne Oakley Mozee challenged touring marksman Frank Butler to a shooting contest; her victory made her his protégée and then his wife. Under Butler's management, she became a star attraction of BUFFALO BILL's touring WILD WEST SHOW (1885–1902), shooting cigarettes from volunteers' lips and dimes from the air. Fellow Wild West employee SITTING BULL is said to have given her the nickname Little Sure Shot. The Irving BERLIN musical *Annie Get Your Gun* (1946) was based on her life.

oater   See HORSE OPERA.

Obie Awards   See OFF-BROADWAY.

Ochs, Adolph   See NEW YORK TIMES.

O'Connor, Flannery   (1925–64) Writer. Georgia-born O'Connor achieved fame in the 1960s for quirky, pathos-ridden stories of her native South, collected in *A Good Man Is Hard to Find* (1955) and *Everything That Rises Must Converge* (1965). She also produced two novels, *Wise Blood* (1952) and *The Violent Bear It Away* (1960), before succumbing to lupus at the age of thirty-nine.

Odd Couple, The   A 1965 play by Neil SIMON that became a 1968 movie and then a television series (1970–75). The role of slovenly sportswriter Oscar Madison was created on Broadway by Walter Matthau, with Art Carney as his finicky housemate, Felix Unger. Matthau also starred in the movie, with Jack Lemmon as Unger. The TV series starred Jack Klugman (Madison) and Tony Randall (Unger).

Odets, Clifford   (1906–63) A founder of the left-wing Group Theater (1931), Odets was the most successful "proletarian playwright" of the 1930s. His major plays for the Group were *Waiting for Lefty* (1935), about a taxi drivers' strike; *Awake and Sing* (1935), about the trials of a working-class Bronx family; and *Golden Boy* (1937), a boxing drama whose film version (1939) made an overnight star of actor William HOLDEN. Odets also wrote *The Country Girl* (1950; film 1954), a story about an alcoholic's marriage that won Grace KELLY a best actress Oscar.

Of Mice and Men   (1937) A short novel by John STEINBECK about the friendship of two California migrant workers who dream of owning a farm of their own. The book ends tragically after strong, slow-witted Lennie accidentally kills his boss's daughter-in-law. Dramatized by Steinbeck, the story was made into movies starring Lon Chaney, Jr. (1940) and John Malkevich (1992).

"Of the people, by the people, and for the people"   Probably the most succinct definition of democracy ever devised, this phrase became widely known after Abraham Lincoln used it in his GETTYSBURG ADDRESS; the speech ended with the hope "that government of the people, by the people, and for the people shall not perish from the earth." Lincoln did not invent the phrase, but borrowed it from abolitionist minister Theodore Parker (1810–60).

Of Thee I Sing   A musical comedy (1931) written by Morrie Ryskind, George S. Kaufman (see KAUFMAN AND HART), and George and Ira GERSHWIN. A satire on American political campaigns, it won a 1932 Pulitzer Prize.

Off-Broadway   Blanket term for a diffuse array of experimental drama productions which, in the 1950s, began to provide innovative alternatives to the BROADWAY theater. Groups like the Living Theater and the Open Theater successfully challenged the mainline theater's hegemony, although within a decade Off-Broadway theater had itself become so expensive that it spawned an even less commercial splinter "movement," Off-Off-Broadway. The Obie Awards, sponsored by *The Village Voice*, have since 1956 honored Off-Broadway achievements.

"Oh Dem Golden Slippers"   One of the most popular turn-of-the-century MINSTREL SHOW tunes. It was written in 1879 by James Bland.

"Oh How I Hate to Get Up in the Morning"   A humorous song written by Irving BERLIN (1918), about an Army recruit's doleful reaction to reveille. It was popular, especially with the troops, in both world wars.

"Oh say can you see"   See "THE STAR-SPANGLED BANNER."

"Oh, Susanna"   (1848) One of Stephen FOSTER's best-known songs. An unofficial theme of the FORTY-NINERS, it has been a sing-along favorite for a century and a half.

> *Oh it rained all night the day I left,*
> *The weather it was dry;*
> *The sun so hot I froze to death,*
> *Susanna, don't you cry,*
> *Oh, Susanna, don't you cry for me;*
> *I come from Alabama with my banjo on my knee.*

O'Hara, John   (1905–70) Writer. Known for his realistic dialogue and insight into American social relations, O'Hara set many of his stories and novels in the fictional town of Gibbsville, Pennsylvania. His most famous novel, *Butterfield 8* (1935), was a character study of a big-city call girl; the film version (1960) earned Elizabeth TAYLOR her first Oscar. O'Hara's other books included *Appointment in Samarra* (1934), *From the Terrace* (1958), and PAL JOEY, which inspired a Richard RODGERS and Lorenz HART musical.

O'Hara, Scarlett   See GONE WITH THE WIND.

OK   A ubiquitous American slang term for "all right." Its etymology has been much debated, with one often cited story calling it an illiterate Andrew JACKSON abbreviation for "oll korrect." A more plausible origin is Old Kinderhook, the nickname of Jackson's vice president, Martin Van Buren, whose supporters in the 1840s formed "OK Clubs." Also seen as "O.K.," "okay," and (from the 1930s) "okey-doke."

O.K. Corral   A TOMBSTONE, Arizona, cattle pen which, on October 26, 1881, became the site of the most famous gunfight in western history. On one side were Wyatt EARP, his brothers Morgan and Virgil, and their friend, shotgun-toting Doc HOLLIDAY. On the other were two pairs of brothers, Ike and Billy Clanton and Tom and Frank McLaury, members of a prominent ranching (and, many said, rustling) outfit which later legend called the Clanton gang. In the brief exchange of gunfire, the McLaurys and Billy Clanton were killed, the Earp quartet escaping with minor wounds. Historians still debate whether the battle was the ambitious Earps' legal murder of political rivals or their justified excision of an unwelcome element. The Earp version got full play in Wyatt's biography and in John Ford's *My Darling Clementine* (See "My Darling Clementine" [2]). A less hagiographic treatment appeared in John Sturges's 1957 *Gunfight at the O.K. Corral*.

O'Keefe, Georgia   (1887–1986) Painter. An avant-garde abstractionist whose work eventually entered the popular canon, O'Keefe was best known for her starkly lyrical representations of flowers, the southwestern landscape, and parched animal skulls. She was married to the photographer Alfred STIEGLITZ.

"Okie from Muskogee"   See Merle HAGGARD.

Okies   Bankrupt farm families who fled Oklahoma in the 1930s to seek work as migrant laborers on the West Coast. Traveling in jalopies piled high with their belongings, they epitomized the ravages of the DUST BOWL. Their plight, recorded by such government photographers as Dorothea LANGE, also inspired John STEINBECK's novel THE GRAPES OF WRATH.

Oklahoma   (1) The forty-sixth state in the Union, formed out of land that from 1830 to 1889 had been INDIAN TERRITORY. See SOONER; TRAIL OF TEARS. (2) As *Oklahoma!:* a 1943 Broadway musical by Richard RODGERS and Oscar HAMMERSTEIN II. It broke the record for musical runs and introduced three classic tunes: "Oh What a Beautiful Morning," "The Surrey with the Fringe on Top," and "People Will Say We're in Love."

"Ol' Man River"   A moodily philosophical tune by Oscar HAMMERSTEIN II and Jerome KERN, written in black dialect for the original production of *Show Boat* (see SHOWBOAT [2]).

> *I gets weary and sick of tryin',*
> *Tired of livin' but feared of dyin',*
> *But Ol' Man River he just keeps rolling along.*

Old Abe   Nickname for Abraham LINCOLN.

Old Betsy   Davy Crockett's pet name for his rifle. Legend has him swinging it like a club in his last desperate moments at the ALAMO.

"Old Black Joe"   Song by Stephen FOSTER (1860). The plaintive lyrics reflect the supposed nostalgia of an elderly slave for his plantation youth.

Old Blood and Guts   Nickname for General George S. PATTON (1885–1945), the tactically brilliant, irascible World War II tank commander whose Third Army led the final assault on occupied Europe.

Old Blue Eyes   See Frank SINATRA.

"Old Chisholm Trail"   See CHISHOLM TRAIL.

old college try   One's best effort, given even in the face of adversity. From the early days of college football.

Old Colony   See PLYMOUTH COLONY.

"Old Dan Tucker"   A minstrel tune written in the 1840s by Dan EMMETT. It became a fiddler's favorite in square dances and other rural gatherings.

"Old Dog Tray"   A sentimental song written by Stephen FOSTER. It was once his third best-known tune, after "OLD FOLKS AT HOME" and "MY OLD KENTUCKY HOME."

Old Dominion   Virginia's STATE NICKNAME.

Old Faithful   A natural landmark and tourist attraction in Wyoming's YEL-LOWSTONE PARK, a geyser that shoots water 150 feet into the air approximately once an hour. It received its nickname from explorer Henry Washburn in 1870.

Old Farmer's Almanac   Established in 1793 by Robert Bailey Thomas, the *Old Farmer's Almanac* is the oldest existing almanac in the United States. Like English antecedents, it contains daily weather predictions, herbal remedies, and farming advice. Like its famous American predecessor, POOR RICHARD'S ALMANACK, it also features humor and proverbial sayings.

"Old Folks at Home"   Typically wistful, and enormously popular, song by Stephen FOSTER (1851). Also known as "Swanee River," from its opening line, "Way down upon the Swanee River." It is the state song of Florida.

Old Fuss and Feathers   Nickname of General Winfield Scott (1786–1866), from his dandified appearance and emphasis on discipline. An able soldier in the WAR OF 1812 and the Indian wars of the 1830s, he became overall army commander in the MEXICAN WAR and ran unsuccessfully for president in 1848.

Old Glory   The United States flag. The term was coined by Massachusetts sea captain William Driver in 1831 and applied initially to his ship's colors. See also Betsy ROSS; STARS AND STRIPES; "THE STAR-SPANGLED BANNER."

"Old Gray Mare, The"   A song written in 1915 by Frank Panella. It was a popular marching song in World War I and in AMERICAN LEGION posts thereafter.

Old Hickory   Andrew JACKSON. For his reputed toughness.

Old Ironsides   The frigate U.S.S. *Constitution*, which saw action against the BARBARY PIRATES and in the WAR OF 1812. She earned the nickname from her oak-timbered hull, which made her virtually impervious to enemy shot. Commissioned in 1797, the ship was to be scrapped in 1830 when Oliver Wendell HOLMES's poem "Old Ironsides" galvanized public opinion to have her restored. The vessel is now a national monument in Boston harbor.

Old Joe   See CAMEL.

"Old Joe Clark"   A play-party song from the southern mountains that became a fiddler's standard. Protagonist Joe Clark has not been certainly identified. Humorous stanzas celebrating his adventures number in the hundreds.

> *Old Joe Clark, the preacher's son,*
> *He preached all over the plain.*
> *The only text he ever knew*
> *Was high, low, Jack and the game.*

Old John and Old Master   The main characters in a cycle of slave stories from plantation days. John is an elderly slave who, by his cunning, continuously gets the better of Old Master (or, as his name is often spelled, Old Massa). Old

John brings the ingenuity of African trickster figures into the peculiarly straitened milieu of slave society.

Old Kinderhook Nickname for Martin Van Buren (1782–1862), eighth president of the United States, who was born in Kinderhook, New York. See also OK.

"Old MacDonald Had a Farm" A children's song published under the title "Ohio" in 1917 but popular for several decades before that. It follows a conventional "chain" pattern, as singers itemize animals on the old man's farm.

> *Old MacDonald had a farm, ee-eye, ee-eye, oh.*
> *And on this farm he had a duck, ee-eye, ee-eye, oh.*
> *With a quack-quack here and a quack-quack there;*
> *Here a quack, there a quack, everywhere a quack-quack;*
> *Old MacDonald had a farm, ee-eye, ee-eye, oh.*

Old Man and the Sea, The (1952) A short novel by Ernest HEMINGWAY about the desperate battle of an aging fisherman to save his catch from marauding sharks. Probably Hemingway's most accessible work, it became a standard school text and a 1958 movie starring Spencer TRACY.

"Old Mill Stream, The" See "DOWN BY THE OLD MILL STREAM."

Old Miss Nickname for the University of Mississippi, whose main, or Oxford, campus is in Oxford. Formerly a nickname for the state itself.

Old North Church See "PAUL REVERE'S RIDE."

Old Northwest See NORTHWEST TERRITORY.

"Old Oaken Bucket, The" A sentimental song (1843) by Samuel Woodworth and George Kiallmark. The country well that the lyrics celebrate, supposedly located near Boston, was depicted in the 1860s by CURRIER & IVES. The tune was adopted as the Brown University alma mater.

Old Rough and Ready Nickname for General Zachary Taylor (1784–1850), earned for his exploits during the Seminole War (1835–42). It stuck with him through the MEXICAN WAR and through the campaign that won him the presidency in 1848.

"Old Rugged Cross, The" Gospel song written in 1913 by George Bennard. In a modern poll of Protestant churchgoers, it was chosen the most popular hymn of all time.

"Old Smokey" See "ON TOP OF OLD SMOKEY."

"Old soldiers never die. They just fade away" The most famous line in Douglas MACARTHUR'S farewell speech to Congress (1951). The general was quoting from an old army ballad.

Old South The pre–Civil War South. The term, which dates from the Reconstructionist 1870s, often connotes romanticized gentility and bucolic charm. See also "DIXIE"; LOST CAUSE.

Old Stormalong A legendary "deepwater sailorman" popularized by Frank Shay's 1930 tall-tale collection *Here's Audacity!* A giant in the Paul BUNYAN mold, "Stormie" drank whale soup out of a dory and bested octopuses by tying their tentacles into knots; his ship was so huge that its masts swung down on hinges to avoid the moon, while young salts who went aloft "came down as greybeards." Shay and others promoted the character as a folk hero, although like Bunyan he shows the signs of literary invention.

"Old Swimming Hole, The" An 1883 poem by James Whitcomb RILEY which helped to make his reputation as a professional HOOSIER. The image of the unsupervised swimming hole, in which boys could engage in "skinny dipping," or naked swimming, remained a stock image of country innocence into this century.

"Old Time Religion" (or **"Gimme That Old Time Religion"**) A black American spiritual from the 1860s. It remains a standard in Christian revivals.

Old West Broadly, the trans-Mississippi West of the nineteenth century. More narrowly, the legendary Wild West of cowboys and Indians, gunfights and cattle drives, depicted in popular novels and Hollywood movies. The historical period referred to stretched from approximately the end of the Civil War to the turn of the century.

"Old Zip Coon" See "TURKEY IN THE STRAW."

Oldenburg, Claes See POP ART.

Oldfield, Barney (1878–1946) Race car driver. Berna Eli Oldfield was a headline-making racer in the sport's formative years. He was the first driver to reach sixty miles per hour, and the first to run a 100-mile-per-hour lap at the Indianapolis Speedway. In 1910, he set a world record of just under 132 miles per hour.

O'Leary's cow, Mrs. According to legend, the immediate cause of the great CHICAGO FIRE (1871). The cow was said to have kicked over a kerosene lantern, igniting straw in the O'Leary barn.

Olmsted, Frederick Law (1822–1903) Landscape architect. One of the pioneers of city planning, Olmstead is best known as the chief architect of New York City's Central Park. He also designed parks for Boston, Chicago, and Montreal, as well as the grounds of Stanford University and the 1893 Chicago WORLD'S FAIR.

"On the Banks of the Wabash Far Away" An 1899 song by Paul DRESSER, one of the best-loved parlor songs of the 1900s. It became the state song of Indiana.

on the fritz See KATZENJAMMER KIDS.

On the Road (1957) A vaguely autobiographical novel by Jack KEROUAC which became an unofficial manifesto of the BEAT GENERATION. It describes the hedonistic travels of the author and a friend.

On the Waterfront An intense, realistic film about corruption on the New York City docks which won the best picture Academy Award for 1954. It also took Oscars for director Elia KAZAN, screenwriter Budd SCHULBERG, and actor Marlon BRANDO, for his gritty portrayal of ex-boxer Terry Malloy. In one poignant scene, Terry charges his gangster brother (Rod STEIGER) with having used him in fixed fights "for the short-end money." When the brother protests that Terry got well paid, he responds with the film's best-known speech: "You don't understand. I coulda been a contender. I coulda had class and been somebody ... instead of a bum, let's face it, which is what I am."

"On Top of Old Smokey"   An old ballad popularized in the 1950s by, among others, Gene AUTRY and Pete SEEGER. The opening line,

> *On top of Old Smokey, all covered in snow,*
> *I lost my true lover by courting too slow,*

is the target of a common children's parody:

> *On top of spaghetti, all covered in cheese,*
> *I lost my poor meatball when somebody sneezed.*

Onassis, Jackie   (1929–94) As John F. KENNEDY's First Lady, the former Jacqueline Bouvier set fashion trends and helped to create the stylish CAMELOT White House. Five years after Kennedy's death, she wed Greek shipping tycoon Aristotle Onassis (1906–75), making her one of the world's wealthiest women and a favorite target of paparazzi and tabloid writers. As Onassis's widow, she was sometimes referred to as Jackie O.

One Flew over the Cuckoo's Nest   A 1962 novel by Ken KESEY about an inmate's fight with an oppressive mental institution. The 1975 film version swept the Academy Awards, winning Oscars for best picture, best direction (Milos Forman), best actor (Jack Nicholson as Randle McMurphy), and best actress (Louise Fletcher as Nurse Ratched).

"One-Hoss Shay, The"   See "THE DEACON'S MASTERPIECE."

"One if by land, and two if by sea"   See "PAUL REVERE'S RIDE."

One Man's Family   A radio series about a California family, the Barbours. Inspired by John Galsworthy's *The Forsyte Saga,* its creator, Carlton Morse, made it one of the medium's most enduring domestic dramas. It ran from 1932 to 1959.

"One small step for [a] man"   See Neil ARMSTRONG.

Oneida   (1) An Indian nation of the IROQUOIS LEAGUE. During the Revolution, it was the only one of the five to side with the Americans. (2) The most successful of nineteenth-century American UTOPIAN COMMUNITIES. It was founded at Oneida, New York, in 1848, by "perfectionist" preacher John Humphrey Noyes (1811–86), whose prescriptions included industrial enterprise (the community manufactured bear traps and silverware), "biblical communism," and "complex marriage." Under threat of prosecution for this latter, free-love practice, Noyes fled to Canada in 1879, and the Oneida Community was reorganized as a joint-stock company. Its principal commercial legacy is Oneida silverware.

O'Neill, Eugene   (1888–1953) Widely held to be America's greatest dramatist, O'Neill was the son of actors James O'Neill and Ella Quinlan. After a peripatetic youth, he began writing one-acts for the PROVINCETOWN PLAYERS, building on his own experiences as a merchant seaman in *The Long Voyage Home* (1917) and other "sea plays." He turned to full-length plays with *Beyond the Horizon* (1920), a study of thwarted dreams, which won him a Pulitzer Prize. For the next three decades O'Neill brought bitter insights and technical wizardry to a wide range of subjects. The maritime drama *Anna Christie* (1921) earned him a second Pulitzer. *The Emperor Jones* (1920) and *The Hairy Ape* (1922) introduced a fascination with the dialectic of order and "uncivilized" passion. A similar focus appeared in *Desire Under the Elms* (1924) and his third Pulitzer play, *Strange Interlude* (1928). The psychological costs of success were revealed in *The Great God Brown* (1926) and *Marco Millions* (1928). The trilogy *Mourning Becomes Electra* (1931) recast Aeschylus's *Oresteia* in New England.

After winning the Nobel Prize for literature in 1936, O'Neill was virtually silent for a decade. He returned to Broadway in 1946, with a moving study of derelicts, *The Iceman Cometh.* In 1956 appeared a searing portrayal of domestic turmoil, *Long Day's Journey into Night,* which earned him a fourth, posthumous, Pulitzer Prize. Written fifteen years earlier, it examined the manifold illusions of an Irish theater family that was clearly modeled on O'Neill's own. Actor Jason Robards, Jr. (1922–   ), who had forged a career out of his performance in *The Iceman Cometh,* shone again in this autobiographical drama as the drunken father. The film version (1962) was a triumph for him and for Katharine HEPBURN.

"only good Indian is a dead Indian, The"   Racist adage usually attributed to Philip SHERIDAN. The general's actual words, uttered in 1869, were "The only good Indians I ever saw were dead." A decade later, with the western tribes nearly defeated, he reflected more generously, "We took away their country and their means of support, broke up their mode of living, their habits of life, introduced disease and decay among them, and it was for this and against this that they made war. Could anyone expect less?"

"only thing we have to fear is fear itself, The"   President Franklin D. ROOSEVELT's most famous nostrum, delivered in his 1933 inaugural address. It became a keynote summary of NEW DEAL optimism.

Open Door   See "SPLENDID LITTLE WAR"

"Orange Blossom Special"   A spirited fiddle tune written in the 1930s by E. T. Rouse and later recorded by, among others, Johnny CASH. It was named for the Orange Blossom Special railroad train, which ran from Miami to New York.

Orbison, Roy   (1936–88) Singer. Texas-born Orbison's plaintive vocal style, punctuated by a characteristic falsetto, made him a major star of the early 1960s and an éminence grise to later country-rock performers. His chief hits, all made between 1960 and 1964, were "Only the Lonely," "Crying," "Running Scared," "Dream Baby," and the chart-topping "Pretty Woman." Orbison's death preceded by months the release of a collaborative album, *The Traveling Wilburys,* on which he performed with Ricky Scaggs, Tom Petty, George Harrison, and Bob DYLAN.

Oregon Question   See "FIFTY-FOUR FORTY OR FIGHT."

Oregon Trail   A trail from Missouri to Oregon territory which, in the 1840s and 1850s, became the major COVERED WAGON conduit for westward expansion. The first wagon train reached Oregon in 1843, the last probably in the 1870s, by which time the RAILROAD had made the trail obsolete. Historian Francis Parkman (1823–93) wrote his first and most famous book, *The Oregon Trail* (1849), about such a journey.

Oreo   (1) A sandwich-style cookie sold by the National Biscuit Company (Nabisco). Because the cookie is composed of chocolate wafers sandwiching a white cream center, the term was adopted by black radicals in the 1960s to mean (2) an accommodationist black, because he is black on the outside but white within (see UNCLE TOM'S CABIN).

Orr, Bobby   (1948–) Hockey player. Before his career (1967–79) was cut short by injuries, Ontario-born Orr set numerous records as a defenseman for the Boston Bruins. He was the first defenseman to lead the National Hockey League in scoring, eight years in a row the league's top defenseman, and three years in a row its most valuable player.

Oscars   See ACADEMY AWARDS.

Osceola   (ca. 1803–38) War leader of the SEMINOLE Indians who, in 1835, refused a U.S. government "offer" to repatriate them from their homeland in northern Florida to Oklahoma. Working out of isolated sanctuaries in the Everglades, he waged a guerrilla war against federal troops for two years, until a duplicitous general, Sidney Jessup, captured him under a flag of truce and sent him to a South Carolina prison, where he died. Osceola's people continued the struggle until 1842, when all but a few hundred were shipped west. Today's Seminoles live in Florida and Oklahoma.

O'Sullivan, John   See MANIFEST DESTINY.

Oswald, Lee Harvey   (1939–63) The reputed killer of President John F. KENNEDY. An ex-Marine with ties to the Soviet Union, Oswald was identified by the WARREN COMMISSION, which investigated the presidential assassination, as the "lone gunman" responsible for the Dallas tragedy. Since he himself was killed two days later by nightclub owner Jack Ruby, he never received the benefit of a trial, and students of the assassination continue to debate the commission's findings. A large body of opinion sees Oswald as either the cat's-paw or the fall guy for a wider conspiracy.

Our American Cousin   (1858) A comedy by English dramatist Tom Taylor (1817–80). It was playing at the national capital's FORD'S THEATRE on April 14, 1865, when Abraham LINCOLN went to his fateful appointment with John Wilkes BOOTH.

"Our country, right or wrong"   A toast given by war hero Stephen DECATUR at a Norfolk, Virginia, dinner in 1815, shortly after his return from the BARBARY COAST. The full salute was "Our country! In her intercourse with foreign nations may she always be in the right. But our country, right or wrong.'' English writer G. K. Chesterton compared the sentiment to that of ''My mother, drunk or sober.''

Our Gang comedies   Short, comic films made first by the Hal ROACH studio, then by MGM, from 1922 to 1944. They starred an ensemble of child actors named for the initial vehicle, *Our Gang* (1922), and concerned the repercussions of the youngsters' endearing mischievousness. The major characters included freckled Alfalfa, ''love interests'' Mary and Darla, token ''darkies'' Farina and Buckwheat, and the gang leader, chubby Spanky McFarland. On television in the 1950s, the films appeared under the title *The Little Rascals*.

Our Town   (1938) A Pulitzer Prize play by Thornton WILDER. Set in fictional Grover's Corners, New Hampshire, it reveals the simple, poignant beauty of small-town life. Wilder's innovations included a nearly bare set and a character called the Stage Manager, who commented in asides on the action. The play is frequently revived in amateur productions.

"Outcasts of Poker Flat, The"   (1869) Bret HARTE's best-known story. A quartet of rogues, banished from a mining camp, heroically give their lives for an innocent woman, who perishes with them, in spite of their sacrifice, in a mountain blizzard.

outlaws   In popular films and fiction, the ''good bad man'' has been a durable, if questionable, hero for over a century. Appearing sometimes as a renegade reformed by love, sometimes as a Robin Hood–style avenger, and sometimes as an adolescent rebel, the western bandit has consistently embodied the fearfully attractive ideal of uncivilized freedom. Exemplars of the type include Sam BASS, BILLY THE KID, BLACK BART, Butch CASSIDY, Jesse JAMES, and Joaquín MURIETA. Gangster films of the 1930s borrowed the motif, usually with less sympathy for the urban renegades. See BONNIE AND CLYDE; Pretty Boy FLOYD.

"Over the Rainbow"   Song by E. Y. ''YIP'' HARBURG and Harold ARLEN, written for the 1939 movie THE WIZARD OF OZ. A deliciously wistful ballad, it won the best song Oscar and became young Judy GARLAND's theme song.

"Over There"   George M. COHAN's 1917 salute to the American doughboy, just committed to the war overseas. It became the hit of the year. President Wilson praised it as ''a genuine inspiration to all American manhood'' and it earned Cohan a congressional medal in 1941.

Owen, Robert   See UTOPIAN COMMUNITIES.

Owens, Buck   (1929–) Singer, songwriter. Texas-born Alvis Edgar Owens was a country music superstar in the 1960s, topping the singles charts over two dozen times. His biggest songs included ''Excuse Me (I Think I've Got a Heartache),'' ''Together Again,'' ''I've Got a Tiger by the Tail,'' ''Waitin' on Your Welfare Line,'' and a song later covered by the Beatles, ''Act Naturally.'' For almost twenty years (1969–86) he cohosted the syndicated television variety show HEE HAW, with his backup group, the Buckaroos, serving as the house band. A longtime resident of Bakersfield, California, Owens was so popular by 1970 that a tongue-in-cheek campaign was mounted there to have the spelling changed to ''Buckersfield.''

Owens, Jesse   (1913–80) As an Ohio State University student, black athlete James Cleveland Owens swept the National Collegiate Athletic Association's championships in 1935, and at the following year's Berlin Olympics performed the feat for which he is most remembered, taking gold medals in the 100- and 200-meter dashes, the broad jump, and the 400-meter relay. His virtuosity so embarrassed "master race" host Adolf Hitler that he left the stadium to avoid presenting the medals. Sportswriters' polls consistently place Owens among the top ten athletes of all time.

Ox-Bow Incident, The   A 1940 novel by Walter van Tilburg Clark (1909–71) about a hysterical posse's lynching of three innocent cowboys. A powerful film version (1942), directed by William WELLMAN, earned a best picture Academy Award nomination. Many see the story as a comment on fascism.

Oz   See THE WIZARD OF OZ.

Ozarks   A mountain system centered in northwestern Arkansas and stretching into Missouri, Kansas, and Oklahoma. The region's isolation from population centers nurtured a unique backwoods culture and folklore heritage, including tall tales, superstitions, and homespun remedies. See also "THE ARKANSAS TRAVELER"; BEVERLY HILLBILLIES; HILLBILLY; L'IL ABNER.

Ozzie and Harriet   Short for *The Adventures of Ozzie and Harriet,* the second-longest-running (1952–66) domestic sitcom in television history (after THE HONEYMOONERS). It starred the four members of the Nelson family as themselves, abetted by a large ensemble playing friends and neighbors. Ozzie Nelson (1907–75) had been a popular bandleader in the 1930s, and his wife, Harriet (1914–   ), had been his vocalist. Their sons David (1936–   ) and Ricky (1940–85), whose voices had been done by actors on radio (1944–52), played themselves when the series moved to television, and soon became the show's dramatic center.

In 1957, Ricky used the show to spark a second career as a rock music performer. Coming out of the squeaky-clean "Nelson family," he was promoted as a "safe" alternative to Elvis PRESLEY, and his melodious style made him a teenage heartthrob. His major hits, which appeared between 1957 and 1961, were "I'm Walking" (done originally by Fats DOMINO), "Poor Little Fool," "Hello, Mary Lou," and "Travelin' Man." After his death in a plane crash, his twin sons continued the family tradition as the rock band Nelson.

"Pack up Your Troubles in Your Old Kit Bag and Smile, Smile, Smile" Song written in 1915 by George Asaf and Fritz Powell. It became a favorite with World War I soldiers for its acclamation of the cheerful Private Perks. A kit bag was a doughboy's knapsack.

"packing the court" See NINE OLD MEN.

Pac-Man See VIDEO GAMES.

paddy Nickname for Patrick; hence an eighteenth-century term for an Irishman. The expression "paddy wagon," for a police van, reflects either their use for conveying Irish wrongdoers to jail or the high percentage of Irish on municipal police forces.

Paige, Satchel (ca. 1906–82) Baseball player. The most famous black player of the pre-integrated era, Leroy Robert Paige acquired the nickname Satchel because of his satchel-size feet. From 1924 to 1948 he played in the Negro Leagues, where he was billed as the World's Greatest Pitcher and where he won over two thousand games, including over forty no-hitters. Joe DiMAGGIO, against whom he threw in exhibition games, called him "the best pitcher I ever faced." Paige was also known for his homespun philosophy, epitomized in the adage "Don't look back. Something might be gaining on you."

Paine, Thomas (1737–1809) The most effective propagandist of the American Revolution, the English-born Paine went to America in 1774 to edit the *Pennsylvania Gazette*. Two years later he produced "COMMON SENSE," a pamphlet that did almost as much as taxes to exacerbate the tension with Mother England. Impressed by Paine's rhetorical skills, George Washington asked him to write something cheering for the army, and Paine responded with sixteen "Crisis" papers (1776–83). The first one, which opens with the famous line "These are the times that try men's souls," was read to the troops on the eve of the Battle of Trenton. After the American victory there (see GEORGE WASHINGTON CROSSING THE DELAWARE), Paine was rewarded with a government post. After the war, he returned to England, wrote a pamphlet praising the French Revolution, fled to France, and was briefly a member of its National Assembly. Heavy drinking and a cantankerous personality blighted his personal life, and he died largely forgotten in New York City.

Pal Joey (1940) A collection of stories by writer John O'HARA about the machinations of a big-city heel. A musical treatment by Richard RODGERS and Lorenz HART contained the ballad "Bewitched, Bothered, and Bewildered." Frank SINATRA starred in the 1957 movie.

Palmer, Arnold   (1929–   ) Golfer. The first golfer to earn a million dollars in his professional career, Palmer was most successful between 1958 and 1964, when he won two British Opens, one U.S. Open, and four Masters tournaments. His engaging personality earned him a following known as Arnie's Army.

Palmer raids   Government raids on suspected Bolsheviks conducted during the "Big Red Scare" of 1919–20. Thousands of alleged subversives were arrested and hundreds deported, among them the anarchist couple Andrew Berkman and Emma GOLDMAN. The raids were named for the U.S. attorney general, Mitchell "The Fighting Quaker" Palmer, who ordered them after a package bomb exploded at his home.

palomino   A golden-coated horse introduced by the Spanish and named for conquistador Juan de Palomino. A famous example was Roy ROGERS's horse, Trigger.

palooka   Since the 1920s, an unsuccessful boxer. The term inspired the boxing comic strip *Joe Palooka,* drawn by Ham Fisher from 1928.

Panama Canal   A ship canal dug across the Isthmus of Panama between 1903 and 1914 and regarded at the time as an engineering marvel: Theodore ROOSEVELT, under whose administration construction on the "Big Ditch" began, called it "the greatest task of its own kind that has ever been performed in the world." Fighting yellow fever and malaria, thousands of workers under chief engineer George Washington GOETHALS completed the passage at a cost of $337 million. The canal, which remains of great commercial and strategic importance, is owned and operated by the U.S. government, which pays an annual rental to the nation of Panama. Current treaties stipulate the U.S. control will end in the year 2000.

pancakes   Flat cakes browned on a griddle and typically served with MAPLE SYRUP for breakfast. Precursors of today's fluffy variety included the seventeenth-century no cake (from the Narraganset *nokehick,* "it is soft"), the eighteenth-century hoe cake (possibly because it was cooked on a hoe), and the New England favorite JOHNNY CAKE—all of which were made with cornmeal. Pancakes have also been called flapjacks, griddle cakes, batter cakes, flannel cakes, and "a string of flats." See also AUNT JEMIMA.

panhandle   A narrow "extension" of a state, resembling a handle. "Texas panhandle," for that state's northernmost counties, is the most common use, although panhandles are also found in Oklahoma, Florida, and Idaho.

Paramount   The product of a merger between Adolph ZUKOR and Jesse Lasky, Paramount was one of the major studios of Hollywood's Golden Age. Its directors in the 1930s and 1940s included Cecil B. DE MILLE, Preston STURGES, and Billy WILDER; Alfred HITCHCOCK was a 1950s addition. Among the actors whose careers were shaped by Paramount were Gary COOPER, Kirk DOUGLAS, Burt LANCASTER, Fredric MARCH, MARTIN AND LEWIS, W. C. FIELDS, Bob HOPE, and Mae WEST.

Parent-Teacher Associations   See PTA.

Park Avenue   An exclusive residential street in New York City. Hence a metaphor for expensive tastes and social standing.

Parker, Bonnie   See BONNIE AND CLYDE.

Parker, Charlie   (1920–55) Jazz musician. Parker's lyrical wizardry on the alto saxophone made him a legend even before his early death; his recordings with Dizzy GILLESPIE in the 1940s pioneered the style known as BEBOP. His nickname Bird, short for "Yardbird," led to the posthumous expression "Bird lives."

Parker, "Colonel"   See Elvis PRESLEY.

Parker, Dorothy   (1893–1967) Writer. The mordantly pessimistic queen of the ALGONQUIN ROUND TABLE, Parker first wrote drama reviews for VANITY FAIR and THE NEW YORKER, in one of which she assessed an early Katharine HEPBURN performance in the withering line "She ran the gamut of emotions from A to B." Parker's fiction included the story "Big Blonde," winner of the 1929 O. Henry Prize. She was best known, however, for her poetry—the bittersweet verse of an Ogden NASH with a hangover. Famous examples were the couplet "News Item" ("Men seldom make passes / At girls who wear glasses") and the quatrain "Résumé":

> *Razors pain you, rivers are damp.*
> *Acids stain you and drugs cause cramp.*
> *Guns aren't lawful, nooses give.*
> *Gas smells awful. You might as well live.*

Parker's edgy humor also revealed itself in often quoted wisecracks about 1920s sexuality. About a woman who had returned from London with a broken leg: "She probably did it sliding down a barrister." On the young women assembled for a college prom: "If all those sweet young things were laid end to end—I wouldn't be a bit surprised."

Parker, "Hanging"   (1839–96) Frontier judge. As the federal magistrate at Fort Smith, Arkansas, Isaac C. Parker ordered so many executions—three or four a year for twenty years—that he became widely known as "Hanging" Parker. He was also known for his gruesomely eloquent death sentences. One victim he promised to hang until he was "dead, dead, dead." To another, who had been convicted of thirteen murders, he sneered, "It is too bad that you have only one life the law can take. Otherwise you would be hanged thirteen times."

Parker, Quanah   See QUANAH.

Parker, Robert Leroy   See Butch CASSIDY.

Parkman, Francis   (1823–93) The first great historian of North America, Parkman achieved fame with his first book, *The Oregon Trail* (1849), based on his experiences among the SIOUX. His magnum opus, *France and England in North America* (1865–92), covered the two powers' colonial rivalry up to the FRENCH AND INDIAN WAR.

Parks, Bert See MISS AMERICA PAGEANT.

Parks, Rosa (1913–) Sometimes called the mother of the civil rights movement, Parks was a black resident of Montgomery, Alabama, who in 1955 defied the city's segregated transportation ordinance by refusing to surrender her bus seat to a white man. Her arrest sparked the Montgomery bus boycott and the emergence of Martin Luther KING, Jr., as its spokesman.

Parsons, Louella (1893–1972) Gossip columnist. Hedda HOPPER's chief rival in the 1940s, Parsons wrote film colony tidbits for the William Randolph HEARST newspaper chain. Her memoirs appeared in *The Gay Illiterate* (1944) and *Tell It to Louella* (1961).

Parton, Dolly (1946–) Singer, songwriter. The glitzy/earthy blend of a showgirl appearance, a piercing soprano, and evocative lyrics made Parton the best-known country star of the 1970s. One of twelve children born in poverty in Tennessee, she wrote tender songs evoking her humble origins, including "Joshua," "Coat of Many Colors," and "My Tennessee Mountain Home." She debuted at the GRAND OLE OPRY at thirteen, began her career as Porter Wagoner's singing partner, and subsequently was often billed with Kenny ROGERS. Her recording of the title song from the 1980 movie *9 to 5* (in which she also starred) was the crossover hit of the year.

Pastor, Tony See VAUDEVILLE.

Patch, Sam (d. 1829) The "Jersey Jumper," Sam Patch became an overnight celebrity in 1827 when he jumped from a cliff overlooking the Passaic River. He amazed crowds for two years with subsequent feats (including a jump at NIAGARA FALLS) until dying in a leap at Genesee Falls in Rochester, New York. His status as a folk hero outlived him for some decades in ballads, tall tales, "sightings," and theatrical melodramas.

Pathfinder, The See (1) Natty BUMPPO and (2) John C. FRÉMONT.

Patton, George S. (1885–1945) General. A tank brigade commander in World War I, West Pointer Patton became the hero of armored warfare in World War II. He fought the German "Desert Fox" Erwin Rommel in 1942, led the Allied invasion of Sicily in 1943, and drove his Third Army in a motorized sweep across France (1944–45) that liberated Europe from German control. Nicknamed Old Blood and Guts, he outraged many in 1943 when he slapped a bedridden soldier he believed to be malingering. A 1970 film portrait, *Patton,* won Academy Awards for best picture, best direction (Franklin Schaffner), and best actor (George C. Scott).

"Paul Revere's Ride" (1863) LONGFELLOW's romanticized version of Paul REVERE's ride "on the 18th of April in '75." It makes the Boston silversmith the sole hero of the night's activities, forgetting that William Dawes and Samuel Prescott also (and more successfully) warned the Massachusetts countryside of the approaching British. The poem's most vivid image is that of Revere's friend hanging signal lamps in the Old North Church:

One if by land, and two if by sea,
And I on the opposite shore will be,
Ready to ride and spread the alarm
To every Middlesex village and farm.

Payne, John Howard   (1791–1852) Actor, playwright. Best known as the author of "HOME, SWEET HOME" (from his 1823 play *Clari, or The Maid of Milan*), Payne wrote over fifty other plays, including the tragedy *Brutus, or The Fall of Tarquin* (1818), a success for the English actor Edmund Kean.

Peace Corps   A foreign-service program established in 1961 by the John F. KENNEDY administration. It sends American volunteers to less developed nations to provide assistance in health, education, community development, farming, and other fields. A domestic version of the program entitled VISTA (Volunteers in Service to America) was begun in 1964.

peace pipe   A reed-stemmed tobacco pipe used by native American peoples for treaty-making and other ceremonial purposes. The term dates from the eighteenth century; in the previous century, it had been called a calumet, from the French word *chalumeau* for "reed."

Peaceable Kingdom, The   Title of a series of paintings by Pennsylvania primitivist Edward Hicks (1780–1849). They depict a natural harmony in which, as Hicks put it, "The beauteous leopard with his restless eye / shall with the kid in perfect stillness lie."

Peacemaker, the   See Samuel COLT.

peacenik   An antiwar protester during the VIETNAM WAR. A derogatory usage derived from "beatnik" (see BEAT GENERATION).

Peale, Norman Vincent   (1898–1994) Preacher. A Methodist minister, Peale was a longtime pastor of a New York City church and a successful author of inspirational writings. His plan for self-improvement, which combined Bible reading with the promotion of a positive attitude, was outlined in *The Power of Positive Thinking* (1952), one of the best-selling self-help books of all time.

peanut butter and jelly   See PEANUTS.

peanut gallery   An audience seating section reserved for children. Used from the 1920s, but popularized especially by HOWDY DOODY.

peanuts   (1) Native to South America, peanuts were brought to the Old World by the Spanish and Portuguese and raised by the latter in West Africa, where they became an inexpensive food for slaves. Early North American terms included "ground nuts," "ground peas," "monkey nuts," and "goobers" or "goober peas" (from the Bantu *nguba*). The popularity of the food was enhanced by the 1890 invention of peanut butter and by the work of black agronomist George Washington CARVER, who showed how to use it literally from soup to nuts. In addition to the hot-roasted peanuts that have been sold at ball games for almost a century, peanuts also give us the hard-candy treat peanut brittle and the children's lunch box favorite, peanut butter and jelly sandwiches. After Carver, the names most commonly associated with peanuts are Planters (the company that dominates the peanut market) and Jimmie Carter, the Georgia peanut farmer and U.S. president (1977–81).

(2) Drawn by Charles Schulz (1922–   ) since 1950, *Peanuts* is the most successful syndicated comic strip in history. In addition to appearing in thousands of newspapers worldwide, its characters—trusting Charlie Brown, acerbic Lucy, blanket-clutching Linus, and the preening, philosophical dog Snoopy—are shown in endless television specials and promotional spin-offs.

Pearl, Minnie   (1912–   ) Entertainer. Country music's most durable comedienne, Sarah Colley portrayed engaging hayseed Minnie Pearl at the GRAND OLE OPRY from 1940 into the 1980s. Audiences' affection for her guileless enthusiasm contributed greatly to the Opry's success. Her trademarks were a floppy straw hat with the price tag still attached and the infectious greeting "How-dee! I'm so proud to be here!"

Pearl Harbor   A U.S. naval base on the island of Oahu, Hawaii. On December 7, 1941, it was the victim of a surprise attack by Japanese bombers that took 2,400 American lives and decimated U.S. battleships and planes. The incident put an end to United States neutrality. The following day President Franklin D. ROOSEVELT, calling the seventh "a date which will live in infamy," got a declaration of war from the U.S. Congress. Hence the Pacific battle slogan "Remember Pearl Harbor."

Peary, Robert E.   (1856–1920) Naval officer, explorer. Although his claim was long disputed, Peary is now generally recognized as the first man to have reached the North Pole. The feat was accomplished on April 6, 1909, with the help of four Eskimo sled drivers and Peary's longtime black colleague, Matthew Henson. The U.S. Navy recognized his claim by making him an admiral.

Peck, Gregory   (1916–   ) Actor. A handsome leading man with a distinctive baritone voice, Peck became a major star in the 1940s after an Oscar nomination for his second film, *The Keys of the Kingdom* (1945). After further nominations for THE YEARLING, *Gentleman's Agreement* (1947), and *Twelve O'Clock High* (1950), he finally won for the racial drama TO KILL A MOCKINGBIRD, in which he played the liberal southern lawyer Atticus Finch. He was also seen as Captain AHAB in MOBY DICK and as F. Scott FITZGERALD in *Beloved Infidel* (1959).

Peck's Bad Boy   A rambunctious or mischievous youngster. From the title character in stories by Midwest journalist George Wilbur Peck (1840–1916), first published in the 1880s in the Milwaukee paper *Peck's Sun* and reprinted in such collections as *Peck's Bad Boy and His Pa* (1883). Peck was also mayor of Milwaukee and governor of Wisconsin.

Pecos Bill   A modern, manufactured folk hero, the cowboy equivalent of Paul BUNYAN. A Texan raised along the Pecos River, Bill fed his horse, Widowmaker, on nitroglycerin and BARBED WIRE; owned a ranch with a yard so big that several way stations dotted the path to the front door; and could ride "anything that had hair and some things that didn't." Once, bucked by a tornado he was riding on a bet, he fell into California, creating DEATH VALLEY. The author of the tales, Edward O'Reilly, introduced them in the *Century* in the 1920s.

"peculiar institution" Slavery. The phrase was used in the OLD SOUTH to mean it was indigenous to that region.

Pegleg Joe (Pegfoot) See "FOLLOW THE DRINKING GOURD."

Penn, William (1644–1718) An English QUAKER, Penn founded the colony of Pennsylvania in 1681 on land given him by royal charter. Intending it as a safe haven for his often persecuted fellow Quakers, he established it as a "Holy Experiment" in toleration, self-governance, and respect for civil liberties, including the rights of the original native inhabitants. Treaties he made with the DELAWARE Indians were honored in his lifetime and for two decades thereafter. His generous vision survives in the name Philadelphia, the "City of Brotherly Love," which he founded.

pennant In baseball, the annual championship of one of the two major leagues. The National League and American League pennant winners meet each other in the WORLD SERIES.

Pennsylvania Dutch Misnomer for descendants of the German (*Deutsch*) immigrants who settled eastern Pennsylvania in the seventeenth and eighteenth centuries. The majority of them, variously known as the Church, "fancy," or Gay Dutch, belong to mainstream Protestant denominations and have been thoroughly absorbed into middle-class society. A visible minority, the pietistic Plain Folk, still adhere to a nonconventional lifestyle, shunning modernity and practicing communal labor; the most famous of these latter folk are the AMISH. The Pennsylvania Dutch country is known for its foods (such as scrapple and shoofly pie), its crafts (including quilts and Fraktur designs), and its HEX SIGNS.

penny press Nineteenth-century New York City newspapers that shaped the reading tastes of a growing population. Short on analysis and long on sensation, they prefigured YELLOW JOURNALISM and twentieth-century TABLOIDS. Publisher Benjamin Day (1810–89) started the trend with his *New York Sun* (1833), which soon outsold all the city's six-penny papers combined. The *Sun* was followed by the *Herald* (1835), published by James Gordon Bennett (1795–1872), and the *Tribune* (1841), edited by reformer Horace GREELEY.

Pentagon A five-sided building in Arlington, Virginia, that houses the U.S. Army, Navy, Air Force, and Defense departments. As the center of the armed services' bureaucracy, it is a common metaphor for military planning. In 1967, it was the target of a massive march and demonstration against the VIETNAM WAR.

Pentagon Papers A secret PENTAGON study that criticized U.S. handling of the VIETNAM WAR and charged the federal government with deceiving the public. In 1971, when former Pentagon employee Daniel Ellsberg leaked the report to the press, the Justice Department sued to have it censored. A Supreme Court ruling denied the suit, and the "papers" were published in book form by the NEW YORK TIMES. Their revelations, along with those of MY LAI, increased opposition to the war.

"People, Yes, The" (1936) A long, patriotic poem by Carl SANDBURG, celebrating the vitality and goodwill of the American people.

Peoria   A small city in Illinois (population about 125,000) that is often invoked as a metaphor for mainstream attitudes. To determine a project's commercial or political feasibility, one asks, "How will it play in Peoria?"

Pepsi-Cola   A carbonated soft drink similar in taste to, and second in sales to, COCA-COLA. Invented by North Carolina pharmacist Caleb Bradham in 1898, Pepsi was sold originally as "Brad's Drink." An early salvo in what came to be known as the cola wars was fired in the 1930s, when the Pepsi company doubled the size of its bottles from six to twelve ounces and chided Coke with this radio jingle:

> *Pepsi-Cola hits the spot;*
> *Twelve full ounces, that's a lot.*
> *Twice as much for a nickel, too;*
> *Pepsi-Cola is the drink for you.*

Pequod   Captain Ahab's ship in MOBY-DICK, on which most of the novel's action takes place. At the end of the story it is rammed and sunk by the white whale.

Perelman, S. J.   (1904–79) Writer. Brooklyn-born Sidney Joseph Perelman wrote humorous pieces for THE NEW YORKER and for Hollywood movies, including the MARX BROTHERS classics *Monkey Business* (1931) and *Horse Feathers* (1932). His Broadway comedy, *One Touch of Venus* (1943; film 1948), was written with Ogden NASH and Kurt Weill. Perelman's satirical fancies were collected in volumes with titles like *Strictly from Hunger* (1937), *Westward Ha!, or Around the World in 80 Clichés* (1948), and *The Swiss Family Perelman* (1950).

Perils of Pauline, The   (1914) The most famous CLIFF-HANGER of the silent era. It made Pearl White (1889–1938), as the damsel forever in distress, the most popular actress of her day. White also starred in other serials (*The Exploits of Elaine, Perils of Paris*) as well as feature films.

Perkins, Carl   (1932–   ) Singer, songwriter. One of the original rockabilly stars on Sam PHILLIPS's Sun label, Perkins wrote and recorded "BLUE SUEDE SHOES" several months before Elvis PRESLEY covered it. He also wrote "Matchbox," "Everybody's Trying to Be My Baby," and "Honey Don't"—all recorded successfully by the Beatles. In the 1970s, he toured with Johnny CASH.

Perkins, Ma   See MA PERKINS.

Perry, Matthew C.   (1794–1858) and **Oliver Hazard** (1785–1819) Naval officers. Commodore Matthew Perry, a veteran of the WAR OF 1812 and the MEXICAN WAR, led the 1853–54 expedition to the Far East that opened isolationist Japan to American trade. His older brother Oliver commanded the U.S. fleet in the Battle of Lake Erie in 1813. When that battle ended with a British surrender, Perry reported the victory in a famous dispatch: "We have met the enemy and they are ours." See also POGO.

Perry Mason   A long-running (1957–74) television series starring Raymond Burr as sleuth/lawyer Perry Mason, assisted by his legman, Paul Drake, and his secretary, Della Street. A defense attorney who never lost a case, Mason was the creation of writer Erle Stanley Gardner (1889–1970), who featured him in a series of mysteries beginning with *The Case of the Velvet Claws* (1933). The books routinely sold in the millions worldwide, making Gardner the most frequently translated American author and the most successful detective novelist after Mickey SPILLANE. The books also inspired a Perry Mason radio show which ran from 1943 to 1955.

Pershing, John J. (1860–1948) General. "Black Jack" Pershing, after serving effectively in the Spanish-American War and the punitive expedition against Pancho VILLA, commanded the AMERICAN EXPEDITIONARY FORCE (AEF) in World War I. His success earned him promotion to general of the armies—a rank that only George Washington had previously held—and to army chief of staff until his retirement. Pershing acquired his nickname from commanding black cavalrymen early in his career. His memoir *My Experiences in the World War* won the 1932 Pulitzer Prize for history.

pet in the oven A modern legend of domestic tragicomedy, a version of the "stupid baby-sitter" (or "stupid newlywed") theme. A household pet is roasted alive when its caretaker, confusing it with a pizza, places it in an oven. Recent variants have the creature microwaved, exploding within the appliance as a result of the error. For other "urban legends," see SPIDER IN THE HAIRDO; VANISHING HITCHHIKER.

Peter Pan A play (1904) by English writer Sir James Barrie about a boy who refuses to grow up, Peter Pan, and his adventures in a timeless Never-Never-Land; other major characters include the Darling children, Wendy, Michael, and John; Peter's fairy companion, Tinker Bell; and his adversary, the pirate Captain Hook. Maude ADAMS created the title role on Broadway, and the story's American audience expanded greatly thanks to two treatments of the 1950s. The first, a Walt DISNEY animated feature, appeared in 1953. The second, a Broadway musical starring Mary MARTIN, opened in 1954 and was televised in 1955, winning EMMY AWARDS for Martin and for the show itself as the best single program of the year. At its dramatic turning point, Peter begs the audience to clap their hands if they believe in fairies so that Tinker Bell's life, which depends on faith, can be saved. The moment was a brilliant (and for the period rare) example of interactive television.

Peter, Paul, and Mary The most popular folk group of the 1960s. Peter Yarrow (1937–), Paul Stookey (1937–), and Mary Travers (1938–) began singing together in GREENWICH VILLAGE folk clubs, had an initial hit with Pete SEEGER's "If I Had a Hammer" in 1962, and the following year covered "BLOWIN' IN THE WIND" in a version that brought Bob DYLAN his first acclaim. The sweetly harmonious trio was also associated with the children's song "Puff the Magic Dragon," weirdly interpreted by some as a psychotropic anthem.

Peter Principle "In a hierarchy individuals tend to rise to the level of their incompetence"—as in the gifted teacher becoming an inept principal. The title of a 1969 book by Laurence J. Peter and Peter Hull. See also MURPHY'S LAW.

Petrified Forest (1) A national park in eastern Arizona that contains the an extensive assortment of petrified trees. (2) As *The Petrified Forest*: a play (1935;

film 1936) by Robert SHERWOOD about the frustrated dreams of characters who meet in an Arizona roadhouse. Humphrey BOGART's portrayal of the villain Duke Mantee made him a star both on Broadway and on film.

Petty, Richard (1937–) Stock car racer. The son of Lee Petty, a three-time winner of the national stock car championship and the first-ever winner of the Daytona 500, Richard Petty is commonly known as the King in driving circles. He broke practically every NASCAR record available in the 1960s and 1970s, including winning seven grand championships and six Daytona runs.

Peyton Place A 1956 novel by Grace Metalious (1924–64) about scheming and extramarital affairs in a New England town. The blockbuster novel of the decade, it sold over 10 million copies and set a fashion for steamy family sagas. A television version ran throughout the 1960s, becoming the first successful prime-time SOAP OPERA.

PG, PG13 See RATING.

Phantom, The A comic strip created in 1936 by Lee Falk. The superhero protagonist, a kind of TARZAN in tights, is a masked defender of justice who lives in a jungle cave and is known by his friends, the pygmies, as the Ghost Who Walks. As "Mr. Walker," he rights the wrongs of civilization. The strip has great appeal internationally. At its fiftieth anniversary, its distributor, King Features, called it "the most widely read superhero comic on earth today."

Phantom of the Opera, The A silent film (1925) starring Lon CHANEY as a mysterious, grotesque figure who haunts the Paris Opera House. The story, from a 1911 novel by Gaston Leroux, also inspired a 1943 remake (with Claude Rains as the Phantom) and a 1986 musical by Andrew Lloyd-Webber.

Phi Beta Kappa An academic honorary society founded at the College of WILLIAM AND MARY in 1776. Originally a social club, it evolved into the nation's most prestigious organization of undergraduate scholars, with chapters on hundreds of college campuses. The Greek letters φ, β, and κ, which appear on members' coveted gold keys, stand for *philosophia biou kubernetes,* "philosophy the guide of life."

Philadelphia The largest city in Pennsylvania and the fifth largest in the United States. Founded by William PENN, it became the center of colonial politics in the eighteenth century: the home of the Continental Congress, INDEPENDENCE HALL, and the Constitutional Convention. From 1790 to 1800 it was the nation's capital. Penn's Greek name means the "City of Brotherly Love."

Philadelphia lawyer A shrewd attorney. An eighteenth-century term that may derive from Philadelphian Alexander HAMILTON's successful defense of John Peter Zenger in 1835 (see ZENGER TRIAL). An old New England adage says that three Philadelphia lawyers are a match for the devil.

Philadelphia Story, The A comedy (1939) by playwright Philip Barry (1896–1949) about the conflict between love and propriety among the idle rich. Katharine HEPBURN, who played the female lead onstage, also starred in director

George CUKOR's 1940 film version, one of the most successful SCREWBALL COMEDIES. It won James STEWART an Oscar for best actor, another for Donald Ogden Stewart for best screenplay. A 1956 remake, *High Society,* with songs by Cole PORTER, starred Bing CROSBY, Grace KELLY, and Frank SINATRA.

Phillips, Sam (1923–) Record producer. A former disc jockey, Phillips recorded black BLUES and RHYTHM AND BLUES artists in the late 1940s, then midwifed rockabilly into existence single-handedly from his Sun Studios on Memphis's Union Avenue. Stars who began on the Sun label included Johnny CASH, Elvis PRESLEY, Jerry Lee LEWIS, and Carl PERKINS.

Phillips, Wendell See ABOLITIONISTS.

Phyfe, Duncan (1768–1854) Cabinetmaker. The undisputed American master of both Georgian and Empire furniture styles, the Scottish-born Phyfe worked for half a century out of a workshop in lower Manhattan. Known especially for his mahogany veneers, lyre-backed chairs, and ornamental carvings, he furnished fashionable homes from Baltimore to Boston.

Pickett's Charge On the final day of the Battle of GETTYSBURG (July 3, 1863), Virginia General George E. Pickett (1825–75) led fifteen thousand of his men in a frontal assault that briefly threatened to break the Union line. Pickett's Charge, even though it failed, was thenceforth eulogized as a shining moment of Confederate glory.

Pickford, Mary (1893–1979) Actress. Toronto-born Gladys Smith, a stage baby at the age of five, relied on an angelic appearance and an infectious personality to become, in Ephraim Katz's words, "the most popular star in screen history." Dubbed Mary Pickford by David BELASCO, she became "Little Mary" under the tutelage of D. W. GRIFFITH, who provided her first starring roles. These, and those she performed for various companies thereafter, so successfully capitalized on her innocent aura that she was universally idolized as "America's Sweetheart." Highlights of her screen career (1909–33) were roles in *Little Red Riding Hood* (1911), *Poor Little Rich Girl* and *Rebecca of Sunnybrook Farm* (both 1917), *Daddy Long Legs* (1919), *Pollyanna* (1920), and *Little Lord Fauntleroy* (1921).

  A savvy businesswoman, Pickford gained control over her properties early in her career, successfully negotiated ever-increasing salaries, and in 1919 formed her own production company, UNITED ARTISTS, with Griffith, Charlie CHAPLIN, and Douglas FAIRBANKS. Her second marriage, to Fairbanks (1920–36), was a press agent's dream; the couple's mansion, Pickfair, a Hollywood salon. Pickford received a special Oscar in 1975, acknowleging her legacy to the world of the movies.

pie in the sky A metaphor for vain promises, especially religious ones. Popularized by Joe HILL's song "The Preacher and the Slave," a parody of the hymn "In the Sweet Bye and Bye."

> *You will eat, bye and bye,*
> *In that glorious land above the sky.*
> *Work and pray, live on hay.*
> *You'll get pie in the sky when you die.*

pig Latin   A "secret" children's language in which initial consonants, plus the "ay" sound, are moved to the ends of words: "Go to the store" becomes "Oh-gay oo-tay uh-thay or-stay."

pig woman   See HALL-MILLS CASE .

Pike, Zebulon   (1779–1813) Explorer. A U.S. Army officer, Pike led two major expeditions into the American West. On the first (1805–6), he explored the north of the LOUISIANA PURCHASE. On the second (1806–7), a trek through the Southwest and Rocky Mountains, he sighted a 14,000-foot Colorado peak that bears his name. Pike died in the WAR OF 1812.

"Pikes Peak or Bust"   A slogan of the 1858 GOLD RUSH that brought thousands of would-be miners to the Rocky Mountains. The disappointed ones sometimes returned East displaying banners that read "Busted, by God!"

Pilgrims   English religious dissenters who, in 1608, fled England for Holland to avoid persecution. Twelve years later, under elders William Brewster and William Bradford, they embarked on the MAYFLOWER for the New World, there to found Massachusetts's PLYMOUTH COLONY. The colony's leaders are sometimes called the Pilgrim Fathers. The term "Pilgrim" arose in the nineteenth century; what the dissenters called themselves was Saints. See also PURITANS, THANKSGIVING.

pill, the   Shorthand for oral contraceptives or that method of birth control. From the 1960s; "birth control pill" dates from the previous decade. A woman "on the pill" is one practicing such contraception.

Pillsbury Doughboy   An advertising icon of the Pillsbury food conglomerate. Used since 1965, the doughboy (his name is actually Poppin' Fresh) has a baker's cap, a constant smile, and a characteristic giggle.

pinball   An arcade game in which players accumulate points by propelling steel balls to scoring areas by means of "flippers." The name comes from the placement of guiding pins in the original models from the beginning of the century. The heyday of pinball machines was the 1950s; since the 1970s, they have lost ground to VIDEO GAMES.

Ping-Pong   A type of miniature tennis played on a table (hence the official designation "table tennis") with small wooden paddles and plastic balls. The name, which comes from the sound of the paddles hitting the balls, was trademarked by the game company Parker Brothers.

Pink Panther, The   A 1964 movie directed by Blake Edwards and starring Peter Sellers as inept Inspector Clouseau. Its credit sequences, and those of its sequels, featured an animated panther slinking along to music by Henry MANCINI. The cat became as well known as the human participants, starring in animated shorts and a children's TV show.

Pinkertons   Men employed by the nation's first detective firm, the Pinkerton Agency, founded in 1850 by Allen Pinkerton (1819–84). They foiled a plot to assassinate Abraham Lincoln, spied for the Union during the Civil War, and were thereafter active in the suppression of labor unrest. See FINK (2); HOMESTEAD STRIKE; MOLLY MAGUIRES.

pinko   One with communist or leftist sympathies that are not blatant enough to label him a RED. A cold war term from the 1940s.

Pinocchio   An animated feature film (1940) by Walt DISNEY. Based on a story by Italian author Carlo Collodi, it is the tale of a woodcarver's puppet who comes to life. A central dramatic conceit is that Pinocchio's nose grows longer every time he tells a lie. The idea has provided grist for numerous satirists. In casting doubt on President Bill Clinton's veracity, for example, one magazine portrayed him in a long-nosed caricature under the legend "The Adventures of Clinocchio."

Pinta   See Christopher COLUMBUS.

pinup   A photograph of a sexually appealing woman, typically in a bathing suit or other revealing dress. Such photographs of movie actresses and models were distributed free by their employers to World War II servicemen, who pinned them up in their barracks and workstations. The G.I.s' favorite pinup girl was Betty GRABLE. A LIFE magazine photo of a close second, Rita HAYWORTH, was attached to a test atomic bomb dropped on the island of Bikini.

pioneers   Common term for the settlers of the American frontier in the eighteenth- and nineteenth-century westward expansion. *The Pioneers* (1823) was the first of James Fenimore Cooper's LEATHERSTOCKING TALES. *O Pioneers!* (1913) was Willa Cather's first Nebraska novel. The Sons of the Pioneers are SINGING COWBOYS.

pirates   See BLACKBEARD; CAPTAIN KIDD; Jean LAFITTE; Sir Henry MORGAN.

Pit, The   See Frank NORRIS.

"Pit and the Pendulum, The"   A horror story (1842) by Edgar Allan POE. It describes the torture of the narrator by the Spanish Inquisition. Vincent PRICE starred in a 1961 movie version.

Pitcher, Molly   Revolutionary War heroine. At the Battle of Monmouth in 1778, Mary Hays provided water to her husband and his comrades and, when he was incapacitated (by heat or injury, depending on the source), she stood in for him as cannoneer. The Pennsylvania legislature granted her a pension until her death in 1832, and the nickname Molly Pitcher remained so associated with heroic rescue that ABOLITIONISTS later applied it to Harriet TUBMAN.

Pittsburgh   The second largest city in Pennsylvania (after PHILADELPHIA). It sits at the confluence of the Allegheny and Monongahela rivers, a spot that young surveyor George Washington suggested as ideal for a fort. Both the French and English followed his suggestion, and the name Pittsburgh evolved from the English Fort Pitt. Since the 1880s, it has been the center of U.S. steel manufacturing, hence a byword for industrial growth and accompanying pollution.

pizza   A flat, usually round pie with a dough crust and covered with tomato sauce, cheeses, and sundry toppings. Pizza was invented in Naples, first made in the United States by Italian immigrants, and enjoyed a boost in popularity in the 1950s thanks to the acquired taste of returning Italian-campaign G.I.s and the concurrent rise of the FAST FOOD industry. Family pizzerias, which proliferated in the 1960s, now compete for the huge pizza market with national restaurant chains, delivery services, and frozen-food companies.

plantation   (1) Among English settlers since the sixteenth century, a synonym for "colony," "planted" both with and by settlers: Governor William Bradford wrote a history of "Plimouth Plantation." (2) In the OLD SOUTH, a large estate on which slaves, and sometimes indentured servants, farmed crops of cotton, tobacco, indigo, rice, and sugar. The plantation system, run by wealthy landowners collectively known as the planter aristocracy, was in decline by the end of the eighteenth century, when Eli WHITNEY's cotton gin gave it a new lease on life. Southern plantations were thereafter, until the Civil War, inexorably linked to cotton and to slavery.

Platters, the   Vocal group that specialized in moodily sentimental lyrics and rich harmonies. Between 1955 and 1960, they made the RHYTHM AND BLUES and pop charts with "The Great Pretender," "Twilight Time," and "Smoke Gets in Your Eyes."

"Play it, Sam"   See CASABLANCA; Dooley WILSON.

Playboy   A slick girlie magazine founded in 1953 by Hugh Hefner (1926–   ), an early sign of the so-called sexual revolution. The magazine's first issue contained a nude photograph of Marilyn MONROE, and each subsequent issue featured a "Playmate of the Month" whose similarly au naturel likeness was a stapled-in "centerfold." Because the magazine also contained quality writing, interviews with celebrities, and Hefner's own rambling "Playboy Philosophy," it became a joke to say that one bought it "for the articles." With the magazine's success, Hefner adopted a playboy lifestyle, posing with Playmates in his Chicago mansion, and opened up a string of Playboy key clubs whose skimpily uniformed waitresses were known as bunnies. The bunny logo of the Playboy empire is now internationally known, while the pathway blazed by Hefner for the appreciation of female nudity has been followed with lubricious glee by *Hustler* and *Penthouse*.

Play-Doh   A modeling clay developed in 1955 by Cincinnati inventor Joseph McVicker. Cleaner and more versatile than normal clay, it is marketed by that city's Kenner Products, which has sold over 800 million cans.

player piano   A mechanical piano in which the keys are operated by forced air. The air, produced by a foot bellows, passes through a pattern of holes in a roll of paper—each pattern corresponding to a specific tune. Player pianos, invented just before the turn of the century, remained popular into the 1920s, when radio gradually made them a thing of the past.

Pledge of Allegiance   A pledge to the American flag written for the COLUMBUS quadricentennial in 1892. The probable author was children's magazine editor Francis Bellamy. It was common until recently for American schoolchildren to begin each morning's classes by reciting the pledge. The wording, changed slightly from Bellamy's version, is "I pledge allegiance to the flag of the United

States of America, and to the republic for which it stands, one nation, under God, indivisible, with liberty and justice for all.''

Plessy v. Ferguson   An 1896 Supreme Court decision that upheld a Louisiana law requiring railroad passengers in the state to be separated by race (Homer Plessy, the law's black challenger, was the loser). The decision made ''separate but equal'' accommodations legal nationwide, and in the South paved the way for JIM CROW laws.

plumbers   See WATERGATE.

Pluto   In Walt DISNEY cartoons since 1930, Pluto is MICKEY MOUSE's dog.

Plymouth Colony   The first lasting English colony north of Virginia. Settled by the MAYFLOWER passengers in 1620, it survived a devastating ''Generall Sickness'' in its first New England winter, profited from the aid of Indians such as Samoset and SQUANTO, and in 1621 celebrated the so-called first THANKSGIVING. Thanks to Henry Wadsworth LONGFELLOW, the colony's most famous members are John ALDEN, Priscilla Mullins, and Miles STANDISH. Its hardiness also survives in the automobile name Plymouth, whose long-standing trademark was an iconic figure of the *Mayflower*. In 1691, Plymouth was absorbed into the larger Massachusetts Bay Colony, whereupon its holdings became known as the Old Colony.

Plymouth Rock   A shoreline boulder marking the traditional landing site of the MAYFLOWER Pilgrims, and supposed to be the actual rock they used as a stepping-stone to the New World. Although no contemporary source verifies the designation, the rock, protected by a canopy, has been a Plymouth, Massachusetts, tourist attraction for generations.

Pocahontas   (ca. 1595–1617) Known to schoolchildren as the Indian princess who saved Captain John SMITH's life, Pocahontas was actually named Matoaka (the nickname Pocahontas means ''playful one''), and she was the daughter of the leader Powhatan, head of Virginia's Powhatan confederacy. The rescue tale, told in Smith's history of Virginia, has been questioned by historians, but they agree that the girl was helpful to the Jamestown colony in persuading her father to furnish them with food. She also married the colonist John ROLFE—not Smith himself, as the legend claims—ushering in a period of interracial harmony that lasted from 1614 to 1622. Her trip to London as the christianized Lady Rebecca Rolfe created a sensation, but it also brought on the illness from which she died.

Podunk   A dull, provincial small town or rural area. From the Mohegan word for ''neck of land.''

Poe, Edgar Allan   (1809–49) Writer. The American master of gothic horror, Poe wrote the eerie classics ''THE FALL OF THE HOUSE OF USHER,'' ''THE PIT AND THE PENDULUM,'' and ''THE TELL-TALE HEART.'' On the basis of ''The Murders in the Rue Morgue'' (1841) and ''The Purloined Letter'' (1845), starring the amateur sleuth C. Auguste Dupin, he is also credited with inventing the detective story. His literary criticism and musical verse—best represented by the onomatopoetic ''The Bells'' (1849), the elegiac ''Annabel Lee'' (1849), and ''THE RAVEN''—were much admired by European literati; Baudelaire in particular acknowledged his mastery.

Poe's personal life was as chaotic as his writing was polished. Forced out of West Point and the University of Virginia for misconduct, he suffered throughout his life from alcoholism, improvidence, and personal tragedy (his child bride, Virginia, died at twenty-five), while his finances forever lagged behind his esteem. After a binge that left him unconscious in a Baltimore street, he succumbed to "congestion of the brain" at the age of forty. See also Roger CORMAN, Vincent PRICE.

Pogo   Comic strip created in the 1940s by Walt Kelly (1913–73). Its title character, a kindly, philosophical opposum, comments obliquely on the political scene from his swampland home. He uttered his most famous line, a takeoff on Oliver Hazard PERRY, during the VIETNAM WAR: "We have met the enemy and he is us."

pogo stick   A toy invented in 1909 by George B. Hansburg. The stick, usually of metal, is equipped with footrests; standing on these rests, the user jumps up and down, activating a spring that enables him to hop from place to place.

Poitier, Sidney   (1924–   ) Actor. Poitier's charm, good looks, and theatrical sensitivity made him the first black movie star to transcend racial stereotyping. His first major success was as an escaped convict in *The Defiant Ones* (1958). He won an Oscar nomination for that role and took the award itself for *Lilies of the Field* (1963). His best-known work with all-black casts was in PORGY AND BESS and A RAISIN IN THE SUN. He broke new ground in two films about interracial romance—*A Patch of Blue* (1965) and *Guess Who's Coming to Dinner?* (1967)— and he galvanized audiences in the troubled 1960s as the no-nonsense professional Virgil Tibbs (see IN THE HEAT OF THE NIGHT).

poker   A card game that evolved from the British game Brag. The name may derive from the German *pochen,* "to boast," or from a similar French game, *pogue.* Originating in New Orleans around 1800, it moved up the Mississippi River with riverboat gamblers to become a well-known betting game. It exists in numerous variants. In the most common one, five-card draw, players receive five cards face down, exchange up to four from the remaining deck, and bet on their resulting hands for an accumulating pot of "chips." The possible hands, arranged in order from highest to lowest, are as follows:

straight flush	five cards of the same suit in order
four of a kind	four cards of the same rank
full house	three of a kind and a pair
flush	five cards of the same suit
straight	five cards in order
three of a kind	three cards of the same rank
two pair	two cards of one rank, two of another
one pair	two cards of the same rank
high card	the highest rank card of all hands (used when no player has at least a pair)

Because players must "see" previous bets—that is, place an equal amount of money in the pot to stay in the hand—bluffing is a critical strategy; if the holder of a good hand will not see another player's bet, he must "fold," that is, withdraw from that round, even though his hand could have beaten the other's. In the words of the Paul NEWMAN character in the 1967 movie *Cool Hand Luke:* "Sometimes nothing can be a real cool hand."

"See the bet" and "fold" are only two of many expressions that poker has contributed to American slang. To have an "ace up one's sleeve" means to cheat. A "blue chip" stock is a valuable one, like the most expensive-colored chips in a poker game. "To cash in one's chips" means to leave the game, that is, to die. "To call one's bluff" means to demand that he show what he has or (to use another betting expression) that he "put up or shut up." One begins a project by doing or saying something "for openers," like a player who "opens the bet" on a given hand. A "poker face" is the type of impassive expression that a good poker bluffer needs, while someone who is believed to be less than he pretends to be may be called a "fourflusher." A "jackpot" is a pot with major winnings, and the "joker" was the first innovative "wild card," an unknown quantity that adjusted the odds. Poker purists have never cottoned to wild cards; for amateurs, the favorites are deuces and one-eyed jacks. See also ACES AND EIGHTS.

Police Gazette   Popular name for the *National Police Gazette,* a weekly magazine (1845–1937) that prefigured the modern TABLOID in its fondness for stories laced with sex and gore. Ostensibly devoted to covering crime, it played heavily on the duress—and undress—of nubile women.

political parties   In the United States as in Great Britain, politics runs on the dynamic tension between competing major parties—usually, although not always, two at a time. The most important parties have been the following.

Federalist party   The nation's first major party, formed by defenders of the federal CONSTITUTION of 1787. The party of the first two presidents, it favored centralism, support for business, and government by what John ADAMS called "the rich, the well-born, and the able."

Democratic-Republican party   Thomas JEFFERSON's party, which came to power in the "revolution of 1800." Hostile to the Federalists' central power, Democratic-Republicans generally supported revolutionary France and were suspicious of the controlling merchant class. Riven by factionalism, they split into the Democratic and Whig parties.

Democratic party   Formed by backers of Andrew JACKSON, who elected him to the presidency in 1828. The oldest continuously existing party in the world, it stands for popular rights against government and industrial power and has been notable for forging alliances of disparate groups. Its southern, agrarian base contributed to the extension of the franchise under JACKSONIAN DEMOCRACY and later to an affection for STATES' RIGHTS and prolabor legislation. Under FDR's NEW DEAL and LBJ's GREAT SOCIETY, the Democrats created the modern welfare state.

Whig party   A coalition of northern industrialists and southern STATES' RIGHTS advocates who opposed the dominant, JACKSON wing of the Democratic-Republicans. They elected Presidents William Henry Harrison (1840) and Zachary Taylor (1848) before succumbing to internal dissension over slavery.

Republican party   Formed in 1854 to oppose the extension of slavery, the Republican Party elected Abraham LINCOLN in 1860, imposed RECONSTRUCTION on the South after the Civil War, and became gradually identified with business interests. As the Grand Old Party of the nineteenth century, they supervised industrial growth and national expansion. Generally seen as conservative, the Republicans also had a Progressive wing, as exemplified by Theodore ROOSEVELT and Robert LA FOLLETTE (see PROGRESSIVISM). They remain the Democrats' chief rivals for government power.

Less powerful third parties have also played important roles, sometimes providing a critical "swing" effect in national elections. See FREE-SOILERS; POPULISTS; BULL MOOSE PARTY; Eugene V. DEBS; Norman THOMAS.

Pollock, Jackson   (1912–56) Painter. After studying in New York City with Thomas Hart BENTON, Pollock went on to develop a personal style that was as celebrated for its active process as for its products. Dripping and throwing paint onto unstretched canvases, he produced distinctive effects of swirling, textured color that made him an instant hero of abstract expressionism.

Pollyanna   A novel (1913) by Massachusetts writer Eleanor Hodgman Porter (1868–1920). Its perky heroine, a devotee of "the glad game," became a byword for irrepressible optimism. She was portrayed on film by Mary PICKFORD (1920) and, in an Oscar-winning performance, by Hayley Mills (1960).

Ponce de León, Juan   (ca. 1460–1521) Explorer. After sailing with COLUMBUS on his second voyage to the New World, Ponce de León subdued the native peoples of Borinquén (Puerto Rico) in 1508 and governed the island for the following three years. In 1513, he sailed north seeking the island of Bimini, which legends claimed contained a "fountain of youth." He landed instead in Florida, which, because he got there in April, he named for the Easter season, *pascua florida*. He died, the victim of a Carib arrow, in Havana.

Pontiac   (ca. 1720–69) Indian leader. Faced by the threat of British encroachment after the FRENCH AND INDIAN WAR, the Ottawa chief Pontiac led an alliance of tribes in attacks on frontier settlements throughout the Great Lakes region and the Ohio Valley. "Pontiac's Rebellion" ended in 1766 with a treaty promising to keep white settlers east of the Alleghenies; breaches of the promise by frontier colonials created tension not only with the Indians but also with the Crown. The leader's most visible legacy, the Pontiac automobile, uses a warrior's head as its trademark.

Pony Express   A horseback mail delivery system which, in its year and a half of operation (1860–61), became a high point of Old West romance. It linked St. Joseph, Missouri, to Sacramento, California, by a series of relay stations at which riders changed mounts. With the typical rider averaging five horses and seventy-five miles a day, the pony express made the 2,000-mile trip in about ten days—less than half the time of the typical stagecoach. With exhaustion and hostile Indians constant problems, the freight company that organized the service advertised for "daring young men, preferably orphans." Most of the riders were barely out of their teens, and the most famous one, the future BUFFALO BILL, was fifteen. The service folded with the completion of the transcontinental telegraph.

Poor Richard's Almanack   The collective name for a series of almanacs written from 1732 to 1757 by Benjamin FRANKLIN. In addition to the practical information typical of almanacs, they contained many of the maxims for which Franklin was known, such as "God helps those that help themselves" and "Early to bed, early to rise, makes a man healthy, wealthy, and wise." Franklin wrote under the pen name Richard Saunders. See also BONHOMME RICHARD.

poor white trash Slovenly or shiftless white people, especially in the South. Stuart Berg Flexner, who dates it to the 1830s, suggests it may originally have been a slave term describing whites who were willing to work like slaves. Heard since the 1850s as "white trash," and sometimes in this century simply as "trash."

pop art A loose-knit movement of artists, based chiefly in New York City, who experimented with popular-culture icons to produce visually arresting, self-consciously "vulgar" artworks that mocked the aesthetic borders between "high" and "kitsch." Perhaps the most famous examples of pop art were Andy WARHOL's silk screens of Marilyn MONROE photographs and CAMPBELL's soup cans. Other notable pop art jeux d'esprit were Roy LICHTENSTEIN's (1923–   ) parodic comic book panels, Jaspar Johns's (1930–   ) paintings of American flags, and Claes Oldenburg's (1929–   ) giant replicas of household objects.

Pop Warner football A football league for children (chiefly boys) from seven to fifteen. Although not as well known as baseball's LITTLE LEAGUE, it is actually an older organization, having been founded in 1929. It was named for college coach Glen "Pop" WARNER.

popcorn Introduced to white settlers by native Americans (including the guests at the first THANKSGIVING), popcorn now accounts for a major slice of the snack food industry, with Americans eating an estimated forty quarts per person every year. It is especially popular in movie theaters and at sporting events. See also CORN; CRACKER JACK.

Popeye Cartoon character created in 1929 by E. C. Segar and adapted four years later by the FLEISCHER BROTHERS as part of their BETTY BOOP series. Popeye, a good-hearted, brawling sailor, got his own animated series in September 1933, with the short whose title became a signature phrase: *I Yam What I Yam*. The appearances that followed (in media ranging from comic books to movies) revolved around the hero's rivalry with villain Bluto for the attentions of spindly, squeaky-voiced Olive Oyl. Popeye's inevitable victory follows his ingestion of spinach; hence his other signature line: "I'm strong to the finish, 'cause I eats me spinach. I'm Popeye the Sailor Man."

popsicle Flavored ice on a stick. From the trademark Popsicle, owned by New Jersey–based Popsicle Industries, but now applied generically to any such treat. The idea came by accident to an eleven-year-old boy, Frank Epperson, who in 1905 left a container of soda and a stirrer outside overnight and discovered them in the morning frozen together. See also ICE CREAM.

popular sovereignty Stephen A. DOUGLAS's proposed solution to the slavery issue. In drafting the KANSAS-NEBRASKA ACT of 1854, Douglas suggested that each territory be allowed to decide for itself whether or not it wished to permit slavery within its borders. Abraham Lincoln countered the idea in the famous Lincoln-Douglas debates of 1858 by observing, "A HOUSE DIVIDED AGAINST ITSELF CANNOT STAND."

Populists Agrarian reformers who mounted serious third-party campaigns for the White House in 1892 and 1896. The Populist party, or National People's party, wanted labor reforms, low-interest loans, an income tax, regulation of railroads, and most of all free silver. See also William Jennings BRYAN; "FREE SILVER."

Porgy and Bess   A "folk opera" (1935) with music by George GERSHWIN and words by his brother, Ira, and DuBose Heyward, from whose 1925 novel, *Porgy,* the story was adapted. The best-loved and most down-to-earth of American operas, it is a tale of love and death among the poor black residents of South Carolina's Catfish Row. Its best-known tunes are "I Got Plenty o' Nothin'," "It Ain't Necessarily So," and "SUMMERTIME." Sidney POITIER played the lead in a 1959 film.

Porky Pig   Cartoon character. The first LOONEY TUNES star, Porky made his debut in the 1935 short *I Haven't Got a Hat.* He met his nemeses DAFFY DUCK and BUGS BUNNY in *Porky's Duck Hunt* (1937) and *Porky's Hare Hunt* (1938). His stutter, provided by Mel BLANC, ended many Warner Brothers cartoons with the line "Tha . . . Tha . . . Tha . . . That's all, folks."

Porter, Cole   (1892–1964) Songwriter. An elegantly witty lyricist, Porter composed YALE UNIVERSITY's fight song, "Bulldog Yale," while an undergraduate there, then wrote show tunes for almost twenty Broadway musicals, including *Night and Day* (1932), *Anything Goes* (1934), and *Kiss Me Kate* (1948). Among his best-known songs—dozens of them now staples of the nightclub circuit—are "Begin the Beguine," "You're the Top," "I Love Paris," "Just One of Those Things," "Let's Do It," and a tongue-in-cheek country-western tune, "Don't Fence Me in." Cary GRANT played Porter in a 1946 film biography, *Night and Day.*

Porter, Edwin S.   (1869–1941) Film director. As an employee of the EDISON film company, Porter pioneered the close-up, intercutting, and narrative continuity. Although he directed dozens of short films, making him the first name director before D. W. GRIFFITH, he is best remembered for two works of 1903: the ingeniously edited *Life of an American Fireman* and the first "full length" story film, THE GREAT TRAIN ROBBERY.

Porter, William Sydney   See O. HENRY.

Portia Faces Life   A radio SOAP OPERA that ran on NBC from 1941 to 1952. Its hero, widowed attorney Portia Blake, fought political corruption in boss-ridden Parkerstown while juggling the claims of motherhood and romance. The character was named for Portia in *The Merchant of Venice.*

Post, C. W.   See BREAKFAST CEREALS.

Post, Emily   (1873–1960) Etiquette authority. A product of Baltimore high society, Emily Post was for nearly four decades the final word on "proper" behavior. Her guide to the social graces, *Etiquette: the Blue Book of Social Usage* (1922), entered ninety printings before her death, and her advice was also dispensed through newspapers and radio. While her writing sometimes reflected her precious upbringing—defining, for example, the need for a gold stud with a cutaway— much of it was generously commonsensical. In a 1950 edition, she urged her readers to ask not what is "correct," but what will "make the social machinery run more smoothly."

potato chips   Potatoes sliced thin and fried. One of the commonest American snacks, they were originally called Saratoga chips because of their invention, around 1853, in a Saratoga Springs, New York, restaurant.

Potomac   A river forming the border between the Virginias and Maryland. On its banks lie the family estates of Robert E. LEE and George Washington (see MOUNT VERNON); the tiny town of Harpers Ferry, West Virginia (see John BROWN); and the city of WASHINGTON, D.C. In the Civil War it was the northeastern border of the Confederacy, and the Union force assigned to protect the capital was known as the Army of the Potomac. "On the Potomac" and "down on the Potomac" are metaphors for Washington and the federal government.

Pound, Ezra   (1885–1972) Poet. A major force in modern poetry not only for his own verse but for his editing of W. B. Yeats and T. S. ELIOT, the Idaho-born Pound left the United States for Europe in 1908 to become an eccentric major-domo of the expatriate avant-garde. His poetry—metrically inventive and densely allusive—was collected in several volumes including *Hugh Selwyn Mauberley* (1920) and *The Pisan Cantos* (1948). The latter book he wrote while in a U.S. Army prison camp, where he was incarcerated for making broadcasts in favor of Mussolini. Pound spent from 1945 to 1958 in a mental hospital, and upon his release returned to his home in Italy.

Power, Tyrone   (1913–58) Actor. A handsome leading man of the 1930s and 1940s, Power was cast in romances, swashbucklers, and historical dramas that in general underutilized his talents. Among his best parts were that of the philosophic pilgrim Larry Darrell in *The Razor's Edge* (1946) and that of the tortured carnival "geek" in *Nightmare Alley* (1947). He also played Jake Barnes in THE SUN ALSO RISES and the title roles in *Jesse James* (1939) and *The Mark of Zorro* (1940).

Power of Positive Thinking, The   See Norman Vincent PEALE.

Powhatan   (ca. 1547–1618) Indian leader. The head of a confederacy uniting dozens of tidewater peoples, Powhatan befriended the English colonists at JAMESTOWN and, in spite of his suspicion of their expansionism, made a peace with them that lasted his lifetime. See also POCAHONTAS.

prairie   The grasslands stretching from the MISSISSIPPI RIVER to the foothills of the ROCKY MOUNTAINS; roughly, a synonym for the Great Plains. The word, which is French for "meadow," is used in numerous combinations, including prairie dog, for the region's gopherlike rodent, prairie fire, PRAIRIE OYSTER, and prairie schooner. *The Prairie* (1827), the third of James Fenimore Cooper's LEATHERSTOCKING TALES, tells of the old age and death of Natty Bumppo. Illinois is the Prairie State. See also "BURY ME NOT ON THE LONE PRAIRIE."

prairie oyster   (1) MOUNTAIN OYSTERS. (2) A drink of raw egg, salt, pepper, and either vinegar or whiskey; also called a prairie cocktail.

prairie school   See Frank Lloyd WRIGHT.

prairie schooner   See COVERED WAGON.

"Praise the Lord and pass the ammunition"   Catchphrase that emerged from the Japanese attack on PEARL HARBOR in 1941. The speaker was U.S. Navy chaplain Howell M. Forgy. It was the title of a 1942 popular song.

President of the United States   Title of the nation's chief executive, chosen by election every four years. In theory any "natural born" citizen over thirty-five and with fourteen years' residency is eligible. In practice all the presidents have been white males experienced in either politics or the military, and all but John F. KENNEDY have been, at least nominally, Protestants. Until Franklin D. ROOSEVELT, no president ran more than twice; FDR's breaking of that precedent led to the twenty-second Constitutional Amendment, limiting the chief to two terms (or a total of ten years) in office.

PRESIDENT	PARTY	TERM
1. George Washington	Federalist	1789–97
2. John Adams	Federalist	1797–1801
3. Thomas Jefferson	Democratic-Republican	1801–9
4. James Madison	Democratic-Republican	1809–17
5. James Monroe	Democratic-Republican	1817–25
6. John Quincy Adams	Democratic-Republican	1825–29
7. Andrew Jackson	Democratic	1829–37
8. Martin Van Buren	Democratic	1837–41
9. William Henry Harrison	Whig	1841
10. John Tyler	Whig	1841–45
11. James K. Polk	Democratic	1845–49
12. Zachary Taylor	Whig	1849–50
13. Millard Fillmore	Whig	1850–53
14. Franklin Pierce	Democratic	1853–57
15. James Buchanan	Democratic	1857–61
16. Abraham Lincoln	Republican	1861–65
17. Andrew Johnson	Republican	1865–69
18. Ulysses S. Grant	Republican	1869–77
19. Rutherford B. Hayes	Republican	1877–81
20. James A. Garfield	Republican	1881
21. Chester A. Arthur	Republican	1881–85
22. Grover Cleveland	Democratic	1885–89
23. Benjamin Harrison	Republican	1889–93
24. Grover Cleveland	Democratic	1893–97
25. William McKinley	Republican	1897–1901
26. Theodore Roosevelt	Republican	1901–9
27. William Howard Taft	Republican	1909–13
28. Woodrow Wilson	Democratic	1913–21
29. Warren G. Harding	Republican	1921–23
30. Calvin Coolidge	Republican	1923–29
31. Herbert C. Hoover	Republican	1929–33
32. Franklin D. Roosevelt	Democratic	1933–45
33. Harry S Truman	Democratic	1945–53
34. Dwight D. Eisenhower	Republican	1953–61
35. John F. Kennedy	Democratic	1961–63
36. Lyndon B. Johnson	Democratic	1963–69
37. Richard M. Nixon	Republican	1969–74
38. Gerald R. Ford	Republican	1974–77
39. James E. Carter, Jr.	Democratic	1977–81

40. Ronald Reagan	Republican	1981–89
41. George Bush	Republican	1989–93
42. Bill Clinton	Democratic	1993–

Presley, Elvis (1935–77) Singer. Although he did not invent ROCK MUSIC—better candidates for that honor are Chuck BERRY and LITTLE RICHARD—Elvis Aaron Presley did become its first superstar and the first major embodiment of its social significance. In 1956 alone, he had five number-one singles: "Heartbreak Hotel," "I Want You, I Need You, I Love You," "Don't Be Cruel," "Love Me Tender," and the song that became his signature tune, "HOUND DOG." For the next two decades his popularity remained unfaded, and when he died, his title of "King" was secure.

Born in Mississippi, Presley moved to Memphis as a teenager. He was a truck driver there in 1954 when Producer Sam PHILLIPS, seeking "a white man with the Negro sound," recorded his version of an Arthur Crudup blues, "That's All Right, Mama." That local hit was followed by "Mystery Train," which topped the country charts and presaged rockabilly. Under the management of "Colonel" Tom Parker, Presley left Phillips's Sun label for RCA, recording "Heartbreak Hotel" there as his first national hit. By 1957, he had become the biggest teen idol since Frank SINATRA, as famous for his gyrating stage act as for his singing. As "Elvis the Pelvis," he so shocked conservative America that he was filmed on *The Ed* SULLIVAN *Show* from the waist up. The 1957 hits "All Shook Up," "Teddy Bear," and "Jailhouse Rock" filled out the vintage years of his legend.

From 1958 to 1960, Presley served with the U.S. Army in Germany. There he met teenager Priscilla Beaulieu, an officer's daughter, who returned with him to his Memphis mansion, Graceland; they were married in 1967 in Las Vegas. Presley's 1960s hits—from "It's Now or Never" and "Are You Lonesome Tonight?" (both 1960) to "Suspicious Minds" (1969)—emphasized his skill with romantic ballads, although the decade also saw him chained to Hollywood in a series of lucrative musical/romance clunkers, from *G.I. Blues* (1960) to *Viva Las Vegas* (1964) to *Change of Habit* (1969).

In the 1970s Presley became increasingly reclusive and obese. His marriage to Priscilla ended in 1973. In 1977, just days before his death, three members of his personal entourage, the so-called Memphis Mafia, published a book detailing his chemical dependencies, and drugs were clearly a factor in his early death. When he died, Graceland became a shrine. Opened to the public in 1982, it is the second most visited building in the United States (after the WHITE HOUSE).

In some ways Presley is even more visible in death than he was in life. Elvis impersonators blanket the nightclub circuit; curios fill antique and souvenir shops; the "young Elvis" appears on a postage stamp; and the TABLOIDS swell with tales of Elvis "sightings" and of messages from "the King" beyond the grave. For an entire generation, he remains, like John F. KENNEDY, a tragic emblem of dreams doomed to die.

Preston, Sergeant See SERGEANT PRESTON OF THE YUKON.

Price, Vincent (1911–93) Actor. Price was a respected stage star—he played opposite Helen HAYES on Broadway—who became best known in the 1950s for his horror films, may of them adaptations by Roger CORMAN of tales by Edgar Allan POE. Highlights of his elegantly gruesome portrayals included *House of*

Wax (1953), *The Fly* (1958), *The House of Usher* (1960), *The Pit and the Pendulum* (1961), *The Raven* (1963), and *The Masque of the Red Death* (1964).

Pride, Charley (1938–   ) Country singer. Famous for breaking the color barrier in country music, Mississippi-born Pride became one of its major stars, black or white, in the 1970s. Among his hits were "Just Between You and Me" (1966), "Amazing Love" (1973), "I'll Be Leavin' Alone" (1977), and "Burgers & Fries" (1978). The trade magazine *Cash Box* in 1980 named him the top male country artist of the decade.

Princeton University Founded in 1746 as the College of New Jersey, Princeton was established to train clergymen. Today, along with HARVARD UNIVERSITY and YALE UNIVERSITY, it forms the "big three" of the eastern IVY LEAGUE. For several months during the Revolutionary War, when the town of Princeton was the national capital, the college building, Nassau Hall, was the capitol. Alumni included Aaron BURR, James MADISON, and the university's first lay president, Woodrow WILSON.

Profiles in Courage (1956) A collection of biographies of political figures by then Massachusetts Senator John F. KENNEDY. It won him a Pulitzer Prize and increased visibility.

Progress and Poverty See Henry GEORGE.

Progressivism The reformism of the so-called Progressive Era, roughly 1900–20, during which the federal government, following the lead of western states, passed laws regarding child labor, railroads, the food industry, senatorial elections, women's suffrage, and workmen's compensation. See BULL MOOSE PARTY; Robert LaFOLLETTE; MUCKRAKERS.

Prohibition The period between 1920 and 1933, when the Eighteenth Amendment prohibited the "manufacture, sale, or transportation of intoxicating liquors." The Noble Experiment, as Herbert Hoover called it, exacerbated rather than quelled the nation's drinking, as BOOTLEGGING took over the liquor industry and the appeal of forbidden fruit supported thousands of SPEAKEASIES. Disregard for the law was universal, as President Warren G. Harding drank in the White House and gangsters like Al CAPONE ran the ROARING TWENTIES. In addition to giving organized crime a lift, the period also popularized the terms "bathtub gin," "home brew," and "near beer."

Promontory Point See GOLDEN SPIKE CEREMONY.

Provincetown Players A theater group founded in 1915 in Provincetown, Massachusetts, and based from 1916 to 1929 in New York City. Formed to encourage native talent, it produced almost one hundred plays while giving a start to playwright Eugene O'NEILL.

Prufrock, J. Alfred See T. S. ELIOT.

Prynne, Hester See THE SCARLET LETTER.

Psycho (1960) A murder mystery directed by Alfred HITCHCOCK. Famous for its bloody "shower scene," in which heroine Janet Leigh is dispatched by a madman, and for Anthony Perkins's portrayal of edgy Norman Bates, proprietor of the creepy Bates Motel.

PTA   Parent-Teacher Associations, a national network of local groups that promote the educational and social welfare of American children; the "PTA meeting" is a common feature of U.S. schooling. The current umbrella organization, the National Congress of Parents and Teachers, grew out of the National Congress of Mothers, founded in 1897.

"The public be damned"   Railroad executive William H. Vanderbilt's 1883 response to a news reporter who asked him what responsibility he felt for the "public benefit." "Railroads are not run on sentiment," he explained, "but on business principles, and to pay." Often cited as an example of ROBBER BARON arrogance. See VANDERBILT FAMILY.

public enemy   (1) A notorious criminal. The term gained currency in the 1930s with the popularity of William WELLMAN's 1931 film *The Public Enemy,* in which James CAGNEY plays gangster Tom Powers. A couple of years later, the FBI named John DILLINGER public enemy number one. Hence (2) a RAP group of the 1980s that capitalized on the "tough guy" image.

Pueblo   A generic term for several Indian peoples of the Southwest, among them the HOPI and the ZUÑI. The Spanish name, meaning "town," reflects their architecture: adobe buildings grouped in village clusters.

Pulitzer, Joseph   (1847–1911) Publisher. Hungarian immigrant Pulitzer founded two of the nineteenth century's most successful newspapers, the *St. Louis Post-Dispatch* (1878) and the *New York World* (1883), in which he introduced such circulation boosters as COMICS, sports coverage, and banner headlines. Pulitzer's rivalry with William Randolph HEARST led to the YELLOW JOURNALISM of the 1890s, a contributory cause of the SPANISH-AMERICAN WAR. His will funded the Columbia University School of Journalism and the PULITZER PRIZES.

Pulitzer Prizes   Annual awards in journalism, literature, and music provided by a stipend established in Joseph PULITZER's will. First given in 1917, they are now awarded in nineteen separate categories. In spite of their modest cash value ($1,000), Pulitzers are second only to the Nobel Prize in prestige and are therefore coveted signs of success in the world of writing. Novelists and poets who have received them constitute a who's who of American letters.

Pullman car   A railroad sleeping car patented in 1864 by industrialist George M. Pullman (1831–97). Its use in President Lincoln's funeral train gave it notoriety, and the Pullman Palace Car Company, founded in 1867, became the world's largest railroad car concern. "Pullman" became a generic term for any berth car and "Pullman porter" for a black railroad attendant (see A. Philip RANDOLPH).

Pullman strike   An 1894 strike against the Pullman Palace Car Company sparked by a 25 percent wage cut. It was led by Eugene V. DEBS and broken by the intervention of federal troops, although not before a spate of sympathetic riots and the killing, in Chicago, of seven workers.

pulp magazines   Cheap fiction magazines printed on pulpwood paper and sold at newsstands from the 1890s to the 1930s. Picking up where the DIME NOVEL left off, the "pulps" provided adventure and romance to a mass audience until the advent of radio and comic books. The first pulp, *Argosy,* was started by publisher Frank Munsey in 1896. Famous pulp writers included Max BRAND and Edgar Rice BURROUGHS. See also BLACK MASK.

pumpkin   A large gourd indigenous to the Americas. Its pulp is used in making pumpkin pie, a traditional THANKSGIVING dish since colonial times. Pumpkin shells, carved in grotesque faces, become the jack-o'-lanterns of the American Halloween.

punk rock   See ROCK MUSIC.

Puritans   English religious dissenters who founded New England. They included the PILGRIM settlers of PLYMOUTH COLONY, the Cotton MATHER family of Massachusetts Bay, and the eighteenth-century preacher Jonathan EDWARDS. Puritan theology, which stressed the absolute dependence of human beings on God's grace, had an enduring impact on American literature, especially in the works of Nathaniel HAWTHORNE. More frequently vilified than understood, their lifestyle has been travestied as "puritanical," meaning narrow-minded and fearful of sexuality. H. L. MENCKEN reflected this simplistic view when he defined Puritanism as "the haunting fear that someone, somewhere, might be happy." See also SALEM WITCH TRIALS.

"Purple Cow, The"   A nonsense poem by humorist Gelett Burgess (1866–1951). It first appeared (1895) in the San Francisco literary journal *The Lark.*

> *I never saw a purple cow;*
> *I never hope to see one.*
> *But I can tell you anyhow*
> *I'd rather see than be one.*

Purple Heart   A decoration given to members of the armed forces wounded in battle or, if they die, to their next of kin. Created by George Washington as the Badge of Military Merit (1782), it is a purple-enameled, gold-bordered heart with a profile of Washington in the center.

Pyle, Ernie   (1900–45) War correspondent. Pyle's vivid reports from the front in World War II earned him a 1944 Pulitzer Prize and the affection of the common soldier whose perspective he shared. His European coverage appeared in *Here Is Your War* (1943) and *Brave Men* (1944). When he was killed by Japanese fire near Okinawa, servicemen marked the spot with a sign: "Here the American fighting man lost a buddy—Ernie Pyle."

Q

quadroon A person of one-fourth African heritage or, more broadly, any light-skinned mulatto. From Spanish *cuarterón,* meaning roughly "quarter-er." At "quadroon balls," held in antebellum New Orleans, white men danced with quadroon mistresses or companions.

Quakers English Protestants who formed a Religious Society of Friends in the 1640s and who followed the teachings of George Fox on the "inner light"; they were called Quakers from their trembling in its presence. Persecuted in England, they settled throughout the eastern seaboard, finding a special haven in William PENN's Pennsylvania, established as a "Holy Experiment" in Quaker living. Known as the "peculiar people" because of their pacifism, plain dress, and archaic pronouns ("thee" and "thou"), American Quakers were also peculiar in their progressivism. They were among the few settlers to establish amity with the neighboring Indians, and they had banished slavery from their communities by 1787—the same year the CONSTITUTION wrote it into law.

Philadelphia was known since Penn's time as the Quaker City. The Quaker man who appears on Quaker Oats cereal boxes goes back to 1877, when he was the trademark of an Ohio milling firm. One of the firm's founders saw in the figure the embodiment of qualities he wanted in his product—"the purity of the lives of the people, their sterling honesty, their strength and manliness."

Quanah Comanche leader. The son of Comanche chief Nokoni and a white captive, Cynthia Ann Parker, Quanah refused to sign a reservation treaty in 1867, led raids against Texas settlements in the 1870s, and finally reconciled himself to reservation life in 1875. Along with GERONIMO, he rode in Teddy ROOSEVELT's inaugural parade.

Quantrill's Raiders The South's most famous guerrillas in the Civil War. Their leader, William Clarke Quantrill (1837–65), earned his spurs fighting abolitionists in "BLEEDING KANSAS." After 1861, he went official and, with a Confederate commission, attacked Union encampments in the Midwest; in 1863, he burned Lawrence, Kansas. Before being killed by Union troops in Kentucky, he gave a start to the career of Frank and Jesse JAMES.

quarterback The play initiator on a football team. Hence "to quarterback" as a synonym for "to direct events" and MONDAY-MORNING QUARTERBACK for someone with twenty-twenty hindsight.

Quebec The name of a Canadian province and its capital city—founded by the French and still officially French-speaking. The struggle for Quebec city in September 1759 was a famous engagement of the FRENCH AND INDIAN WAR. It took place on the nearby Plains of Abraham between troops under British General James Wolfe and French General Louis de Montcalm. Both of them died in the battle, and the symbolically and strategically important site passed to the British. French separatist sentiments periodically surface within the province.

Queeg, Captain   See THE CAINE MUTINY.

Queen, Ellery   A detective hero introduced in the 1929 novel *The Roman Hat Mystery*. His creators, cousins Frederic Dannay (1905–82) and Manfred Lee (1905–71), wrote numerous other books and stories starring the contemplative sleuth as well as founding and editing *Ellery Queen's Mystery Magazine*. Queen also appeared in films and radio and television series.

Queen for a Day   Television series. Female contestants told hard-luck stories about their lives, with the "neediest" ones (as determined by the audience) being given prizes. The show ran from 1956 to 1964.

Queen's College   The original name of Rutgers University, chartered in 1766 by George III. The Queen in question was his wife, Charlotte. The college was renamed for philanthropist Henry Rutgers in 1825. See also KING'S COLLEGE.

Queequeg   See MOBY-DICK.

Quetzalcoatl   The feathered serpent god of ancient Mexico. Worshipped by the AZTECS as a creator and culture hero, he was also conflated with various historical kings. The banishment in the twelfth century of one such king led to legends of Quetzalcoatl's eventual return. These worked to the advantage of Hernando CORTÉS in 1519, when he reached Mexico and was taken for the god.

quilts   Heavy bedcoverings used in Europe since the Middle Ages and brought to a peak of aesthetic design in the United States. At "quilting parties" or "bees" held since the early nineteenth century, women cooperated in piecing together quilts with traditional designs, such as the Bear's Paw, Tree of Life, Wedding Ring, Log Cabin, and free-form "crazy quilt" patterns. Once viewed as pretty but basically utilitarian, quilts are now seen as museum-worthy examples of American folk art.

Quimby, Phineas Parkhurst   (1802–66) Faith healer. Originally a clockmaker, Parkhurst turned to hypnotism and then "mental healing" as part of a lifelong investigation of "mind over matter." One of his disciples, Julius Dresser, founded the California-based NEW THOUGHT movement (1894). Another one, Mary Baker EDDY, founded CHRISTIAN SCIENCE.

Quivira   See CÍBOLA.

Quiz Kids   A QUIZ SHOW that ran on radio in the 1940s and television in the 1950s. A panel of youngsters, ranging in age from six to sixteen, answered questions prepared by the producers and the viewing audience. The show's most famous panelist, nine-year-old science whiz Robert Strom, eventually "graduated" to THE $64,000 QUESTION. "Quiz kid" became a tag for any precocious youngster.

quiz shows   Television shows in which contestants compete for prizes by demonstrating either general or select knowledge or both. A staple of the medium since its inception, quiz shows suffered from the ''rigging'' scandals of the 1950s (see TWENTY-ONE), but came back strong in the 1960s and have remained so. Among the most popular quiz shows have been *Twenty Questions* (1949–55), THE $64,000 QUESTION, YOU BET YOUR LIFE (1950–61), and JEOPARDY!

Quonset hut   A prefabricated metal building, semicylindrical in design, first used for troop shelters during World War II. It was named for its place of origin, Quonset Point, Rhode Island.

R See RATING.

R & B See RHYTHM AND BLUES.

radio Commercial radio broadcasting began in the 1920s, with the Radio Corporation of America (RCA) the initial supplier of both programs and radio sets. With David SARNOFF's encouragement, RCA founded the first network, the National Broadcasting Company (NBC), and by the 1930s, network programming was in full swing. In the so-called Golden Age of Radio (roughly 1930–50), it aired not only news and music ranging from SWING MUSIC to the GRAND OLE OPRY but also entertainment formats that made it ubiquitous in American homes.

The earliest such format was the variety show, adapted from VAUDEVILLE most successfully by Rudy VALLEE. A Vallee skit evolved into a spin-off show, THE ALDRICH FAMILY, which prompted other radio SITCOMS such as THE GOLDBERGS, FIBBER MCGEE AND MOLLY, and the phenomenally popular AMOS 'N' ANDY; comedy also shone in the ostensible feud between medium stars Jack BENNY and Fred ALLEN. Radio invented the SOAP OPERA with enduring hits such as STELLA DALLAS and ROAD OF LIFE, while for children there was a raft of daily adventures patterned on the SERIALS of the silver screen. The best known included JACK ARMSTRONG, THE ALL-AMERICAN BOY; THE SHADOW; and a trio out of WXYZ in Detroit: THE LONE RANGER, THE GREEN HORNET, and SERGEANT PRESTON OF THE YUKON.

Perhaps the most famous single broadcast of the Golden Age was Orson WELLES's 1938 WAR OF THE WORLDS, an event that showed the dramatic reach of the medium. That reach began to shorten in the 1950s, as television effectively cannibalized radio's formats and absorbed successful personalities like Benny. At the same time, however, the advent of ROCK MUSIC afforded a chance for radio to recapture its musical roots, and it did so, with increasing success, in the 1960s. DISC JOCKEYS continue to reach enormous audiences by playing not only rock music but classical selections, "new country," and "middle of the road" (MOR).

A more recent development has been "talk radio," in which host/interviewers invite their listeners to participate by calling in their comments and questions for guests. This interactive format, an electronic version of the TOWN MEETING, has been ably handled by hosts in local markets; nationally known hosts include Larry King and Rush Limbaugh, both of whom have also expanded into television.

Radio City Music Hall The largest indoor theater in the world, built in 1932 in ROCKEFELLER CENTER. Designed by Donald Deskey, it includes 6,000 seats, a nearly 10,000-square-foot stage, and a huge Art Deco foyer. A venue for both movies and stage shows, it is also known for its precision chorus line, the Rockettes.

Raft, George   (1895–1980) Actor. Originally a dancer, Raft was typecast in the 1930s and 1940s as a dapper gangster after a memorable performance as Guido Rinaldi in SCARFACE. His flipping of a coin in that film became a common gesture of movie hoods. As "Spats" Colombo in SOME LIKE IT HOT (1959), Raft reacts to a fellow gangster's performing it by asking witheringly, "Where'd you learn that cheap trick?" His dancing appeared to good effect in *Bolero* (1934).

Ragged Dick   See Horatio ALGER.

Raggedy Ann   A cheery, redheaded rag doll invented in stories by John Gruelle in 1918 and first marketed by Marshall FIELD in 1920. Gruelle adapted the name from the James Whitcomb RILEY poems "Little Orphant Annie" and "The Raggedy Man." The doll, along with her brother Raggedy Andy, has been a favorite with children for generations.

ragtime   A syncopated, or rhythmically "ragged," music that, between the 1890s and 1920s, was the most popular style in the United States. Closely associated with the jaunty pianos of GAY NINETIES saloons, it fused the dance rhythms of the MINSTREL SHOW with European harmonies and structure. The most famous composers of rag tunes, or "rags," were Scott JOPLIN and Joseph Lamb (1887–1960). See also "ALEXANDER'S RAGTIME BAND."

railroads   In 1850, there were fewer than ten thousand miles of railroad track in the United States. Spurred by the Civil War and by an influx of cheap Irish and Chinese labor, railroads became the growth industry of the century, leading to the industrial fortunes of the VANDERBILT and STANFORD clans and providing transcontinental service by 1869 (see GOLDEN SPIKE CEREMONY). By World War I, there were over a quarter of a million track miles coast to coast, and the "romance of the rails" had become an indelible part of the American scene. See also John HENRY, Casey JONES; "THE PUBLIC BE DAMNED"; Jimmie RODGERS; TOM THUMB.

Railsplitter, the   Nickname for Abraham LINCOLN. From his early experience splitting logs for rail fences.

rain check   (1) In baseball since the 1880s, a voucher for free admission to a future game given to patrons attending one that is rained out. Hence (2) a voucher given customers by a retailer when a discounted item has been sold out; it entitles them to the lower price when stock is replenished. To "take a rain check" is to defer one's acceptance of an invitation.

Rainey, Gertrude   (1886–1939) Blues singer. Sometimes called the mother of the blues, she was born in Georgia to minstrel performers Thomas and Ella Pridgett. After her 1904 marriage to another trouper, William "Pa" Rainey, she was known as "Madame" or "Ma" Rainey. With her husband and such other singers as Bessie SMITH and Thomas A. DORSEY, she toured extensively until 1935. Her blend of "down-home" blues, jazz, and provocative lyrics made her a major influence on Smith and other performers. Dorsey called her "the greatest of blues singers."

Raisin in the Sun, A   A play (1959) by Lorraine Hansberry about a black family in a white Chicago suburb. The first Broadway production written by a black woman, it won the New York Drama Critics' Circle Award and became a 1961 movie starring Sidney POITIER.

Raleigh, Sir Walter (ca. 1552–1618) An English courtier and favorite of Elizabeth I, Raleigh promoted English colonization of North America and was the force behind the ill-fated ROANOKE COLONY. He also named the tidewater area Virginia, after his patroness, the "Virgin Queen." Court intrigue led to his arrest by Elizabeth's successor James I, a long imprisonment in the Tower of London, and his execution.

Rambo John Rambo, an ex–GREEN BERET portrayed in a series of 1980s action movies by Sylvester STALLONE: The series began in 1982 with *First Blood*. Unable to adjust to civilian life and hounded by authorities, Rambo reflects the demobilization problems of the Vietnam veteran. At the same time, because of his quietness and zest for violence, he symbolizes American machismo in the tradition of John WAYNE.

Ramona An 1884 novel by Helen Hunt JACKSON about the mistreatment of California Indians. The mixed-blood heroine was played by Mexican actress Dolores Del Rio (1905–83) in a 1928 film. A song written by Wolfe Gilbert and Mabel Wayne to exploit the movie became a hit for the Paul WHITEMAN band.

Rand, Ayn (1905–82) Writer. Championing a philosophy of enlightened self-interest she dubbed Objectivism, the Russian-born Rand garnered a large following during the cold war with her haughtily clever sneers at "collectivism." Her libertarian views, expressed in numerous essays, are best known from her novels THE FOUNTAINHEAD and *Atlas Shrugged* (1957).

Rand, Sally (1903–79) A minor actress in the 1920s, Helen Gould Beck achieved overnight success in 1933 when she was arrested for doing an "obscene" dance at a Chicago world's fair. Performing coquettishly with the aid of huge fans, she became the world's most celebrated fan dancer and was still performing into the 1970s.

Randolph, A. Phillip (1889–1979) Labor leader. Randolph founded the Brotherhood of Sleeping Car Porters in 1925 to promote the welfare of the PULLMAN CAR company's black employees. A powerful voice against racism, he also elicited an antidiscrimination order from Franklin ROOSEVELT and helped to direct a 1963 March on Washington for Jobs and Freedom.

rangers See Robert ROGERS; TEXAS RANGERS.

rap To talk or converse. A nineteenth-century underworld term adopted, possibly through jazz, by hippies and black radicals in the 1960s. Hence "rap session," a lengthy discussion; "rap music," a 1980s pop form in which rhythmically insistent poetry is spoken to minimal orchestration; and the nickname of the voluble SNCC leader "Rap" Brown.

Rapp, George See UTOPIAN COMMUNITIES.

Rathbone, Basil (1892–1967) Actor. The American screen's most famous Sherlock Holmes, the South African–born Rathbone also personified snarling urbanity in adventure films of the 1930s and 1940s. One of the few movie swash-bucklers who actually could fence, he displayed his skill effectively against Errol FLYNN in *Captain Blood* (1935) and *The Adventures of Robin Hood* (1938). The first of his fourteen Holmes roles was in *The Hound of the Baskervilles* (1939).

rating   The film rating system established in 1968—a successor to the old HAYS OFFICE code—classifies motion pictures according to content. The original ratings set by the Motion Picture Association of America were G for General (all ages admitted); PG for Parental Guidance (all ages); R for Restricted (to adults and those accompanied by them); and X (for those over seventeen). As on-screen sex and violence increased, the MPAA set two new ratings. A PG-13 rating carries the suggestion that preteens be accompanied by an adult; an NC-17 rating (for "no children under seventeen") was devised to accommodate marginally pornographic films that formerly would have received X ratings.

rattlesnake   Any of a number of pit vipers indigenous to the Americas whose tails are composed of horny "rattles." The rattler's deadly venom makes it among the most feared of serpents (although the bite, contrary to legend, is not always fatal), while its distinctive feature has given rise to the folk belief that it "warns" its victims by rattling before it strikes. Benjamin FRANKLIN employed the snake symbolically in a famous cartoon urging colonial unity: a snake cut into thirteen segments with the legend "Join or Die." Rattlers also figure prominently in western lore, as in the tale of the freighter whose wagon tongue, struck by a rattler, had to be chopped off to save the vehicle's life. A contemporary beer, Old Rattler, is jokingly called the "beer that bites you back." See also DON'T TREAD ON ME.

"Raven, The"   (1945) Edgar Allan POE's most famous poem, a dirge on the poet's deceased beloved. In it he vainly seeks solace from a giant bird whose only utterance is the gloomy "Nevermore." The poem inspired Roger CORMAN's 1963 movie.

Rawhide   A television western (1959–66) about nineteenth-century cattle drives. It started the career of Clint EASTWOOD, who played assistant trail boss Rowdy Yates.

Rawlings, Marjorie Kinnan   Author of THE YEARLING.

Ray, James Earl   Assassin of Martin Luther KING, Jr.

Rayburn, Sam   (1882–1961) A Democratic congressman from Texas, Rayburn served as Speaker of the House of Representatives for seventeen years—longer than anyone else in U.S. history. "Mr. Sam's" rule of the House began in 1940 and ended only with his death. His protégé was fellow Texan Lyndon B. JOHNSON.

Raye, Martha   (1916–   ) Singer, comedienne. Onstage from the age of three, Margaret O'Reed capitalized on a large, plastic mouth and booming voice to forge a successful career in vaudeville, Broadway, and Hollywood. Her USO tours in three wars earned her a 1969 special Academy Award.

razorback   A type of hog associated with the southern states, and especially with the Arkansas pinewoods. Noted for its pugnaciousness and indestructibility, it is the mascot of the University of Arkansas football team and the hero of anecdotes suggesting regional toughness. In one tale, a razorback that has swallowed a stick of dynamite is kicked by a mule. After the explosion, its owner laments to a neighbor, "Killed my mule, wrecked my barn, broke every window out of one side of my house, and, brother, I've got an awful sick hog."

"Read my lips. No new taxes" A pledge given by Republican candidate George Bush during his 1988 campaign for the presidency. Once elected, he signed an unpopular tax bill, and his failure adequately to explain this reneging on his promise contributed to his reelection loss to Bill Clinton.

Reader's Digest A monthly magazine founded in 1922 by DeWitt and Lila Acheson Wallace. It contains a mixture of original and reprinted articles on many subjects, with a penchant for homey anecdotes, inspiring stories, and centrist politics. With a circulation exceeding 16 million and editions published abroad in a dozen languages, it is the most widely read periodical in the world.

Reagan, Ronald (1911–) Actor, politician. In a fairly humdrum Hollywood career, Reagan turned in one notable performance in *King's Row* (1942) and served six terms as president of the Screen Actors Guild. His turn to politics in the 1960s involved a switch from Democratic liberalism to conservative Republicanism and earned him the California governorship in 1966. His success there as a tight-money, law-and-order boss made him a favorite with the GOP leadership, and he easily defeated incumbent Jimmy Carter in 1980 to become the fortieth president of the United States. In his eight-year administration, the "Reagan Revolution" rolled back progressive policies of the previous forty years, built up the nation's defense system, and generated intense feelings of both affection and distaste for the personable, stridently anticommunist president. See also "WIN ONE FOR THE GIPPER."

real McCoy See MCCOY, THE REAL.

Rebecca of Sunnybrook Farm (1903) A juvenile novel by Kate Douglas Wiggin (1856–1923) about ten-year-old Rebecca Randall, once described as the "nicest child in American literature." A perennial girls' favorite, it was filmed in 1917 with Mary PICKFORD, then twenty-four, playing the lead.

Rebel Without a Cause (1955) A film directed by Nicholas Ray about generational conflict and peer pressure among modern teens. James DEAN's portrayal of sensitive but misunderstood Jim Stark made him the instant epitome of "troubled youth."

Rebels Also seen as "Rebs" and "Johnny Rebs." A northern term for Confederate soldiers during the Civil War, known in the North as the War of the Rebellion. Hence a slang tag for any southerner, adopted by southerners themselves as a label of pride. The "Rebel yell," used by Confederate troops in battle, has been similarly adopted by civilian enthusiasts, notably drunks and fans of sporting events.

Reconstruction A decade (1867–77) following the CIVIL WAR during which the defeated South was ruled by martial law under the Military Reconstruction

Act of 1867. Congressional laws passed to protect the rights of newly enfranchised blacks established a regime that was as progressive in its voting and social policies as it was vindictive in its attitude toward former Confederates. The result was an intensification rather than amelioration of racial tensions, and the reactive passage in the 1890s of JIM CROW laws. See also CARPETBAGGERS; SCALAWAG.

red   Slang for "communist," used both as a noun and as an adjective. In Europe, the color was associated since the mid-nineteenth century with radical republicanism, anarchism, and other revolutionary philosophies. The periods of the PALMER RAIDS and of Joseph McCARTHY's reign were both referred to as red scares. See also PINKO.

Red Badge of Courage, The   (1895) Stephen CRANE's most popular novel, a "psychological study of fear" in a Civil War soldier. It is a standard text in high school literature classes.

Red Emma   See Emma GOLDMAN.

Red River Valley   A traditional song set to the melody of James Kerrigan's "In the Bright Mohawk Valley" (1896). Some sources say the words refer to the Red River that flows from North Dakota into Lake Winnipeg. Given the song's long association with COWBOYS, a more likely candidate is the one that divides Texas from Oklahoma.

> Come and sit by my side if you love me;
> Do not hasten to bid me adieu.
> But remember the Red River Valley
> And the cowboy who loves you so true.

redcoats   British soldiers in the American Revolution. From their scarlet uniforms. A British term from the sixteenth century. See "THE BRITISH ARE COMING, THE BRITISH ARE COMING."

Redding, Otis   (1941–67) Singer, songwriter. After James BROWN, the impassioned, energetic Redding was the most popular male SOUL singer of the 1960s. His RHYTHM AND BLUES hits included "Mr. Pitiful," "Fa Fa Fa Fa Fa," and "Dock of the Bay" (all written with Steve Cropper); "I've Been Loving You Too Long" (with Jerry Butler); and his most famous composition, "Respect," which was a major success for Aretha FRANKLIN. He died in a plane crash with four members of his band.

redeye   (1) Cheap whiskey. From the link between alcohol and bloodshot eyes. (2) An overnight plane flight that arrives early in the morning. Such a flight may be called the red-eye special—a term that referred to whiskey in the 1920s.

Redford, Robert   (1937–) Actor. The most popular male film star of the 1970s, Redford is known for his rugged good looks, lean, infectious acting, and liberal politics. His portrayal of a charming con artist in *The Sting* (1973) won him an Oscar nomination. Other major roles have included the Sundance Kid in *Butch Cassidy and the Sundance Kid* (1969), Jay Gatsby in *The Great Gatsby* (1974), and reporter Bob Woodward (of WOODWARD AND BERNSTEIN) in *All the*

President's Men (1976). Redford's production company, Sundance, provides artistic and financial assistance to young filmmakers. He won the best-director Oscar for *Ordinary People* (1980).

redneck   Since the 1830s, a poor, rural white southerner. From the sunburned necks of outdoor laborers. The term gradually acquired the connotations of loutish, backward, and racist, although by the 1970s, these class markers were being reversed by GOOD OLD BOYS defensively lauding their roots. President Jimmy Carter's brother Billy, who enlivened the decade with his homespun humor, called a book of his "wit and wisdom" *Redneck Power* (1977). Texan Jerry Jeff Walker wryly eulogized the redneck in a 1973 song:

> *Up against the wall, redneck mother,*
> *A mother who has raised a son so well.*
> *He's thirty-four and drinking in a honky-tonk,*
> *Kicking hippies' asses and raising hell.*

"Remember Pearl Harbor"   See PEARL HARBOR.

"Remember the Alamo"   See ALAMO.

"Remember the Maine"   See U.S.S. MAINE.

Remington, Frederic   (1861–1909) The best-known artist of the Old West, Remington was an easterner who found his métier after a youthful trip to the frontier. Attention to detail and an obvious affection for his subject imparted realism to his studies of cowboys, cavalrymen, and Indians. In addition to working in oils and sculpture, he also illustrated books and periodicals. Sent to Cuba by William Randolph HEARST on the eve of the SPANISH-AMERICAN WAR, Remington reported that conditions there did not warrant a war, which is said to have elicited Hearst's famous quip "You furnish the pictures and I'll furnish the war." Among the pictures he furnished was one of Spanish officials strip-searching an American woman—an invention that got full play in Hearst's jingoistic *Journal.* See also YELLOW JOURNALISM.

Renwick, James   (1818–95) Architect. The driving force of the American Gothic revival, Renwick is best known for designing New York City's ST. PATRICK'S CATHEDRAL. He also did that city's Grace Church (1846), the original building of the SMITHSONIAN INSTITUTION (1844–55), and the Main Hall at Vassar College (1860).

Republican party   See POLITICAL PARTIES.

Revere, Paul   (1735–1818) Patriot, silversmith. Thanks to Longfellow's poem "PAUL REVERE'S RIDE," Bostonian Revere became known as the sole herald of the British advance on the eve of the Battle of LEXINGTON. That the poet ignored the contributions of his fellow riders William Dawes and Samuel Prescott testifies to Revere's significance before that event. A member of the SONS OF LIBERTY, he had already published an engraving of the BOSTON MASSACRE that helped to inflame anti-British feeling; carried messages for the underground Committees of Correspondence; and participated in the BOSTON TEA PARTY. Acquitted of charges of cowardice during the Revolutionary War, he retired honorably to become a prominent silversmith; his Revere ware is highly prized among collectors.

revivals Religious awakenings that have periodically animated American social life, calling Protestant Christians to deepen their faith. Generally hostile to ritual and doctrinal complexity, revivalists stress a personal commitment to God. See Billy GRAHAM; GREAT AWAKENING; GREAT REVIVAL; Aimee Semple McPHERSON; Dwight Lyman MOODY; Oral ROBERTS; Billy SUNDAY.

Revolutionary War (1775–83) The war that secured independence for Great Britain's thirteen North American colonies erupted out of colonial resentment over taxes that began just after the FRENCH AND INDIAN WAR. To pay for that war, the British Parliament had passed first the STAMP ACT and then the TOWNSHEND ACTS. Resistance to these measures, outrage at the BOSTON MASSACRE, and a growing perception that the mother country was insensitive to colonial opinion led in quick succession to the BOSTON TEA PARTY, the retaliatory INTOLERABLE ACTS, and the convening in 1774 of a Continental Congress. The colonies were thus poised against further encroachments when in April of 1775 an army of British regulars under Thomas Gage moved on CONCORD to commandeer colonial arms. The resulting skirmish at the Battle of LEXINGTON AND CONCORD was the first engagement of the Revolution.

By the summer of 1776, American "rebels" had captured British positions at Crown Point and FORT TICONDEROGA as well as mounting a sturdy defense of BUNKER HILL. A second Continental Congress made George WASHINGTON commander in chief of colonial forces and, in 1776, adopted the DECLARATION OF INDEPENDENCE, which transformed the fighting into a war for autonomy. Although hampered by ill-prepared troops and congressional parsimony, Washington turned his "rabble" into an army that weathered half a decade of buffeting by a force that was then thought the finest in the world. He lost New York to the British later that summer and was forced to beat a winter retreat across New Jersey, but he rebounded with a daring attack at Trenton (see GEORGE WASHINGTON CROSSING THE DELAWARE) while in upstate New York, American General Horatio Gates decisively stopped a British advance at Saratoga.

After spending a bitter winter at VALLEY FORGE, Washington's army was heartened in the spring of 1778 by French recognition of the infant republic and by the ongoing labor of the Marquis de LAFAYETTE to secure his countrymen's support for the American cause. Between 1778 and 1781, battles were joined on many fronts, with George Rogers Clark commanding American forces in the Ohio Valley; Anthony WAYNE taking a British fort at Stony Point, New York; and Nathanel Greene directing operations in the South with the able assistance of SWAMP FOX Francis Marion. The last major battle occurred at YORKTOWN, where on October 19, 1781, British General Lord Cornwallis surrendered to Washington. The Peace of Paris was signed two years later, marking British recognition of the United States.

There is an immense patriotic lore associated with the Revolution, from the lyrics of "YANKEE DOODLE" to Nathan HALE's final words; from the stolidness of the MINUTEMEN to that of John Paul JONES. Although the war split the colonists momentarily into "Patriots" and LOYALISTS, the outcome erased most memory of this division, as victorious Washington became a national hero and the American success inspired republicans everywhere.

For figures particularly associated with the Revolution, see also Ethan ALLEN;

John ANDRÉ; Benedict ARNOLD; Benjamin FRANKLIN; Philip FRENEAU; GEORGE III; John HANCOCK; Patrick HENRY; Thomas JEFFERSON; Thomas PAINE; Paul REVERE; and John TRUMBULL.

RFD   Rural free delivery, a mail service established in 1896 after years of lobbying by the National GRANGE. It was resisted by small-town businesses, who predicted, correctly, that it would help mail-order businesses at their expense. The immediate beneficiaries of the new system were SEARS, ROEBUCK and Montgomery WARD.

Rhapsody in Blue   An orchestral piece by George GERSHWIN. First performed in 1924 by the Paul WHITEMAN band, it was an inventive fusion of jazz and classical idioms which helped to popularize jazz in the United States. Also the title of a 1945 film biography of the composer.

rhythm and blues   Broadly, a 1940s euphemism for black popular music, formerly known as race music. More specifically, that decade's urban blues, which utilized electric guitars, wailing saxophones, and backup harmonies to create a fuller, more driving sound than country blues. Masters of the R&B sound, which strongly influenced both ROCK MUSIC and SOUL, include Ray CHARLES, B. B. KING, and Ike and Tina TURNER.

Rice, "Daddy" Thomas   (1808–60) Minstrel performer. Often called the father of American minstrelsy, Rice created the character of JIM CROW, the prototypical dancing plantation darky, and portrayed him to international acclaim in the 1830s. He also developed the blackface song-and-skit genre that became known as Ethiopian opera and, following the success of Harriet Beecher STOWE's novel, was one of the many stage Uncle Toms (see UNCLE TOM'S CABIN) of the 1850s.

Rice, Dan   (1823–1900) Clown. Rice was to the nineteenth century what Emmett KELLY was to the twentieth—the epitome of the comic circus professional. After youthful experience as a gambler and strongman, Rice donned whiteface in the 1840s and become so popular in the next thirty years that he was able to buy and sell several circuses of his own. He ran unsuccessfully for the presidency in 1868, wearing a "flag suit" on which Thomas NAST is said to have modeled his depiction of UNCLE SAM; Rice milked the likeness for laughs in subsequent appearances.

Rice, Grantland   (1880–1954) Sportswriter. Writing in a widely syndicated column in the interwar years, Rice reached an estimated 100 million readers with his effusive commentaries on sports events. He was the announcer at the first broadcast World Series (1922) and the originator of the football tag FOUR HORSEMEN. He also wrote a famous quatrain on competition:

> *For when the One Great Scorer comes*
> *To write against your name,*
> *He marks—not that you won or lost—*
> *But how you played the game.*

Richardson, Henry Hobson   (1838–86) Architect. The most successful architect of his day, Richardson created a massive yet elegant mock-medieval style that came to be called Richardsonian Romanesque. It showed to full advantage in Boston's Trinity Church (1877), Chicago's Marshall FIELD warehouse (1887), and numerous railway depots and private mansions.

Rickenbacker, Eddie (1890–1973) The most successful flying ace of World War I, Rickenbacker shot down twenty-two German planes and four balloons. He later served as president (1938–53) and chairman of the board (1954–63) of Eastern Airlines.

Rickey, Branch (1881–1965) Baseball executive. As president of the St. Louis Cardinals in the 1920s and 1930s, Rickey introduced a farm system that helped to bring the club five pennants. As general manager of the Brooklyn Dodgers (1942–50), he not only turned them into a world-class team but broke the color barrier by hiring Jackie ROBINSON.

Riis, Jacob See HOW THE OTHER HALF LIVES.

Riley, James Whitcomb (1849–1916) Poet. A master of his native Indiana's dialect, the "Hoosier poet" achieved immense success with his first book, *The Old Swimmin' Hole and 'Leven More Poems* (1883). Income from this book and from subsequent lecturing made him the wealthiest American writer of his day. The best known of his homey verses are "Little Orphant Annie," "The Raggedy Man," and "When the Frost is on the Pumpkin."

Rin Tin Tin The stage name of a series of German shepherds that starred in adventure stories in silent films, radio, and television. The model for the films, which ran in the 1920s, was a homeless puppy found in a World War I trench by an American serviceman. The television series (1954–59), which was set on a frontier cavalry outpost, made "Rinty" the second most popular dog of the decade (after LASSIE).

Ringling Brothers Five Wisconsin brothers who in 1884 established a traveling wagon show that grew into a major circus. After the acquisition of P. T. BARNUM's and James Anthony Bailey's circus in 1907, the combined Ringling Brothers, Barnum & Bailey Circus was billed, immodestly but accurately, as "The Big One." It toured under a huge tent, the "big top," until the 1950s, when it began to limit shows to indoor venues.

Rio Grande The river dividing Mexico from Texas. The name is Spanish for "big river," although the Mexicans themselves—in whose territory it lay before the Texas Revolution—called it the Rio Bravo del Norte. In the PECOS BILL stories, Bill digs it to irrigate his ranch during a drought. As a largely unpatrolled international border, it serves as a crossing point into the United States for undocumented laborers (see WETBACK).

"Rip Van Winkle" A story by Washington IRVING, contained in his 1819 *Sketch Book*. Rip is a lazy, henpecked New York stater who falls asleep for twenty years under the influence of drink and magic and awakes to find he has slept through the American Revolution. Irving's most popular tale, it was brought to the stage by actor Joseph JEFFERSON.

Ripley's Believe It or Not!   A newspaper feature created in 1918 by New York cartoonist Robert Ripley (1893–1947). It focused on oddities of custom and chance around the world, such as extraordinary coincidences, narrow escapes from death, and the ritual behavior of "exotic" peoples. Picked up by the HEARST syndicate in 1929, it ran in three hundred papers, a significant precursor to the modern TABLOID. It also inspired a popular radio series and two relatively short-lived (1949–50 and 1982–86) television shows.

Ritter, Tex   (1905–74) Singing cowboy. A folksinger and Broadway actor in the early 1930s, Texan Woodward Maurice Ritter turned to films in 1936, with the first of many low-budget westerns, *Song of the Gringo*. They made him, according to his billing, "America's Most Beloved Cowboy," and fostered a recording career that included the title track for the film HIGH NOON. Ritter was the only person elected to both the Country Music and the Cowboy halls of fame. His son John became a comedy star on the television sitcom *Three's Company* (1977–84).

Ritz crackers   Brand name for round, buttery crackers developed in 1934 by the National Biscuit Company. Used chiefly as snacks and for canapés, they are also the main ingredient in mock apple pie.

riverboats   See KEELBOATS; SHOWBOATS; STEAMBOATS.

Roach, Hal   (1892–1992). Filmmaker. As director, producer, and writer, Roach was to the 1930s what Mack SENNETT had been to the 1920s: Hollywood's king of comedy. The company he formed in 1915 developed the careers of LAUREL AND HARDY, Harold LLOYD, and the kids of the OUR GANG COMEDIES. Two of his shorts, Laurel and Hardy's *The Music Box* (1932) and the Our Gang *Bored of Education* (1936), won Academy Awards.

Road Less Traveled, The   (1978) An inspirational book by "born again" psychiatrist M. Scott Peck. Its fusion of practical advice and Christian spirituality made it an astonishingly durable success; it was still on the best-seller lists in the 1990s. See "THE ROAD NOT TAKEN."

"Road Not Taken, The"   (1915) One of Robert FROST's most often quoted poems, a reflection of the ambiguous consequences of choice.

> *Two roads diverged in a wood, and I—*
> *I took the one less travelled by,*
> *And that has made all the difference.*

A blockbuster inspirational book of the 1980s, M. Scott Peck's THE ROAD LESS TRAVELED, takes its title from Frost's poem.

Road of Life   A radio SOAP OPERA that pioneered the medical milieu that was later to be used on TV's *General Hospital*. Featuring the adventures of surgeon Jim Brent, it had a faithful audience for over twenty years (1937–59).

Road Runner and Coyote   A WARNER BROTHERS cartoon created in 1948 by Chuck Jones and Michael Maltese. Road Runner is an elusive bird whose single utterance, "Beep! Beep!," was supplied by Mel BLANC. Wile E. Coyote, the "villain" who chases him in vain, is, in Jones's words, "victimized by his own ineptitude."

Roanoke Colony   The first English colony in the New World, established tentatively in 1585 and more solidly two years later. Its founder, Sir Walter RALEIGH, sent over one hundred settlers there in 1587, but when fellow adventurers returned to the settlement from England in 1591, they found abandoned dwellings and no signs of life. The word "Croatan" was carved into a tree, but that nearby island proved just as forlorn as Roanoke itself. No one has ever determined what happened to Raleigh's "Lost Colony" or its most famous resident, the infant Virginia DARE.

roarer   A boaster; one given to hyperbolic, often humorous self-promotion. The folk type was represented by the historical figures Davy CROCKETT and Mike FINK and by two literary creations of the 1830s. The first, Colonel Nimrod Wildfire, was the "raw Kentuckian" hero of James Paulding's play *The Lion of the West* (1831), depicted by actor James Hackett for twenty years. The second, Roaring Ralph Stackpole, was a blustery horse thief in Robert Montgomery Bird's 1837 novel *Nick of the Woods.*

Roaring Twenties   The 1920s, so called because of the decade's PROHIBITION-inspired excesses: sexual license, SPEAKEASIES, and gangland killings. Director Raoul WALSH's 1939 film *The Roaring Twenties* starred James CAGNEY as a World War I veteran who turns to bootlegging when legitimate work fails him. In the movie's last scene, after he dies on the steps of a church, his girlfriend utters the famous eulogy "He used to be a big shot."

robber barons   Derogatory term for the business leaders, formerly called captains of industry, who ran the American economic system at the turn of the century. Resentment at their abuses of power led to muckraking, the Progressive movement, and trust-busting. See MUCKRAKERS; PROGRESSIVISM; TRUSTS.

Robbins, Harold   (1916–   ) Novelist. As consistently derided by the literati as he is devoured by the masses, Robbins produces sex-and-violence sagas that have made him among the most widely read novelists in the world. Combined sales of his top three books alone—*The Carpetbaggers* (1961), *Never Love a Stranger* (1948), and *The Adventurers* (1966)—are in the neighborhood of 20 million copies, with sales of his entire oeuvre about ten times that. Many of his books have been made into feature films.

Robbins, Jerome   (1918–   ) Choreographer. Revered by balletomanes for his work with the New York City Ballet, Robbins also achieved popular success with his staging of dance numbers for the Broadway musicals *The King and I* (1951), PETER PAN, WEST SIDE STORY, *Gypsy* (1959), and FIDDLER ON THE ROOF. His work on the film version of *West Side Story* (1961) earned him an Academy Award for codirection.

Robbins, Marty   (1925–83) Country singer. A versatile performer from Arizona, Robbins recorded sentimental songs in the 1950s that earned him the nickname Mr. Teardrop. A childhood fan of Gene AUTRY, he cultivated a SINGING COWBOY image and had his single greatest hit with the ballad "El Paso."

Roberts, Oral   (1918–   ) Evangelist. After recovery from illness convinced him of the power of prayer, Roberts traveled widely as a revivalist and faith healer, founded the Oral Roberts Evangelistic Association in 1948, and reached millions with his television specials in the 1950s and 1960s. He founded Oral Roberts University in Tulsa, Oklahoma.

Robert's Rules of Order   A widely used handbook of parliamentary procedure, adapted from the customs of the U.S. House of Representatives. It was written in 1876 by an army engineer, Henry Martyn Robert.

Robertson, Oscar   (1938–   ) Basketball player. The 6'5" Robertson, known as Big O, played for the Cincinnati Royals and Milwaukee Bucks in the 1960s, averaging over twenty-five points a game throughout his career. He made the NBA All-Star Team nine times.

Robeson, Paul   (1898–1976) Singer, actor. Born in New Jersey, Robeson was a PHI BETA KAPPA member and All-American football player at Rutgers before scoring his first triumph in Eugene O'NEILL's *The Emperor Jones* (1925; film 1933). His other plays included *Show Boat* (1928; film 1936), which featured his extraordinary baritone in a famous rendition of "OL' MAN RIVER"; and *Othello* (1943), which broke the Broadway record for a Shakespearean run. Robeson's commitment to civil rights for his fellow blacks and to international socialism served his career poorly in the cold war years, and in 1950, his U.S. passport was revoked. He died, secluded and ill, in New York's Harlem.

Robin   See BATMAN.

Robinson, Bill   (1878–1949) Dancer, actor. Under the nickname Bojangles, Robinson danced as a child in vaudeville, becoming internationally known after appearing in the Shirley TEMPLE films *The Little Colonel* (1935), *The Littlest Rebel* (1935), and *Rebecca of Sunnybrook Farm* (1938).

Robinson, Edward G.   (1893–1973) Actor. An actor of considerable range, Robinson is remembered chiefly for his tough-guy characterizations in gangster films, notably LITTLE CAESAR and *Key Largo* (1948). He also gave solid performances in the FILMS NOIRS *Double Indemnity* (1944), *The Woman in the Window* (1944), and *Scarlet Street* (1945).

Robinson, Edwin Arlington   (1869–1935) Poet. In terse, lugubrious verse, Robinson described the residents of tiny Tilbury Town, modeled on his childhood home of Gardiner, Maine. He won the Pulitzer Prize three times: for his *Collected Poems* (1921), for the blank-verse narrative *The Man Who Died Twice* (1926) and for the Arthurian romance *Tristram* (1927), which brought him popular acclaim. His most cited poems, about Tilbury Town outcasts, are "Richard Corey" and "Miniver Cheevy."

> *Miniver Cheevy, born too late,*
> *Scratched his head and kept on thinking;*
> *Miniver coughed, and called it fate,*
> *And kept on drinking.*

Robinson, Frank (1935–) Baseball player, manager. In a twenty-year career with various clubs, Robinson earned the distinction of being the only player ever elected most valuable player in both the National (1961) and American (1966) leagues. In 1974, simultaneously playing and managing for the Cleveland Indians, he became the first major league black manager.

Robinson, Jackie (1919–72) Baseball player. Robinson made history in 1947 when he became the first black player in the major leagues. Excelling at the plate and on the field, he played for ten years with the Brooklyn Dodgers, leading them to the National League pennant in his rookie year and the World Series championship in 1955. In 1949, when he led the league in batting and stolen bases, he was voted its most valuable player. In 1962, he became the first black member of the Hall of Fame.

Robinson, Smokey (1940–) Singer, songwriter. One of MOTOWN's most prolific writers, Robinson headed a Detroit vocal group, the Miracles, that had great success in the 1960s. Among their hits were "Shop Around," "You've Really Got a Hold on Me," "The Tracks of My Tears," and "I Second That Emotion." Robinson also wrote for other groups, including THE TEMPTATIONS.

Robinson, Sugar Ray (1920–) Boxer. Born Walker Smith in Detroit, Robinson won the welterweight title in 1946, and in the 1950s won the middleweight title five times. His dogged ability to come back from defeat, as well as his rapid, elegant style, made him one of the sport's most popular champions. He won 175 of his 202 professional bouts.

Rock, The See (1) ALCATRAZ and (2) Rocky MARCIANO.

"Rock a Bye, Baby" A lullabye based on an old Mother Goose rhyme and set to music in 1887 by Bostonian Effie Crockett. Its allegedly soothing qualities are belied by the lyrics.

> *Rock a bye, baby, on the treetop.*
> *When the wind blows the cradle will rock.*
> *When the bough breaks the cradle will fall,*
> *And down will come baby, cradle and all.*

"Rock Around the Clock" See Bill HALEY.

"Rock Island Line" A traditional folk song about a railroad line. Often attributed to, and movingly performed by, LEADBELLY, it was also effectively recorded by Johnny CASH.

rock music The dominant musical idiom of the BABY BOOM generation, rock is a driving, danceable music with wide social influence. Fusing RHYTHM AND BLUES and COUNTRY MUSIC styles, the first rockers were Memphis producer Sam PHILLIPS's "rockabilly" artists, the most famous of which was Elvis PRESLEY. His early recordings, as well as those of Bill HALEY, Buddy HOLLY, and more BLUES-oriented singers like Chuck BERRY and LITTLE RICHARD, were identified by the late 1950s as "rock 'n' roll"—a term that in black slang had referred to sexual intercourse and that was first applied to music (by his own account) by

Alan FREED. In spite of its mild lyrical content, this "first wave" of rock music was controversial because of its intimation of sexual license and social rebellion.

By 1960, rock 'n' roll had entered a period of relative sobriety, with the pleasantly sonorous "Philly sound," but the rest of the decade brought a spate of innovations that made "rock" a potpourri term for a plethora of styles. British groups like the Beatles and the Rolling Stones resuscitated the music's blues and rockabilly roots. California groups injected the previously eastern-dominated charts with "surfer music" (see BEACH BOYS) and "acid rock" (see JEFFERSON AIRPLANE). The FOLK REVIVAL produced "folk rock" stars like THE BYRDS and Bob DYLAN, while black artists, especially at MOTOWN, created SOUL music. By the 1970s, the original rock 'n' roll formula had been variously transformed, and young audiences—the baby boomers' children—were listening to theatrical "glitter rock," mechanically danceable "disco," deafeningly virtuosic "heavy metal," and self-consciously antisocial "punk."

A chief chronicler of the rock revolution has been the magazine *Rolling Stone* (see ROLLING STONE [2]). Its major celebration was the WOODSTOCK festival.

rockabilly   See ROCK MUSIC.

Rockefeller, John D.   (1839–1937) Industrialist. Once the richest man in the world, Rockefeller was founder and president of the Standard Oil Company (1870), a vast system of wells, refineries, and distribution centers that, until it was dissolved by the U.S. Supreme Court in 1911, held a worldwide monopoly of the petroleum industry. Objectively, Rockefeller's success stemmed from hard work, favorable railroad rates, and ruthlessness in eliminating competitors. In his own view, it came from providence; he once explained, "God gave me my money." Much of that money he himself gave away toward the end of his life, in funding for the University of Chicago and the Rockefeller Foundation. The foundation was long run by Rockefeller's son John D., Jr. (1874–1960). His grandson Nelson (1908–79) was four times governor of New York and vice president of the United States under Gerald Ford.

Rockefeller Center   An office and entertainment complex in New York City, built in the 1930s with money administered by John D. Rockefeller, Jr. Composed of several skyscrapers of which the most famous is the RCA Building, it includes broadcasting studios, RADIO CITY MUSIC HALL, and an outdoor skating rink.

Rockne, Knute   (1888–1931) Football player, coach. Norwegian-born Rockne made Notre Dame a powerhouse in college football. Playing there in a 1913 game against Army, he caught so many forward passes from quarterback Gus Dorias that the tiny school scored a 35–13 upset—and in the process transformed what had been an oddity into one of the principal elements of the modern game. As his alma mater's coach in the 1920s, Rockne developed stunning backfields, the most famous being 1924's FOUR HORSEMEN. Before his early death in a plane crash, he won 105 out of 122 games, the highest-winning percentage of any college coach. See also "WIN ONE FOR THE GIPPER."

rock 'n' roll   See ROCK MUSIC.

Rockwell, Norman   (1894–1978) The twentieth century's most famous magazine illustrator, Rockwell specialized in nostalgic scenes of small-town America, as appreciated by the masses as they were derided by cynics. In addition to over three hundred covers for THE SATURDAY EVENING POST, he also did calendars for the BOY SCOUTS OF AMERICA and a quartet of paintings, The FOUR FREEDOMS, that were widely seen as posters during World War II.

Rockettes   See RADIO CITY MUSIC HALL.

Rocky   A 1976 movie written and directed by Sylvester STALLONE, who played the lead character Rocky Balboa. A small-time boxer (the "Italian stallion"), he challenges the black champion Apollo Creed and, after a bloody battle, is narrowly defeated. The film, which won the best picture Oscar, skillfully twisted the racist motif of the GREAT WHITE HOPE into a poignant study of courage and the AMERICAN DREAM. It produced three sequels lacking the punch of the original. The flamboyant Creed is modeled roughly on Muhammad ALI, while the laconic Balboa's namesake is Rocky MARCIANO. Shot in Philadelphia, the film became so popular there that a Rocky statue now graces the steps of its art museum.

Rocky Horror Picture Show, The   (1975) A cult movie based on a 1973 British "glitter rock" musical by Richard O'Brien. An elaborate spoof of Hollywood musicals, horror films, and sexual conventions, it stars Tim Curry as Dr. Frank N. Furter, a vampiric transvestite from another galaxy. Typically shown in late-night screenings, it is attended by hordes of devotees who dress as the film's characters, echo the dialogue, and bombard each other with water, banter, and projectiles.

Rocky Mountains   A rugged mountain system that extends from Alberta to New Mexico, containing the most spectacular ranges in the United States. First explored by the LEWIS AND CLARK EXPEDITION, they were later exploited by the fur-trapping MOUNTAIN MEN of the Rocky Mountain Fur Company and American Fur Company (see ASTOR FAMILY). Pioneers passed through them on the OREGON TRAIL beginning in the 1840s, and in 1858 thousands of gold-seekers braved them under the banner PIKES PEAK OR BUST.'' The central Rockies now contain numerous ski resorts, especially in Wyoming and Colorado.

rodeo   A western entertainment in which cowboys compete for prize money by demonstrating their skills in bronco busting, bull riding, calf roping, and steer wrestling (known as bulldogging). Mexican VAQUEROS held the first such events at their annual roundups (*rodeos*) in the 1800s, and the idea spread during the cattle drives of the nineteenth century. Prescott, Arizona, was the first municipality to charge spectators an admission fee (1888), and Cheyenne, Wyoming—whose "Frontier Days" remains one of the largest rodeos—brought tourists in by train in the 1890s. Major rodeos are held under the jurisdiction of the Professional Rodeo Cowboys Association. Multiple winners of the "All Around Cowboy" title have included Jim Shoulders, Larry Mahan, and Tom Ferguson.

Rodeo Drive   An elegant shopping street in BEVERLY HILLS; a favorite with entertainment celebrities and wealthy tourists.

Rodgers, Jimmie   (1897–1933) Country singer. In a career that lasted less than a decade, Rodgers became the first major star of "hillbilly" music. Known as the Singing Brakeman because of his youthful work on railroad gangs and as the

Blue Yodeler because of his introduction of the yodel into the country repertoire, he sang songs ranging from TIN PAN ALLEY tunes to hymns, although his success rested mainly on sentimental, regional, and "rambling" songs such as "Blue Yodel," "When the Cactus Is in Bloom," and "Waiting for a Train." Born in Mississippi, he moved to Texas to alleviate the symptoms of the tuberculosis that eventually killed him, and he is strongly associated with the Southwest. Rodgers influenced the styles of countless younger performers, notably Gene AUTRY, Hank SNOW, and Ernest TUBB.

Rodgers, Richard   (1902–79) Composer. Rodgers was the musical collaborator for two of Broadway's finest lyricists. With his college friend Lorenz HART, he wrote the shows *A Connecticut Yankee* (1927), *Babes in Arms* (1937), and PAL JOEY. With Oscar HAMMERSTEIN II, he did The King and I (1951), OKLAHOMA!, THE SOUND OF MUSIC, and SOUTH PACIFIC. Rodgers's best-known tunes included (with Hart) "Blue Moon," "My Funny Valentine," and "Where or When"; and (with Hammerstein) "Hello, Young Lovers," "If I Loved You," "Oh, What a Beautiful Morning," "People Will Say We're in Love," "Some Enchanted Evening," "The Surrey with the Fringe on Top," and "You'll Never Walk Alone."

Roe v. Wade   A 1973 Supreme Court decision striking down a Texas law restricting abortions. In establishing a "right to privacy" over the previously acknowledged fetal right to life, the Roe decision legalized most abortions, sparking the most divisive social debate since slavery days. Proponents of "abortion rights" are called "pro-choice." Their "pro-life" opponents include Operation Rescue, which blocks abortion clinics, and nonconventional feminists like Women Exploited by Abortion and Feminists for Life.

Rogers, Fred   See MR. ROGERS' NEIGHBORHOOD.

Rogers, Ginger   See ASTAIRE AND ROGERS.

Rogers, John   (1829–1904) Sculptor. The Norman ROCKWELL of sculpture, Rogers produced small figure groups on patriotic, literary, and domestic themes that were copied in plaster and sold through mail-order catalogues. Ranging in price from five to fifty dollars, the Rogers Groups sold in the tens of thousands, becoming a significant element in the democratization of art.

Rogers, Kenny   (1941–) Country singer. The most popular American singer of the late 1970s, Texas-born Rogers sang in the 1960s with a soft folk band, the First Edition, whose major hit was "Ruby, Don't Take Your Love to Town." As a solo singer, combining what Bill Malone accurately calls a country mood and Las Vegas production, he scored pop hits with "Lucille," "The Gambler," "Lady," and (in a duet with Dolly PARTON), "Islands in the Stream." The success of "The Gambler" led to television movies exploiting the theme.

Rogers, Robert   (1731–95) Army officer. Fighting for the British in the FRENCH AND INDIAN WAR, Rogers commanded a guerrilla company, Rogers's Rangers, that gained fame by burning an Indian village allied with the French. Rogers's buckskin-clad, stealthy wilderness fighters were a prototype for later elite forces such as the Army Rangers and Special Forces, the Navy Seals, and British commandos. Rogers fought for the British in the American Revolution.

Rogers, Roy   (1912–   ) Singer, actor. Billed as "King of the Cowboys," Cincinnati-born Leonard Slye succeeded Gene AUTRY in the 1940s as the most popular of the SINGING COWBOYS. In the 1930s, he used his milk-and-honey tenor and ingratiating smile to forge a singing career with the Sons of the Pioneers. Signed in 1937 by Republic, Slye became Roy Rogers, the easygoing, straight-shooting hero of dozens of westerns. By the 1950s, he had his own television show and had made millions in investments. In 1947, he married Dale Evans (1912–   ), his leading lady since *The Cowboy and the Senorita* (1944). She frequently acted with him on both the big and small screens. Their duet "Happy Trails to You" was the TV show's sign-off tune. The Rogers/Evans sidekick was Gabby HAYES; their horses were Trigger and Buttermilk.

Rogers, Will   (1879–1935) Entertainer. A former cowboy and WILD WEST SHOW trick roper, Oklahoman Rogers expressed a grittily humorous, populist viewpoint in films, onstage, and in the press that made him the most beloved CRACKER-BARREL PHILOSOPHER of the century. He served as mayor of Beverly Hills, stumped for Franklin D. ROOSEVELT in 1932, and summed up his partisanship in the droll announcement "I belong to no organized party; I'm a Democrat." The line most commonly attributed to him is "I never met a man I didn't like." He died in a plane crash in Alaska.

Rolfe, John   (1585–1622) English colonist. The enterprising Rolfe developed tobacco as the Virginia colony's leading cash crop. His marriage to POCAHONTAS helped secure a period of peace between the races, but he himself was killed in an Indian attack.

Rolling Stone   (1) O. HENRY's first literary venture, a humor magazine that he edited in 1894–95 in Austin, Texas. (2) An entertainment periodical founded in 1967 in New York City. Originally focused on ROCK MUSIC, it now brings its fashionable iconoclasm to the broader realms of national culture and politics. The name echoed that of the British rock band the Rolling Stones and the title of Bob DYLAN's song "Like a Rolling Stone."

Romance of Helen Trent, The   Radio SOAP OPERA. One of the first and most successful of the breed, it chronicled the trials of glamorous, lovelorn Helen Trent as she fended off suitors and attacks on her life with equal dexterity. She managed this for twenty-seven years (1933–60).

Romberg, Sigmund   (1887–1951) Composer. Born in Hungary, Romberg wrote light operas for the American stage. The best known—all later adapted for the movies—were *Maytime* (1917), *The Student Prince* (1924), *The Desert Song* (1926), and *The New Moon* (1928).

Ronald McDonald   A trademark clown representative of the McDONALD'S restaurant chain. "Ronald McDonald Houses" (founded in 1974) are company-supported "homes away from home" for familes of children undergoing hospital care.

Rooney, Mickey   (1920–   ) Actor. Born Joe Yule in Brooklyn, Rooney made his name in 1935 as Puck in the film version of *A Midsummer Night's Dream.* Two years later, in *A Family Affair,* he created the character of Andy Hardy, a small-town teenager, which he played in over a dozen subsequent films. The Hardy series, coupled with his performances in BOYS TOWN and in his first of several films with Judy GARLAND, *Thoroughbreds Don't Cry* (1937), made him, by 1939, the biggest box-office draw in America (a distinction he took over from Shirley TEMPLE). Service in World War II interrupted a momentum he never really regained, although he gave fine character performances in several subsequent films, notably *National Velvet* (with Elizabeth TAYLOR, 1944), *Baby Face Nelson* (1957), and *Breakfast at Tiffany's* (1961). He made his Broadway debut, approaching sixty, in *Sugar Babies* (1979). Rooney's first of several wives was Ava GARDNER.

Roosevelt, Eleanor   (1884–1962) As the country's first activist First Lady, FDR's wife spoke widely on humanitarian concerns and civil rights. Her public appearances and her newspaper column "My Day" made her one of the world's most admired women. After her husband's death, she served eight years as U.S. delegate to the United Nations, helping to draft its Declaration of Human Rights.

Roosevelt, Franklin D.   (1882–1945) U.S. president. One of the most fiercely loved and fiercely hated of chief executives, wealthy New Yorker Franklin Delano Roosevelt took office in 1933, promising a "new deal" for the "forgotten man" of the Great Depression. His subsequent legislative package (see NEW DEAL) provided more symbolic than real relief to the economically strapped country, although it undeniably lifted the national mood while laying the groundwork for the welfare state. FDR, who had campaigned with the song "HAPPY DAYS ARE HERE AGAIN," periodically fanned the flames of hope in his FIRESIDE CHATS. His exuberance and mastery of the media earned him an unprecedented four terms in office.

In his final term, with the Depression behind him, Roosevelt shepherded the country through World War II—a conflict that America had entered following his famous "DATE WHICH WILL LIVE IN INFAMY" speech. With Great Britain's Winston Churchill and the Soviet Union's Joseph Stalin, he formed the Big Three junta of the Allied effort and was a major voice at the Teheran and Yalta conferences. Crippled by polio since the age of forty, FDR died of an unrelated brain hemorrhage just four months before the war's end. Actor Ralph Bellamy gave a memorable portrait of his dynamic personality in the play *Sunrise at Campobello* (1958; film 1960).

Roosevelt, Theodore   (1858–1919) U.S. president. A sickly child who transformed himself by sheer will into an indefatigable exemplar of the robust life, Teddy Roosevelt had been a New York City police commissioner, organizer of the ROUGH RIDERS, and his state's governor before being "kicked upstairs" into the vice presidency by political bosses who feared his independence and reformism. Their plans backfired when, on William MCKINLEY'S assassination, he became the nation's twenty-sixth chief executive (for the bosses' reaction, see Mark HANNA). TR's presidency was marked by trust-busting (see TRUSTS) at home and the BIG STICK abroad. Critical of those he called "malefactors of great wealth," he used the newly created Department of Commerce to rein in ROBBER BARONS, established the Interstate Commerce Commission to regulate railroads, and passed a Pure Food and Drug Act to protect consumers. Internationally, he beefed up the MONROE DOCTRINE by threatening U.S. "police power" in the Caribbean (the so-called Roosevelt Corollary), sent the GREAT WHITE FLEET on a world tour, and supported a Central American revolution that gave the United States the PANAMA CANAL.

An outspoken big-game hunter and outdoorsman, Roosevelt strongly supported the infant conservation movement, set aside millions of acres of national forest reserves, and established the U.S. Park Service. His writings included a history of the WAR OF 1812 and the four-volume *Winning of the West* (1889–96). See also BULL MOOSE PARTY; "BULLY!"; SAN JUAN HILL; TEDDY BEAR.

root beer A soft drink popularized by Philadelphia druggist Charles Hires (1852–1937), who adapted a herbal tea recipe of a New Jersey inn. Originally marketed as Hires herb tea, it became root beer at the suggestion of Russell Conwell (see ACRES OF DIAMONDS) and was promoted at the 1876 Philadelphia Centennial.

Rootabaga Stories A book (1922) of children's stories by Carl SANDBURG.

Roots A partly fictionalized saga (1976) by Alex Haley (1921–92) that traces the genealogy of his family back to its African progenitor, Kunta Kinte, a young Gambian who was abducted into slavery in the eighteenth century. A television miniseries made from the book became the media phenomenon of the 1970s; nearly half the population of the United States watched its final episode (1978). Haley also wrote *The Autobiography of* MALCOLM X.

Rose, Billy (1899–1966) Lyricist. Rose wrote the words to several popular ballads, notably "It's Only a Paper Moon," "Me and My Shadow," "That Old Gang of Mine," and "Tonight You Belong to Me."

Rose, Louis (or Moses) See ALAMO.

Rose, Pete (1941–) Baseball player. Cincinnati Reds fielder Rose, known as Charlie Hustle, made more hits in his career than anyone else in the history of the game: His lifetime record was 4,256. In 1989, he was barred from baseball for life after revelations of his gambling improprieties, but before that ignominious end, he had three times won the National League batting title and twice been voted most valuable player.

Rose Bowl A football stadium in Pasadena, California, where successful college teams compete in postseason play; hence, by extension, the game itself. Such games had been played in Pasadena, as part of its Tournament of Roses, since 1902, but the current Rose Bowl was not built until 1923. The game, with its accompanying parade, is now a major television event, and its success has led to equally popular imitations, notably the Orange Bowl (Miami), Sugar Bowl (New Orleans), Cotton Bowl (Dallas), and Gator Bowl (Jacksonville).

"Rose is a rose is a rose is a rose" See Gertrude STEIN.

Rose Marie An operetta (1924) with music by Rudolf Friml and words by Otto Harbach and Oscar HAMMERSTEIN II. In a 1936 film version, the leads were sung by Nelson EDDY and Jeanette MacDonald. The title song was an independent hit.

Rosebud The enigmatic last word of protagonist Charles Foster Kane in CITIZEN KANE. The search for its meaning is the movie's theme.

Rosenberg case Julius Rosenberg (1918–53) and his wife, Ethel (1915–53), were communist sympathizers executed in 1953 for passing secrets about the atomic bomb to the Soviet Union. They never confessed their guilt, and their conviction inspired pleas for clemency which President EISENHOWER refused. Liberal orthodoxy continues to depict them as innocent victims of COLD WAR zealotry.

"Rosie the Riveter" A popular song of the 1940s, celebrating women's industrial contribution to the war effort. Rosie became a symbol first of women's emancipation from traditional roles and then, once returning G.I.s took back their old factory jobs, of their expendability.

Ross, Betsy (1752–1836) A Philadelphia seamstress who, according to tradition, sewed the first American flag—with thirteen stripes and a circle of thirteen stars—at the request of George Washington. Ross did make flags for the Pennsylvania Navy, but there is no evidence that the Stars and Stripes story (first proposed in the 1870s by her grandson) was anything more than a family legend.

Ross, Diana See THE SUPREMES.

Ross, Harold (1892–1951) Editor. Ross founded THE NEW YORKER in 1925 and ran it until his death. Largely responsible for its reputation as a sophisticate's refuge, he promoted the work of Dorothy PARKER, James THURBER, and E. B. WHITE.

Rotary Clubs An association of business and professional men formed to promote better business practices, encourage community service, and sponsor scholarships. The first was founded in 1905 by Paul Harris, a Chicago lawyer. In 1922, the organization changed its name to Rotary International. H. L. MENCKEN, responding to early members' hearty boosterism, snapped, ''The first Rotarian was the first man to call John the Baptist 'Jack.' ''

ROTC Reserve Officers' Training Corps, pronounced *rot-see*. A U.S. Army program on college campuses which offers graduating seniors a commission for taking military coursework and training. The Navy and Air Force have similar campus programs (NROTC and AFROTC).

Rough Riders A cavalry unit whose daring at the Battle of SAN JUAN HILL made their second-in-command, Theodore ROOSEVELT, a household name. An unlikely mix of eastern socialites and western roughnecks, they were described by one observer as ''the society page, financial column, and Wild West Show all wrapped up in one.'' Their nominal commander, Roosevelt's superior, was Colonel Leonard WOOD.

Roughing It (1872) A travel book by Mark TWAIN. It recounts his youthful experiences as a Nevada silver miner.

Route 66 (1) A highway that runs from Chicago to Los Angeles. A major route west before the advent of the Interstate Highway System, it is affectionately known as the mother road. (2) A song written in 1946 by Bob Troup. It was a hit for Nat ''King'' COLE and the Rolling Stones.

If you ever plan to motor west,
Take my way, the highway that's the best;
Get your kicks on Route 66.

(3) A television series (1960–64) about two young men touring the country in search of adventure.

Rover Boys   See Edward STRATEMEYER.

Rowlandson, Mary   (1635–78) A Massachusetts minister's wife who was captured by Indians in 1676, Rowlandson wrote an account of her travail that became the first colonial best-seller. Published in 1682, it was entitled *The Sovereignty and Goodness of God, Together with the Faithfulness of His Promises Displayed.*

Royal Canadian Mounted Police   Canada's federal police force. Known for their scarlet uniforms and reputation for "always getting their man," the Mounties were formed in 1873 as the North-West Mounted Police. Their stock was high among American children in the 1950s thanks to the television series SERGEANT PRESTON OF THE YUKON.

rube   A country bumpkin; a hick. Originally "Rustic Reuben," then (by the 1840s) "Reuben," and finally (by the 1880s) just "rube."

Rube Goldberg contraption   See Rube GOLDBERG.

Rubin, Jerry   See YIPPIES.

Rudolph the Red-nosed Reindeer   The hero of a poem written in 1939 by Robert May as a Christmas promotion for his employer, Montgomery WARD. In a twist on the ugly-duckling motif, Rudolph is mocked by his fellow reindeer for his red nose until it comes in handy on a foggy Christmas Eve, lighting Santa's way on his nocturnal rounds. A Johnny Marks song on the same theme was a huge hit for Gene AUTRY in 1949.

"Rum, Romanism, and rebellion"   An 1884 campaign slur describing the heritage of the Democratic party. The speaker, Rev. Samuel Burchard, was referring to the party's perceived courting of drunken Irishmen and former REBELS. Republican candidate James Blaine's failure to denounce the remark helped to lose him the election to Grover Cleveland. See also "MA, MA, WHERE'S MY PA?"

Runyon, Damon   (1884–1946) Writer. Runyon wrote stories about colorful, often shady Broadway characters in an idiom that was distinguished for its slang. His most famous book was GUYS AND DOLLS.

Rushmore, Mount   A granite cliff in South Dakota into which, beginning in 1927, sculptor Gutzon Borglum (1871–1941) carved sixty-feet-high heads of four presidents: Washington, Jefferson, Lincoln, and Teddy Roosevelt. The four were meant to represent, respectively, the country's founding, philosophy, unity, and expansion. Mount Rushmore is now a National Memorial. Borglum also carved a monumental tribute to Confederate leaders at Stone Mountain, Georgia.

Russell, Bill   (1934–   ) Basketball player. After leading the U.S. basketball team to a gold medal in the 1956 Olympics, Russell played for the Boston Celtics for thirteen years. In that period the team won eleven NBA titles, and the center himself was most valuable player five times. He retired with a career record of 14,522 points.

Russell, Charles   (1) Charles M. Russell (1864–1926) was a cowboy turned artist whose paintings of the Old West are as vivid, and almost as well known, as those of Frederic REMINGTON. Like Remington, he also sculpted action figures. (2) Charles Taze Russell (1852–1916) was an eloquent purveyor of Bible tracts who in 1872 started the millenarian sect that would evolve into the JEHOVAH'S WITNESSES. He also founded their journal, THE WATCHTOWER.

Russell, Jane   (1921–   ) Actress. A competent, if undistinguished, performer, Russell shocked the country in her movie debut as BILLY THE KID's girlfriend in *The Outlaw* (1943). Producer Howard HUGHES's come-ons for the film included posters of the buxom starlet in disarray over the caption "How'd you like to tussle with Russell?" Sound character work in *His Kind of Woman* (1951) and GENTLEMEN PREFER BLONDES offset the sexpot image, although in the 1980s she was still doing brassiere ads on TV.

Russell, Lillian   (1861–1922) Singer, actress. The most renowned beauty of the gaslight era, Helen Louise Leonard appeared for over three decades in burlesque and comic operas. Married four times, she was also romantically linked to Diamond Jim BRADY.

Russell, Rosalind   (1908–76) Actress. Known for her crisp, vibrant presence, "Roz" Russell played Hildy Johnson in HIS GIRL FRIDAY and received Academy Award nominations for *My Sister Eileen* (1942), *Sister Kenny* (1946), *Mourning Becomes Electra* (1947), and *Auntie Mame* (1958)—the last in a role that had earned her acclaim on Broadway.

Ruth, Babe   (1895–1948) Baseball player. The "Sultan of Swat" was born George Herman Ruth in Baltimore and shone for six years as a Boston Red Sox pitcher before being sold in 1920 to the New York YANKEES. In fifteen years with that club, he helped to restore fans' faith after the BLACK SOX SCANDAL, brought in enough gate receipts to finance Yankee Stadium, and became the highest-paid athlete of his time. The American League home run champion for all but two years of the 1920s, Ruth set a single-season (1927) record of sixty homers that was not broken until 1961. His lifetime total of 714 home runs stayed intact until 1974 (see Hank AARON).

Ruth's genial, exuberant personality generated legends that made him seem superhuman. One has him hitting four for four on a day he has left a speakeasy at dawn. In another, he promises a desperately ill child to hit him a homer—and ends up hitting him two. In a third, he points accurately to a spot in the stands where he will wallop the next incoming pitch. Such tales enlivened film biographies of "the Bambino" starring William Bendix (1948) and John Goodman (1992).

Ryan, Nolan   (1947–   ) Pitcher. A durable Texas right-hander, Ryan holds the major league records for career strikeouts (5,714) and most strikeouts in this century in a single season (383 in 1973). In a career spanning almost three decades (1966–93), he played for the New York Mets, California Angels, and Houston Astros.

Sacajawea (ca. 1787–1812) A Shoshone Indian woman who, as a teenager, guided the LEWIS AND CLARK EXPEDITION through the Rocky Mountains. Wife of a French trapper, Toussaint Charbonneau, she traveled with him and their son Jean-Baptiste, born en route. Their presence helped protect the expedition from war parties, and the girl also served effectively as an interpreter. One explorer called her "time and again the genius of the occasion."

Sacco and Vanzetti case Anarchists executed for robbery. Born in Italy, Nicola Sacco (1891–1927) and Bartolomeo Vanzetti (1888–1927) were philosophical anarchists and World War I draft evaders who, in 1920, were arrested for a Massachusetts factory robbery in which two company employees were shot to death. When they were convicted the following year, liberals rallied to their defense, claiming that they were the victims of anticommunist hysteria (see PALMER RAIDS). Support for their cause increased when another condemned man implicated the "Morelli gang," but they went to the electric chair anyway in 1927. The ballistics evidence against them is still contested. See also ROSENBERG CASE.

sad sack In the 1930s, an unpopular student, a NERD. Popularized in the 1940s by a comic strip, *Sad Sack,* about a bumbling, constantly put-upon soldier. It was created by cartoonist George Baker for an armed forces paper.

Sadie Hawkins Day The first Saturday in November, on which an invented custom obliges single men to accept any interested woman's proposal of marriage. The idea, which builds on the leap year proposals of European tradition, came from Al Capp's comic strip LI'L ABNER, where Hawkins was a "man-hungry" spinster.

"St. James Infirmary" A traditional blues ballad of thwarted love. A gambler mourns the death of his beloved, "stretched out on a long white table" in New Orleans's St. James Infirmary.

> *Let her go, let her go, God bless her,*
> *Wherever she may be.*
> *She may search this wide world over*
> *And never find a man as sweet as me.*

"St. Louis Blues" A song written in 1914 by W. C. HANDY. After achieving phenomenal success in sheet music and recordings, it was interpolated in several motion pictures, including the film biography of the composer, *St. Louis Blues* (1958), in which Handy was portrayed by Nat "King" COLE.

St. Patrick's Cathedral   The largest Roman Catholic cathedral in the United States. Designed by James RENWICK in a combination of French and English Gothic, it was constructed between 1858 and 1879. It is a principal tourist attraction of New York's FIFTH AVENUE.

St. Valentine's Day massacre   A Chicago gangland killing that happened on February 14, 1929. The killers, who impersonated policemen, were Al CAPONE henchmen. The victims, seven hoods of rival bootlegger "Bugs" Moran, were machine-gunned from behind while they were facing a wall. The gory scene was reproduced in numerous movies, notably SOME LIKE IT HOT.

Salem witch trials   Trials for witchcraft that took place in the town of Salem, Massachusetts, in 1692. Many of the suspected bewitched were teenage girls whose strange behavior—possibly prankish, possibly delusional—was interpreted by the Puritan elders as evidence of "possession." They accused a slave, Tituba, of causing their maladies. Under the lash she confessed and named two accomplices, touching off a frenzy of accusations that ended with the execution of twenty "witches." Contrary to popular legend, none were burned; nineteen women were hanged and a male victim, Giles Corey, was crushed with stones. The Cotton MATHER family repudiated the court's findings, and the episode is now generally seen as a collective delusion. Arther MILLER'S 1953 play *The Crucible* suggested analogies between the Salem and Joseph MCCARTHY hearings.

Salinger, J. D.   (1919–) Writer. New Yorker Jerome David Salinger is an accomplished short story writer whose quirky Glass family was introduced in "A Perfect Day for Bananafish" (1949) and who later figured in *Franny and Zooey* (1961) and *Raise High the Roof-Beam, Carpenters* (1963). His most famous work is THE CATCHER IN THE RYE.

Salvation Army   An international charity organization founded by English evangelist William Booth (1829–1912) in 1865. It opened its first U.S. mission in 1879 and achieved a notable victory four years later, when its "soldiers" reformed BOWERY drunk "Ashbarrel Jimmy." Known especially for its work among the poor, the Salvation Army is also involved in disaster relief, children's aid, and prison work. Its traces in American popular culture include Vachel LINDSAY's eulogy "General William Booth Enters into Heaven" (1913), the Salvation Army heroine of GUYS AND DOLLS, and the red kettles that bell-ringing members use at Christmas to collect donations for the underprivileged.

Sambo   Since the early 1900s, a condescending term for a black male. Probably from a West African term for "second son," although possibly influenced by Spanish *Zambo*, for one of black and Indian parentage. Its distastefulness to blacks was intensified in 1899, when British author Helen Bannerman published the illustrated children's book *Little Black Sambo,* about a black child who outwits a quartet of tigers and, when they turn into butter by chasing each other around a tree, uses it on a monstrous stack of pancakes. Civil rights groups, including the NAACP, denounced the story as racially condescending, but it continued to sell into the 1970s.

San Francisco   The jewel of Northern California's noted Bay Area, "Frisco" is a port city noted for its international flavor and unconventional lifestyles.

Founded by the Spanish in 1776, it was a tiny outpost until the 1840s, when GOLD RUSH hopefuls changed it into a boomtown and made its waterfront Barbary Coast an entertainment mecca. Its 1990 population was 1.6 million, with over 6.5 million in the Bay Area as a whole. Situated on steep hills over the San Andreas Fault, it has a reputation for precipitous beauty and imminent collapse: the SAN FRANCISCO EARTHQUAKE of 1906 was only one of many tremors to rock the city. In the 1960s HIPPIES flocked to its HAIGHT-ASHBURY district, while nearby Oakland spawned the BLACK PANTHER party; since the 1970s it has been known as a haven for homosexuals. Tourist attractions include CABLE CARS, CHINATOWN, GOLDEN GATE BRIDGE, ALCATRAZ, and a world-famous restaurant row on Fisherman's Wharf.

San Francisco earthquake A massive quake that hit San Francisco on April 18, 1906. It leveled countless buildings, started a fire that lasted three days, and took hundreds of lives.

San Juan Capistrano A Spanish mission in Orange County, California. Founded in 1776, it was nearly destroyed by an earthquake in 1812. Swallows that nest in the ruin are said to follow a peculiarly ecclesiastical migrating pattern. They fly south each year on October 23 (St. John's Day) and return the following spring on March 19 (St. Joseph's Day).

San Juan Hill A hill overlooking Santiago Harbor in Cuba. It was the putative site of the most famous battle of the Spanish-American War—the ROUGH RIDERS' storming of the heights in the face of withering Spanish fire. Actually, this battle, like that of BUNKER HILL, was misnamed, as nearby Kettle Hill was the troops' secured objective. Also distinguished for their bravery that day (June 22, 1898) were black troops under the command of John J. PERSHING.

San Salvador An island in the Bahamas, also called Watlings Island. It is believed to have been the 1492 landfall of Christopher COLUMBUS, who gratefully named it Holy Savior. The native Arawak called it Guanahani.

Sand Creek Massacre An 1864 slaughter of peaceful Cheyenne Indians by Colorado militia under the command of John Chivington. The Indians, led by Black Kettle, had been led to believe they were under U.S. Army protection; the treachery strengthened the resolve of militant leaders who rightly put no faith in such assurances.

Sandburg, Carl (1878–1967) Poet, folksinger. Illinois-born Sandburg, the "people's poet," wrote colloquial, experimental verse on American themes. His most famous poem, "Chicago" (1914), evokes the bustling energy of the midwestern city. "The People, Yes" (1936) reflects his intense populism. He won Pulitzer Prizes for his *Complete Poems* (1950) and for *Abraham Lincoln: The War Years* (1939), part of a long biography of the president. Much in demand as a folksinger, Sandburg collected his favorites tunes in *The American Songbag* (1927).

Sanders, Colonel See KENTUCKY COLONEL.

Sankey, Ira D. (1840–1908) Songwriter. An accomplished organist and singer, Sankey was the musical right-hand man of Dwight L. MOODY, accompanying him on a triumphal tour of England (1873–75) and providing hymns for the Moody revivals. Many of these were collected in *Gospel Hymns*.

Santa Anna, Antonio López de   (1794–1876) Mexican soldier and politician. Santa Anna styled himself the Napoleon of the West, and was so popular with his countrymen that they elected him Mexico's president four times. In the United States, he is best known as the commander of the Mexican forces that took the ALAMO and, several weeks later, surrendered to Texan Sam HOUSTON. See also CHEWING GUM.

Santa Claus   The American counterpart of the Dutch St. Nicholas, or "Sinter Klaas," a legendary character who rewards good children at Christmas. In the New World normative ritual, he visits children's houses on Christmas Eve, arriving in a sleigh drawn by reindeer and descending through the chimney to leave gifts. Although his red suit may reflect ecclesiastical garb (the original Nicholas was a fourth-century bishop), the chimney and reindeer tropes are modern innovations. Current images of Santa Claus derive from Clement Moore's "THE NIGHT BEFORE CHRISTMAS" and drawings by Thomas NAST.

Santa María   See Christopher COLUMBUS.

Sargent, John Singer   (1856–1925) Painter. A fashionable portraitist at the turn of the century, Sargent specialized in flattering depictions of wealthy patrons. His unconventionality, however, showed dramatically in an 1884 portrait of "Madame X," a socialite whom he painted in a low-cut dress. Popular on both sides of the Atlantic, Sargent refused a British knighthood rather than sacrifice his American citizenship.

Sarnoff, David   (1891–1971) Broadcasting executive. Born in Russia, Sarnoff became an overnight celebrity in 1912, when he was the sole wireless operator to broadcast the rescue of *Titanic* survivors. A few years later he proposed to his employer, the Marconi Company, that they market a "radio music box" for home enjoyment. The idea inspired the modern broadcasting industry and positioned the imaginative immigrant as one of its leaders. He served as RCA president beginning in 1930 and was the founder of the first RADIO network, NBC. He was also among the pioneers of commercial TELEVISION.

Saroyan, William   (1908–81) Writer of homey, sentimental stories and plays. He is best known for the story collection *The Daring Young Man on the Flying Trapeze* (1934), the Pulitzer Prize play *The Time of Your Life* (1939), and the novel *The Human Comedy* (1943).

Sasquatch   A large, hairy hominid believed by some to inhabit the wilds of the Pacific Northwest. The name comes from the Salish term for "wild man." Sightings of the creature (or creatures) have been reported for decades, and believers offer the incredulous such evidence as fuzzy photographs, eyewitness testimony, and mammoth footprints. The animal is also called Bigfoot.

Satchmo   See Louis "Satchmo" ARMSTRONG.

Saturday Evening Post, The   A general interest magazine founded in Philadelphia in 1821. It achieved wide appeal under editor George H. Lorimer (1899–1936) and was long identified by the cover art of Norman ROCKWELL.

Saturday Night Fever   A 1977 movie starring John Travolta as a young Brooklynite who dreams of escape to Manhattan and beyond. Its settings in New York dance clubs made it the quintessential movie of the disco scene (see ROCK MUSIC).

Saturday Night Live   A late-night television comedy show first aired by NBC in 1975. It features skits by a repertory ensemble and celebrity hosts as well as musical interludes by popular performers. The show has been a training ground for comics, among them Chevy Chase, Billy Crystal, and Eddie Murphy.

Saturday night special   Slang term for an inexpensive handgun, from their popularity as the firearms of choice for weekend troublemakers. They are the frequent targets of gun control bills.

sawbuck   A ten-dollar bill. From the Roman numeral X, resembling the X of a sawhorse end. A "double sawbuck" is a twenty-dollar bill.

Sawyer, Tom   See TOM SAWYER.

Say Hey Kid   Nickname for Willie MAYS.

"Say it ain't so, Joe"   See BLACK SOX SCANDAL.

scalawag   A person of low moral character. Applied during RECONSTRUCTION to those southerners who cooperated for their own advantage with the federal system. See also CARPETBAGGERS.

scalping   Since the seventeenth century, this has meant the removal of the hair and scalp of a defeated enemy. The taking of scalps as trophies was a relatively rare custom among native peoples until white governors began to offer bounties for Indian scalps. Henceforth the practice spread on both sides. Scalping, accomplished with a "scalping knife," was often, although not always, fatal. Eastern warriors, who shaved their heads, sometimes left a topknot, or "scalplock," as a taunting invitation to their enemies.

Scarface   (1932) A gangster film produced by Howard HUGHES, written by Ben HECHT, and directed by Howard HAWKS. It starred Paul Muni as Tony Camonte, a violent psychotic modeled roughly on recently incarcerated Al CAPONE. The character's brutality and intimations of incest made the movie shocking for its time, just two years before the HAYS OFFICE code took effect.

Scarlet Letter, The   A novel (1850) by Nathaniel HAWTHORNE. Set in seventeenth-century New England, it is the story of unwed mother Hester Prynne, who refuses to divulge to the Puritan elders the identity of her lover, the minister Arthur Dimmesdale. A classic study of guilt and expiation, it is required reading in many high schools. The scarlet letter of the title is a large red A, which Hester wears on her dress as an emblem of adultery.

scat singing   The singing of nonsense syllables to music, especially JAZZ music. The technique has been traced to Louis ARMSTRONG, although its most famous practitioner is Ella FITZGERALD.

Schulberg, Budd   (1914–) Writer. Schulberg made his name with *What Makes Sammy Run?* (1941), a novel about a scheming Hollywood tycoon that became a television play (1949) and a Broadway musical (1964). He also explored the dark side of success in *The Harder They Fall* (1947; film 1956) and "A Face in the Crowd" (1953; film 1957). He received an Oscar for the screenplay of ON THE WATERFRONT.

Schultz, Dutch   (1902–35) Gangster. Bootlegger Arthur Flegenheimer was one of the charter members of the underworld syndicate "Murder, Inc." He was killed by rival mobsters in a New Jersey restaurant.

Schulz, Charles   See PEANUTS (2).

Scientology   A self-help movement with quasi-religious overtones that evolved from the writings of science fiction writer L. Ron Hubbard (1911–86). Its members' basic goal, as established in his 1950 book *Dianetics,* is to free the mind from self-defeating impressions ("engrams") and thus achieve a state of "clear" awareness. Incorporated in 1965 as the Church of Scientology, the movement has a significant international following.

Scopes trial   The so-called monkey trial took place in the Dayton, Tennessee, county courthouse in the summer of 1925. The defendant, schoolteacher John T. Scopes, was accused of violating a state law prohibiting the teaching of evolution in public schools. The clash between his defense attorney, Clarence DARROW, and the chief prosecutor, William Jennings BRYAN, became a lively debate on biblical fundamentalism. Scopes was convicted, but his fine was voided on a technicality. In Stanley Kramer's 1960 film of the trial, *Inherit the Wind,* Darrow and Bryan were played brilliantly by, respectively, Spencer TRACY and Fredric MARCH.

Scott, Dred   See DRED SCOTT DECISION.

Scott, Randolph   (1903–87) Actor. Born Randolph Crane, Scott was a reliable star of B westerns for thirty years. He played Natty BUMPPO in *The Last of the Mohicans* (1936), Wyatt EARP in *Frontier Marshal* (1939), and—for veteran western director Budd Boetticher—the strong, silent hero of *The Tall T* (1957), *Buchanan Rides Alone* (1958), and *Comanche Station* (1960).

Scott, Winfield   (1786–1866) General. "Old Fuss and Feathers" was general in chief of the U.S. Army from 1841 to 1861 and was best known for his success in the MEXICAN WAR. He ran for president unsuccessfully in 1852.

Scottsboro Boys   A celebrated civil rights case of the 1930s. Nine black youngsters, arrested for rape in Alabama in 1931, were convicted, and all but one (who was twelve) were sentenced to death. Supreme Court reviews of the case, sparked by international protests, overturned their convictions on the grounds of racial bias in jury selection and inadequate counsel.

Scrabble   A crossword-puzzle-type game invented in the 1930s by Alfred M. Butts and marketed since the 1950s by Selchow and Righter. Players use "tiles" marked with letters to accumulate points by spelling words on a patterned board. Scrabble is, after MONOPOLY, the best-selling board game in the world.

screwball comedies   Film comedies of the 1930s that featured wacky (or "screwy") characters, fast-paced dialogue, and plots satirizing social and economic conventions. "Screwball" was a baseball term for a type of curve pitch, hence for a person who was similarly "off center." The genre's prince of players was Cary GRANT, its notable directors Frank CAPRA and Howard HAWKS. Examples included IT HAPPENED ONE NIGHT, *My Man Godfrey* (1936), TOPPER, YOU CAN'T TAKE IT WITH YOU, *Bringing Up Baby* (1938), HIS GIRL FRIDAY, and THE PHILADELPHIA STORY.

scrimshaw Carved or engraved whalebone or ivory. A folk art among nineteenth-century whalers, and now a staple of New England tourist shops.

Scruggs, Earl See FLATT AND SCRUGGS.

SDS Students for a Democratic Society. See NEW LEFT.

Sears, Roebuck A retail chain founded in 1893 by Richard Sears (1863–1914) and his partner Alvah Roebuck. The company originally specialized in selling watches, but under Sears's leadership it grew into the nation's largest mail-order house, with the "Sears catalog" offering everything from suits to nuts. Sears retired in 1909, leaving behind a company that would grow into the leading retailer of the twentieth century.

Sears Tower The tallest building in the world. A Chicago landmark erected between 1970 and 1984, it was built to house the world headquarters of the Sears retail company.

Second City Nickname for Chicago. From its long standing as the nation's second most populous city, after New York. (It is now third, behind Los Angeles.)

Seeger, Pete (1919–) Folksinger. The grand old man of the FOLK REVIVAL, Seeger helped to found the leftist Almanac Singers in the 1930s and then the WEAVERS, whose 1950s hits included the ballad "ON TOP OF OLD SMOKEY" and LEADBELLY's signature "GOOD NIGHT IRENE." The son of a musicologist, he was a major force in the preservation of traditional styles; his casual, throaty voice and expert banjo-picking made him a concert favorite for fifty years. Blacklisted as a socialist in the 1950s, he was rediscovered in the 1960s by youthful protesters, who warmed especially to his antiwar anthem "Where Have All the Flowers Gone?" and the hymnlike "Turn Turn Turn." With fellow Weaver Lee Hays he wrote "IF I HAD A HAMMER." He toured both with Woody GUTHRIE and with Guthrie's son Arlo GUTHRIE.

Selznick, David O. (1902–65) Movie producer. Selznick worked for Paramount, RKO, and MGM before becoming an independent producer in 1936. Three years later he supervised his greatest triumph, GONE WITH THE WIND. Selznick was also involved in producing KING KONG, the 1937 version of A STAR IS BORN, and Alfred HITCHCOCK's American debut, the Oscar-winning *Rebecca* (1940).

Seminoles One of the FIVE CIVILIZED TRIBES, the Seminoles settled in the eighteenth century in Florida. They engaged in two wars with the advancing whites (1817–19 and 1835–42), the second of which resulted in their removal to Indian Territory (see TRAIL OF TEARS). Several hundred descendants still live in Florida.

"Semper Fidelis" Latin for "always faithful." (1) An 1888 march by John Philip SOUSA. (2) The motto of the United States Marine Corps. Since the 1980s, seen shortened to "Semper Fi."

Senate See CONGRESS.

Seneca Falls convention (1848) The nation's first women's rights convention, held at Seneca Falls, New York. It adopted a Declaration of Sentiments detailing discrimination against women and called for reforms including WOMEN'S SUFFRAGE.

Sennett, Mack (1880–1960) Director, producer. Canadian-born Michael Sinnott started as an actor under D. W. GRIFFITH, then in 1912 formed his own film company, Keystone, which was to dominate movie slapstick for almost two decades. In addition to developing the company's namesake KEYSTONE KOPS, Sennett also inaugurated the careers of Harry Langdon, Fatty ARBUCKLE, and Charlie CHAPLIN.

"separate but equal" See PLESSY V. FERGUSON.

Sequoyah (ca. 1773–1843) A Cherokee Indian linguist, Sequoyah developed an 86-character syllabary for his native tongue that is a unique example of a transcription system for speech. The *Cherokee Phoenix* newspaper (1828) was written in this system, and the sequoia tree of California was named for its inventor.

Sergeant Preston of the Yukon An adventure series about a Canadian Mountie and his husky companion, Yukon King, the "swiftest and strongest lead dog in the Northwest." Set in the KLONDIKE gold rush period, it was created by the same team—George Trendle and Fran Striker—who had done THE LONE RANGER and THE GREEN HORNET. First on radio (1947–55) and then on television (1955–58), it was known for the doughty hero's exhortation "On, King! On, you huskies!"

Sergeant York See Alvin YORK.

serials Short films produced from the silent era into the 1940s and released in episodes from one week to the next. The earliest serials, many of them westerns or suspense yarns, were known as CLIFF-HANGERS. Later ones featured the derring-do of heroes like THE GREEN HORNET and FLASH GORDON. The 1981 blockbuster *Raiders of the Lost Ark* (see INDIANA JONES) pays homage to the hectic charm of these early thrillers.

Serra, Junipero (1713–84) Missionary. A Franciscan monk, Father Serra was a pioneer in the conversion of California's Indians. He founded the first California mission, San Diego, in 1769. His other settlements—eight in all—stretched as far north as San Francisco.

Service, Robert W. (1874–1958) A Canadian poet, Service earned wide popularity throughout North America for his vigorous doggerel celebrating the KLONDIKE gold rush. His best-known poems were "The Shooting of Dan McGrew" and "The Cremation of Sam McGee," both from his first book, *The Spell of the Yukon* (1907). The opening of the latter poem typifies what a fellow writer called Service's "very good newspaper verse."

> There are strange things done in the midnight sun
>   By the men who moil for gold.
> The Arctic trails have their secret tales
>   That would make your blood run cold.
> The Northern lights have seen queer sights,
>   But the queerest they ever did see
> Was that night on the marge of Lake Lebarge
>   I cremated Sam McGee.

Like Ernest HEMINGWAY, Service drove an ambulance in World War I. His verse recollections of his war experiences, *Rhymes of a Red Cross Man* (1916), topped the American best-seller lists for two years.

Sesame Street   A children's television show that first aired in 1969. Designed as a corrective to the medium's vapidity and violence, it attempts to stimulate its preschool audience with educational though entertaining fare. The Sesame Street of the title is a fictional neighborhood inhabited by real-life and cartoon characters, including the MUPPETS.

Seuss, Dr.   See DR. SEUSS.

Seven Cities of Cíbola   See CÍBOLA.

Seven Little Foys   See FOY FAMILY.

Seven Mules   See FOUR HORSEMEN.

Seven Sisters   A consortium of elite women's colleges established in 1915 to coordinate goals and admissions policies. Generally taken as the female equivalent of the IVY LEAGUE, the group is composed of Mount Holyoke (founded 1836), VASSAR (1861), Wellesley (1870), Smith (1871), Bryn Mawr (1880), Barnard (1889), and Radcliffe (1894).

7-Up   A soft drink introduced in 1929 as "Bib Label Lithiated Lemon Lime Soda." Its citruslike flavor and lack of coloring inspired the 1970s ad slogan "The Uncola." Previous slogans had been "Fresh Up with 7-Up" and "You Like It—It Likes You."

Seventh Cavalry   A U.S. Army regiment. It was George Armstrong CUSTER's outfit at the Battle of the LITTLE BIGHORN.

Seward's Folly   A derisive term for Alaska. From President Andrew Johnson's secretary of state, William Henry Seward (1801–72), who arranged the purchase of the territory from the Russians. Also seen as "Seward's Icebox."

Shadow, The   A long-running (1930–54) radio show about vigilante crime-fighter Lamont Cranston's battles with greed and corruption. As the unseen

Shadow—"a man of wealth, a student of science, and a master of other people's minds"—he devoted his life to "protecting the innocent and punishing the guilty." His eerie calling card, which opened each episode, was a cackling laugh and a knowing leer: "Who knows what evil lurks in the hearts of men? The Shadow knows."

Shakers A millenarian sect founded in England in 1747, led by "Mother" Ann Lee (1736–84) and brought by her to America in 1774. Based first in upstate New York and then in several communities throughout the Midwest, the Shakers believed in celibacy, equality of the sexes, and common property. Renowned for the simple elegance of their furniture, they were called Shakers from the ecstatic movement of their communal services. The most famous of many Shaker hymns, "Simple Gifts," was incorporated into Aaron Copland's *Appalachian Spring*. The movement declined after the Civil War. See also REVIVALISM; UTOPIAN COMMUNITIES.

"Shall We Gather at the River?" A Methodist hymn written in 1864 by Robert Lowry. The imagery is from Ezekiel and Revelation.

> *Yes, we will gather at the river,*
> *The beautiful, the beautiful river;*
> *Gather with the saints at the river*
> *That flows by the throne of God.*

Shane A western (1953) directed by George Stevens. Based on Jack Schaefer's 1949 novel, it cast Alan Ladd as a gunslinger with a heart of gold who protects a community of farmers against cattle barons. A classic morality tale of good versus evil, it romantically reflects the conflict between "sheepmen" and "cowboys" that historically presaged the closing of the frontier.

shanghai To kidnap someone for work on an oceangoing ship, usually after drugging him unconscious. The practice was common in the nineteenth century as a means of securing crews for the China trade; hence the term, from the principal Chinese port. Shanghaiers were also known as crimps, from a seventeenth-century British term for blackguard. Their unsavory work was encouraged by numerous captains, who paid them hefty fees for the hapless personnel. The most famous of BARBARY COAST crimps was "Shanghai" Kelly.

"Share the Wealth" See Huey P. LONG.

Sharp, Zerna See DICK AND JANE.

sharpshooter An expert marksman. From the accuracy of the Sharps buffalo gun, produced in the 1850s by Connecticut gunsmith Christian Sharps (1811–74).

Shays's Rebellion An armed revolt of debtor farmers in western Massachusetts. Led by Revolutionary War veteran Daniel Shays (ca. 1747–1825), it lasted for less than six months (1786–87), but it so shook the confidence of the infant federal government that a Constitutional Convention was called in 1787 to revise or do away with the ARTICLES OF CONFEDERATION.

Shazam! See CAPTAIN MARVEL.

"She Wore a Yellow Ribbon" (1) A traditional U.S. cavalry song dating from about the 1830s. Soldiers' sweethearts wore such ribbons as signs of their devotion. (2) A 1949 western filmed in luscious color in Utah's Monument Valley. The second of John FORD's cavalry trilogy, it stars John WAYNE as an aging frontier officer attempting to forestall an Indian uprising. See also YELLOW RIBBONS.

Shearer, Norma (1900–83) Actress. Born in Montreal, Shearer was billed by her studio, MGM, as the "First Lady of the Screen." Married to, and groomed by, Irving THALBERG, she won an Oscar for her work in *The Divorcee* (1930) and was nominated five other times for the best actress award. Her skill in classical roles showed in her title performances in *Romeo and Juliet* (1936) and *Marie Antoinette* (1938).

Sheik, The (1921) A silent film starring Rudolph VALENTINO as an Arab sheik. It contributed greatly to his image as a mysterious lover and was responsible for a Middle Eastern vogue in design. Valentino's last film was *The Son of the Sheik* (1926).

"She'll Be Comin' Round the Mountain" A parody of an old camp meeting song that was popular with railroad crews in the nineteenth century and then, thanks partly to its humorous sound effects, with schoolchildren. The "she" has been interpreted as a locomotive, its "six white horses" as the engine's power. This explanation, however, fails to explain why she is "wearing pink pajamas" in one verse and is obliged to "sleep with Grandma" in the last.

"Shenandoah" A folk song expressing the singer's longing for a distant love. The verse references are inconsistent, although most versions have the beloved as an Indian maiden. The song was originally an 1820s sea chantey.

Sheridan, Philip (1831–88) General. An effective Union leader in the Civil War, Sheridan helped to drive Lee's army to surrender at APPOMATTOX COURTHOUSE and in the late 1860s commanded frontier troops in the Indian Wars. Known as Little Phil, he was made general in chief of the army for the last four years of his life. See also "THE ONLY GOOD INDIAN IS A DEAD INDIAN."

Sherman, William T. (1820–91) General. At the end of the Civil War, "Sherman" was the most hated name in the South. In 1864, the West Point–trained soldier led Union troops in a devastating attack on the city of ATLANTA and thence on an even more crippling "march to the sea," destroying everything in their path from Atlanta to Savannah. Sherman's thoroughness helped hasten the end of the war and earned him a promotion to head of the army in 1869. When he surrendered that post to Philip SHERIDAN in 1883, Republican Party hacks urged him to run for president. He responded, "If nominated I will not run. If elected I will not serve." See also "WAR IS HELL."

Sherwood, Robert (1896–1955) Playwright. A World War I veteran, Sherwood devoted much of his literary life to attacks on militarism. Two of his four Pulitzer Prizes came for plays with war themes: *Idiot's Delight* (1936; film 1939) and *There Shall Be No Night* (1940). The others were for *Abe Lincoln in Illinois* (1938; film 1940) and a New Deal biography, *Roosevelt and Hopkins* (1948). Sherwood's most enduring popular works were *The Petrified Forest* (see Petrified Forest [2]) and the Oscar-winning screenplay for The Best Years of Our Lives.

shingling the fog   A weather lie told from New England to the Great Plains. The fog is so thick that a man shingling his roof is out past the edge before he sees that he is driving nails into the fog.

Shirelles   Vocal group. One of the earliest doo-wop "girl groups," the Shirelles were New Jersey teenagers who scored rhythm and blues and pop hits in the early 1960s. The biggest were "Will You Love Me Tomorrow?," "Dedicated to the One I Love," "Mama Said," "Baby It's You," and "Soldier Boy."

Shirley Temple   A nonalcoholic drink served to children in adult establishments. Made to resemble a cocktail, it usually consists of 7-Up or ginger ale with a dash of grenadine. Named for the child actress; when served to boys, it is called a Roy Rogers.

shmoo   A creature created by Al Capp in the comic strip Li'l Abner and probably named after the Yiddish *schmo*, for "loser." The shmoo was a roly-poly, eternally smiling figure who gave both milk and eggs, tasted like chicken, and thrived on abuse. Bottom-weighted inflatable toys that spring back when punched are often called shmoos in the creature's honor.

Shoeless Joe   See Black Sox scandal.

Shoemaker, Willie   (1931–) Jockey. The most successful rider in racing history, "the Shoe" won over 200 races his first year out and set a season record of 485 in 1953. His lifetime wins total over 7,000.

"Shoo Fly, Don't Bother Me"   A song by Billy Reeves and Frank Campbell, according to Sigmund Spaeth "the most popular nonsense song of the Civil War." The opening verses announce "Shoo fly, don't bother me," "I belong to Company G," and "I feel like a morning star." Spaeth observes that "there were serious discussions at the time as to whether one could feel like a morning star."

shoofly pie   A Pennsylvania Dutch dessert made with molasses and brown sugar. When pies were set to cool on windowsills, flies had to be "shooed" from their sticky fillings.

"Shortin' Bread"   A traditional black folksong about the miraculous curing powers of "Mammy's" baking.

> *Two little children lying in bed;*
> *One of them sick and one most dead.*
> *Went to the doctor, the doctor said,*
> *Feed them children on shortnin' bread.*

shot heard round the world, the   (1) The first shot of the American Revolution. See Concord. (2) A home run hit by New York Giants batter Bobby

Thomson in the 1951 National League pennant race. Hit in the bottom of the ninth inning, it gave the Giants a 5–4 victory over the Brooklyn Dodgers, sending them into the World Series against the YANKEES. The Giants lost the Series, but the Thomson homer is still cited among baseball buffs as one of the most exciting moments in sports history.

showboat   (1) In the nineteenth century on the Mississippi and other rivers, showboats were large, often steam-propelled vessels that carried actors and other entertainers to isolated communities. The largest of them, the Floating Circus Palace, could seat 3,400 patrons for onboard shows. (2) As *Show Boat*: a novel about such traveling shows written by Edna Ferber in 1926. It inspired a smash Broadway musical, with lyrics by Oscar HAMMERSTEIN II and music by Jerome KERN. Filmed three times, the play included the songs "Bill," "Can't Help Lovin' That Man of Mine," and "OL' MAN RIVER."

Show-Me State   Missouri. From its residents' reputation for incredulity.

Siamese twins   Twins whose bodies are joined by a congenital abnormality. From the first widely known American example, Chang and Eng Bunker (1811–74), for many years attractions at the P. T. BARNUM show.

"Sic semper tyrannis"   Latin for "Thus ever to tyrants." See also John Wilkes BOOTH.

sideburns   Male hairstyle. The temple hair is allowed to grow long, over the cheekbones, without an accompanying beard. Originally called burnsides for their popularizer, Union general Ambrose Burnside (1824–81), they were revived in the 1950s by Elvis PRESLEY.

"Sidewalks of New York, The"   A song written in 1894 by Charles Lawlor and James Blake. It became a Gay Nineties favorite and the theme song for the presidential campaign of New York Governor Al SMITH.

silent generation   A derisive term for the adults of the 1950s, applied to them in retrospect by their children. Allegedly, they were blindly industrious, sexually repressed, and politically complacent—unimaginative paragons of middle-class respectability. See also BABBITT.

silent majority   A Nixon administration catchphrase from 1969, referring to the supposedly overwhelming numbers of American citizens who, by their lack of protest, were tacitly supporting the war in Vietnam. It gradually came to mean the "average American"—one in general agreement with government policies.

Silly Putty   A chemical compound invented in 1945 by engineer James Wright and packaged in plastic eggs as a children's toy. Its chief attraction is its versatility. As well as being broken, molded, and bounced, it can also pick up the ink from newspapers and comics.

Silly Symphonies   A series of DISNEY cartoon shorts in which the animation was synchronized to prerecorded music—a reversal of the technique then in use. The first Silly Symphony cartoon was *The Skeleton Dance* (1929), the most famous one THREE LITTLE PIGS.

silver (1) See "FREE SILVER." (2) Name of the LONE RANGER's horse, a white stallion.

silver bullet The LONE RANGER's signature ammunition.

(Simon, Neil (1927–) Playwright. The author of bright, sophisticated comedies about the middle class, Simon is among the most successful writers in Broadway history. His biggest hits, all turned into major films, include *Barefoot in the Park* (1963), THE ODD COUPLE, *Plaza Suite* (1968), *The Sunshine Boys* (1973), *The Goodbye Girl* (1977), *Brighton Beach Memoirs* (1984), and *Lost in Yonkers* (1991). His 1993 play *Laughter on the Twenty-third Floor* recalls his early days as a sketch writer for Sid CAESAR's *Your Show of Shows.*

Simon and Garfunkel A folk-rock duo that achieved immense success in the 1960s with inventive harmonies and Simon's sensitive lyrics. Childhood friends, Paul Simon (1942–) and Art Garfunkel (1942–) had their first number-one single with "The Sounds of Silence" (1965), a second with "Mrs. Robinson" (1967), a third with "Bridge over Troubled Water" (1970). Their albums placed consistently in the pop charts, with the biggest sellers being *Parsley, Sage, Rosemary, and Thyme* (1966), *Bookends* (1967), and *Bridge Over Troubled Water* (1970). After their breakup in 1971, both singers pursued successful solo careers, with Simon recording several more Top-10 songs. The title song from his album *Graceland* received a best song Grammy in 1988.

Simpson, O. J. (1947–) Football player. Orenthal James Simpson, known as Juice (from "OJ" for orange juice) was a running back for eleven years (1969–79) with the Buffalo Bills. He set a record for most yards gained in a single season (1973) and retired with an 11,236-yard career total. He later appeared in films and as a sports commentator. In 1994, after the stabbing death of his ex-wife, he was arrested and charged with her murder.

Sinatra, Frank (1915–) Singer, actor. No performer between Rudolph VALENTINO and Elvis PRESLEY commanded such a passionate following as New Jersey–born crooner Frank Sinatra. In the 1940s, his honeyed voice and meticulous phrasing made him the darling of millions of swooning coeds, while his radio work with the Tommy Dorsey band (see Jimmy and Tommy DORSEY) made him the most successful male vocalist of the decade. His star status, somewhat diminished by 1950, was revived by his Oscar-winning performance in FROM HERE TO ETERNITY and an Oscar-nominated follow-up in *The Man with the Golden Arm* (1955). By the 1960s, he was a frequent Las Vegas headliner and had graduated from being "Frankie" and "the Voice" to the more mature "Old Blue Eyes" and the "Chairman of the Board." His treatment of SWING MUSIC tunes and TORCH SONGS by "old standard" songsmiths—including George GERSHWIN, Cole PORTER, and Irving BERLIN—set a standard of excellence that has not been surpassed.

In a career encompassing half a century, Sinatra recorded nearly one hundred hit singles. The highlights included "All or Nothing at All" (1943), "Young at Heart" (1954) "All the Way" (1957), "Witchcraft" (1958), "Strangers in the Night" (1966), and "My Way" (1968). He also appeared in over fifty films, including the musicals *On the Town* (1949) and GUYS AND DOLLS (1955) and the Las Vegas caper film *Ocean's Eleven* (1960), in which he shared billing with

Hollywood friends known as the Rat Pack, a group that included Sammy DAVIS, Jr., and Dean Martin (see MARTIN AND LEWIS). His second of several wives was Ava GARDNER. His daughter Nancy was a minor pop star in the 1960s.

Sinclair, Upton   (1878–1968) Writer. Best known as the author of THE JUNGLE, Sinclair expressed his socialist philosophy in dozens of books, including novels about the TEAPOT DOME scandal (*Oil,* 1927) and the SACCO AND VANZETTI CASE (*Boston,* 1928). Proceeds from *The Jungle* enabled him to found a short-lived cooperative community in New Jersey (1907), and he ran for governor of California (1934) on an antipoverty platform. His antifascist novel *Dragon's Teeth* won a 1944 Pulitzer Prize.

Sing Sing   A penitentiary built around 1830 at Sing Sing, New York—a Hudson River community whose name was later changed to Ossining. Its location "up the river" from New York City gave us that slang equivalent for "prison."

Singer, Isaac   (1811–75) Sewing machine manufacturer. A former machinist, Singer patented the first commercially successful sewing machine in 1851. Patent suits from Elias HOWE forced him into a sizable settlement three years later, but his company grew thanks to such business innovations as installment buying, postsales service, trade-in allowances, and advertsising. Singer remains the most recognized name in the sewing machine field.

Singin' in the Rain   (1952) An MGM musical directed by Stanley Donen and Gene KELLY about the transition from silent to sound films. Kelly's dance in the rain to the title song is perhaps the best-known sequence in any musical. The story was based on songs written twenty years earlier by Nacio Herb Brown and the film's producer, Arthur Freed.

singing cowboys   In the 1920s, this term meant COUNTRY MUSIC singers who dressed in western garb to perform cowboy tunes. Some, like Jules Verne Allen ("Lonesome Luke"), had actually been cowboys, although many—including the most influential example, Jimmie RODGERS—had not. In the 1930s, the term came to refer to performers who developed movie careers with the same persona. Of these, the first was RODEO rider Ken Maynard (1895–1973), who sang in the 1930 film *Song of the Caballero.* The most famous, Gene AUTRY, was billed as the "Nation's Number One Singing Cowboy." Tex RITTER and Roy ROGERS copied the Autry model of the hero who, as Bill Malone puts it, "was equally adept with a gun and guitar." Also known as singing cowboys were vocal groups who exploited the cowboy image on stage and screen. The best known was the Sons of the Pioneers (formed in 1933), who sang with Rogers on radio and in films.

singing telegram   The delivery of a telegram by a singing messenger. Introduced in 1933 by a New York City cable company and used chiefly for birthday and other congratulations.

Sioux   A native American people of the Great Plains, traditionally divided into three large groups (Lakota, Dakota, and Nakota) but called jointly Sioux by the French. Buffalo hunters renowned for their horsemanship and valor, they were the chief architects of George Armstrong CUSTER's defeat at the LITTLE BIGHORN and later the hapless victims of the WOUNDED KNEE massacre. The Sioux warrior's colorful costumes, including coup sticks and feather headdresses, made him the archetypal "Indian" in popular culture, and Indian curio shops as far east as New England employ the figure anomalously as an advertising icon. See also CRAZY HORSE; GHOST DANCE; SITTING BULL; SUN DANCE.

sister Like BROTHER, a term of address and reference indicating solidarity. Most often used today by church groups, college sororities, feminists, and young black women. In the 1920s, it was a casual, dismissive term for any woman; it is heard in this sense in 1930s gangster movies. About the same time, a "sob sister" was a woman journalist specialzing in sensational or emotional stories ("sob stories"). Nineteenth-century terms for a timid male included "weak sister," "sissy," and "sissy pants."

Sister Carrie (1900) Theodore DREISER's first novel, a bleak, naturalistic study of a girl forced to sleep her way to success. The theme caused its banning for over a decade.

sitcom Abbreviation for "situation comedy," commercial television's most durable genre. Distantly related to the English comedy of manners, the TV sitcom had more immediate roots in radio, with the comic misadventures of AMOS 'N' ANDY, Jack BENNY, THE GOLDBERGS, and Chester Riley (see LIFE OF RILEY [2]). Until the advent of *All in the Family* (see Archie BUNKER), the genre usually treated domestic misunderstandings in a lighthearted, noncontroversial manner; since then, socially sensitive subjects have become more common. For the longest running sitcoms, see TELEVISION.

Sitting Bull (1831–90) Indian leader. A medicine man of the Hunkpapa SIOUX (part of the Lakota group), Sitting Bull was the elder chief of the Indian resistance that was victorious at the LITTLE BIGHORN. After that battle, he fled to Canada, but returned in the 1880s to tour the country with Buffalo Bill's WILD WEST SHOW. Suspected as a leader of the GHOST DANCE revival, he was arrested in 1890 and killed by police.

60 Minutes A "news magazine" show that first aired in 1968. It covers politics, entertainment, sports, and human interest stories in a breezy but hard-hitting investigative style. Among the top reporters associated with the show have been Dan Rather, Harry Reasoner, and Mike Wallace.

$64,000 Question, The (1955–58) The first big-money television QUIZ SHOW. It offered prizes ranging up to $64,000 for answering questions in diverse fields. It was known for attracting guests with unusual interests, such as the New York shoemaker who won $32,000 for his knowledge of opera and a young psychologist, Joyce Brothers, who was an expert on boxing (she went on to become a popular media personality). The show folded during the quiz-show "rigging" scandal of 1958. See TWENTY-ONE.

Skelton, Red (1913–) Comedian. After starting in radio, Richard Skelton hosted a comedy variety show that lasted on network television for twenty years (1951–71). He was known for his creation of humorous characters such as the speechless tramp Freddie the Freeloader, the country bumpkin Clem Kadiddlehopper, and the "mean widdle kid" who announced his mischief with "I do'd it!"

Skinner, B. F. (1904–90) Psychologist. A pioneer in behavior modification research, Harvard psychologist Burrhus Frederic Skinner developed the reinforcement technique known as operant conditioning. He applied it in his celebrated "Skinner box" for the conditioning of test animals with rewards for learning—such as food dispensed with the pushing of a lever. Skinner's novel *Walden Two* (1948), about a fictional society built on behaviorist principles, became a minor utopian classic in the 1960s.

"Skip to My Lou" A traditional children's tune from the 1840s and used commonly in the nineteenth century as a play-party song. "Lou" is Scottish dialect for "love" or "sweetheart."

skraelings See VINLAND.

skyscraper Multistoried, steel-framed buildings that are the prinicipal American contribution to modern architecture. The tall structures, made possible by the invention of elevators and the use of metal rather than masonry for support, transfigured what are now known as urban skylines. The first skyscraper, the ten-story Home Insurance Building, rose in Chicago in 1883–85. Subsequent landmarks that, when completed, were the tallest structures in the world included Chicago's Masonic Temple Building (1891); New York's American Surety Building (1895), Woolworth Building (1913), Chrysler Building (1930), Empire State Building (1931), and World Trade Center (1973); and the current topper, Chicago's Sears Tower (1974).

Sleepy Hollow See "THE LEGEND OF SLEEPY HOLLOW."

Slick, Grace See JEFFERSON AIRPLANE.

Slick, Sam A prototype of the CONNECTICUT YANKEE, a peddler who takes delight in conning the foolish. He was the creation of Canadian humorist Thomas Haliburton (1796–1865), who introduced him in the newspaper *The Novascotian*. He became known as a Yankee stereotype through books beginning with *The Clockmaker, or The Sayings and Doings of Sam Slick, of Slickville* (1836).

Slinky Brand name for a coiled spring that "walks" down stairs if started at the top. The toy, which has sold in the millions, was invented in the 1940s by engineer Richard James.

Smith, Al (1873–1944) Politician. A four-term reform governor of New York, Smith became the first Roman Catholic ever nominated for president by a major party when he ran for that office as a Democrat in 1928. Proud of his humble background, he used to boast of his "F.F.M. degree," earned while working in New York's Fulton Fish Market. Franklin Roosevelt called him "the happy warrior." See WHISPERING CAMPAIGN.

Smith, Bessie (1894–1937) "Empress of the Blues." Born in Chattanooga, Tennessee, Smith was the most accomplished blues singer of her generation. She sang frequently with jazz musicians (among them Louis ARMSTRONG) and was as well known for her improvisatory skills as for her earthy delivery. She died of injuries sustained in an automobile accident after being refused treatment at an all-white hospital.

Smith, Jed (1799–1831) Mountain man. Jedediah Smith had as good a claim to the title of "Pathfinder" as the man who acquired it, John C. FRÉMONT. An extraordinary trapper who took a record 668 beaver pelts in one season, he opened Wyoming's South Pass through the Rockies and was the first white man to trek from those mountains to California, to cross the Great Salt Lake Desert, and to blaze a West Coast trail from California into Oregon. A pious New Englander described by a companion as "half grizzly and half preacher," Smith was killed by COMANCHE Indians on the Santa Fe Trail.

Smith, John (ca. 1580–1631) Soldier. A restless adventurer who began his career fighting the Turks, Captain John Smith became, in 1609, the man who was chiefly responsible for the survival of JAMESTOWN. As council president that year, he built up defenses, secured food from local Indians, and forced the gold-obsessed colonists to attend to planting with the dictum "He that will not work shall not eat." An avid explorer, he mapped both Virginia and New England and wrote a history of the English settlements. It was there that he told the tale most often associated with him. Captured by POWHATAN's warriors, he said, he was at the exact point of being brained to death when the girl POCAHONTAS threw herself across his body. The rescue is the most famous incident in Virginia history, and it contributed to the belief—quite unfounded—that the "Indian princess" and Smith were later married.

Smith, Joseph (1805–44) Religious patriarch. Smith founded the Church of Jesus Christ of Latter-Day Saints in 1830 and that same year published its basic scripture, *The Book of Mormon*. He headed a steadily growing congregation of believers at various settlements from New York to Illinois until non-Mormon authorities, outraged as much by the sect's prosperity as by its polygamy, had the leader arrested and thrown in jail. He was dragged from there by a lynch mob and shot to death. See MORMONS.

Smith, Kate (1909–86) Singer. A radio singer in the 1930s, Smith hosted both daytime and evening television shows in the 1950s. She was identified with the songs "When the Moon Comes over the Mountain" and "GOD BLESS AMERICA."

Smith, Seba (1792–1868) Writer. A Maine journalist, Smith created the pundit Major Jack Downing, who cast a shrewdly humorous eye on JACKSONIAN DEMOCRACY in various papers throughout the 1830s. Downing was a precursor of such YANKEE rube savants as Sam SLICK and Artemus WARD. Smith himself also wrote "YOUNG CHARLOTTE."

Smith, Snuffy See BARNEY GOOGLE.

Smithsonian Institution A U.S. government institute of learning established in 1846 and made possible by a gift from British scientist James Smithson (1765–1829). The Washington-based Smithsonian, which supports a wide spectrum of research projects and publications, also runs national museums of natural history, history and technology, and art. Its National Air Museum contains the WRIGHT BROTHERS' original biplane as well as Charles LINDBERGH's *Spirit of St. Louis.*

Smokey Bear (1) An advertising symbol of the U.S. Forest Service, a gentle bear dressed in a forest ranger's uniform. After rangers found a bear cub orphaned by a 1945 forest fire in New Mexico, the cartoon bear was created to encourage fire safety. His common refrain is "Remember—only you can prevent forest fires." (2) In CB parlance, a "Smokey" or "Smokey the Bear" is a state patrolman. From the similarity of their hats to those of forest rangers.

Smothers Brothers   Musician comedians Tom (1937–) and Dick (1939–) Smothers hosted an irreverent TV variety show beginning in 1967. Their thinly veiled antiwar stance and their willingness to twit sacred cows forced them off the air in 1969, when CBS replaced them with the safer HEE HAW. The show touted the tongue-in-cheek presidential candidate Pat Paulsen, who announced, quoting William T. SHERMAN, "If nominated I will not run and if elected I will not serve."

Smurfs   Elfin cartoon characters created in 1957 by French artist Pierre Culliford. Beginning in 1981, they became one of the fixtures of Saturday morning children's television and the inspiration for countless dolls and other tie-ins.

snafu (or SNAFU)   A confused situation or mistake. A U.S. service acronym from World War II, it stands for "situation normal, all fucked up" or (in the sanitized version) "situation normal, all fouled up."

"Snap, Crackle, and Pop"   Advertising slogan for the breakfast cereal Rice Krispies. Supposedly mimicking the sound of the cereal in milk, the three words are personified on packaging by miniature bakers.

SNCC   Student Nonviolent Coordinating Committee. Pronounced *snick*. A civil rights organization in the early 1960s. Originally dedicated to voter registration, sit-ins, and freedom rides, SNCC members—under the leadership first of Stokely Carmichael and then of H. "Rap" Brown—eventually broke with the integrationist tactics of Martin Luther KING, Jr., to promote the radical economic separatism of BLACK POWER.

Snead, Sam   (1912–) Golfer. Known for his long drives, "Slammin' Sammy" was one of the finest players of the 1940s and 1950s. He was player of the year in 1949, the top moneymaker in 1949 and 1950, and the Masters winner in 1949, 1952, and 1954.

Snoopy   The most widely recognized member of the *Peanuts* cast, a beagle with both literary and swashbuckling pretensions—the Walter MITTY of the canine set. Snoopy's most common adventures are writing a mystery novel that begins invariably, "It was a dark and stormy night"; and fighting the Red Baron in the skies over war-torn France. Stuffed Snoopy dolls are as popular with American children as the RAGGEDY ANN dolls of former generations. See also PEANUTS (2).

Snow, Hank   (1914–) Singer. Born in Nova Scotia, Clarence E. Snow was a country star of the 1950s. Modeling himself on Jimmie RODGERS, he began as the "Yodeling Ranger" and became the "Singing Ranger" with his success on radio. Snow's biggest hit was the train song "I'm Moving on" (1950). He also wrote and performed the romantic tunes "Brand on My Heart" and "Marriage Vow." He was a regular featured performer on the GRAND OLE OPRY.

Snow White and the Seven Dwarfs (1937) The first animated feature film. Walt Disney adapted the story from the Grimm Brothers' fairy tale and employed hundreds of cartoonists on the project despite snickers that it would be "Disney's Folly." His ambition paid off. The hour-and-a-half cartoon grossed millions in its first of many releases and earned the studio a special Academy Award. The voice of Snow White was supplied by Adriana Caselotti, that of the wicked Queen by Lucille LaVerne. The seven dwarfs were Happy, Grumpy, Sleepy, Sneezy, Bashful, Dopey, and Doc.

"Snowbound" (1886) A nostalgic evocation of rural New England by the poet John Greenleaf Whittier, describing the security of a country home in the dead of winter. It brought him national renown.

Snuffy Smith See Barney Google.

soap operas Episodic melodramas that follow the personal complications of multiple characters' lives through story lines that may last many years. First aired during the 1930s on radio and beginning in the 1950s on daytime television, they are called soap operas, or simply soaps, because the early versions were sponsored by soap companies. Originally seen as housewives' escapism, they have accumulated a huge, diverse audience that follows their intricate plots, both on air and in print synopses, with religious intensity. With the faithful numbering in the tens of millions, soap viewers now have their own superstars, fanzines, and media awards.

   Radio soaps, which soared to popularity during the Great Depression, began in 1930 with *Painted Dreams*. The decade's most successful examples included The Romance of Helen Trent, Stella Dallas, and the first "medical soap," Road of Life. Several 1930s soaps made a successful transition to television. Radio's *Love of Life* (which began on television in 1951) and *Search for Tomorrow* (1951), for example, became among the new medium's most enduring "weepies." Other hardy TV series include *As the World Turns* (1956), *The Edge of Night* (1956), and the longtime medical leader, *General Hospital* (1963). A 1981 *General Hospital* episode depicting the wedding of the characters Luke and Laura Spencer drew the largest daytime audience in television history. Such success led in the 1970s to so-called prime-time soaps such as *Dallas* (see Dallas [2]) and Knots Landing.

soapbox racing Competitive racing of unpowered, homemade vehicles that are drawn by gravity down an inclined track. From their early construction (beginning in the 1930s) out of soapboxes. Contestants, who are eleven to fifteen years old, now usually make their cars out of fiberglass. They compete at the annual Soap Box Derby in Akron, Ohio.

sock hop A party or dance where participants shed their shoes. From the 1950s. The image was memorialized in the Danny and the Juniors song "At the Hop" (1958).

soda jerk One who serves sodas at an ice-cream parlor or soda fountain. An early 1900s term from such a person's pulling on a tap.

Solid South A political term indicating the tendency of the Deep South states, beginning with Reconstruction, to vote solidly Democratic. The pattern was broken in 1928 by anti-Catholic prejudice against Al SMITH (see WHISPERING CAM-PAIGN), in 1952 by Dwight D. EISENHOWER's landslide victory, and by the 1980 "swing to the right" of Ronald REAGAN.

"Solidarity Forever" A pro-union song written to the tune of JOHN BROWN's BODY by Ralph Chaplin of the INDUSTRIAL WORKERS OF THE WORLD. The stirring chorus is three lines of "Solidarity forever" followed by "For the union makes us strong." Music historian John Greenway called it "the greatest song yet produced by American labor."

Some Like it Hot (1959) A film comedy directed by Billy WILDER. It starred Tony Curtis and Jack Lemmon as jazz musicians who, to elude pursuing gangsters, dress as women in a female band. The romantic lead was played by Marilyn MONROE.

Son of Sam The psychotic persona of mass murderer David Berkowitz, who killed six New Yorkers in 1976–77. He believed he was acting on divine instruction, transmitted to him through a neighbor, Sam Carr.

Sondheim, Stephen (1930–) Songwriter. Beginning as a lyricist on WEST SIDE STORY and *Gypsy* (1959), Sondheim turned in the 1960s to writing both words and music. His first Broadway effort was *A Funny Thing Happened to Me on the Way to the Forum* (1962). It was followed by the popular *Company* (1970) and the operettas *A Little Night Music* (1973) and *Sweeney Todd* (1979). Sondheim's best known song, from *Night Music,* is "Send in the Clowns."

"Song of Hiawatha" See HIAWATHA (2).

"Song of Myself" A long ecstatic poem by Walt WHITMAN, the centerpiece of his 1855 LEAVES OF GRASS. It fuses introspection with an expansive catalogue of natural wonders in experimental, modernistic verse. Simultaneously ribald and reverent, particularist and transcendental in its scope, it is a central testament to the poet's vitality.

> *Do I contradict myself?*
> *Very well then I contradict myself,*
> *(I am large, I contain multitudes.)*

Song of the South A 1946 film by Walt DISNEY. Based on the UNCLE REMUS stories, it used an innovative combination of live action and animated figures. The score contained the popular song "Zip-a-Dee-Doo-Dah."

Sons of Liberty Secret organizations of anti-British radicals that flourished in the colonies on the eve of the Revolutionary War. Formed in response to the 1765 STAMP ACT, the groups were strongest in New York and Boston, where they burned stamps and government buildings and intimidated tax collectors. Led in Boston by John HANCOCK and Samuel ADAMS, the Sons were prominent in the 1773 BOSTON TEA PARTY.

Sons of the Pioneers See SINGING COWBOYS.

Sooner A resident of Oklahoma (the Sooner State) or a member of a University of Oklahoma athletic team. When Oklahoma was opened to white settlement on

April 22, 1889, some settlers literally jumped the gun, sneaking into the territory before the official opening. These original "Sooners" gave the state its nickname.

soul A quality of emotional intensity and authenticity attributed by black musicians to each other and also touted generically as an "essence" of blackness. Similar in meaning to the less ethnically marked term "spirit," it may derive distantly from the title of W.E.B. DU BOIS's *The Souls of Black Folk* (1903), although its widespread use dates from the 1960s. In that decade "black pride" led to the use of the terms "soul brother" and "soul sister" for fellow blacks; "soul food" for traditional black cuisine; and "soul music" for the work of many black performers, notably James BROWN, Ray CHARLES, Aretha FRANKLIN, Otis REDDING, Smokey ROBINSON, and the MOTOWN clan. *Soul on Ice* (1968) was a book of essays by BLACK POWER leader Eldridge Cleaver. "Soul City" was an epithet for HARLEM.

Sound of Music, The A musical play (1959) with songs by Richard RODGERS and Oscar HAMMERSTEIN II. Based on the life story of Austria's Trapp Family singers, it had over fourteen hundred Broadway performances. The film version (1965), starring Julie Andrews as Maria Trapp, won Oscars for best picture and best direction (Robert WISE). In addition to the title song, it contains the tunes "Climb Every Mountain," "My Favorite Things," and the round "Do-Re-Mi."

sourdough Bread made from a "starter" portion of dough rather than dry ingredients. Its use among KLONDIKE gold rushers gave us "sourdough" as a synonym for prospector. A specialty to this day of San Francisco.

Sousa, John Philip (1854–1932) The "March King." The nation's premier composer of marching tunes, Sousa conducted the U.S. Marine Band for twelve years (1880–92) and his own band from 1892 until his death. Its concert tours made him world-renowned and laid the foundations of the American concert band. Of his 136 marches, the best known are "Semper Fidelis" (1888), "The Washington Post March" (1889), and "The Stars and Stripes Forever" (1896). Sousa also wrote songs and operettas.

South Pacific A musical play (1949) based on James MICHENER's *Tales of the South Pacific*. It ran for five seasons on Broadway and was made into a 1958 film. Among its Richard RODGERS and Oscar HAMMERSTEIN II songs are "I'm Gonna Wash That Man Right Outa My Hair," "Some Enchanted Evening," and "There Is Nothing like a Dame."

"South shall rise again, The" A stock southern phrase, suggesting the region's resilience after RECONSTRUCTION. It survives in the twentieth century as a semihumorous anti-YANKEE taunt.

southern belle A young, attractive woman from the South. Partly because of Scarlett O'Hara's portrayal (see GONE WITH THE WIND) of the type's duplicity, the term often connotes hyperfemininity and calculated helplessness.

southern fried chicken Chicken pieces dipped in batter and fried. A traditional dish in the southern states, now internationally available through FAST FOOD chains, the most successful of which is Kentucky Fried Chicken. In Texas and other parts of the Southwest, batter-dipped beef is called chicken-fried steak.

southpaw Broadly, a left-handed person. Specifically, a left-handed pitcher. Possibly from the early-twentieth-century custom of laying out baseball diamonds so that the batter faces east—with his eyes away from the afternoon sun. A pitcher facing him would then have his throwing arm to the south.

Spade, Sam See THE MALTESE FALCON.

spaghetti westerns Westerns made by Italian film companies in the 1960s, characterized by minimal dialogue and maximum violence. Director Sergio Leone, who started the trend, made Clint EASTWOOD an international star by casting him as the "Man With No Name" in *A Fistful of Dollars* (1964) and two sequels.

Spam A Hormel Company brand name for a canned, processed meat product that was developed in 1937 and became staple G.I. fare in World War II. The name allegedly comes from sp for "spices" and am for "ham." The subject of frequent gourmet jibes, it is widely sold as a breakfast and luncheon meat, and "Spamorama" cooking contests showcase its versatility.

Spanish-American War (1898) A brief but geopolitically crucial conflict between Spain and the United States. It was precipitated by an 1895 Cuban rebellion against Spanish rule. With American sympathies already with the rebels, William Randolph HEARST and other purveyors of YELLOW JOURNALISM fanned the flames of outrage with stories of Spanish atrocities against both Cubans and Americans. War fever spread when a Spanish minister impugned President McKINLEY's integrity in a letter leaked to Hearst's *Journal* and when the American battleship MAINE exploded in Havana harbor; two months after the tragedy, Congress declared war. The fighting, which lasted less than four months, gave the United States stunning victories at Manila Bay in Spain's Philippines (see George DEWEY) and on rebellious Cuba's own SAN JUAN HILL. The peace treaty signed at Paris in 1899 made Cuba a U.S. protectorate and gave the United States control over the remaining Spanish empire, including the Philippines, Guam, and Puerto Rico. Thus the "splendid little war," as Secretary of State John Hay called it, made the United States an international power.

"Speak softly and carry a big stick" See BIG STICK.

speakeasy An illegal drinking establishment. Probably from customers' sotto voce requests for admittance and possibly related to the English "speak softly shop" for a smugglers' den. From dry Kansas in the 1890s and popularized, often as "speak," during PROHIBITION.

Speaker, Tris (1888–1958) Baseball player. In 1916, the Cleveland Indians' Tristram Speaker broke Ty COBB's nine-year streak to become the American League batting champion. Although he never again took that spot, he was distinguished for hitting consistency throughout his career (1907–28). Playing mainly for Cleveland and Boston, he led the league in doubles eight times and retired with 3,515 total hits. He also established several fielding records.

Spector, Phil (1940–) Rock record producer. Spector pioneered a thick, overdubbed orchestration known as the Wall of Sound. His skill in shaping the musical texture of vocal groups led to multiple hits for the Crystals and the

Ronettes in the early 1960s. He also produced the Ike and Tina Turner classic "River Deep, Mountain High" (1966).

spider in the hairdo From the 1950s, a common rumor or "urban legend." A woman consults a doctor about a headache and discovers that it is caused by a pack of spiders that has nested in her thickly sprayed bouffant. See also PET IN THE OVEN; VANISHING HITCHHIKER.

Spider-Man A cartoon character created in 1962 by Marvel Comics' Stan Lee and Steve Ditko. Peter Parker, transformed by the bite of a radioactive spider into the "Amazing Spider-Man," vanquishes villains with the aid of newly acquired arachnid skills (including wall-climbing) and phenomenal strength. "Spidey" has starred in newspapers, comic books, and films.

Spielberg, Steven (1947–) Film director. Spielberg became known as the boy wonder of Hollywood when he directed the film version of JAWS. That film, the INDIANA JONES trilogy, E.T., and a "living dinosaur" shocker, *Jurassic Park* (1993), gave him the distinction of having directed half of the top ten box-office hits of all time. A master of the adventure and thriller genres, Spielberg also directed the science fiction fantasy *Close Encounters of the Third Kind* (1977) and a study of the Hitlerian Holocaust, *Schindler's List* (1993), which won him Oscars for best picture and best direction.

Spillane, Mickey (1918–) Mystery writer. Spillane carried the tough-guy conventions of the HARD-BOILED FICTION school to sadistic extremes in novels starring detective Mike Hammer. The progenitor for such later vigilante heroes as DIRTY HARRY, Hammer first appeared in *I, the Jury* (1947; film 1953). Other Spillane novels that have sold well (over 5 million copies each) are *My Gun Is Quick* (1950), *Kiss Me, Deadly* (1952), and *Vengeance Is Mine* (1959).

Spirit of St. Louis, The See Charles LINDBERGH.

Spirit of '76, The A painting by Archibald Willard (1836–1918) done on the occasion of the national centennial (1876). It depicts three musicians—a fifer and two drummers—marching through a Revolutionary War battlefield.

spirituals Religious songs that emerged before the Civil War among slaves who fused blues-style melodies with African call-and-response structures and Christian lyrics to create a uniquely African-American musical genre. Many of these songs—also called Negro spirituals, slave songs, and plantation hymns—appeared in an 1867 collection, *Slave Songs of the United States;* they were carried beyond the South in the 1870s by the FISK JUBILEE SINGERS and other choirs. Famous examples include "Roll, Jordan, Roll," "Go Down, Moses," and "Swing Low, Sweet Chariot." Scholars continue to debate the coded political significance of the genre to slaves who may have conflated "Heaven" and "freedom." As popular expressions of black Christianity, the spirituals gradually gave way to GOSPEL MUSIC.

Spitz, Mark (1950–) Swimmer. Spitz dominated the lanes and the headlines at the 1972 summer Olympic Games, bringing home an unprecedented seven gold medals. He was a member of the U.S. freestyle and medley relay teams and also took personal firsts in freestyle and butterfly. Between 1967 and his retirement later in 1972, he set over thirty world records.

"splendid little war, A" The SPANISH-AMERICAN WAR, in the estimation of William McKINLEY's secretary of state, John Hay (1838–1905). Hay was also the architect of the Open Door policy, which paved the way for U.S. trade with China.

Spock (1) "Dr. Spock" was Benjamin Spock, M.D. (1903–) Author of *The Common-Sense Book of Baby and Child Care* (1946), a "spare the rod" guide to child-rearing that has taught understanding of children's needs to three generations of parents and has sold more copies than any book other than the Bible. In the 1960s, he was an anti–Vietnam War activist. (2) "Mr. Spock" was a half-breed Vulcan/Earthling officer on the U.S.S. *Enterprise* of STAR TREK. His surface emotionlessness masked a puckish charm that made him the series's most popular character. He was played by the actor Leonard Nimoy.

spoils system The awarding of government jobs and contracts to those who have helped place a candidate, or a party, in power. The custom is as old as politics itself, but is identified particularly with Andrew JACKSON's administration. See "TO THE VICTOR BELONG THE SPOILS."

Spoon River Anthology (1915) A collection of poems by midwesterner Edgar Lee Masters (1869–1950). The verses, presented as posthumous monologues by "Spoon River" residents, revealed the narrow complacency of small-town life.

"Springfield Mountain" A mournful ballad of the 1760s about a Massachusetts youth who dies after being bitten by a snake and who is followed by his lover after she tries to suck the poison out. Its sentimentality made it a favorite among parodists.

Springsteen, Bruce (1949–) Singer, songwriter. Born in New Jersey, Springsteen became the ROCK MUSIC success story of the 1970s with his driving, passionate songs about blue-collar angst. Originally billed as the new Bob DYLAN, he developed such a following with his stage presence that he was transformed into "the Boss," the quintessential rocker. His biggest hits have been "Born to Run," "Hungry Heart," "Born in the U.S.A.," and "Streets of Philadelphia," which won an Oscar as part of the soundtrack of *Philadelphia* (1993).

Squanto A Pawtuxet Indian whose abduction by English sailors was to prove an incomparable boon to the PILGRIMS. Having learned English while in captivity abroad (ca. 1605–18), Squanto fortuitously returned to his New England home two years before the Pilgrims' landing. He served them as translator and also assisted them in fishing and the planting of corn. Plymouth historian William Bradford called him "a special instrument sent of God," and his death in 1622 was mourned throughout the colony.

square Conventional, unimaginative, "straight." Originally a black musicians' term, it was picked up in the 1950s by rebellious teens. Used both as an adjective and as a substantive, as in "The squares don't dig it." "Squaresville" was any place inhabited by squares.

square dance   A folk dance form in which four couples, arranged in an open square, perform designated steps to the instructions of a "caller." Popular since colonial times, square dancing is now preserved by "old-timey" dance groups, many of whom also perform "contra" dances, where the couples face each other in parallel lines.

Square Deal   Theodore ROOSEVELT's term for the reform program he offered voters during the 1904 presidential election. "If elected I shall see to it that every man has a square deal, no more and no less."

stage-door Johnny   See JOHN.

stagecoach   (1) A four-wheeled, horse-drawn vehicle that carried mail, freight, and passengers from the colonial period until the burgeoning of railroads in the nineteenth century. Stagecoaches, or "stages," were the principal public transport in the American West. They figure in countless western movies, including (2) *Stagecoach,* a 1939 film directed by John FORD. It features a chase by Indians through Utah's Monument Valley and was the movie that brought stardom to John WAYNE. Thomas Mitchell won an Oscar for his drunken-doctor role.

Stagg, Amos Alonzo   (1862–1965) Football coach. A star end at Yale under Walter CAMP, Stagg coached the University of Chicago team for over forty years (1892–1933), during which they won six Big Ten titles and had five undefeated seasons. He then coached at smaller colleges into his eighties, becoming known as the Grand Old Man of Football. He is credited with introducing the end run, the hidden ball play, the tackling dummy, varsity letters, and cheerleading.

Stagolee   A famous bad man of African-American oral tradition. Boastful, lustful, pugnacious, and yet possessed of enormous charm and comic bravado, he typifies the social ambivalence of the so-called bad nigger. The hero of numerous ballads and tall tales, he was also celebrated in the 1959 popular song "Stagger Lee," by New Orleans rhythm and blues singer Lloyd Price. Also seen as "Stackolee" and "Stack."

Stallone, Sylvester   (1946–   ) Writer, actor, and director who created two memorable American types: John RAMBO and ROCKY Balboa.

Stamp Act   A British revenue measure imposed on the American colonies in 1765 to help pay the debt incurred by the FRENCH AND INDIAN WAR. It required government stamps to be affixed to many printed documents, and was so unpopular that Parliament repealed it within a year—but not before it had swelled the ranks of the SONS OF LIBERTY and greatly intensified colonial resentment at British authority.

"Stand By Your Man"   See Tammy WYNETTE.

Standish, Miles   (ca. 1584–1656) The military leader of New England's PLYMOUTH COLONY, Standish is remembered chiefly as the spurned suitor of Longfellow's romance "THE COURTSHIP OF MILES STANDISH." His supposed affection for Priscilla Mullins was a poetic invention, but his contributions were real enough. As soldier and interpreter to the local Indians, he secured the colony's safety in its fledgling years.

Stanford, Leland (1824–93) Railroad executive. Stanford founded the Central Pacific Railroad in 1861, served as its first president, and supervised the "joining of the rails" in 1869 when his company's tracks met those of the Union Pacific (see GOLDEN SPIKE CEREMONY). Briefly governor of California, he served as the state's senator from 1885 until his death. He also founded (and funded) Stanford University.

Stanton, Elizabeth Cady (1815–1902) Women's rights advocate. The wife of a prominent ABOLITIONIST who deleted the word "obey" from her wedding vows. Stanton organized the SENECA FALLS CONVENTION, fought tirelessly for women's voting and property rights, and served as first president of the National Woman Suffrage Association. She also mothered a six-volume history of women's suffrage and seven children.

Stanwyck, Barbara (1907–90) Actress. A former ZIEGFELD FOLLIES chorus girl, Brooklyn-born Ruby Stevens became one of the hottest stars of the 1940s. Her skill at portraying winningly assertive, no-nonsense women won her four Academy Award nominations: for STELLA DALLAS, *Ball of Fire* (1942), *Double Indemnity* (1944), and *Sorry, Wrong Number* (1948). From 1965 to 1969, she played matriarch Victoria Barkley on the TV western *Big Valley*.

"Star Dust" A song written in 1927 by Hoagy CARMICHAEL, with words added two years later by Mitchell Parish. It has been recorded in hundreds of versions and was especially popular in the Big Band era. Artie Shaw's recording sold 2 million copies alone, and it also appeared in a unique two-sided format, with Tommy Dorsey's band on one side (see Jimmy and Tommy DORSEY) and Benny GOODMAN's on the other.

Star Is Born, A The title of three Hollywood movies about the personal dramas beneath the veneer of celebrity. The skeletal story is that of a fading star who promotes a young woman's career, marries her, and commits suicide. All three films derived ultimately from a 1932 movie, *What Price Hollywood?* The first, made by William WELLMAN in 1937, starred Fredric MARCH and Janet Gaynor. The second and most famous version, directed in 1954 by George CUKOR, starred James Mason and Judy GARLAND; it was distinguished by her rendition of the Harold ARLEN torch song "The Man That Got Away" and by her Oscar-nominated performance. A third, rock music version (1976) starred singers Kris Kristofferson and Barbra STREISAND.

"Star-Spangled Banner, The" (1814) The national anthem of the United States. The words were written by Washington lawyer Francis Scott Key (1779–1843) to the music of an English drinking song, "To Anacreon in Heaven." Key was inspired by the sight of an American flag (the "star-spangled banner"), still flying after a night bombardment of FORT MCHENRY by British forces during the WAR OF 1812. The song was adopted by Congress as the national anthem in 1931. Its first verse, sung before baseball games and other sporting events, is as follows:

Oh say can you see by the dawn's early light
What so proudly we hailed at the twilight's last gleaming?
Whose broad stripes and bright stars through the perilous fight

O'er the ramparts we watched were so gallantly streaming?
And the rockets' red glare, the bombs bursting in air
Gave proof through the night that our flag was still there.
Oh say does that star-spangled banner yet wave
O'er the land of the free and the home of the brave?

Star Trek A science fiction series that enjoyed modest success on television from 1965 to 1969 but became a cult smash among "Trekkies" in 1970s reruns. It starred William Shatner as Captain James Kirk, commander of the twenty-third-century starship *Enterprise;* Leonard Nimoy as his deadpan Vulcan colleague, Mr. Spock (see SPOCK [2]); and DeForest Kelley as the ship's doctor, "Bones" McCoy. Growing interest in the crew's galactic adventures inspired *Star Trek: The Movie* in 1979, three sequels, a second TV series (1987–94), and a vast sales, convention, and trading network for Star Trek paraphernalia. See "BEAM ME UP, SCOTTY."

Star Wars (1) The first film (1977) of a proposed nine-film cycle developed and directed by George Lucas (1945–). Its enormous success led to the sequels *The Empire Strikes Back* (1980) and *Return of the Jedi* (1983), constituting a trilogy that has brought Lucas and his company, Lucasfilms, earnings in excess of half a billion dollars. The Star Wars films, set in "a galaxy far, far away," are space epics with densely mythological textures and Oscar-winning special effects. They have made household names of "Jedi Knight" Luke Skywalker (played by Mark Hamill), his sister Princess Leia (Carrie Fisher), daredevil rocket jockey Han Solo (Harrison Ford), aging Jedi Obi-Wan-Kenobi (Alec Guinness), the humanlike robots R2D2 and C3PO, and the faceless, ominous villain, Darth Vader. The films' action turns frequently on Luke's wavering ability to harness the good aspect (rather than "dark side") of a universal Force; hence the stock expression "May the Force be with you." (2) A derisive term for Strategic Defense Initiative (SDI), a high-tech, orbital missile-defense system pushed unsuccessfully by the Ronald REAGAN administration.

Starr, Belle (1848–89) Outlaw. Transformed by dime novelists into the West's notorious "Bandit Queen," Starr was a Missouri-born renegade who practiced sundry varieties of thievery first with the Jesse JAMES gang, then with lesser stalwarts in Texas and Oklahoma. She survived a short prison term imposed on her by "Hanging" PARKER in 1883, but returned to her customary activities upon her release. She was shot by an unknown assassin in 1889.

Stars and Bars The Confederate battle flag. The design was a red field with a white St. Andrew's cross, a blue one superimposed on it, and a cross of white stars on top of that. Also known as the Rebel flag.

Stars and Stripes (1) The United States flag. The term dates from the REVOLUTIONARY WAR period and was the inspiration for John Philip SOUSA's march "The Stars and Stripes Forever" (1896). (2) A U.S. armed services newspaper, popular in World War II as the vehicle for Bill MAULDIN's cartoons.

Stars Fell on Alabama The title of (1) a popular song by Mitchell Parish and Frank Perkins and (2) a book on Alabama folklore by Carl Carmer, both published in 1934. The Carmer book reported the folk belief that the state's alleged aura of dark mystery could be traced to a meteor shower. There had been major showers visible there in 1833 and 1867.

state nicknames The rationale behind many state nicknames is obvious: They reflect distinctive natural resources. Others, such as Arkansas's "Land of Opportunity," are booster labels. The following list explains some of the terms that are not self-evident.

Alabama	Yellowhammer
Alaska	Land of the Midnight Sun
Arizona	GRAND CANYON
Arkansas	Land of Opportunity
California	Golden (see GOLD RUSHES)
Colorado	Centennial (from 1876 admission to the Union)
Connecticut	Nutmeg
Delaware	First (from 1787 ratification of the Constitution)
Florida	Sunshine
Georgia	Peach; Empire State of the South
Hawaii	ALOHA
Idaho	Gem; Spud; Panhandle
Illinois	Prairie; Land of Lincoln
Indiana	HOOSIER
Iowa	Hawkeye
Kansas	Sunflower; Jayhawk (see JAYHAWKER)
Kentucky	BLUEGRASS
Louisiana	Pelican; CREOLE; Sportsman's Paradise
Maine	Pine Tree
Maryland	Free; Old Line
Massachusetts	Bay
Michigan	Wolverine
Minnesota	North Star; Gopher; Land of 1000 Lakes
Mississippi	Magnolia
Missouri	SHOW-ME
Montana	Treasure
Nebraska	Cornhusker
Nevada	Sagebrush; Silver
New Hampshire	Granite
New Jersey	Garden
New Mexico	Land of Enchantment
New York	Empire
North Carolina	TARHEEL
North Dakota	SIOUX; Flickertail
Ohio	Buckeye
Oklahoma	SOONER
Oregon	BEAVER
Pennsylvania	Keystone
Rhode Island	Ocean
South Carolina	Palmetto
South Dakota	Sunshine; COYOTE
Tennessee	Volunteer
Texas	LONE STAR

Utah	Beehive
Vermont	Green Mountain
Virginia	Old Dominion
Washington	Evergreen; Chinook
West Virginia	Mountain
Wisconsin	Badger
Wyoming	Equality (from 1869 women's suffrage law)

states' rights (1) The rights of the individual states of the United States as distinct from those of the federal government. Hence (2) the political viewpoint that resists centralized government in favor of local control. Architects of the U.S. states' rights philosophy included James MADISON and Thomas JEFFERSON. It was used in the 1880s to defend slavery and opposed in the 1950s by members of the CIVIL RIGHTS MOVEMENT who saw it as a southern euphemism for segregation.

Statue of Liberty A large, copper-sheathed statue in New York Harbor designed by French sculptor Frédéric Bartholdi (1834–1904) and presented to the American people by the French as an emblem of Franco-American unity. Unveiled in 1886, it became a symbol of American freedom to European immigrants, who passed it on their way to ELLIS ISLAND. An Emma LAZARUS poem inscribed on its pedestal added to its power as a national icon. The figure—a woman holding a book and a torch—is often called Miss Liberty. Bartholdi's title was *Liberty Enlightening the World.*

Staubach, Roger (1942–   ) Football player. As quarterback of the Dallas Cowboys in the 1970s, Staubach led them to four conference championships and two SUPER BOWL victories (1972 and 1978). In his eleven-year career, he threw for 22,700 yards and completed 153 touchdown passes.

"Steal Away" A nineteenth-century SPIRITUAL, also called "Steal Away to Jesus." Important in the folklore of the UNDERGROUND RAILROAD because Harriet TUBMAN was said to have used it as a signal to slaves awaiting her help to escape.

Steamboat Willie (1928) The first sound cartoon. It starred MICKEY MOUSE, who had just been created by Walt DISNEY and his chief animator, Ub Iwerks. Disney himself provided the characters' voices.

steamboats Although Europeans experimented with steamboats as early as the 1780s, the first commercially practical model was Robert Fulton's CLERMONT, built in 1807 for the Hudson River. Its success heralded the end of the KEELBOAT (and, in the long run, of the CLIPPER SHIP) while inaugurating the era of the Mississippi River paddle wheelers recalled vividly by Mark TWAIN in *Life on the Mississippi* (1883). These large, flat-bottomed vessels were the principal form of river transportation, both freight and passenger, in the mid-nineteenth century, their heyday giving rise to numerous legends about somnambulist pilots and oily onboard gamblers. In spite of bans against it, racing was common. When the *Robert E. Lee* beat the *Natchez* in a New Orleans to St. Louis race in 1870, their progress was telegraphed to bettors around the world. See also SHOWBOAT.

Steffens, Lincoln (1866–1936) Journalist. One of the principal MUCKRAKERS, Steffens was managing editor of *McClure's* magazine (1901–6), where he published exposés of municipal corruption. The most famous of them in book form was *The Shame of the Cities* (1904). Strongly affected by the possibility of socialist reform, he returned from a 1919 trip from the new Soviet Union with the famous encomium "I have seen the future and it works."

Steichen, Edward   (1879–1983) Photographer. Working with Alfred STIEGLITZ on the Photo-Secession journal *Camera Work,* Steichen was a principal force in the acceptance of photography as a fine art. After mastering the soft-focus techniques admired by the Stieglitz circle, he did fashion work for VOGUE and VANITY FAIR in the 1920s and 1930s, and for fifteen years (1947–62) headed the New York Museum of Modern Art's photography section. The museum's Family of Man exhibit, which he organized in 1955, was the most widely seen photography show (and coffee-table book) of the decade.

Steiger, Rod   (1925–   ) Actor. Steiger's training at the Actors' Studio in New York made him an accomplished method actor (see METHOD ACTING). After a live television triumph in MARTY, he won Academy Award nominations for his work in ON THE WATERFRONT and *The Pawnbroker* (1965), finally winning for IN THE HEAT OF THE NIGHT (1967), where he played a small-town southern sheriff struggling with racism. He took the title roles of the Chicago gangster in *Al Capone* (1959) and the screen comedian in *W.C. Fields and Me* (1976).

Stein, Gertrude   (1874–1946) Writer. Born in Pennsylvania and educated at Radcliffe, the independently wealthy Stein became a permanent expatriate in 1903, establishing a literary salon on Paris's Left Bank. There she amassed a famous art collection; entertained the likes of Pablo Picasso, Ernest HEMINGWAY, and F. Scott FITZGERALD; and wrote elliptical, experimental works that fit Mark TWAIN's definition of a classic: "a work that everyone admires and nobody reads." These include the novel *The Making of Americans* (1906–8), the opera libretto *Four Saints in Three Acts* (1929), and her most accessible work, *The Autobiography of Alice B. Toklas* (1933), a memoir written in the voice of her longtime companion. To the public at large, Stein remains the doyenne of enigma, known for two famous toss-off lines: "You are all a LOST GENERATION" and "Rose is a rose is a rose is a rose." The latter appeared in "Sacred Emily" (1922), which also contained the similarly deathless nuggets "It is rose in hen" and "which is pretty which is pretty which is pretty."

Steinbeck, John   (1902–68) Writer. Winner of the 1962 Nobel Prize and of a Pulitzer for his 1940 novel THE GRAPES OF WRATH, Steinbeck wrote sympathetically about the working poor of his native California. He achieved his first success with *Tortilla Flat* (1935), about a band of Mexican-American outcasts. It was followed by OF MICE AND MEN, and a story collection, *The Long Valley* (1938), which contained his classic tale "The Red Pony." Steinbeck worked as a war correspondent in World War II, then returned to his familiar terrain in *Cannery Row* (1945), about California fish-packers; and *The Pearl* (1947), about a pearl that brings a Mexican family misfortune. Of his later works, the best remembered are EAST OF EDEN and *Travels with Charley* (1962), a memoir of a cross-country truck tour.

Stella Dallas   One of the great "weepies" of American culture, *Stella Dallas* was a 1923 novel by Olive Higgins Prouty about the sacrifices of a working-class mother for her daughter. A best-seller as a book, it was made into a 1937 movie that earned Barbara STANWYCK, as the mother, an Oscar nomination. The movie's success that year inspired a radio SOAP OPERA that ran until 1955.

Stengel, Casey   (1890–1975) Baseball manager. The "Old Professor," Charles Stengel played the outfield for over a decade (1912–25) and managed four teams, but gained fame as the crusty headman of the New York YANKEES. In twelve years (1949–60) as their manager, he brought them to ten American League pennants and seven World Series titles while delighting the public with quasi-grammatical quips that became known as examples of "Stengelese." His best-known press conference line, used as the title of a 1979 biography, was "You could look it up." His nickname came from the initials of his hometown, Kansas City, Missouri.

Sternberg, Josef von   (1894–1969) Film director. Sternberg discovered Marlene DIETRICH in a Berlin theater, directed her in *The Blue Angel* (1930), then brought her to Hollywood, where he cast her in six more films. It was this sextet, including *Blonde Venus* (1932) and *The Devil Is a Woman* (1935), that established the mystique of the German star as a femme fatale. The director's fondness for soft focus, veils, and shadows give his pictures a "Sternbergesque" expressionist aura.

stetson   Common name for a broad-brimmed, high-peaked hat, the typical "cowboy hat" of western movies. John B. Stetson (1830–1905) was a Philadelphia hatmaker who produced a broad line of men's headgear with a western flair. Those with outsize crowns were sometimes called, hyperbolically, ten-gallon hats.

Stewart, James   (1908–   ) Actor. Distinguished by his nasal Hoosier drawl and shambling charisma, Stewart was a major star for forty years. Probably best known for his tongue-in-cheek comic roles, he won an Oscar as an engaging drunk in THE PHILADELPHIA STORY and was nominated for his work in four other films: MR. SMITH GOES TO WASHINGTON, IT'S A WONDERFUL LIFE, HARVEY, and *Anatomy of a Murder* (1959). His historical roles included those of Glenn MILLER in *The Glenn Miller Story* (1954), Charles LINDBERGH in *The Spirit of St. Louis* (1957), and Wyatt EARP in John FORD's *Cheyenne Autumn* (1964). Alfred HITCHCOCK starred him in *Rear Window* (1954) and *Vertigo* (1958), and he gave the best of many western performances in *Destry Rides Again* (1939), *Bend of the River* (1952), and *The Man Who Shot Liberty Valance* (1962).

Stieglitz, Alfred   (1864–1946) Photographer. The chief proponent of "art photography" in the twentieth century, Stieglitz edited the journal *Camera Notes* (1897–1902) and its successor *Camera Work* (1903–17), using them to promote the pictorialist masters Edward STEICHEN, Gertrude Käsebier, and Clarence White. As the manager of several New York galleries, he showed not only Photo-Secession pictures but also the work of European avant-garde artists and of such "straight" photographers as Ansel ADAMS. Stieglitz's own work ranged from pictorialist studies of New York immigrants to photographs of clouds that he considered psychological "equivalents." He was married to the painter Georgia O'KEEFE.

stogie   See CONESTOGA.

Stone, Irving   (1903–89) Novelist. Stone writes best-selling fictionalizations of famous lives. His 1961 book on Michelangelo, *The Agony and the Ecstasy,* sold close to 3 million copies and inspired a 1965 movie with Charlton HESTON as the artist. Stone has also done "biographical novels" on Clarence DARROW, Eugene V. DEBS, and Jack LONDON.

Stone, Lucy   (1818–93) Abolitionist, women's rights advocate. Stone was co-founder, with Julia Ward HOWE, of the American Woman Suffrage Association. Known for her oratory, she married a fellow abolitionist, Henry Blackwell, in 1855. Her refusal to adopt his name inspired the expression "Lucy Stoner" for any woman so disinclined.

Stooges, Three   See THREE STOOGES.

Stormalong   See OLD STORMALONG.

"Stormy Weather"   (1) A 1933 romantic ballad by Ted Koehler and Harold ARLEN. It became a theme song for both Lena HORNE and Ethel WATERS. Horne sang it in (2) *Stormy Weather,* a 1943 musical that also included performances by Fats WALLER and Dooley WILSON.

Storyville   A section of New Orleans, rich in brothels and honky-tonks, where Jelly Roll MORTON and others created JAZZ. Its main artery was world-famous Basin Street.

Stout, Rex   (1886–1975) Mystery writer. Stout created the character of Nero Wolfe, a rotund, beer-loving sleuth whose mind is just as taut as his frame is flaccid. Working from a New York brownstone that he never leaves, Wolfe relies on a wisecracking legman, Archie Goodwin, for the clues he uses to beat the police to solutions. Wolfe made his debut in *Fer-de-Lance* (1934) and subsequently appeared in nearly fifty other novels.

Stowe, Harriet Beecher   (1811–96) The author of UNCLE TOM'S CABIN. She came from a staunch antislavery family, her father and two brothers being noted abolitionists. Born in Connecticut, she based her famous book on a long residence in Ohio (just across the river from slaveholding Kentucky), where she lived with her husband, Calvin Stowe, a biblical scholar. Two of her later novels—*The Minister's Wooing* (1859) and *Oldtown Folks* (1869)—are set in her native New England.

Strasberg, Lee   (1901–82) Actor, director. The Austrian-born Strasberg helped to found the leftist Group Theater in 1931 and the Actors Studio in 1947. As artistic director of the latter and of its successor, the Strasberg Institute of the Theater, he trained three generations of performers in METHOD ACTING. Among those whom he influenced were Marlon BRANDO, James DEAN, and Rod STEIGER.

Stratemeyer, Edward   (1863–1930) Writer. Under various pen names, Stratemeyer produced perhaps 150 juvenile novels between the turn of the century and his death. As Arthur Winfield, he wrote twenty books (1899–1917) about the prep school and college adventures of the Rover Boys, as well as forty volumes on a youthful inventor, Tom Swift. He was also the "Laura Lee Hope" behind the BOBBSEY TWINS and the founder (1906) of the Stratemeyer Syndicate, which produced the HARDY BOYS and NANCY DREW series.

Strauss, Levi   See BLUE JEANS.

Streetcar Named Desire, A   A 1947 play by Tennessee WILLIAMS. It concerns the conflict between a self-deluding SOUTHERN BELLE, Blanche Du Bois, and her aggressively vulgar brother-in-law, Stanley Kowalski. The play's mature themes (including nymphomania and rape), coupled with Marlon BRANDO's riveting performance as Kowalski, made it a popular Broadway shocker. The play's director, Elia KAZAN, brought it to the screen four years later, and it nearly swept the 1951 acting Oscars, with awards going to Vivien Leigh (as Blanche), Karl Malden, and Kim Hunter. Brando's screen Kowalski earned him a best actor nomination, but he lost the award to Humphrey BOGART (for THE AFRICAN QUEEN).

"Streets of Laredo, The"   See "THE COWBOY'S LAMENT."

Streisand, Barbra   (1942–) Singer, actress, director. Streisand became a Broadway sensation in 1964 as Fanny BRICE in the title role of *Funny Girl*; a film version made in 1968 earned her an Academy Award. Her exuberance and searing vocals made her simultaneously one of the decade's top singers, enormously successful in recordings and live performances. Streisand has also acted in the films HELLO, DOLLY!, *The Way We Were* (1973), and A STAR IS BORN (1976), winning a second Oscar for writing its theme, "Evergreen." She turned to film direction in the 1980s, earning acclaim for *The Prince of Tides* (1991).

Stroheim, Erich von   (1885–1957) Actor, director. Stroheim made his reputation in silent films playing stiff-necked Prussian military types—roles that made him known as the Man You Love to Hate. His directing skills showed to good effect in *Blind Husbands* (1919) and other dark romances, but those skills did not include frugality, and he was embroiled for years with studio executives who saw his subsequent scenarios as budget-breaking fiascos. His most famous film, the endless *Greed* (1923), was drastically cut by others once the print was in, while the almost equally elaborate *Queen Kelly* (1928) signaled the end of his directorial career. He made a famous appearance as former director Max von Mayerling in Billy WILDER's somber SUNSET BOULEVARD.

Stuart, Gilbert   (1755–1828). Portraitist. A student of Benjamin WEST, Stuart did likenesses of the first five American presidents and is best known for three studies of George Washington. One of them, commissioned by Martha Washington around 1796, is reproduced on the U.S. dollar bill.

Stuart, Jeb   (1833–64) Confederate officer. The South's most brilliant cavalry leader, James Ewell Brown (J.E.B.) Stuart was expert at conducting long-range intelligence raids behind enemy lines. The facility backfired during the Battle of GETTYSBURG, when his information reached Robert E. Lee too late to be useful. Stuart was killed at the Battle of Yellow Tavern.

Student Nonviolent Coordinating Committee See SNCC.

Studs Lonigan Popular term for a trilogy of novels by James T. Farrell (1904–79) about a young man, William "Studs" Lonigan, in the tough, violent milieu of blue-collar Chicago. The novels were *Young Lonigan* (1932), *The Young Manhood of Studs Lonigan* (1934), and *Judgment Day* (1935).

Sturges, Preston (1898–1959) Writer, director. After writing successful plays and screenplays, Sturges had a brief though brilliant career as a director of fast-paced satires. *The Great McGinty* (1940) looks at the lives of the unemployed. *The Lady Eve* (1941) and *The Miracle of Morgan's Creek* (1944) are sparkling comedies of the sexes. *Sullivan's Travels* (1941), his best-known work, is a trenchant fantasy about a Hollywood director who is wrongly imprisoned on a CHAIN GANG.

Stuyvesant, Peter (1610–72) Governor of New Netherland, which later became New York. Known for his silver-adorned peg leg (he had lost a leg in battle) and his autocratic temper, he imposed taxes, befriended the Indians, and encouraged trade. More effective than popular, he was forced to surrender the colony to the English in 1664 when the good burghers he had offended refused to fight.

Styne, Jule (1905–) Composer. Born in London, Styne went to Hollywood in the 1930s, where he was a voice coach for, among others, Shirley TEMPLE. With lyricist Sammy CAHN he wrote "I've Heard That Song Before" (1942) and the Oscar-winning title song from THREE COINS IN THE FOUNTAIN. He also did the music for the Broadway plays GENTLEMEN PREFER BLONDES, *Gypsy* (1959), and *Funny Girl* (1964).

Styron, William (1924–) Novelist. Styron's fictionalized treatment of the Nat TURNER rebellion, *The Autobiography of Nat Turner* (1967), earned him a Pulitzer Prize. He also wrote two disturbing novels about domestic tragedy, *Lie Down in Darkness* (1951) and *Sophie's Choice* (1979).

suffragettes Women who fought for the right to vote. Although the struggle for WOMEN'S SUFFRAGE dates at least from the 1848 SENECA FALLS CONVENTION, the term "suffragette" first emerged in the 1900s, when it meant the followers of British leader Emmeline Pankhurst.

Sullivan, Ed (1902–74) Television host. A former news reporter and radio emcee, Sullivan dominated Sunday night television for two decades (1948–71) with a variety show entitled first *Toast of the Town* and, after 1955, *The Ed Sullivan Show*. With a fare ranging from the sublime to the idiotic, it introduced the American viewing public to such durable stars as MARTIN AND LEWIS, Lena HORNE, and the Beatles as well as nine-day novelties like ventriloquist "Señor Wences," one of whose "dummies" was concealed in a tiny box. The host himself was the butt of endless joking, not only for his dour, stoop-shouldered appearance but also for delivering, week after week, an opening promise of a "reealy big shew."

Sullivan, John L. (1858–1918) Boxer. Last of the great bare-knuckle fighters, "John L" (also called the Boston Strong Boy) became heavyweight champion in

1882 by knocking out title-holder Paddy Ryan. Seven years later, he made the last bare-knuckle defense of his crown in a 75-round bout against Jake Kilrain. He lost the title to Gentleman Jim CORBETT in 1892. Sullivan was portrayed with great dignity by Ward Bond in the film *Gentleman Jim* (1942).

Sullivan, Louis (1856–1924) Architect. A pioneer of the famed "Chicago school," Sullivan worked with the firm of William Le Baron Jenney, which designed the Home Insurance Building (see SKYSCRAPER); built the Wainwright Building (1890–91) in St. Louis; and produced other buildings that imaginatively fused modern angularity with his characteristic curvilinear ornamentation. Sullivan's dictum "Form follows function" was adopted as a credo by the succeeding generation, including his most famous disciple, Frank Lloyd WRIGHT.

Sultan of Swat Nickname of Babe RUTH.

Summer of Love The summer of 1967, when HIPPIES in San Francisco's HAIGHT-ASHBURY district first garnered wide media attention. Press coverage stressed the pacific aspects of the drug COUNTERCULTURE, including participants' penchant for "love-ins" and "flower power."

"Summertime" The most famous song from the 1935 "folk opera" PORGY AND BESS. An instant classic, it was subsequently performed by everyone from BIG BAND chanteuses to Janis JOPLIN.

> *Summertime, and the living is easy;*
> *Fish are jumping, and the cotton is high.*
> *Your daddy's rich and your mama's good looking,*
> *So hush, little baby, don't you cry.*

Sumter, Fort See FORT SUMTER.

Sun Also Rises, The (1926) Ernest HEMINGWAY's first novel, a picture of doomed romance among American expatriates. The book's epigraph popularized Gertrude STEIN's observation "You are all a lost generation." Errol FLYNN gave a moving performance in the 1957 film as hero Jake Barnes's rival, the drunk Mike Campbell.

sun dance A traditional Plains Indian ceremony designed to induce visions by fasting and pain. In its most extreme form, participants hooked their flesh by thongs to a central pole and pulled or "danced" away until the hooks tore out. A depiction of the ritual in the film *A Man Called Horse* (1970) stresses its secondary characteristics as a warrior's ordeal.

sundae See ICE CREAM.

Sundance Kid See Butch CASSIDY.

Sunday, Billy (1862–1935) Revivalist. A professional baseball player for almost a decade, Sunday got religion in the 1890s and became the most successful evangelist of his day. His traveling, circus-style meetings elicited audience enthusiasm with the help of marching bands, huge choirs, and Sunday's inimitable, slang-slugging sermons. As well as converting an estimated 1 million listeners, he was also a factor in the passage of PROHIBITION. Actor Burt LANCASTER reportedly used him as a model in his creation of the title character in ELMER GANTRY.

Sunset Boulevard   (1950) A moody FILM NOIR by Billy WILDER about a ménage of convenience between a struggling writer and an aging star who hires him to write her comeback film. Gloria SWANSON, in an unnervingly autobiographical role, plays the fading beauty Norma Desmond to William HOLDEN's fatally compromised Joe Gillis. The movie's central in-joke is the casting of Erich von STROHEIM, a former Swanson director, as Desmond's director turned chauffeur, Max von Mayerling.

Super Bowl   A postseason professional football game played between the champions of the National and American football conferences. It has become a one-day equivalent of the WORLD SERIES and among the most avidly watched events on national television. The first Super Bowl (January 15, 1967) was won by Vince LOMBARDI's Green Bay Packers, in a 35–10 victory over the Kansas City Chiefs.

Superman   Mass media superhero. One of the most successful characters in popular culture history, Superman was the creation of artist Joe Shuster and writer Jerry Siegel, who introduced him in a 1938 comic book. His popularity in that medium spanned six decades and spawned a host of imitators, including BATMAN and CAPTAIN MARVEL. The Man of Steel has also starred in a newspaper strip (1939–67), a radio series (1940–51), a television series (1951–57), and several feature films.

The Shuster/Siegel legend began on the planet Krypton, where Superman was born as Kal-El. Shot to Earth in a rocket just before Krypton explodes, the infant lands outside Smalltown, U.S.A., where he is adopted by the kindly Kents and named Clark. In Earth's atmosphere he is found to have superhuman powers, notably X-ray vision, phenomenal strength, virtual indestructibility, and the ability to fly: In the words of the television voiceover, he is "faster than a speeding bullet ... more powerful than a locomotive ... able to leap tall buildings at a single bound." Determined to use these powers for good, he dons a red-and-blue costume and sallies forth into Metropolis, where he fights a "never-ending battle for truth, justice, and the American way."

Superman appears as the hero only in times of distress, when he is required to rescue the innocent or foil the wicked. At other times he is "disguised" as Clark Kent, a timid, bespectacled reporter for the *Daily Planet*. The character's driving tension is thus the contrast between a mousy, conventional exterior and the "real man" within. This contrast is not lost on Kent's colleague Lois Lane, who tolerates him while pining for his alter ego. Major secondary characters include the evil genius Lex Luthor; cub reporter Jimmy Olson, who idolizes both Kent *and* Superman; and the bluff, excitable editor Perry White, known for his exclamation "Great Caesar's ghost!"

Superman's Achilles heel is his susceptibility to kryptonite, a green rock that can render him instantly powerless. This chink in his armor is as well known to American children as his ability to change into costume at a moment's notice (in such unlikely dressing rooms as corner phone booths) and his ingenuity in concealing his identity from Lane. The character was popularized on television by actor George Reeves (1914–59) and in a 1978 Hollywood film (and three sequels) by Christopher Reeve. Recent TV spinoffs have included *Superboy* (1988–91) and *Lois and Clark* (1993–).

supermarket A large, self-service grocery store that also sells a wide range of domestic products. The prototype was a Piggly Wiggly established in Memphis, Tennessee, in 1916. Supermarkets, along with department stores, gradually supplanted the MOM-AND-POP STORES and general stores of the nineteenth century.

Supreme Court The highest federal court of the United States. It was established by Article III of the CONSTITUTION and is particularly concerned with the "constitutionality" of laws. The Constitution does not stipulate the court's size, although since the 1870s it has remained stable at nine judges, or "justices," with the presiding one known as the chief justice. As the nation's final board of appeal, the court either "upholds" or "strikes down" federal and state laws, giving it considerable power in the setting of legal precedent and thus in the implementation of social standards. Notable chief justices have included John JAY, John MARSHALL, William Howard Taft, and Earl WARREN. For significant social decisions, see BROWN v. BOARD OF EDUCATION, DRED SCOTT DECISION, MIRANDA DECISION, PLESSY v. FERGUSON, and ROE v. WADE.

Supremes, the The most successful of MOTOWN's female groups, the original Supremes were Diana Ross (1944–), Mary Wilson (1944–), and Florence Ballard (1943–76). Carefully groomed by Motown president Berry Gordy, they dominated the pop-soul scene with their upbeat harmonies. Between 1964 and 1967, the trio had ten number-one singles, including "Where Did Our Love Go?," "Baby Love," "Stop! In the Name of Love," "Back in My Arms Again," and "Love Is Here and Now You're Gone." With Ballard replaced in 1968 by Cindy Birdsong (1939–), they scored again with "Love Child" and "Someday We'll Be Together." Ross left in 1969 for a solo career that included movie roles as well as continued record success. She played Billie HOLIDAY in *Lady Sings the Blues* (1972) and Dorothy in the all-black musical *The Wiz* (1978), adapted from the original WIZARD OF OZ.

surfing Riding an incoming wave to shore by lying or standing on a flat, keeled board ("surfboard"). Popular especially in California and Hawaii, it became a national fad in the 1960s, encouraged by the music of Jan and Dean ("Surf City," 1963) and the BEACH BOYS and by the 1966 movie *The Endless Summer,* which followed the adventures of surfers seeking the "perfect wave." "Hang ten," in surfer parlance, was to ride the board standing with all ten toes over the forward edge; it became a voguish metaphor for derring-do. "Wipe out," meaning to be toppled by a wave, similarly became a synonym for failure.

Surratt, Mary See Abraham LINCOLN.

Susann, Jacqueline (1921–74) Novelist. Susann's best-selling books might have been subtitled "sleazy lifestyles of the rich and famous." Her biggest seller, *Valley of the Dolls* (1966; film 1967), explored pill-popping among affluent housewives. Two subsequent steamers, *The Love Machine* (1969; film 1971) and *Once Is Not Enough* (1973; film 1975), also sold in the millions.

Sutter, John (1803–80) Settler. Gold discovered on his land in 1848 led to the following year's California GOLD RUSH. A wealthy landowner and cattle baron before the find, he lost much of his property to pilfering prospectors, and he died while petitioning Congress to redress his bankruptcy.

Sutton, Willie   (1901–80) Bank robber. Sutton turned to robbery in the 1920s, was caught and imprisoned several times, but managed so many escapes, often in disguise, that he was known in underworld folklore as Willie the Actor. Asked by an interviewer why he robbed banks, he gave the classic reply "That's where the money is."

SWAK   Sealed with a kiss. Sometimes written on envelopes as a sign of affection.

Swamp Fox   Nickname of the guerrilla general Francis Marion (ca. 1732–95), who harassed British troops during the Revolutionary War from hiding places in the South Carolina backcountry. His elusiveness and Spartan ways made him a Robin Hood–style hero in southern folklore.

"Swanee"   A 1919 song by Irving Caesar and George GERSHWIN. It was popularized by Al JOLSON.

"Swanee River"   See "OLD FOLKS AT HOME."

Swanson, Gloria   (1897–1983) Actress. The epitome of Hollywood glamour and excess, Swanson dazzled silent film fans with her exotic wardrobe, many husbands, and passionate acting. She rose to stardom at PARAMOUNT in Cecil B. DE MILLE bedroom comedies, lost a fortune bankrolling the Erich von STROHEIM debacle *Queen Kelly* (1928), but bounced back to win Oscar nominations for best actress two years in a row, for *Sadie Thompson* (1928) and *The Trespasser* (1929). She got a third for her stunning portrayal of Norma Desmond in SUNSET BOULEVARD.

Swedish Nightingale   Nickname for Jenny LIND.

"Sweet Adeline"   A love song (1903) by Richard Gerard and Henry Armstrong, the title referring to opera singer Adelina Patti. It became a favorite with BARBERSHOP QUARTETS, and female quartets now call themselves Sweet Adelines.

"Sweet Betsy from Pike"   A humorous song about the California GOLD RUSH, written around 1855 by miner John Stone and published in that year's *Original California Songster*. Stone, who styled himself "Old Put," set the words to a popular melody, "Villikins and His Dinah."

> *Oh don't you remember sweet Betsy from Pike,*
> *Who crossed the big mountains with her lover Ike,*
> *With two yoke of cattle, a large yellow dog,*
> *A tall shanghai rooster and one spotted hog.*

"Sweet Georgia Brown"   A 1925 song by Kenneth Casey and Maceo Pinkard. It became the theme of the HARLEM GLOBETROTTERS.

"Swing Low, Sweet Chariot"   A SPIRITUAL from the 1870s. It was one of several included by black singer Harry Burleigh in a celebrated 1917 compilation.

> *I looked over Jordan and what did I see*
>   *Coming for to carry me home.*
> *A band of angels coming after me,*
>   *Coming for to carry me home.*

swing music   The dominant popular music of the 1930s and 1940s, a lushly textured, rhythmically invigorating JAZZ that was played for ballroom dancing by BIG BANDS. Swing vastly broadened the appeal of jazz by bringing it out of the honky-tonk and onto the radio. It also had a subtle influence on racial attitudes, since the white-led dance hall orchestras were often integrated. Benny GOODMAN, who pioneered this progressivism, was known as the King of Swing. *Swing Time* (1936) was the sixth film pairing of ASTAIRE AND ROGERS. See also WESTERN SWING.

Sylvester and Tweety   Cartoon characters. The continually frustrated cat Sylvester first appeared in animator Friz Freleng's 1945 *Life with Feathers*. His nemesis, Tweety the canary, followed two years later, in *Tweety Pie*. Sylvester, who has roughly the same relationship with the bird as Wile E. Coyote has with the ROAD RUNNER, is known for his exasperated splutter "Sufferin' succotash!" Tweety's stock observation is "I taut I taw a puddy tat!"

Symbionese Liberation Army   A radical group that in 1973–74 killed a California school superintendent and kidnapped William Randolph HEARST's granddaughter Patricia. Her alleged defection to their cause as gun-wielding "Tania" captured headlines through the spring of 1974. Several SLA members were killed in a Los Angeles police raid when the house in which they were hiding was burned to the ground. Hearst herself, convicted of armed robbery, served part of a seven-year sentence before being pardoned by President Jimmy Carter.

T-Bird See THUNDERBIRD (2).

"Ta-Ra-Ra-Boom-Dee-Ay" A nonsense song of the 1890s. It was said to have originated in a St. Louis nightclub, where it was sung with suggestive lyrics. Cleaned up by showbiz publicist Henry Sayers, it took first London, then New York, by storm.

tabloid A small-format newspaper, usually one that favors sensationalist reporting. The term dates from the early 1900s, when it was used to characterize papers in London and New York. From the 1920s, the *New York News* and the *New York Mirror* (sometimes chided as the "New York Noose" and the "New York Murder") were leading examples. More recently, "tabloid" has described similarly formatted papers such as the *National Enquirer* and *Star*, which stress celebrity scandals, UFO sightings, and other "creative" newsmaking. "Tabloid television" employs similar tactics in that medium.

"Take Me out to the Ball Game" A 1908 song by Jack Norworth and Albert VON TILZER. It is baseball's unofficial theme song.

> *Let me root, root, root for the home team;*
> *If they don't win it's a shame.*
> *For it's one, two, three strikes, "You're out"*
> *At the old ball game.*

"Take the A Train" The theme song of the Duke ELLINGTON band, written by the group's arranger, Billy Strayhorn (1941). The A train is a subway line that connects midtown New York City with uptown HARLEM.

take the Fifth See FIFTH AMENDMENT.

"Take This Hammer" A traditional work song, common with southern prison gangs into this century. LEADBELLY made it familiar to northern audiences.

> *Take this hammer, take it to the captain.*
> *Tell him I'm gone, tell him I'm gone.*

A similar sensibility is evident in the 1977 country song written by David Allen Coe and popularized by Johnny Paycheck: "Take This Job and Shove It."

talk shows   See RADIO; TELEVISION.

tall tale   An anecdotal exaggeration, a "windie." The folk form is common worldwide, although it flourished particularly in the American nineteenth century, as settlers added inventions of their own humorous design to the already daunting hazards of frontier life. Many tall tales stress the prodigiousness of frontier beasts and weather (see SHINGLING THE FOG). Others, in the Baron Münchhausen tradition, celebrate the exploits of heroes like Mike FINK, Davy CROCKETT, and other ROARERS. Literary inventions may also be referred to as tall tales; for this genre, see PECOS BILL, Paul BUNYAN, Febold FEBOLDSON, Joe MAGARAC, and OLD STORMALONG.

Tammany Hall   Nickname for the Democratic political machine in New York City. Founded in 1789, the Society of Tammany stood generally for reform—supporting both Thomas JEFFERSON and Andrew JACKSON—until the 1860s, when the reign of Boss TWEED made "Tammany" a synonym for corruption. It retained its hold on city politics until the election of Fiorello LA GUARDIA in 1934. The term is a variant of Tamanend, the chief Indian negotiator in William PENN's 1683 treaty with the Delaware.

tap dancing   An American form of step dancing in which performers use shoes with metal plates or "taps" to amplify their rhythmic heel and toe work. Influenced by the clog dances of the British Isles, it grew out of the nineteenth-century slave community, whose creativity was adopted in quick succession by MINSTREL SHOWS, VAUDEVILLE, and MUSICAL COMEDY. The leading vaudeville dancer, Bill ROBINSON, specialized in tap dancing on stairs—a trick he passed on to Shirley TEMPLE in their first of four films, *The Little Colonel* (1936). Other notable film tappers were ASTAIRE AND ROGERS, Ray Bolger, and Gene KELLY.

"Taps"   A military bugle call signaling "Lights out." It was written in 1862 by Union General Daniel Butterfield.

tar and feathers   A punishment extended in the colonial and Revolutionary periods to British government officials and their sympathizers. Victims were drenched in hot tar, sprinkled with feathers, and often "ridden" out of their communities on fence rails. The procedure, while extremely painful, was seldom fatal. See LYNCHING.

Tar Baby   The mute centerpiece of an UNCLE REMUS story. The "baby" is a tar doll whose silence so infuriates Brer Rabbit that he strikes the thing until he is stuck fast. The story, which has African prototypes, appeared in Joel Chandler HARRIS's first (1880) collection of sketches.

Tara   The O'Hara family plantation in GONE WITH THE WIND. Named for the seat of the ancient Irish kings.

Tarbell, Ida   (1857–1944) Muckraker. Tarbell's father, a small oil producer, was ruined by John D. ROCKEFELLER's monopolistic Standard Oil. In revenge she wrote a lengthy exposé of Rockefeller's tactics that aroused public opinion against the TRUSTS. Her "History of the Standard Oil Company" first appeared in *McClure's* in 1903.

Tarheel A native of North Carolina. From the production there of pine tar and resins.

Tariff of Abominations A protective tariff passed in 1828 under John Quincy Adams's administration. Its unpopularity lost him the White House to Andrew JACKSON and inspired John C. CALHOUN's so-called NULLIFICATION doctrine, which said that states had the right to invalidate federal laws.

Tarkenton, Fran (1940–) Football player. As a quarterback for the Minnesota Vikings and New York Giants (1961–78), Tarkenton became professional football's most accomplished passer. He holds the records for career yardage (47,003), most passes completed (3,686), and most touchdown passes (342).

Tarkington, Booth (1869–1946) Writer. Tarkington warmly evoked midwestern adolescence in the juvenile novels *Penrod* (1914) and *Seventeen* (1916). His more sobering accounts of the heartland included the Pulitzer Prize novels *The Magnificent Ambersons* (1918) and *Alice Adams* (1921). Orson WELLES filmed the first as his follow-up (1942) to CITIZEN KANE; the second, filmed by George Stevens (1935), earned an Oscar nomination for Katharine HEPBURN.

Tarzan The title character in a series of pulp novels by British writer Edgar Rice Burroughs (1875–1950). Tarzan is an English nobleman, Lord Greystoke, who is orphaned in the African bush as an infant, raised by apes, and grows up to be "Lord of the Jungle." Burroughs's *enfant sauvage* fantasy earned him millions of readers around the world, none more dedicated than those in America, where the "Ape Man" has appeared in every conceivable medium, from Hollywood films to radio and TV to comics. Of the actors who have portrayed him on film, the best known remains the swimmer Johnny WEISMULLER. His famous 1932 greeting to his "mate," Jane Porter, "Me Tarzan, you Jane," has become a mock-serious slang expression of male robustness.

Taylor, Elizabeth (1932–) Actress. Born in London to American parents, Taylor starred as a girl in LASSIE films and in *National Velvet* (1944), then emerged as an MGM superstar as well known for her offscreen romances as for her violet-eyed beauty. The steamiest of her early sex-kitten roles were as prostitutes in CAT ON A HOT TIN ROOF and *Butterfield 8* (1960), for the latter of which she won an Academy Award. She won again as the tortured harridan, Martha, in *Who's Afraid of Virginia Woolf?* (1966), where her costar (also nominated) was Richard BURTON, the fifth of her several husbands. Taylor and Burton, the most highly paid acting duo of the decade, also appeared in the financially disastrous *Cleopatra* (1963) and the more restrained *Taming of the Shrew* (1967).

Taylor, Zachary See MEXICAN WAR.

"Tea for Two" A romantic ditty written in 1924 by Irving Caesar and Vincent Youmans and introduced the following year in the Broadway musical *No, No, Nanette*.

Teach, Edward See BLACKBEARD.

Teapot Dome Site of a federal oil reserve in Wyoming. In 1922, President Warren G. Harding's interior secretary, Albert Fall, accepted bribes from developers to grant them leasing rights. By the time the news broke, Harding was dead, but it still cast a retroactive pall over his already scandal-ridden administration. Upton SINCLAIR used the episode in his novel *Oil!* (1927).

Tecumseh   (1768–1813) Shawnee leader. Tecumseh, along with his brother the Shawnee Prophet, attempted to unite the native peoples of the NORTHWEST TERRITORY into a grand alliance against the whites. After his hopes were dashed at the Battle of Tippecanoe (1811), he joined forces with the British in the WAR OF 1812. He was killed at the Battle of the Thames.

teddy bear   A stuffed toy bear. Teddy bears have been popular children's bedtime companions since 1903, when the first ones were manufactured by a New York couple, Rose and Morris Michtom. They were named for Theodore ROOSEVELT after a 1902 hunting trip on which he publicly refused to shoot a captured bear cub.

telegraph   See Samuel F. B. MORSE; WESTERN UNION.

telephone   See Alexander Graham BELL; MA BELL.

television   The technology for the industrialized world's most pervasive entertainment medium was in place by the late 1930s, but commercial programming remained sporadic for almost a decade with only about 1 million U.S. families owning TV sets by 1948. The 1950s saw an explosion of the medium, as 90 percent of the country gained access to reception. In the ensuing decade, major networks adapted RADIO genres such as the SITCOM and the SOAP OPERA, the action-adventure series and the variety show, while blazing new ground in the coverage of news and sports events. During the early 1950s, the immediacy and unpredictability of live broadcasts typified a so-called Golden Age, and the medium's most durable and beloved personalities—among them Milton BERLE, Ed SULLIVAN, and Jack BENNY—became universal fixtures in American living rooms. The end of the decade saw the rise of the QUIZ SHOW and the first stirrings of the interview format "talk show," of which THE TODAY SHOW and THE TONIGHT SHOW were the pioneering models. That format took a sensationalist turn in the 1970s and 1980s, as daytime hosts such as Phil Donahue, Geraldo Rivera, and Sally Jesse Raphael fused racy themes with current events to create "infotainment." This TABLOID-style journalism was further exploited by news shows ranging from the durable 60 MINUTES to the frothier, celebrity-oriented *A Current Affair*.

In a listing that considered both popularity and longevity, Tim Brooks and Earle Marsh determined that the following shows were the top twenty prime-time series in television history.

SHOW	GENRE	DATES
1. *60 Minutes*	News	1968–
2. *Gunsmoke*	Western	1955–75
3. *Red Skelton Show*	Comedy/variety	1951–71
4. *Bonanza*	Western	1959–73
5. *All in the Family*	Sitcom	1971–83
6. *Walt Disney*	Juvenile variety	1954–90
7. *Ed Sullivan Show*	Variety	1948–71
8. *The Lucy Show*	Sitcom	1962–74

9. *M*A*S*H*	Sitcom	1972–83
10. *Dallas*	Drama	1978–91
11. *Andy Griffith Show*	Sitcom	1960–68
12. *The Cosby Show*	Sitcom	1984–92
13. *Jack Benny Show*	Comedy/variety	1950–65
14. *Cheers*	Sitcom	1982–93
15. *Three's Company*	Sitcom	1977–85
16. *I Love Lucy*	Sitcom	1951–61
17. *The Danny Thomas Show*	Sitcom	1953–71
18. *Beverly Hillbillies*	Sitcom	1962–71
19. *You Bet Your Life*	Quiz show	1950–61
20. *Happy Days*	Sitcom	1974–84

"Tell-Tale Heart, The" A short story (1843) by Edgar Allan POE. A murderer is maddened into confession by what he supposes to be the beating of his victim's heart.

temperance movement National agitation for the banning of alcohol. It began in the early 1800s as a true "temperance" movement, but by midcentury had evolved into a teetotalers' crusade, with Maine passing the first prohibition law in 1851. Many of the early temperance workers were also champions of women's suffrage; Susan B. ANTHONY was among those who formed the Women's Christian Temperance Union (WCTU) in 1874. It was followed by the Anti-Saloon League (1893), the well-publicized raids of Carry NATION, and the passage, in 1919, of PROHIBITION.

Temple, Shirley (1928–) The most famous child star of the century. In the midst of the Great Depression, "Curly Top" Shirley Temple—singing, dancing, and displaying her dimples—became the nation's number-one Hollywood attraction. She made her first film at the age of four, and by 1938, when she was ten, had appeared in two dozen winning roles, including *Little Miss Marker* (1934), *The Little Colonel* (1935), *Poor Little Rich Girl* (1936), *Wee Willie Winkie* (1937), *Heidi* (1937), and *Rebecca of Sunnybrook Farm* (1938). She later served in Republican administrations as a delegate to the United Nations and chief of protocol.

Temptations, the Vocal group. Tight stage choreography and exciting harmonies made the Temptations MOTOWN's top male act of the 1960s. Their hit songs—many of them written by Smokey ROBINSON—included "My Girl," "Get Ready," "Beauty's Only Skin Deep," "I'm Losing You," "All I Need," "I Wish It Would Rain," and "Just My Imagination."

Ten Commandments, The The title of two successful biblical epics, a silent version filmed in 1923, a talking spectacular (with Charlton HESTON as Moses) in 1956. Both were directed by Cecil B. DE MILLE.

ten-gallon hat See STETSON.

"Ten Nights in a Barroom" (1854) A short story by Timothy Shay Arthur (1809–85). A best-selling temperance tale, it was dramatized in 1858 by William Pratt, becoming second only to UNCLE TOM'S CABIN in stage popularity.

Tender Is the Night   (1934) A novel by F. Scott FITZGERALD. Like A STAR IS BORN, it concerns a seesaw relationship in which one's character's fortunes climb as another's decline. The characters here, no doubt influenced by the author's troubled alliance with his wife, Zelda, are psychiatrist Dick Diver and his patient Nicole Warren. They were played in a 1962 movie by Jason Robards and Jennifer Jones.

tenderfoot   (1) In western slang, a novice, especially an eastern newcomer, a "dude." Possibly from such a person's sensitivity to tight-fitting cowboy boots. Hence (2) the lowest rank in the BOY SCOUTS OF AMERICA.

tenderloin   Usually seen as "tenderloin district." An area of a city dedicated to vice and amusement. From the 1880s in New York City, because such a district afforded police officers the "juiciest" graft.

tepee   Also seen as "teepee," "tipi." A conical tent used by the nomadic Plains Indians. From a SIOUX word for "dwelling." Like other things Sioux, it has been widely and recklessly taken as generically "Indian."

Terry, Sonny, and Brownie McGhee   Blues musicians. Harmonica player Teddell Terry (1911–86) and guitarist Walter McGhee (1914–) were independent itinerant musicians until 1939, when they met at a North Carolina concert. Together they became the most recognized folk-blues duo of the century, performing traditional songs as well as originals like "Fox Hunt" and "Stranger Blues." They electrified a New York audience at a 1950 memorial concert to LEADBELLY, and they were much in demand during the FOLK REVIVAL.

Terry and the Pirates   A comic strip about American adventurers in the Far East. It was begun by Milton Caniff (1907–88) in 1934. Its alluring villain, the Dragon Lady, was a popular PINUP with World War II G.I.s, and it made "Dragon Lady" a slang expression for an intimidating woman.

Tex-Mex   Produced in Texas but displaying Mexican origins or characteristics. Most commonly applied to music and food.

Texas   Long known as the largest state in the Union, Texas was originally a northern province of Mexico; it gained its independence during the 1836 Texas Revolution, remembered for the battle of the ALAMO and for Sam HOUSTON's subsequent victory over SANTA ANNA. The quintessential COWBOY state since the nineteenth century, it has been the setting for countless westerns, as well as dramas that exploit its fame as the home of Big Oil, such as Edna FERBER's *Giant* (1952) and the TV series *Dallas* (see DALLAS [2]). When Alaska was admitted to the Union in 1959, Texas became the second largest of the United States, although its residents' reputation for boastfulness was undiminished by the acquisition. The Lone Star State's brash good-heartedness was typified by its native son President Lyndon B. JOHNSON.

Texas Guinan   See Texas GUINAN.

Texas Rangers   Formed in the 1820s as a volunteer home guard against Indian attacks, the Texas Rangers evolved gradually into a frontier militia that saw action in the MEXICAN WAR and then, after 1874, into a statewide law enforcement agency. Their reputation for brave efficiency, especially under Commander Jack Coffee Hays (1817–84), was unparalleled, as exemplified in the often repeated story of the single Ranger sent to quell a riot. When frightened citizens asked, "They only sent one of you?" he calmly replied, "There's only one riot, ain't there?" In the 1930s, the Rangers merged with the Highway Patrol. See also THE LONE RANGER.

TGIF   Thank God it's Friday.

Thalberg, Irving   (1899–1936) Movie executive. Hollywood's "Boy Wonder," Thalberg was MGM's chief of production from 1924 until his early death. His concern for detail and his institution of the sneak preview to test audience reaction were important factors in the studio's success. He was intimately involved in the production of the film classics BEN-HUR, *Anna Christie* (1930), MUTINY ON THE BOUNTY, *A Night at the Opera* (1935), and *The Good Earth* (1937). He was married to the actress Norma SHEARER.

Thanksgiving   An American harvest holiday held on the fourth Thursday in November. European "Harvest Home" antecedents are abundant, although tradition identifies the First Thanksgiving as a 1621 feast held in PLYMOUTH COLONY to celebrate the PILGRIMS' surviving their first year in the New World. Ad hoc "Thanksgivings" were proclaimed by colonial and state governors for two centuries thereafter, but the holiday did not become nationally established until 1863, when Sarah Josepha HALE, after a thirty-year campaign, convinced President Abraham Lincoln to make it annual and official. Thanksgiving is traditionally observed with a family meal of stuffed TURKEY, cranberry sauce, and PUMPKIN pie (the Pilgrims' supposed menu). The feast is also marked by "Turkey Day" sales and by the celebration (now televised) of football spectaculars.

"Thar she blows!"   A whaler's cry, indicating he has sighted a whale. "Blow" refers to the spouting of surfacing whales.

"that damned cowboy"   See Mark HANNA.

Thatcher, Becky   See TOM SAWYER.

"That's all, folks"   See LOONEY TUNES.

Thaw, Harry K.   See Stanford WHITE.

Thayer, Ernest   Author of "CASEY AT THE BAT."

"There'll Be a Hot Time in the Old Town Tonight"   A song written in 1886 by the conductor of a minstrel group, Theodore Metz. The lyrics by Joseph Hayden indicated a pious intent ("And when you gets religion you want to shout and sing"), but it was adopted during the SPANISH-AMERICAN WAR as a marching tune and used later by Theodore ROOSEVELT as a campaign song.

"There's a Long Long Trail Awinding"   A song written in 1913 by Yale students Stoddard King and Zo Elliott, who presented it at a fraternity banquet.

Picked up by TIN PAN ALLEY, it became a favorite among American soldiers in World War I.

"There's a sucker born every minute"   See P. T. BARNUM.

"There's No Business like Show Business"   The unofficial theme song of the entertainment industry. It was written in 1946 by Irving BERLIN for the musical *Annie Get Your Gun,* a show that made it an Ethel MERMAN theme song. Marilyn MONROE sang it in the motion picture *There's No Business like Show Business* (1954).

"There's no place like home"   In THE WIZARD OF OZ, the "magic formula" that Dorothy utters to bring herself and Toto back to Kansas. From the song "HOME, SWEET HOME."

"These are the times that try men's souls"   See Thomas PAINE.

Thin Man, The   A 1932 mystery novel by Dashiell HAMMETT. It introduced the debonair sleuthing couple Nick and Nora Charles. Played by William Powell and Myrna Loy in a 1934 movie, they became as well known for their banter as for their brainstorming. The "thin man" of the title was a murder victim, but the phrase became associated with Charles/Powell, and it appeared, anachronistically, in the titles of five sequels.

Thirteen Colonies   The British colonies that, after the Revolutionary War, combined to form the United States of America. They were represented on the original U.S. flag by thirteen stripes and a circle of thirteen stars; hence the designation STARS AND STRIPES. Given in the order in which they ratified the CONSTITUTION, they were Delaware (1787), Pennsylvania (1787), New Jersey (1787), Georgia (1788), Connecticut (1788), New Hampshire (1788), Virginia (1788), New York (1788), North Carolina (1789), and Rhode Island (1790).

38th parallel   The border between North and South Korea, established in 1948. General Douglas MACARTHUR's crossing of this line drew Chinese troops into the KOREAN WAR in support of the North Korean communist regime. It was reestablished as the national boundary in the 1953 armistice.

"This is the place"   See Brigham YOUNG.

This Is Your Life   A television show hosted by Ralph Edwards from 1952 to 1961. It told the life stories of guests ranging from celebrities to average Joes, who were reunited on the air with bygone acquaintances. They were not told in advance that they were going to be honored, and the charm of the show was in the teary reunions.

"This Land Is Your Land"   Woody GUTHRIE's most famous folk song, a celebration of the communal treasures of the American people.

> *This land is your land, this land is my land,*
> *From California to the New York island.*
> *From the redwood forests to the Gulf Stream waters*
> *This land was made for you and me.*

Thomas, Danny (1914–91) Singer, actor. The Lebanese-American performer Amos Muzyad Jahoob was a nightclub comedian in the 1940s before becoming a perennial on family television with the SITCOM *The Danny Thomas Show* (1953–71). It concerned the mild domestic trials of entertainer Danny Williams. Thomas's daughter Marlo (1937–   ) starred in *That Girl* (1966–71), a precursor of "independent woman" sitcoms like *The Mary Tyler* MOORE *Show*.

Thomas, Norman (1884–1968) Political leader. A Presbyterian minister, Thomas opposed U.S. entry into World War I, helped to found the American Civil Liberties Union, and in 1928 became head of the American Socialist party. For the next twenty years he ran as that party's candidate in every presidential election, gradually becoming socialism's elder statesman. His books included *A Socialist's Faith* (1951) and *The Great Dissenters* (1961).

Thoreau, Henry David (1817–62) A New England original, Thoreau is remembered most for writing WALDEN, the record of his two-year "experiment" in rustic living. He was also the author of the essay "Civil Disobedience" (1849), in which he explained his one-night imprisonment for tax evasion (he had refused to pay a poll tax that supported the MEXICAN WAR) and applauded the primacy of conscience over the state. The humanistic radicalism that he expounded there was also evident in 1859, when he publicly defended abolitionist John BROWN. Among modern protesters influenced by his writings were Mahatma Gandhi and Martin Luther KING, Jr.
A native of CONCORD, Massachusetts, Thoreau spent most of his life there ("I have traveled a good deal in Concord," he wryly boasted), where his friends included EMERSON and HAWTHORNE. His studies of the New England countryside appear in a mammoth journal and in essays on the Concord and Merrimack rivers, Cape Cod, and the Maine woods. Part child of the forest and part public scold, he remains a paragon of the individualistic YANKEE, intent on marching to "a different drummer." His last sentence, as he died of tuberculosis, was entirely in character. Asked whether he had made his peace with God, he responded, "I am not aware that we ever quarreled." See also TRANSCENDENTALISM.

Thornton, Big Mama (1926–84) Blues singer. Alabama-born Willie Mae Thornton toured the South as a teenager with the Hot Harlem Revue and began recording RHYTHM AND BLUES in the 1950s. She played with Chicago artists such as Muddy WATERS and was the first person to record the rock classic "HOUND DOG." Her own song "Ball and Chain" was a hit for Janis JOPLIN.

Thorpe, Jim (1888–1953) Athlete. Born in Oklahoma of mixed Indian and white parentage, James Francis Thorpe is commonly called the greatest male athlete of the century. After an All-American football career at the tiny Indian School in Carlisle, Pennsylvania, he won the decathlon and the pentathlon at the 1912 Olympic Games. The following year, when it was revealed that he had played professional baseball, he lost his gold medals and turned professional full-time, playing for the New York Giants and Boston Braves until 1919. He also founded a pro football team in 1915 and served as first president of what would become the National Football League.

"Three Coins in the Fountain" A romantic song by Sammy CAHN and Jule STYNE. Written for the 1954 motion picture of the same name, it won an Academy

Award for best song. The reference was to Rome's Trevi Fountain, which the movie made a major tourist attraction.

Three Little Pigs   (1933) The best-known of Walt DISNEY's "Silly Symphony" cartoons, a fable about the importance of preparedness. Three pigs, two shiftless and one practical, build houses against the maraudings of a wolf; only the practical builder's brick house survives. Appearing in the middle of the GREAT DEPRESSION, it taught a curiously unrosy lesson about deferred gratification. The film's reassuring theme song, "Who's Afraid of the Big Bad Wolf?," was widely popular.

Three Stooges   A comedy act that began in vaudeville and made roughly two hundred short films between 1934 and 1958. Specialists in witless banter and violent slapstick, the team underwent occasional personnel changes, although the sustaining trio were Moe Howard (1897–1975), his brother Jerome, known as Curly (1906–52), and Larry Fine (1911–75). They also appeared in several feature films.

thunderbird   (1) In the mythology of various native American peoples, thunderbirds are supernatural creatures who cause thunder and frequently do battle with underwater snakes. Depictions of the creatures in spread-eagle poses are found from the eastern woodlands to the Great Plains. (2) Capitalized, a sports car developed by the Ford Motor Company and fashionable since the 1950s as the "T-Bird." (3) Brand name of an inexpensive, fortified wine.

Thurber, James   (1894–1961) Writer. The deftest American humorist of the interwar years, Thurber wrote frequently for THE NEW YORKER from its early days until his death. Although he produced essays on diverse topics, including the HALL-MILLS CASE, he was at his best skewering the follies of everyday life. His short sketches—many of them illustrated by his own mordant cartoons—reveal men and women trapped by fate and each other in the webbing of their own too-human designs. Among his best works are the story of Walter MITTY, the fractured fairy tales in *Fables for Our Time* (1940), and the retrospective collection *The Thurber Carnival* (1945).

Ticonderoga, Fort   See FORT TICONDEROGA.

"Tie a Yellow Ribbon Round the Ole Oak Tree"   See YELLOW RIBBONS.

Tiffany's   A jewelry store on New York City's FIFTH AVENUE. Famed both for its original creations and for its imports, it was founded in 1837 by Charles Lewis Tiffany (1812–1902). His son Louis Comfort Tiffany (1848–1933) was an interior decorator and glassmaker who brought Art Nouveau to the attention of the middle class. His stained-glass creations—ranging in size from lampshades to huge windows—are masterpieces of fin-de-siècle design. *Breakfast at Tiffany's,* a 1958 novel by Truman Capote, was filmed with Audrey Hepburn in the lead in 1961.

Tilden, Bill   (1893–1953) Tennis player. "Big Bill" Tilden dominated men's tennis in the 1920s. He won the U.S. singles title six years in a row (1920–25) and a seventh time in 1929. He also led the American team to seven consecutive Davis Cup victories (1920–26) and was the Wimbledon singles champion three times (1920–21 and 1930).

Tillman, "Pitchfork Ben" (1847–1918) Politician. The South's most vocal white supremacist for thirty years, Benjamin Tillman served as the staunchly JIM CROW governor of South Carolina from 1890 to 1894. A U.S. senator from 1895 until his death, he fought for farmers' rights and the regulation of railroads. His nickname came from a senatorial campaign promise that, if elected, he would stick a pitchfork into President Grover Cleveland.

Time Founded in 1923 by Henry LUCE and Briton Hadden, *Time* was the nation's first modern newsmagazine. With approximately 4 million readers, it is the circulation leader, comfortably ahead of its closest copy, NEWSWEEK. A cover featuring a man or woman of the year is an annual feature. The staff's crisply clever style has become known as Timese.

Times Square A midtown MANHATTAN intersection in the heart of both the theater and the commercial districts. Its high level of activity has made "Times Square," like GRAND CENTRAL STATION, a shorthand expression for urban bustle.

Tin Lizzie Nickname for the MODEL T Ford. Probably a contradiction of "tin limousine."

Tin Pan Alley A metaphor for the American music industry from the 1890s to the 1940s. The period corresponded roughly to the "piano era," when the parlor (or player) piano was a common feature of middle-class homes and when sheet music, promoted by song "pluggers," sold in the millions. The term referred originally to an area of New York City (centered on West 28th Street) where songwriters worked in music publishers' offices; "tin pan" was a variant of "tinny piano." In common usage, it implies "blatantly commercial"—music that is lyrically and melodically formulaic. This pejorative sense is singularly unapt for describing a fraternity that includes Harold ARLEN, Irving BERLIN, George M. COHAN, George GERSHWIN, Oscar HAMMERSTEIN II, and Jerome KERN.

Tinker Bell See PETER PAN.

Tinker to Evers to Chance A metaphor for precision teamwork. From the Chicago Cubs infielders Joe Tinker (1880–1948), Johnny Evers (1881–1947), and Frank Chance (1877–1924), who were celebrated in the 1900s for their double plays.

Tinseltown Hollywood. From its reputation for superficiality. Composer Oscar Levant once defended it tongue in cheek with the observation "Strip away the phony tinsel and you can find the real tinsel underneath."

Tiomkin, Dimitri (1899–1979) Composer. Born in Russia and trained in a St. Petersburg conservatory, Tiomkin was the most successful film composer of Hollywood's Golden Age. He scored everything from westerns to HITCHCOCK thrillers to CAPRA comedies, and was several times nominated for Academy Awards. He won for the scores of HIGH NOON, *The High and The Mighty* (1954), and THE OLD MAN AND THE SEA.

"Tippecanoe and Tyler Too" Whig slogan in the 1840 presidential campaign. The winner, "Old Tippecanoe" William Henry Harrison, had become a national hero in 1811 by defeating a force of warriors under the Shawnee Prophet on the Tippecanoe River in Indiana. His running mate, Virginian John Tyler, inherited the office on Harrison's death in April 1841.

Tituba   See SALEM WITCH TRIALS.

Tlingit   An Indian people native to Alaska. They subsisted on a largely maritime economy, building seagoing canoes for fishing and whaling and living in multi-family plankwood houses. Expert woodcarvers and weavers of stunningly dyed woolen robes, they were also, like their near neighbors the KWAKIUTL, devotees of the potlatch.

To Have and Have Not   A novel (1937) by Ernest HEMINGWAY about the troubles and demise of a Florida boat owner. According to legend, Howard HAWKS produced his movie version in 1944 to prove he could make a good movie out of his friend's worst book. The result was a sparkling antifascist romp in which the main characters—bearing little relation to Hemingway's originals—were played by Humphrey BOGART and Lauren BACALL. The fact that the two fell in love on the set added to the movie's sexual chemistry, while the script, written by Jules Furthman and William FAULKNER, included some of the decade's most quoted one-liners. Best known was Bacall's double entendre to a bewildered Bogart. If you want me, she instructs him, "just whistle. . . . You know how to whistle, don't you, Steve? You just put your lips together and blow."

To Kill a Mockingbird   A best-selling novel by Harper Lee (1926–   ) that won the Pulitzer Prize for fiction in 1961 and became an equally admired movie in 1962. It concerns the rape trial and subsequent murder of an innocent black man. The title refers to the irony of such violence in the Deep South, where it is "a sin to kill a mockingbird." Gregory PECK won an Academy Award for his portrayal of the victim's lawyer, Atticus Finch.

To Tell the Truth   Television QUIZ SHOW. Celebrity panels asked questions of three contestants, all of them claiming to be the same person, in an attempt to deduce which one was telling the truth. The show, which ran for eleven years (1956–67), made a household phrase out of host Bud Collyer's final instruction, "Will the real _____ please stand up?"

"To the victor belong the spoils"   Democratic politician William Marcy's (1786–1857) defense of the SPOILS SYSTEM. He saw "nothing wrong in the rule," he claimed in an 1831 talk, "that to the victor belong the spoils of the enemy."

tobacco   A plant indigenous to the Americas that the Caribbean peoples smoked in rolled cigars. It reached Europe in the 1490s with Christopher COLUMBUS's sailors—not, as is often said, with Sir Walter RALEIGH. Raleigh popularized pipe smoking in England, copying a custom he had learned in Virginia. By the seventeenth century, thanks to John ROLFE, it had become the main cash crop of that colony. Connecticut and North Carolina soon followed it as growing areas for what James I called the "loathsome" plant. Cigarette smoking flourished in the late nineteenth century, especially after James B. Duke (1856–1925) introduced rolling machines as the foundation of his American Tobacco TRUST. Before the discovery of smoking's hazards in the 1960s, cigarettes were widely advertised by movie stars, promising everything from sophistication to virility. See also CAMEL; MARLBORO MAN; PEACE PIPE; "YOU'VE COME A LONG WAY, BABY."

Tobacco Road A novel (1932) by Erskine CALDWELL. Its titillating theme—degeneracy among Georgia sharecroppers—made it a best-seller, and its audience was further expanded in 1933, when Jack Kirkland adapted it for the stage. It ran on Broadway for eight years, holding the record for performances until being edged out by LIFE WITH FATHER in the 1940s.

Tocqueville, Alexis de (1805–59) A French magistrate, Tocqueville was sent by his government in 1831 to study the United States prison system. His resulting "report," *Democracy in America* (1835, 1840), described the possibilities and dangers of JACKSONIAN DEMOCRACY with a keenness that has never been surpassed. To Tocqueville, the basic feature of American life, a passion for equality, at once nurtured and potentially threatened liberty because of the "tyranny of the majority." His book remains fundamental to an understanding of American culture. He also wrote on the French Revolution.

Toklas, Alice B. See Gertrude STEIN.

Tokyo Rose The nickname given by U.S. servicemen to various women who broadcast Japanese propaganda during World War II. One of them, Iva D'Aquino, was an American citizen who after the war was imprisoned for treason. The European theater equivalent was AXIS SALLY.

Toland, Gregg (1904–48) Hollywood cameraman. Developer of the "deep focus" technique, Toland won an Academy Award for his work on William WYLER's *Wuthering Heights* (1939). He also photographed THE GRAPES OF WRATH, CITIZEN KANE, and THE BEST YEARS OF OUR LIVES.

Toll House cookie A chocolate chip cookie created in the 1930s by Ruth Wakefield, proprietor of the Whitman, Massachusetts, Toll House Inn. Its popularity was enhanced when the Nestlé company began printing Wakefield's recipe on its chocolate chip packaging.

Tom, Uncle See UNCLE TOM'S CABIN.

Tom and Jerry (1) A cartoon duo created by HANNA AND BARBERA for the 1940 film *Puss Gets the Boot*. Tom was an alley cat, Jerry his antagonist, an ingenious mouse. They appeared together in numerous MGM cartoons, winning their creators seven Academy Awards. (2) The original stage name of SIMON AND GARFUNKEL. They had a modest hit with "Hey, Schoolgirl" (1957).

"Tom Dooley" A mournful folk song supposedly composed as a gallows confession by an embittered Civil War veteran, Tom Dula, who killed his sweetheart over her affections for a rival suitor. It became a hit for the KINGSTON TRIO in 1958.

Tom Sawyer The main character in Mark TWAIN's novel *The Adventures of Tom Sawyer* (1876). Clever and mischievous, he must contend in this juvenile classic with the gentility of his Aunt Polly and the less tender ministrations of

Injun Joe, a murderer whose crime Tom witnesses with his friend Huck Finn. In the book's most endearing set piece, Tom gets neighbor children to whitewash a fence for him by convincing them of his reluctance to abandon such "fun." In its suspenseful finale, Tom and his sweetheart, Becky Thatcher, are nearly caught by the villain while lost in a cave. The book inspired three sequels, including HUCKLEBERRY FINN.

Tom Thumb   (1) A small locomotive built in 1830 by inventor Peter Cooper to demonstrate the possibilities of steam-powered railroads. Even though it lost its first race with a horse-drawn train, rail officials were convinced of its potential. Cooper's "teakettle on a truck" pointed the way to the future. (2) "General Tom Thumb" was the stage name of Charles Stratton (1838–83), a midget transformed by P. T. BARNUM into one of the most famous curiosities of the century. Both uses derive from a diminutive nursery character, Tom Thumb, whose "history" was published in 1621.

tomahawk   A stone club or hatchet used in warfare and hunting by native American peoples. The Indian term means roughly "that which cuts." It was later applied to metal axes sold as trade goods. Hence "to bury the hatchet" as a metaphor for making peace and "Uncle Tomahawk" as an Indian equivalent of "Uncle Tom."

Tomb of the Unknown Soldier   A memorial in ARLINGTON NATIONAL CEMETERY to the unidentified dead of World War I. It was dedicated in 1921 as the resting place of a single, symbolically representative U.S. soldier. Known since 1958 as the Tomb of the Unknowns, it now also contains the bodies of servicemen who died in the nation's subsequent military engagements.

Tombstone   A small Arizona town whose violent heritage makes it an OLD WEST tourist site. Its principal draws are BOOT HILL and the O.K. CORRAL. A short-lived television western, *Tombstone Territory* (1957–59), advertised it as "the Town Too Tough to Die." A 1993 movie, *Tombstone,* was a recounting of the Wyatt EARP legend.

tommy gun   A submachine gun developed for military use by World War I small-arms specialist John T. Thompson (1860–1949). A favorite weapon with PROHIBITION-era gangsters, it was sometimes called a Chicago violin because it could be carried in a violin case.

Tonight Show, The   Television's second longest-running series, a late night interview show that has been carried by NBC since 1954. The format, which has varied only moderately over the years, includes comic sketches and live music performances, but focuses chiefly on casual chatter between host and guests. In spite of its insomniacal scheduling (it airs after the late evening news), it remains a prime venue for celebrity self-promotion. The show's chief hosts have been Steve Allen (1954–56), Ernie Kovacs (1956–57), Jack Paar (1957–62), Johnny CARSON (1962–92), and Jay Leno (since 1992).

Tonkin Gulf Resolution   See VIETNAM WAR.

Tonto   The "faithful Indian companion" in THE LONE RANGER series. In the original radio legend, Tonto revives the hero, John Reid, after he has been

wounded and left for dead by the Cavendish gang. They are henceforth inseparable. Tonto, who belongs to no designated Indian nation, was played on-screen by Mohawk actor Jay Silverheels (1919–80). The character's inexpert grasp of English grammar always irritated some viewers, who pointed out that Spanish *tonto* means "foolish" and who relished an often repeated joke about the two companions being caught in an Indian ambush. The Lone Ranger, seeing that they are doomed, says, "Well, old friend, it looks like we're goners this time." Tonto replies, "What do you mean *we,* white man?"

Tony Awards Annual awards given since 1947 to honor achievement in the theater arts. Presented to actors, directors, and other stage professionals by the American Theater Wing, they are named for that organization's former chair, the actress and producer Antoinette Perry (1888–1946).

tooth fairy A mythical creature who gives children money in exchange for lost teeth. Typically, the tooth is placed under the child's pillow and is miraculously replaced by coins by the following morning. The ritual, which dates from the first half of this century, reflects European tooth-exchange customs in which the usual benefactor is a mouse. The spread of the custom in the 1950s was likely the result of media encouragement: Popular culture fairies of midcentury included Glinda of THE WIZARD OF OZ, the Blue Fairy of Walt Disney's PINOCCHIO, the fairy godmother of his *Cinderella* (1950), and the Tinker Bell of his PETER PAN.

Tootsie Roll A chocolate fudge candy created in 1896 by Leo Hirschfield. "Tootsie" was his daughter Clara's nickname. Tootsie Roll Pops—lollipops with a fudge center—were developed in 1930.

Top Hat A 1935 musical starring ASTAIRE AND ROGERS. The fourth, and one of the most successful, of their dance vehicles, it included two memorable Irving BERLIN songs: the title song and "Cheek to Cheek."

"Top of the world, Ma!" See WHITE HEAT.

Topper A 1923 novel by Thorne Smith (1892–1934) about a stuffy banker whose life is transformed by two fun-loving ghosts. Cary GRANT and Constance Bennett played the ghosts, Roland Young the banker, in a 1937 movie version. *Topper* was also a bright, if brief, television series (1953–56). (2) HOPALONG CASSIDY's horse.

Topsy A black child in UNCLE TOM'S CABIN, remembered for a single observation. When asked to explain her existence in the absence of either mother or father, she replied, "I 'spect I grow'd."

torch song A moody romantic ballad, such as might be sung by one "carrying a torch" for a lost love. The term dates from the 1930s.

Tories See LOYALISTS.

tornado A small, violent storm that resembles a snake twisting from the clouds to the ground; hence the slang term "twister." Tornadoes, which are common in the Great Plains between Texas and Nebraska ("Tornado Alley"), can have wind speeds over one hundred miles per hour and be phenomenally destructive in a brief period. One that "touched down" in Missouri and neighboring states in 1925 is estimated to have killed nearly seven hundred people. For fictional treatments, see PECOS BILL and THE WIZARD OF OZ.

Toscanini, Arturo (1867–1957) Conductor. The Italian-born Toscanini conducted the Metropolitan Opera orchestra (1908–14), the New York Philharmonic (1926–36), and the NBC Symphony Orchestra (1937–54). His records greatly expanded the classical music audience; among twentieth-century conductors, only Leonard BERNSTEIN was as well known.

totem poles Tall carved posts that were used by the KWAKIUTL, TLINGIT, and other Northwest Coast peoples as grave markers and heraldic family memorials. The name is a misnomer, for the figures carved on them usually represent clan members and tutelary spirits rather than the animal ancestors that anthropologists call totems. The "stacking" of figures one on top of another led to the expressions "top (or bottom) man on the totem pole" for one in a superior (or lowly) position.

Toto In THE WIZARD OF OZ, Dorothy's dog. She is searching for him at the beginning of the story when both of them are caught up in the tornado, and it is to him that she speaks upon landing in Oz: "Toto, I've a feeling we're not in Kansas anymore."

touchdown In football, the scoring of a goal, worth six points. Abbreviated "TD." Hence a metaphor for any significant victory.

town meeting A durable example of grassroots or (as SDS literature called it) "participatory" democracy. Town meetings are periodic assemblies of all town citizens, who use them to debate and vote on municipal business. They originated in colonial Massachusetts and still survive in small New England communities. Thomas JEFFERSON called them "elementary republics."

Townshend Acts (1767) Acts designed to raise colonial revenues by taxing articles of everyday use, including paint, paper, and tea. They also provided for the quartering of British soldiers in private homes and for the seizure of smuggled goods through writs of assistance. Named for the chancellor of the exchequer, Charles Townshend, they were universally unpopular and were repealed in 1770—with one exception. The retention of the tax on tea led eventually to the BOSTON TEA PARTY.

TR Theodore ROOSEVELT. He was also commonly called Teddy.

Tracy, Dick See DICK TRACY.

Tracy, Spencer (1900–67) Actor. Unglamorous, versatile, and reliable, Tracy was one of Hollywood's most admired leading men. His sparse style earned him the nickname Prince of Underplayers, while his love affair with Katharine HEPBURN was an open secret for over twenty years. He earned Academy Awards for *Captains Courageous* (1937) and BOYS TOWN and nominations for seven other films, including THE OLD MAN AND THE SEA, *Inherit the Wind* (1960), and *Guess Who's Coming to Dinner?* (1967), his final film and the ninth with Hepburn. The

Hepburn/Tracy chemistry was at its best in *Adam's Rib* (1949), *Pat and Mike* (1952), and *Desk Set* (1957). Tracy also played the title roles in *Edison the Man* (1940) and *Dr. Jekyll and Mr. Hyde* (1941).

Trail of Tears   Under the Indian Removal Act of 1830, native peoples of the FIVE CIVILIZED TRIBES were driven from their homes in the fertile Southeast and resettled in distant INDIAN TERRITORY. Most of the CHEROKEE were "escorted" there in 1838–39. Their hardships along the way, during which thousands died of exhaustion and disease, gave the march the title "Trail of Tears."

transcendentalism   An unofficial "school" of American Romanticism that stressed intuition over rationalist authority and sought to make society "naturally" harmonious. Drawing on Kantian idealist philosophy and European Romantic poetry, the movement is usually dated from 1836, when Boston minister George Ripley (1802–80) founded a Transcendentalist Club and Ralph Waldo EMERSON published the credo *Nature*. Kindred spirits were Louisa May ALCOTT's father, Bronson (1799–1888); feminist writer Margaret Fuller (1810–50), who edited the movement magazine *The Dial;* and Henry David THOREAU. See also BROOK FARM.

transcontinental railroad   An indirect result of the Civil War, whose military needs encouraged the building of railroads, the first spanning of the continent occurred on May 10, 1869, at the much celebrated GOLDEN SPIKE CEREMONY. Joined that day were lines of the Union Pacific, building westward from Omaha, Nebraska, and the Central Pacific, building eastward from Sacramento, California. See also IRON HORSE.

Traveller   Robert E. LEE's horse, a dappled gray stallion that carried him throughout the Civil War. The general himself described it as "a Confederate gray."

Traven, B.   See THE TREASURE OF THE SIERRA MADRE.

Travis, Merle   (1917–83) Country singer, songwriter. Born in Kentucky, Travis was the author of two classic coal mining ballads, "Dark as a Dungeon" and "Sixteen Tons," the latter of which was a 1955 pop hit for Ernie Ford. He also wrote the novelty tune "Smoke, Smoke, Smoke That Cigarette" (1947) and developed the two-finger guitar style known as Travis picking.

Travis, William B.   (1809–36) Commander of the ALAMO garrison, Travis was a South Carolina lawyer who contributed a major set piece to the Alamo legend by supposedly drawing a line in the mission's sand, over which the defenders stepped, signaling readiness to die. He was played in John WAYNE's movie (1960) by Laurence Harvey. The popularity of "Travis" as a Texas boy's name may be traced to his heroic death.

Treasure of the Sierra Madre, The   A novel written in German by the intensely private B. Traven (1890–1969). A story of greed among gold-seekers in the Mexican mountains, it was translated into English in 1934 and brought to the screen by John HUSTON in 1948. The picture won Oscars for Huston as director and screenwriter and for his father, Walter, who played Howard, a grizzled prospector. It is also notable for Humphrey BOGART's portrayal of treasure-maddened Fred C. Dobbs, for Max Steiner's stirring score, and for a much quoted exchange between Dobbs and a bandit leader impersonating a lawman. Asked by Dobbs to display his posse's badges, the bandit splutters indignantly, "Badges? We ain't got no badges. We don't need no badges! I don't have to show you any stinking badges!"

"Trees"   Joyce KILMER's most famous poem (1913), a sentimental ode to a giant oak that stood in his hometown of New Brunswick, New Jersey. It plays on the contrast between natural and artistic creation, beginning with "I think that I shall never see / A poem as lovely as a tree," and ending with the modest disclaimer "Poems are made by fools like me / But only God can make a tree."

Trent, Helen   See THE ROMANCE OF HELEN TRENT.

trick or treat   A Halloween ritual in which costumed children beg candy "treats" from householders with the implied promise that the generous will not be "tricked." Similar begging customs are common worldwide. The American version evolved in the 1930s as a means of redirecting the holiday energy of mischievous youngsters, whose vandalism was seen as the "Halloween problem." The children's formulaic doorstep requests are "Trick or treat?" and "Anything for Halloween?"

Tricky Dick   See Richard NIXON.

Trigger   Roy ROGERS's horse. See also PALOMINO.

Triple Crown   (1) A collective term for horse racing's three biggest races: the KENTUCKY DERBY, the Preakness Stakes, and the Belmont Stakes. Since 1919, when the latter two races were established, only eleven horses have taken the Triple Crown, that is, won all three races in the same year. (2) In baseball, a player's achievement, in the same season, of his league's highest number of home runs, highest runs-batted-in average, and highest overall batting average. See Ted WILLIAMS.

trolley cars   Also known as trolleys and streetcars. Street railways, originally horse-drawn, then electrified, that were common modes of public transport in the nineteenth century. The first one was used in New York City in 1833. They were superseded by buses, subways, and private vehicles, although one surviving example—San Francisco's CABLE CAR system—remains a popular tourist attraction.

Tropic of Cancer   See Henry MILLER.

Trudeau, Garry   (1948–   ) Cartoonist. Trudeau is the creator of *Doonesbury,* a satirical comic strip that won the 1974 Pulitzer Prize for editorial cartooning. Syndicated in hundreds of newspapers, it traces the life stories of 1960s commune members into the political and personal tangles of middle age. Trudeau is married to television newswoman Jane Pauley.

Truman, Harry S   (1884–1972) U.S. president. Crusty, colorful, and outspoken, Missouri-born "Give 'Em Hell Harry" was perhaps the last "man of the people" president. He had been a haberdasher and U.S. senator before becoming Franklin

ROOSEVELT's vice president in 1945. Three months later FDR was dead, and Truman inherited the burden of World War II. His use of the atomic bomb to end it was the first of many controversial actions that made his presidency the forcing ground for the COLD WAR. In his first term, he established the Truman Doctrine, providing aid for countries threatened by communist expansion; its principal components were NATO and the MARSHALL PLAN. Domestically, his economic interventionism and his support of civil rights alienated many voters, and his 1948 reelection victory was unexpected.

Truman's second term saw the ROSENBERG CASE and HISS trial, the first of Joseph MCCARTHY's attacks on the government, and the KOREAN WAR. Truman's most notorious decision in that conflict was to fire his commanding general, Douglas MACARTHUR, for actions that Truman felt would widen the war. Although he was eligible for a third term, he retired to Missouri in 1952, announcing his decision with characteristic bluntness: "I have had all of Washington that I want." See also "THE BUCK STOPS HERE"; "DEWEY DEFEATS TRUMAN!"; "GIVE 'EM HELL, HARRY."

Trumbull, John (1756–1803) "Painter of the Revolution." Trumbull was the son of Connecticut Governor Jonathan Trumbull (1710–85), the only colonial governor to support independence from England. He carried on the family's patriot tradition in large canvases celebrating the Revolution. These included *The Battle of Bunker's Hill, The Surrender of Cornwallis,* and *The Declaration of Independence.*

trusts The huge industrial monopolies of the late nineteenth and early twentieth centuries. The first was John D. ROCKEFELLER's Standard Oil, founded in 1879; its success in controlling oil prices prefigured similar monopolistic ventures by captains of other industries, making the United States, by 1890, the home of big business. In that year, Congress sought to limit business power with the Sherman Anti-Trust Act, which prohibited "combinations in restraint of trade," but it was not until 1904, when the Supreme Court dissolved the Northern Securities holding company, that the law really began to have an effect (see J. P. MORGAN). That case established Theodore ROOSEVELT's reputation as a trust-buster, although his ostensibly more conservative successor, William Howard Taft, actually prosecuted twice as many trusts.

Truth, Sojourner (ca. 1797–1883) A pioneering feminist and abolitionist, Sojourner Truth was born a slave in New York State, fled her master in 1827, experienced a religious conversion, and began calling for emancipation in the 1840s. Her slave name was Isabella Baumfree; she changed it to acknowledge her spiritual calling.

Tubb, Ernest (1914–84) Country singer, songwriter. Texas-born Tubb, a fervent admirer of Jimmie RODGERS, was helped by Rodgers's widow in the 1930s to his first recordings in a fifty-year career. His first big hit, "Walking the Floor over You," came in 1941, and the following year he debuted on the GRAND OLE OPRY. He wrote a string of country favorites in the 1940s, including "Slippin' Around" and "Warm Red Wine," and continued to record into the 1980s. His influence on younger musicians was incalculable, because he was a pioneer in the use of electric instruments and their attendant style, the HONKY-TONK sound. A tribute album released on his sixty-fifth birthday included tracks by, among others, Merle HAGGARD, George JONES, Loretta LYNN, Willie NELSON, and Conway TWITTY.

Tubman, Harriet (ca. 1821–1913) Abolitionist. The most famous "conductor" on the UNDERGROUND RAILROAD, Tubman was born a slave, fled north in 1849, and risked her safety on numerous return trips south, escorting roughly three hundred slaves to freedom. Legend credits her with the use of the hymn "STEAL AWAY" as a signal and of a pistol to "encourage" reluctant escapees. Tubman's efforts earned her the nickname Moses.

Tucker, Sophie (1884–1966) "Last of the Red Hot Mamas." Born in Russia, Tucker came to New York in 1906 and parlayed an ample frame and equally ample voice into a singing career that spanned half a century. In vaudeville, nightclubs, and occasional films, she specialized in the comic brassiness reflected in her nickname. She is known too for a pithy comment on success: "I've been poor and I've been rich. Believe me, rich is better."

tumbleweed A plant that has been dislodged from arid soil and is being blown about, or "tumbled," by the wind. Tumbleweeds are a common feature of western landscapes and as such have acquired symbolic value. *Tumbleweeds* (1925) was William S. HART's last film, *Tumbling Tumbleweeds* (1935) Roy ROGERS's first.

"Tunney, Gene (1897–1978) Boxer. James Joseph Tunney was heavyweight champion from 1926, when he took the crown from Jack DEMPSEY, until 1928, when he retired. In 1927, he was the victor in a controversial "long count" rematch with Dempsey. Knocked down in the seventh round, he spent more than ten seconds on the canvas, yet was able to come up and win because Dempsey had been slow to retire to a neutral corner, and the referee held the count until he did so.

Tupperware party A social gathering sponsored by a representative of the Tupperware company, who uses the occasion to sell its wares to the guests. The wares are plastic household containers invented by Earl Tupper (1907–83). The representatives are known as hostesses.

turkey A large game bird indigenous to the Americas, named for Turkey by Europeans ignorant of its origins. Wild turkeys were abundant in colonial times, and their supposed although unproven use at the first THANKSGIVING made domesticated varieties a traditional main dish on that holiday; the celebration itself is known as Turkey Day. Benjamin FRANKLIN coyly nominated the turkey, and not the eagle, as the national bird, in that it was a "true native original," and John James AUDUBON chose it as the opening plate in his celebrated *Birds of America*. The use of "turkey" as a synonym for "dolt" or "loser" derives from the alleged stupidity of domestic breeds; the wild turkey, by contrast, is a paragon of cunning. Wild Turkey is a popular brand of BOURBON.

"Turkey in the Straw" A traditional fiddle tune set to the melody of the MINSTREL SHOW song "Zip Coon" or "Old Zip Coon." Zip Coon was a stereotypical "dandified darky."

"Turn on, tune in, drop out" A catchphrase of the 1960s COUNTERCULTURE. Its chemical salvation message may be traced to Timothy LEARY.

Turner, Ike and Tina   Musicians. Ike Turner (1931–) played in Mississippi blues clubs as a child and by the 1950s was a top session guitarist. Singer Tina, born Annie Mae Bullock (1938–), joined his band the Kings of Rhythm in 1956, married him two years later, and was soon the center of a rhythm and blues revue featuring her sexually charged dancing with the backup Ikettes. The group's hits included "I Think It's Gonna Work Out Fine," "River Deep, Mountain High," and "Proud Mary." Ike's abusive treatment of his protégée precipitated a 1976 divorce. Tina's solo career took off in the 1980s, with the album *Private Dancer* (1985) and a 1985 Grammy Award as pop singer of the year. Her hit "What's Love Got to Do with It?" was also the title of a feature film (1993) about her life.

Turner, Lana   (1920–) Actress. According to legend, Julia Jean Turner was discovered at the soda fountain of Hollywood's Schwab's Drugstore and soon promoted as a promising "sweater girl." Her rather chilly allure and lack of range made her more of a movie star than an actress, but she did solid work in *The Postman Always Rings Twice* (1946), *Peyton Place* (1957), and *Madame X* (1966).

Turner, Nat   (1800–31) Leader of the largest slave revolt in U.S. history. Turner was born in Virginia, became a self-ordained preacher in the 1820s, and in 1831 incited a rebellion in which dozens of whites were killed in a four-day rampage. Turner and sixteen followers were hanged in retribution, and other, innocent slaves were also killed. Fear of further risings hardened the South; the rebellion's immediate impact was to tighten the "codes" that kept the servile population uneducated and immobile. See also Denmark VESEY.

Turner, Tina   See Ike and Tina TURNER.

Turner thesis   Also known as the frontier thesis. The idea that, throughout U.S. history, the presence of open western land provided a "safety valve" for social tensions and nurtured a spirit of democratic individualism among settlers who sought to exploit its promise of freedom. The thesis was proposed by historian Frederick Jackson Turner (1861–1932) in an 1893 address to the American Historical Association. Turner taught at Wisconsin and Harvard. His book *The Significance of Sections in American History* won a 1933 Pulitzer Prize.

Turpin, Ben   (1874–1940) A silent film comedian whose trademark was his permanently crossed eyes, Turpin worked for Mack SENNETT from 1917. He was particularly adept at parodying romantic heroes, as in his faux-VALENTINO portrait, *The Shriek of Araby* (1923).

Tuskegee Institute   See Booker T. WASHINGTON.

TV   See TELEVISION.

TV dinners   Frozen complete dinners meant to be heated and eaten while watching television. Introduced (1953) by the Swanson company.

TV Guide   A weekly magazine (founded 1953) of television program listings. It also carries feature stories and soap opera summaries. With over 15 million readers, it is second only to the READER'S DIGEST in circulation.

Twain, Mark   (1835–1910) Writer. The premier American humorist of the nineteenth century, Samuel Langhorne Clemens is best known as the author of TOM SAWYER and HUCKLEBERRY FINN. His ear for dialect, narrative control, and sensitivity to detail, however, also enabled him to produce other accomplished novels, fine travel books, and the essays in the posthumously published *Letters from the Earth,* which reveals the pessimism beneath his comic mask.

Born in Missouri, he worked for a time as a Mississippi River pilot, which gave him his nickname Mark Twain (a boatman's expression for "two fathoms deep") and the recollection *Life on the Mississippi* (1883). A trip west produced the memoir *Roughing It* (1872) and his first national success, the story "THE CELEBRATED JUMPING FROG OF CALAVERAS COUNTY." He satirized class hierarchy in the historical romances *The Prince and the Pauper* (1882) and *A Connecticut Yankee in King Arthur's Court* (1889) while attacking social ills more directly in THE GILDED AGE. Twain's darker later works, doubtless influenced by the death of his wife and daughter, include "The Man That Corrupted Hadleyburg" and "The Mysterious Stranger" (both 1898).

Twain's fame in his own day was extraordinary: For decades he was *the* American lecturer. It has survived him thanks to the limpidity of his prose and the adaptation of his works by Hollywood studios. Many of his novels have been filmed, and he himself was played in *The Adventures of Mark Twain* (1944) by a suitably witty, white-suited Fredric MARCH.

Tweed, "Boss"   Democratic kingpin William Marcy Tweed (1823–78) ran New York City's TAMMANY HALL political machine during the graft-ridden post–Civil War GILDED AGE. Through patronage and "creative" expense accounting, he defrauded taxpayers of tens of millions of dollars while exerting influence on the state as well as municipal level. Skewered in cartoons by Thomas NAST and investigated by reformer Samuel Tilden, Tweed was ousted from office in 1873 and died five years later in prison.

Tweety Pie   See SYLVESTER AND TWEETY.

20th Century-Fox   A movie production company formed in 1935 as a merger between companies started by William Fox, Joseph Schenck, and Darryl ZANUCK. It has been a production giant for nearly six decades. Its directors included Elia KAZAN, Ernst Lubitsch, and Otto Preminger, its stars Henry FONDA, Betty GRABLE, Gregory PECK, Tyrone POWER, Marilyn MONROE, and Shirley TEMPLE.

Twenty-One   (1) A card game also known as blackjack, in which players accumulate cards whose combined face values are ideally as close as possible to twenty-one; a player who exceeds that number loses the hand. (2) A fashionable New York City restaurant and nightclub. It began in the 1920s as a SPEAKEASY. (3) A television QUIZ SHOW modeled roughly on the card game. It was popular for two years (1956–58) until a disgruntled contestant on another quiz show initiated investigations of the entire genre. *Twenty-One* was revealed to have been rigged, with the producers providing answers in advance to popular players. One of these, Columbia University English professor Charles Van Doren, lost his teaching job as a result of the scandal.

Twilight Zone, The   A television science fiction series hosted by Rod Serling from 1959 to 1965. It featured offbeat, often gruesomely ironic endings, and its musical theme became a shorthand for eeriness. The concept was carried over into a movie (1983) and a second TV series (1985–87).

Twinkies   A cream-filled cake invented in 1930 by a Chicago bakery manager, James Dewar. The full name, Hostess Twinkies, is a registered trademark of the Continental Baking Company. Dewar came up with the name upon seeing a factory sign for Twinkle Toe shoes. Twinkies are perhaps the ultimate JUNK FOOD. In the 1979 murder trial of Dan White, who had killed two of his superiors in the San Francisco city government, the defense contended that he had been deranged by eating Twinkies. This unsuccessful "Sugar made me do it" plea was called the Twinkie defense.

Twist, the   A dance crazy of the early 1960s. It was inspired by Chubby Checker's 1960 cover of "The Twist," which had previously been recorded by Hank Ballard. Checker, born Ernest Evans (1941–   ) in Philadelphia, followed the hit with similar dance-related songs. Joey Dee and the Starlighters recorded another chart-topper, "The Peppermint Twist," in 1961, helping to make New York City's Peppermint Lounge a brief sensation.

twister   See TORNADO.

Twitty, Conway   (1933–93) Singer, songwriter. Born Harold Lloyd Jenkins in Mississippi (and named for the movie comic Harold LLOYD), Twitty took his stage name from the towns of Conway, Arkansas, and Twitty, Texas. He had a rock 'n' roll hit in 1958 with "It's Only Make Believe," then went on to become country music's most successful record seller, with over fifty number-one songs to his credit. Among them were "I Love You More Today," "Hello Darlin'," "After the Fire is Gone" (recorded with Loretta LYNN), and "I Can't Stop Loving You." He owned a theme park near Nashville, Twitty City, that drew hundreds of thousands of tourist fans a year.

2001: A Space Odyssey   A 1968 film directed by Stanley KUBRICK from a story by science fiction writer Arthur Clarke. Visually striking and tantalizingly ambiguous, it concerns the conflict between a crew of human spacemen and an onboard computer, Hal, that aborts their mission. It was an early foray into themes that flourished a decade later: the possibility of extraterrestrial life and the "humanity" of robots. See E.T., STAR WARS (1).

Two Years Before the Mast   (1840) A narrative by Richard Henry Dana (1815–82) based on his experience as a sailor on the vessel *Pilgrim* (1836–38). It exposed the harsh treatment of sailors by tyrannical captains and led to successful calls for maritime reform.

Tyler, Royall   (1757–1826) Lawyer, playwright. Author of *The Contrast,* Tyler is sometimes considered the father of American drama. He studied law under John ADAMS, fought in the Revolutionary War, and was chief justice of the Vermont supreme court (1807–13). He also wrote *The Algerine Captive* (1797), a novel.

Typhoid Mary   Nickname of Mary Mallon (1868–1938), an Irish cook who infected dozens of people with typhoid fever in the 1910s. Health officials identified her as the source of contagion as early as 1907, but they were unable to isolate her until 1915. A "carrier" who was evidently immune to the disease herself, she repeatedly broke her promises to keep out of kitchens until she was forcibly confined to a New York hospital. She died there a quarter of a century later.

Uncas An Indian hero in James Fenimore Cooper's Leatherstocking Tales. He is the "last of the Mohicans" of that series.

Uncle Abe Nickname for Abraham Lincoln.

Uncle Remus The fictional narrator of a series of stories by Georgia writer Joel Chandler Harris (1848–1908). As a boy, Harris had heard black field hands telling African folktales, and his collections, beginning with *Uncle Remus: His Songs and Sayings* (1880), reflect his memories. Because Uncle Remus is a seemingly contented slave, and because he tells the tales in a plantation dialect, Harris has been occasionally castigated as condescending. Folklorist Richard Dorson, on the other hand, called the Uncle Remus figure "a well-rounded carrier of Negro lore," true in sensibility, if not in speech, to the African heritage.

The popular reception of the Uncle Remus stories has been less divided. In Harris's hands, the rivalry between the ever-hungry Brer Fox and the ever-resourceful Brer Rabbit quickly entered the mainstream of children's literature, while his Tar Baby and "Briar Patch" tales became regional classics. The Uncle Remus stories filled several volumes and inspired the Walt Disney animated feature *Song of the South* (1946).

Uncle Sam A personification of the U.S. federal government and more broadly of the nation itself. Fanciful attempts have been made to identify the eponymous prototype as "Uncle" Sam Wilson (1768–1854), a government inspector during the War of 1812, but his name probably became attached to "U.S." long after the letters had stood for "United States." Uncle Sam is usually seen as a white-goateed, top-hatted gentleman with stars, stripes, or both as part of his attire (see Stars and Stripes). This image was established by James Montgomery Flagg in his World War I recruiting posters. Flagg had modeled the figure on Thomas Nast's cartoons, and Nast in turn had looked to Dan Rice, whose "flag suit" may have been the original Uncle Sam costume.

Uncle Tom See Uncle Tom's Cabin.

Uncle Tomahawk A subservient native American male. See tomahawk.

Uncle Tom's Cabin An antislavery novel (1852) by Harriet Beecher Stowe. Its main character are the aged, kindly slave Uncle Tom; Little Eva, the daughter of Tom's owner; the slave child Topsy, the young mulatto woman Eliza; and Simon Legree, a northern-born overseer who beats Tom to death. Subtitled "Life Among the Lowly," the book had a tremendous impact on opinion about the "peculiar institution." Sold to 300,000 readers in the first year and translated into twenty languages, it was also staged throughout Europe and America, winning wide sympathy for the ABOLITIONIST cause. In 1862, Abraham LINCOLN addressed Stowe, in a telling exaggeration, as "the little woman who wrote the book that started this great war." "Uncle Tomitude" soon came to mean sympathy with blacks. The pejorative meaning of Uncle Tom—a happily submissive black male—did not arise until the 1940s. In this sense it is also seen simply as "Tom."

Unconditional Surrender   A nickname for Ulysses S. GRANT, acquired in 1862 after he had demanded "an unconditional and immediate surrender" of a Confederate fort. It stuck partly because of the chance concurrence between the general's initials and those of the expression.

"Under the spreading chestnut tree"   See "VILLAGE BLACKSMITH, THE"

underground railroad   The network of hiding places and escape routes that brought fugitive slaves to freedom before the Civil War. The railroad metaphor was preserved in the names Liberty Line and North Star Line and in coded references to safe houses, "railroad" workers, and transported slaves as respectively "stations," "conductors," and "packages" or "goods." The network received ABOLITIONIST support, but was run chiefly by escaped slaves themselves, of whom the most famous was Harriet TUBMAN. See also "FOLLOW THE DRINKING GOURD."

"Union Maid"   (1947) A song written by Woody GUTHRIE to the tune of a traditional folk tune, "Redwing." Like Joe HILL's "Rebel Girl," it applauds a young woman's prolabor spirit.

> *Oh you can't scare me, I'm sticking to the union,*
> *Sticking to the union till the day I die.*

Union Pacific   A rail line authorized by Congress in 1862. The eastern portion of the TRANSCONTINENTAL RAILROAD, it stretched from Omaha, Nebraska, to Promontory Point, Utah. The discovery of graft in its finances led to the Crédit Mobilier scandal of the Ulysses S. GRANT administration.

Unitas, Johnny   (1933–   ) Football player. Playing for the Baltimore Colts from 1956 to 1973, Unitas was one of professional football's greatest quarterbacks. He set records for total yardage, passes completed, touchdown passes, and touchdown passes completed in consecutive games; the final record (forty-seven) still stands. Unitas led the Colts to three National League championships.

United Artists   A film production company formed in 1919 by Charlie CHAPLIN, Douglas FAIRBANKS, D. W. GRIFFITH, and Mary PICKFORD. It began by releasing their films, then expanded to handle the work of other artists, including Buster KEATON and Rudolph VALENTINO. It is still a going concern in the 1990s.

Universal Pictures   A film production company founded in 1912 by Carl Laemmle. Its stars included the monster mafia of Lon CHANEY, Boris KARLOFF, and Bela LUGOSI as well as the comedy duo ABBOTT AND COSTELLO. A recent association with Steven SPIELBERG has proved immensely profitable.

unreasonable searches and seizures   One of the potential abuses of government power against which the BILL OF RIGHTS provides protection. The Fourth Amendment requires that law officers searching for evidence of a crime have "probable cause" for the search and be in possession of a search warrant. The principle became contested in the 1960s, with "law and order" citizens claiming that it crippled the police in their attempts to protect society. Police zealotry in response to this encouragement eventually swung the pendulum in the other direction, and "evidence illegally obtained" is a common technicality upon which otherwise solid indictments are thrown out of court.

Unser, Al and Bobby   Race car drivers. Brothers Al (1939–   ) and Bobby (1934–   ) Unser, the sons of a driver, were perennial contenders for the INDIANAPOLIS 500 title in the 1970s. Since 1967, Al has placed seven times, winning the race in 1970, 1971, 1978, and 1987. Bobby, with four places, won in 1968, 1975, and 1981. Al's son Al Jr. was second in the 1989 run.

Untouchables, The   (1) FBI agents under the direction of Special Agent Eliot Ness (1903–57), referring to the belief that his G-MEN could not be bought. Ness had been influential in breaking the back of the Al CAPONE mob. His exploits inspired two exceptionally violent media productions also called *The Untouchables:* (2) a television series (1959–63) starring Robert Stack and (3) a feature film (1987) starring Kevin Costner.

Up from Slavery   See Booker T. WASHINGTON.

up the river   See SING SING.

Updike, John   (1932–   ) Writer. Long associated with THE NEW YORKER, Updike writes stories and novels that explore the intermingling of middle-class reality and spiritual yearning. His first popular novel, *Rabbit, Run* (1960), was followed by sequels, one of which, *Rabbit Is Rich* (1981), won a Pulitzer Prize. The steamier *Couples* (1968) is his biggest seller.

Uris, Leon   (1924–   ) Writer. Uris specializes in novels of contemporary political interest. *Exodus* (1958), about the founding of Israel, sold over 5 million copies and inspired a 1960 movie starring Paul NEWMAN. He has also written a novel on the 1962 Cuban missile crisis and the screenplay for John Sturges's 1957 film *Gunfight at the O.K. Corral* (see O.K. CORRAL).

U.S.A.   (1) The United States of America. Seen infrequently as "US of A." Hence (2) The "U.S.A." trilogy, a massive novel by John DOS PASSOS. Often cited as the GREAT AMERICAN NOVEL, it uses a wide range of experimental prose techniques to explore American life in the early twentieth century. Its component volumes—all of which can be read alone—are *The 42nd Parallel* (1930), *1919* (1932), and *The Big Money* (1936).

USO   United Service Organizations. A civilian-run network of social and educational centers that cater to U.S. military personnel. Founded in 1941, the USO is best known as the sponsor of troop entertainment shows in World War II, the Korean conflict, and Vietnam. See also Bob HOPE.

utopian communities   The idea of utopia as an ideal community goes back thousands of years, to Plato's *Republic;* the name itself derives from Thomas More's *Utopia* (1516), a famous description of a perfect *ou-topos* ("no place"). The belief that perfection might actually be seen on earth was a grounding sentiment for many settlers of the New World. The PURITANS of New England believed that God had chosen them to establish a new, righteous social order—what elder John Winthrop called "a city upon a hill." Roger WILLIAMS's Rhode Island revised this basic dream, while communities of the AMISH and the SHAKERS also reflected the conviction that religious discipline might transform "no place" into reality.

That conviction was still strong in the nineteenth century. Between 1805 and 1824 the German pietist George Rapp (1757–1847) founded three celibate and communistic "Rappite" communities; the first one, at Harmony, Pennsylvania, lasted until 1847 (the same year that, half a continent away, the MORMONS were founding Salt Lake City). A more secular idealism informed other nineteenth-century experiments. In the early 1800s, the Welsh-born Robert Owen (1771–1858) used remarkably modern ideas of environmental conditioning to create a model "factory town" at Scotland's New Lanark; with his profits, he bought one of Rapp's sites and founded short-lived (1825–27) New Harmony, Indiana, where private property and "irrational religion" were abolished.

The 1840s saw a wave of similar experiments, many of them, like BROOK FARM, Bronson Alcott's Fruitlands (1844), and New Jersey's North American Phalanx (1843–55), inspired by the writings of French socialist Charles Fourier on the "scientific" virtues of cooperation. A handful proved quite durable. The most stable of several Icarian communities founded by disciples of another French visionary, Etienne Cabet, lasted almost a quarter of a century (1860–84). John Humphrey Noyes's "perfectionist" Oneida (see ONEIDA [2]) made it from 1848 to 1879, and the Iowa "Christian communist" town of Amana, founded in 1855, still exists today in modified form; outsiders know it as the home of Amana appliances.

Communalism rose again in the 1960s, when HIPPIES and others disenchanted with society formed "back to the land" communes in rural areas; and in the 1970s, as religious "cult" leaders—most tragically, Jim Jones of JONESTOWN— attempted to revive the dream of a heaven on earth. See also LOOKING BACKWARD; B. F. SKINNER.

Valentino, Rudolph (1895–1926) Actor. The prototype of the "Latin lover," the Italian-born Rodolfo d'Antonguolla was the silent screen's greatest romantic idol. Coming to Hollywood in 1917, he was a bit player until 1921, when he became an "overnight" sensation with two films: *The Four Horsemen of the Apocalypse* and *The Sheik*. Men expressed contempt for his Mediterranean preening—a Chicago paper called him the "Pink Powder Puff"—but women found him irresistible, and showings of *The Sheik* were filled with swooners. Valentino's other box-office hits were *Blood and Sand* (1922), *Monsieur Beaucaire* (1924), *The Eagle* (1925), and *Son of the Sheik* (1926). When a perforated ulcer suddenly ended his life on August 23, 1926, 100,000 mourners came to his wake. For decades afterward, a veiled "woman in black" made headlines each August 23 by laying a wreath of flowers on his grave.

Vallandigham, Clement L. (1820–71) Politician. During the Civil War, Ohio Congressman Vallandigham was the North's most notorious COPPERHEAD. His speeches denouncing President Lincoln and extolling STATES' RIGHTS got him tried for treason in 1863 and banished, by Lincoln's order, to the Confederacy. He went from there to Canada and then, in 1864, back to Ohio, where his political influence gradually waned. He is thought to have been the model for Philip Nolan, the banished protagonist of THE MAN WITHOUT A COUNTRY.

Vallee, Rudy (1901–86) Singer. The nation's first "crooner," Hubert Prior Vallee was idolized in the 1920s for his renditions of "Good Night, Sweetheart" and his signature tune, "I'm Just a Vagabond Lover." Beginning in 1929, he hosted radio's first variety hour, helping to launch Edgar BERGEN and THE ALDRICH FAMILY. He did minor parts in films into the 1970s.

Valley Forge A site in eastern Pennsylvania where the Continental Army endured disease and privation in the winter of 1777–78. The troops, ill-fed and ill-clothed, reluctantly stayed with commanding General George Washington although one in four of them never saw the spring. Washington's concern for them was the subject of a Parson WEEMS anecdote, depicted in numerous works of art, about the general kneeling in prayer in the snow.

valley girl A stereotypically empty-headed young woman from California's San Bernardino Valley. The type became a national joke in the 1980s following Frank ZAPPA's novelty tune "Valley Girl" (1982), in which his teenage daughter parodied valley girl slang, including the derisive "Gag me with a spoon."

Valley of the Dolls See Jacqueline SUSANN.

vamoose To go; to depart in a hurry. Western slang from the Spanish *vamos* or *vámonos*, "Let's go."

vamp   A dangerously seductive woman, a femme fatale. As a verb, it means "to entice or seduce." From Theda Bara's portrayal of the "vampirish" woman in *A Fool There Was* (1915).

Van Buren, Abigail   See "Dear Abby."

Van Buren, Martin   (1782–1862) U.S. president from 1837 to 1841, Van Buren had been Andrew Jackson's vice president and before that a party leader of such conciliatory skills that his nicknames included the Little Magician and the Fox of Kinderhook. His birthplace, Kinderhook, New York, is the probable origin of the expression OK.

Van Doren, Charles   See Twenty-One (3).

Van Heusen, Jimmy   (1913–90) Songwriter. Van Heusen composed the music to songs made popular by Bing Crosby and Frank Sinatra. With lyricist Johnny Burke he wrote the Academy Award "Swinging on a Star" for Crosby's hit movie *Going My Way* (1944). With Sammy Cahn he won Oscars for the Sinatra hits "All the Way," "Call Me Irresponsible," and "High Hopes." Sinatra also recorded their "My Kind of Town" and "Second Time Around."

Vanderbilt family   The Vanderbilt family saga was a classic rags-to-riches story. In 1810, young Cornelius Vanderbilt (1794–1877) invested $100 borrowed from his father to establish a ferry service between Manhattan and Staten islands. From that base he gradually expanded his operations and his ambition, first securing a monopoly of the Hudson River shipping trade, then moving to ocean-going vessels and international success. After the Civil War, he did on land what he had already done on water, turning a failing New York rail line into gold and making "Vanderbilt" a byword for prosperity. When "the Commodore" died, he left a fortune of over $100 million and a lasting legacy in the university that bears his name. His railroad interests were run after his death by his son William (1821–85), an able manager who is remembered for his Fifth Avenue mansion and the regrettable line "The public be damned." William's sons Cornelius and William K., also involved in the family business, helped to make Newport, Rhode Island, socially fashionable; the best known of its many mansions is Cornelius's The Breakers.

vanishing hitchhiker   The most widely known example of the modern or "urban" legend. A driver picks up a young woman hitchhiker, drops her at her house, and discovers that she has left some personal item in his car. Going to the door to return it, he discovers that the item had belonged to the owner's daughter—who was killed in an accident years before at the precise spot where he had picked the girl up. Variants of this "mysterious passenger" rumor are discussed in folklorist Jan Harold Brunvand's *The Vanishing Hitchhiker* (1981).

Vanity Fair   The title of three New York magazines. The first (1859–63) was a humor weekly which occasionally published the work of Artemus Ward. The second (1868–1936) exhibited a more socially incisive editorial policy, critiquing politics, literature, and the arts until it was absorbed by Vogue. The third, a slick monthly ballyhooed as the revival of the second, first appeared in 1983.

Vanzetti, Bartolomeo   See SACCO AND VANZETTI.

vaquero   Spanish for COWBOY. The West's riding and roping skills were developed in the early 1800s by these horsemen, who were usually Indian riders employed on Southwest ranches. Their "roundups" gave us the term RODEO, their name itself the expression "buckaroo."

Variety   A weekly trade paper of the New York theater world. Founded in 1905, it includes feature stories and promotional material as well as reviews, and has long been noted for its slang-rich style.

Vassar College   Founded in 1861, Vassar was the first U.S. college to promote women's education on a par with that of men. Good women's schools were already in existence (Mount Holyoke, for example, since 1836), but their curricula tended to reinforce female "differentness." When Poughkeepsie, New York, brewer Matthew Vassar funded his namesake, he intended it to be "a college for women that shall be to them what Yale and Harvard are to young men." The college paved the way for the other women's schools that were to become known as the SEVEN SISTERS. It has been coeducational since 1970.

vaudeville   Variety theater which, between 1890 and 1930, was the United States' chief form of stage entertainment. Its precursors were the MINSTREL SHOW and, beginning in the 1870s, burlesque shows that featured provocatively clad women in dance routines. The so-called father of American vaudeville, Tony Pastor (1837–1908), opened a New York City theater in 1881 that was dedicated to less racy entertainment, and the vogue for "straight, clean variety" soon caught on. By 1910, Pastor's theater had thirty competitors. The best known of these, the Palace Theater, was every vaudevillian's dream venue. Literally hundreds of others blanketed the country, the most successful managed on the famous "Keith circuit" by the partners Benjamin Keith and Edward Albee.

Vaudeville theaters, often open from midmorning to late evening, offered audiences a wide array, from mime to acrobatics to song and dance, from dramatic monologues to rapid-patter comedy. Their stages were particularly fertile ground for comics. Among those who started there were Jack BENNY, Milton BERLE, BURNS AND ALLEN, W. C. FIELDS, Bob HOPE, and the MARX BROTHERS. The genre was gradually replaced by movies; its closest approximation at midcentury was *The Ed* SULLIVAN *Show*.

Vaughan, Sarah   (1924–90) Jazz singer. The "Divine One," Vaughan began singing jazz with Earl Hines and emerged in the 1940s as a BEBOP stylist, known for her work with Charlie PARKER and Dizzy GILLESPIE. She turned more mainstream in the 1960s, singing at the White House and recording the songs of Henry MANCINI.

VC   Vietcong. See VIETNAM WAR.

Veblen, Thorstein   (1857–1929) Social scientist. In his witty, trenchant analysis of Gilded Age society (see THE GILDED AGE), *The Theory of the Leisure Class* (1899), Veblen excoriated the idle rich for their disinterest in honest craftsmanship and their "conspicuous consumption." The book added a psychological component to economic theory. In *The Theory of Business Enterprise* (1904), he developed his belief that it was the engineer, not the entrepreneur, who created progress.

Vegas   See LAS VEGAS.

Venturi, Robert   (1925–   ) Architect. In the 1960s, Venturi revolted against the severity of the International Style to champion an eclectic, often whimsical architecture that came to be called postmodern. His radical, and increasingly visible, ideas are presented in *Complexity and Contradiction in American Architecture* (1966) and *Learning from Las Vegas* (1972).

Vernon, Mount   See MOUNT VERNON.

Verrazano, Giovanni da   (ca. 1485–ca. 1528) The Italian navigator Verrazano, while on a 1524 search for the NORTHWEST PASSAGE, explored the East Coast from the Carolinas to Canada's Maritimes. He was the first European to enter New York Bay and to see what would become MANHATTAN and Staten islands and the Hudson River. New York City's Verrazano-Narrows Bridge, once the longest suspension bridge in the world, is named in his honor.

Vesey, Denmark   (1767–1822) Leader of a foiled slave uprising, Vesey was a slave until 1800, when he used his winnings from a lottery to purchase his freedom. For two decades he worked as a carpenter and preacher in Charleston, South Carolina. Then, in 1822, he planned a revolt that was to kill slaveowners and take over the city. His plot revealed by an informer, he was executed with over thirty of his followers. See also Nat TURNER.

Vespucci, Amerigo   See AMERICA.

Veterans Day   November 11, a holiday honoring veterans of U.S. wars. As Armistice Day, it was first observed on November 11, 1919, the anniversary of the end of World War I. The current name was established in 1954. See also MEMORIAL DAY.

VFW   Veterans of Foreign Wars. The oldest, and second largest, U.S. veterans' organization. It was founded in 1913 by veterans of the Spanish-American War. The VFW maintains hundreds of posts around the country. The paper "poppies" its members sell as fund-raisers reflect the profusion of those flowers in World War I graveyards. See also AMERICAN LEGION.

victory gardens   Home gardens planted during World War II. The government encouraged them so that the food industry could dedicate more of its resources to feeding the troops.

Vidal, Gore   (1925–   ) Writer. The versatile Vidal's first popular successes came with the satirical dramas *Visit to a Small Planet* (1957) and *The Best Man* (1960). His novel about a Hollywood transsexual, *Myra Breckinridge* (1968; film 1970), made him a household name. An astute observer of the U.S. political tradition, he has also published several essay collections and the best-selling historical novels *Burr* (1973), *1876* (1976), *Lincoln* (1984), *Empire* (1987), and *Hollywood* (1990).

video games   Electronic arcade games which, beginning in the 1970s, gradually replaced PINBALL as teenage obsessions. The first popular game, Pong, was invented by California engineer Nolan Bushnell; it sold well in bars and made the name of Bushnell's company, Atari. Pong, basically an updated version of PING-PONG, was outpaced by Japanese imports like Space Invaders, which established a high-tech, combat-oriented design that remains the industry's essential marketing mode. During the Gulf War of 1991, media wags commented only half jokingly that the precision bombing of Baghdad military installations had been accomplished by pilots who had been "trained" as youngsters on the video simulators Pac-Man and Asteroids. Many video games can be adapted for home television.

videos   Short films made to accompany pop music recordings. They were pioneered by MTV in the 1980s and soon became indispensable marketing tools. Few would-be hits are now released by record companies without an accompanying, made-for-TV video, and channels such as MTV (Music Television) and CMTV (Country Music Television) program hours every day of these mixed-media productions. As DISC JOCKEYS have long promoted recorded music, "video jockeys" (video jocks, VJs) now do the same for videos.

Vidor, King   (1894–1982) Film director. The visually inventive Vidor first scored a hit with the World War I romance *The Big Parade* (1923). He followed it with a wrenching study of urban anomie, *The Crowd* (1928); the emotionally intense, all-black family drama *Hallelujah* (1929); and a hymn to agrarian cooperation, *Our Daily Bread* (1934). His engagement with class tensions appeared vividly in STELLA DALLAS, *Ruby Gentry* (1952), and the shockingly sensual western *Duel in the Sun* (1947). Vidor also filmed Ayn Rand's THE FOUNTAINHEAD.

Vietcong   See VIETNAM WAR.

Vietnam War   (ca. 1960–75) The least popular war in American history. It began slowly in the early 1960s, with U.S. advisers supporting a South Vietnamese regime under attack by local Vietcong guerrillas (the "VC") and their communist backers, the North Vietnamese government of HO CHI MINH. Lyndon JOHNSON inherited the problem—and the cold war fear of communism that got it rolling—after John F. KENNEDY's death, and he supervised the rapid escalation of U.S. involvement, especially after an alleged attack on American warships convinced Congress to pass the Gulf of Tonkin Resolution (1964), giving wide executive powers to the commander in chief. By the close of the decade, hundreds of thousands of U.S. troops had been sucked into LBJ's "quagmire," and television carried nightly reports of their suffering and deaths.

   Public outcry against further U.S. involvement reached a fever pitch in the late 1960s, becoming a principal factor in the development of the COUNTERCULTURE. Outraged particularly by military atrocities against civilians (see MY LAI), "peaceniks" engaged in frequent clashes with police and sponsored a huge peace march on the PENTAGON in 1967. Public rancor forced Johnson from office the following year. His decision not to seek reelection transferred the management of the war to President NIXON, who inherited the rancor as well as the responsibility. Nixon's policy—a combination of peace feelers and intensified bombing—led to U.S. withdrawal by 1973; two years later, the embattled South capitulated to Ho's forces. By that time, the conflict had permanently scarred not only tiny Vietnam but America as well. Frustration and embarrassment at the debacle remained so high that it was years before a war memorial was erected in Washington to the 58,000 U.S. troops who lost their lives there.

See also CHICAGO EIGHT; PENTAGON PAPERS.

Vikings A warlike Scandinavian people who between the ninth and eleventh centuries ravaged much of Europe in raiding parties. Among the places that their expansionist tendencies brought them to was the Western Hemisphere. See LEIF ERICSSON; VINLAND.

Villa, Pancho (1878–1923) Mexican revolutionary. During the Mexican Revolution of 1910, guerrilla General Francisco "Pancho" Villa controlled the large northern region of Chihuahua. Of his many alliances during this turbulent period, the most solid was with Emiliano ZAPATA, with whom he shared a commitment to land reform. Villa's raids across the RIO GRANDE—during one of which he killed several Americans—precipitated a U.S. invasion of Mexico (1916) under John J. PERSHING; it failed to bring the bandit leader to heel. He was killed by political rivals while in retirement.

Village, the See GREENWICH VILLAGE.

"Village Blacksmith, The" A poem (1839) by Henry Wadsworth LONGFELLOW describing the simple, robust life of a rural laborer. Once widely quoted, it begins

> Under the spreading chestnut tree
> The village smithy stands;
> The smith a mighty man is he,
> With large and sinewy hands.

Village People A spoof-rock group of the 1970s that parlayed stereotypical images of "macho" males into disco hits with homosexual double meanings. The name referred to sexually tolerant GREENWICH VILLAGE. The group's most successful songs were "Macho Man" and "YMCA."

Village Voice, The A New York City newspaper begun in 1955 in GREENWICH VILLAGE. Radically COUNTERCULTURE in the 1960s, it gradually developed a tone of respectable reformism. Its original staff included Norman MAILER.

Vinland A VIKING settlement in North America—the first, albeit short-lived, European colony in the New World. Its exact location is unknown, although scholarly consensus puts it near Newfoundland. It was founded by LEIF ERICSSON around 1000 and was abandoned roughly fifteen years later because of the hostile reception of the native "skraelings."

VIP Very important person. The letters are pronounced separately: *vee-eye-pea*.

Virginia Named for the "Virgin Queen," Elizabeth I, Virginia was the first permanent English colony in North America. The earliest settlements were Walter Raleigh's ill-fated ROANOKE COLONY and the more successful JAMESTOWN. Virginia was the first colony to have a representative assembly (House of Burgesses, 1619) and slavery (also 1619), the second to have a college of higher learning

(William and Mary, 1693). It was extremely influential during the Revolution, giving rise to the Continental Congress, Patrick HENRY, and Thomas JEFFERSON, and was equally central to the formation of the Confederacy: It was the home of Robert E. LEE; the Confederate capital, Richmond; and APPOMATTOX COURT-HOUSE. The "Mother of Presidents," Virginia gave birth to eight chief executives, including the so-called Virginia Dynasty of WASHINGTON, JEFFERSON, MADISON, and MONROE.

Virginia Slims   See "YOU'VE COME A LONG WAY, BABY."

Virginian, The   A 1902 novel by Owen Wister (1860–1938), a Philadelphia lawyer who went west for his health in the 1880s and built on his experiences there for the story. It pits a nameless Virginian against the antagonist Trampas in the first WESTERN novel in American literature. Wister dedicated it to his former Harvard classmate Theodore ROOSEVELT. Adapted as a stage play, a movie (1929) starring Gary COOPER, and a television show (1962–71), it established many of the cowboy movie conventions, including the laconic hero and the showdown with the villain. Insulted by Trampas, the Virginian delivers the book's most famous line: "When you call me that, smile!"

"Visit from St. Nicholas, A"   See "THE NIGHT BEFORE CHRISTMAS."

VISTA   See PEACE CORPS.

Vogue   A fashion magazine founded in 1892. Its photographs made "straight out of Vogue" a catchphrase for stylishness.

Voice of America   A radio station run by the federal government out of the United States Information Agency in Washington, D.C. Founded in 1942 as part of the Office of War Information, it broadcasts American descriptive and promotional programs around the world. It especially targeted communist countries during the COLD WAR.

Volstead Act   (1919) The congressional act that enforced the Eighteenth Amendment and made the federal government the official watchdog for PROHIBITION. It was named for its sponsor, Minnesota Congressman Andrew J. Volstead (1860–1947).

von Sternberg, Josef   See Josef von STERNBERG.

von Stroheim, Erich   See Erich von STROHEIM.

Von Tilzer, Harry   (1872–1946) Songwriter. One of TIN PAN ALLEY's most prolific writers, Von Tilzer exercised what Sigmund Spaeth called "a species of hypnotism" on the public of his day. Working out of his own New York publishing firm, he produced COON songs like "Alexander," the immensely popular vacation ditty "On a Sunday Afternoon," and many songs about romance. The most durable of these were "A BIRD IN A GILDED CAGE," "I WANT A GIRL JUST LIKE THE GIRL," and "WAIT TILL THE SUN SHINES, NELLIE." Von Tilzer's most effective lyricists were Arthur Lamb and Andrew Sterling. His brother Albert (1878–1956) wrote "I'll Be with You in Apple Blossom Time" and "TAKE ME OUT TO THE BALL GAME."

Vonnegut, Kurt   (1922–   ) Writer. Extremely popular in the 1960s, especially with college students, Vonnegut writes novels that blend eccentric humor with an often dark vision of human frailty. His best-known works include *Cat's Cradle* (1963) and *Slaughterhouse Five* (1969).

voodoo   A folk religion of the West Indies, particularly Haiti, whose influence is also felt in Louisiana. It blends elements of African, native Caribbean, and Roman Catholic worship into a unique amalgam that stresses possession by spirits and the working of magic by the manipulation of their powers. For example, "voodoo dolls" made in the image of an enemy are said to be able to harm him when stuck with pins. Voodoo's most striking feature is its worshippers' fascination with the dead; a zombie is a corpse that has been revived by the magical activity of a voodoo adept. This latter concept has given us countless "living dead" horror films as well as the name of a mind-deadening cocktail.

"Vote Yourself a Farm"   A political slogan of the 1850s. Promoted by Horace GREELEY and other champions of westward expansion, it bore its fruit in the passage of the HOMESTEAD ACT.

voyageurs   French-Canadian canoers in the eighteenth-century FUR TRADE, many of them the sons of Indian mothers. They were hired by the large fur companies to transport trappers' pelts to dispatch points. The word is French for "traveler."

"Wabash Cannonball" A traditional song about a train that spirits the disadvantaged away from their miseries. Associated with the CARTER FAMILY'S A.P. Carter (who is often credited with writing it) and Roy ACUFF.

Wagner, Honus (1874–1955) Baseball player. An expert fielder and base stealer, the Pittsburgh Pirates' John "Honus" Wagner was also one of the game's most consistent hitters. The National League's answer to Ty COBB, he led the league in batting seven times between 1900 and 1911, retiring after twenty-one years with a .329 career average. He was one of the first members of the Hall of Fame. His base-stealing gave him the nickname "Flying Dutchman."

wagon train A caravan of COVERED WAGONS. The term was used for the title of a television WESTERN (1957–65), which was inspired by John FORD'S epic movie *Wagonmaster* (1950); both vehicles starred veteran Ford player Ward Bond.

"Wait till the Sun Shines, Nellie" (1905) A romantic song, advertised as a "novelty march," written by Harry VON TILZER and lyricist Andrew Sterling. One of the major hits of the 1900s.

Waiting for Lefty (1935) A play about a taxi drivers' strike written by Clifford ODETS for the Group Theater. It was a well-known "workers' play" of the Depression years.

Walden (1854) Henry David THOREAU's meditative account of a stay (1845–47) at CONCORD's Walden Pond, where he went to "front only the essential facts of life." Often erroneously described as a retreat, the stay was rather an experiment in fruitful privation. Thoreau visited the village almost daily, yet at Walden he followed the maxim "Simplify, simplify"—farming, fishing, reading, and writing the manuscript that would become *A Week on the Concord and Merrimack Rivers* (1849). *Walden,* subtitled "Life in the Woods," is rich in observations of the author's sylvan surroundings. These, along with Thoreau's spirited rejection of conventional lives' "quiet desperation," make it the most influential "nature" book in American history. Its underlying self-improvement message inspired the title of B. F. SKINNER's *Walden Two.*

Wall Street (1) A street in the financial district of lower MANHATTAN that contains numerous banks and the New York Stock Exchange. It took its name from a defensive wall built there in the 1650s. Hence (2) a metaphor for U.S. brokerage and financial activity. Often personified: "Wall Street is bullish on microchips."

Wall Street Journal, The   A newspaper aimed chiefly at the business community but noted also for its incisive general reporting. Tucked under an American executive's arm, the *Journal* is as much an emblem of success as his British counterpart's bowler and umbrella.

Wallace, George   (1919–   ) Politician. The voice of segregation in the 1960s, Wallace was governor of Alabama in 1963–67 and again in 1971–78. He gained national attention in 1963 by attempting to block the admission of black students to the University of Alabama. In 1968 and 1972 he ran for the White House; during the second campaign a would-be assassin's bullet left him partially paralyzed, and he ran his state in the 1970s from a wheelchair.

Wallace, Lew   See BEN-HUR; BILLY THE KID.

Wallendas   The "Flying Wallendas" were aerialists who emigrated from Bohemia in 1928 to perform with the Ringling Brothers and Barnum & Bailey Circus. Led by Karl Wallenda (1905–78), they dazzled audiences for decades until a series of fatal falls reduced their numbers. Karl himself was killed in a high-wire accident.

Waller, Fats   (1904–43) Musician. Thomas Waller, who was playing piano in nightspots when he was sixteen, helped to develop the "stride" keyboard style that influenced all succeeding generations of JAZZ players. He accompanied Bessie SMITH, was the first to use the organ in jazz, and was a successful composer of popular songs, many of them written with lyricist Andy Razaf. He is known especially for "Honeysuckle Rose" and "Ain't Misbehavin'."

Wallis, Hal   (1899–1986) Movie producer. Wallis oversaw production at WARNER BROTHERS in the 1930s, supervising the studio's crime and swashbuckler successes, from LITTLE CAESAR and *Captain Blood* (1935) to THE MALTESE FALCON and *The Sea Hawk* (1940). After 1944 he ran his own company, which produced hits ranging from westerns (*Gunfight at the O.K. Corral*, 1957) to Elvis PRESLEY musicals (*G.I. Blues*, 1960) to costume dramas (*Becket*, 1964).

Walsh, Raoul   (1887–1980) Director. Hollywood's best-known action director, Walsh helped to shape the virile images of Humphrey BOGART, James CAGNEY, Douglas FAIRBANKS, and Errol FLYNN. In a career spanning half a century, he directed over one hundred films, among them Fairbank's *The Thief of Bagdad* (1924), Bogart's *The Roaring Twenties* (1939) and *High Sierra* (1940), Flynn's *They Died with their Boots On* (1941) and *Gentleman Jim* (1942), and Cagney's WHITE HEAT.

Waltons, The   A television drama (1972–81) about a rural Virginia family during the Depression. Like LITTLE HOUSE ON THE PRAIRIE, it was a family saga that applauded backwoods traditions.

wampum   Beadwork made by Indian peoples of the eastern woodlands. Because it sometimes served as a medium of exchange, it has been stereotyped as "Indian money." In fact, wampum served several purposes, including intertribal identification, status, and the recording of treaties.

War Hawks In the months preceding the WAR OF 1812, Americans who favored declaring war on England. See also HAWKS AND DOVES.

"War is hell" General William T. SHERMAN's comment on his chosen profession. This succinct version was attributed to him by reporters. When he spoke to a boys' military school in 1879, he was more voluble: ''I am sick and tired of war. Its glory is all moonshine. It is only those who have never fired a shot nor heard the shrieks and groans of the wounded who cry aloud for more blood, more vengeance, more desolation. Some say that war is all glory, but I tell you, boys, it is all hell.''

War of 1812 (1812–15) Known as Mr. Madison's war by its critics, the War of 1812 was precipitated chiefly by the British practice of forcibly recruiting, or ''impressing,'' American sailors suspected to be deserters from His Majesty's navy. Subsidiary causes were the Royal Navy's seizure of U.S. contraband thought to be intended for Napoleon's France; and the belief, firmly held by so-called War Hawks like Henry CLAY and John C. CALHOUN, that the crown was encouraging Indian attacks on the frontier. This trio of grievances came to a head in 1812, when President James MADISON signed a declaration of war.

The conflict was fought both on land and at sea. Among the naval battles, Stephen DECATUR was victorious against the British ship *Macedonian;* OLD IRONSIDES sank the *Guerrière* and the *Java;* and Oliver Hazard PERRY triumphed on Lake Erie. Significant land battles were fought at Detroit and other points along the Canadian border, while the opposing forces also succeeded in burning each other's political nerve centers, the Americans razing York (now Toronto) in 1813, the British retaliating at Washington one year later.

The Treaty of Ghent, ratified in 1815, ended the war without an exchange of territory, causing some to deride the conflict as pointless. It did, however, stop the high-seas impressment and give a considerable boost to American nationalism. Especially potent in this regard was Francis Scott KEY's writing of ''THE STAR-SPANGLED BANNER'' at the defense of Fort McHenry; and Andrew JACKSON's victory at the Battle of NEW ORLEANS—fought, ironically, two weeks after the treaty signing.

War of the Worlds, The An 1898 novel by English writer H. G. Wells about the invasion of the earth by predatory Martians. On October 30, 1938, Orson WELLES dramatized it on radio's *Mercury Theater of the Air.* The vividly realistic broadcast, supposedly emanating from the Martians' touchdown spot, Grover's Mills, New Jersey, created a panic among listeners who had not heard the opening announcement and who believed the Halloween entertainment was the real thing. The incident made young Welles's reputation.

"war to end war, the" Sometimes seen as ''the war to end all wars.'' A contemporary description of World War I. Often attributed, wrongly, to Woodrow WILSON. Probably from the title of H. G. Wells's book *The War That Will End War* (1914).

Warbucks, Daddy See DADDY WARBUCKS.

Ward, Artemus (1834–67) Pseudonym of writer Charles Farrar Browne, who wrote humorous sketches for the *Cleveland Plain Dealer* in 1858–60. ''Artemus

Ward's Sayings'' relied on the down-home, Down East humor of his native Maine, including faux-dialect spelling that influenced Josh BILLINGS and Mark TWAIN. Twain, who met Ward in Nevada, also learned much from the New Englander's slyly deadpan lecture style. Among Ward's other admirers was Abraham Lincoln.

Ward, Montgomery   (1843–1913) Businessman. Ward revolutionized retailing in the 1870s by starting the nation's first mail-order house. His wares, advertised by catalog, brought consumer goods within reach of rural families and were the foundation of a department store chain. Among those who followed his example was Richard Sears (see SEARS, ROEBUCK). Ward also introduced the money-back guarantee.

Warhol, Andy   (1928–87) Artist. The most widely known figure in the POP ART movement, Warhol made large silkscreen reproductions of mass-media images, such as commercial labels, comic strip panels, and famous faces, including those of Elizabeth TAYLOR and Marilyn MONROE. The lengthy experimental films that he produced in his New York studio, the Factory, starred a cadre of photogenic amateurs who became briefly famous. Warhol's comment on celebrity, of which he himself was a classic example, coyly summarized the legacy of his fashionable circle: ''In the future everyone will be famous for fifteen minutes.''

Warner, Pop   (1871–1954) Football coach. Glenn Scobey Warner, after whom POP WARNER FOOTBALL is named, coached college ball from the 1890s to the 1930s. He accumulated a lifetime record of over three hundred wins. Warner coached at his alma mater, Cornell, and at Stanford, Pittsburgh, Temple, and the Carlisle, Pennsylvania, Indian School; his most famous player at Carlisle was Jim THORPE.

Warner Brothers   A film company that began as a distribution company in the 1910s and was incorporated as a studio in 1932—five years after it made movie history by releasing the first major ''talkie,'' THE JAZZ SINGER. In its heyday, Warner Brothers was known for its costume dramas, crime and detective films, and musicals. Its major stars were Humphrey BOGART, James CAGNEY, Bette DAVIS, Errol FLYNN, and Edward G. ROBINSON. The brothers of the title were Harry (1881–1958), Albert (1884–1967), Sam (1888–1927), and the studio head, Jack (1892–1978).

Warren, Earl   (1891–1974) Chief justice of the Supreme Court from 1953 to 1969. Warren had previously served as governor of California (1942–53) and been Thomas E. Dewey's vice presidential candidate in his 1948 run against Harry S TRUMAN. The Warren Court was noted for its liberal readings, especially in BROWN V. BOARD OF EDUCATION and the MIRANDA DECISION. See also WARREN COMMISSION.

Warren, Robert Penn   (1905–89) Writer. Kentucky-born Warren helped to found the literary journals *The Fugitive* (1922) and *The Southern Review* (1935), wrote widely on southern themes, and lived to become the dean of regional writing. He won Pulitzer Prizes for the novel ALL THE KING'S MEN and the poetry volume *Promises* (1957). A professor of English at Yale for two decades (1950–73), he wrote popular texts on poetry and fiction as well as critical essays on Theodore DREISER, John Greenleaf WHITTIER, and segregation.

Warren Commission   A federal commission formed to investigate the John F. KENNEDY assassination and named for its chairman, Chief Justice Earl WARREN. The commission concluded that the president had been killed by a single gunman, Lee Harvey OSWALD, acting alone. Americans who suspected a wider conspiracy denounced the Warren Report as either duplicitous or sloppy—in the words of one prominent critic, a "rush to judgment." Its validity is still debated today.

Washington, Booker T.   (1756–1915) Educator. The best-known black leader of his day, Booker Taliaferro Washington was born in slavery, graduated from Hampton Institute in 1875, and became an eloquent champion of vocational training for his fellow blacks. In 1881, he became president of Tuskegee Institute, an Alabama trade school, and by his retirement in 1915 had turned it into one of the nation's most respected black colleges. His moderate approach to civil rights won him enemies in the black community—notably, W.E.B. DU BOIS—even as white liberals supported his work with hefty contributions. His moving autobiography is *Up from Slavery* (1901).

Washington, George   (1832–99) First president of the United States. No figure in American history was more widely revered than the Virginia farmer-soldier George Washington. A lifetime of managing his ancestral estate, Mount Vernon, made him a paragon of the country gentleman, while his service as commander in chief of the Continental Army and as the nation's first chief executive earned him the title Father of His Country. When he died, his former comrade Henry Lee called him "first in war, first in peace, and first in the hearts of his countrymen." The accolade has survived the reassessments of two centuries.

Born in Virginia, Washington practiced surveying as a young man, joined the colonial militia, and in the French and Indian War served under Edward Braddock (see BRADDOCK'S DEFEAT), gaining valuable experience in frontier tactics. In the 1760s, married to the wealthy widow Martha Custis, he grew tobacco at Mount Vernon and, as a member of the Virginia House of Burgesses, joined the chorus of opponents to British taxation. In 1774, he was a delegate to the Continental Congress, which the following year made him head of the army. Under his command, citizen soldiers defeated the best-disciplined army in the world, with Washington himself directing notable victories at Trenton, Princeton, and YORKTOWN. The Trenton victory over Hessian mercenaries followed a nighttime crossing of the icy Delaware River; it was memorialized in a famous painting by Emanuel LEUTZE, where the general assumes an unlikely standing pose. Washington's dignity at VALLEY FORGE was similarly embellished by a popular image of him praying in the snow.

As president, Washington—himself a Federalist—attempted to reconcile the competing philosophies of the strong centralist Alexander HAMILTON (who became his secretary of the treasury) and the STATES' RIGHTS champion Thomas JEFFERSON (who served as secretary of state). His administration (1789–97) saw the passage of the BILL OF RIGHTS, the establishment of the federal court system (with John JAY serving as first chief justice), and the growth of a partisan contentiousness that Washington himself, in his celebrated Farewell Address (1796), denounced as inimical to civil harmony. In his handling of the nation's first civil revolt, the 1794 WHISKEY REBELLION, Washington confirmed the power of the federal government. Although his reputation endured a drastic shock when he pushed for the highly unpopular Jay's Treaty, he became in his retirement "the godlike

Washington,'' an American Cincinnatus whose air of reserve only added to his aura of integrity.

That aura was enhanced upon his death by the publication of Parson WEEMS's biography. Widely reprinted, it contained "moral tales" about the leader's childhood intended to inspire emulation among young readers. The most famous of these was the "cherry tree" story, in which young George, having injured a tree with his "little hatchet," is lauded by his father for confessing the deed. In a similar tale, the youthful Virginian hurls a silver dollar across the Rappahannock River—commonly misremembered as the POTOMAC.

Modern historians have pecked away at the Washington myth, highlighting his personal severity, his fiscal caginess, and his alleged infatuation with a friend's wife, Sally FAIRFAX. None of this has seriously tarnished his image. Washington has lent his name to one state, numerous physical landmarks, and hundreds of townships and cities, including the nation's capital—which includes his famous memorial, the WASHINGTON MONUMENT. His face appears on the quarter and the dollar bill (see Gilbert STUART) as well as on the PURPLE HEART and Mount RUSHMORE. What John Adams called his "superstitious veneration" may have subsided, but he remains the single most respected figure in the nation's history.

Washington, D.C.   The national capital of the United States, a site chosen by George Washington and named for him. Although the city sits on the Potomac River in eastern Maryland, technically it is in the District of Columbia (D.C.), federal land whose residents are voting citizens but whose representation in Congress is only nominal. The government section of the city, planned by French engineer Pierre-Charles L'Enfant (1791), includes such buildings as the U.S. CAPITOL, the LINCOLN MEMORIAL, the SMITHSONIAN INSTITUTION, the WHITE HOUSE, and the WASHINGTON MONUMENT. Washington is also the home of many other federal buildings, national museums, libraries, and universities.

Washington Monument   A stone obelisk honoring George Washington that is a principal tourist attraction of WASHINGTON, D.C. Designed by Robert Mills (1781–1855), it was begun in 1848 and completed forty years later. From the top of the 555-feet-tall shaft, visitors may see the city and surrounding states.

Washington Post   (1) A national newspaper published since 1877 in WASHINGTON, D.C. Editorially liberal, it took a suspicious view of U.S. Vietnam War policy and was chiefly responsible for covering the WATERGATE story. (2) "The Washington Post March" is an 1889 composition by John Philip SOUSA.

WASP   White Anglo-Saxon Protestant. Like ANGLO, a generic, often negative term for the "nonethnic" majority. Pronounced, and sometimes spelled, *wasp*.

"Waste Land, The"   A 1922 poem by T. S. ELIOT. It explores the themes of spiritual decay and possible rebirth in an experimental format thick with literary allusions. Eliot dedicated the poem to Ezra POUND, who provided valuable help in trimming it. The poem begins with the line "April is the cruellest month" and ends with the Sanskrit word for peace, "Shantih."

Watchtower, The   The principal periodical of the JEHOVAH'S WITNESSES, a Bible pamphlet that is handed out door-to-door. Founded in 1879, it is now published in dozens of languages and reaches millions of readers worldwide.

water moccasin   A pit viper of the southwestern United States; also known as the cottonmouth from its mouth's white interior. Although its poison is seldom fatal, its menacing appearance and painful bite have engendered a widespread folklore about its deadliness. In one common tale, a swimmer warned away from a body of water dives in and emerges torn to shreds, having landed in the snakes' underwater nest.

Watergate   A political scandal of the NIXON administration. During the 1972 presidential campaign, five men were caught breaking into the Democratic party headquarters in Washington's Watergate building. When a connection emerged between them and Nixon's reelection committee, federal prosecutors began investigating White House staffers, including the president's closest aides and his personal counsel. Nixon was reelected in November, but by year's end—thanks partly to probing by WOODWARD AND BERNSTEIN—a bewildering array of White House skulduggery had come to light, including the existence of a "plumbers" group formed to plug press leaks, the payment of "hush money" to one of the burglars, and another burglary, of an antiwar psychiatrist's office.

   In the following months, the president first appointed and then fired special prosecutors, withheld information from the judiciary, released heavily edited tapes of White House conversations, and eventually was forced to admit that he himself had participated in the obstruction of justice. Under threat of impeachment, he resigned in August 1974—and was immediately pardoned by incoming President Gerald Ford. The term "Watergate" became inseparable from political wrong-doing—so much so that subsequent scandals often acquired the damning suffix "-gate."

watermelon   A vine of the cucumber family, native to Africa and introduced into North America in the 1500s. The green-hulled fruit contains a soft, usually pink or red center that is a child's treat, especially in the South. Iconographically, the watermelon is also linked with the stereotype of the "happy darky."

Waters, Ethel   (1900–77) Singer, actress. The first black woman to get first-line billing in the American theater, Waters began as a recording star in the 1920s; she was associated with the songs "Dinah" and "STORMY WEATHER." Onstage she did straight dramatic roles as well as musicals, later carrying this versatility onto the screen with the musical *Cabin in the Sky* (1943) and the dramas *The Member of the Wedding* (1952) and *Pinky* (1949)—the latter of which won her an Oscar nomination. Waters also originated the role of the savvy maid Beulah in the television sitcom of that name (1950–53).

Waters, Muddy   (1915–83) Blues musician. Mississippi singer and guitarist McKinley Morganfield played country-style blues until the 1940s, when his shift to electric guitar in a small, driving combo helped to forge the sound called Chicago blues. His rhythm and blues hits—often tinged with sexual implications—included "Honey Bee," "Hoochie Coochie Man" "Got My Mojo Working," and "I Just Wanna Make Love to You." His influence on rock 'n' roll was considerable. The Rolling Stones in particular looked to his example, choosing their name from his song "Rollin' Stone."

Wayfaring Stranger   Nickname of Burl IVES.

Wayne, Anthony   (1745–96) General. Known as Mad Anthony because of his daring, Wayne led a 1779 attack on a British garrison at Stony Point, New York, which was one of the Revolutionary War's most talked-about victories. In 1794, he commanded the troops that defeated a large Shawnee and Miami force at Fallen Timbers, Ohio, thus opening the NORTHWEST TERRITORY to white settlement.

Wayne, John   (1907–79) Actor. Born Marion Morrison in Iowa, "Duke," Wayne became, in the course of a fifty-year career, the archetypal image of the American hero. His work in 1930s low-budget westerns prepared him for his first major role, that of the Ringo Kid in *Stagecoach* (see STAGECOACH [2]). His association with director John FORD on that film shaped his work for decades. Ford cast him in many of his best pictures, including the westerns FORT APACHE, SHE WORE A YELLOW RIBBON, *The Searchers* (1956), and *The Man Who Shot Liberty Valance* (1962); the war drama *They Were Expendable* (1945); and the rollicking Irish romance *The Quiet Man* (1952). Most firmly associated with cowboy roles, Wayne also starred in Howard HAWKS's *Red River* (1948) and *Rio Bravo* (1959) and won an Oscar as an aging marshal in *True Grit* (1969).

One of Hollywood's superpatriots, Wayne also directed a 1960 epic, *The Alamo,* in which he himself played Davy CROCKETT; and a 1968 war film, *The Green Berets,* which cast the unpopular Vietnam War as a righteous crusade. After he survived an initial cancer operation in the 1960s, he said that he had "licked the Big C." Three years before cancer finally killed him, he gave a fine portrayal of a similarly afflicted gunfighter in his last film, Don Siegel's *The Shootist* (1976).

"We have met the enemy and they are ours"   See Oliver Hazard PERRY.

"We hold these truths to be self-evident"   A line from the DECLARATION OF INDEPENDENCE announcing its basic philosophy. The truths were "that all men are created equal," "that they are endowed by their Creator with certain unalienable rights," "that among these are life, liberty, and the pursuit of happiness," that government is designed to ensure these rights, and that, when it fails to do so, the people may "alter" or "abolish" it.

"We Shall Overcome"   The anthem of the modern CIVIL RIGHTS MOVEMENT. Originally a Baptist hymn, it had also been used as a union song before being adapted by Freedom Riders in the 1960s.

> *Deep in my heart, I do believe*
> *We shall overcome someday.*

"We the people"   The opening words of the preamble to the U.S. CONSTITUTION. In suggesting the sovereignty of the citizenry over government structures, they reflected the same view of democratic principles as are implied in the DECLARATION OF INDEPENDENCE's "consent of the governed." In an 1830 debate with STATES' RIGHTS proponent Robert Hayne, Daniel WEBSTER invoked them as a federalist argument: It was the people, he said, and not the states, who had framed the Constitution.

"We was robbed"   When heavyweight boxing champion Max Schmeling lost his title on June 21, 1932, to Jack Sharkey, Schmeling's manager, Joe Jacobs, shouted this classic of outrage into the radio microphone. Three years later, after leaving a sickbed to place a losing bet on the World Series, Jacobs gave reporters another chestnut: "I should of stood in bed."

Weavers, The   A folksinging group formed in 1949 by Ronnie Gilbert, Lee Hays, Fred Hellerman, and Pete SEEGER. Blacklisted because of their politics in the Joseph McCARTHY era, they were a major force in the FOLK REVIVAL. Their hits included "Kisses Sweeter than Wine," "ON TOP OF OLD SMOKEY," and "WHEN THE SAINTS GO MARCHING IN." Hays and Seeger later wrote "IF I HAD A HAMMER."

Webb, Jack   See DRAGNET.

Weber and Fields   Comedians. Pudgy Joe Weber (1867–1942) and lean Lew Fields (1867–1941) started in vaudeville as children and became that venue's most successful slapstick team. Their contrasting appearances gave them a MUTT AND JEFF quality that prefigured that of LAUREL AND HARDY. The team did several films in the silent era. Fields was the father of lyricist Dorothy FIELDS.

Webster, Daniel   (1782–1852) Politician. Known as the godlike Daniel from his commanding presence and oratory, Webster was the chief voice of American nationalism before the Civil War. He represented first his native New Hampshire, then Massachusetts, in Congress in a career that lasted almost forty years (1813–50). There he vigorously opposed NULLIFICATION, giving the unionists a famous slogan in 1830 when he proclaimed, "Liberty *and* Union, now and forever, one and inseparable!" He served two terms as secretary of state (1841–43 and 1850–52) and was a chief supporter of the 1850 Compromise, which postponed southern secession by appeasing slaveholders (see also John C. CALHOUN and Henry CLAY). His legendary persuasiveness was the subject of "THE DEVIL AND DANIEL WEBSTER."

Webster, Noah   (1758–1843) Born in Connecticut and educated at Yale, Webster was the first lexicographer to identify American usage as a unique vernacular rather than a poor copy of "true" English. He promoted standardized spelling in a best-selling "blue-backed speller" as well as in the volume most associated with him, *An American Dictionary of the English Language* (1828). Because of his far-reaching influence, "Webster's" sometimes means any dictionary. He was also a founder of Amherst College.

Weems, Parson   (1759–1825) Mason Locke Weems was an itinerant parson and bookseller who wrote a famous, fanciful biography of the first president. *The Life and Memorable Actions of George Washington,* first published in 1800, went into over fifty editions by midcentury. It is the source of many "moral fables" of its subject's life, notably the cherry tree tale, which Weems claimed he heard from a Washington acquaintance. He also wrote lives of Benjamin FRANKLIN and William PENN and moral pamphlets such as *God's Revenge Against Adultery.*

Weismuller, Johnny   (1904–84) Athlete, actor. A gold medalist in swimming at the 1924 and 1928 Olympics, Weismuller became a pop culture demigod in the 1930s, as TARZAN in MGM adventure films. In the first of these, *Tarzan the Ape Man* (1932), he addresses his leading lady, Maureen O'Sullivan, with the immortal line "Me Tarzan, you Jane." After the Tarzan fad faded, he starred as white hunter Jungle Jim in movies and television, then left Hollywood to exploit his name in a variety of businesses.

Welch, Raquel   (1940–   ) Actress. The principal sex goddess of the 1960s, Welch came to public attention in 1963, when she played a semiclad "cave-woman" in *One Million B.C.* Even though the roles that followed were indifferent, she maintained a high visibility through poster sales and was able to command attention on voluptuousness alone. Her films include *Myra Breckinridge* (1970) and *The Three Musketeers* (1974).

Welk, Lawrence   (1903–92) Bandleader. The king of "champagne music," Welk hosted a network television music show that lasted from 1955 to 1971, then aired for another decade in syndication. His musical taste was old-fashioned and his Polish accent the butt of frequent jokes, yet he ultimately surpassed Ed SULLIVAN for variety show longevity. The show's big band arrangements of romantic standards were regularly leavened by the accordion wizardry of Myron Floren and the sweet harmonies of a female quartet, "da lovely Lennon Sisters."

Welles, Orson   (1915–85) Actor, director. Shortly after founding the Mercury Theater with John Houseman, Welles aired a 1938 broadcast of THE WAR OF THE WORLDS that made him a household name. He followed it with the film that is widely considered not only his but the American film industry's finest achievement, CITIZEN KANE. His next films fell understandably short of that pinnacle, although his society drama *The Magnificent Ambersons* (1942) and his dark mysteries *The Lady from Shanghai* (1948) and *Touch of Evil* (1958) were critical successes. Welles's fascination with Shakespeare produced *Macbeth* (1948), *Othello* (1952), and the cinematic collage *Chimes at Midnight/Falstaff* (1966), in all of which he himself took the lead. A master of extravagant characterization, he also acted in *Jane Eyre* (1944), *The Third Man* (1949), and many historical dramas. From the 1950s he worked mostly in Europe.

Wellman, William   (1896–1975) Film director. Known as Wild Bill for his rambunctious personality, Wellman served in the French Foreign Legion and the LAFAYETTE ESCADRILLE before becoming a filmmaker. He drew on the first experience for the 1939 *Beau Geste,* on the second for the 1927 WINGS. His concern with social problems was explored vividly in THE PUBLIC ENEMY and THE OX-BOW INCIDENT. He also did the first version of A STAR IS BORN and a World War II classic, *The Story of G. I. Joe* (1945).

Wells, Kitty   (1919–   ) The first singer to earn the title Queen of Country Music. Born Muriel Deason in Nashville, she started recording in the 1940s and made her breakthrough in 1952 with "It Wasn't God Who Made Honky Tonk Angels." Capitalizing on a straightforward country charm, she had best-selling records throughout the 1960s. Among them were "A Woman Half My Age" and "Heartbreak U.S.A."

Wells, Fargo   A stagecoach company founded in 1852 by Henry Wells and William Fargo. It provided banking as well as transportation and mail service to

the trans-Mississippi West. Its stages were frequent targets of bandit attacks—episodes that were often reenacted in western movies.

"We're in the Money"   Popular title for "The Gold-Diggers' Song," written in 1933 by Al Dubin and Harry Warren. It was a highlight of the movie *Gold Diggers of 1933*. The lyrics were infectiously, if prematurely, optimistic:

> *We're in the money, the skies are sunny.*
> *Old man Depression, you are through, you done us wrong.*

West, Benjamin   (1738–1820) The first internationally known American artist. A Pennsylvania Quaker, he moved to Europe in the 1760s and took up permanent residence in London. There he helped to found the Royal Academy and became the official history painter to GEORGE III. He worked in numerous genres, including portraiture and religious tableaus, but is best known for his large historical canvases, among them *The Death of General Wolfe* and *Penn's Treaty with the Indians*. His London studio received such students as Samuel F. B. MORSE, Gilbert STUART, and John TRUMBULL.

West, Mae   (1892–1980) Actress. West was the cutting edge of public sexuality for almost three-quarters of a century. As the "Baby Vamp" in burlesque and vaudeville, she introduced the provocative "shimmy" to the stage. Her first play, *Sex* (1926), earned her ten days in jail on obscenity charges. *Drag* (1927) concerned the taboo subject of homosexuality. *Diamond Lil* (1928) got her noticed by Hollywood and was transformed into her first hit film, *She Done Him Wrong* (1933). She brought her gift for double entendre to several other films, the best known being *My Little Chickadee* (1940), with W. C. FIELDS. In the 1940s, she toured Europe and the States with a stage revival of *Diamond Lil,* and in the 1950s, she starred in a nightclub act. In 1970, as she was approaching eighty, she made her last major film, *Myra Breckinridge.*

West was known to the public by her hourglass figure, outlandish costumes, and suggestive delivery. Little known was the fact that she wrote or cowrote most of her properties, from her first play, *Sex,* to her last, *Sextette* (1978). Once the highest-paid woman in the country, she is remembered especially for her throaty one-liners. Examples are "COME UP AND SEE ME SOMETIME," "Is that a pistol in your pocket or are you just real happy to see me?," and "Beulah, peel me a grape." The title of her 1959 autobiography came from her film response to the exclamation "Thank goodness": *Goodness Had Nothing to Do with It.*

West, Nathanael   (1903–40) Pen name of Nathan Weinstein, whose few novels, largely unnoticed in his lifetime, are considered masterpieces of savage disillusionment. MISS LONELYHEARTS was released in 1933. It was followed by *A Cool Million* (1934), which twits the Horatio ALGER story; and *The Day of The Locust* (1939), which satirizes Hollywood. West's brother-in-law was S. J. PERELMAN.

West Point   Site of the U.S. Military Academy in upstate New York; hence a popular name for the academy itself. Founded in 1802, West Point trains students, called cadets, for second-lieutenant commissions in the U.S. Army. For the site's earlier importance, see Benedict ARNOLD.

West Side Story   A musical comedy (1957) with a script by Arthur Laurents, songs by Leonard BERNSTEIN and Stephen SONDHEIM, and choreography by

Jerome ROBBINS. It transposed the story of Romeo and Juliet to the world of New York City street gangs. After a successful Broadway run, it became the best picture of 1961, also winning Oscars for Robbins, director Robert WISE, and supporting players George Chakiris and Rita Moreno. It featured the songs "America," "Tonight," "I Feel Pretty," and "Maria."

western A dramatic and literary genre celebrating the westward expansion of the United States; it highlights conflicts between white and red, "good guys" and "bad guys," farmers and ranchers. Owen Wister's 1902 novel THE VIRGINIAN is usually taken as the first written western, although western tales had earlier figured in the DIME NOVEL. The movie western arose about the same time, with THE GREAT TRAIN ROBBERY, and has remained a staple of the film and television industries ever since. The best-known western writers were Max BRAND, Louis L'AMOUR, and Zane GREY. Prominent names in the film western include Gary COOPER, Clint EASTWOOD, John FORD, William S. HART, Howard HAWKS, Tom MIX, Randolph SCOTT, James STEWART, and John WAYNE. See also COWBOY; SINGING COWBOYS; SPAGHETTI WESTERNS.

western swing A type of country music developed in Texas in the 1930s and still a dominant style in Southwest dance halls. It fused the standard fiddle and guitar sound of hillbilly music with the dance rhythms—and occasionally the brass accompaniments—of big band jazz. The earliest groups were the Light Crust Doughboys and the Musical Brownies. The undisputed "King of Western Swing" was Doughboy veteran and expert fiddler Bob Wills (1905–75). With his band the Texas Playboys he brought the style national recognition. Among the Wills standards that still enliven Texas dance halls are "COTTON-EYED JOE," "Take Me Back to Tulsa," and "San Antonio Rose." The last song was a 1941 hit for Bing CROSBY.

Western Union A telegraph company founded in 1856. Its network spanned the continent by the Civil War; the story of its construction was told in *Western Union,* a 1941 film directed by Fritz Lang. Western Union messengers hand-delivered telegrams and, beginning in the 1930s, SINGING TELEGRAMS.

wetback A Mexican citizen who enters the United States illegally in search of work. From swimming or fording the RIO GRANDE to escape border patrols. An Anglo term from the 1940s.

"What do you mean we, white man?"   See TONTO.

"What hath God wrought?"   See Samuel F. B. MORSE.

What Price Glory?   A 1924 play by Maxwell Anderson and Laurence Stallings. Famous for its profane, realistic treatment of World War I. Director Raoul WALSH filmed it in 1926.

"What this country needs is a good five-cent cigar"   This tongue-in-cheek solution to the nation's ills was proposed during a long Senate debate by Woodrow WILSON's vice president, Thomas Marshall (1854–1925). Marshall, who had been governor of his native Indiana, served eight years as Wilson's second-in-command.

"What Was Your Name in the States?"   A miner's song from the California GOLD RUSH. It suggests a hidden reason for the prospecting migration.

> *What was your name in the States?*
> *Was it Thompson or Johnson or Bates?*
> *Did you murder your wife and fly for your life?*
> *Say, what was your name in the States?*

What's My Line?   A television game show hosted by John Daly from 1950 to 1967. A celebrity panel, by asking yes or no questions, attempted to guess the occupations of guests. The appeal of the show was in the wit of the panel, which included media personality Arlene Francis, columnist Dorothy Kilgallen, and publisher Bennett Cerf. To determine products manufactured by guests, panelists often resorted to the stock query "Is it bigger than a breadbox?"

"What's up, doc?"   See BUGS BUNNY.

Wheaties   A breakfast cereal introduced in 1922 and pitched to the fitness-conscious as "The Breakfast of Champions." Youngsters who were visibly fit or growing rapidly were sometimes congratulated with the line "I see you've been eating your Wheaties."

Wheatley, Phillis   (ca. 1755–84) Poet. Born in Africa, she was brought to New England as a slave and educated by her master, John Wheatley. Her volume of conventional verse, *Poems on Various Subjects, Religious and Moral* (1733), was the first poetry book by an American black woman. It made her a celebrity on both sides of the Atlantic.

Wheel of Fortune   A television show which, since its debut in 1975, has become the medium's most watched daytime quiz show. Contestants spin a giant wheel to "purchase" letters, enabling them to spell out a phrase and win prizes. Hosted by Pat Sajak, the show made his decorative assistant, Vanna White, a surprise celebrity.

When Johnny Comes Marching Home Again"   A Civil War song (1863) by military bandmaster Patrick S. Gilmore (1829–92). Popular then and in the Spanish-American War.

> *When Johnny comes marching home again, Hurrah! Hurrah!*
> *We'll give him a hearty welcome then, Hurrah! Hurrah!*
> *The men will cheer, the boys will shout,*
> *The ladies they will all turn out,*
> *And we'll all feel gay when Johnny comes marching home.*

"When Lilacs Last in the Dooryard Bloom'd"   An elegy by Walt WHITMAN on the death of Abraham LINCOLN. First published in 1866, it later became part of LEAVES OF GRASS. See also "O CAPTAIN! MY CAPTAIN!"

"When the Saints Go Marching In"   A well-known Dixieland jazz tune, adapted from an earlier gospel song (1896) written by Katherine Purvis and James Black.

"When You and I Were Young, Maggie"   A nostalgic ballad (1866) by George Washington Johnson. The aged singer recounts his courting days.

"When you call me that, smile!"   See THE VIRGINIAN.

"When You Were Sweet Sixteen"   (1890) A romantic ballad by James Thornton. A major "lost love" hit of the gaslight era and a perennial favorite of BARBERSHOP QUARTETS.

Whigs   See POLITICAL PARTIES.

Whiskey Rebellion   A 1794 revolt by Pennsylvania farmers who objected to an onerous tax on whiskey. It was put down by the order of President Washington, providing the first incontrovertible evidence of federal power.

Whiskey Ring   A scandal of the Ulysses S. GRANT administration. It involved an agreement between federal officials and whiskey distillers—known collectively as the Whiskey Ring—to transfer liquor taxes to the Republican Party. The most famous conspirator, Orville Babcock, was Grant's personal secretary. The ring was exposed in 1875.

whispering campaign   In 1928, Al SMITH became the first Roman Catholic to run for president on a major party ticket. Anti-Catholic rumor-mongering by, among others, the KU KLUX KLAN, fueled the belief that he would be a papal proxy. This "whispering campaign" kept him from the White House.

whistle Dixie   To speak with unrealistic bravado or optimism, like an unregenerate defender of the Confederacy. See "DIXIE;" LOST CAUSE; "THE SOUTH SHALL RISE AGAIN."

whistle-stop   An isolated small town. From the fact that trains would stop there on an irregular basis, such stops being announced by the engineer's whistle. The term became well known during Harry S TRUMAN's 1948 reelection run, when he campaigned from train platforms throughout small-town America.

Whistler, James McNeill   (1834–1903) Painter. Born in Massachusetts and educated for a time at WEST POINT, Whistler left the United States as a young man and made his reputation in Paris and London. Influenced by the Impressionists and Japanese prints, he produced works that were not widely appreciated until after his death. The art critic John Ruskin, who accused him of "flinging a pot of paint in the public's face," was only one of the acerbic expatriate's many antagonists; others were noted in his memoir *The Gentle Art of Making Enemies* (1890). As famous for his wit as for his brushwork, he traded quips with the likes of Oscar Wilde and was a dapper darling of the London dinner set.

Whistler's most famous painting, commonly known as *Whistler's Mother,* was an 1872 portrait of his mother officially entitled *Arrangement in Grey and Black, No. 1.* It shows a primly posed New England matron in a straight-backed chair, and is among the best known of all American artworks. For its revelation of regional character, it compares favorably with Grant Wood's AMERICAN GOTHIC.

White, E. B.   (1899–1985) Writer. Elwyn Brooks White wrote the "Talk of the Town" column for THE NEW YORKER in the 1920s and 1930s. With fellow *New*

Yorker regular James THURBER, he produced the humorous pieces in *Is Sex Necessary?* (1929). Two of his children's stories, *Stuart Little* (1945) and *Charlotte's Web* (1952), became instant classics, and the handbook that he authored with William Strunk, Jr., *The Elements of Style* (1959), is unsurpassed as an introduction to the craft of writing.

White, George (1890–1968) Entrepreneur. Canadian-born White started as a song-and-dance man and became widely known for *George White's Scandals*, Broadway revues of the 1920s and 1930s. They introduced many popular songs of the period and were, like ZIEGFELD'S FOLLIES, precursors of MUSICAL COMEDY.

White, Pearl See THE PERILS OF PAULINE.

White, Stanford (1853–1906) Architect. White studied under Henry Hobson RICHARDSON; helped to found the influential firm of McKim, Mead, and White; and designed public and private buildings in neo-Renaissance style. Most active in New York, he gave that city the Washington Square arch, the Century Club, and a lavish MADISON SQUARE GARDEN on whose rooftop he was murdered in 1906. His killer was a jealous husband, Harry K. Thaw, whose wife's affections White had once enjoyed. Thaw's trial became a gold mine for the press, especially after Mrs. Thaw, the former showgirl Evelyn Nesbit, revealed the amorous games she had played at the architect's mansion. Her recollection of one of them led to the sniggering epithet the "girl in the red velvet swing."

White, Vanna See WHEEL OF FORTUNE.

white bread Bread made with whitened flour, that is, with the bran and germ removed. In African-American slang, an equivalent for SQUARE or lacking in SOUL. Used as an adjective and a derogatory term of address. See also GRAHAM CRACKER.

"White Christmas" A 1942 song by Irving BERLIN. Written for the movie *Holiday Inn,* in which it was sung by Bing CROSBY, it won an Oscar for best song of the year and immediately became a classic of seasonal nostalgia. With sheet music sales in the millions and record sales topping 100 million, it is the single most successful song in music history.

> *I'm dreaming of a white Christmas,*
> *Just like the ones I used to know.*
> *Where the treetops glisten and children listen*
> *To hear sleighbells in the snow.*

White City See WORLD'S FAIRS.

White Fang (1) A 1905 novel by Jack LONDON about the domestication of a wild dog; it was the sequel to THE CALL OF THE WILD. (2) Ben HECHT's telling nickname for Harry COHN.

White Fleet See GREAT WHITE FLEET.

White Heat A 1949 gangster movie directed by Raoul WALSH and starring James CAGNEY as the psychotic mama's boy Cody Jarrett. In its gripping blend

of action and tortured psychology, it fuses the conventions of the WARNER BROTH-
ERS crime drama with those of FILM NOIR. In the final sequence, Jarrett is trapped
atop an oil tank. As he fires into the tank, blowing himself up, he screeches
wildly, "Top of the world, Ma!"

White House   (1) The official residence of the president of the United States.
A neoclassical mansion designed by the Irish-born James Hoban (1762–1831), it
was expanded in the 1800s by Benjamin LATROBE and rebuilt in 1815–17 by
Hoban himself after its burning by British troops in the War of 1812. Its address
is 1600 Pennsylvania Avenue, Washington, D.C. (2) A metonym for the executive
branch of government. The congressional equivalent is "the Hill."

white lightning   See CORN LIQUOR.

white slavery   Enforced prostitution. The term derived from the 1882 melodrama *The White Slave,* by Bartley Campbell (1843–88). See MANN ACT.

white trash   See POOR WHITE TRASH.

Whiteman, Paul   (1890–1967) Orchestra conductor. Originally a classical vio-
list, Whiteman became famous in the 1920s for his orchestra's fusion-style "symphonic jazz." At a much discussed concert in New York City (1924), he
introduced a Victor HERBERT suite and George Gershwin's RHAPSODY IN BLUE.
Before the advent of the BIG BANDS, he was known as the King of Jazz.

Whitman, Walt   (1819–92) Denounced as an immoralist and lionized as "the
good gray poet," Whitman was the most revolutionary American poet of the
nineteenth century. Rejecting moral and literary canons, he wrote rambling, experimental verse in natural rhythms that displayed with equal fervor his transcendentalist wonder, personal individualism, and love of democracy. He published his
first book, LEAVES OF GRASS, in 1855, and continued to issue revisions until his
death. *Drum Taps* (1865) built on his experience nursing Civil War soldiers; its
sequel (1866) contained two elegies for Abraham LINCOLN, "O CAPTAIN! MY
CAPTAIN!" and "WHEN LILACS LAST IN THE DOORYARD BLOOM'D." The prose
volume *Democratic Vistas* (1871) lamented the Gilded Age's "hollowness of
heart." Whitman strongly influenced members of the BEAT GENERATION and other
poetic rebels.

Whitney, Eli   (1765–1825) Inventor. Whitney was responsible for two inventions that revolutionized society. His cotton gin (1793) simplified the removal of
COTTON from its seed and thus paved the way for the Old South's cotton economy.
His "uniformity method" of manufacturing muskets (1798) used identically
tooled, interchangeable parts instead of unique, hand-made ones; the technique
was the foundation of modern mass production.

Whittier, John Greenleaf   (1807–92) Poet. A Massachusetts Quaker, Whittier
devoted much energy to the abolitionist cause, but is remembered chiefly as the
poetic voice of rural New England. Among his most successful poems were
"BARBARA FRIETCHIE," "MAUD MILLER," and "SNOWBOUND." California's
Whittier College (the alma mater of fellow Quaker Richard NIXON) was named
for him.

"Who's Afraid of the Big Bad Wolf?" See THREE LITTLE PIGS.

"Why don't you speak for yourself, John?" See "THE COURTSHIP OF MILES STANDISH."

Wicked Witch of the West The hapless villain of THE WIZARD OF OZ. She tries in vain to dispatch Dorothy after the girl inadvertently kills her sister, the Wicked Witch of the East. She was played unforgettably by Margaret Hamilton (1902–85) in the 1939 movie. She expires with the famous curtain line "I'm melting!"

Widowmaker See PECOS BILL.

Wieland, or The Transformation A novel (1798) by Charles Brockden Brown (1771–1810) involving spontaneous human combustion, unearthly voices, and familial madness. Brooding and gruesome, it was the first gothic novel written in America.

Wiggin, Kate Douglas Author of REBECCA OF SUNNYBROOK FARM.

Wigglesworth, Michael Author of THE DAY OF DOOM.

Wild Bunch (1) The outlaw gang headed by Butch CASSIDY. (2) As *The Wild Bunch*: A 1969 western directed by Sam Peckinpah (1925–84) about a band of outlaws caught up in the Mexican Revolution. Denounced for excessive violence upon its release, it has gradually been accepted as the director's masterpiece and, in more than one critic's estimation, as the greatest western ever made.

Wild West See OLD WEST.

Wild West Show A combination RODEO, traveling theater, and cowboy circus founded in 1883 by BUFFALO BILL. It included stock tableaus such as stage hold-ups and buffalo hunts as well as regular appearances by Annie OAKLEY and SITTING BULL. A highlight was the owner's reenactment of his fight with Yellow Hand, a Cheyenne chief he had killed in hand-to-hand combat. The show successfully romanticized the OLD WEST at precisely the moment when modernization was erasing it. It toured the United States and Europe for thirty years.

Wilder, Billy (1906–) Film director. A Viennese Jew, Wilder left Europe in 1933, leaving behind a family that Hitler exterminated. The tragedy gave his direction a unique style, combining grimness and offsetting humor. He won Academy Awards for two films—THE LOST WEEKEND and *The Apartment* (1960)— both of which also won for best picture. His other notable films included the FILM NOIR classics *Double Indemnity* (1944) and SUNSET BOULEVARD and the Marilyn MONROE sex comedy SOME LIKE IT HOT.

Wilder, Laura Ingalls See LITTLE HOUSE ON THE PRAIRIE.

Wilder, Thornton (1897–1975) Writer. Wilder won the first of three Pulitzer Prizes for his novel *The Bridge of San Luis Rey* (1972), which examined the concept of fate in the lives of five people who perish together in a bridge collapse.

He is better known as a playwright, with two of his plays, OUR TOWN and *The Skin of our Teeth* (1942), also winning Pulitzers. His 1954 drama *The Matchmaker* (1954) was the basis for the musical comedy HELLO, DOLLY!

Wilderness Road   A trail through the Cumberland Gap blazed in 1775 by Daniel BOONE and thus sometimes called Boone's Trace. It was a major artery for westward expansion.

Wildfire, Nimrod   See NIMROD WILDFIRE; ROARER.

"Will the Circle Be Unbroken?"   A religious song from the southern mountains. Because the CARTER FAMILY helped to make it famous, it is often said to have been written by A. P. Carter.

> *Will the circle be unbroken*
> *By and by, Lord, by and by?*
> *There's a better home a-waiting*
> *In the sky, Lord, in the sky.*

William and Mary   The College of William and Mary, founded in 1693, is the second oldest college in the United States. Named for the reigning British monarchs and established at WILLIAMSBURG, Virginia, it was the alma mater of Presidents Thomas JEFFERSON, James MONROE, and John Tyler. PHI BETA KAPPA was founded there in 1776; three years later, it opened the nation's first law and medical schools.

William Tell Overture   See THE LONE RANGER.

Williams, Esther   (1923–   ) Actress. A swimming star in her teens, Williams capitalized on her talents in *Bathing Beauty* (1944), a musical comedy with ample water scenes. Similar productions followed into the 1950s, giving Williams the title Hollywood's Mermaid. She left the screen in the 1960s to manufacture swimming pools.

Williams, Hank   (1923–53) Singer, songwriter. The biggest country music star of the 1950s and still a dominant influence in the field, Hiram "Hank" Williams was born in rural Alabama, sang in his teens with a black street musician, Rufus Payne, and won an amateur contest around 1935 with "WPA Blues." For ten years he worked the honky-tonks, fusing gospel, blues, and western swing into a uniquely passionate style he called "moaning the blues." His break came in the late 1940s, when he was signed by Nashville's Acuff-Rose publishing company and began singing on Shreveport radio's *Louisiana Hayride.* By 1949, he had joined the GRAND OLE OPRY and had his first national hit, "Lovesick Blues."

Over the next four years, plagued by marital troubles and a weakness for the bottle, Williams became a country music legend. Before dying of a heart attack just short of his thirtieth birthday, he had written "Jambalaya," "I'm So Lonesome I Could Cry," "Hey, Good Lookin'," and "Your Cheatin' Heart"—all of which became standards after his death. To most fans, he remains the prototypical "hard livin' " country star, a poignantly imperfect embodiment of his own witticism: "You got to have smelt a lot of mule manure before you can sing like a hillbilly."

Williams's son Hank, Jr. (1949–   ), is also a successful country singer. He began doing his father's material, including the gold-record sound track to the 1964 film biography *Your Cheatin' Heart*. His more rock-oriented, southern "outlaw" image, which emerged in the 1970s, was reflected in "Whiskey Bent and Hell Bound," "A Country Boy Can Survive," "All My Rowdy Friends Have Settled Down" and the wry tribute "It's a Family Tradition."

Williams, Roger (ca. 1603–83) PURITAN leader. The Anglican minister Williams came to America in 1631, ran congregations in PLYMOUTH COLONY and Salem, and in 1635 was banished from Massachusetts for his liberal politics and theology. Leading a small flock south, he founded the colony of Rhode Island, whose tolerance made it a haven for Puritan dissenters, QUAKERS, and Jews. Williams explained his latitudinarianism in *The Bloody Tenent of Persecution* (1644). A vocal defender of native American land rights, he also wrote a guide to the local tongue, *A Key into the Language of America* (1643).

Williams, Ted (1918–   ) Baseball player. A Boston Red Sox outfielder, Williams was one of baseball's great power hitters. In 1941, he won the American League batting title with a season average of .406, making him the last major leaguer to pass the .400 mark. He went on to win five more batting championships, two most valuable player awards, and three Triple Crowns (see TRIPLE CROWN [2]). He retired in 1960 with a career record of 521 home runs and a .344 batting average.

Williams, Tennessee (1911–83) Playwright. Thomas Lanier Williams, born in Mississippi, wrote moody, often shocking plays about emotional and sexual maladjustment. After his first success, THE GLASS MENAGERIE, he earned Pulitzer Prizes for A STREETCAR NAMED DESIRE and CAT ON A HOT TIN ROOF. His interest in social outcasts and personal violence also appeared in *Suddenly Last Summer* (1958; film 1960), *Sweet Bird of Youth* (1959; film 1960), and *The Night of the Iguana* (1962; film 1964).

Williamsburg The capital of Virginia in the eighteenth century. Restored in the 1930s, it is now a historic site known as Colonial Williamsburg. It is also the site of the College of WILLIAM AND MARY.

Willie and Joe See Bill MAULDIN.

Wills, Bob See WESTERN SWING.

Wills, Helen Newington (1905–   ) Tennis player. The greatest woman player of the 1920s, Wills won her first title as a teenager in 1921. Between 1923 and her retirement in 1938, she took seven U.S. women's singles titles, eight British singles titles, and four French. She also won nine doubles championships. In the 1930s, she played under her married name, Helen Wills Moody.

Wilson, Dooley (1894–1953) The black actor Arthur "Dooley" Wilson was the piano player Sam in CASABLANCA; he sings the film's theme song "As Time Goes By." A drummer and singer who had played nightclubs and vaudeville, he later appeared in the all-black musical STORMY WEATHER.

Wilson, Sam See UNCLE SAM.

Wilson, Woodrow (1856–1924) U.S. president (1913–21). Arguably one of the nation's greatest presidents, and unarguably one of its most visionary and articulate, Wilson was a Virginian educated at the College of New Jersey (now PRINCETON UNIVERSITY) who served as that school's president from 1902 to 1910. His inspired leadership and scholarly works—including a mammoth history of the United States—recommended him to Democratic kingmakers, and he became the state's governor in 1910. Both as governor and as U.S. president, he was an effective champion of PROGRESSIVISM, fighting the TRUSTS and reducing their power over labor.

  In foreign affairs, Wilson desperately promoted American neutrality until the sinking of the LUSITANIA and the ZIMMERMANN NOTE made the stance untenable. His 1917 speech to Congress asking for war against Germany proclaimed that "the world must be made safe for democracy" and called for the immediate conscription of half a million men. With the 1918 armistice, Wilson again became a peacemaker, proposing FOURTEEN POINTS for an amicable postwar recovery, among which was a draft of the League of Nations. While campaigning in vain for the League, he suffered a stroke that left him partially paralyzed for the rest of his term. He received the Nobel Peace Prize in 1919—just months before the Congress rejected his dream.

"Win one for the Gipper" A line from Knute ROCKNE's pep talk to the 1928 Notre Dame football team as it was about to take the field against undefeated Army. "The Gipper" was George Gipp, a Notre Dame All-American who had died in 1920, allegedly expiring with the request that his teammates win a game in his honor. Rockne's pathos was effective, as Notre Dame beat the cadets 12 to 6. The line reappeared in the 1940 movie *Knute Rockne, All-American,* with Ronald REAGAN playing the part of George Gipp. Reagan revived it wryly during his presidency as a means of marshaling support for his policies.

Winchell, Walter (1897–1972) Columnist, radio commentator. Originally a vaudeville performer, Winchell reached a huge audience in the 1930s and 1940s with a blend of political comment and celebrity gossip. His *New York Daily Mirror* column was syndicated in hundreds of papers, and his Sunday evening radio broadcasts to "Mr. and Mrs. America" had approximately 20 million listeners. He was strongly pro–Franklin ROOSEVELT and, later, pro–Joseph McCARTHY.

Winchester rifle A lever-action repeating rifle developed by Oliver Winchester (1810–60) and sold by his Winchester Arms Company. Widely seen in western movies, it was the model for the popular Daisy air rifle. Its almost magical significance is explored in *Winchester '73,* a 1950 movie directed by Anthony Mann.

Windy City Chicago. From the prevalence of gusts off Lake Michigan.

Winesburg, Ohio The best-known work of Ohio writer Sherwood Anderson (1876–1941), a collection of short stories set in a small midwestern town. The characters reveal themselves to a young reporter, George Willard.

Wings   (1927) A World War I air battle picture directed by William WELLMAN. It won the Academy of Motion Picture Arts and Sciences' first best picture award and was rereleased as a sound film in 1929.

"Winning isn't everything"   See Vince LOMBARDI.

wipe out   See SURFING.

Wise, Robert   (1914–   ) Film director. After starting as an editor on Orson Welles's CITIZEN KANE, Wise did commendable work in several genres, including horror (*The Body Snatcher,* 1945), boxing (*The Set-Up,* 1949; *Somebody up There Likes Me,* 1956), and science fiction (*The Day the Earth Stood Still,* 1951; STAR TREK, 1979). Wise won Oscars for the musicals WEST SIDE STORY and THE SOUND OF MUSIC.

Wister, Owen   Author of THE VIRGINIAN.

witch-hunt   The persecution of an innocent person. Commonly applied to (1) the SALEM WITCH TRIALS and (2) Joseph MCCARTHY's anticommunist crusade.

Wizard of Oz, The   Popular name for a juvenile fantasy that is the principal American contribution to the fairy tale. It concerns the adventures of a farm girl, Dorothy Gale, and her dog, Toto, in magical Oz, whence they are transported by a Kansas tornado. Accompanied by a scarecrow, a cowardly lion, and a tin woodsman, they follow a yellow brick road to the Emerald City of Oz, where they enlist the help of the Wizard to foil the Wicked Witch of the West and make their way safely back to Kansas. The characters were created by journalist L. Frank Baum (1865–1919) in his book *The Wonderful Wizard of Oz* (1900), which he also adapted as a musical play. Baum's dozens of children's books included several Oz sequels.
  Baum's story became the basis for the 1939 MGM musical *The Wizard of Oz,* directed by Victor Fleming and starring Judy GARLAND. The perennial favorite features the Academy Award song ''OVER THE RAINBOW'' as well as ''We're Off to See the Wizard'' and ''Follow the Yellow Brick Road''; the Harold ARLEN–E.Y. ''Yip'' HARBURG score also won an Oscar. Novel touches included the dramatic combination of black-and-white and color film, the use of singing midgets to play the Munchkins, and special effects that showed a bicyclist in midair. The movie might have taken the Oscar for best picture, but it lost to another Fleming film, GONE WITH THE WIND. The story was reprised as *The Wiz* in 1978, with an all-black cast headed by Diana Ross of THE SUPREMES.

Wobblies   See INDUSTRIAL WORKERS OF THE WORLD.

Wolfe, James   (1727–59) The British general who won Canada for the British by capturing Quebec in 1759. He and his French counterpart, Louis-Joseph de Montcalm, both lost their lives in the battle. *The Death of General Wolfe* is a Benjamin WEST painting.

Wolfe, Nero   See Rex STOUT.

Wolfe, Thomas   (1900–38) Writer. Born in North Carolina, Wolfe wrote sprawling, exuberant prose that gave him a posthumous reputation as one of the century's finest novelists. *Look Homeward, Angel* (1929) and its sequel, *Of Time and the River* (1935), were autobiographical stories of Eugene Gant, whose personal pilgrimage reflected Wolfe's own. The published volumes were the result of heavy editing by Scribner's editor Maxwell Perkins. Two further books, *The Web and the Rock* and YOU CAN'T GO HOME AGAIN, emerged from a mammoth Wolfe manuscript after his death, thanks to similar work by Harper's editor Edward Aswell.

Wolfe, Tom   (1931–) Writer. The principal star of the 1960s "new journalism," Wolfe brought an inventive, colloquial style and dramatic flair to the examination of popular culture and social life. *The Electric Kool-Aid Acid Test* (1968) examined the drug-and-music wing of the COUNTERCULTURE. *The Right Stuff* (1979) told the story of the Mercury ASTRONAUTS. *The Bonfire of the Vanities* (1987) explored racial tensions.

women's liberation   Known colloquially as women's lib. A 1960s term for the women's rights movement, which brought feminist concerns to the issue of gender inequity. Sparked partly by the appearance of Betty Friedan's book *The Feminine Mystique* (1963), women joined "consciousness-raising" groups to support each other and resist male privilege; formed the National Organization for Women (1966) to promote women's issues; and fought for the passage of an Equal Rights Amendment (ERA) that would have made gender discrimination unconstitutional. The effects of the movement included a burgeoning of college-based women's studies programs, an increase in female professionals, and the emotionally divisive endorsement of "abortion rights" (see ROE v. WADE).

women's suffrage   The right of women to vote. The chief focus of the nineteenth-century women's movement. See Susan B. ANTHONY; SENECA FALLS CONVENTION; Elizabeth Cady STANTON; Lucy STONE; SUFFRAGETTES; Victoria WOODHULL.

Wonder, Stevie   (1950–) Musician. Blind from birth, Steveland Morris Hardaway was a MOTOWN prodigy at the age of ten, when, as "Little Stevie Wonder," he sang and played harmonica on "Fingertips." Hits in his teen years included "I Was Made to Love Her," "For Once in My Life," and "My Cherie Amour." As an adult, under a contract that gave him complete artistic control, he displayed a wide range of musical talents, playing numerous instruments on such best-selling records as "Superstition," "You Are the Sunshine of My Life," and (in a duet with Paul McCartney) "Ebony and Ivory."

Wonder Woman   A 1940s comic book character by William Moulton Marston. After being raised among Amazons, Wonder Woman becomes an American superhero, complete with a red, white, and blue costume, great strength, and magic bracelets that can deflect bullets. A 1970s television version of the adventure starred former beauty queen Lynda Carter.

Wood, Grant   (1892–1942) Painter. The creator of AMERICAN GOTHIC, Wood was an Iowa regionalist whose work shows the influence of Flemish painting, which he studied on a 1920s European visit. His *Daughters of Revolution* (1932) is a satirical group portrait of DAUGHTERS OF THE AMERICAN REVOLUTION members.

Wood, Leonard   (1860–1927) Army officer. Wood was the official commander of the ROUGH RIDERS. He later became governor of Cuba (1899–1902) and of the Philippines (1921–27) and narrowly lost the 1920 Republican nomination to Warren G. Harding.

wooden nickels   Counterfeit coins. From the mid-nineteenth century, when con men also sold wooden nutmegs. Hence the humorously monitory farewell "Don't take any wooden nickels." A "plugged nickel," as in the expression "not worth a plugged nickel," is one whose center has been replaced by a base metal "plug."

Woodhull, Victoria   (1838–1927) Pioneering feminist. With her sister Tennessee Claflin, Woodhull published *Woodhull and Claflin's Weekly* (1870–76), which printed the first English translation of the *Communist Manifesto;* promoted free love, women's suffrage, and birth control; and caused a major scandal by accusing preacher Henry Ward Beecher (Harriet Beecher STOWE's brother) of adultery. In 1872, she ran for the U.S. presidency on the Equal Rights party platform; her running mate was abolitionist Frederick DOUGLASS.

"Woodman, Spare That Tree"   A sentimental song written around 1830 by New York literati George Morris and Henry Russell. It asks a lumberjack to spare an old tree that had sheltered the singer in his youth. New York University student John Love wrote an 1868 parody called "Barber, Spare Those Hairs."

Woodstock   A rock music festival held near Woodstock, New York, in August 1969. Described as "Three Days of Peace and Music," it featured performances by Jimi HENDRIX, JEFFERSON AIRPLANE, and numerous other bands for an audience that was estimated at half a million. The COUNTERCULTURE's shining moment, the event was endlessly evoked after the fact as the best of times. It was the subject of Joni Mitchell's song "Woodstock" and the documentary movie *Woodstock* (both 1970).

Woodward and Bernstein   Bob Woodward (1943–   ) and Carl Bernstein (1944–   ) were the WASHINGTON POST reporters who covered the WATERGATE story. Their investigation, which contributed to Richard NIXON's downfall, was recorded in their 1974 book *All the President's Men*. A movie version (1976) starred Robert REDFORD and Dustin HOFFMAN.

Woody Woodpecker   A cartoon character created by animator Walter Lantz (1900–94). A fun-loving, slightly manic bird, Woody first appeared in *Knock Knock* (1940).

Woollcott, Alexander   (1887–1943) Writer. A charter member of the ALGONQUIN ROUND TABLE, Woollcott wrote theater criticism, hosted the gossipy radio show *The Town Crier* (1929–42), and was the model for egotistical Sheridan Whiteside, the convalescing hero of THE MAN WHO CAME TO DINNER.

Woolworth, F. W.   (1852–1919) Businessman. Creator of the FIVE-AND-DIME, Frank Winfield Woolworth opened his first store in Lancaster, Pennsylvania, in 1879. By his death, he had built an empire of one thousand stores, and "Woolworth's" was a common feature of American main streets. The WOOLWORTH BUILDING is named for him.

Woolworth Building   A New York City SKYSCRAPER in neo-Gothic style. Designed by Cass Gilbert, it was built between 1909 and 1913 with funds provided by retailer F. W. WOOLWORTH. Until 1930 it was the tallest building in the world.

wop   Derogatory slang for an Italian. Probably from Italian dialect *guappo*, "bully." See also DAGO.

Work, Henry Clay   (1832–84) Songwriter. Work's first hit was the temperance song "Come Home, Father" (1864), which appeared in the dramatized "TEN NIGHTS IN A BARROOM." He also wrote "MARCHING THROUGH GEORGIA" and the sentimental "GRANDFATHER'S CLOCK," which in sheet music sold 800,000 copies.

Works Progress Administration   The major job-relief agency of the NEW DEAL. Between 1935 and 1943, the WPA provided over 8 million jobs, mainly in construction and the arts.

World Series   An end-of-season play-off, held since 1903, between the leading teams (or "pennant winners") of baseball's American and National leagues. The Series comprises a maximum of seven games, with the winner being the first to win four. The record for numbers of Series won is held by the New York YANKEES (33); they are followed by the St. Louis Cardinals (15) and the New York Giants (14).

World Trade Center   Twin skyscrapers built in lower Manhattan between 1968 and 1973 to a design by Emery Roth and Minoru Yamasaki. Before the erection of Chicago's SEARS TOWER, they were the tallest buildings in the world. In a 1976 remake of KING KONG, they are the site of the lovestruck ape's fatal climb.

World War I   The international conflict known originally as the World War, the Great War, and the European War began in 1914, sparked by the assassination of an Austrian archduke, Franz Ferdinand, whose nation, joined with Italy and Germany, formed the Triple Alliance. With Britain, France, and Russia composing the Triple Entente, Europe was split into factions of colonialist competitors well before 1914, and the assassination triggered a series of mobilizations—encouraged by passionate nationalism—that led by summer's end to open war. The ensuing hostilities transformed European society, scarring a generation with memories of carnage and adding to humanity's stock of horrors the innovations of aerial combat, tank and trench warfare, poison gas, high-explosive shells, and the machine gun.

The United States was slow to enter the war. Up until 1917, President Woodrow WILSON, reflecting the nation's isolationist consensus, followed an official policy of neutrality, even after the sinking of the LUSITANIA had revealed the threat to Americans of German U-boats. Reelected in 1916 on the slogan "He kept us out of war," the president maintained this stance until the spring of 1917, when German attacks on U.S. merchant vessels, coupled with the release of the ZIMMERMANN NOTE, made neutrality an increasingly fruitless posture. On April 2, Wilson, proclaiming that "the world must be made safe for democracy," asked Congress for a declaration of war. The resolution was approved four days later.

To the strains of George M. Cohan's "OVER THERE," American DOUGHBOYS trooped to the European front, where for a year and a half they were an important component in Allied strategy. Under the overall command of General John J.

PERSHING, they distinguished themselves particularly at the battles of Belleau Wood, St.-Mihiel, and the Meuse-Argonne. Casualties were severe—130,000 lost to battle and disease—although minuscule compared to European tallies. In total, the "war to end war" took 8 million soldiers' lives and 6.6 million civilian ones.

The Great War ended with an armistice late in 1918 and the Treaty of Versailles, signed the following year. To avoid similar devastation in the future, the major powers also established a League of Nations, based on Wilson's peace proposal, the FOURTEEN POINTS. The U.S. Congress, however, failed to ratify the League, and the nation retreated again into isolationism.

See also "LAFAYETTE, WE ARE HERE"; LAFAYETTE ESCADRILLE; LOST GENERATION; Eddie RICKENBACKER; Alvin YORK.

World War II In the 1930s, the rise of fascism in Europe and of imperialism in Japan alerted the western democracies to the threat of war. In spite of prodigious attempts to forestall it by "appeasing" an expansionist Germany, that threat finally materialized in 1939, when Hitler's Blitzkrieg stormed eastward into Poland. In the ensuing conflict, the original lines were drawn between the Axis triad of Germany, Italy, and Japan and an Allied pact between Great Britain and France. After Germany abrogated a nonaggression pact with the Soviet Union by invading that country in 1941, Stalin's nation joined the anti-Axis effort.

As had been the case during WORLD WAR I, the United States initially avoided military involvement by limiting itself to supplying the Allies with arms—in this case within the provisions of the Lend-Lease Act, which permitted this indirect support of the Allied cause. In thus transforming America into "the arsenal of democracy," however, President Franklin D. ROOSEVELT only prepared the way for deeper involvement, and it came on December 7, 1941, when Japan attacked the U.S. Navy base at PEARL HARBOR. Within a day the United States had joined the Allies, and American industrial resources became totally committed to the war effort (finally breaking the back of the GREAT DEPRESSION). By 1945, when the conflict ended, U.S. factories had supplied nearly 300,000 planes and over 2 million trucks.

The involvement of U.S. armed forces was worldwide, with arduous campaigns fought on both the European and the Pacific fronts. In the North Atlantic, where Allied convoys brought supplies through submarine-infested waters, the loss of sailors' lives was considerable: U-boats sank over 13 million tons of Allied vessels, while almost eight hundred of the subs themselves were sunk by "subchasers." On the European mainland, American forces spearheaded the invasion of Italy in 1943 and the massive D-day operation of June 6, 1944, in which forces under the command of Dwight D. EISENHOWER began a final assault on the crumbling Third Reich.

The Pacific theater, too, was an amphibious arena. Costly "island hopping" by U.S. Marines (see, for example, IWO JIMA) gradually pushed Japanese defenses back to the Asian mainland, while fleets of battleships and aircraft carriers struggled for control of the vast ocean. In one critical battle (1942) near the island of Midway, American naval forces halted the imperial advance by destroying four Japanese carriers and over three hundred planes; the war continued, however, for another three years, with vessels enduring attacks not only from torpedoes but also from suicidal "kamikaze" pilots.

Eleven months after D-day, the German Reich finally surrendered to the Allies. Four months later, after the United States dropped atomic bombs on the Japanese cities of Hiroshima and Nagasaki, Japan signed an "instrument of surrender" on the deck of the U.S. battleship *Missouri,* officially ending the most devastating war in history. Its aftermath included the Nuremberg war crimes trials, in which Nazi officials were tried for the extermination of European Jews; the establishment of the United Nations; and the opening of the COLD WAR between the United States and the Soviet Union over the spoils of the conflict they had fought together.

The valor and grim romance of this momentous event was recorded in countless works of fiction. Among the American novels it inspired were THE CAINE MUTINY, FROM HERE TO ETERNITY, MISTER ROBERTS, and THE NAKED AND THE DEAD. The war also figured in many popular films, notably the Oscar winners THE BEST YEARS OF OUR LIVES, CASABLANCA, and *Patton* (1970). See also "I SHALL RETURN"; Douglas MACARTHUR; "NUTS!"; George S. PATTON.

world's fairs International fairs that exhibit scientific, industrial, and artistic productions in an atmosphere that is half amusement park, half trade show. The pattern was established by the Great Exhibition of 1851, held in London's specially designed Crystal Palace. The first major U.S. fair, the 1876 Philadelphia Centennial Exposition, introduced the work of Alexander Graham BELL and Thomas EDISON. The World's Columbian Exhibition, held in Chicago in 1893, marked the quadricentennial of Columbus's voyages in an architecturally lavish, electrically lit "White City." The 1901 Pan-American Exposition in Buffalo, New York, was the site of President MCKINLEY's assassination. Fairs entitled "A Century of Progress" in Chicago (1933) and "The World of Tomorrow" in New York (1939) placed a heavy emphasis on scientific advances. More recent U.S. fairs have been held in Seattle (1962), New York (1964–65), Spokane (1974), Knoxville (1982), and New Orleans (1984).

Wouk, Herman (1915–) Novelist. Wouk won a Pulitzer Prize for THE CAINE MUTINY and scored a second success with *Marjorie Morningstar* (1955; film 1958), about a Jewish woman's search for romance. He returned to World War II themes in *The Winds of War* (1971) and *War and Remembrance* (1978), which were made into television miniseries.

Wounded Knee A creek on the Pine Ridge Sioux reservation in South Dakota. On December 29, 1890, a group of Sioux led by Big Foot were surrounded there and slaughtered in a U.S. cavalry cross fire. The massacre, whose victims included many women and children, is often called the last "battle" of the Plains Indian wars. The phrase "Bury My Heart at Wounded Knee," from a Stephen Vincent BENÉT poem, became the title of Dee Brown's 1971 "Indian History of the American West." Two years after its publication, the Pine Ridge reservation was briefly occupied by Sioux activists, reviving Wounded Knee as a symbol of resistance.

WPA See WORKS PROGRESS ADMINISTRATION.

Wray, Fay (1907–) Actress. The "girl in the hairy paw," Wray played Ann Darrow in 1933's KING KONG; she is the young woman whose beauty causes the beast's destruction. She played mostly in action-adventure and horror films before retiring from the screen in 1958.

"Wreck of the Hesperus, The" An 1841 poem by Henry Wadsworth LONGFELLOW. It recounts the breakup on a Massachusetts reef of the schooner *Hesperus.* Hence looking "like the wreck of the *Hesperus*" as a metaphor for dishevelment.

"Wreck of the Old 97, The" A railroad ballad from the 1920s, adapted from folk tradition by Henry Whitter and Vernon Dalhart. One of several songs about a 1903 Virginia train wreck, it made Dalhart a "hillbilly music" star.

Wright, Frances (1795–1852) Reformer. Born in Scotland, "Fanny" Wright first toured America in 1818–20, publishing the appreciative *Views of Society and Manners in America* in 1821. In 1825, she founded the Nashoba community for emancipated slaves in Tennessee and after it failed joined Robert Owen's New Harmony (see UTOPIAN COMMUNITIES). Her advocacy of equal rights, public education, and free love earned her the epithet Harlot of Infidelity. Many of her sentiments were later espoused by Victoria WOODHULL.

Wright, Frank Lloyd (1867–1959) The most famous American architect of the twentieth century. Wright was born in Wisconsin, studied under Louis SULLIVAN, and while still at Sullivan's firm developed his own, innovative "prairie style," characterized by horizontal lines, huge overhangs, and expanses of glass. As a proponent of "organic architecture," he strove to integrate his buildings with the natural landscape and to incorporate its forms in their construction. Among his large projects were the Imperial Hotel in Tokyo (1922); his own studio residence, Taliesin West, in Arizona (1936); and the Guggenheim Museum in New York City (1959). See also THE FOUNTAINHEAD.

Wright, Richard (1908–60) Writer. The first great black novelist of the twentieth century, best known for the psychologically penetrating NATIVE SON. His story collection *Uncle Tom's Children* (1938), based on his Mississippi boyhood, won a fiction prize from his sponsor, the Federal Writers Project (part of the WORKS PROGRESS ADMINISTRATION). *Black Boy* (1945) was also autobiographical. *White Man, Listen!* (1957) compiled essays on racial issues.

Wright Brothers Inventors. Wilbur (1867–1912) and Orville (1871–1948) Wright were Ohio bicycle manufacturers when they began experimenting in the 1890s with kites and gliders. On December 17, 1903, at Kitty Hawk, North Carolina, Orville flew a biplane of their design over 120 feet of sand dunes. The short hop was the first flight of a heavier-than-air, self-propelled aircraft. Within two years, they were making twenty-mile circuits, and by the end of the decade, they were delivering planes to the U.S. Army.

Wrigley, William, Jr. (1861–1932) Businessman. Wrigley founded the company bearing his name in 1891. A maverick enterprise that refused to cooperate with the Adams Chicle Company TRUST, it became the world's leading manufacturer of CHEWING GUM. Popular Wrigley gum flavors include Spearmint, Doublemint, and Juicy Fruit. The Chicago Cubs baseball team's home field, Wrigley Field, carries his name.

Wyeth, N. C. and Andrew Artists. Newell Convers Wyeth (1882–1945) was a book illustrator who worked for the publisher Charles Scribner's Sons. His major legacy is his work for children's classics such as *Robinson Crusoe* and TOM SAWYER. His son Andrew (1917–   ), like his father a master of technical realism, is known for studies of rural locales and their people. *Christina's World* (1948) has been widely reproduced. The so-called Helga pictures, published in 1986, are frank yet enigmatic portraits of a neighbor done over the previous fifteen years.

Wyler, William   (1902–81) Film director. Born in Germany, Wyler came to Hollywood in the 1920s. In a fifty-year career, he acquired a reputation for fastidiousness that inspired the nickname Ninety-Take Wyler. Bette DAVIS was among many who resented, and profited from, his dictatorial style; he directed her in *Jezebel* (1938), *The Letter* (1940), and *The Little Foxes* (1941). Wyler won best director Oscars for three movies that were also best pictures: *Mrs. Miniver* (1942), THE BEST YEARS OF OUR LIVES, and the 1959 BEN-HUR.

Wynette, Tammy   (1942–   ) Country singer. Born in Mississippi, Virginia Wynette Pugh is known for her tempestuous marriage to George JONES (1968–75) as well as the mournful savvy of "D-I-V-O-R-C-E," "Your Good Girl's Gonna Go Bad," and the song most identified with her, "Stand By Your Man." Released in 1968, it became the biggest-selling woman's single ever recorded.

X

X, Malcolm   See MALCOLM X.

X-rated   Sexually explicit. Applied originally to pornographic or other feature films that earned this RATING from the Motion Picture Association of America. Now descriptive of anything erotic.

X-ray vision   One of SUPERMAN's extraordinary powers. It allowed him to identify wrongdoers by peering through walls. The talent was also acquired by Ray Milland, playing an unstable scientist, in Roger CORMAN's 1963 film *X—The Man with the X-ray Eyes.*

Xanadu   The palatial home of Charles Foster Kane in CITIZEN KANE. The name comes from Samuel Taylor Coleridge's poem "Kubla Khan," which begins "In Xanadu did Kubla Khan / A stately pleasure dome decree." The supposed real-world model was San Simeon, the California mansion of William Randolph HEARST.

Xerox   A trademarked name of the company that pioneered this reproduction process, Xerox is commonly used as a verb instead of "photocopy"—to the consternation of the Xerox company.

XIT Ranch   A Texas cattle ranch that in the 1880s covered roughly 3 million acres. Part of the holdings lay in distant Montana, and a trail between the spreads crossed several states. The ranch's fifteen hundred miles of fencing used so much BARBED WIRE that fastening staples alone were ordered by the carload. See also KING RANCH.

XYZ Affair   A diplomatic tiff between the United States and France that caused the so-called Quasi-War of 1798–1800. It occurred in 1797, when French ships were routinely searching American vessels suspected of supplying France's enemy, Great Britain. Three U.S. envoys sent to Paris to negotiate an end to the practice were met by a counterpart French trio, identified in dispatches as Minister X, Minister Y, and Minister Z. When these emissaries stated their government's demands—including a $10-million loan and a huge bribe for Foreign Minister Talleyrand—American outrage led to open conflict. In the first year of the war, South Carolina Congressman Robert Harper gave the obscure affair a memorable tag line by toasting the American legation with "Millions for defense but not one cent for tribute."

Y Common designation for the YMCA (Young Men's Christian Association) or YWCA (Young Women's Christian Association), which run athletic, social, and educational programs worldwide. Both were started in England in the mid-nineteenth century. YMHAs and YWHAs (Young Men's Hebrew Associations and Young Women's Hebrew Associations), which arose at the same time, are usually linked to Jewish community centers.

"Yahoo!" Western expression of jubilation, common among both real and DRUGSTORE cowboys. Not to be confused with Jonathan Swift's Yahoos, a race of all-too-human brutes in *Gulliver's Travels*. In the latter sense the word is sometimes used to refer to people of alleged backwardness or insensitivity.

Yale University The nation's third oldest institution of higher learning, founded in 1701 by Congregational ministers and named Yale College to honor benefactor Elihu Yale. With PRINCETON UNIVERSITY and longtime rival HARVARD UNIVERSITY, Yale forms the Big Three of the IVY LEAGUE. Undergraduates founded the country's oldest college literary magazine (1836) and daily paper (1878); the faculty granted its first Ph.D. (1861). Famous Yale graduates include Nathan HALE, Cole PORTER, Noah WEBSTER, and Presidents William Howard Taft and George Bush.

y'all You all. Southern dialect for plural "you," as in the common storekeeper's farewell, "Y'all hurry back, hear?" Pronounced *yawl*.

Yankee (1) In the seventeenth century, a derogatory English term for a Dutchman, traced fancifully to an eponymous Jan Kees. (2) By the eighteenth century, a Dutch-born American colonist, then any American colonist. The British preserve this usage today with "Yank." (3) A New Englander, especially one thought to be guilelessly humorous (like BROTHER JONATHAN) or humorously devious (like Sam SLICK); see also CONNECTICUT YANKEE. (4) Because of the connection to New England, "Yankee" eventually came to mean any northerner. Still a term of abuse among die-hard REBELS. An old southern joke divides people into three classes: southerners, Yankees, and "damyankees."

"Yankee Doodle" The Revolutionary War soldier's best-known marching song. Legend says it was written by a British army doctor, Richard Shuckberg, to mock the ragged uniforms of American troops in the French and Indian War; and that, after the Battle of CONCORD, the colonials adopted it as their own, using it to chide the retreating redcoats. The "macaroni" of the refrain meant a fop.

X, Malcolm   See MALCOLM X.

X-rated   Sexually explicit. Applied originally to pornographic or other feature films that earned this RATING from the Motion Picture Association of America. Now descriptive of anything erotic.

X-ray vision   One of SUPERMAN's extraordinary powers. It allowed him to identify wrongdoers by peering through walls. The talent was also acquired by Ray Milland, playing an unstable scientist, in Roger CORMAN's 1963 film *X—The Man with the X-ray Eyes.*

Xanadu   The palatial home of Charles Foster Kane in CITIZEN KANE. The name comes from Samuel Taylor Coleridge's poem "Kubla Khan," which begins "In Xanadu did Kubla Khan / A stately pleasure dome decree." The supposed real-world model was San Simeon, the California mansion of William Randolph HEARST.

Xerox   A trademarked name of the company that pioneered this reproduction process, Xerox is commonly used as a verb instead of "photocopy"—to the consternation of the Xerox company.

XIT Ranch   A Texas cattle ranch that in the 1880s covered roughly 3 million acres. Part of the holdings lay in distant Montana, and a trail between the spreads crossed several states. The ranch's fifteen hundred miles of fencing used so much BARBED WIRE that fastening staples alone were ordered by the carload. See also KING RANCH.

XYZ Affair   A diplomatic tiff between the United States and France that caused the so-called Quasi-War of 1798–1800. It occurred in 1797, when French ships were routinely searching American vessels suspected of supplying France's enemy, Great Britain. Three U.S. envoys sent to Paris to negotiate an end to the practice were met by a counterpart French trio, identified in dispatches as Minister X, Minister Y, and Minister Z. When these emissaries stated their government's demands—including a $10-million loan and a huge bribe for Foreign Minister Talleyrand—American outrage led to open conflict. In the first year of the war, South Carolina Congressman Robert Harper gave the obscure affair a memorable tag line by toasting the American legation with "Millions for defense but not one cent for tribute."

Y Common designation for the YMCA (Young Men's Christian Association) or YWCA (Young Women's Christian Association), which run athletic, social, and educational programs worldwide. Both were started in England in the mid-nineteenth century. YMHAs and YWHAs (Young Men's Hebrew Associations and Young Women's Hebrew Associations), which arose at the same time, are usually linked to Jewish community centers.

"Yahoo!" Western expression of jubilation, common among both real and DRUGSTORE cowboys. Not to be confused with Jonathan Swift's Yahoos, a race of all-too-human brutes in *Gulliver's Travels*. In the latter sense the word is sometimes used to refer to people of alleged backwardness or insensitivity.

Yale University The nation's third oldest institution of higher learning, founded in 1701 by Congregational ministers and named Yale College to honor benefactor Elihu Yale. With PRINCETON UNIVERSITY and longtime rival HARVARD UNIVERSITY, Yale forms the Big Three of the IVY LEAGUE. Undergraduates founded the country's oldest college literary magazine (1836) and daily paper (1878); the faculty granted its first Ph.D. (1861). Famous Yale graduates include Nathan HALE, Cole PORTER, Noah WEBSTER, and Presidents William Howard Taft and George Bush.

y'all You all. Southern dialect for plural "you," as in the common storekeeper's farewell, "Y'all hurry back, hear?" Pronounced *yawl*.

Yankee (1) In the seventeenth century, a derogatory English term for a Dutchman, traced fancifully to an eponymous Jan Kees. (2) By the eighteenth century, a Dutch-born American colonist, then any American colonist. The British preserve this usage today with "Yank." (3) A New Englander, especially one thought to be guilelessly humorous (like BROTHER JONATHAN) or humorously devious (like Sam SLICK); see also CONNECTICUT YANKEE. (4) Because of the connection to New England, "Yankee" eventually came to mean any northerner. Still a term of abuse among die-hard REBELS. An old southern joke divides people into three classes: southerners, Yankees, and "damyankees."

"Yankee Doodle" The Revolutionary War soldier's best-known marching song. Legend says it was written by a British army doctor, Richard Shuckberg, to mock the ragged uniforms of American troops in the French and Indian War; and that, after the Battle of CONCORD, the colonials adopted it as their own, using it to chide the retreating redcoats. The "macaroni" of the refrain meant a fop.

Yankee Doodle went to town riding on a pony;
Stuck a feather in his cap and called it macaroni.
Yankee Doodle keep it up, Yankee Doodle dandy;
Mind the music and the step and with the girls be handy.

"Yankee Doodle Boy"   A patriotic song (1904) by George M. COHAN, the title adapted from "YANKEE DOODLE."

I'm a Yankee Doodle Dandy, Yankee Doodle do or die,
A real live nephew of my Uncle Sam, born on the 4th of July.

Yankee Doodle Dandy   A 1942 film biography of George M. COHAN for which James CAGNEY won an Academy Award. It was released by director Michael Curtiz in the same year as his very different but equally patriotic CASABLANCA.

Yankees   A New York City baseball team that, for much of this century, dominated American League play from its home field at Yankee Stadium. Between the 1920s and the present, the club played in over thirty World Series and won over twenty, including five in a row (1949–53) under manager Casey STENGEL. Famous Yankee players have included Yogi BERRA, Joe DiMAGGIO, Lou GEHRIG, Mickey MANTLE, and Babe RUTH. Rival fans' resentment of their leadership was reflected in the title of the 1955 musical *Damn Yankees,* which had been adapted from Douglas Wallop's 1954 novel *The Year the Yankees Lost the Pennant.*

Yearling, The   A Pulitzer Prize novel (1938) by Florida writer Marjorie Kinnan Rawlings (1896–1953) about a boy's affection for an orphaned fawn that must be killed to protect the family crops. Gregory PECK gave an Oscar-nominated performance as the boy's father in a 1946 film.

yellow   (1) Cowardly. An old connotation, possibly from the color's symbolic value in medieval lore. Hence "yellow belly" for "coward," "yellow streak" for a coward's fatal flaw. (2) Lighter than average. Said of a black person's skin color. "High yellow" usually refers to an appealing woman, as in the expression "high-yaller girl." See also "YELLOW ROSE OF TEXAS."

yellow brick road   The road to Oz in THE WIZARD OF OZ. In the movie version, Dorothy and her friends dance down it to the song "Follow the Yellow Brick Road."

yellow-dog contract   A worker's agreement not to join a union, usually signed as a condition of employment. So called because, according to unionists, only a yellow dog would sign one. Such contracts, common in the early part of this century, were outlawed in 1932.

Yellow Hand   A Cheyenne warrior whom BUFFALO BILL killed in hand-to-hand combat in 1876. The event was much embellished in DIME NOVELS and regularly reenacted in the WILD WEST SHOWS.

yellow journalism   Sensationalist reporting. The term dates from the 1890s, when a circulation war between Joseph PULITZER's *New York World* and William Randolph HEARST's *Journal* produced an escalation of such writing. "Yellow" referred to the comic strip *The Yellow Kid,* drawn by separate artists for the rival papers; the papers themselves were called the yellow press. This initial yellow journalism had a jingoistic tinge, in encouraging indignation at Spanish atrocities in Cuba; the immediate result was the SPANISH-AMERICAN WAR. The heirs of the tradition—the contemporary TABLOIDS—give relatively more space to sex and scandal.

Yellow Kid   See YELLOW JOURNALISM.

yellow pages   A commercial advertising section in municipal phone directories. Printed on yellow paper, it is promoted as an effortless way to shop; hence the slogan "Let your fingers do the walking."

yellow press   See YELLOW JOURNALISM.

yellow ribbons   Expressions of solidarity with U.S. service personnel abroad, first displayed on homes during the Iran hostage crisis (1979–81) and instantly "traditionalized" (as well as commercialized) during the GULF WAR. Cavalry-men's sweethearts had worn ribbons in the nineteenth century, and a 1973 popular song, "Tie a Yellow Ribbon Round the Ole Oak Tree," suggested the idea of displaying them in the Iranian crisis. During the Gulf War, they were nearly as common on the home front as American flags.

"Yellow Rose of Texas, The"   A folk song from the 1830s expressing a black man's longing for his YELLOW, that is, mulatto, lover. It was first published in 1858, served as a Civil War marching song and a MINSTREL SHOW tune, appeared frequently in songsters, and became a hit recording for Mitch Miller in the 1950s—with the racial connotations effectively muted. Legend identifies the original "yellow rose" as Emily Morgan, a mulatto slave whose amorous distraction of SANTA ANNA led to Sam HOUSTON's victory at San Jacinto, the battle that won the Texas Revolution.

> *You may talk about your Clementine and sing of Rosalie,*
> *But the Yellow Rose of Texas beats the belles of Tennessee.*

Yellowhair   See George Armstrong CUSTER.

Yellowstone Park   Established in 1872, Yellowstone was the United States's first national park. It is also the largest park outside of Alaska, covering nearly 3,500 square miles in Idaho, Wyoming, and Montana. It is known for its striking vistas, wildlife (including BUFFALO, BEAR, and moose), and abundant geysers (see OLD FAITHFUL).

Yerby, Frank   (1916–91) Novelist. Once the most commercially successful black writer in America, Yerby produced southern "romances" that effectively challenged antebellum stereotypes. The first of these, still his best-known title, was *The Foxes of Harrow* (1946). Also adept at swashbucklers, Yerby had a new book on the best-seller lists every year but one between 1946 and 1954.

"Yes, Virginia, there is a Santa Claus"   In 1897, a young New Yorker, Virginia O'Hanlon, wrote the following letter to the *New York Sun:*

I am eight years old. Some of my little friends say there is no Santa Claus. Papa says, "If you see it in The Sun, *it's so." Please tell me the truth. Is there a Santa Claus?*

Editor Frank Church gave a response that was reprinted, thanks to popular demand, every Christmas until the paper's demise in 1949. "Yes, Virginia, there is a Santa Claus," he assured her. "He exists as certainly as love and generosity and devotion exist. . . . No Santa Claus! Thank God! He lives and lives forever. A thousand years from now, Virginia, nay ten times 10,000 years from now, he will continue to make glad the heart of childhood."

"Yes, We Have No Bananas"   A nonsense song written in 1923 by Frank Silver and Irving Cohn, who claimed they heard the title from a fruit vendor. It was turned into a hit by Eddie CANTOR.

yippies   Members of the Youth International Party (YIP), an impromptu group formed around 1968 by "cultural revolutionaries" Jerry Rubin and Abbie Hoffman. The name was an exultant variant of HIPPIE. The "party's" political platform included running a pig for president. Rubin and Hoffman soon became two of the CHICAGO EIGHT. See also YUPPIE.

YMCA, YMHA, YWCA, YWHA   See Y.

yo-yo   (1) A child's toy modeled on a Filipino hunting tool and popularized in the 1920s by manufacturer Donald Duncan. Enthusiasts have devised a plethora of yo-yo maneuvers, although the basic trick remains a simple one: The user flips the toy out to the end of a string, and a rewinding action returns it to his hand. (2) A stupid or indecisive person. Perhaps because such a person, like a yo-yo, does not "stay in one place" for very long.

yodel   A singing technique in which normal and falsetto notes "warble" alternately. The principal American examples are found in Jimmie RODGERS's singing and the movie TARZAN's jungle call.

Yogi Bear   A HANNA AND BARBERA cartoon character that first appeared in the "Huckleberry Hound" series in 1958. A voracious but lovable resident of "Jellystone Park" (see YELLOWSTONE), he spends his time plotting to steal food. The name is a pun on Yogi BERRA.

Yogi-ism   See Yogi BERRA.

Yoknapatawphah County   A fictional Mississippi county that is the principal setting of William FAULKNER's writings; fourteen novels and many stories take place there.

Yokum family   See LI'L ABNER.

York, Alvin   (1887–1964) The most highly decorated U.S. soldier of World War I. Originally a conscientious objector, York enlisted in 1917. At the Battle of the Argonne, his unit captured a German machine-gun nest, and he personally took 132 prisoners. He received, among other awards, the MEDAL OF HONOR. Howard

HAWKS told his story in *Sergeant York* (1941), with Gary COOPER winning an Oscar for the title role.

Yorktown Site on the Atlantic coast of Virginia where, on October 19, 1781, British overall commander Lord Cornwallis surrendered his besieged troops to George Washington. The surrender marked the end of the REVOLUTIONARY WAR.

Yosemite Park A national park (1890) in northern California that contains the highest waterfalls in North America. It is also known for its sequoia stands and for landscapes brilliantly photographed by Ansel ADAMS. The Indian name Yosemite means "grizzly bear."

Yosemite Sam A Warner Brothers cartoon character. Sam is a red-whiskered, gun-toting wild westerner whose occasional nemesis is BUGS BUNNY. He first appeared in *Hare Trigger* (1945).

"You ain't heard nothing yet" See THE JAZZ SINGER.

"You Are My Sunshine" See Jimmie DAVIS.

You Bet Your Life A television quiz show (1950–61) hosted by Groucho Marx (see MARX BROTHERS). The format was unimaginative, with contestants winning money for answering simple questions, but Marx's banter and mildly risqué humor kept its ratings high. One amusing feature was a $100 bonus awarded to contestants who said a "secret word," with the bonus delivered to them by a stuffed duck. Another was Groucho's consolation questions: Contestants who got nothing right would still leave with money in their pockets by answering, "Who is buried in Grant's Tomb?"

You Can't Go Home Again (1940) A novel by Thomas WOLFE. It concerns the disillusionment of hero George Webber upon returning home after a stay in Europe.

You Can't Take It with You (1936) A Pulitzer Prize play by KAUFMAN AND HART about the madcap eccentricities of the Sycamore family, which includes a would-be playwright, a candymaker, a fireworks manufacturer, and an iceman who came to deliver but never left. It was the best picture of 1938 and won a second Oscar for Frank CAPRA's direction.

"You could look it up" See Casey STENGEL.

"You dirty rat" James CAGNEY's best-known and most often parodied gangster line. Like "Play it again, Sam," it is actually a misquotation. In *Taxi* (1932), Cagney plays cab driver Matt Nolan, whose brother is killed by a taxi syndicate's gunman. Cornering the culprit in a locked room, he yells, "Come out and take it, you dirty, yellow-bellied rat, or I'll give it to you through the door."

You Know Me, Al See Ring LARDNER.

"You may fire when you are ready, Gridley" See George DEWEY.

Young, Brigham (1801–77) Religious leader. After the death of founder Joseph SMITH in 1844, Young became the head of the MORMON church. His first major decision was to isolate his flock from contaminating Gentile influence. To that end, he led them west from Illinois to the barren flats surrounding the Great Salt Lake. Legend says that, when he first saw the spot in 1847, he proclaimed simply, "This is the place." Under Young's leadership the desert bloomed, and Mormons so completely dominated Utah's territorial politics that the prophet himself was appointed its first governor (1850–57). Young also directed the settling of Mormon colonies throughout the West. He is believed to have had about twenty wives.

Young, Chic   The creator of BLONDIE.

Young, Cy   (1867–1955) Pitcher. Denton T. Young played baseball at the turn of the century (1890–1911), retiring with a still untouched record of 511 wins. He struck out over 2,800 batters, pitched three no-hitters, and in 1904 threw a perfect game. The Cy Young Award, given since 1956, honors baseball's best pitcher of the year.

Young, Lester   (1909–59) Saxophone player. Young played tenor with Count BASIE in the 1940s, developing a fluid, light style that prepared the way for the "cooler" BEBOP sound. He was responsible for Billie HOLIDAY's nickname Lady Day.

Young, Loretta   (1913–   ) Actress. Born Gretchen Young, she was a reliable, elegant leading lady in films of the 1930s and 1940s. She won an Oscar for the title role in *The Farmer's Daughter* (1947) and three EMMY Awards for *The Loretta Young Show,* a television drama series (1953–60) on which she was star and hostess.

Young, Robert   (1907–   ) Actor. Capitalizing on his wholesome appearance and easy charm, Young played in dozens of MGM movies from the 1930s on, yet achieved his greatest success on television when he was cast as Jim Anderson, the easygoing patriarch of FATHER KNOWS BEST. He scored again in the title role of *Marcus Welby, M.D.,* a medical drama that lasted seven seasons (1969–76).

"Young Charlotte"   A sentimental ballad of the 1840s about a young girl who freezes to death on her way to a party. It has been attributed to political humorist Seba Smith (1792–1868) and was once known from his native New England to the Far West.

"Young Man Who Wouldn't Hoe Corn, The"   A traditional farm song warning against idleness. A young man whose crops go to weed fails to win the woman he loves—"all because he wouldn't hoe corn." For similar sentiments, see "HE THAT WILL NOT WORK SHALL NOT EAT" and THREE LITTLE PIGS.

Younger Brothers   Outlaws. Missourians Cole and Jim Younger were Confederate guerrillas in the Civil War. When it ended, they joined the Jesse JAMES gang with two other brothers, John and Bob. John died in 1874. The remaining three, captured in the Northfield, Minnesota, bank fiasco, were sent to prison in 1876.

"Your Cheatin' Heart"   (1952) One of Hank WILLIAMS's most famous songs. It became the title of a movie (1964) based on the singer's life, the score of which was provided by his son, Hank, Jr.

Your Hit Parade   See HIT PARADE.

Your Show of Shows   See Sid CAESAR.

"You're a Grand Old Flag"   A patriotic song by George M. COHAN. He first presented it in the musical *George Washington, Jr.* (1906).

"You've Come a Long Way, Baby"   A 1970s advertising slogan for Virginia Slims cigarettes, designed to appeal to the liberated woman. It was often accompanied by sepia-toned photo tableaus depicting preliberated women kept from smoking by their husbands. The perhaps unintentional condescension of the apostrophe ''Baby'' made the campaign a target of feminist criticism.

Yukon King   See SERGEANT PRESTON OF THE YUKON.

Yukon Territory   A Canadian province between the Northwest Territories and Alaska. It was the site of the 1896 KLONDIKE gold rush. SERGEANT PRESTON OF THE YUKON was a radio (1947–55), then a television (1955–58) series about an officer with the ROYAL CANADIAN MOUNTED POLICE.

yuppie   From the 1980s acronym YUP, for ''young upwardly mobile professional'' or ''young urban professional.'' A journalistic invention suggesting the baby boomers' acquisitiveness and drive for status. A pun, both linguistically and conceptually, on YIPPIE.

Z

Zaharias, "Babe" Didrikson (1914–56) Widely considered the finest woman athlete of the century, Mildred Didrikson was a high school basketball star before turning to track and field and winning two gold medals (javelin and 80-meter hurdles) in the 1932 Olympics. In the 1930s, after marrying wrestler George Zaharias, she concentrated on golf; she was the U.S. Women's Open champion in 1948, 1950, and 1954. Before her early death from cancer, the Associated Press six times voted her woman athlete of the year.

Zangwill, Israel See MELTING POT.

Zanuck, Darryl F. (1902–79) Movie executive. After working as a screenwriter in the 1920s—on, among other things, RIN TIN TIN films—Zanuck was WARNER BROTHERS studio head for five years (1928–33), then formed his own company, which evolved into 20TH CENTURY-FOX. As its chief of production (1934–56), he supervised the film classics THE GRAPES OF WRATH, *How Green Was My Valley* (1941's best picture), and ALL ABOUT EVE. Later, as an independent producer, he triumphed with *The Longest Day* (1962), a story of the Normandy D-day landings. Zanuck's son Richard (1934–), also a film executive, produced the blockbusters JAWS and *The Sting* (1973).

Zapata, Emiliano (1879?–1919) Mexican revolutionary. An eloquent defender of peasant land claims, Zapata helped to overthrow dictator Porfirio Díaz, joined Pancho VILLA in the Mexican Revolution, and tirelessly promoted a land-redistribution scheme that he came to believe the revolution had betrayed. A dashing "people's leader," he became a folk hero after his betrayal and assassination. Marlon BRANDO won an Oscar nomination for his title role in *Viva Zapata!* (1952).

Zappa, Frank (1941–93) Musician. Zappa combined expert musicianship with political disenchantment and a penchant for outrage to produce unusual examples of California "freak rock." With his band the Mothers of Invention, he sniped at American conventions in the albums *Freak Out* (1966), *Lumpy Gravy* (1967), and *Uncle Meat* (1969). A subsequent solo career also displayed his antic virtuosity. See also VALLEY GIRL.

Zenger trial A 1735 libel trial that laid the foundations for freedom of the press. Publisher John Peter Zenger (1697–1746), imprisoned for attacking colonial Governor William Cosby in his *New York Weekly Journal,* was defended by Alexander HAMILTON on the grounds that, since the published statements were true, they could not be considered libelous. The jury agreed and Zenger was released. The trial has been called the "germ of American freedom."

Ziegfeld Follies   Annual variety shows staged in New York by impresario Florenz Ziegfeld (1869–1932). They secured the careers of stars like Fanny BRICE, W. C. FIELDS, and Will ROGERS, but were best known for their statuesque "Ziegfeld girls," a chorus line personally selected by the showman. Begun in 1907, the shows thrived into the 1930s. Ziegfeld's second wife, Billie Burke (1885–1970), played Glinda, the good witch, in THE WIZARD OF OZ. MGM's *The Great Ziegfeld,* with William Powell and Myrna Loy as the couple, won the 1936 Academy Award for best picture.

Zimmerman, Robert   See Bob DYLAN.

Zimmermann note   (1917) A secret message from German Foreign Minister Arthur Zimmermann to his ambassador in Mexico City, instructing him to offer Mexico financial aid in exchange for its invasion of the United States. The note, which also promised to restore the lost Southwest to Mexico, was intercepted by the British and given to President Woodrow WILSON. Made public in March, it readied the American people for war with Germany.

Zinnemann, Fred   (1907–   ) Film director. Vienna-born Zinnemann won the first of three Oscars for the short "historical mystery" *That Mothers Might Live* (1938). He also won for FROM HERE TO ETERNITY and for the biography of Sir Thomas More, *A Man for All Seasons* (1966). His best-known film, however, was HIGH NOON.

"Zip-a-Dee-Doo-Dah"   See SONG OF THE SOUTH.

ZIP code   A five-(now nine-) digit postal routing code, introduced by the U.S. Postal Service in 1963. Small communities have individual codes; large cities are divided into several zip code zones. ZIP is an acronym for Zone Improvement Plan.

"Zip Coon"   A MINSTREL SHOW song about a dandified northern black man. It lent its melody to "TURKEY IN THE STRAW."

zip gun   A homemade handgun, typically using nails or .22–caliber bullets. Since the 1950s among teenage gangs.

zombie   See VOODOO.

zoot suit   A dress style fashionable among convention-bucking males, especially ghetto dandies, in the 1940s. It consisted of a bulky, padded frock coat, baggy trousers pegged at the ankles, a broad-brimmed hat, and a long, dangling key chain. Those who favored the style were known as zoot-suiters.

Zorro   Western hero. A Southwest version of the Scarlet Pimpernel, Zorro was a "masked avenger" figure in Spanish California, posing as foppish Don Diego de la Vega to hide his true identity, Zorro ("the Fox"). The swashbuckling swordsman, created by Johnston McCulley (1883–1958) in his 1920 novel *The Mark of Zorro,* inspired movies starring Douglas FAIRBANKS (1920) and Tyrone POWER (1940) as well as a Walt DISNEY television series (1957–59).

Zs Sleep. "To catch," "cop," or "get some Zs" is to go to sleep. Probably from cartoonists' equating the sounds of snoring and sawing wood, both conventionally represented by a series of Zs.

Zukor, Adolph (1873–1976) Movie producer. A Hungarian immigrant and former furrier, Zukor made a fortune in the 1910s with his "Famous Players in Famous Plays," a series of filmed productions of Broadway stage hits. President of PARAMOUNT Pictures from its founding until 1936, he was honored in 1949 with a special Academy Award.

Zuñi A native American pueblo in western New Mexico. Its people, named for the site, engage in farming, herding, and jewelry making. In the sixteenth century, their homeland was rumored to be CÍBOLA. Their winter Shalako Festival is a KACHINA celebration.

zydeco A black musical style that developed in Louisiana and east Texas in the 1950s. A fusion of BLUES and CAJUN elements, it is typified by accordionist Clifton Chenier. "Zydeco" may be a version of *haricots,* French for "beans."